TEACH YOURSELF BOOKS

WELSH DICTIONARY

TEACH YOURSELF BOOKS

WELSH DICTIONARY

Edwin C. Lewis
M.Ed., Ph.D.
Consultant Editor Cennard Davies M.A.

Long-renowned as *the* authoritative source for self-guided learning – with more than 30 million copies sold worldwide – the *Teach Yourself* series includes over 200 titles in the fields of languages, crafts, hobbies, sports, and other leisure activities.

This edition was first published in 1993 by NTC Publishing Group, 4255 West Touhy Avenue, Lincolnwood (Chicago), Illinois 60646 – 1975 U.S.A. Originally published by Hodder and Stoughton Ltd.

Library of Congress Catalog Card Number: 92–80868

Printed and bound in Great Britain by
Cox & Wyman Ltd, Reading, Berkshire.

CYNNWYS
CONTENTS

FOREWORD
RHAGAIR

The *Teach Yourself Welsh Dictionary* is a modern dictionary specifically designed for use by Welsh learners. The Welsh-English section is based on a basic vocabulary formulated to meet their particular needs. It differs significantly from the traditional type of dictionary, in as much as it also contains mutated forms of nouns, verbs, adjectives and prepositions integrated into the main alphabetical structure. Learners thereby are able to trace the standard form of a mutated word without difficulty. Irregularly formed plural nouns are systematically included, and each Welsh verb is complete with its first person singular form in the present tense. In addition, many of the prepositions governed by various verbs are included.

An attempt has been made to supply sufficient grammatical detail with each entry in the English-Welsh section to facilitate cross-reference and easy access to the fuller definition in the Welsh-English section.

Throughout, the dictionary is well illustrated with examples of language in action, with an emphasis on Welsh idiomatic usage.

The supplement contains a short introduction to some of the salient features of Welsh grammar including the conjugation of verbs and prepositions, the comparison of adjectives, forms of personal pronouns, and a summary of the main rules of consonantal mutation.

I am indebted to Mr Cennard Davies, M.A., for his sustained interest and encouragement during the preparation of the work, for reading the manuscript, and for his many valuable suggestions.

I gratefully acknowledge that a section of the dictionary was awarded First Prize at the 1989 Llanrwst National Eisteddfod. Its completion was commissioned by the Eisteddfod Council, and it is now published by kind permission of the National Eisteddfod Court.

Edwin C. Lewis.

August 1992.
Llangyfelach,
SWANSEA.

GEIRIADUR
Cymraeg–Saesneg

BYRFODDAU
ABBREVIATIONS

a.	ansoddair	*adjective*
a.b.	ansoddair benywaidd	*feminine adjective*
ad.	adferf	*adverb*
a.g.	ansoddair gwrywaidd	*masculine adjective*
ardd.	arddodiad	*preposition*
At.	Atodiad	*Supplement, Appendix*
b.	benywaidd	*feminine*
be.	berfenw	*verb-noun* (followed in brackets by the first person present form)
bf.	berf	*verb*
c.	cysylltair	*conjunction*
D.C.	De Cymru	*South Wales (S.W.)*
e.b.	enw benywaidd	*feminine noun*
**e.b.g.*	enw benywaidd/gwrywaidd	*feminine/masculine noun*
ebych.	ebychiad	*interjection*
e.e.	er enghraifft	*for example*
e.g.	enw gwrywaidd	*masculine noun*
* *e.g.b.*	enw gwrywaidd/benywaidd	*masculine/feminine noun*
e.ll.	enw lluosog	*plural noun*
e.torf.	enw torfol	*collective noun*
g.	gwrywaidd	*masculine*
G.C.	Gogledd Cymru	*North Wales (N.W.)*
geir.	geiryn	*particle*
geir. gof.	geiryn gofynnol	*interrogative particle*
geir. perth.	geiryn perthynol	*relative particle*
gw.	gweler	*see*
lit.		*literally*
ll.	lluosog	*plural*
N.W.		*North Wales dialect*
[pron.]		*[pronounced]*
rhag.	rhagenw	*pronoun*
rhagdd.	rhagddodiad	*prefix*
rhag. gof.	rhagenw gofynnol	*interrogative pronoun*
rhag. perth.	rhagenw perthynol	*relative pronoun*
S.W.		*South Wales dialect*
S.W.W.		*South West Wales dialect*
y fan.	Y fannod	*definite article*
ymad. ad.	ymadrodd adferfol	*adverbial phrase*

* The gender of some nouns varies in different dialects. e.g. munud (*minute*); llygad (*eye*)

a *geir. gof. o flaen berf (interrogative particle before a verb);* **A oes heddwch?** Is there peace?
a *rhag. perth. (followed by soft mutation)* who, whom, which, (**a** *is often omitted in everyday speech, but the mutated form of the verb remains):* **Y ferch a welais** The girl whom I saw; **y llyfr a ddarllenais** the book which I read.
a:ac [**ac** *pron.* **ag**] *c.* (**a** *before a consonant,* **ac** *before a vowel;* **a** *followed by spirant mutation)* and: **du a gwyn** black and white. **pensil a phapur** pencil and paper. **afal ac oren** apple and orange.
â *bf.* he/she/it goes; *gw.* **mynd.**
â: ag 1 *ardd.* (**â** *before a consonant,* **ag** *before a vowel;* **â** *followed by spirant mutation)* with (*an instrument*), by means of: **torri cig â chyllell** cutting meat with a knife; **crynu ag ofn** shivering with fear. 2 *c.* (**â** before a consonant, **ag** before a vowel; **â** followed by spirant mutation) as; **cyn goched â thân** as red as fire; **mor ysgafn â phluen** as light as a feather; **mor wyn ag eira** as white as snow.
aber *e.g.b.* *ll.* **-oedd** estuary, mouth of river; confluence; stream.
aberth *e.g.b.* *ll.* **-au** sacrifice.
aberthu *be.* **(aberthaf)** to sacrifice.
absennol *a.* absent.
ac *gw.* **a.**
acen *e.b.* *ll.* **-nau, -ion** accent; intonation.
act *e.b.* *ll.* **-au** act; statute.
actio *be.* **(actiaf)** to act.
acw: cw *ad.* (**cw** *in everyday speech)* there, yonder.
achlysur *e.g.* *ll.* **-on** occasion; cause, opportunity.
achos 1 *e.g.* *ll.* **-ion** reason, cause; action; case, factor. 2 *ardd.* because, for.
achosi *be* **(achosaf)** to cause.
achub *be.* **(achubaf)** to save: **achub bywyd** to save life; **achub cyfle** to seize an opportunity.
adael *gw.* **gadael.**
adain *e.b.* *ll.* **adanedd** wing; *gw.* **aden.**
adanedd *gw.* **adain.**
adar *gw.* **aderyn.**
adeg *e.b.* *ll.* **-au** opportunity; period of time; **adeg y Nadolig** Christmas time; **ar adegau** at (certain) times.
adeilad *e.g.* *ll.* **-au** building.
adeiladu *be.* **(adeiladaf)** to build, to construct.
adeiladwr *e.g.* *ll.* **adeiladwyr** builder.
aden *e.b.* *ll.* **-ydd** wing; *gw.* **adain.**
adenydd *gw.* **aden.**
aderyn *e.g.* *ll.* **adar** bird.
adfer *be.* **(adferaf)** to return; to revive; to restore *(to health, former condition, etc.).*
adferf *e.b.* *ll.* **-au** adverb.
adlais *e.g.* *ll.* **adleisiau** echo.
adleisiau *gw.* **adlais.**
adloniannau *gw.* **adloniant.**
adloniant *e.g.* *ll.* **adloniannau** entertainment; recreation.
adnabod *be.* **(adnabyddaf)** to recognise; to be familiar with; to identify; to know *(person or place)*; to diagnose.
adnod *e.b.* *ll.* **-au** verse *(in Bible);* clause; section
adran *e.b.* *ll.* **-nau** division, section; department: **Adran Addysg** Education Department.
adref *ad.* homewards.
adrodd *be.* **(adroddaf)** to relate; to recite; to report.
adroddiad *e.g.* *ll.* **-au** account, report; recitation; narration.
addas *a.* fitting, suitable, proper.
addewid *e.g.b.* *ll.* **-ion** promise.
addo (i), *be.* **(addawaf)** to promise: **Addewais iddo y byddwn yn mynd.** I promised him that I would go.
addoldai *gw.* **addoldy.**
addoldy *e.g.* *ll.* **addoldai** place of worship.

addoli *be* **(addolaf)** to worship.
addoliad *e.g. ll.* **-au** worship; religious service.
addysg *e.b. ll.* **-au** learning, knowledge; education, instruction: **addysg grefyddol** religious education; **addysg gynradd** primary education; **addysg uwchradd** secondary education.
aeaf *gw.* **gaeaf.**
aeddfed *a.* ripe, mature.
ael *e.b. ll.* **-iau** brow.
aelod *e.g. ll.* **-au** limb; member: **Aelod Seneddol** Member of Parliament.
aelodaeth *e.b.* membership.
aelwyd *e.b. ll.* **-ydd** hearth; home.
aer 1 *e.g.* air, atmosphere. **2** *e.g. ll.* **-(i)on** heir.
aeres *e.b. ll.* **-au** heiress.
aerion *gw.* **aer.**
aeron *gw.* **aer, aeronen.**
aeronen *e.b. ll.* **aeron** berry, fruit.
aeth *gw.* **mynd.**
afael *gw.* **gafael.**
afal *e.g. ll.* **-au** apple.
afan(s)en *e.b. ll.* **afan(s)** raspberry *(S.W.).*
afiach *a.* unhealthy, sick; dirty, unwholesome.
afiechyd, *e.g. ll.* **-on** disease, illness.
afon, *e.b. ll.* **-ydd** river; straits: **Afon Tawe** River Tawe; **Afon Menai** Menai Straits.
afonydd *gw.* **afon.**
afr *gw.* **gafr.**
agor *be.* **(agoraf)** to open.
agored *a.* open; unobstructed; liable.
agoriad, *e.g. ll.* **-au** key *(N.W.)*; opening, aperture: **agoriad llygad** eye-opener.
agos *a.* **(at** *person,* **i** *place)* near; *gw. At. Ansoddeiriau.*
agosach *gw.* **agos.**
agosaf, *gw.* **agos.**
agosáu (at, i) *be.* **(agosâf)** to draw near to, to approach; **agosáu at** *(person);* **agosáu i** *(place).*
agosed *gw.* **agos.**
angau *e.g. ll.* **angheuoedd** death.
angel *e.g. ll.* **angylion, engyl** angel;
angenrheidiau *gw.* **anghenraid.**
angenrheidiol *a.* necessary.
anghenraid *e.g. ll.* **angenrheidiau** necessity.
angheuoedd *gw.* **angau.**
anghofio *be.* **(anghofiaf)** to forget.
anghyfarwydd *a.* unfamiliar, unaccustomed; **anghyfarwydd â** unfamiliar with, unaccustomed to.
anghywir *a.* inaccurate, wrong; false.
angladd *e.g.b. ll.* **-au** funeral.
angylion *gw.* **angel**
ai 1 *geir. gof. heb dreiglad ar ei ôl, a geir o flaen enw, rhagenw, berfenw ac ansoddair (interrogative particle not followed by mutation, and used before a noun, pronoun, verb-noun, or adjective)* (**ai** *is often omitted in spoken Welsh)*: **Ai te sy'n y cwpan?** Is it tea in the cup? **Ai Twm sy yno?** Is it Twm that's there? **2** *c.* either . . . or; **naill ai Marc neu Ioan** Either Marc or Ioan.
âi *bf.* he/she/it was going/would go/ used to go; *gw.* **mynd.**
ail *a. (followed by soft mutation)* second; like, similar: **yr ail fachgen** the second boy; **yr ail dŷ** the second house; **yr ail gadair** the second chair; **heb (ei) ail** unequalled; **bob (yn) ail** alternate, alternately.
ail *rhagdd.* re-, second; secondary; **ail achos** secondary cause; **ailadroddiad** repetition; **ailfeddwl** second thought, afterthought; **ailgyfrif** a recount; **ail-law** second-hand; **ailystyried** to reconsider.
ailgylchu *be.* **(ailgylchaf)** to recycle.
air *gw.* **gair.**
alar *gw.* **galar.**
alarch *e.g. ll.* **-od, elyrch** swan.
alaw *e.b. ll.* **-on.** music; air, melody, tune; lily: **alaw werin** folk tune.
Alban, Yr *eb.* Scotland.
Almaen, Yr *eb.* Germany.
alw *gw.* **galw.**
alwad *gw.* **galwad.**
alwyn *gw.* **galwyn.**
allan *ad.* out, outside.
allanfa *e.b. ll.* **allanfeydd** exit.
allanfeydd *gw.* **allanfa.**
allanol *a.* external, outward, exterior.
allt *e.b. ll.* **elltydd** hill *(N.W.)*; cliff *(N.W.)*; wood *(N.W.).*
alltud *e.g. ll.* **-ion** exile; alien.
alltudion *gw* **alltud.**
allu *gw.* **gallu.**
alluog *gw.* **galluog.**
allwedd *e.b. ll.* **-au, -i** key *(S.W.)*; cleff.
allweddell *e.b. ll.* **-au** keyboard.
am 1 *ardd. (followed by soft*

mutation) (personal forms: **amdana, amdanat, amdano/amdani, amdanon, amdanoch, amdanyn***)* about, at, around, for, on: **am ddeg o'r gloch** at ten o'clock; **Galwodd am Emyr** He called for Emyr; **am y tro** for the time being; *gw. At. Arddodiaid.* **2** *c.* because, for, since; provided that.
amaethwr *e.g. ll.* **amaethwyr** farmer; *gw.* **ffarmwr: ffermwr.**
amaethyddiaeth *e.b.* agriculture.
amau 1 *be.* **(amheuaf)** to doubt; to suspect; to dispute. **2** *e.g. ll.* **amheuon** doubt.
ambell *a. (followed by soft mutation)* occasional; **ambell waith** occasionally, sometimes; **ambell un** an occasional one.
ambiwlans *e.g. ll.* **-ys** ambulance.
amcan *e.g. ll.* **-ion** purpose, notion, guess.
amcanion *gw.* **amcan.**
amddiffyn 1 *be.* **(amddiffynnaf)** to defend; to protect. **2** *e.g. ll.* **-ion** defence.
Americanwr *e.g. ll.* **Americanwyr** an American.
amgaeëdig *a.* enclosed.
amgáu *be.* **(amgaeaf)** to enclose; to envelop
amgueddfa *e.b. ll.* **amgueddfeydd** museum: **Amgueddfa Genedlaethol** National Museum; **Amgueddfa Werin** Folk Museum.
amgueddfeydd *gw* **amgueddfa.**
amgylch *e.g. ll.* **-oedd** circuit, environs; **o amgylch** round about, about.
amgylchedd *e.g. ll.* **-au, -ion** environment.
amharod *a.* unprepared, unready, unwilling.
amherffaith *a.* imperfect.
amheuon *gw.* **amau.**
amhosibl *a.* impossible.
aml *a. (followed by soft mutation)* frequent, abundant; **aml (i) gyfle** frequent opportunity; **gan amlaf** most often, mostly.
amlen *e.b. ll.* **-ni** envelope.
amlenni *gw.* **amlen.**
amlosgfa *e.b. ll.* **amlosgfeydd** crematorium.
amlosgfeydd *gw.* **amlosfga.**
amlosgi *be.* **(amlosgaf)** to cremate.
amlwg, *a.* evident, clear, plain; famous; prominent.
amod *e.g.b. ll.* **-au** condition; term; proviso.
amryw *a. (followed by soft mutation)* several; various: **amryw fath** various kinds.
amrywiaeth *e.g. ll.* **-au** variety; variation.
amser *e.g. ll.* **-au, -oedd** time, period; season; tense; rhythm, measure *(in music and poetry).*
amserau *gw.* **amser.**
amserlen *e.b. ll.* **-ni** timetable.
amseroedd *gw.* **amser.**
amynedd *e.g.* patience.
amyneddgar *a.* patient.
anabl *a.* disabled.
anabledd *eg.* disability.
anadl *[pron.* **anal** *in S.W.] e.g.b. ll.* **-au, -on** breath.
anadlu *be.* **(anadlaf)** to breathe.
anaddas *a.* unfit, unsuitable.
anafu *be.* **(anafaf)** to receive hurt or injury; to injure, to wound, to mutilate.
anaml *a.* infrequency; scarce, rare.
anarferol *a.* unusual.
anawsterau *gw.* **anhawster.**
aneffeithiol *a.* ineffectual.
aneglur *a.* obscure.
anerchion *gw.* **annerch.**
anferth *a.* huge, gigantic, monstrous, prodigious.
anfodlon *a.* unwilling, discontented.
anfoesgar *a.* rude, ill-mannered.
anfon *be.* **(i** *place,* **at** *person***)** **(anfonaf)** to send; to transmit.
anffodus *a.* unfortunate.
anhapus *a.* unhappy; unlucky.
anhawster *e.g. ll.* **anawsterau** difficulty.
anhwyldeb *e.g. ll.* **-au** sickness.
anhwylder *e.g. ll.* **-au** sickness.
anhwylus *a.* unwell; inconvenient.
anialwch *e.g.* desert, wilderness.
anifail *e.g. ll.* **anifeiliaid** animal, beast.
anifeiliaid *gw.* **anifail.**
anlwcus *a.* unlucky.
annerch 1 *be.* **(anerchaf)** to greet; to address. **2** *e.g. ll.* **anerchion** greetings
anerchiadau addresses, speeches.
annhebyg *a.* unlike, dissimilar, different.
annheg *a.* unfair, unjust.
annheilwng *a.* unworthy.
anniben *a.* untidy.
annibyniaeth *e.b.* independence.
Annibynnwr *e.g. ll.* **Annibynwyr** Independent, Congregationalist.
annoeth *a.* unwise.

annwyd *e.g.* *ll.* **-au, -on** cold, chill: **Mae annwyd arno fe(fo)** He has a cold.
annwyl *a. (when the adjective precedes the noun soft mutation occurs)* dear, beloved; precious. **Annwyl Blant** Dear Children. **Annwyl Gyfaill** Dear Friend *(used to begin a speech or a letter);* **anwylyd** darling.
anochel *a.* unavoidable, inevitable.
anodd *a.* difficult, hard.
anos *a.* more difficult, harder.
anrheg *e.b.* *ll.* **-ion** gift, present.
anrhydedd *e.g.* *ll.* **-au** honour.
ansicr *a.* uncertain, doubtful.
ansicrwydd *e.g.* uncertainty, doubt.
ansoddair *e.g.* *ll.* **ansoddeiriau** adjective.
ansoddeiriau *gw.* **ansoddair.**
antur *e.g.b.* *ll.* **-iau, -iaethau** adventure; danger, risk.
anturus *a.* adventurous.
anweledig *a.* invisible, unseen.
anwes *e.g.* *ll.* **-au** fondness, pampering, fondling; indulgence: **anifail anwes** pet.
anwesu *be.* **(anwesaf)** to fondle, to cherish
anwiredd *e.g.* *ll.* **-au** untruth, iniquity.
anwyd *gw.* **ganwyd.**
anwylaf 1 *a.* dearest. 2 *e.g.* beloved one.
anwyliaid *e.ll.* beloved ones.
ar *ardd. (followed by soft mutation) (personal forms:* **arna, arnat, arno/ arni, arnon arnoch, arnyn**). on, upon; by, in, at: **ar fynydd Epynt** on Epynt mountain; **ar lawr y gegin** on the kitchen floor; **ar hap a damwain** by chance; *gw. At. Arddodiaid.*
araf *a.* slow, leisurely. **yn araf deg** slowly, gently; by degrees.
arafu *be.* **(arafaf)** to slow, to retard, to decelerate.
araith *e.b.* *ll.* **areithiau** speech, address.
arall *a.* *ll.* **eraill** another, other, else: **bachgen arall** another boy; **bechgyn eraill** other boys.
arbed *be.* **(arbedaf)** to spare, to save; **arbed amser** to save time.
arbennig *a.* specialist, distinct.
arch 1 *e.b.* *ll.* **eirchion** request, petition. 2. *e.b.* *ll.* **eirch.** coffin, ark.
arch- *rhagdd.* chief, principal, high, arch-; worst: **archesgob** archbishop; **archdderwydd** archdruid; **archoffeiriad** chief priest; **archelyn** worst enemy.
archeb *e.b.* *ll.* **-ion** order *(especially for goods).*
archebu *be.* **(archebaf)** to order.
archfarchnad *e.b.* *ll.* **-oedd** hypermarket.
ardal *e.b.* *ll.* **-oedd** region, district, area.
ardd *gw.* **gardd.**
arddangosfa *e.b.* *ll.* **arddangosfeydd** show, exhibition.
ardderchog *a.* excellent, splendid.
arddio *gw.* **garddio.**
arddodiad *e.g.* *ll.* **arddodiaid** preposition.
arddodiaid *gw.* **arddodiad.**
arddwr *gw.* **garddwr.**
arddwrn *e.g.* *ll.* **arddyrnau** wrist.
areithiau *gw.* **araith.**
arf *e.g.b.* *ll.* **-au** weapon; tool; **arfau** arms.
arfer 1 *be.* **(arferaf)** to use; to practise; to accustom; to partake of. 2 *e.g.b.* *ll.* **- ion** usage, custom, practice; rule; habit.
arferion *gw.* **arfer.**
arferol *a.* usual, customary.
arfog *a.* armed.
arfordir *e.g.* *ll.* **-oedd** sea-coast, maritime district.
arglwydd *e.g.* *ll.* **-i** lord: **Tŷ'r Arglwyddi** House of Lords.
arglwyddes *e.b.* *ll.* **-au** lady.
arglwyddi *gw.* **arglwydd.**
argraff *e.b.* *ll.* **-iadau, -au** impression, imprint.
argraffiad *e.g.* *ll.* **-au** edition.
argraffu *be.* **(argraffaf)** to print, to impress.
argymell *be.* **(argymhellaf)** to urge.
arholiad *e.g.* *ll.* **-au** examination: **arholiad llafar** oral examination; **arholiad ysgrifenedig** written examination; **sefyll arholiad** to take *(sit)* an examination.
arian *e.g.* silver; money, coin, cash: **arian byw** quicksilver, mercury; **arian gleision** small change, **arian parod** cash; **arian pen** exact money; **arian poced** pocket money.
arllwys *be.* **(arllwysaf)** to pour, to empty: **arllwys y glaw** to pour with rain *(S.W.).*
arogl *e.g.* *ll.* **-au** scent, perfume *(N.W.).*
arogli: aroglu *be.* **(aroglaf)** to scent,

to smell *(N.W.)*.
aros (am) *be.* **(arhosaf)** to wait (for), to stay; to stop, to remain.
arth *e.g.* *ll.* **eirth** bear.
arw *gw.* **garw.**
arwain *be.* **(arweiniaf)** to lead, to guide, to conduct.
arweinydd *e.g.* *ll.* **-ion** leader, guide, conductor.
asesu *be.* **(asesaf)** to assess.
asgellwr *e.g.* *ll.* **asgellwyr** wing: **blaenasgellwr** flanker *(rugby).*
asgwrn *e.g.* *ll.* **esgyrn** bone.
asiant *e.g.* *ll.* **-au** agent.
asiantaeth *e.b.* *ll.* **-au** agency.
asyn *e.g.* *ll.* **-nod** ass, donkey.
asynnod *gw.* **asyn.**
at *ardd. (followed by soft mutation) personal forms:* **ata, atat, ato/ati, aton, atoch, atyn)** to, towards, for, at, by; *gw. At. Arddodiaid.*
atal *(rhag), be.* **(ataliaf)** to stop; to prevent; to withhold: **atal dweud** to stammer.
ateb 1 *be.* **(atebaf)** to answer, to reply. 2 *e.g.* *ll.* **-ion** answer, reply.
atebion *gw.* **ateb.**
atgoffa *be.* **(atgoffaf)** to recall, to remind.
atodiad *e.g.* *ll.* **-au.** appendix.
atyniadol *a.* attractive.
athrawes *e.b.* *ll.* **-au** female teacher.
athrawon *gw.* **athro.**
athro *e.g.* *ll.* **athrawon** teacher; professor: **yr Athro Thomas Parry** Professor Thomas Parry.
aur *e.g.* gold.
awdur *e.g.* *ll.* **-on** author.
awduraeth *e.b.* *ll.* **-au** authorship.
awdurdod *e.g.b.* *ll.* **-au** authority: **awdurdod iechyd** health authority.
awduron *gw.* **awdur.**
awel *e.b.* *ll.* **-on** breeze.
awelon *gw.* **awel.**
awgrymu *be.* **(awgrymaf)** to suggest.
awn *bf.* we go. *gw.* **mynd.**
awr *e.b.* *ll.* **oriau** hour; time.
Awst *e.g.* August.
awyddus *a.* desirous, eager, zealous: **yn awyddus i fynd** eager to go.
awyr *e.b.* air; sky: **awyr agored** open air; **awyr iach** fresh air.
awyren *e.b.* *ll.* **-nau** aeroplane.

ba *gw.* **pa.**
bab *gw.* **pab.**
baban *e.g.* *ll.* **-od** baby.
babanaidd *a.* babyish, childish, puerile.
babell *gw.* **pabell.**
babi *e.g.* baby; *gw.* **pabi.**
babydd *gw.* **pabydd.**
bac *gw.* **pac.**
baced *gw.* **paced.**
bacio *be.* **(baciaf)** to back; to move backward; to bet (on): **bacio car** to reverse a car; **bacio ceffyl** to bet on success of a horse; *gw.* **pacio.**
bach 1 *e.g.* *ll.* **-au** hook, hinge. **2** *a.* small, little; dear: **araf bach** slowly, very slow; **bore bach** very early morning, crack of dawn.
bachau *gw.* **bach; bachyn.**
bachgen *e.g.* *ll.* **bechgyn** boy.
bachgennaidd *a.* boyish, childish, puerile.
bachu *be.* **(bachaf)** to hook, to grapple.
bachyn *e.g.* *ll.* **bachau** hook.
bad *e.g.* *ll.* **-au** boat; **bad achub** lifeboat.
badell *gw.* **padell.**
bader *gw.* **pader.**
bae *e.g.* *ll.* **-au** bay; **Bae Abertawe** Swansea Bay.
baent *gw.* **paent.**
bafiliwn *gw.* **pafiliwn.**
bafin *gw.* **pafin.**
bag *e.g.* *ll.* **-iau** bag.
bagan *gw.* **pagan.**
bagiau *gw.* **bag.**
bai *e.g.* *ll.* **beiau** fault, blame; defect.
baich *e.g.* *ll.* **beichiau** load, burden.
bais *gw.* **pais.**
bâl *gw.* **pâl.**
balas *gw.* **palas.**
balch *a.* proud, fine, stately; glad: **Roedd e'n falch ein gweld ni** He was glad to see us.
balchder *e.g.* pride, glory.
baled *e.b.* *ll.* **-i** ballad.
baledwr *e.g.* *ll.* **baledwyr** composer of ballads, ballad-monger.
balot *e.g.* *ll.* **-au** ballot.
balu *gw.* **palu.**
balŵn *e.b.* *ll.* **balwnau** balloon.
ballu *gw.* **pallu.**
bamffled *gw.* **pamffled.**
ban *e.g.b.* *ll.* **-nau** peak, mountain, beacon, height; top, summit; corner, quarter; arm, branch; verse, section of line: **Bannau Brycheiniog** Brecon Beacons; **o bedwar ban y byd** from the four corners of the world.
banana *e.g.* *ll.* **-s, bananâu** banana.
banasen *gw.* **panasen.**
banc 1 *e.g.* *ll.* **-iau** bank; **gŵyl banc** bank holiday. **2** *e.g.* *ll.* **bencydd** mound, bank, hillock.
bancio *be.* **(banciaf)** to bank.
band *e.g.* *ll.* **-au, -iau** band: binding: **band pres** brass band.
banel *gw.* panel.
baner *e.b.* *ll.* **-i** banner, flag.
bannas *gw.* **panasen.**
bannau *gw.* **ban.**
bannod *e.b.* *ll.* **banodau 1** line, clause, part; **2** definite article *gw.* **y, yr, 'r.**
banodau *gw.* **bannod.**
bant *gw.* **pant.**
bapur *gw.* **papur.**
bapuro *gw.* **papuro.**
bar *e.g.* *ll.* **-rau** bar.
bâr *gw.* **pâr.**
bara *e.g.* bread: **bara brith** currant bread; **bara lawr** laver bread; **bara menyn** bread and butter; *gw.* **para.**
baragraff *gw.* **paragraff.**
baratoi *gw.* **paratoi.**
barc *gw.* **parc.**
barch *gw.* **parch.**
barchedig *gw.* **parchedig.**
barchu *gw.* **parchu.**
barchus *gw.* **parchus.**
bardwn *gw.* **pardwn.**
bardd *e.g.* *ll.* **beirdd** bard, poet.
barddoniaeth *e.b.* poetry.
barf *e.b.* *ll.* **-au** beard.
barhad *gw.* **parhad.**
barhau *gw.* **parhau.**
barn *e.b.* *ll.* **-au** opinion, judgement:

Dydd y Farn the Day of Judgement.
barnwr *e.g.* *ll.* **barnwyr** judge.
barod *gw.* **parod.**
barrau *gw.* **bar.**
barsel *gw.* **parsel.**
barti *gw.* **parti.**
bas 1 *e.g.* bass (*voice*); base; **2** *a.* shallow.
Basg, Gwlad y *e.b.* the Basque Country; *gw.* **Pasg.**
basged *e.b.* *ll.* **-i** basket; **basgedaid** basketful.
basiant *gw.* **pasiant.**
basn *e.g.* *ll.* **-au, -ys** basin; **basn siwgr** sugar basin.
basnau *gw.* **basn.**
basnys *gw.* **basn.**
baswn i *bf.* I would (be); *gw.* **bod.**
baswr *e.g.* *ll.* **baswyr** bass (*singer*)
bat *e.g.* *ll.* **-iau** bat.
batrwm *gw.* **patrwm.**
batrymau: batrynau *gw.* **patrwm.**
bath 1 *e.g.* *ll.* **-au** kind; bath; such a; **Dim byd o'r fath** nothing of the kind; **Welais i erioed y fath le** I never saw such a place. **2** *a.* minted.
bathdai *gw.* **bathdy.**
bathdy *e.g.* *ll.* **bathdai** mint.
bathodyn *e.g.* *ll.* **-nau** badge.
bathu *be.* **(bathaf)** to form, to shape, to coin, to mint: **bathu gair** to coin a word.
baw *e.g.* dirt (*S.W.*), dung, filth, mucus.
bawb *gw.* **pawb.**
bawd *e.g.* *ll.* **bodiau** thumb; big toe; **bys bawd** thumb, big toe.
bawen *gw.* **pawen.**
becso *be.* **(becsaf)** to worry, to vex (*S.W.*).
becyn *gw.* **pecyn.**
bechadur *gw.* **pechadur.**
bechan *a.b.* little, small; *gw.* **bychan.**
bechgyn *gw.* **bachgen.**
bechod *gw.* **pechod.**
bechu *gw.* **pechu.**
bedair *gw.* **pedair.**
bedol *gw.* **pedol.**
bedw *gw.* **bedwen.**
bedwar *gw.* **pedwar.**
bedwaredd *gw.* **pedwaredd.**
bedwen *e.b.* *ll.* **bedw** birch; **gwialen fedw** birch-rod.
bedwerydd *gw.* **pedwerydd.**
bedyddio *be.* **(bedyddiaf)** to baptise.
Bedyddiwr *e.g.* *ll.* **Bedyddwyr** Baptist: **Ioan Fedyddiwr** John the Baptist.
bedd *e.g.* *ll.* **-au** grave, tomb.
beg *gw.* **peg.**
begwn *gw.* **pegwn.**
beiau *gw.* **bai.**
Beibl *e.g.* *ll.* **-au** Bible: **Y Beibl Cymraeg Newydd** The New Welsh Bible.
beic *e.g.* *ll.* **-iau** bicycle.
beicio *be.* **(beiciaf)** to cycle.
beichiau *gw.* **baich.**
beichiog *a.* pregnant; burdened.
beidio *gw.* **peidio (â).**
beiddio *be.* **(beiddiaf)** to dare, to venture.
beilot *gw.* **peilot.**
beint *gw.* **peint.**
beintio *gw.* **peintio.**
beintiwr *gw.* **peintiwr.**
beio *be.* **(beiaf)** to blame, to accuse, to censure.
beirdd *gw.* **bardd.**
beiriant *gw.* **peiriant.**
beirniad *e.g.* *ll.* **beirniaid** adjudicator, critic.
beirniadu *be.* **(beirniadaf)** to adjudicate, to criticise.
beirniaid *gw.* **beirniad.**
beisiau *gw.* **pais.**
bêl *gw.* **pêl.**
belydr *gw.* **pelydr.**
bell *gw.* **pell.**
bellach *ad.* now, at length, further; *gw.* **pell.**
bellaf *gw.* **pell.**
belled *gw.* **pell.**
bellter *gw.* **pellter.**
ben *gw.* **pen.**
benaethiaid *gw.* **pennaeth.**
benawdau *gw.* **pennawd.**
ben-blwydd *gw.* **pen-blwydd.**
bencadlys *gw.* **pencadlys.**
bencampwr *gw.* **pencampwr.**
bencydd *gw.* **banc.**
bendant *gw.* **pendant.**
benderfyniad *gw.* **penderfyniad.**
benderfynol *gw.* **penderfynol.**
benderfynu *gw.* **penderfynu.**
bendigedig *a.* blessed, glorious, wonderful.
bendith *e.b.* *ll.* **-ion** blessing.
bendithio *b.e.* **(bendithiaf)** to bless.
benelin *gw.* **penelin.**
benfoel *gw.* **penfoel.**
ben-glin *gw.* **pen-glin.**
benigamp *gw.* **penigamp.**
benillion *gw.* **pennill.**
ben-lin *gw.* **pen-glin.**
benlinio *gw.* **penlinio.**
bennaeth *gw.* **pennaeth.**

bennaf *gw.* **pennaf.**
bennau *gw.* **pen.**
bennawd *gw.* **pennawd.**
bennill *gw.* **pennill.**
bennod *gw.* **pennod.**
benodau *gw.* **pennod.**
benodi *gw.* **penodi.**
benodiad *gw.* **penodiad.**
benrhyn *gw.* **penrhyn.**
bensaer *gw.* **pensaer.**
bensil *gw.* **pensil.**
bensiwn *gw.* **pensiwn.**
bensiynau *gw.* **pensiwn.**
bensiynwr *gw.* **pensiynwr.**
benteulu *gw.* **penteulu.**
bentref *gw.* **pentref.**
bentwr *gw.* **pentwr.**
bentyrrau *gw.* **pentwr.**
benthyca *be.* **(benthycaf)** to borrow, to lend.
benyw *e.b.* *ll.* **-od** woman, female.
benywaidd *a.* female, feminine.
ber *a.b.* short, brief; *gw.* **byr.**
bêr *gw.* **pêr.**
berchen: berchennog *gw.* **perchen.**
beren *gw.* **peren.**
bererin *gw.* **pererin.**
berf *e.b.* *ll.* **-au** verb.
berfa *e.b.* *ll.* **berfâu** wheelbarrow (*N.W.*); *gw.* **whilber.**
berfedd *gw.* **perfedd.**
berfenw *e.b.* *ll.* **-au** verb-noun.
berffaith *gw.* **perffaith.**
berffeithio *gw.* **perffeithio.**
beri *gw.* **peri.**
berl *gw.* **perl.**
berllan *gw.* **perllan.**
bersli *gw.* **persli.**
berson *gw.* **person.**
bersonol *gw.* **personol.**
bersonoliaeth *gw.* **personoliaeth.**
bert *gw.* **pert.**
berth *gw.* **perth.**
berthnasau *gw.* **perthynas.**
berthnasol *gw.* **perthnasol.**
berthyn *gw.* **perthyn.**
berthynas *gw.* **perthynas.**
berw 1 *e.g.* boiling, tumult, turmoil. 2 *a.* boiling, seething; **dŵr berw** boiling water. 3 *e.g.* cress: **berw'r dŵr** water cress.
berwi *be.* **(berwaf)** to boil.
beryg: berygl *gw.* **peryg.**
beryglus *gw.* **peryglus.**
beswch *gw.* **peswch.**
besychiad *gw.* **pesychiad.**
betrol *gw.* **petrol.**
beth *rhag.* what?: **beth am ginio?** what about dinner?; **beth mae e'n wneud?** what's he doing?; **beth sydd yma?** what's here?; **beth ydy ei enw?** what's his name?; *gw.* **peth.**
biano *gw.* **piano.**
bianydd *gw.* **pianydd.**
bib *gw.* **pib.**
biben *gw.* **piben.**
bicil: bicl *gw.* **picil.**
bictiwr *gw.* **pictiwr.**
bicwnen *gw.* **picwnen.**
bigfain *gw.* **pigfain.**
bigiad *gw.* **pigiad.**
bigo *gw.* **pigo.**
bigog *gw.* **pigog.**
bil *e.g.* *ll.***-iau** bill; *gw.* **pil.**
biler *gw.* **piler.**
bilio *gw.* **pilio.**
bilion *gw.* **pil.**
bili-pala *gw.* **pili-pala.**
bilsen *gw.* **pilsen.**
bilyn *gw.* **pilyn.**
bin *e.g.* *ll.* **-iau** bin; *gw.* **pin.**
bîn *gw.* **pîn.**
binc *gw.* **pinc.**
binnau *gw.* **pin.**
binsio *gw.* **pinsio.**
binwydden *gw.* **pinwydden.**
bioden *gw.* **pioden.**
bioleg *e.b.* biology.
bisged *e.b.* *ll.* **bisgedi** biscuit.
bisgïen *e.b.* *ll.* **bisgis** biscuit.
bisyn *gw.* **pisyn.**
biti *gw.* **piti.**
bitw *a.* tiny; **bws bitw** minibus.
blaen 1 *e.g.* *ll.* **-au, -ion** point, end, top, tip; front, van; edge; source, limit, lead. 2 *a.* foremost, front, first.
blaenor *e.g.* *ll.* **-iaid** leader; deacon; predecessor.
blaenwr *e.g.* *ll.* **blaenwyr** forward (*rugby and soccer*); leader (*of orchestra*).
blaguro *be.* **(blaguraf)** to bud.
blaguryn *e.g.* *ll.* **blagur** bud.
blaid *gw.* **plaid.**
blaidd *e.g.* *ll.* **bleiddiaid, bleiddiau** wolf.
blan *gw.* **plan.**
blanced *e.b.* *ll.* **-i** blanket: **blanced wlân** woollen blanket; **blanced drydan** electric blanket.
blanhigyn *gw.* **planhigyn.**
blannu *gw.* **plannu.**
blant *gw.* **plant.**
blas *e.g.* taste, flavour; fervour, zest: **colli blas ar** to lose one's taste for; *gw.* **plas.**

blasty *gw.* **plasty.**
blasu *be.* **(blasaf)** to taste, to relish.
blasus *a.* tasty, delicious, savoury.
blât *gw.* **plât.**
blawd *e.g.* *ll.* **blodiau, blodion** flour, meal: **blawd codi** self-raising flour; **blawd llif** sawdust.
ble *rhag.* where?
bleidiau *gw.* **plaid.**
bleidlais *gw.* **pleidlais.**
bleidleisio *gw.* **pleidleisio.**
bleidleisiwr *gw.* **pleidleisiwr.**
bleiddiaid: bleiddiau *gw.* **blaidd.**
blentyn *gw.* **plentyn.**
blentynnaidd *gw.* **plentynnaidd.**
bleser *gw.* **pleser.**
bleserus *gw.* **pleserus.**
blesio *gw.* **plesio.**
blew *gw.* **blewyn.**
blewyn *e.g.* *ll.* **blew** hair (*on body, not on head*), fur; small fish bone: **hollti blew** to split hairs.
blin *a.* tired, tiresome, cross; sorry.
blinder *e.g.* *ll.* **-au** weariness, trouble, adversity.
blinedig *a.* wearisome, tired.
blino *be,* **(blinaf)** to tire, to vex, to weary: **Rydw i wedi blino** I am tired; **Mae e wedi blino** he is tired; **blino ar** to grow tired of.
blisgyn *gw.* **plisgyn.**
blisman: blismon *gw.* **plisman.**
blith *gw.* **plith.**
blodau *gw.* **blodyn.**
blodeugerdd *e.b.* *ll.* **-i** anthology.
blodfresychen *e.b.* *ll.* **blodfresych** cauliflower.
blodiau: blodion *gw.* **blawd.**
blodyn *e.g.* *ll.* **blodau** flower, blossom, bloom.
bloedd *e.g.* *ll.* **-iau, -iadau** shout.
bloeddio *be.* **(bloeddiaf)** to shout (*N.W.*).
blows *e.b.* *ll.* **-ys** blouse.
blu *gw.* **pluen.**
bluen *gw.* **pluen.**
bluf *gw.* **plufyn.**
blufyn *gw.* **plufyn.**
blwc *gw.* **plwc.**
blwch *e.g.* *ll.* **blychau** box, chest.
blwg *gw.* **plwg.**
blwm *gw.* **plwm.**
blwydd 1 *e.b.* *ll.* **-i** year-old, year of age: **tair blwydd oed** three years of age. 2 *a.* year old; *gw. At. Treiglad Trwynol.*
blwyddyn *e.b.* *ll.* **blynyddoedd** year; *ll.* **blynedd** years (*used usually after cardinal numbers*): **dwy flynedd** two years; **tair blynedd** three years; **pedair blynedd** four years; **pum mlynedd** five years; *gw. At. Treiglad Trwynol.*
blwyf *gw.* **plwyf.**
blychau *gw.* **blwch.**
blygu *gw.* **plygu.**
blynedd *gw.* **blwyddyn.**
blynyddoedd *gw.* **blwyddyn.**
bob *gw.* **pob: bob bore** every morning; **bob nos** every night; **bob dydd** every day.
bobi *gw.* **pobi.**
bobl *gw.* **pobl.**
boblogaeth *gw.* **poblogaeth.**
boblogaidd *gw.* **poblogaidd.**
bobman *gw.* **pobman.**
bobydd *gw.* **pobydd.**
boced *gw.* **poced.**
bocs *e.g.* *ll.* **-ys** box.
boch *e.b.* *ll.* **-au** cheek.
bod 1 *e.g.* *ll.* **-au** existence; being: **Y Bod Mawr** God. 2 *be.* **(rydw i)** to be; **rydw i** I am, **rwyt ti** you are, **mae e/o** he/it is, **mae hi** she/it is, *etc; gw. At. Berfau.*
bodau *gw.* **bod.**
bodiau *gw.* **bawd.**
bodio *be.* **(bodiaf)** to thumb, to finger.
bodlon: boddlon *a.* willing, pleased, content; **bodlon ar** satisfied with.
bodloni *be.* **(bodlonaf)** to please, to satisfy, to be contented.
bodd *e.g.* will, pleasure; consent; **rhyngu bodd** to please: **trwy fodd** with consent or permission; **wrth ei fodd** happy, contented.
boddhad *e.g.* satisfaction, pleasure.
boddi *be.* **(boddaf)** to drown, to be drowned, to flood.
boddlon *gw.* **bodlon.**
boen *gw.* **poen.**
boeni *gw.* **poeni.**
boenus *gw.* **poenus.**
boenydio *gw.* **poenydio.**
boer: boeri *gw.* **poer, poeri.**
boeth *gw.* **poeth.**
boethi *gw.* **poethi.**
bol *e.g.* *ll.* **-iau** belly, stomach, abdomen.
bola *e.g.* *ll.* **bolâu, boliau** belly, stomach, abdomen.
bolâu *gw.* **bola.**
boliau *gw.* **bol.**
bolion *gw.* **polyn.**
boliticaidd *gw.* **politicaidd.**
bolyn *gw.* **polyn.**
bollt *e.g.b.* *ll.* **-au, byllt** bolt, dart; thunderbolt.

bolltau *gw.* **bollt.**
bolltio *be.* **(bolltiaf)** to bolt.
bom *e.g. ll.* **-iau** bomb.
bôn *e.g. ll.* **bonau, bonion** base, trunk, stump: **yn y bôn** basically, in reality; counterfoil.
boneddiges *e.b. ll.* **-au** lady.
boneddigion *gw.* **bonheddwr.**
bonheddig *a.* noble, gentle.
bonheddwr *e.g. ll.* **bonheddwyr, boneddigion** gentleman, nobleman: **Foneddigion a Boneddigesau** Ladies and Gentleman *(in addressing an audience).*
bonion *gw.* **bôn.**
bont *gw.* **pont.**
bontydd *gw.* **pont.**
bopeth *gw.* **popeth.**
bopty *gw.* **popty.**
bord *e.b. ll.* **-ydd, -au** table (*S.W.*), board (*S.W.*).
bordau: bordydd *gw.* **bord.**
bore *e.g. ll.* **-au** morning: **yn fore** early.
borfa *gw.* **porfa.**
borfeydd *gw.* **porfa.**
borffor *gw.* **porffor.**
bori *gw.* **pori.**
bortread *gw.* **portread.**
borth *gw.* **porth.**
borthladd *gw.* **porthladd.**
bos *e.g. ll.* **-ys** boss, chief: **Pwy ydy'r bos yma?** Who's the boss here?
bôs *gw.* **pôs.**
bosibilrwydd *gw.* **posibilrwydd.**
bosibl *gw.* **posibl.**
bost *gw.* **post.**
bostio *gw.* **postio.**
bostman: bostmon *gw.* **postman.**
bostmyn *gw.* **postman.**
bostyn *gw.* **postyn.**
bosys *gw.* **bos.**
botel *gw.* **potel.**
botwm *e.g. ll.* **botymau** button.
botymu *be.* **(botymaf)** to button.
bowdr: bowdwr *gw.* **powdr.**
bowdrau *gw.* **powdr.**
bowlen: powlen *e.b. ll.* **-ni, bowliau: powliau** bowl.
braf *a.* fine, nice, pleasant: **bore braf** a fine morning; **Mae hi'n braf** (*no mutation*), it is fine (*weather-wise*).
braich *e.b.g. ll.* **breichiau** arm.
braidd *ad.* near, almost, just, rather, scarcely: **o'r braidd** hardly; *gw.* **praidd.**
brain *gw.* **brân.**
braint *e.b. ll.* **breintiau, breiniau** privilege, right, honour, status.
bram *gw.* **pram.**
brân *e.b. ll.* **brain** crow.
bras *a.* thick, fat; greasy; coarse; rich; rough, approximate.
braslun *e.g. ll.* **-iau** outline, sketch.
braster *e.g. ll.* **-au** grossness, fat.
braw *e.g. ll.* **-iau** terror, fright; *gw.* **prawf.**
brawd *e.g. ll.* **brodyr** brother.
brawddeg *e.b. ll.* **-au** sentence.
brawf *gw.* **prawf.**
brawiau *gw.* **braw.**
brecwast *e.g. ll.* **-au** breakfast; **i frecwast** for breakfast.
brech *e.b. ll.* **-au** eruption, vaccination, pox: **brech goch** measles; **brech yr ieir** chickenpox.
brechdan *e.b. ll.* **-au** slice of buttered bread, sandwich.
brechiad *e.g. ll.* **-au** inoculation, vaccination.
bregeth *gw.* **pregeth.**
bregethu *gw.* **pregethu.**
bregethwr *gw.* **pregethwr.**
breichiau *gw.* **braich.**
breichled *e.b. ll.* **-au** bracelet, bangle.
breiddiau *gw.* **praidd.**
breifat *gw.* **preifat.**
breiniau: brientiau *gw.* **braint.**
bren *gw.* **pren.**
brenhines *e.b. ll.* **breninesau** queen.
brenhinoedd *gw.* **brenin.**
brenhinol *a.* royal.
brenin *e.g. ll.* **brenhinoedd** king.
brennau *gw.* **pren.**
brentis *gw.* **prentis.**
brentisiaeth *gw.* **prentisiaeth.**
bres *e.g. ll.* **-i, -ys** brace; *gw.* **pres.**
breseb *gw.* **preseb.**
bresennol *gw.* **presennol.**
bresenoldeb *gw.* **presenoldeb.**
bresgripsiwn *gw.* **presgripsiwn.**
brest *e.b. ll.* **-iau** breast; chest.
breswyl: breswylfod *gw.* **preswyl.**
breswylfeydd *gw.* **preswyl.**
bresychen *e.b. ll.* **bresych** cabbage.
brethyn *e.g. ll.* **-nau** cloth; **brethyn cartref** home-spun cloth.
breuddwyd *e.b.g. ll.* **-ion** dream.
breuddwydio *be.* **(breuddwydiaf)** to dream.
breuddwydion *gw.* **breuddwyd.**
bridwerth *gw* **pridwerth.**
bridd *gw.* **pridd.**

brif *gw.* **prif.**
brifardd *gw.* **prifardd.**
brifathrawes *gw.* **prifathrawes.**
brifathro *gw.* **prifathro.**
brifddinas *gw.* **prifddinas.**
brifeirdd *gw.* **prifardd.**
brifio *gw.* **prifio.**
brifo *be.* **(brifaf)** to hurt, to wound; to crumble (*N.W.*).
brifysgol *gw.* **prifysgol.**
briffordd *gw.* **priffordd.**
briffyrdd *gw.* **priffordd.**
brig *e.g. ll.* **-au** top, summit; outcrop; twig(s): **brig y don** crest of the wave; **brig y goeden** the tree top; **brig y nos** dusk; **brig y to** the roof-top; **o'r brig i'r bôn** from top to bottom; **glo brig** open-cast coal.
brigau *gw.* **brig, brigyn.**
brigyn *e.g. ll.* **brigau** twig.
brin *gw.* **prin.**
brinder *gw.* **prinder.**
brintio *gw.* **printio.**
briod *gw.* **priod.**
briodas *gw.* **priodas.**
briodi *gw.* **priodi.**
briodol *gw.* **priodol.**
bris *gw.* **pris.**
briwsionyn *e.g. ll.* **briwsion** crumb, fragment.
bro *e.b. ll.* **bröydd** region, country, vale, lowland: **bro a bryn** vale and hill; **Bro Morgannwg** Vale of Glamorgan.
broblem *gw.* **problem.**
brodor *e.g. ll.* **-ion** native.
brodorol *a.* native.
brodyr *gw.* **brawd.**
brofi *gw.* **profi.**
brofiad *gw.* **profiad.**
brofiadol *gw.* **profiadol.**
brofion *gw.* **profion.**
broffid *gw.* **proffid.**
broffidiol *gw.* **proffidiol.**
broffwyd *gw.* **proffwyd.**
broffwydo *gw.* **proffwydo.**
broga *e.g. ll.* **-od** frog *gw.* **ffroga.**
bron 1 *e.b. ll.* **-nau** breast. **2** *e.b. ll.* **-nydd** breast of hill. **3** *ad.* almost, nearly.
bronfraith *e.b. ll.* **bronfreithod** thrush.
bronnau: bronnydd *gw.* **bron.**
Brotestant *gw.* **Protestant.**
brown *a.* brown.
bröydd *gw.* **bro.**
brudd *gw.* **prudd.**
brwdfrydig *a.* enthusiastic.
brwnt *a.* dirty *(S.W.)*, foul, cruel *(N.W.)*.
brws: brwsh *e.g. ll.* **brwsys: brwshys** brush, broom.
brwsio: brwshio *be.* **(brwsiaf: brwshiaf)** to sweep, to brush.
brwsys: brwshys *gw.* **brws.**
brwydr *e.b. ll.* **-au** battle, conflict.
brwydrau *gw.* **brwydr.**
bryd *e.g. ll.* **-iau** mind, thought, intent; *gw.* **pryd.**
Brydain *gw.* **Prydain.**
brydau *gw.* **pryd.**
Brydeinig *gw.* **Prydeinig.**
bryder *gw.* **pryder.**
bryderu *gw.* **pryderu.**
bryderus *gw.* **pryderus.**
brydferth *gw.* **prydferth.**
brydferthwch *gw.* **prydferthwch.**
brydiau *gw.* **bryd, pryd.**
brydlon *gw.* **prydlon.**
bryf: bryfedyn: bryfyn *gw.* **pryf.**
bryfed *gw.* **pryf.**
bryfocio *gw.* **profocio.**
bryfyn *gw.* **pryf.**
bryn *e.g. ll.* **-iau** hill.
brynhawn *gw.* **prynhawn.**
bryniau *gw.* **bryn.**
brynu *gw.* **prynu.**
brynwr *gw.* **prynwr.**
brys *e.g.* haste, hurry: **ar frys** in haste, hurriedly; **ar frys gwyllt** in a mad rush.
brysio *be.* **(brysiaf)** to hasten, to hurry.
brysurdeb *gw.* **prysurdeb.**
brysuro *gw.* **prysuro.**
brysur *gw.* **prysur.**
buan *a* swift, quick, fast; soon; *gw. At. Ansoddeiriau.*
buarth *e.g. ll.* **-au** farmyard, yard.
buchod *gw.* **buwch.**
budr *a.* dirty (*N.W.*), nasty (*N.W.*), foul (*N.W.*), vile (*N.W.*): **bachgen budr** a bit of a lad (*S.W.*).
buddugol *a.* victorious, winning.
buddugoliaeth *e.b. ll.* **-au** victory.
bues i *bf.* I was, I have been; *gw.* **bod.**
bugail *e.g. ll.* **bugeiliaid** shepherd; pastor.
bugeiliaid *gw.* **bugail.**
bugeilio *be.* **(bugeiliaf)** to shepherd, to watch.
bulpud *gw.* **pulpud.**
bum: bump *gw.* **pump.**
bûm: bues *bf.* I was, I have been; *gw.* **bod.**
b'un *gw.* **p'un.**
bunnau: bunnoedd *gw.* **punt.**
bunt *gw.* **punt.**

bupur *gw.* **pupur.**
bur *gw.* **pur.**
burfa *gw.* **purfa.**
buro *gw.* **puro.**
busnes *e.g.b.* *ll.* **-ion, -au** business, affairs.
buwch *e.b.* *ll.* **buchod, da** cow (*S.W.*).
bwced *e.g.b.* *ll.* **-i** bucket.
bwdin *gw.* **pwdin.**
bwdr *gw.* **pwdr.**
bwdryn *gw.* **pwdryn.**
bwdu *gw.* **pwdu.**
bwlch *e.g.* *ll.* **bylchau** gap, pass.
bŵer *gw.* **pŵer.**
bwll *gw.* **pwll.**
bwmp *gw.* **pwmp.**
bwnc *gw.* **pwnc.**
bwrdd *e.g.* *ll.* **byrddau** table (*N.W.*); board, plank; deck: **bwrdd brecwast** breakfast table; **bwrdd du** blackboard.
bwriad *e.g.* *ll.* **-au** purpose, intention, resolution.
bwriadu *be.* **(bwriadaf)** to intend.
bwrpas *gw.* **pwrpas.**
bwrs *gw.* **pwrs.**
bwrw *be.* **(bwriaf)** to cast; to shed; to strike: **bwrw glaw** to rain.
bws *e.g.* *ll.* **bysiau, bysys** bus.
bwthyn *e.g.* *ll.* **bythynnod** cottage, cabin.
bwy *gw.* **pwy.**
bwyd *e.g.* *ll.* **-ydd** food.
bwyda *gw.* **bwydo.**
bwydlen *e.b.* *ll.* **-ni** menu.
bwydo: bwyda *be.* **(bwydaf)** to feed, to nourish: **bwydo'r adar** to feed the birds.
bwydydd *gw.* **bwyd.**
bwyll *gw.* **pwyll.**
bwyllgor *gw.* **pwyllgor.**
bwyllo *gw.* **pwyllo.**
bwynt *gw.* **pwynt.**
bwys *gw.* **pwys.**
bwysedd *gw.* **pwysedd.**
bwysig *gw.* **pwysig.**
bwysigrwydd *gw.* **pwysigrwydd.**
bwyslais *gw.* **pwyslais.**
bwyso *gw.* **pwyso.**
bwyta: byta *(S.W.) be.* **(bwytâf)** to eat; to consume, to ravage; to corrode (*S.W.*): **Bwytâf ginio bob dydd** I eat dinner every day; *gw. At. Berfau.*
bwyth *gw.* **pwyth.**
bychan *a. g.* little, small, petty; *gw.* **bechan.**
byd *e.g.* *ll.* **-oedd** world; life; state: **byd caled** a hard struggle; **byd da** good living, a sumptuous life; **byd o wahaniaeth** a world of difference; **gwyn ei fyd** blessed is he, how fortunate!; **beth yn y byd . . .?** what in the world . . .? what on earth . . .?
bydoedd *gw.* **byd.**
bydru *gw.* **pydru.**
bydd (e /hi), *bf.* he/she/it will be: **Bydd Mair yno** Mair will be there; **Bydd plant yno hefyd** Children will be there also; *gw.* **bod.**
byddar 1 *e.g.* *ll.* **-iaid** deaf person. 2 *a.* deaf.
byddin *e.b.* *ll.* **-oedd** army, host.
byddinoedd *gw.* **byddin.**
bylchau *gw.* **bwlch.**
byllau *gw.* **pwll, pyllyn.**
byllt *gw.* **bollt.**
byllyn *gw.* **pyllyn.**
bymtheg: bymtheng *gw.* **pymtheg.**
bymthegfed *gw.* **pymthegfed.**
bynciau *gw.* **pwnc.**
bynnag *rhag.* -ever, -soever: **beth bynnag** whatsoever; **ble bynnag** wherever; **pryd bynnag** whenever; **pwy bynnag** whoever.
byped *gw.* **pyped.**
byr *a.g.* *ll.* **-ion** short, brief: **dyn byr** a short man; **stori fer** a short story; **straeon byrion** short stories; *gw.* **ber.**
byrbryd *e.g.* *ll.* **-iau** snack.
byrddaid *e.g.* *ll.* **byrddeidiau** tableful.
byrddau *gw.* **bwrdd.**
byrfodd *e.g.* *ll.* **-au** abbreviation.
byrsau *gw.* **pwrs.**
byrth *gw.* **porth.**
bys *e.g.* *ll.* **-edd** finger: **bys bawd** thumb, big toe; **bysedd y blaidd** lupins; **bysedd y cŵn** foxgloves; *gw.* **pysen.**
bysedd *gw.* **bys.**
bysen *gw.* **pysen.**
bysgod *gw.* **pysgodyn.**
bysgodyn *gw.* **pysgodyn.**
bysgota *gw.* **pysgota.**
bysgotwr *gw.* **pysgotwr.**
bysiau *gw.* **bws.**
byst *gw.* **post, postyn.**
bysys *gw.* **bws.**
byta *(S.W.) gw.* **bwyta.**
byth 1 *ad.* ever, still, always; **am byth** for ever; **byth a hefyd** continually; 2 **(byth** *is frequently used in negative sentences*

in the present, future, imperfect and conditional tense to convey the meaning never). **Ddaw e byth** He will never come; **Doedd hi byth yn hwyr** She was never late; 3 *e.g. ll.* **-oedd** eternity: **byth bythoedd** for ever and ever, world without end.
bythefnos *gw.* **pythefnos.**
bythynnod *gw.* **bwythyn.**
byw 1 *be.* **(bywiaf)** to live, to exist, to dwell, to inhabit; to animate, to revive, to restore to life: **byw a bod** to be habitually present; **Mae e'n byw yma** He lives here, 2 *a.* alive, living: **Ydy e'n fyw?** Is he alive?; 3 *e.g.* life; **yn fy myw** for the life of me.
bywiog *a.* lively, vivacious.
bywyd *e.g. ll.* **-au** life, existence.
bywydeg *e.b.* biology.

caban *e.g.* *ll.* **-au** booth, cabin, hut.
cacen *e.b.* *ll.***-nau, -ni** cake *(N.W.).*
cacwn *gw.* **cacynen.**
cacynen *e.b.* *ll.***cacwn** wasp *(N.W.)*: **yn gacwn gwyllt** furious.
cadach *e.g.* *ll.* **-au** cloth, rag; handkerchief, bandage *(N.W.)*: **cadach llawr** cloth for wiping floor; **cadach llestri** dish-cloth.
cadair *e.b.* *ll.* **cadeiriau** chair: **cadair esmwyth** easy chair; **cadair freichiau** arm chair.
cadeirio *be.* **(cadeiriaf)** to chair.
cadeiriol *a.* chaired: **eglwys gadeiriol** cathedral.
cadeirydd *e.g.* *ll.* **-ion** chairman.
cadno *e.g.* *ll.* **cadnoaid, cadnawon** fox; **cadnawes: cadnöes** vixen *(S.W.).*
cadw *(rhag.) be.* **(cadwaf)** to keep, to preserve (from): **cadw ar gof** to keep on record; **cadw draw** to stay away; **cadw sŵn** to make a noise, to complain; **cadw-mi-gei** money box; **cyfrif cadw** deposit account.
cadwyn *e.b.* *ll.* **-au, -i** chain; series.
cadwyno *be.* **(cadwynaf)** to chain, to enslave.
cae *e.g.* *ll.* **-au** field.
caeau *gw.* **cae.**
cael *be.* **(caf)** to have, to find; **ar gael** in existence, available; **cael annwyd** to catch cold; **cael blas ar** to enjoy; **cael a chael** a close call; *gw. At. Berfau*
caer *e.b.* *ll.* **-au, ceyrydd** fort, castle.
Caer *e.b.* Chester.
Caerdydd *e.b.* Cardiff.
Caeredin *e.b.* Edinburgh.
Caerfyrddin *e.b.* Carmarthen.
Caergybi *e.b.* Holyhead.
Caerloyw *e.b.* Gloucester.
Caersalem: Jerwsalem *e.b.* Jerusalem.
caets *e.g.* *ll.* **-ys** cage.
caf *bf.* I have, I shall have; *gw.* **cael.**
cafodd *bf.* he/she/it had; *gw.* **cael.**
caffe *e.g.* *ll.* **-s** café.
cangen *e.b.* *ll.* **canghennau** branch.
canghennau *gw.* **cangen.**
caiff *bf.* he/she/it will have; *gw.* **cael.**
cais *e.g.* *ll.* **ceisiadau, ceisiau** attempt; try *(rugby)*; request; application; **gwneud cais** to make an application, to apply.
calan *e.g.* *ll.* **-nau, -ni** first day *(of month or season)*: **Dydd Calan** New Year's Day; **Calan Gaeaf** All Saint's Day; **Calan Mai** May Day.
caled *a.* hard, hardy, difficult; *gw. At. Ansoddeiriau.*
caledi *e.g.* hardship, severity.
caledu *be.* **(caledaf)** to harden; to dry; **caledu dillad** to air clothes; **caledu gwely** to air a bed.
caledwch *e.g.* hardness; difficulty.
calendr *e.g.* *ll.* **-au** calendar.
calenigion *gw.* **calennig.**
calennig *e.g.* *ll.* **calenigion** New Year's Gift.
caletach *gw.* **caled.**
caletaf *gw.* **caled.**
caleted *gw.* **caled.**
calon *e.b.* *ll.* **-nau** heart: **diolch o galon** heartfelt thanks; **calon lân** pure heart; **calon y gwir** the absolute truth.
call *a.* wise, sensible; **hanner call a chrac** foolish, stupid; *gw. At. Ansoddeiriau.*
callach *gw.* **call.**
callaf *gw.* **call.**
called *gw.* **call.**
cam 1 *e.g.* *ll.* **-au** stride, step; injury: **o gam i gam** step by step. **2** *a.* crooked, false; **coesgam** bandy-legged.
camarwain *be.* **(camarweiniaf)** to mislead.
camddeall *be.* **(camddeallaf)** to misunderstand.
camera *e.g.* *ll.* **camerâu** camera.
camp *e.b.* *ll.* **-au** feat, game; excellence; **campau** sports.
campfa *e.b.* *ll.* **campfeydd** gymnasium.
campfeydd *gw.* **campfa.**
campus *a.* excellent, splendid.
campwaith *e.g.* *ll.*

campweithiau masterpiece.
campweithiau *gw.* **campwaith.**
camsyniad *e.g. ll.* **-au** mistake *(S.W.).*
camu *be* **(camaf)** to step, to stride; to bend, to stoop.
cân *e.b. ll.* **caniadau, caneuon** song, poem; **cân actol** action song; **cân bop** pop song; **cân serch** love song; **cân werin** folk song; **cân ysgafn** ballad
can 1 *a.* white; hundred; **canpunt** a hundred pounds (sterling); **canmlwydd** a hundred years old; **canmil** a hundred thousand; **canrif** a century; *gw.* **cant.** 2 *e.g.* white flour, flour; **bara can** white bread. 3 *e.g. ll.* **-iau** *(tin)* can.
caneuon *gw.* **cân.**
canfed *a.* hundredth.
canhwyllau *gw.***cannwyll.**
canhwyllbren *e.g. ll.* **-nau, -ni** candlestick.
caniad *e.g. ll.* **-au** song, singing; ring *(telephone)*: **Rhowch ganiad i fi** Telephone me.
caniadaeth *e.b.* music, singing; **Caniadaeth y Cysegr** Songs of Praise.
caniadau *gw.* **cân, caniad.**
caniatâd *e.g.* permission, consent.
caniatáu *be.* **(caniatâf)** to allow.
caniedydd *e.g. ll.* **-ion** song-book, hymn-book.
canmlwydd *e.ll.* ac *e.b. ll.***-i** a hundred years old, hundred years; century.
canmlwyddiannau *gw.* **canmlwyddiant.**
canmlwyddiant *e.g.* **canmlwyddiannau** centenary.
canmol 1 *be.* **(canmolaf)** to praise. 2 *e.g.* praise.
canmoliaeth *e.b. ll.* **-au** praise.
cannoedd *gw.* **cant.**
cannwyll *e.b. ll.* **canhwyllau** candle: **cannwyll y llygad** pupil of the eye; apple of the eye.
canol 1 *e.g. ll.* **-au** centre, middle; **canol dydd** midday; **canol nos** midnight. 2 *a.* middle.
canolbarth *e.g. ll.* **-au** midland; **Canolbarth Cymru** Mid Wales; **Canolbarth Lloegr** The Midlands; **Canolbarth Ffrainc** Central France.
canolbwyntio (ar) *be.* **(canolbwyntiaf)** to concentrate, to focus (on).
canoldir *e.g. ll.* **-oedd** inland region; **Y Môr Canoldir** Mediterranean Sea.
canolfan *e.b. ll.* **-nau** centre; **canolfan ddinesig** civic centre; **canolfan hamdden** leisure centre.
canolwr *e.g. ll.* **-wyr** referee, umpire.
canradd *a.* centigrade.
canran *e.b. ll.* **-nau** percentage.
canrif *e.b. ll.* **-au, -oedd** century.
canrifau: canrifoedd *gw.* **canrif.**
cant: can *e.g. ll.* **cannoedd** hundred: **cant a mil** a hundred and one, a large number; **cant y cant** hundred per cent; **deg y cant** ten per cent; **can diolch** many thanks; **canwaith** a hundred times.
cantor *e.g. ll.* **-ion** precentor; *gw.* **cantores; canwr.**
cantores *e.b. ll.* **-au** female singer, female vocalist; *gw.* **cantor; canwr.**
canu *be.* **(canaf)** to sing, to play: **canu cloch** to ring a bell; **canu'n iach** to bid goodbye; **canu'r piano** to play the piano; **wedi canu ar** too late, all up; *gw. At. Berfau.*
canŵ *e.g. ll.* **-od** canoe.
canŵio *be.* **(canŵiaf)** to canoe.
canwr *e.g. ll.* **canwyr** male singer, vocalist; *gw.* **cantor; cantores.**
canwriad *e.g. ll.* **canwriaid** centurion.
cap *e.g. ll.* **-iau** cap.
capel *e.g. ll.* **-i, -au** chapel.
capteiniaid *gw.* **capten.**
capten *e.g. ll.* **-iaid, capteiniaid** captain.
capteniaid *gw.* **capten.**
car *e.g. ll.* **ceir** car: **car heddlu** police car; **car rasio** racing car; **car llusg** sled.
carafán *e.b. ll.* **-au** caravan.
carafana *be.* **(carafanaf)** to go caravanning.
carco *be.* **(carcaf)** to take care of *(S.W.).*
carcus *a.* careful *(S.W.).*
carchar *e.g. ll.* **-au** prison.
carcharor *e.g. ll.* **-ion** prisoner.
carcharu *be.* **(carcharaf)** to imprison.
cardiau *gw.* **cerdyn.**
caredig *a.* kind.
caredigrwydd *e.g.* kindness.
cariad *e.g.b. ll.* **-on** love, lover; **Dere 'ma, cariad!** Come here, love!
cariadon *gw.* **cariad.**
cariadus *a.* beloved; loving.
cario *be.* **(cariaf)** to carry.
carol *e.b. ll.* **-au** carol: **carol Nadolig** Christmas carol.

carped *e.g.* ll. **-i** carpet.
carreg *e.b. ll.* **cerrig** stone: **carreg aelwyd** hearthstone; **carreg fedd** tombstone; **carreg filltir** milestone; **carreg y drws** doorstep; **cerrig mân** pebbles, chippings.
cartref *e.g. ll.* **-i** home; **gartref** at home; **adref** homewards.
cartrefi *gw.* **cartref.**
cartrefu *be.* **(cartrefaf)** to dwell.
caru *be.* **(caraf)** to love, to like, to court.
cas 1 *e.g.* enmity, hated person or thing; case. 2 *a.* nasty.
casáu *be.* **(casâf)** to detest.
casgen *e.b. ll.* **-ni** barrel.
casgenni *gw.* **casgen.**
casgliad *e.g. ll.* **-au** collection; gathering; conclusion: **Fe ddaeth i'r casgliad** He came to the conclusion.
casglu *be.* **(casglaf)** to collect, to infer; **casglu dros** to collect on behalf of.
Cas-gwent *e.b.* Chepstow.
Casllwchwr *e.b.* Loughor.
Casnewydd *e.b.* Newport *(Gwent).*
castell *e.g. ll.* **cestyll** castle.
Castell-nedd *e.b.* Neath.
cath *e.b. ll.* **-od** cat; **cath fach** kitten; **cwrcath, cwrcyn** tomcat.
cau 1*be.* **(caeaf)** to close. 2 *a.* enclosed; hollow.
cawl 1 *e.g.* soup, broth: **cawl cennin** leek broth; **cawl pys** pea soup. 2 *e.g.* mess; **Fe wnaeth e gawl o'r trefniadau** He made a mess of the arrangements.
cawod *e.b. ll.* **-ydd** shower; **cawodydd Ebrill** April showers.
cawr *e.g. ll.* **cewri** giant; **cawr o wleidydd** a great politician.
caws *e.g.* cheese: **caws Caer** Cheshire cheese; **caws Caerffili** Caerffili cheese; **cael caws o fola ci** to get blood out of a stone; *gw.* **cosyn.**
cefn *e.g. ll.* **-au** back; ridge; support: **cefn gwlad** heart of the countryside; **Roedd e'n gefn i'r teulu** He was a great help to the family.
cefnder *e.g. ll.* **-wyr, cefndyr** cousin *(male); gw.* **cyfnither.**
cefnderwyr *gw.* **cefnder.**
cefndir *e.g. ll.* **-oedd** background.
cefndiroedd *gw.* **cefndir.**
cefndyr *gw.* **cefnder.**
cefnu (ar) *be.* **(cefnaf)** to turn one's back upon, to forsake.
cefnwr *e.g. ll.* **cefnwyr** back, full-back.
ceffyl *e.g. ll.* **-au** horse: **ceffyl blaen** leading horse, pushy person; **ceffyl brith** piebald horse; **ceffyl gwinau** bay (horse); **ceffyl siglo** rocking horse; **ar gefn ei geffyl** on his high horse, exultant.
ceg *e.b. ll.* **-au** mouth; (cael, rhoi) **llond ceg** *(to receive, to give)* a telling off.
cegin *e.b. ll.* **-au** kitchen; **cegin fach** kitchenette; **cegin gefn** back kitchen.
cei *e.g. ll.* **ceiau** quay; *gw.* **cael.**
ceidwad *e.g. ll.* **ceidwaid** keeper.
ceiliog *e.g. ll.* **-od** cockerel; **ceiliog y gwynt** weathercock; **ceiliog y rhedyn** grasshopper.
Ceinewydd *e.b.* Newquay.
ceiniog *e.b. ll.* **-au** penny: **heb geiniog goch** without a brass farthing or penny.
ceir *gw.* **car.**
ceisiadau: ceisiau *gw.* **cais.**
ceisio *be.* **(ceisiaf)** to seek, to ask; **ceisio am** to try for, to apply for.
celf *e.b. ll.* **-au** art, craft; **Adran Celf** Art Department.
celfi *gw.* **celficyn.**
celficyn *e.g. ll.* **celfi** a piece of furniture; a tool.
celwydd *e.g. ll.* **-au** lie, untruth: **celwydd golau** white lie; **celwydd noeth** barefaced lie; **celwyddgi** a liar.
celwyddog *a.* untruthful.
celyn *gw.* **celynnen.**
celynnen *e.b. ll.* **celyn** holly; **llwyn celyn** holly bush.
cell *e.b. ll.* **-oedd, -au** cell.
cellau: celloedd *gw.* **cell.**
cemeg *e.b.* chemistry.
cenadaethau *gw.* **cenhadaeth**
cenedl *e.b. ll.* **cenhedloedd** nation; species, kind; gender *(grammar):* **Cenedl y Cymry** the Welsh nation; **Y Cenhedloedd** the Gentiles; **y Cenhedloedd Unedig** the United Nations; **cenedl enwau** gender of nouns.
cenedlaethau *gw.* **cenhedlaeth.**
cenedlaethol *a.* national: **Llyfrgell Genedlaethol Cymru** National Library of Wales.
cenedlaetholdeb *e.b.* nationalism.
cenedlaetholwr *e.g. ll.* **cenedlaetholwyr** a nationalist.
cenedlaetholwyr *gw.*

cenedlaetholwr.
cenedligrwydd *e.g.* nationality.
cenfigennus *a.* jealous
cenhadaeth *e.b.* *ll.* **cenadaethau** mission; embassy.
cenhadol *a.* missionary.
cenhadon *gw.* **cenhadwr.**
cenhadu *be.* **(cenhadaf)** to conduct a mission; to allow.
cenhadwr *e.g.* *ll.* **cenhadon** a missionary; **cenhades** a female missionary.
cenhedlaeth *e.b.* *ll.* **cenedlaethau** generation; nation.
cenhedloedd *gw.* **cenedl.**
cenhinen *e.b.* *ll.* **cennin** leek; **cenhinen Bedr** daffodil.
cennin *gw.* **cenhinen.**
cer *bf.* go! *(singular); gw.* **mynd.**
cerdyn *e.g.* *ll.* **cardiau** card: **cerdyn Nadolig** Christmas card; **cerdyn pen-blwydd** birthday card.
cerdd *e.b.* *ll.* **-au, -i** song, poem; music; **cerdd dafod** poetic art, poetry; music; **cerdd dant** instrumental music; penillion singing.
cerdded *be.* **(cerddaf)** to walk.
cerddi *gw.* **cerdd.**
cerddor *e.g.* *ll.* **-ion** musician.
cerddorfa *e.b.* *ll.* **cerddorfeydd** orchestra; **Cerddorfa Ieuenctid** Youth Orchestra.
cerddorfeydd *gw.* **cerddorfa.**
cerddoriaeth *e.b.* music.
cerddorol *a.* musical.
cerddwr *e.g.* *ll.* **cerddwyr** walker: **Cymdeithas Cerddwyr Dyfed** Dyfed Ramblers Association.
cerddwyr *gw.* **cerddwr.**
cerflun *e.g.* *ll.* **-iau** statue.
cerrig *gw.* **carreg.**
cerwch *bf.* go! *(plural); gw.* **mynd.**
ces *bf.* I had; *gw.* **cael.**
cesair *e. torf.* hailstones *(S.W.).*
cestyll *gw.* **castell.**
ceubren *e.g.* *ll.* **-nau** hollow tree.
cewri *gw.* **cawr.**
cewyn *e.g.* *ll.* **-nau, -ion** napkin *(S.W.).*
ceyrydd *gw.* **caer.**
ci *e.g.* *ll.* **cŵn** dog; **ci bach** pup, **ci defaid** sheepdog; **ci hela** hound; **corgi** corgi; **milgi** greyhound.
cig *e.g.* *ll.* **-oedd** meat; gum: **cig eidion** beef; **cig oen** lamb; **cig moch** bacon.
cigydd *e.g.* *ll.* **-ion** butcher.
cigyddion *gw.* **cigydd.**
cilio (i) *(rhag.) be.* **(ciliaf)** to flee; to retreat (to, from): **cilio i** to flee towards; **cilio rhag** to flee from, to retreat from.
ciniawau *gw.* **cinio.**
cinio *e.g.b.* *ll.* **ciniawau** dinner.
cipolwg *e.g.* *ll.* **cipolygon** glance.
cist *e.b.* *ll.* **-iau** chest, coffer.
claf 1 *eg.* *ll.* **cleifion** sick person. **2** *a.* ill.
clai *e.g.* *ll.* **cleiau, cleion** clay; **traed o glai** mortal.
clasur *e.g.* *ll.* **-on** a classic.
clasurol *a.* classical.
clawdd *e.g.* *ll.* **cloddiau** wall made of earth, ditch: **Clawdd Offa** Offa's Dyke.
clawr *e.g.* *ll.* **cloriau** cover, lid; **ar glawr** on record.
clebran *be.* **(clebraf)** to chatter.
cledr *e.b.* *ll.* **-au** pole, rafter; rail; palm *(of hand);* **cledrau** rails *(of railway).*
clefyd *e.g.* *ll.* **-au, -on** sickness: **clefyd melyn** jaundice; **clefyd melys/siwgr** diabetes.
cleifion *gw.* **claf.**
clêr *gw.* **cleren.**
clerc *e.g.* *ll.* **-od** clerk.
cleren *e.b.* *ll.* **clêr** fly *(S.W.)*: **cleren lwyd** horse-fly.
clir *a.* clear.
clirio *be.* **(cliriaf)** to clear.
clo *e.g.* *ll.* **-eau, -eon** lock: **ar glo** locked; **dan glo** locked, locked up, under lock and key; **yng nghlo** locked; **twll y clo** keyhole.
cloc *e.g.* *ll.* **-iau** clock: **cloc larwm** alarm-clock.
cloch *be.* *ll.* **clychau** bell; **cloch y llan** church-bell; **clychau'r gog** bluebells; **dau o'r gloch** two o'clock.
clod *e.g.b.* *ll.* **-ydd** praise.
clodfori *be.* **(clodforaf)** to praise.
cloddiau *gw.* **clawdd.**
cloeau *gw.* **clo.**
cloeon *gw.* **clo.**
cloff *a.* lame.
cloffi 1 *be.* **(cloffaf)** to become lame; **cloffi rhwng dau feddwl** to hesitate. **2** *eg.* lameness.
clogwyn *e.g.* *ll.* **-au, -i** cliff, crag.
clogwyni: clogwynau *gw.* **clogwyn.**
clogyn *e.g.* *ll.* **-au** cloak.
cloi *be.* **(cloaf, clof)** to lock; to conclude: **cloi allan** to lock out, to exclude; **cload allan** lock-out; **Nawr i gloi** Now to conclude.

clorian *e.b. ll.* **-nau** scales.
cloriau *gw.* **clawr.**
clown *e.g. ll.* **-iaid** clown.
clun *e.b. ll.* **-iau** hip; thigh; leg.
clust *e.b. ll.* **-iau** ear; **bonclust** box on the ear.
clustog *e.b. ll.* **-au** pillow, cushion.
clwm *e.g. ll.* **clymau** knot; tie; *gw.* **cwlwm.**
clwtyn *e.g. ll.* **clytiau** rag *(S.W.)*: **clwtyn llawr** floor cloth; **clwtyn llestri** dish cloth; **clwtyn ymolch** face cloth; **ar y clwt** stranded, abandoned; without work.
Clwyd *e.b.* County in N.E. Wales.
clwyd *e.b. ll.* **-i, -au** gate.
clwydi: clwydau *gw.* **clwyd.**
clwyf *e.g. ll.* **-au** wound, injury: **clwyf y traed a'r genau** foot and mouth disease.
clychau *gw.* **cloch.**
clymau *gw.* **clwm, cwlwm.**
clymu *be.* **(clymaf)** to tie.
clytiau *gw.* **clwtyn.**
clyw 1 *e.g.* hearing, earshot: **trwm ei glyw** hard of hearing; **yn fy nghlyw** within my hearing. 2 *bf.* hear! *(singular),* listen! *(singular); gw.* **clywed.**
clywed (am, oddi wrth) *be.* **(clywaf)** to hear (of, from); to feel; to taste; to smell; **Clywch, clywch!** Hear, hear!
cnau *gw.* **cneuen.**
cneuen *e.b. ll.* **cnau** nut.
cnoc *e.g.b. ll.* **-au** a knock; a fool *(S.W.)*: **tipyn o gnoc:** quite a fool; **cnocell y coed** woodpecker.
cnocio: cnoco *be.* **(cnociaf: cnocaf)** to knock, to strike.
cnoi *be.* **(cnoaf)** to bite, to chew; **cnoi cil** to chew the cud; to mull over.
coban *e.b. ll.* **cobannau** night-shirt.
cobannau *gw.* **coban.**
coch *a. ll.* **-ion** red: **yn goch** obscene; of poor quality; **coch y berllan** bullfinch; *gw. At. Ansoddeiriau.*
cochach *gw.* **coch.**
cochaf *gw.* **coch.**
coched *gw.* **coch.**
cochen *e.b.* red-haired female.
cochyn *e.b.* red-haired male.
codi *be.* **(codaf)** to rise, to erect, to pick up; to withdraw *(money)*, to charge (fee).
coed *gw.* **coeden.**
Coed-duon Blackwood.
coeden *e.b. ll.* **coed** tree.
coedwig *e.b. ll.* **-oedd** forest, wood.
coes *e.b. ll.* **-au** leg: **tynnu coes** to leg pull.
cof *e.g. ll.* **-ion** memory; remembrance: **er cof am** in memory of; **o fewn cof** within living memory; **o'i gof** angry; mad; **ar gof a chadw** recorded and preserved, on record; **cofion cynnes** warmest regards.
cofio (am) *be.* **(cofiaf)** to remember.
cofion *gw.* **cof.**
cofleidio *be.* **(cofleidiaf)** to embrace.
cofrestr *e.b. ll.* **-au, -i** register.
cofrestru *b.e.* **(cofrestraf)** to register.
coffi *e.g.* coffee; **noson goffi** coffee evening.
cog 1 *e.b. ll.* **-au** cuckoo; *gw.* **cwcw.** 2 *e.g. ll.* **-au** cook.
coginio *be.* **(coginiaf)** to cook.
cogydd *e.g. ll.* **-ion** cook.
coleg *e.g. ll.* **-au** college.
coler *e.g.b. ll.* **-au, -i** collar.
colofn *e.b. ll.* **-au** column, pillar.
coluro *be.* **(coluraf)** to colour, to make up.
colled *e.g.b. ll.* **-ion** loss: **Roedd colled arni** She was angry.
collen *e.b. ll.* **cyll** hazel; **cnau cyll** hazelnuts.
colli *be.* **(collaf)** to lose, to spill, to fail, to miss; **ar goll** lost, missing, mislaid.
copïo *be.* **(copïaf)** to copy.
copyn *e.g. ll.* **-nau, -nod** spider; **pryf copyn** spider.
côr *e.g. ll.* **corau** choir: **côr cymysg** mixed choir; **côr merched** ladies' choir.
corau *gw. côr.*
cordyn *e.g. ll.* **-ion** cord, string.
corff *e.g. ll.* **cyrff** body; corpse; capital: **Yr Hen Gorff** Calvanistic Methodists.
corfforol *a.* bodily, physical; **Addysg Gorfforol** physical education.
corgi *e.g. ll.* **corgwn** corgi.
corn *e.g. ll.* **cyrn** horn; corn; cairn; chimney: **corn simdde** chimney stack; **Siôn Corn** Father Christmas.
cornel *e.b.g. ll.* **-au, -i** corner.
coron *e.b. ll.* **-au** crown.
coroni *be.* **(coronaf)** to crown; **i goroni'r cwbl** to cap it all.
corryn *e.g. ll.* **corynnod** spider *(S.W.)*.
corynnod *gw.* **corryn.**
cosb *e.b. ll.* **-au** punishment,

penalty: **y gosb eithaf** capital punishment; **cic gosb** penalty kick.
cosbi *be.* **(cosbaf)** to punish.
cosi 1 *be.* **(cosaf)** to itch. 2 *e.g.* itch.
costus *a.* expensive.
cosyn *e.g.* *ll.* **-nau** a small cheese; *gw.* **caws.**
cot: côt *e.b.* *ll.* **cotau: cotiau** coat: **cot fawr** overcoat; **cot law** raincoat.
cotau: cotiau *gw.* **cot.**
cotwm *e.g.* *ll.* **cotymau** cotton.
crac 1 *e.g.* *ll.* **-au, -iau** crack. 2 *a.* angry *(S.W.).*
crachach *e.ll.* snobs *(S.W.).*
crafu 1 *be.* **(crafaf)** to scratch; to scrape. 2 *e.g.* itch.
crafiad *e.g.* *ll.* **-au** scratch.
cragen *e.b.* *ll.* **cregyn** shell.
craig *e.b.* *ll.* **creigiau** rock, cliff: **Mae e'n graig o arian.** He's very wealthy.
cras *a.* *ll.* **creision** baked; scorched; harsh: **llai cras** not so highly baked; **tafod cras** a harsh tongue; **llais cras** a raucous voice; *gw.* **creisionyn.**
crasu *be.* **(crasaf)** to bake; to scorch.
credu (yn) *be.* **(credaf)** to believe, to trust (in).
crefydd *e.b.* *ll.* **-au** religion.
crefft *e.b.* *ll.* **-au** skill, craft.
crefftwr *e.g.* *ll.* **crefftwyr** craftsman.
crefftwyr *gw.* **crefftwr.**
cregyn *gw.* **cragen.**
creigiau *gw.* **craig.**
creigiog *a.* rocky.
creision *gw.* **cras, creisionyn.**
creisionyn *e.g.* *ll.* **creision** crisp, flake: **creision ŷd** corn flakes.
crempog *e.b.* *ll.* **-au** pancake *(N.W.).* *gw.* **ffroesen.**
creulon *a.* cruel.
creulondeb *e.g.* *ll.* **-au** cruelty.
cri *e.g.b.* *ll.* **-au** cry, lament.
crib *e.b.* *ll.* **-au** comb; bird's comb; crest, summit, ridge: **crib y ceiliog** the cock's comb; **crib y mynydd** the mountain's ridge; **mynd â chrib fân** to examine minutely.
cribo *be.* **(cribaf)** to comb; to card.
criced *e.g.* cricket (game).
cricedwr *e.g.* *ll.* **cricedwyr** cricketer.
cricsyn *e.g.* *ll.* **criciaid, crics** a cricket *(insect).*
crio (am, ar) *be.* **(criaf)** to shout, to weep *(N.W.).*
Cristion *e.g.* *ll.* **Cristnogion** Christian.
criw *e.g.* *ll.* **-iau** crew, crowd; **criw o bobl ifainc** a gang of young people.
croen *e.g.* *ll.* **crwyn** skin, hide; peel: **croendenau** thin-skinned; sensitive; **croendew** thick-skinned; insensitive; **croenddu** black-skinned; negroid; **croen ei din ar ei dalcen** in a bad mood.
croes *e.b.* *ll.***-au** cross: **croes Crist** Christ's cross.
croesair *e.g.* *ll.* **croeseiriau** crossword; **pôs croeseiriau** crossword puzzle.
croesau *gw.* **croes.**
croesawu *be.* **(croesawaf)** to welcome.
croesawus *a.* hospitable.
croeseiriau *gw.* **croesair.**
croesfan *e.g.* *ll.* **-nau** crossing.
croesffordd *e.b.* *ll.* **croesffyrdd** cross-road.
croeshoelio *be.* **(croeshoeliaf)** to crucify.
croesholi *be.* **(croesholaf)** to cross-examine; **croesholiad** a cross-examination.
croesi *be.* **(croesaf)** to cross, to oppose.
croeso *e.g.* welcome: **y Bwrdd Croeso** the Welsh Tourist Board.
Croesoswallt *e.b.* Oswestry.
cronfa *e.b.* *ll.* **cronfeydd** reservoir; fund.
cronfeydd *gw.* **cronfa.**
crud *e.g.* *ll.* **-au, -iau** cradle.
crwst *e.g.* *ll.* **crystiau** crust; *gw.* **crystyn.**
crwyn *gw.* **croen.**
cryd *e.g.* *ll.* **-iau** shivering, fever: **Mae'r cryd arna i** I've got the shivers; **cryd y cymalau** rheumatism.
cryf *a.* *ll.* **-ion** strong, powerful, *gw.* *At. Ansoddeiriau.*
cryfach *gw.* **cryf.**
cryfaf *gw.* **cryf.**
cryfed *gw.* **cryf.**
crynhoi *be.* **(crynhoaf)** to collect, to gather, to summarise: **i grynhoi** to sum up.
cryno *a.* tidy; suitable; compact: **ffurfiau cryno'r ferf** compact forms of the verb; **cryno ddisg** compact disc.
crynodeb *e.g.b.* *ll.* **-au** precis, summary; tidiness.
crynu *be* **(crynaf)** to shiver, to quake; **daeargryn** earthquake.
crys *e.g.* *ll.* **-au** shirt: **crys T** T-shirt; **Y Crysau Cochion** The Welsh Rugby Team.

crystiau *gw.* **crwst, crystyn.**
crystyn *e.g. ll.* **crystiau** crust; *gw.* **crwst.**
cu *a.* dear, fond, beloved; **mam-gu** grandmother *(S.W.).* **tad-cu** grandfather *(S.W.).*
cuddio *(rhag.) be.* **(cuddiaf)** to hide (from), to cover, to bury.
cul *a. ll.* **-ion** narrow, narrow-minded. **culfor** *e.g.* strait, channel.
curo *be.* **(curaf)** to strike, to knock, to defeat: **curo dwylo** to clap hands.
cusan *e.g.b. ll.* **-au** kiss.
cusanu *be.* **(cusanaf)** to kiss.
cw *gw.* **acw.**
cwb *e.g. ll.* **cybiau** kennel, coop.
cwbl 1 *a.* all, complete, entire: **cwbl iach** completely healthy; **cwbl gyfan** quite complete; **cwbl sicr** completely certain. 2 *e.g. ll. (used with the definite article)* all, everything; **y cwbl** everything, all: **y cwbl oll** everything, the whole lot; **dim o gwbl** nothing at all; **dyna'r cwbl** that's all; **Prynodd e'r cwbl** He bought everything.
cwcw *e.b. ll.* **cwcŵod** cuckoo *(S.W.); gw.* **cog.**
cwch *e.g. ll.* **cychod** boat; hive; **cwch hwylio** sailing boat; **cwch modur** motor boat; **cwch pysgota** fishing boat; **cwch rhwyfo** rowing boat; **cwch gwenyn** beehive.
cwd *e.g. ll.* **cydau** bag; purse; sack.
cwdyn *e.g. ll.* **cydau** bag; purse; sack.
cweryl *e.g. ll.* **-au, -on** quarrel.
cweryla (â) *be.* **(cwerylaf)** to quarrel (with).
cwerylau: cwerylon *gw.* **cweryl.**
cwestiwn *e.g. ll.* **cwestiynau** question.
cwestiyna *be.* **(cwestiynaf)** to question.
cwestiynau *gw.* **cwestiwn.**
cwlwm *e.g. ll.* **clymau** knot; bunch; *gw.* **clwm.**
cwm *e.g. ll.* **cymoedd** valley; **Cwm Tawe** Swansea Valley.
cwmni *e.g. ll.* **cwmnïau, cwmnïoedd** company; **cwmni yswiriant** insurance company.
cwmnïau *gw.* **cwmni.**
cwmnïoedd *gw.* **cwmni.**
cwmwl *e.g. ll.* **cymylau** cloud.
cŵn *gw.* **ci.**
cwningen *e.b. ll.* **cwningod** rabbit.
cwningod *gw.* **cwningen.**
cwpan *e.g.b. ll.* **-au** cup.
cwpla *be.* **(cwplâf)** to finish *(S.W.).*
cwpwrdd *e.g. ll.* **cypyrddau** cupboard; **cwpwrdd cornel** corner cupboard.
cwr *e.g. ll.* **cyrrau, cyrion** corner, end; edge, border; outskirts. **ar gwr y dref** on the outskirts of the town.
cwrdd 1 *e.g. ll.* **cyrddau** meeting *(S.W.),* religious service, congregation: **cwrdd gweddi** prayer-meeting; **cyrddau mawr** special preaching meetings; **tŷ cwrdd** chapel *(nonconformist).* 2 *be.* **(cwrddaf)** to meet, to come together; to touch: **cwrdd â** to meet, meeting.
cwrs *e.g. ll.* **cyrsau, cyrsiau** course.
cwrtais *a.* courteous.
cwrw *e.g. ll.* **-au** beer.
cwsg 1 *e.g.* sleep; numbness. 2 *a.* asleep; numb; **ynghwsg** asleep; lifeless, numb.
cwsmer *e.g. ll.* **-iaid** customer.
cwstwm *e.g. ll.* **cystymau** custom, patronage.
cwt *e.b.g. ll.* **cytiau** hut, sty, wound; tail; queue; **cwt ieir** chicken coop.
cwta *a.* short, abrupt.
cwymp *e.g. ll.* **-au, -iau** fall, slope; collapse.
cwympo *be.* **(cwympaf)** to fall; to fell.
cwyn *e.b.g. ll.* **-au, -ion** complaint.
cwyno (am, i) *be.* **(cwynaf)** to complain (about, to).
cwyr *e.g. ll.* **-au** bees-wax; wax.
cychod *gw.* **cwch.**
cychwyn 1 *e.g.* beginning, start. 2 *be.* **(cychwynnaf)** to begin, to start: **ar y cychwyn** at first, at the start.
cydadrodd *be.* **(cydadroddaf)** to recite together: **parti cydadrodd** choral speaking party.
cydau *gw.* **cwd, cwdyn.**
cydio (yn) *be* **(cydiaf)** to join, to connect, to couple, to take hold (of).
cydnabod 1 *be.* **(cydnabyddaf)** to acknowledge; to honour, to remunerate 2 *e.g.* acquaintance.
cyfaill *e.g. ll.* **cyfeillion** friend, companion.
Annwyl Gyfeillion Dear Friends *(form of address); gw.* **cyfeilles.**
cyfan *e.g. ll.* **-ion** all, total, entirety; **y cyfan** all, the lot, everything: **ar y cyfan** on the whole; **wedi'r cyfan** after all.

cyfangwbl *a.* altogether, complete, whole: **yn gyfangwbl** completely, wholly; **Roedd e'n gyfangwbl ddu** He was completely black.
cyfansoddi *be.* **(cyfansoddaf)** to compose; to establish.
cyfansoddwr *e.g. ll.* **cyfansoddwyr** composer.
cyfanswm *e.g. ll.* **cafansymiau** total, amount.
cyfarch *be.* **(cyfarchaf)** to greet.
cyfarchion *e.ll.* greetings.
cyfarfod 1 *e.g. ll.* **-ydd** meeting. **2** *be.* **(cyfarfyddaf)** to meet, to encounter; **cyfarfod â** to meet.
cyfarfodydd *gw.* **cyfarfod.**
cyfarth *be.* **(cyfarthaf)** to bark.
cyfarwyddiadur *e.g. ll.* **-on** directory.
cyfarwyddo (â) *be.* **(cyfarwyddaf)** to familiarise, to instruct.
cyfarwyddwr *e.g. ll.* **cyfarwyddwyr** director.
cyfeilles *e.b. ll.* **-au** female friend; *gw.* **cyfaill.**
cyfeillgar *a.* friendly, sociable; *gw. At. Ansoddeiriau.*
cyfeillgarwch *e.g.* friendship.
cyfeillion *gw.* **cyfaill.**
cyfeiriad *e.g. ll.* **-au** direction, reference, address.
cyfeirio (at, i) *be.* **(cyfeiriaf)** to direct, to refer.
cyfenw *e.g. ll.* **-au** surname.
cyferbyn (â) *a.* opposite, contrary; **cyferbyn â** opposite.
cyfiawn *a.* righteous, just.
cyfiawnder *e.g. ll.* **-au** righteousness, justice.
cyfieithiad *e.g. ll.* **-au** translation.
cyfieithu *be.* **(cyfieithaf)** to translate.
cyfieithydd *e.g. ll.* **-ion** translator, interpreter.
cyfle *e.g. ll.* **-oedd** opportunity, chance.
cyfleu *be.* **(cyfleaf)** to convey, to imply.
cyfleus *a.* convenient, expedient.
cyflog *e.b. ll.* **-au** salary, wages, hire.
cyflogi *be.* **(cyflogaf)** to employ, to hire.
cyflogwr *e.g. ll.* **cyflogwyr** employer.
cyflwr *e.g. ll.* **cyflyrau** state, condition, case.
cyflwyno (i) *be.* **(cyflwynaf)** present (to), to dedicate (to).
cyflym *a.* quick, swift, speedy; *gw. At. Ansoddeiriau.*
cyflymach *gw.* **cyflym.**
cyflymaf *gw.* **cyflym.**
cyflymder *e.g. ll.* **-au** speed, velocity, swiftness.
cyflymed *gw.* **cyflym.**
cyflymu *be.* **(cyflymaf)** to accelerate, to hasten.
cyflymydd *e.g. ll.* **-ion** accelerator.
cyflyrau *gw.* **cyflwr.**
cyfnither *e.b. ll.* **-oedd** female cousin; *gw.* **cefnder.**
cyfoeth *e.g.* wealth, riches.
cyfoethog *a.* rich, wealthy.
cyfradd *e.b. ll.* **-au** rate; **cyfraddau llog** interest rates.
cyfraith *e.b. ll.***cyfreithiau** law.
cyfrannu (i, at) *be.* **(cyfrannaf)** to contribute; to impart.
cyfreithiwr *e.g. ll.* **cyfreithwyr** solicitor, lawyer.
cyfreithwyr *gw.* **cyfreithiwr.**
cyfres *e.b. ll.* **-au, -i** series, suite *(musical);* **drama gyfres** a serial.
cyfresau: cyfresi *gw.* **cyfres.**
cyfrif 1 *be.* **(cyfrifaf)** to count, to reckon. **2.** *e.g.* account, reckoning; **cyfrif trafod** current account; **cyfrif cadw** deposit account.
cyfrifiadur *e.g. ll.* **-on** computer.
cyfrifiannell *e.g. ll.* **-au** calculator.
cyfrifol *a.* responsible; calculable: **cyfrifol am** responsible for.
cyfrifoldeb *e.g. ll.* **-au** responsibility.
cyfrifydd *e.g. ll.* **-ion** accountant.
cyfrinach *e.b. ll.* **-au** secret, mystery.
cyfrinachol *a.* secret, confidential, private.
cyfrol *e.b. ll.* **-au** volume, book.
cyfrwng *e.g. ll.* **cyfryngau** agent; agency; medium; means: **trwy gyfrwng** through the medium of; **y cyfryngau** the media.
cyfrwys *a.* cunning, crafty.
cyfryngau *gw.* **cyfrwng.**
cyfun *a.* agreeing, comprehensive, united; **Ysgol Gyfun Treforys** Morriston Comprehensive School.
cyfuwch *gw.* **uchel.**
cyfweld (â) *be.* **(cyfwelaf)** to interview.
cyfweliad *e.g. ll.* **-au** interview.
cyfyng *a.* narrow, confined, restricted: **Mae hi'n gyfyng arni** She is in dire straits.
cyfyngu (ar) *be.* **(cyfyngaf)** to narrow, to confine, to restrict.
cyfystyr 1 *e.g. ll.* **-on** synonym. **2** *a.* synonymous; **cyfystyr â** synonymous with.

cyfforddus: cyffyrddus *a.* comfortable *(S.W.).*
cyffredin *a.* common, ordinary, vulgar: **enw cyffredin** common noun; **pobl gyffredin** ordinary people.
cyffrous *a.* exciting, moving.
cyffur *e.g.* *ll.* **-iau** drug, medicine.
cyffwrdd (â) *be.* **(cyffyrddaf)** to touch, to contact, to meet.
cyngerdd *e.g.b.* *ll.* **cyngherddau** concert.
cyngherddau *gw.* **cyngerdd.**
cynghori (i) *be.* **(cynghoraf)** to advise, to counsel, to exhort.
cynghorion *gw.* **cyngor.**
cynghorwr *e.g.* *ll.* **cynghorwyr** adviser, councillor.
cynghrair *e.g.* *ll.* **cynghreiriau** alliance, league.
cynghreiriad *e.g.* *ll.* **cynghreiriaid** ally.
cynghreiriau *gw.* **cynghrair.**
cyngor 1 *e.g.* *ll.* **cynghorion** advice, counsel. 2 *e.g.* *ll.* **cynghorau** council: **Cyngor Cymuned** community council; **Cyngor Dosbarth** District Council; **Cyngor Sir** County Council; **Cyngor y Celfyddydau** the Arts Council.
cyhoedd 1 *a.* public. 2 *e.g.* public: **ar gyhoedd, ar goedd** publicly; **y cyhoedd** the public.
cyhoeddi *be.* **(cyhoeddaf)** to announce, to proclaim; to publish.
cyhoeddiad *e.g.* *ll.* **-au** publication; announcement; engagement.
cyhoeddus *a.* public: **neuadd gyhoeddus** public hall; **cyfarfod cyhoeddus** public meeting.
cyhoeddusrwydd *e.g.* publicity.
cyhoeddwr *e.g.* *ll.* **cyhoeddwyr** publisher; announcer.
cyhyd *gw.* **hir.**
cyhyrog *a.* muscular, strong.
cylch *e.g.* *ll.* **-au, -oedd** circle, hoop; class; region: **o gylch** around.
cylchfan *e.g.* *ll.* **-nau** roundabout.
cylchgrawn *e.g.* *ll.* **cylchgronau** magazine, periodical.
cylchgronau *gw.* **cylchgrawn.**
cylchlythyr *e.g.* *ll.* **-au, -on** a circular.
cyll *bf.* he/she/it loses; *gw.* **collen, colli.**
cyllell *e.b.* *ll.* **cyllyll** knife: **cyllell boced** penknife; **cyllell fara** bread knife.
cyllyll *gw.* **cyllell.**
cymaint *gw.* **mawr.**
cymal *e.g.* *ll.* **-au** joint; clause, phrase.
cymanfa *e.b.* *ll.***-oedd** assembly, singing festival.
cymanfaoedd *gw.* **cymanfa.**
cymdeithas *e.b.* *ll.* **-au** society, association.
cymdogion *gw.* **cymydog.**
cymeriad *e.g.* *ll.* **-au** character.
cymryd *be.* **(cymeraf)** to accept, to take; **cymryd ar** to pretend *(N.W.).*
cymharu (â) *be.* **(cymharaf)** to compare.
cymhleth *a.* complex, involved.
cymhlethod *e.g.* *ll.* **-au** complication, complexity.
cymhlethu *be.* **(cymhlethaf)** to complicate.
cymhorthion *gw.* **cymorth.**
cymoedd *gw.* **cwm.**
cymorth *e.g.* *ll.* **cymhorthion** aid, assistance; **cymorth cyntaf** first aid.
Cymraeg 1 *e.b.g.* Welsh *(language).* 2 *a.* Welsh *(in language)*: **Y Gymraeg** The Welsh Language; **yn Gymraeg** in Welsh; **Cymraeg da** good *(spoken or written)* Welsh.
Cymraes; Cymreiges *e.b.* *ll.* **-au** Welshwoman.
Cymreictod *e.g.* Welsh quality, Welshness.
Cymreig *a.* Welsh, pertaining to Wales or to the Welsh: **arferion Cymreig** Welsh traditions; **brethyn Cymreig** Welsh woollen cloth; **Swyddfa Gymreig** The Welsh Office.
Cymreiges *gw.* **Cymraes.**
Cymro *e.g.* *ll.* **Cymry** Welshman: **Cymro i'r carn** thorough Welshman; **Cymro uniaith** monglot Welshman; **Cymry alltud** exiled Welsh; **Cymry Llundain** London Welsh.
Cymru *eb.* Wales.
Cymry *gw.* **Cymro.**
cymryd *gw.* **cymeryd.**
cymwynas *e.b.* *ll.* **-au** favour, kindness; **talu'r gymwynas olaf** to pay the last respects *(attendance at funeral).*
cymydog *e.g.* *ll.* **cymdogion** neighbour.
cymylau *gw.* **cwmwl.**
cymylog *a.* cloudy.
cymysg *a.* mixed.
cymysgu (â) *be.* **(cymysgaf)** to mix, to confuse.

cymysgwch 1 *e.g.* jumble, medley. 2 *bf.* mix! *(plural); gw.* **cymysgu.**
cyn 1 *ardd.* before, previous to: **Dewch cyn cinio** Come before dinner. 2 *rhagdd.* (followed by soft mutation) first, former, ex-; **cyn-brifathro** former headteacher; **cyn-löwr** former miner; **cyn-weinidog** former minister. 3 *c. & ad.* (followed by soft mutation) as; **cyn dewed â mochyn** as fat as a pig; **cyn ddued â'r frân** as black as the crow; **cyn goched â thân** as red as fire; *gw. At. Treigladau.*
cynaeafau *gw.* **cynhaeaf.**
cynddrwg *gw.* **drwg.**
cynffon *e.b. ll.* **-nau** tail *(N.W.);* **cynffonnau ŵyn bach** hazel catkins; *gw.* **cwt.**
cynhadledd *e.b. ll.* **cynadleddau** conference.
cynhaeaf *e.g. ll.* **cynaeafau** harvest.
cynhesu *be.* **(cynhesaf)** to warm, to get warm.
cynhwysion *gw.* **cynnwys.**
cynhyrfus *a.* exciting, agitated.
cynigion *gw.* **cynnig.**
cynilion *e.ll.* savings.
cynilo *be.* **(cynilaf)** to save, to ecnomise.
cynllun *e.g. ll.* **-iau** plan, design, scheme, project.
cynllunio *be.* **(cynlluniaf)** to plan, to design.
cynlluniwr: cynllunydd *e.g. ll.* **cynllunwyr** planner, designer, architect.
cynnal *be.* **(cynhaliaf)** to support, to hold, to maintain: **gwaith cynnal a chadw** maintenance work.
cynnar *a.* early, soon; *gw. At. Ansoddeiriau.*
cynnes *a.* warm.
cynnig 1 *be.* **(cynigiaf)** to attempt, to try, to propose; **rhoi cynnig ar** to attempt to. 2 *e.g. ll.* **cynigion** attempt; offer, proposal; motion, bid.
cynnwys 1 *eg. ll.* **cynhwysion.** content, contents. 2 *be.* **(cynhwysaf)** to contain, to include; **gan gynnwys** including.
cynorthwy-ydd *e.g. ll.* **cynorthwywyr** helper, assistant.
cynorthwywr *e.g. ll.* **cynorthwywyr** helper, assistant.
cynradd *a.* primary: **ysgol gynradd** primary school.
cynrychioli *be.* to represent.
cynt: gynt *ad.* formerly, previously, *née:* **Siân Owen, gynt Lewis** Siân Owen, *née* Lewis; **y flwyddyn gynt** the previous year; *gw.* **buan, cynnar.**
cyntaf *a.* first, chief, earliest *gw.* **cynnar.**
cynted *gw.* **cynnar.**
cyntedd *e.g. ll.* **cynteddau, cynteddoedd** porch, court, lobby, hall.
cynteddau: cynteddoedd *gw.* **cyntedd.**
cynulleidfa *e.b. ll.* **-oedd** congregation.
cypyrddau *gw.* **cwpwrdd.**
cyrddau *gw.* **cwrdd.**
cyrff *gw.* **corff.**
cyrion *gw.* **cwr.**
cyrliog *a.* curly.
cyrn *gw.* **corn.**
cyrraedd *be.* **(cyrhaeddaf)** to reach, to arrive, to attain: **Cyrhaeddodd y tŷ** He arrived at the house.
cyrrau *gw.* **cwr.**
cyrsau *gw.* **cwrs.**
cyrsiau *gw.* **cwrs.**
cysglyd *a.* sleepy.
cysgod *e.g. ll.* **-ion, -au** shadow; shelter.
cysgodau *gw.* **cysgod.**
cysgodi *(rhag.) be.* **(cysgodaf)** to shade; to shelter.
cysgodion *gw.* **cysgod.**
cysgu *be.* **(cysgaf)** to sleep.
cystadlaethau *gw.* **cystadleuaeth.**
cystadleuaeth *e.b. ll.* **cystadlaethau** competition.
cystadleuwr: cystadleuydd *e.g. ll.* **cystadleuwyr** competitor.
cystadleuwyr *gw.* **cystadleuwr.**
cystadlu (â) *be.* **(cystadlaf)** to compete.
cystal *gw.* **da.**
cystymau *gw.* **cwstwm.**
cysur *e.g. ll.* **-on** comfort, consolation.
cysuro *be.* **(cysuraf)** to comfort, to console.
cysurus *a.* comfortable.
cyswllt *e.g. ll.* **cysylltau** joint, junction, connection.
cytgan *e.b. ll.* **-au** chorus.
cytsain 1 *e.b. ll.* **cytseiniaid** consonant. 2 *e.b. ll.* **cytseiniau** harmony.
cytseiniaid *gw.* **cytsain.**
cytseiniau *gw.* **cytsain.**
cytundeb *e.g. ll.* **-au** agreement, pact, contract.

cytuno (â) *be.* **(cytunaf)** to agree (with), consent (to).
cyw *e.g.* *ll.* **-ion** chick; **cyw iâr** chicken *(N.W.); gw.* **ffowlyn.**
cywaith *e.g.* *ll.* **cyweithiau** project; collective work.
cyweithiau *gw.* **cywaith.**
cywion *gw.* **cyw.**
cywir *a.* correct, sincere, true, honest.
cywiriad *e.g.* *ll.* **-au** correction.
cywiro *be.* **(cywiraf)** to correct, to amend, to verify.

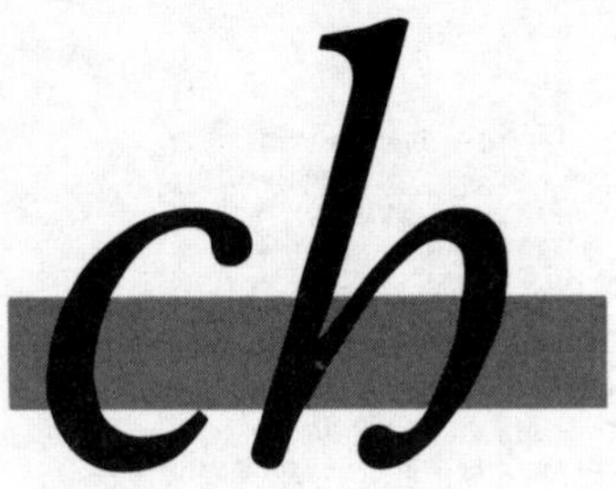

'ch *rhag.* you, your; *gw. At. Rhagenwau Personol.*
chaban *gw.* **caban.**
chacen *gw.* **cacen.**
chacwn *gw.* **cacwn.**
chacynen *gw.* **cacynen.**
chadach *gw.* **cadach.**
chadair *gw.* **cadair.**
chadeirio *gw.* **cadeirio.**
chadeiriol *gw.* **cadeiriol.**
chadeirydd *gw.***cadeirydd.**
chadnawes *gw.* **cadno.**
chadno *gw.* **cadno.**
chadnoaid *gw.* **cadno.**
chadw *gw.* **cadw.**
chadwyn *gw.* **cadwyn.**
chadwyno *gw.* **cadwyno.**
chae *gw.* **cae.**
chael *gw.* **cael.**
chaer *gw.* **caer.**
Chaerdydd *gw.* **Caerdydd.**
Chaerfyrddin *gw.* **Caerfyrddin.**
Chaergybi *gw.* **Caergybi.**
chaets *gw.* **caets.**
chaf *gw.* **caf.**
chafodd *gw.* **cafodd.**
chaffe *gw.* **caffe.**
changen *gw.* **cangen.**
changhennau *gw.* **cangen.**
chaiff *gw.* **caiff.**
chais *gw.* **cais.**
chalan *gw.* **calan.**
chaled *gw.* **caled.**
chaledi *gw.* **caledi.**
chaledu *gw.* **caledu.**
chaledwch *gw.* **caledwch.**
chalendr *gw.* **calendr.**
chalenigion *gw.* **calennig.**
chalennig *gw.* **calennig.**
chaletach *gw.* **caled.**
chaletaf *gw.* **caled.**
chaleted *gw.* **caled.**
chalon *gw.* **calon.**
chall *gw.* **call.**
challach *gw.* **call.**
challaf *gw.* **call.**
challed *gw.* **call.**
cham *gw.* **cam.**
chamarwain *gw.* **camarwain.**
chamddeall *gw.* **camddeall.**
chamera *gw.* **camera.**
champ *gw.* **camp.**
champfa *gw.* **campfa.**
champfeydd *gw.* **campfa.**
champus *gw.* **campus.**
champwaith *gw.* **campwaith.**
chamsyniad *gw.* **camsyniad.**
chamu *gw.* **camu.**
chân *gw.* **cân.**
chan *gw.* **can, gan.**
chaneuon *gw.* **cân.**
chanfed *gw.* **canfed.**
chanhwyllau *gw.* **cannwyll.**
chanhwyllbren *gw.* **canhwyllbren.**
chaniad *gw.* **caniad.**
chaniadaeth *gw.* **caniadaeth.**
chaniadau *gw.* **cân, caniad.**
chaniatâd *gw.* **caniatâd.**
chaniatáu *gw.* **caniatáu.**
chaniedydd *gw.* **caniedydd.**
chanmlwydd *gw.* **canmlwydd.**
chanmlwyddiannau *gw.* **canmlwydd.**
chanmol *gw.* **canmol.**
chanmoliaeth *gw.* **canmoliaeth.**
channoedd *gw.* **cant.**
channwyll *gw.* **cannwyll.**
chanol *gw.* **canol.**
chanolbarth *gw.* **canolbarth.**
chanolbwyntio *gw.* **canolbwyntio.**
chanoldir *gw.* **canoldir.**
chanolfan *gw.* **canolfan.**
chanolwr *gw.* **canolwr.**
chanradd *gw.* **canradd.**
chanran *gw.* **canran.**
chanrif *gw.* **canrif.**
chanrifau: chanrifoedd *gw.* **canrif.**
chant *gw.* **cant.**
chantor *gw.* **cantor.**
chantores *gw.* **cantores.**
chanu *gw.* **canu.**
chanŵ *gw.* **canŵ.**
chanŵio *gw.* **canŵio.**
chanwr *gw.* **canwr.**
chap *gw.* **cap.**
chapel *gw.* **capel.**
chapteiniaid *gw.* **capten.**
chapten *gw.* **capten.**
chapteniaid *gw.* **capten.**

char *gw.* **car.**
charafán *gw.* **carafán.**
charafana *gw.* **carafana.**
charco *gw.* **carco.**
charcus *gw.* **carcus.**
charchar *gw.* **carchar.**
charcharor *gw.* **carcharor.**
charcharu *gw.* **carcharu.**
chardiau *gw.* **cerdyn.**
charedig *gw.* **caredig.**
charedigrwydd *gw.* **caredigrwydd.**
chariad *gw.* **cariad.**
chariadon *gw.* **cariad.**
chariadus *gw.* **cariadus.**
chario *gw.* **cario.**
charol *gw.* **carol.**
charped *gw.* **carped.**
charreg *gw.* **carreg.**
chartref *gw.* **cartref.**
chartrefi: chartrefydd *gw.* **cartref.**
chartrefu *gw.* **cartrefu.**
charu *gw.* **caru.**
chas *gw.* **cas.**
chasáu *gw.* **casáu.**
chasgen *gw.* **casgen.**
chasgenni *gw.* **casgen.**
chasgliad *gw.* **casgliad.**
chasglu *gw.* **casglu.**
Chas-gwent *gw.* **Cas-gwent.**
Chasllwchwr *gw.* **Casllwchwr.**
Chasnewydd *gw.* **Casnewydd.**
chastell *gw.* **castell.**
Chastell-nedd *gw.* **Castell-nedd.**
chath *gw.* **cath.**
chau *gw.* **cau.**
chawl *gw.* **cawl.**
chawod *gw.* **cawod.**
chawr *gw.* **cawr.**
chaws *gw.* **caws.**
chefn *gw.* **cefn.**
chefnder *gw.* **cefnder.**
chefndir *gw.* **cefndir.**
chefndiroedd *gw.* **cefndir.**
chefndyr *gw.* **cefnder.**
chefnu *gw.* **cefnu.**
chefnwr *gw.* **cefnwr.**
chefnwyr *gw.* **cefnwr.**
cheffyl *gw.* **ceffyl.**
cheg *gw.* **ceg.**
chegin *gw.* **cegin.**
chei *gw.* **cael, cei.**
cheidwad *gw.* **ceidwad.**
cheiliog *gw.* **ceiliog.**
Cheinewydd *gw.* **Ceinewydd.**
cheiniog *gw.* **ceiniog.**
cheisio *gw.* **ceisio.**
chelf *gw.* **celf.**
chelfi *gw.* **celficyn.**
chelficyn *gw.* **celficyn.**
chelwydd *gw.* **celwydd.**
chelwyddog *gw.* **celwyddog.**
chelyn *gw.* **celynnen.**
chelynnen *gw.* **celynnen.**
chell *gw.* **cell.**
chellau: chelloedd *gw.* **cell.**
chemeg *gw.* **cemeg.**
chenadaethau *gw.* **cenhadaeth.**
chenedl *gw.* **cenedl.**
chenedlaethau *gw.* **cenhedlaeth.**
chenedlaethol *gw.* **cenedlaethol.**
chenedlaetholdeb *gw.* **cenedlaetholdeb.**
chenedlaetholwr *gw.* **cenedlaetholwr.**
chenedlaetholwyr *gw.* **cenedlaetholwr.**
chenfigennus *gw.* **cenfigennus.**
chenhadaeth *gw.* **cenhadaeth.**
chenhadol *gw.* **cenhadol.**
chenhadon *gw.* **cenhadwr.**
chenhadu *gw.* **cenhadu.**
chenhadwr *gw.* **cenhadwr.**
chenhedlaeth *gw.* **cenhedlaeth.**
chenhedloedd *gw.* **cenedl.**
chenhinen *gw.* **cenhinen.**
chennin *gw.* **cenhinen.**
cher *gw.* **mynd.**
cherdyn *gw.* **cerdyn.**
cherdd *gw.* **cerdd.**
cherdded *gw.* **cerdded.**
cherddor *gw.* **cerddor.**
cherddorfa *gw.* **cerddorfa.**
cherddorfeydd *gw.* **cerddorfa.**
cherddoriaeth *gw.* **cerddoriaeth.**
cherddorol *gw.* **cerddorol.**
cherddwr *gw.* **cerddwr.**
cherddwyr *gw.* **cerddwr.**
cherflun *gw.* **cerflun.**
cherrig *gw.* **carreg.**
cherwch *gw.* **mynd.**
ches *gw.* **ces.**
chesair *gw.* **cesair.**
chestyll *gw.* **castell.**
chewri *gw.* **cawr.**
chewyn *gw.* **cewyn.**
cheyrydd *gw.* **caer.**
chi: chwi *rhag.* you; *gw.* **ci.**
chig *gw.* **cig.**
chigydd *gw.* **cigydd.**
chigyddion *gw.* **cigydd.**
chilio *gw.* **cilio.**
chiniawau *gw.* **cinio.**
chinio *gw.* **cinio.**
chipolwg *gw.* **cipolwg.**
chist *gw.* **cist.**
chithau: chwithau *rhag.* you also.
chlaf *gw.* **claf.**
chlai *gw.* **clai.**

chlasur *gw.* **clasur.**
chlasurol *gw.* **clasurol.**
chlawdd *gw.* **clawdd.**
chlawr *gw.* **clawr.**
chlebran *gw.* **clebran.**
chledr *gw.* **cledr.**
chlefyd *gw.* **clefyd.**
chleifion *gw.* **claf.**
chlêr *gw.* **cleren.**
chlerc *gw.* **clerc.**
chleren *gw.* **cleren.**
chlir *gw.* **clir.**
chlirio *gw.* **clirio.**
chlo *gw.* **clo, cloi.**
chloc *gw.* **cloc.**
chloch *gw.* **cloch.**
chlod *gw.* **clod.**
chlodfori *gw.* **clodfori.**
chloff *gw.* **cloff.**
chloffi *gw.* **cloffi.**
chlogwyn *gw.* **clogwyn.**
chlogyn *gw.* **clogyn.**
chloi *gw.* **cloi.**
chlorian *gw.* **clorian.**
chloriau *gw.* **clawr.**
chlown *gw.* **clown.**
chlun *gw.* **clun.**
chlust *gw.* **clust.**
chlustog *gw.* **clustog.**
chlwm *gw.* **clwm.**
chlwtyn *gw.* **clwtyn.**
Chlwyd *gw.* **Clwyd.**
chlwyd *gw.* **clwyd.**
chlwydau: chlwydi *gw.* **clwyd.**
chlwyf *gw.* **clwyf.**
chlychau *gw.* **cloch.**
chlymau *gw.* **clwm.**
chlymu *gw.* **clymu.**
chlytiau *gw.* **clwtyn.**
chlyw *gw.* **clyw.**
chlywed *gw.* **clywed.**
chnau *gw.* **cneuen.**
chneuen *gw.* **cneuen.**
chnoc *gw.* **cnoc.**
chnocio *gw.* **cnocio.**
chnoi *gw.* **cnoi.**
choban *gw.* **coban.**
chobannau *gw.* **coban.**
choch *gw.* **coch.**
chochach *gw.* **coch.**
chochaf *gw.* **coch.**
choched *gw.* **coch.**
chodi *gw.* **codi.**
Choed-duon *gw.* **Coed-duon.**
choeden *gw.* **coeden.**
choedwig *gw.* **coedwig.**
choes *gw.* **coes.**
chof *gw.* **cof.**
chofio *gw.* **cofio.**
chofion *gw.* **cof.**
chofleidio *gw.* **cofleidio.**
chofrestr *gw.* **cofrestr.**
chofrestru *gw.* **cofrestru.**
choffi *gw.* **coffi.**
chog *gw.* **cog.**
choginio *gw.* **coginio.**
chogydd *gw.* **cogydd.**
choleg *gw.* **coleg.**
choler *gw.* **coler.**
cholofn *gw.* **colofn.**
choluro *gw.* **coluro.**
cholled *gw.* **colled.**
chollen *gw.* **collen.**
cholli *gw.* **colli.**
chopïo *gw.* **copïo.**
chopyn *gw.* **copyn.**
chôr *gw.* **côr.**
chorau *gw.* **côr.**
chordyn *gw.* **cordyn.**
chorff *gw.* **corff.**
chorfforol *gw.* **corfforol.**
chorgi *gw.* **corgi.**
chorn *gw.* **corn.**
chornel *gw.* **cornel.**
choron *gw.* **coron.**
choroni *gw.* **coroni.**
chorryn *gw.* **corryn.**
chorynnod *gw.* **corryn.**
chosb *gw.* **cosb.**
chosbi *gw.* **cosbi.**
chostus *gw.* **costus.**
chot *gw.* **cot.**
chotau: chotiau *gw.* **cot.**
chotwm *gw.* **cotwm.**
chrac *gw.* **crac.**
chrachach *gw.* **crachach.**
chrafu *gw.* **crafu.**
chragen *gw.* **cragen.**
chraig *gw.* **craig.**
chras *gw.* **cras.**
chrasu *gw.* **crasu.**
chredu *gw.* **credu.**
chrefydd *gw.* **crefydd.**
chrefft *gw.* **crefft.**
chrefftwr *gw.* **crefftwr.**
chrefftwyr *gw.* **crefftwr.**
chregyn *gw.* **cragen.**
chreigiau *gw.* **craig.**
chreigiog *gw.* **creigiog.**
chreision *gw.* **creisionyn.**
chrempog *gw.* **crempog.**
chreulon *gw.* **creulon.**
chreulondeb *gw.* **creulondeb.**
chri *gw.* **cri.**
chrib *gw.* **crib.**
chribo *gw.* **cribo.**
chriced *gw.* **criced.**
chricedwr *gw.* **cricedwr.**

chrio *gw.* **crio.**
Christion *gw.* **Cristion.**
Christnogion *gw.* **Cristion.**
chriw *gw.* **criw.**
chroen *gw.* **croen.**
chroes *gw.* **croes.**
chroesair *gw.* **croesair.**
chroesau *gw.* **croes.**
chroesawu *gw.* **croesawu.**
chroesawus *gw.* **croesawus.**
chroeseiriau *gw.* **croesair.**
chroesfan *gw.* **croesfan.**
chroesffordd *gw.* **croesffordd.**
chroesholi *gw.* **croesholi.**
chroesi *gw.* **croesi.**
chroeso *gw.* **croeso.**
chronfa *gw.* **cronfa.**
chronfeydd *gw.* **cronfa.**
chrud *gw.* **crud.**
chrwst *gw.* **crwst.**
chryd *gw.* **cryd.**
chryf *gw.* **cryf.**
chryfach *gw.* **cryf.**
chryfaf *gw.* **cryf.**
chryfed *gw.* **cryf.**
chrynhoi *gw.* **crynhoi.**
chryno *gw.* **cryno.**
chrynodeb *gw.* **crynodeb.**
chrynu *gw.* **crynu.**
chrys *gw.* **crys.**
chrystiau *gw.* **crwst, crystyn.**
chrystyn *gw.* **crystyn.**
chu *gw.* **cu.**
chuddio *gw.* **cuddio.**
chul *gw.* **cul.**
churo *gw.* **curo.**
chusan *gw.* **cusan.**
chusanu *gw.* **cusanu.**
chwaer *e.b.* *ll.* **chwiorydd** sister, maiden.
chwain *gw.* **chwannen.**
chwaith: ychwaith *ad.* neither, nor . . . either, not . . . either.
chwalu *be.* **(chwalaf)** to crumble; to scatter, to disperse; **chwalu cartref** to break up a home.
chwaneg: ychwaneg *a. & e.g.* more, additional.
chwanegu *gw.* **ychwanegu.**
chwannen *e.b.* *ll.* **chwain** flea.
chwant *e.g.* *ll.* **-au** desire, appetite; lust: **Mae chwant bwyd arnaf i** I desire food; **Does dim chwant mynd arni** She doesn't feel like going.
chwap *a. & ad.* at once, instantly.
chwarae: 1 *be.* **(chwaraeaf)** to play, to perform. 2 *e.g.* *ll.* **-on** game, sport; play: **amser chwarae** play-time; **chwarae teg** fair play; **meysydd chwarae** playing fields.
chwaraewr *e.g.* *ll.* **chwaraewyr** player, actor.
chwaraewyr *gw.* **chwaraewr.**
chwarddaf *gw.* **chwerthin.**
chwarel 1 *e.b.g.* *ll.* **-i, -au** quarry. 2 *e.g.b.* *ll.* **-au, -i** pane of glass.
chwarelau: chwareli *gw.* **chwarel.**
chwareus *a.* playful.
chwarter *e.g.* *ll.* **-au, -i** quarter.
chwb *gw.* **cwb.**
chwbl *gw.* **cwbl.**
chwcw *gw.* **cwcw.**
chwch *gw.* **cwch.**
chwd *gw.* **cwd.**
chwdyn *gw.* **cwdyn.**
chwe: chwech *a.* six; **chwe** *before singular nouns (followed by spirant mutation)*; **chwe bachgen, chwe llyfr; chwech** *on its own or with* **o** + *plural noun* **chwech o dai, chwech o blant; chwe deg** sixty.
chweched *a.* sixth.
chwedl *e.b.* *ll.* **-au, -euon** story, legend, fable; report, rumour; saying.
chwedlau: chwedleuon *gw.* **chwedl.**
Chwefror *e.g.* February.
chwerthin 1 *be.* **(chwarddaf)** to laugh, to smile; **chwerthin am ei ben** to laugh at him. 2 *e.g.* laughter.
chwerthinllyd *a.* laughable.
chwerw *a.* bitter; severe, sharp, spiteful.
chweryl *gw.* **cweryl.**
chweryla *gw.* **cweryla.**
chwerylau: chwerylon *gw.* **cweryl.**
chwestiwn *gw.* **cwestiwn.**
chwestiyna *gw.* **cwestiyna.**
chwestiynau *gw.* **cwestiwn.**
chwi *gw.* **chi.**
chwiban *e.g.* *ll.* **-au** a whistling, whistle.
chwiban: chwibanu (ar) *be,* **(chwibanaf)** to whistle.
chwifio (at) *be.* **(chwifiaf)** to wave.
chwilen *e.b.* *ll.* **chwilod** beetle; **Mae chwilen yn ei ben** He has a bee in his bonnet.
chwilio (am) *be.* **(chwiliaf)** to search (for), to examine.
chwiliwr *e.g.* *ll.* **chwilwyr** investigator, searcher.
chwilod *gw.* **chwilen.**
chwilota *be.* **(chwilotaf)** to rummage, to pry.
chwilwyr *gw.* **chwiliwr.**
chwilotwr *e.g.* *ll.* **chwilotwyr**

rummager, one engaged in research.
chwiorydd *gw.* **chwaer.**
chwip 1 *e.b.g.* *ll.* **-au, -iau** whip. 2 *a.* swift, quick. 3 *ad.* instantly.
chwipio *be.* **(chwipiaf)** to whip.
chwistrelliad *e.g.* *ll.* **-au** injection.
chwith *a.* left; strange; sad: **o chwith** the wrong way about, awkwardly; **tu chwith** inside out.
chwithau *gw.* **chithau.**
chwithig *a.* strange; awkward.
chwlwm *gw.* **cwlwm.**
chwm *gw.* **cwm.**
chwmni *gw.* **cwmni.**
chwmnïau *gw.* **cwmni.**
chwmnïoedd *gw.* **cwmni.**
chwmwl *gw.* **cwmwl.**
chŵn *gw.* **ci.**
chwningen *gw.* **cwningen.**
chwningod *gw.* **cwningen.**
chwpan *gw.* **cwpan.**
chwpla *gw.* **cwpla.**
chwpwrdd *gw.* **cwpwrdd.**
chwr *gw.* **cwr.**
chwrdd *gw.* **cwrdd.**
chwrs *gw.* **cwrs.**
chwrtais *gw.* **cwrtais.**
chwrw *gw.* **cwrw.**
chwsg *gw.* **cwsg.**
chwsmer *gw.* **cwsmer.**
chwstwm *gw.* **cwstwm.**
chwt *gw.* **cwt.**
chwta *gw.* **cwta.**
chwydu *be.* **(chwydaf)** to vomit.
chwyddiant *e.g.* *ll.* **chwyddiannau** inflation; inflammation.
chwyddo *be.* **(chwyddaf)** to swell, to increase.
chwyddwydr *e.g.* *ll.* **-au** magnifying glass.
chwyldro: chwyldroad *e.g.* *ll.* **chwyldroadau** revolution: **y Chwyldro Diwydiannol** the Industrial Revolution; **y Chwyldro Ffrengig** the French Revolution.
chwymp *gw.* **cwymp.**
chwympo *gw.* **cwympo.**
chwyn *e. torf.* weeds; *gw.* **cwyn;** *gw.* **chwynnyn.**
chwynladdwr *e.g.* weed-killer.
chwynnyn *e.g.ll. & e.torf.* **chwyn** weed.
chwynnu *be.* **(chwynnaf)** to weed.
chwyno *gw.* **cwyno.**
chwyro *gw.* **cwyro.**
chwyrnru *be.* **(chwyrnaf)** to snore, to snarl; to whirl.
chwys *e.g.* perspiration, sweat; **yn chwys domen** dripping with perspiration.
chwysu *be.* **(chwysaf)** to perspire, to sweat.
chwythu *be.* **(chwythaf)** to blow.
chychod *gw.* **cwch.**
chychwyn *gw.* **cychwyn.**
chydadrodd *gw.* **cydadrodd.**
chydau *gw.* **cwd; cwdyn.**
chydio *gw.* **cydio.**
chydnabod *gw.* **cydnabod.**
chyfaill *gw.* **cyfaill.**
chyfan *gw.* **cyfan.**
chyfangwbl *gw.* **cyfangwbl.**
chyfansoddi *gw.* **cyfansoddi.**
chyfansoddwr *gw.* **cyfansoddwr.**
chyfanswm *gw.* **cyfanswm.**
chyfarch *gw.* **cyfarch.**
chyfarfod *gw.* **cyfarfod.**
chyfarfodydd *gw.* **cyfarfod.**
chyfarwyddiadur *gw.* **cyfarwyddiadur.**
chyfarwyddo *gw.* **cyfarwyddo.**
chyfarwyddwr *gw.* **cyfarwyddwr.**
chyfeilles *gw.* **cyfeilles.**
chyfeillgar *gw.* **cyfeillgar.**
chyfeillgarwch *gw.* **cyfeillgarwch.**
chyfeiriad *gw.* **cyfeiriad.**
chyfeirio *gw.* **cyfeirio.**
chyfenw *gw.* **cyfenw.**
chyferbyn *gw.* **cyferbyn.**
chyfiawn *gw.* **cyfiawn.**
chyfiawnder *gw.* **cyfiwnder.**
chyfieithiad *gw.* **cyfieithiad.**
chyfieithu *gw.* **cyfieithu.**
chyfieithydd *gw.* **cyfieithydd.**
chyfle *gw.* **cyfle.**
chylfeu *gw.* **cyfleu.**
chyfleus *gw.* **cyfleus.**
chyflog *gw.* **cyflog.**
chyflogi *gw.* **cyflogi.**
chyflogwr *gw.* **cyflogwr.**
chyflwr *gw.* **cyflwr.**
chyflwyno *gw.* **cyflwyno.**
chyflym *gw.* **cyflym.**
chyflymach *gw.* **cyflymach.**
chyflymaf *gw.* **cyflymaf.**
chyflymder *gw.***cyflymder.**
chyflymed *gw.* **cyflymed.**
chyflymu *gw.* **cyflymu.**
chyflymydd *gw.* **cyflymydd.**
chyflyrau *gw.* **cyflywr.**
chyfnither *gw.* **cyfnither.**
chyfoeth *gw.* **cyfoeth.**
chyfoethog *gw.* **cyfoethog.**
chyfraith *gw.* **cyfraith.**
chyfrannu *gw.* **cyfrannu.**
chyfreithiwr *gw.* **cyfreithiwr.**
chyfreithwyr *gw.* **cyfreithiwr.**
chyfres *gw.* **cyfres.**

chyfresau: chyfresi *gw.* **cyfres.**
chyfrif *gw.* **cyfrif.**
chyfrifiadur *gw.* **cyfrifiadur.**
chyfrifiannell *gw.* **cyfrifiannell.**
chyfrifol *gw.* **cyfrifol.**
chyfrifoldeb *gw.* **cyfrifoldeb.**
chyfrifydd *gw.* **cyfrifydd.**
chyfrinach *gw.* **cyfrinach.**
chyfrinachol *gw.* **cyfrinachol.**
chyfrol *gw.* **cyfrol.**
chyfrwng *gw.* **cyfrwng.**
chyfrwys *gw.* **cyfrwys.**
chyfryngau *gw.* **cyfrwng.**
chyfun *gw.* **cyfun.**
chyfuwch *gw.* **uchel.**
chyfweld *gw.* **cyfweld.**
chyfweliad *gw.* **cyfweliad.**
chyfyng *gw.* **cyfyng.**
chyfyngu *gw.* **cyfyngu.**
chyfystyr *gw.* **cyfystyr.**
chyfforddus *gw.* **cyfforddus.**
chyffredin *gw.* **cyffredin.**
chyffrous *gw.* **cyffrous.**
chyffur *gw.* **cyffur.**
chyffwrdd *gw.* **cyffwrdd.**
chyffyrddus *gw.* **cyffyrddus.**
chyngerdd *gw.* **cyngerdd.**
chyngherddau *gw.* **cyngerdd.**
chynghori *gw.* **cynghori.**
chynghorion *gw.* **cyngor.**
chynghorwr *gw.* **cynghorwr.**
chynghrair *gw.* **cynghrair.**
chynghreiriad *gw.* **cynghreiriad.**
chyngor *gw.* **cyngor.**
chyhoedd *gw.* **cyhoedd.**
chyhoeddi *gw.* **cyhoeddi.**
chyhoeddiad *gw.* **cyhoeddiad.**
chyhoeddus *gw.* **cyhoeddus.**
chyhoeddusrwydd *gw.* **cyhoeddusrwydd.**
chyhoeddwr *gw.* **cyhoeddwr.**
chyhyd *gw.* **cyhyd.**
chyhyrog *gw.* **cyhyrog.**
chylch *gw.* **cylch.**
chylchfan *gw.* **cylchfan.**
chylchgrawn *gw.* **cylchgrawn.**
chylchgronau *gw.* **cylchgrawn.**
chylchlythyr *gw.* **cylchlythyr.**
chyll *gw.* **collen; colli.**
chyllell *gw.* **cyllell.**
chyllyll *gw.* **cyllell.**
chymaint *gw.* **cymaint.**
chymal *gw.* **cymal.**
chymanfa *gw.* **cymanfa.**
chymanfaoedd *gw.* **cymanfa.**
chymdeithas *gw.* **cymdeithas.**
chymdogion *gw.* **cymydog.**
chymeriad *gw.* **cymeriad.**
chymeryd *gw.* **cymryd.**
chymharu *gw.* **cymharu.**
chymhleth *gw.* **cymhleth.**
chymhlethdod *gw.* **cymhlethdod.**
chymhlethu *gw.* **cymhlethu.**
chymhorthion *gw.* **cymorth.**
chymoedd *gw.* **cwm.**
chymorth *gw.* **cymorth.**
Chymraeg *gw,* **Cymraeg.**
Chymraes *gw.* **Cymraes.**
Chymreictod *gw.* **Cymreictod.**
Chymreig *gw.* **Cymreig.**
Chymreiges *gw.* **Cymreiges.**
Chymro *gw.* **Cymro.**
Chymru *gw.* **Cymru.**
Chymry *gw.* **Cymro.**
chymryd *gw.* **cymryd.**
chymwynas *gw.* **cymwynas.**
chymydog *gw.* **cymydog.**
chymylau *gw.* **cwmwl.**
chymylog *gw.* **cymylog.**
chymysg *gw.* **cymysg.**
chymysgu *gw.* **cymysgu.**
chymysgwch *gw.* **cymysgwch.**
chyn *gw.* **cyn.**
chynaeafau *gw.* **cynhaeaf.**
chynddrwg *gw.* **cynddrwg.**
chynffon *gw.* **cynffon.**
chynhadledd *gw.* **cynhadledd.**
chynhaeaf *gw.* **cynhaeaf.**
chynhesu *gw.* **cynhesu.**
chynhyrfus *gw.* **cynhyrfus.**
chynigion *gw.* **cynnig.**
chynilion *gw.* **cynilion.**
chynilo *gw.* **cynilo.**
chynllun *gw.* **cynllun.**
chynllunio *gw.* **cynllunio.**
chynlluniwr *gw.* **cynlluniwr.**
chynllunydd *gw.* **cynlluniwr.**
chynnal *gw.* **cynnal.**
chynnar *gw.* **cynnar.**
chynnes *gw.* **cynnes.**
chynnig *gw.* **cynnig.**
chynnwys *gw.* **cynnwys.**
chynorthwywr *gw.* **cynorthwywr.**
chynorthwy-ydd *gw.* **cynorthwy-ydd.**
chynradd *gw.* **cynradd.**
chynt *gw.* **cynnar.**
chyntaf *gw.* **cyntaf, cynnar.**
chynted *gw.* **cynnar.**
chyntedd *gw.* **cyntedd.**
chynteddau *gw.* **cyntedd.**
chynteddoedd *gw.* **cyntedd.**
chynulleidfa *gw.* **cynulleidfa.**
chypyrddau *gw.* **cwpwrdd.**
chyrddau *gw.* **cwrdd.**
chyrff *gw.* **corff.**
chyrion *gw.* **cwr.**
chyrliog *gw.* **cyrliog.**
chyrn *gw.* **corn.**

chyrraedd *gw.* **cyrraedd.**
chyrrau *gw.* **cwr.**
chyrsau *gw.* **cwrs.**
chyrsiau *gw.* **cwrs.**
chysglyd *gw.* **cysglyd.**
chysgod *gw.* **cysgod.**
chysgodau *gw.* **cysgod.**
chysgodi *gw.* **cysgodi.**
chysgodion *gw.* **cysgod.**
chysgu *gw.* **cysgu.**
chystadlaethau *gw.* **cystadleuaeth.**
chystadleuaeth *gw.* **cystadleuaeth.**
chystadleuwr *gw.* **cystadleuwr.**
chystadleuwyr *gw.* **cystadleuwr.**
chystadleuydd *gw.* **cystadleuwr.**
chystadlu *gw.* **cystadlu.**
chystal *gw.* **cystal.**
chystymau *gw.* **cwstwm.**
chysur *gw.* **cysur.**
chysuro *gw.* **cysuro.**
chysurus *gw.* **cysurus.**
chyswllt *gw.* **cyswllt.**
chytgan *gw.* **cytgan.**
chytsain *gw.* **cytsain.**
chytseiniaid *gw.* **cytsain.**
chytseiniau *gw.* **cytsain.**
chytundeb *gw.* **cytundeb.**
chytuno *gw.* **cytuno.**
chyw *gw.* **cyw.**
chywaith *gw.* **cywaith.**
chyweithiau *gw.* **cywaith.**
chywion *gw.* **cyw.**
chywir *gw.* **cywir.**
chywiriad *gw.* **cywiriad.**
chywiro *gw.* **cywiro.**

da 1 *a.* good, well; **bore da** good morning; **da iawn** very good, very well (*in health*); **Mae'n dda gen i weld** I'm glad to see; *gw. At. Ansoddeiriau.* **2** *e.g.* good, goodness. **3** *e. torf.* goods, stock; cattle (*S.W.*).
dabl *gw.* **tabl.**
dablet *gw.* **tablet.**
dacl *gw.* **tacl.**
daclo *gw.* **taclo.**
daclu *gw.* **taclu.**
daclus *gw.* **taclus.**
dacluso *gw.* **tacluso.**
daclwr *gw.* **taclwr.**
dacw *ad.* There is/are, behold (*far away*) (*followed by soft mutation*).
Dachwedd *gw.* **Tachwedd.**
dad *gw.* **tad.**
dadansoddi *be.* **(dadansoddaf)** to analyse.
dad-cu *gw.* **tad-cu.**
dadl *e.b. ll.* **-euon** debate, argument, dispute.
dadlau *be.* **(dadleuaf)** to argue, to debate, to dispute.
daear *e.b. ll.* **-oedd** earth, ground, soil, land: **Beth ar y ddaear ydy e?** What on earth is it?; **Ble ar y ddaear mae e?** Where on earth is he/it?
daeareg *e.b.* geology.
daeargryn *e.g.b. ll.* **-fâu, -feydd** earthquake.
daearyddiaeth *e.b.* geography.
daeth *bf.* he/she/it came; *gw.* **dod.**
dafad *e.b. ll.* **defaid** sheep, ewe; wart.
dafarn *gw.* **tafarn.**
dafarnwr *gw.* **tafarnwr.**
dafell *gw.* **tafell.**
daflegryn *gw.* **taflegryn.**
daflen *gw.* **taflen.**
daflu *gw.* **taflu.**
dafod *gw.* **tafod.**
dafodiaith *gw.* **tafodiaith.**
dafol *gw.* **tafol.**
dagfa *gw.* **tagfa.**
dagrau *gw.* **deigryn.**
dagu *gw.* **tagu.**
dangnefedd *gw.* **tangnefedd.**
daid *gw.* **taid.**
dail *gw.* **dalen, deilen.**
daioni *e.g.* goodness: **er daioni** for the good of; *gw.* **da.**
dair *gw.* **tair.**
daith *gw.* **taith.**
dal *gw.* **tal.**
dal: dala (*S.W.*) *be.* **(daliaf, dalaf)** to hold, to capture, to seize, to catch; to maintain; to keep, to wager, to bet; to continue; to rely, to trust: **dal annwyd** to catch a cold; **dal ati** to persevere, to stick at it; **dal dŵr** to hold water; **dal dig** to bear or retain a grudge; **dal ei dir** to hold his ground; **dal i fyny** to bear up, to uphold; **dal i lawr** to subjugate; **dal perthynas â** to be related to; **dal sylw** to take notice; **dal wrth/at** to adhere to, to persevere in; **dal y slac yn dynn** to pretend to work; **does dim dal arno** He cannot be relied upon; **Ydy e'n dal i ganu?** Does he still sing?
dâl *gw.* **tâl.**
dalai *gw.* **talai.**
dalaith *gw.* **talaith.**
dalcen *gw.* **talcen.**
daleb *gw.* **taleb.**
daleion *gw.* **talai.**
dalen *e.b. ll.* **dail, -nau** leaf (*of a book*); sheet (*of paper*); leaf (*of tree, plant, etc.*): **troi dalen newydd** to turn over a new leaf; **ymyl y ddalen** margin of a page; *gw.* **deilen, tudalen.**
dalent *gw.* **talent.**
dalentog *gw.* **talentog.**
dalgylch *e.g. ll.* **-oedd** catchment area.
dalu *gw.* **talu.**
dalwr *gw.* **talwr.**
dalwrn *gw.* **talwrn.**
dall 1 *a.* blind. **2** *e.g. ll.* **deillion, deilliaid** blind person(s).
dallu *be.* **(dallaf)** to blind, to dazzle.
damaid *gw.* **tamaid.**
dameg *e.b. ll.* **damhegion** parable.
dameidiau *gw.* **tamaid.**
damhegion *gw.* **dameg.**

damwain *e.b.* *ll.* **damweiniau** accident; chance; **ar ddamwain, trwy ddamwain, wrth ddamwain** by chance.
dan: tan *ardd.* **(dana, danat, dano/ dani, danon, danoch, danyn)** under, until, as far; (*followed by soft mutation*) *gw. At. Arddodiaid.*
dân *gw.* **tân.**
danau *gw.* **tân.**
dancer *gw.* **tancer.**
danddaear *gw.* **tanddaear.**
danfon *be.* **(danfonaf)** to send, to dispatch; to conduct, to accompany; *gw.* **anfon.**
danfor *gw.* **tanfor.**
dangos (i) *be.* **(dangosaf)** to show, to reveal.
danio *gw.* **tanio.**
danlinellu *gw.* **tanlinellu.**
danlwybr *gw.* **tanlwybr.**
danllyd *gw.* **tanllyd.**
dannau *gw.* **tant.**
dannedd *gw.* **dant.**
dannoedd *e.b.* toothache.
danseilio *gw.* **tanseilio.**
dant *e.g.* *ll.* **dannedd** tooth; cog; tyne; **dant blaen** front tooth; incisor; **dannedd gosod/dodi** false teeth; **at ei ddant** to his taste; **dant y llew** dandelion; *gw.* **tant.**
danwydd *gw.* **tanwydd.**
dap *gw.* **tap.**
dâp *gw.* **tâp.**
daran *gw.* **taran.**
daranu *gw.* **taranu.**
darddiad *gw.* **tarddiad.**
darddu *gw.* **tarddu.**
darfod (i) *be.* **(darfodaf)** to end; to finish, to die; to waste away; to happen (*N.W.*).
darganfod *be.* **(darganfyddaf)** to discover.
darged *gw.* **targed.**
darian *gw.* **tarian.**
darlith *e.b.* *ll.* **-iau** lecture.
darlithio *be.* **(darlithiaf)** to lecture.
darlithiwr: darlithydd *e.g.* *ll.* **darlithwyr** lecturer.
darlun *e.g.* *ll.* **-iau** picture.
darlunio *be.* **(darluniaf)** to describe, to draw, to illustrate.
darlledu *be.* **(darlledaf)** to broadcast.
darllen *be.* **(darllenaf)** to read.
darllenwr: darllenydd *e.g.* *ll.* **darllenwyr** reader.
darn *e.g.* *ll.* **-au** part, piece.
daro *gw.* **taro.**
darw *gw.* **tarw.**
dasg *gw.* **tasg.**
dasgu *gw.* **tasgu.**
datblygiad *e.g.* *ll.* **-au** development, evolution.
datblygu *be.* **(datblygaf)** to develop, to evolve.
daten *gw.* **taten.**
datgan *be.* **(datganaf)** to declare, to recite.
datganiad *e.g.* *ll.* **-au** declaration, rendering.
datganoli *be.* **(datganolaf)** to devolve, to decentralise.
datguddio *be.* **(datguddiaf)** to reveal, to disclose.
dato: datws *gw.* **taten.**
datod *be.* **(datodaf)** to undo, to solve, to loose; to dissolve (*N.W.*).
datrys *be.* **(datrysaf)** to solve, to unravel.
datws *gw.* **taten.**
dathlu *be.* **(dathlaf)** to celebrate.
dau 1 *a.g.* (*followed by soft mutation*) two. 2 *e.g.* *ll.* **deuoedd** two; **y ddau** both; *gw.* **dwy.**
dawel *gw.* **tawel.**
dawelu *gw.* **tawelu.**
dawelwch *gw.* **tawelwch.**
dawelydd *gw.* **tawelydd.**
dawelyn *gw.* **tawelyn.**
dawns *e.b.* *ll.* **-iau** dance; **dawns werin** folk dance.
dawnsio *be.* **(dawnsiaf)** to dance; **dawnsio gwerin** folk dancing.
de 1 *a.* southern; right; **y llaw dde** the right hand. 2 *e.g.* south; **pegwn y de** south pole. 3 *e.b.* right side; **ar y dde** on the right (hand) side; *gw.* **te.**
deall 1 *be.* **(deallaf)** to understand. 2 *e.g.* understanding, intelligence, intellect.
deallus *a.* intelligent.
debot *gw.* **tebot.**
debyg *gw.* **tebyg.**
debygrwydd *gw.* **tebygrwydd.**
decell *gw.* **tegell.**
dechneg *gw.* **techneg.**
dechnegol *gw.* **technegol.**
dechnegwr *gw.* **technegwr.**
dechnoleg *gw.* **technoleg.**
dechrau 1 *be.* **(dechreuaf)** to begin, originate: **Mae e'n dechrau tyfu** He/It is beginning to grow. 2 *e.g.* beginning, origin.
dechreuad *e.g.* beginning; **'Yn y dechreuad . . .'** 'In the beginning . . .'

dedwydd *a.* happy, blessed.
deddf *e.b. ll.* **-au** law, statute, act: **Deddf Gwlad** law of the land; **Deddf Uno 1536** Act of Union 1536; **Deddf yr Iaith** (Welsh) Language Act.
deddfu *be.* **(deddfaf)** to legislate.
defnydd *e.g. ll.* **-iau** material, cloth, fabric; use, purpose.
defnyddio *be.* **(defnyddiaf)** to use.
defnyddiol *a.* useful.
deffro *be.* **(deffroaf)** to awake, to awaken.
deg: deng 1 *a.* ten; **deng mlynedd** ten years, decade; **deng mlwydd** ten years (*of age*); **deng niwrnod** ten days; **a'm deg ewin** (*doing*) my level best; *gw, At. Ansoddeiriau.* 2 *e.g. ll.* **degau** ten; *gw.* **teg.**
degan *gw.* **tegan.**
degawd *e.g. ll.* **-au** decade.
degell *gw.* **tegell.**
degwch *gw.* **tegwch.**
deng *a.* ten; (*used before* **blwydd, blynedd** *and* **diwrnod**) followed by nasal mutation; *gw.* **deg.**
deheuol *a.* southern.
dei *gw.* **tei.**
deialog *e.g.b. ll.* **-au** dialogue.
deiar *gw.* **teiar.**
deidiau *gw.* **taid.**
deigr *gw.* **teigr.**
deigryn *e.g. ll.* **dagrau** tear.
deilen *e.b. ll.* **dail** leaf (*of tree*); *gw.* **dalen.**
deiliwr *gw.* **teiliwr.**
deilsen *gw.* **teilsen.**
deilwng *gw.* **teilwng.**
deilwres *gw.* **teilwres.**
deilyngdod *gw.* **teilyngdod.**
deilliaid: deillion *gw.* **dall.**
deimlad *gw.* **teimlad.**
deimlo *gw.* **teimlo.**
deintydd *e.g. ll.* **-ion** dentist.
deipiadur *gw.* **teipiadur.**
deirgwaith *gw.* **teirgwaith.**
deiseb *e.b. ll.* **-au** petition.
deisen *gw.* **teisen.**
deitl *gw.* **teitl.**
deithio *gw.* **teithio.**
deithiwr *gw.* **teithiwr.**
del *a.* pretty, neat (*N.W.*).
deledu *gw.* **teledu.**
deleffon *gw.* **teleffon.**
delw *e.b. ll.* **-au** image, idol, form, manner; **ar ddelw** in the image of.
delwi *be.* **(delwaf)** to become motionless, to be paralysed with fright.
delyn *gw.* **telyn.**
delyneg *gw.* **telyneg.**
delynor *gw.* **telynor.**
delynores *gw.* **telynores.**
deml *gw.* **teml.**
denau *gw.* **tenau.**
deniadol *a.* attractive, enticing.
denu *be.* **(denaf)** to attract, to entice.
derbyn *be.* **(derbyniaf, derbynnaf)** to receive.
derbynebau: derbynebion *gw.* **derbynneb.**
derbyniol *a.* acceptable, approved, receptive.
derbynneb *e.b. ll.* **derbynebau, derbynebion** receipt, voucher.
derfyn *gw.* **terfyn.**
deri *e. ll.* oak-trees, oak; *gw.* **derwen.**
derm *gw.* **term.**
derw *a.* of oak, oaken; *gw.* **derwen.**
derwen *e.b. ll.* **derw** oak-tree, oak *gw.* **deri, derw.**
des *gw.* **tes.**
desg *e.b. ll.* **-iau** desk.
desog *gw.* **tesog.**
destun *gw.* **testun.**
detholiad *e.g. ll.* **-au** selection, anthology.
deuawd *e.g.b. ll.* **-au** duet.
deuddeg 1 *a.* twelve. 2 *e.g.* twelve.
deuddegfed *a.* twelfth.
deugain 1 *a.* forty; **deugain mlynedd** forty years. 2 *e.g.* forty.
deulu *gw.* **teulu.**
deunaw 1 *a.* eighteen; **deunaw mlynedd** eighteen years. 2 *e.g.* eighteen.
deuoedd *gw.* **dau.**
dew *gw.* **tew.**
dewch *bf.* come! (*plural*); *gw.* **dod.**
dewin *e.g. ll.* **-iaid** magician, wizard, diviner.
dewis 1 *be.* **(dewisaf)** to choose, to select. 2 *e.g. ll.* **-au** choice, desire.
dewr 1 *a. ll.* **-ion** brave, valiant. 2 *e.g. ll.* **-ion** brave man, hero.
deyrnas *gw.* **teyrnas.**
di *gw.* **ti,** *gw. At. Rhagenwau.*
diacon *e.g. ll.* **-iaid** deacon.
diafol *e.g. ll.* **diawliaid** devil.
dial (ar) 1 *be.* **(dialaf)** to avenge; to revenge. 2 *e.g. ll.* **-au, -on** vengeance.
dianc *(rhag.) be.* **(dihangaf)** to escape, to avoid.
diarfogi *be.* **(diarfogaf)** to disarm.
diarhebion *gw.* **dihareb.**
diawl *e.g. ll.* **-iaid** devil. **Cer i'r diawl!** To hell with you! **diawl o**

beth a devil of a thing.
diawledig *a.* devilish.
diawliaid *gw.* **diafol, diawl.**
di-baid *a.* unceasing, constant.
diben *e.g.* *ll.* **-ion** end, object, aim; **di-ben-draw** endless, interminable.
dibennu *be.* **(dibennaf)** to end, to finish, to terminate.
di-blwm *a.* unleaded.
dibynnu (ar) *be.* **(dibynnaf)** to depend (on), to rely (on).
diced *gw.* **ticed.**
diderfyn *a.* unlimited.
diddordeb *e.g.* *ll.* **-au** interest, hobby.
diddorol *a.* interesting, of interest.
dieithr *a.* strange, unfamiliar.
dieithryn *e.g.* *ll.* **dieithriaid** stranger.
diferyn *e.g.* *ll.* **-nau, diferion** drop.
difetha *be.* **(difethaf)** to destroy, to spoil.
diflannu *be.* **(diflannaf)** to vanish, to disappear.
diflas *a.* distasteful, dull.
drifrifol *a.* serious, earnest, solemn.
difyr: difyrrus *a.* pleasant, amusing, entertaining.
difyrru *be.* **(difyrraf)** to amuse, to entertain.
diffiniad *e.g.* *ll.* **-au** definition.
diffinio *be.* **(diffiniaf)** to define.
diffodd *be.* **(diffoddaf)** to extinguish, to quench: **diffodda'r golau, (stof/ tân/teledu)** switch off the light, (stove/fire/television).
diffuant *a.* genuine, sincere: **yr eiddoch yn ddiffuant** yours sincerely.
diffyg *e.g.* *ll.* **-ion** defect, want, lack, failure, flaw.
digon 1 *e.g.* enough, sufficiency; plenty. 2 *a.* enough; plentiful, ample. 3 *ad.* enough, sufficiently, adequately: **Dyna ddigon!** That's enough! **yn ddigon da** good enough (*no mutation*).
digonedd *e.g.* abundance, plenty.
digrif *a.* merry, amusing.
digwydd *be.* **(digwyddaf)** to happen, to occur. **Digwyddodd hi weld y dyn.** She happened to see the man.
digwyddiad *e.g.* *ll.* **-au** happening, event.
dihareb *e.b.* *ll.* **diarhebion** proverb.
diheintydd *e.g.* *ll.* **-ion** disinfectant.
dihuno *be.* **(dihunaf)** to waken, to awaken (*S.W.*).
dileu *be.* **(dileaf)** to delete, to abolish, to exterminate, to erase.
dilyn *be.* **(dilynaf)** to follow, to pursue.
dillad *gw.* **dilledyn.**
dilledyn *e.g.* *ll.* **dillad** garment, dress, item of clothing: **dillad bob dydd** everyday clothes; **dillad diwedydd** clothes changed into after work; **dillad gwaith** working clothes; **dillad gwely** bedclothes; **dillad isa(f)** underclothing; **dillad nos** pyjamas; **dillad parch** Sunday best, best clothes.
dim 1 *e.g.* any, no. **am ddim** for nothing, gratis: **dim byd** nothing at all; **dim ond** nothing but, only, merely; **dim un** not a single one; **i'r dim** exactly.
dîm *gw.* **tîm.**
dinas *e.b.* *ll.* **-oedd** city.
dinasyddion *gw.* **dinesydd.**
dinesig *a.* civic, urban.
dinesydd *e.g.* *ll.* **dinasyddion** citizen.
dinistrio *be.* **(dinistriaf)** to destroy.
diniwed *a.* innocent, harmless, simple.
diod *e.b.* *ll.* **-ydd** drink, beverage; **diod gadarn** strong drink; **diod o ddŵr** a drink of water.
dioddef (o) 1 *be.* **(dioddefaf)** to suffer, to endure, to allow. 2 *e.g.* *ll.* **-au, -iadau** suffering, passion.
diofal *a.* careless.
diog: dioglyd *a.* lazy, sluggish, indolent.
diogel *a.* safe, secure, certain.
diogi 1 *be.* **(diogaf)** to be lazy or idle, to laze. 2 *e.g.* laziness.
dioglyd *gw.* **diog.**
diogyn *e.g.* *ll.* **-nod** idler, sluggard.
diolch (i, am) 1 *be.* **(diolchaf)** to thank, to give thanks. 2 *e.g.* *ll.* **-iadau** thanks; thanksgiving. **diolch byth!** thank heaven! **diolch yn fawr** many thanks (*to you*) **diolch i'r nef (drefn)** thank goodness.
diolchgar *a.* thankful, grateful.
diolchgarwch *e.g.* thankfulness, thanksgiving; **Cwrdd Diolchgarwch** Harvest Thanksgiving Service.
diolchiadau *gw.* **diolch.**
dip *gw.* **tip.**
dipyn *gw.* **tipyn.**
dir *gw.* **tir.**
dirgelwch *e.g.* *ll.* **dirgelychau** mystery, secret, secrecy.
dirion *gw.* **tirion.**
dirlun *gw.* **tirlun.**

diroedd *gw.* **tiroedd.**
dirprwy *e.g. ll.* **-on** deputy, delegate, proxy, substitute: **dirprwy brifathro** deputy headmaster.
dirprwyaeth *e.b. ll.* **-au** deputation, delegation.
dirwy *e.b. ll.* **-on** fine, penalty.
disg *e.g.b. ll.* **-iau** disc, record.
disglair *a.* bright, brilliant.
disgleirio *be.* **(disgleiriaf)** to shine, to glitter.
disgrifiad *e.g. ll.* **-au** description.
disgrifio *be.* **(disgrifiaf)** to describe.
disgwyl (am) *be.* **(disgwyliaf)** to expect, to look, to wait for: **Mae hi'n disgwyl baban** She is expecting a baby. **Mae e'n disgwyl bws.** He is waiting for a bus.
disgybl *g. ll.* **-ion** disciple, pupil, novice, follower, adherent.
disgyblaeth *e.b. ll.* **-au** discipline.
disgyn *be.* **(disgynnaf)** to descend, to fall.
disian *gw.* **tisian.**
distaw *a.* silent, calm, quiet.
distawrwydd *e.g.* silence, quiet.
distewi *be.* **(distewaf)** to silence, to be silent, to calm.
diswyddo *be.* **(diswyddaf)** to dismiss, to depose, to sack.
dithau *gw.* **tithau.**
di-waith *a.* unemployed, idle.
diwallu *be.* **(diwallaf)** to satisfy, to supply.
diwedd 1 *e.g. ll.* **-ion, -au** end, close, conclusion; death; purpose. 2 *a.* last, final. **o'r dechrau i'r diwedd** from start to finish.
diweddar *a.* recent; modern, late *(S.W.)*; late *(of person)*; lately, deceased: **y diweddar Tom Jones** the late Tom Jones **Ydych chi wedi nofio'n ddiweddar?** Have you been swimming lately? **Cymraeg Diweddar** Modern Welsh.
diweddglo *e.g. ll.* **diweddgloeon** conclusion, close, epilogue.
diwerth *a.* worthless.
diwethaf *a.* last; previous; latest; **Rydw i'n dal y trên nesa achos collais yr un diwethaf** I'm catching the next train because I missed the previous one.
diwrnod *e.g. ll.* **-au** day: **diwrnod braf/teg** fine day; **diwrnod gwaith** working day; **diwrnod gŵyl** holy-day, holiday; **diwrnod mawr** red letter day, 'big day'; **diwrnod i'r brenin** a thoroughly enjoyable day; **y diwrnod o'r blaen** the day before, the other day; **ers diwrnodau** for many days *(past)*.
diwydiant *e.g. ll.* **diwydiannau** industry; **diwydiant dur** steel industry; **diwydiant glo** coal industry; **diwydiant ymwelwyr** tourist industry; **diwydiant ysgafn** light industry.
diwygiad *e.g. ll.* **-au** reform, reformation; revival; **Diwygiad Protestannaidd** *(Protestant)* Reformation.
diwygio *be.* **(diwygiaf)** to amend, to reform, to revise.
diwylliant *e.g. ll.* **diwylliannau** culture.
dlawd *gw.* **tlawd.**
dlodi *gw.* **tlodi.**
dlodion *gw,* **tlawd.**
dlos *gw.* **tlos.**
dlws *gw.* **tlws.**
dlysau *gw.* **tlws.**
do *ad.* yes *(affirmative answer to questions using verbs in the past tense)*. **Fuest ti'n siopa heddiw? Do.** Were you shopping today? Yes. **Welaist ti'r dyn? Do.** Did you see the man? Yes. *gw.* **to.**
doc *e.g. ll.* **-iau** dock; **docfa** berth.
doctor *e.g. ll.* **-iaid** doctor (always used in title); **Y Dr Tom Huws** Dr Tom Huws.
docyn *gw.* **tocyn.**
docynnwr *gw.* **tocynnwr.**
dod: dyfod (at, dros, yn, i) *be.* **(deuaf)** to come, to arrive; to occur; to become *gw. At. Berfau.*
dodi *be.* **(dodaf)** to put, to place *(S.W.)*; to give; **dodi ar ddeall** to explain to; **dodi bai ar** to blame; **dodi (un) ar waith** to set (one) to work.
dodrefnyn *e.g. ll.* **dodrefn** piece of furniture *(N.W.)*; *gw.* **celficyn.**
dodwy *be.* **(dodwaf)** to lay eggs.
doddi *gw.* **toddi.**
doe *ad. & e.g.b.* yesterday: **bore ddoe** yesterday morning; **echdoe** the day before yesterday.
does *gw.* **toes.**
doeth *a.* wise: **Y Tri Gŵr Doeth** The Three Wise Men.
doethineb *e.b. ll.* **-au** wisdom, discretion.
dof *a. ll.* **-ion** tame, domesticated.
dogfen *e.b. ll.* **-ni, -nau** document.
doiled *gw.* **toiled.**

dol *e.b. ll.* **-iau** doll.
dôl *e.b. ll.* **dolydd, dolau** meadow; dole; **ar y dôl** on the dole.
dolc *gw.* **tolc.**
dolcio *gw.* **tolcio.**
dolen *e.b. ll.* **-nau, -ni** handle, link, ring; **dolen gydiol** connecting link.
dolur *e.g. ll.* **-iau** hurt, ailment, pain, ache: **dolur rhydd** diarrhoea; **dolur y galon** heart disease.
dolydd *gw* **dôl.**
doll *gw.* **toll.**
don *gw.* **ton.**
dôn *gw.* **dôn.**
donau *gw.* **tôn.**
donfedd *gw.* **tonfedd.**
doniol *a.* witty, humorous.
donnau *gw.* **ton.**
dorch *gw.* **torch.**
doreithiog *gw.* **toreithiog.**
doreth *gw.* **toreth.**
dorf *gw.* **torf.**
dorfeydd *gw.* **torf.**
dorheulo *gw.* **torheulo.**
Dori *gw.* **Tori.**
doriad *gw.* **toriad.**
Doriaid *gw.* **Toriaid.**
Doriaidd *gw.* **Toriaidd.**
dorri *gw.* **torri.**
dors *gw.* **tors.**
dorth *gw.* **torth.**
dosau *gw.* **tosyn.**
dosbarth *e.g. ll.* **-au, -iadau** class, standard; district: **dosbarth canol** middle class; **dosbarth gweithiol** working class; **dosbarth isaf** lower class; **dosbarth uchaf** upper class; **dosbarthiadau meithrin** nursery classes; **cyngor dosbarth** district council; **dosbarth nos** evening class.
dost *gw.* **tost.**
dostrwydd *gw.* **tostrwydd.**
dosyn *gw.* **tosyn.**
drachefn: trachefn *ad.* again.
draddodiad *gw.* **traddodiad.**
draddodiadol *gw.* **traddodiadol.**
draed *gw.* **traed.**
draen *e.b. ll.* **-iau** drain; **draeniau dŵr** water drains.
draen: draenen *e.b. ll.* **drain** thorn: **draenen ddu** black-thorn; **draenen wen** hawthorn; **ar bigau'r drain** on tenterhooks.
draenog *e.g. ll.* **-od, -iaid, -ion** hedgehog.
draeth *gw.* **traeth.**
draethau *gw.* **traeth.**
draethawd *gw.* **traethawd.**
draethodau *gw.* **traethawd.**
drafnidiaeth *gw.* **trafnidiaeth.**
drafod *gw.* **trafod.**
drafferth *gw.* **trafferth.**
drafferthu *gw.* **trafferthu.**
draffordd *gw.* **traffordd.**
draffyrdd *gw.* **traffordd.**
dragwyddol *gw.* **tragwyddol.**
drai *gw.* **trai.**
draig *e.b. ll.* **dreigiau** dragon: **Y Ddraig Goch** the Red Dragon.
drain *e. ll.* thorns; *gw.* **draen.**
drais *gw.* **trais.**
drallod *gw.* **trallod.**
drallwysiad *gw.* **trallwysiad.**
drama *e.b. ll.* **dramâu** drama; **drama radio** radio play; **drama deledu** television play; **drama gyfres** serial; **drama un act** one-act play.
dramodwr: dramodydd *e.g. ll.* **dramodwyr** dramatist.
dramor *gw.* **tramor.**
drannoeth *gw.* **trannoeth.**
drap *gw.* **trap.**
draul *gw.* **traul.**
draw *ad.* yonder, there, beyond. **Mae'r tŷ draw fanna** The house is over there.
drawsblannu *gw.* **trawsblannu.**
drawst *gw.* **trawst.**
drechu *gw.* **trechu.**
dref: dre *gw.* **tref.**
drefi *gw.* **tref.**
drefn *gw.* **trefn.**
drefnu *gw.* **trefnu.**
drefnus *gw.* **trefnus.**
dreigiau *gw.* **draig.**
dreiglad *gw.* **treiglad.**
dreiglo *gw.* **treiglo.**
dreisio *gw.* **treisio.**
drem *gw.* **trem.**
drên *gw.* **trên.**
drenau *gw.* **trên.**
drennydd *gw.* **trennydd.**
dreser: dresel *e.g. ll.* **-i, -ydd** dresser.
dreth *gw.* **treth.**
drethdalwr *gw.* **trethdalwr.**
drethu *gw.* **trethu.**
dreuliau *gw.* **traul.**
dreulio *gw.* **treulio.**
drewdod *e.g.* stink, stench.
drewi (o) 1 *be.* **(drewaf)** to stink. 2 *e.g.* stench.
dri *gw.* **tri.**
driawd *gw.* **triawd.**
dric *gw.* **tric.**
dridiau *gw.* **tridiau.**
drigain *gw.* **trigain.**

drigfan *gw.* **trigfan.**
drigo *gw.* **trigo.**
drigolion *gw.* **trigolion.**
dringo *be.* **(dringaf)** to climb.
dringwr *e.g. ll.* **dringwyr** climber.
drin *gw.* **trin.**
drindod *gw.* **trindod.**
drioedd *gw.* **trioedd.**
driongl *gw.* **triongl.**
drist *gw.* **trist.**
dristwch *gw.* **tristwch.**
dro *gw.* **tro.**
drochi *gw.* **trochi.**
droeau *gw.* **tro.**
droed *gw.* **troed.**
droedfedd *gw.* **troedfedd.**
droedffordd *gw.* **troedffordd.**
dröedig *gw.* **tröedig.**
dröedigaeth *gw.* **tröedigaeth.**
droedio *gw.* **troedio.**
droednoeth *gw.* **troednoeth.**
droeon *gw.* **tro.**
drogylch *gw.* **trogylch.**
droi *gw.* **troi.**
dros: tros *ardd. (followed by soft mutation)* **(drosto, drostot, drosto/drosti, droston, drostoch, drostyn):** over, for, instead of, on behalf of; **drosodd** finished; **drosodd a throsodd** over and over again; **dros ben** exceedingly; **mynd dros ben llestri** to go over the top; **dros dro** temporary; *gw. At. Arddodiaid.*
drosedd *gw.* **trosedd.**
droseddu *gw.* **troseddu.**
droseddwr *gw.* **troseddwr.**
drosgais *gw.* **trosgais.**
drosglwyddo *gw.* **trosglwyddo.**
drosi *gw.* **trosi.**
drosiad *gw.* **trosiad.**
droswr *gw.* **troswr.**
drothwy *gw.* **trothwy.**
drowsus *gw.* **trowsus.**
druan *gw.* **truan.**
drud *a.* expensive, dear, precious, valuable.
drudwy *e.g ll.* **-od** starling.
drueni *gw.* **trueni.**
druenus *gw.* **truenus.**
drugaredd *gw.* **trugaredd.**
drugarhau *gw.* **trugarhau.**
drwbl *gw.* **trwbl.**
drwchus *gw.* **trwchus.**
drwg 1 *e.g.* evil, iniquity, wickedness: **o ddrwg i waeth** from bad to worse; **y drwg yn y caws** the source of the evil. **2** *a.* evil; bad; wicked; rotten: **afal drwg** rotten apple; **wy drwg** rotten egg; *gw. At. Ansoddeiriau.*
drwm *e.g. ll.* **drymiau** drum; *gw.* **trwm.**
drws *e.g. ll.* **drysau** door, entrance, gap: **drws cefn** a back door; **drws nesaf** next door; **wrth y drws** at hand, close, near; **carreg y drws** door-step.
drwser *gw.* **trwser.**
drwsio *gw.* **trwsio.**
drwsiwr *gw.* **trwsiwr.**
drwy: trwy *ardd. (followed by soft mutation)* **(drwyddo, drwyddot, drwyddo/drwyddi, drwyddon, drwyddoch, drwyddyn)** through, by, by means of; *gw. At. Arddodiaid.*
drwydded *gw.* **trwydded.**
drwyn *gw.* **trwyn.**
drwynol *gw.* **trwynol.**
drych *e.g. ll.* **-au** mirror; image, form; spectacle; vision.
drychineb *gw.* **trychineb.**
drychiolaeth *e.b. ll.* **-au** apparition, illusion.
drydan *gw.* **trydan.**
drydanwr *gw.* **trydanwr.**
drydedd *gw.* **trydedd.**
drydydd *gw.* **trydydd.**
drydyddol *gw.* **trydyddol.**
drygioni *e.g.* evil, wickedness; *gw.* **drwg.**
drygionus *a.* bad, wicked; *gw.* **drwg.**
dryloyw *gw.* **tryloyw.**
dryll *e.g.b. ll.* **-iau** gun (*S.W.*), rifle (*S.W.*), cannon.
drysau *gw.* **drws.**
drysor *gw.* **trysor.**
drysorfa *gw.* **trysorfa.**
drysori *gw.* **trysori.**
drysorydd *gw.* **trysorydd.**
drysu *bw.* **(drysaf)** to confuse, to entangle, to disarrange.
dryw *e.g.b. ll.* **-od.** wren.
drywydd *gw.* **trywydd.**
du *a. ll.* **-on** black; dark.
dudalen *gw.* **tudalen.**
dueddiad *gw.* **tueddiad.**
dull *e.g. ll.* **-iau** form, mode, manner.
dun *gw.* **tun.**
dunnell *gw.* **tunnell.**
duo *gw.* **(duaf)** to blacken, to darken.
duon *a.ll.* black *gw.* **du.**
dur 1 *e.g. ll.* **-oedd** steel. **2** *a.* steel.
duw *e.g. ll.* **-iau** god; **Duw Dad** God the Father; **Duw Hollalluog** Almighty God; **Duw Tragwyddol** Eternal God; **bendith Duw** the blessing of God; **Duw Duw!** Good God!

duwies *e.b.* *ll.* **-au** goddess.
dwbl *a.* double, twice.
dweud (am, wrth) *be.* **(dwedaf, dywedaf)** to say, to speak; to mention: **dweud a dweud** to keep on saying; **dweud anwiredd** to tell a lie; **dweud ei feddwl** to say what one thinks; **dweud yn dda** (am) to speak well (of); **dweud yn ddrwg (am)** to speak ill (of); **Dywedais wrtho am gau ei geg** I told him to shut up.
dwfn *a.* deep; profound.
dwfr *gw.* **dŵr.**
dwl *a.* dull, foolish.
dwlc *gw.* **twlc.**
dwll *gw.* **twll.**
dwmpath *gw.* **twmpath.**
dwndis *gw.* **twndis.**
dwnel *gw.* **twnel.**
dwp *gw.* **twp.**
dwpsyn *gw.* **twpsyn.**
dŵr: dwfr *e.g.* *ll.* **dyfroedd** water; **dŵr berw(edig)** boiling water; **dŵr glaw** rain-water; **dŵr golchi llestri** dish-water; **dŵr (y) môr** sea water; **gwneud dŵr** to urinate; *gw.* **tŵr.**
dwr *gw.* **twr.**
dwrci *gw.* **twrci.**
dwristiaeth *gw.* **twristiaeth.**
dwrn *e.g.* *ll.* **dyrnau** fist.
dwrw *gw.* **twrw.**
dwsin *e.g.* *ll.* **-au** dozen.
dwt *gw.* **twt.**
dwy *a.b.* two: **y ddwy** the two, both (feminine); *gw.* **dau.**
dwyieithog *a.* bilingual.
dwyieithrwydd *e.g.* bilingualism.
dwylo *e.ll.* hands; *gw.* **llaw.**
dwyll *gw.* **twyll.**
dwyllo *gw.* **twyllo.**
dwym *gw.* **twym.**
dwymo *gw.* **twymo.**
dwymyn *gw.* **twymyn.**
dwyn *be.* **(dygaf)** to take away, to bear, to convey; to bring; to steal: **dwyn ar gof** to bring to mind; **dwyn i ben** to accomplish, to complete; **dwyn ffrwyth** to bear fruit; **dwgyd** to steal (*S.W.*).
dwyrain *e.g.* east; **y Dwyrain Canol** the Middle East; **y Dwyrain Pell** the Far East.
dwys *a.* grave; intense; profound; thick, dense, concentrated; **cwrs dwys** crash course.
dwywaith *ad.* twice.
dy *rhag (followed by soft mutation)* your (*singular*); **dy chwaer** your sister; **dy lyfr** your book.
dŷ *gw.* **tŷ.**
dybied: dybio *gw.* **tybied.**
dychmygion *gw.* **dychymyg.**
dychmygu *be.* **(dychmygaf)** to imagine, to think, to contrive.
dychrynllyd *a.* frightful, dreadful, horrendous.
dychymyg *e.g.* *ll.* **dychmygion** imagination, fancy; idea; riddle.
dydy e/hi ddim *bf.* he/she/it does not; *gw.* **bod.**
dydd *e.g.* *ll.* **-iau** day: **Dydd da!** Good Day; **o ddydd i ddydd** from day to day; **dyddiau'r wythnos** days of the week; **ers dyddiau** many days ago; **Dydd Nadolig** Christmas Day; **Gŵyl Dewi** St David's Day; **Dydd Gwener y Groglith** Good Friday; **dydd Llun (y) Pasg** Easter Monday.
dyddiad *e.g.* *ll.* **-au** date, dating.
dyddiau *gw.* **dydd.**
dyddio *be.* **(dyddiaf)** to date (*something*).
dyddyn *gw.* **tyddyn.**
dyddynnwr *gw.* **tyddynnwr.**
dyfalu *be.* **(dyfalaf)** to conjecture, to guess; to devise.
dyfarniad *e.g.* *ll.* **-au** verdict, decision.
dyfarnu *be.* **(dyfarnaf)** to adjudicate; to adjudge; to decide.
dyfarnwr *e.g.* *ll.* **dyfarnwyr** judge, umpire.
dyfiant *ge.* **tyfiant.**
dyfnder *e.g.* *ll.* **-au, -oedd** deep, depth.
dyfod *gw.* **dod.**
dyfodol 1 *a.* future, coming. 2 *e.g.* future. **amser dyfodol** future tense; **yn y dyfodol** in the future; **dyfodol disglair** a brilliant future.
dyfroedd *gw.* **dŵr.**
dyfu *gw.* **tyfu.**
dyfyniad *e.g.* *ll.* **-au** quotation.
dyffryn *e.g.* *ll.* **-noedd** valley.
dynged *gw.* **tynged.**
dyngedfennol *gw.* **tyngedfennol.**
dyngu *gw.* **tyngu.**
dylanwad *e.g.* *ll.* **-au** influence.
dyle *gw.* **tyle.**
dyled *e.b.* *ll.* **-ion** debt, due, claim, obligation.
dyledus *a.* due, indebted, obligatory.
dyletswydd *e.b.* *ll.* **-au** duty, obligation.
dylino *gw.* **tylino.**

dylwyth *gw.* **tylwyth.**
dyllau *gw.* **twll.**
dyllu *gw.* **tyllu.**
dylluan *gw.* **tylluan.**
dyma *ad.* here is/are; this is; these are.
dymer *gw.* **tymer.**
dymestl *gw.* **tymestl.**
dymherau *gw.* **tymheredd.**
dymheredd *gw.* **tymheredd.**
dymhestlog *gw.* **tymhestlog.**
dymhorau *gw.* **tymor.**
dymor *gw.* **tymor.**
dymuniad *e.g. ll.* **-au** wish, desire; request: **gyda phob dymuniad da** with all best wishes; **dymuniadau gorau** best wishes.
dymuno *be.* **(dymunaf)** to wish, to desire.
dymunol *a.* desirable, pleasant; desired.
dyn *e.g. ll.* **-ion** man, person: **dyn cyffredin** common man; **dyn dieithr** stranger; **dyn eira** snowman; *gw.* **tyn(n).**
dyna *ad.* there is/are: **dyna chi** there you are; **dyna dro** what bad luck! **dyna drueni** what a pity! **dyna fe** there it is.
dyner *gw.* **tyner.**
dynerwch *gw.* **tynerwch.**
dynes *e.b. ll.* **-au** woman (*N.W.*).
dynion *gw.* **dyn.**
dyn(n) *gw.* **tyn(n).**
dynnu *gw.* **tynnu.**
dyrau *gw.* **tŵr.**
dyrfa *gw.* **tyrfa.**
dyrfau *gw.* **twrw.**
dyrnaid *e.g. ll.* **dyrneidiau** handful, little, few.
dyrnau *gw.* **dwrn.**
dyrneidiau *gw.* **dyrnaid.**
dyrrau *gw.* **twr.**
dysgedig *a.* learned.
dysgl *e.b. ll.* **-au** dish, plate; cup; disk: **dysgl de** tea cup; **dysgl gawl** soup-plate, soup-bowl.
dysgu (i) *be.* **(dysgaf)** to learn, to teach, to educate: **dysgu ar gof** to learn by heart.
dysgwr *e.g. ll.* **dysgwyr** learner.
dysgwyr *gw.* **dysgwr.**
dyst *gw.* **tyst.**
dystio *gw.* **tystio.**
dystiolaeth *gw.* **tystiolaeth.**
dystion *gw.* **tyst.**
dystysgrif *gw.* **tystysgrif.**
dywediad *e.g. ll.* **-au** saying.
dyweddïad *e.g. ll.* **-au** engagement, betrothal.
dywel *gw.* **tywel.**
dywod *gw.* **tywod.**
dywydd *gw.* **tywydd.**
dywyll *gw.* **tywyll.**
dywyllu *gw.* **tywyllu.**
dywyllwch *gw.* **tywyllwch.**
dywys *gw.* **tywys.**
dywysog *gw.* **tywysog.**
dywysoges *gw.* **tywysoges.**

dda *gw.* **da.**
ddadansoddi *gw.* **dadansoddi.**
ddadl *gw.* **dadl.**
ddadlau *gw.* **dadlau.**
ddaear *gw.* **daear.**
ddaeareg *gw.* **daeareg.**
ddaeargryn *gw.* **daeargryn.**
ddaearyddiaeth *gw.* **daearyddiaeth.**
ddaeth *gw.* **daeth.**
ddafad *gw.* **dafad.**
ddagrau *gw.* **deigryn.**
ddail *gw.* **deilen.**
ddaioni *gw.* **daioni.**
ddal: ddala *gw.* **dal.**
ddalen *gw.* **dalen.**
ddalgylch *gw.* **dalgylch.**
ddall *gw.* **dall.**
ddallu *gw.* **dallu.**
ddameg *gw.* **dameg.**
ddamhegion *gw.* **dameg.**
ddamwain *gw.* **damwain.**
ddanfon *gw.* **danfon.**
ddangos *gw.* **dangos.**
ddannedd *gw.* **dant.**
ddannoedd *gw.* **dannoedd.**
ddant *gw.* **dant.**
ddarfod *gw.* **darfod.**
ddarganfod *gw.* **darganfod.**
ddarlith *gw.* **darlith.**
ddarlithio *gw.* **darlithio.**
ddarlithiwr: darlithydd *gw.* **darlithiwr.**
ddarlun *gw.* **darlun.**
ddarlunio *gw.* **darlunio.**
ddarlledu *gw.* **darlledu.**
ddarllen *gw.* **darllen.**
ddarllenwr: ddarllenydd *gw.* **ddarllenwr.**
ddarn *gw.* **darn.**
ddatblygiad *gw.* **datblygiad.**
ddatblygu *gw.* **datblygu.**
ddatgan *gw.* **datgan.**
ddatganiad *gw.* **datganiad.**
ddatganoli *gw.* **datganoli.**
ddatguddio *gw.* **datguddio.**
ddatod *gw.* **datod.**
ddatrys *gw.* **datrys.**
ddathlu *gw.* **dathlu.**
ddau *gw.* **dau.**
ddawns *gw.* **dawns.**
ddawnsio *gw.* **dawnsio.**
dde *gw.* **de.**
ddeall *gw.* **deall.**
ddeallus *gw.* **deallus.**
ddechrau *gw.* **dechrau.**
ddechreuad *gw.* **dechreuad.**
ddedwydd *gw.* **dedwydd.**
ddeddf *gw.* **deddf.**
ddeddfu *gw.* **deddfu.**
ddefnydd *gw.* **defnydd.**
ddefnyddio *gw.* **defnyddio.**
ddefnyddiol *gw.* **defnyddiol.**
ddeffro *gw.* **deffro.**
ddeg: ddeng *gw.* **deg.**
ddegawd *gw.* **degawd.**
ddeheuol *gw.* **deheuol.**
ddeialog *gw.* **deialog.**
ddeigryn *gw.* **deigryn.**
ddeilen *gw.* **deilen.**
ddeilliaid: ddeillion *gw.* **dall.**
ddeintydd *gw.* **deintydd.**
ddeiseb *gw.* **deiseb.**
ddel *gw.* **del.**
ddelw *gw.* **delw.**
ddelwi *gw.* **delwi.**
ddeniadol *gw.* **deniadol.**
ddenu *gw.* **denu.**
dderbyn *gw.* **derbyn.**
dderbyniol *gw.* **derbyniol.**
dderbynneb *gw.* **dderbynneb.**
dderi *gw.* **deri.**
dderw *gw.* **derw.**
dderwen *gw.* **derwen.**
ddesg *gw.* **desg.**
ddetholiad *gw.* **detholiad.**
ddeuawd *gw.* **deuawd.**
ddeuddeg *gw.* **deuddeg.**
ddeuddegfed *gw.* **deuddegfed.**
ddeugain *gw.* **deugain.**
ddeunaw *gw.* **deunaw.**
ddeuoedd *gw.* **deuoedd.**
ddewin *gw.* **dewin.**
ddewis *gw.* **dewis.**
ddewr *gw.* **dewr.**
ddiacon *gw.* **diacon.**
ddiafol *gw.* **diafol.**
ddial *gw.* **dial.**
ddianc *gw.* **dianc.**
ddiarfogi *gw.* **diarfogi.**

ddiawl *gw.* **diawl.**
ddiawledig *gw.* **diawledig.**
ddiawliaid *gw.* **diafol, diawl.**
ddi-baid *gw.* **di-baid.**
ddiben *gw.* **diben.**
ddibennu *gw.* **dibennu.**
ddi-blwm *gw.* **di-blwm.**
ddibynnu *gw.* **dibynnu.**
ddiderfyn *gw.* **diderfyn.**
ddiddordeb *gw.* **diddordeb.**
ddiddorol *gw.* **diddorol.**
ddieithr *gw.* **dieithr.**
ddieithryn *gw.* **dieithryn.**
ddiferyn *gw.* **diferyn.**
ddifetha *gw.* **difetha.**
ddiflannu *gw.* **diflannu.**
ddiflas *gw.* **diflas.**
ddifrifol *gw.* **difrifol.**
ddifyr: ddifyrrus *gw.* **difyr.**
ddifyrru *gw.* **difyrru.**
ddiffiniad *gw.* **diffiniad.**
ddiffinio *gw.* **diffinio.**
ddiffodd *gw.* **diffodd.**
ddiffuant *gw.* **diffuant.**
ddiffyg *gw.* **diffyg.**
ddigon *gw.* **digon.**
ddigonedd *gw.* **digonedd.**
ddigrif *gw.* **digrif.**
ddigwydd *gw.* **digwydd.**
ddigwyddiad *gw.* **digwyddiad.**
ddihareb *gw.* **dihareb.**
ddiheintydd *gw.* **diheintydd.**
ddihuno *gw.* **dihuno.**
ddileu *gw.* **dileu.**
ddilyn *gw.* **dilyn.**
ddillad *gw.* **dilledyn.**
ddilledyn *gw.* **dilledyn.**
ddim *gw.* **dim.**
ddinas *gw.* **dinas.**
ddinasyddion *gw.* **dinesydd.**
ddinesig *gw.* **dinesig.**
ddinesydd *gw.* **dinesydd.**
ddinistrio *gw.* **dinistrio.**
ddiniwed *gw.* **diniwed.**
ddiod *gw.* **diod.**
ddioddef *gw.* **dioddef.**
ddiofal *gw.* **diofal.**
ddiog: ddioglydd *gw.* **diog.**
ddiogel *gw.* **diogel.**
ddiogi *gw.* **diogi.**
ddioglyd *gw.* **diog.**
ddiogyn *gw.* **diogyn.**
ddiolch *gw.* **diolch.**
ddiolchgar *gw.* **diolchgar.**
ddiolchgarwch *gw.* **diolchgarwch.**
ddirgelwch *gw.* **dirgelwch.**
ddirprwy *gw.* **dirprwy.**
ddirprwyaeth *gw.* **dirprwyaeth.**
ddirwy *gw.* **dirwy.**
ddisg *gw.* **disg.**
ddisglair *gw.* **disglair.**
ddisgleirio *gw.* **disgleirio.**
ddisgrifiad *gw.* **disgrifiad.**
ddisgrifio *gw.* **disgrifio.**
ddisgwyl *gw.* **disgwyl.**
ddisgybl *gw.* **disgybl.**
ddisgyblaeth *gw.* **disgyblaeth.**
ddisgyn *gw.* **disgyn.**
ddistaw *gw.* **distaw.**
ddistawrwydd *gw.* **distawrwydd.**
ddistewi *gw.* **distewi.**
ddiswyddo *gw.* **diswyddo.**
ddi-waith *gw.* **di-waith.**
ddiwallu *gw.* **diwallu.**
diwedd *gw.* **diwedd.**
ddiweddar *gw.* **diweddar.**
ddiweddglo *gw.* **diweddglo.**
ddiwerth *gw.* **diwerth.**
ddiwethaf *gw.* **diwethaf.**
ddiwrnod *gw.* **diwrnod.**
ddiwydiant *gw.* **diwydiant.**
ddiwygiad *gw.* **diwygiad.**
ddiwygio *gw.* **diwygio.**
ddiwylliant *gw.* **diwylliant.**
ddoc *gw.* **doc.**
ddoctor *gw.* **doctor.**
ddod: ddyfod *gw.* **dod.**
ddodi *gw.* **dodi.**
ddodrefnyn *gw.* **dodrefnyn.**
ddodwy *gw.* **dodwy.**
ddoe *gw.* **doe.**
ddoeth *gw.* **doeth.**
ddoethineb *gw.* **doethineb.**
ddof *gw.* **dof.**
ddogfen *gw.* **dogfen.**
ddol *gw.* **dol.**
ddôl *gw.* **dôl.**
ddolen *gw.* **dolen.**
ddolur *gw.* **dolur.**
ddoniol *gw.* **doniol.**
ddosbarth *gw.* **dosbarth.**
ddraen: ddraenen *gw.* **draen.**
ddraenog *gw.* **draenog.**
ddraig *gw.* **draig.**
ddrain *gw.* **draen.**
ddrama *gw.* **drama.**
ddramodwr *gw.* **dramodwr.**
ddramodydd *gw.* **dramodwr.**
ddreser: ddresel *gw.* **dreser.**
ddrewdod *gw.* **drewdod.**
ddrewi *gw.* **drewi.**
ddringo *gw.* **dringo.**
ddringwr *gw.* **dringwr.**
ddrud *gw.* **drud.**
ddrudwy *gw.* **drudwy.**
ddrwg *gw.* **drwg.**
ddrwm *gw.* **drwm.**
ddrws *gw.* **drws.**

ddrych *gw.* **drych.**
ddrychiolaeth *gw.* **drychiolaeth.**
ddrygioni *gw.* **drygioni.**
ddrygionus *gw.* **drygionus.**
ddryll *gw.* **dryll.**
ddrylliau *gw.* **dryll.**
ddrysau *gw.* **drws.**
ddrysu *gw.* **drysu.**
ddryw *gw.* **dryw.**
ddu *gw.* **du.**
ddull *gw.* **dull.**
dduo *gw.* **duo.**
ddur *gw.* **dur.**
dduw *gw.* **duw.**
dduwies *gw.* **duwies.**
ddwbl *gw.* **dwbl.**
ddweud *gw.* **dweud.**
ddwfn *gw.* **dwfn.**
ddwfr *gw.* **dŵr.**
ddwl *gw.* **dwl.**
ddŵr *gw.* **dŵr.**
ddwrn *gw.* **dwrn.**
ddwsin *gw.* **dwsin.**
ddwy *gw.* **dwy.**
ddwyieithog *gw.* **dwyieithog.**
ddwyieithrwydd *gw.* **dwyieithrwydd.**
ddwylo *gw.* **dwylo.**
ddwyn *gw.* **dwyn.**
ddwyrain *gw.* **dwyrain.**
ddwys *gw.* **dwys.**
ddwywaith *gw.* **dwywaith.**
ddychmygion *gw.* **dychymyg.**
ddychmygu *gw.* **dychmygu.**
ddychrynllyd *w.* **dychrynllyd.**
ddychymyg *gw.* **dychymyg.**
ddydd *gw.* **dydd.**
ddyddiad *gw.* **dyddiad.**
ddyddiau *gw.* **dydd.**
ddyfalu *gw.* **dyfalu.**
ddyfarniad *gw.* **dyfarniad.**
ddyfarnu *gw.* **dyfarnu.**
ddyfarnwr *gw.* **dyfarnwr.**
ddyfnder *gw.* **dyfnder.**
ddyfod *gw.* **dod.**
ddyfodol *gw.* **dyfodol.**
ddyfroedd *gw.* **dŵr.**
ddyfyniaid *gw.* **dyfyniad.**
ddyffryn *gw.* **dyffryn.**
ddylanwad *gw.* **dylanwad.**
ddyled *gw.* **dyled.**
ddyledus *gw.* **dyledus.**
ddyletswydd *gw.* **dyletswydd.**
ddymuniad *gw.* **dymuniad.**
ddymuno *gw.* **dymuno.**
ddymunol *gw.* **dymunol.**
ddyn *gw.* **dyn.**
ddynes *gw.* **dynes.**
ddyrnaid *gw.* **dyrnaid.**
ddyrnau *gw.* **dwrn.**
ddyrneidiau *gw.* **dyrnaid.**
ddysgedig *gw.* **dysgedig.**
ddysgl *gw.* **dysgl.**
ddysgu *w.* **dysgu.**
ddysgwr *gw.* **dysgwr.**
ddysgwyr *gw.* **dysgwr.**
ddywediad *gw.* **dywediad.**
ddyweddïad *gw.* **dyweddïad.**

e: o *gw.* **ef.**
eang *a.* broad, wide, extensive.
eb: ebe: ebr *bf.* says, said (I, he/she, they, etc.).
ebol *e.g.* *ll.* **-ion** colt; buck.
Ebrill *e.g.* April.
economeg *e.b.* economics.
echdoe *e.g.* *ll.* & *ad.* the day before yesterday.
echnos *e.b.* *ll.*& *ad.* the night before last.
edau *e.b.* *ll.* **edafedd** thread.
edifar: edifeiriol *a.* sorry, penitent, contrite.
Mae'n edifar gen i I regret.
edmygu *be.* **(edmygaf)** to admire.
edrych *be.* **(edrychaf)** to look, to observe, to search, to examine; to expect: **edrych am** to look for, to expect; **edrych ar** to look on, to look upon; **edrych ar ôl** to look after, to mind; **edrych at** to look towards; **edrych dros** to overlook, to survey; **edrych allan** to look out, to seek; **edrych ymlaen** to look forward.
ef: efe: efô *rhag.* he, him, it (*N.W.*).
efallai *ad.* perhaps.
efengyl *e.b.* *ll.* **-au** gospel: **Efengyl Iesu Grist** the Gospel of Jesus Christ.
efo *ardd.* with, by means of (*N.W.*).
efô *gw.* **ef.**
effaith *e.b.* *ll.* **effeithiau** effect.
effeithiau *gw.* **effaith.**
effeithiol *a.* effective.
effro *a.* awake (*N.W.*).
egin *gw.* **eginyn.**
eginyn *e.g.* *ll.* **egin.** shoot, sprout, (young) blade.
eglur *a.* clear, evident, plain.
egluro *be.* **(egluraf)** to reveal; to explain; to manifest.
eglwys *e.b.* *ll.* **-i, -ydd** church, the church.
egni *e.g.* *ll.* **egnïon, egnïoedd** energy, might; effort, endeavour.
egnïoedd *gw.* **egni.**
egnïol *a.* vigorous, energetic.
egnïon *gw.* **egni.**
egwyddor *e.b.* *ll.* **-ion** principle; rudiment; alphabet.
egwyddorol *a.* having principles; *gw.* **gwyddor.**
egwyl *e.b.* *ll.* **-iau, -ion** break, interval; spell.
enghraifft *e.b.* *ll.* **enghreifftiau** example, instance; **er enghraifft** for example.
enghreifftiau *gw.* **enghraifft.**
englyn *e.g.* *ll.* **-ion** an epigrammatic four line stanza in Welsh poetry.
engyl *gw.* **angel.**
ehedydd *e.g.* *ll.* **-ion** lark.
ei *rhag.* his, her, its: *gw. At. Treigladau.*
eich *rhag.* your.
Eidal, Yr *e.b.* Italy.
Eidaleg *e.b.* Italian language.
Eidales *e.b.* *ll.* **-au** Italian woman.
Eidalwr *e.g.* *ll.* **Eidalwyr** Italian man.
eiddo 1 *e.g.* possession(s), property, estate; **ei eiddo** his possessions. **2** *ad.* his, hers, etc.
eifr *gw.* **gafr.**
Eingl-Gymro *e.g.* *ll.* **Eingl-Gymry** Anglo-Welshman.
eiliad *e.g.b.* *ll.* **-au** second, moment.
eilwaith *ad.* again, a second time.
ein *rhag.* our.
eira *e.g.* *ll.* **-oedd** snow.
eirch *gw.* **arch.**
eirchion *gw.* **arch.**
eirfa *gw.* **geirfa.**
eiriadur *gw.* **geiriadur.**
eiriau *gw.* **gair.**
eirin *gw.* **eirinen.**
eirinen *e.b.* *ll.* **eirin** plum, damson; berry: **eirin gwlanog** peaches.
eirio *gw.* **geirio.**
eirlys *e.g.* *ll.* **-iau** snowdrop; *gw.* **tlws yr eira.**
eirth *gw.* **arth.**
eisiau *e.g.* need, want, lack, poverty: **Rydw i eisiau —** I need —, I want — **Mae eisiau — arnaf i** I need —, I want —
eisoes *ad.* already.
eistedd *be.* **(eisteddaf)** to sit, to seat.

eisteddfod *e.b.* *ll.* **-au** eisteddfod.
eisteddfodwr *e.g.* *ll.* **eisteddfodwyr** a frequenter of *eisteddfodau.*
eitem *e.b.* *ll.* **-au** item.
eithaf 1 *e.g.* *ll.* **-ion, -oedd, -edd** end, extremity, uttermost part. 2 *a.* farthest, superlative: **y gosb eithaf** capital punishment. 3 *ad.* very, quite.
eithafol *a.* extreme.
eithr 1 *rhag.* except, besides. 2 *c.* but.
eithrio *be.* **(eithriaf)** to except, to exclude; **ac eithrio** except, excepting.
eleni *ad.* this year.
elfen *e.b.* *ll.* **-nau** element, particle, factor, tendency: **yn fy elfen** in my element.
elfennau *gw.* **elfen.**
elfennol *a.* elementary, constituent, simple.
eliffant *e.g.* *ll.* **-od, -iaid** elephant.
elw *e.g.* *ll.* **-on** profit, gain.
elwa *be.* **(elwaf)** to profit, to gain.
elyn *gw.* **gelyn.**
elltydd *gw.* **allt.**
em *gw.* **gem.**
emyn *e.g.* *ll.* **-au** hymn: **emyn-dôn** hymn-tune.
emynydd *e.g.* *ll.* **emynwyr** hymn-writer.
ên *gw.* **gên.**
enaid *e.g.* *ll.* **eneidiau** soul, spirit; life.
enau *gw.* **genau.**
enedigaeth *gw.* **genedigaeth.**
eneidiau *gw.* **enaid.**
eneth *gw.* **geneth.**
eneuau *gw.* **genau.**
enfawr *a.* enormous, vast, immense, huge.
enfys *e.b.* *ll.* **-au** rainbow.
eni *gw.* **geni.**
enillwr: enillydd *e.g.* *ll.* **enillwyr** earner; victor, winner.
ennill 1 *be.* **(enillaf)** to gain, to profit, to get; to win. 2 *e.g.* *ll.* **enillion** winnings; salary; profit.
ennyd *e.g.b.* a while, moment.
enw *e.g.* *ll.* **-au** name; noun; **enw anwes** pet name; **enw benywaidd** feminine noun; **enw gwrywaidd** masculine noun; **enw torfol** collective noun; **ffugenw** nom de plume, pseudonym.
enwad *e.g.* *ll.* **-au** religious denomination.
enwedig *a.* especial.
enwi *be.* **(enwaf)** to name.
enwog 1 *a.* famous, renowned, eminent. 2 *e.ll.* **-ion.** persons of renown or fame; celebrities.
enwogrwydd *e.g.* fame.
eos *e.b.* *ll.* **-iaid** nightingale.
epa *e.g.* *ll.* **-od** ape.
er *ardd.* because of, for, in order to; since (*a fixed point in time*); despite: **er anrhydedd** in honour; **er bod** although; **er cof** in memory, *in memoriam;* **er gwaethaf** in spite of, despite; **er hynny** yet, since then; **er lles/budd** for the benefit of; **er mwyn** for the sake of, in order to; **er dydd Llun** since Monday.
eraill *gw.* **arall.**
erbyn *ardd.* against, facing, opposite; by, for, in preparation for: **erbyn hyn** by this time, by now; **mynd yn erbyn** to oppose, to go against; **erbyn meddwl** coming to think of it.
erddi *gw.* **gardd.**
erfin *gw.* **erfinen.**
erfinen *e.b.* *ll.* **erfin** turnip, swede.
erfyn 1 *be.* **(erfyniaf)** to beg, to entreat, to pray, to implore. 2 *e.g.* *ll.* **arfau** weapon, tool; *gw.* **arf.**
ergyd *e.g.b.* *ll.* **-ion** blow, knock, shot, hit, bang, detonation.
erioed *ad.* ever.
erlid *be.* **(erlidiaf)** to pursue, to persecute.
erlyn *be.* **(erlynaf)** to prosecute.
erlyniad *e.g.* *ll.* **-au** prosecution.
erlynydd *e.g.* *ll.* **-ion** prosecutor.
ernes *e.b.* *ll.* **-au** security, pledge; deposit.
ers *ardd.* for, since (*a continuing period*): **ers pythefnos** for the last fortnight.
erthygl *e.b.* *ll.* **-au** article, literary composition; clause.
erthyliad *e.g.* *ll.* **-au** abortion, miscarriage.
erthylu *be.* **(erthylaf)** to abort, to miscarry.
erw *e.b.* *ll.* **-au** acre.
eryr *e.g.* *ll.* **-od** eagle.
Eryri *e.b.* Snowdonia.
es i *bf.* I went; *gw.* **mynd.**
esboniad *e.g.* *ll.* **-au** commentary; explanation, exposition.
esbonio (i) *be.* **(esboniaf)** to explain (to).
esgeulus *a.* negligent.
esgeuluso *be.* **(esgeulusaf)** to neglect.

esgeulustod: esgeulustra *e.g.* negligence.
esgid *e.b. ll.* **-iau** boot; shoe: **esgidiau mawr/uchel** high boots; **esgidiau ysgafn** light boots or shoes; **yr esgid yn gwasgu** a difficult financial situation.
esgob *e.g. ll.* **-ion** bishop, **Esgob Tyddewi** Bishop of St David's; **Esgobaeth** diocese: **Esgob!** Oh Lord!
esgus *e.g. ll.* **-ion, -odion** excuse; pretence (*S.W.*): **mae e'n esgus cysgu** he's pretending to sleep.
esgusion *gw.* **esgus.**
esgusodi *be.* **(esgusodaf)** to make an excuse, to excuse; **Esgusodwch fi** Excuse me.
esgusodion *gw.* **esgus.**
esgyrn *gw.* **asgwrn; Esgyrn Dafydd!** Good heavens!
esiampl *e.b. ll.* **-au** example.
esmwyth *a.* soft, easy, comfortable.
estron *e.g. ll.* **-iaid** foreigner, alien, stranger.
estyn *be.* **(estynnaf)** to extend, to reach; to stretch, to lengthen; to give.
estyniad *e.g. ll.* **-au** extension.
etifeddu *be.* **(etifeddaf)** to inherit.
eto, *c. & ad.* again a second time, yet, still, nevertheless.
ethol *be.* **(etholaf)** to elect, to choose, to select.
etholaeth *e.b. ll.* **-au** constituency; electorate.
etholiad *e.g. ll.* **-au** election: **etholiad cyffredinol** general election; **is-etholiad** by-election.
eu *rhag.* (*words beginning with a vowel are aspirated when preceded by* **eu**) their: **eu hafalau** their apples; **eu hemynau** their hymns; **eu hysgolion** their schools; *gw. At. Rhagenwau.*
euog *a.* guilty; **euog neu ddieuog** guilty or not guilty.
euogrwydd *e.g.* guilt.
euraid: euraidd *a.* gold, golden.
ewch *bf.* go! (*plural*); *gw.* **mynd.**
ewin *e.g.b. ll.* **-edd** nail, claw, talon; hoof: **â'i ddeg ewin** with all his might.
ewyllys *e.b. ll.* **-iau, -ion** will; desire; testament; **yn erbyn ei ewyllys** against his will.
ewyn *e.g.* foam, froth; *gw.* **gewyn.**
ewythr *e.g. ll.* **-edd, -od** uncle.

fab *gw.* **mab.**
faban *gw.* **baban.**
fabanaidd *gw.* **babanaidd.**
fabi *gw.* **babi.**
fabolgamp *gw.* **mabolgamp.**
facio *gw.* **bacio.**
fach *gw.* **bach.**
fachau *gw.* **bach, bachyn.**
fachgen *gw.* **bachgen.**
fachgennaidd *gw.* **bachgennaidd.**
fachlud *gw.* **machlud.**
fachu *gw.* **bachu.**
fachyn *gw.* **bach.**
fad *gw.* **bad.**
fadarch *gw.* **madarch.**
fae *gw.* **bae.**
faer *gw.* **maer.**
faeres *gw.* **maeres.**
faes *gw.* **maes.**
faestref *gw.* **maestref.**
fafon *gw.* **mafonen.**
fag *gw.* **bag.**
fagddu, y *e.b.* utter darkness.
fagiau *gw.* **bag.**
fagu *gw.* **magu.**
Fai *gw.* **Mai.**
fai *gw.* **bai.**
faich *gw.* **baich.**
fain *gw.* **main.**
faint *rhag. gof.* how much? how many? *gw.* **maint.**
falch *gw.* **balch.**
falchder *gw.* **balchder.**
faldod *gw.* **maldod.**
faldodi *gw.* **maldodi.**
faled *gw.* **baled.**
faledwr *gw.* **baledwr.**
falot *gw.* **balot.**
falu *gw.* **malu.**
falŵn *gw.* **balŵn.**
falwoden *gw.* **malwoden.**
fam *gw.* **mam.**
fam-gu *gw.* **mam-gu.**
fân *gw.* **mân.**
fan *e.b. ll.* **-iau** van; *gw.* **ban, man.**
fanana *gw.* **banana.**
fanc *gw.* **banc.**
fancio *gw.* **bancio.**
fand *gw.* **band.**
fandal *e.g. ll.* **-iaid** vandal.
fandaleiddio *be.* **(fandaleiddiaf)** to vandalise.
fandaliaeth *e.b.* vandalism.
faneg *gw.* **maneg.**
faner *gw.* **baner.**
fannau *gw.* **ban, man.**
fannod *gw.* **bannod.**
fans *gw.* **mans.**
fantais *gw.* **mantais.**
fanteisio *gw.* **manteisio.**
fanteision *gw.* **mantais.**
fantell *gw.* **mantell.**
fanwl *gw.* **manwl.**
fanylion *gw.* **manylyn.**
fanylu *gw.* **manylu.**
fanylyn *gw.* **manylyn.**
fap *gw.* **map.**
far *gw.* **bar.**
fara *gw.* **bara.**
farc *gw.* **marc.**
farcio *gw.* **marcio.**
farchnad *gw.* **marchnad.**
farchog *gw.* **marchog.**
fardd *gw.* **bardd.**
farddoniaeth *gw.* **barddoniaeth.**
farf *gw.* **barf.**
farn *gw.* **barn.**
farnwr *gw.* **barnwr.**
farrau *gw.* **bar.**
fart *gw.* **mart.**
farw *gw.* **marw.**
farwaidd *gw.* **marwaidd.**
farwol *gw.* **marwol.**
farwolaeth *gw.* **marwolaeth.**
fas *gw.* **bas.**
fasged *gw.* **basged.**
fasn *gw.* **basn.**
fasnach *gw.* **masnach.**
fasnachwr *gw.* **masnachwr.**
fasnau: fasnys *gw.* **basn.**
faswr *gw.* **baswr, maswr.**
fat *gw.* **bat, mat.**
fater *gw.* **mater.**
fatsen: fatsien *gw.* **matsen.**
fath *gw.* **bath, math**
fathdy *gw.* **bathdy.**
fathemateg *gw.* **mathemateg.**
fathemategol *gw.* **mathemategol.**
fathemategwr *gw.* **mathemategwr.**

fathodyn *gw.* **bathodyn.**
fathu *gw.* **bathu.**
faw *gw.* **baw**
fawd *gw.* **bawd.**
fawl *gw.* **mawl.**
fawn *gw.* **mawn.**
fawr *gw.* **mawr.**
fawredd *gw.* **mawredd.**
Fawrth *gw.* **Mawrth.**
fe 1 *rhag.* he, him, it. 2 *geir.* particle *(may be used before verbs (S.W.);* **fe welais; fe glywais; fe gwympodd** *gw. At. Berfau –* **Fe/Mi.**
feallai *ad.* perhaps.
fecso *gw.* **becso.**
fechan *gw.* **bechan.**
fechgyn *gw.* **bachgen.**
fechnïaeth *gw.* **mechnïaeth.**
Fedi *gw.* **Medi.**
fedi *gw.* **medi.**
fedru *gw.* **medru.**
fedrus *gw.* **medrus.**
fedwen *gw.* **bedwen.**
fedyddio *gw.* **bedyddio.**
Fedyddiwr *gw.* **Bedyddiwr.**
fedd *gw.* **bedd, medd.**
feddal *gw.* **meddal.**
feddalu *gw.* **meddalu.**
feddu *gw.* **meddu.**
feddw *gw.* **meddw.**
feddwi *gw.* **meddwi.**
feddwl *gw.* **meddwl.**
feddyg *gw.* **meddyg.**
feddygfa *gw.* **meddygfa.**
feddyginiaeth *gw.* **meddyginiaeth.**
feddylgar *gw.* **meddylgar.**
feddyliau *gw.* **meddwl.**
fefus *gw.* **mefusen.**
Fehefin *gw.* **Mehefin.**
feiau *gw.* **bai.**
feibion *gw.* **mab.**
Feibl *gw.* **Beibl.**
feic *gw.* **beic.**
feicrodon *gw.* **meicrodon.**
feichiau *gw.* **baich.**
feichiog *gw.* **beichiog.**
feiddio *gw.* **meiddio.**
feim *gw.* **meim.**
feinir *gw.* **meinir.**
feio *gw.* **beio.**
feirdd *gw.* **bardd.**
feirioli *gw.* **meirioli.**
feirniad *gw.* **beirniad.**
feirniadu *gw.* **beirniadu.**
feirniaid *gw.* **beirniad.**
feistr *gw.* **meistr.**
feistres *gw.* **meistres.**
feistri: feistriaid *gw.* **meistr.**
feithrin *gw.* **meithrin.**
fel *c.* as, so, like; **fel arfer** usually; **fel pe bai/petai/petasai** as if.
fêl *gw.* **mêl.**
felen *gw.* **melen.**
felin *gw.* **melin.**
felyn *gw.* **melyn.**
felys *gw.* **melys.**
fellten *gw.* **mellten.**
felltith *gw.* **melltith.**
felly *ad.* so, thus.
fendigedig *gw.* **bendigedig.**
fendith *gw.* **bendith.**
fenig *gw.* **maneg.**
fenter *gw.* **menter.**
fentrau *gw.* **menter.**
fentro *gw.* **mentro.**
fentrus *gw.* **mentrus.**
fenthyca *gw.* **benthyca.**
fenyn *gw.* **menyn.**
fenyw *gw.* **benyw, menyw.**
fenywaidd *gw.* **benywaidd, menywaidd.**
fer *gw.* **ber.**
fêr *gw.* **mêr.**
ferch *gw.* **merch.**
Fercher *gw.* **Mercher.**
ferchetaidd *gw.* **merchetaidd.**
ferf *gw.* **berf.**
ferfa *gw.* **berfa.**
ferfenw *gw.* **berfenw.**
ferlod *gw.* **merlyn.**
ferlota *gw.* **merlota.**
ferlotwr *gw.* **merlotwr.**
ferlyn *gw.* **merlyn.**
fersiwn *e.g. ll.* **fersiynau** version.
ferthyr *gw.* **merthyr.**
ferw *gw.* **berw.**
ferwi *gw.* **berwi.**
fes *gw.* **mesen.**
fesen *gw.* **mesen.**
festri *e.b. ll.* **festrïoedd, festrïau** vestry.
fesul *gw.* **mesul.**
fesur *gw.* **mesur.**
fesurydd *gw.* **mesurydd.**
fetel *gw.* **metel.**
fetr *gw.* **metr.**
fetrig *gw.* **metrig.**
fethiant *gw.* **methiant.**
fewn *gw.* **mewn.**
fewnwr *gw.* **mewnwr.**
feysydd *gw.* **maes.**
fi: mi *rhag.* I , me, *gw.* **mi.**
ficer *e.g. ll.* **-iaid** vicar.
ficerdai *gw.* **ficerdy.**
ficerdy *e.g. ll.* **ficerdai** vicarage.
ficrodon *gw.* **microdon.**
figwrn *gw.* **migwrn.**

fil *gw.* **mil.**
filfeddyg *gw.* **milfeddyg.**
filgi *gw.* **milgi.**
filiwn *gw.* **miliwn.**
filoedd *gw.* **mil.**
filwr *gw.* **milwr.**
filltir *gw.* **milltir.**
fin *gw.* **bin.**
fin *gw.* **min.**
finegr *e.g.* *ll.* **-au** vinegar.
finiog *g.w.* **miniog.**
finlliw *gw.* **minlliw.**
finnau *gw.* **minnau.**
fiola *e.b.* *ll.* **-s** viola.
fioled *e.b.* *ll.* **-au** violet.
fioleg *gw.* **bioleg.**
firi *gw.* **miri.**
firws *e.g.* *ll.* **-au** virus.
fis *gw.* **mis.**
fisged *gw.* **bisged.**
fisgïen *gw.* **bisgïen.**
fisglwyf *gw.* **misglwyf.**
fisoedd *gw.* **mis.**
fisol *gw.* **misol.**
fisolyn *gw.* **misolyn.**
fitw *gw.* **bitw.**
fiwsig *gw.* **miwsig.**
flaen *gw.* **blaen.**
flaenor *gw.* **blaenor.**
flaenwr *gw.* **blaenwr.**
flaguro *gw.* **blaguro.**
flaguryn *gw.* **blaguryn.**
flaidd *gw.* **blaidd.**
flanced *gw.* **blanced.**
flas *gw.* **blas**
flasu *gw.* **blasu.**
flasus *gw.* **blasus.**
flawd *gw.* **blawd.**
fleiddiaid *gw.* **blaidd.**
flew *gw.* **blewyn.**
flewyn *gw.* **blewyn.**
flin *gw.* **blin.**
flinder *gw.* **blinder.**
flinedig *gw.* **blinedig.**
flino *gw.* **blino.**
flodau *gw.* **blodyn.**
flodeugerdd *gw.* **blodeugerdd.**
flodfresychen *gw.* **blodfresychen.**
flodyn *gw.* **blodyn.**
floedd *gw.* **bloedd.**
floeddio *gw.* **bloeddio.**
flows *gw.* **blows.**
flwch *gw.* **blwch.**
flwydd *gw.* **blwydd.**
flwyddyn *gw.* **blwyddyn.**
flychau *gw.* **blwch.**
flynedd *gw.* **blwyddyn.**
flynyddoedd *gw.* **blwyddyn.**
fo *rhag.* he, him it *(N.W.).*
focs *gw.* **bocs.**
foch *gw.* **boch, mochyn.**
fochyn *gw.* **mochyn.**
fod *gw.* **bod.**
fodau *gw.* **bod.**
fodfedd *gw.* **modfedd.**
fodiau *gw.* **bodiau.**
fodio *gw.* **bodio.**
fodlon: foddlon *gw.* **bodlon.**
fodloni *gw.* **bodloni.**
fodrwy *gw.* **modrwy.**
fodryb *gw.* **modryb.**
fodur *gw.* **modur.**
fodurwr *gw.* **modurwr.**
fodd *gw.* **bodd, modd.**
foddhad *gw.* **boddhad.**
foddi *gw.* **boddi.**
foddion *gw.* **moddion.**
foel *gw.* **moel.**
foelni *gw.* **moelni.**
foes *gw.* **moes.**
foesol *gw.* **moesol.**
foethus *gw.* **moethus.**
fogi *gw.* **mogi.**
fol *gw.* **bol.**
fola *gw.* **bola.**
foli *gw.* **moli.**
foliau *gw.* **bol.**
follt *gw.* **bollt.**
folltau *gw.* **bollt.**
fom *gw.* **bom.**
Fôn *gw.* **Môn.**
fôn *gw.* **bôn.**
foneddiges *gw.* **boneddiges.**
foneddigion *gw.* **bonheddwr.**
fonheddig *gw.* **bonheddig.**
fonheddwr *gw.* **bonheddwr.**
fonion *gw.* **bôn.**
fôr *gw.* **môr.**
ford *gw.* **bord.**
fordau: fordydd *gw.* **bord.**
forddwyd *gw.* **morddwyd.**
fore *gw.* **bore.**
forfa *gw.* **morfa.**
forfil *gw.* **morfil.**
forgais *gw.* **morgais.**
Forgannwg *gw.* **Morgannwg.**
forgeisiau *gw.* **morgais.**
forgrugyn *gw.* **morgrugyn.**
forio *gw.* **morio.**
fôr-leidr *gw.* **môr-leidr.**
forlo *gw.* **morlo.**
foroedd *gw.* **môr.**
foron *gw.* **moronen.**
foronen *gw.* **moronen.**
forthwyl *gw.* **morthwyl.**
forwr *gw.* **morwr.**
forwyn *gw.* **morwyn.**
fory: yfory *ad.* tomorrow.

fos *gw.* **bos.**
fotwm *gw.* **botwm.**
fotymu *gw.* **botymu.**
fowlen *gw.* **bowlen.**
fraich *gw.* **braich.**
fraint *gw.* **braint.**
frân *gw.* **brân.**
fras *gw.* **bras.**
fraslun *gw.* **braslun.**
fraster *gw.* **braster.**
fraw *gw.* **braw.**
frawd *gw.* **brawd.**
frawddeg *gw.* **brawddeg.**
frecwast *gw.* **brecwast.**
frech *gw.* **brech.**
frechdan *gw.* **brechdan.**
frechiad *gw.* **brechiad.**
freichiau *gw.* **braich.**
freichled *gw.* **breichled.**
freiniau: freintiau *gw.* **braint.**
frenhines *gw.* **brenhines.**
frenhinoedd *gw.* **brenin.**
frenhinol *gw.* **brenhinol.**
frenin *gw.* **brenin.**
fres *gw.* **bres.**
frest *gw.* **brest.**
fresychen *gw.* **bresychen.**
frethyn *gw.* **brethyn.**
freuddwyd *gw.* **breuddwyd.**
freuddwydio *gw.* **breuddwydio.**
freuddwydion *gw.* **breuddwyd.**
frifo *gw.* **brifo.**
frig *gw.* **brig.**
frigau *gw.* **brig, brigyn.**
frigyn *gw.* **brigyn.**
friwsion *gw.* **briwsionyn.**
friwsionyn *gw.* **briwsionyn.**
fro *gw.* **bro.**
frodor *gw.* **brodor.**
frodyr *gw.* **brawd.**
froga *gw.* **broga.**
fron *gw.* **bron.**
fronfraith *gw.* **bronfraith.**
fronnau: fronnydd *gw.* **bron.**
frown *gw.* **brown.**
fröydd *gw.* **bro.**
frwdfrydig *gw.* **brwdfrydig.**
frwnt *gw.* **brwnt.**
frws: frwsh *gw.* **brws.**
frwsio: frwshio *gw.* **brwsio.**
frwsys: frwshys *gw.* **brws.**
frwydr *gw.* **brwydr.**
frwydrau *gw.* **brwydr.**
fryd *gw.* **bryd.**
fryn *gw.* **bryn.**
fryniau *gw.* **bryn.**
frys *gw.* **brys.**
frysio *gw.* **brysio.**
fuan *gw.* **buan.**
fuarth *gw.* **buarth.**
fuchod *gw.* **buwch.**
fud *gw.* **mud.**
fudiad *gw.* **mudiad.**
fudr *gw.* **budr.**
fuddugol *gw.* **buddugol.**
fuddugoliaeth *gw.* **buddugoliaeth.**
fues i *bf.* I was, I have been; *gw.* **bod.**
fugail *gw.* **bugail.**
fugeiliaid *gw.* **bugail.**
fugeilio *gw.* **bugeilio.**
ful *gw.* **mul.**
fûm: fues *bf.* I was, I have been; *gw.* **bod.**
funud *gw.* **munud.**
fur *gw.* **mur.**
fusnes *gw.* **busnes.**
fuwch *gw.* **buwch.**
fwced *gw.* **bwced.**
fwg *gw.* **mwg.**
fwgwd *gw.* **mwgwd.**
fwlch *gw.* **bwlch.**
fwnci *gw.* **mwnci.**
fwrdeistref *gw.* **bwrdeistref.**
fwrdd *gw.* **bwrdd.**
fwriad *gw.* **bwriad.**
fwriadu *gw.* **bwriadu.**
fwrw *gw.* **bwrw.**
fws *gw.* **bws.**
fwstwr *gw.* **mwstwr.**
fwthyn *gw.* **bwthyn.**
fwy *gw.* **mawr.**
fwyaf *gw.* **mawr.**
fwyar *gw.* **mwyaren.**
fwyaren *gw.* **mwyaren.**
fwyd *gw.* **bwyd.**
fwydo: fwyda *gw.* **bwydo.**
fwydlen *gw.* **bwydlen.**
fwydydd *gw.* **bwyd.**
fwydyn *gw.* **mwydyn.**
fwyn *gw.* **mwyn.**
fwynhad *gw.* **mwynhad.**
fwynhau *gw.* **mwynhau.**
fwyta: fyta *gw.* **bwyta.**
fy *rhag. (followed by nasal mutation)* my, of me; *gw. At. Rhagenwau.*
fychan *gw.* **bychan.**
fyd *gw.* **byd.**
fydoedd *gw.* **byd.**
fydd e/o/hi *bf.* he/she/it will be; *gw.* **bod.**
fyddar *gw.* **byddar.**
fyddin *gw.* **byddin.**
fyddinoedd *gw.* **byddin.**
fyfyrdod *gw.* **myfyrdod.**
fyfyrio *gw.* **myfyrio.**
fyfyriwr *gw.* **myfyriwr.**
fyglyd *gw.* **myglyd.**

fygu *gw.* **mygu.**
fygydau *gw.* **mwgwd.**
fylchau *gw.* **bwlch.**
fynach *gw.* **mynach.**
fynachlog *gw.* **mynachlog.**
fynachod *gw.* **mynach.**
fynaich *gw.* **mynach.**
fynd: fyned *gw.* **mynd.**
fynedfa *gw.* **mynedfa.**
fynedfeydd *gw.* **mynedfa.**
fynediad *gw.* **mynediad.**
fynegai *gw.* **mynegai.**
fynegeion *gw.* **mynegai.**
fynegi *gw.* **mynegi.**
fynnu *gw.* **mynnu.**
fynwent *gw.* **mynwent.**
fyny, i *ad.* up, upwards: **oddi fyny** from above; **ar i fyny** upwards; in good spirits, in a cheerful mood.
fynydd *gw.* **mynydd.**
fynyddig: fynyddog *gw.* **mynyddig.**
fyr *gw.* **byr.**
fyrbryd *gw.* **byrbryd.**
fyrddau *gw.* **bwrdd.**
fyrfodd *gw.* **byrfodd.**
fyrr *gw.* **myrr.**
fys *gw.* **bys.**
fysedd *gw.* **bys.**
fystyrau *gw.* **mwstwr.**
fysys *gw.* **bws.**
fyth *gw.* **myth.**
fythynnod *gw.* **bwthyn.**
fyw *gw.* **byw.**
fywiog *gw.* **bywiog.**
fywyd *gw.* **bywyd.**
fywydeg *gw.* **bywydeg.**

ffa *gw.* **ffäen.**
ffäen: ffeuen *e.b. ll.* **ffa.** bean.
ffactor *e.g.b. ll.* **-au** factor.
ffaelu (â) *be.* **(ffaelaf)** to fail, to miss, to mistake *(S.W.)*.
ffafr *e.b. ll.* **-au** favour, respect.
ffair *e.b. ll.* **ffeiriau** fair: **ffair haf** summer fair; **ffair lyfrau** book fair; **ffair sborion** jumble sale; **fel ffair** an utter mess, very busy.
ffaith *e.b. ll.* **ffeithiau** fact.
ffarm: fferm *e.b. ll.* **ffermydd** farm; **tŷ fferm** farmhouse.
ffarmio: ffermio *be.* **(ffarmiaf: ffermiaf)** to farm.
ffarmwr: ffermwr *e.g. ll.* **ffermwyr** farmer, agriculturist.
ffárwel: ffarwél *e.b.* farewell; **Ffárwel haf** Michaelmas daisy.
ffarwelio (â) *be.* **(ffarweliaf)** to bid farwel, to say goodbye.
ffatri *e.b. ll.* **ffatrïoedd** factory.
ffau *e.b. ll.* **ffeuau** den, lair, burrow, set.
ffefryn *e.g. ll.* **-nau** favourite.
ffeiriau *gw.* **ffair.**
ffeithiau *gw.* **ffaith.**
ffel *a.* dear; knowing – especially of a dog.
ffenestr *e.b. ll.* **-i** window.
fferm *gw.* **ffarm.**
ffermdai *gw.* **ffermdy.**
ffermdy *e.g. ll.* **ffermdai** farmhouse.
ffermio *gw.* **ffarmio.**
ffermwr *gw.* **ffarmwr.**
ffermwyr *gw.* **ffarmwr.**
fferyllydd *e.g. ll.* **-ion** pharmacist, chemist.
ffeuau *gw.* **ffau.**
ffeuen *gw.* **ffäen.**
ffiaidd *a.* foul, loathsome, odious.
ffigur *e.g. ll.* **-au** figure, type, form; diagram.
ffin *e.b. ll.* **-iau, -ion** boundary, border, frontier, limit.
ffiniau *gw.* **ffin.**
ffiniol *a.* bordering.
ffinion *gw.* **ffin.**
ffiseg *e.b.* physics.
fflachio *be.* **(fflachiaf)** to flash.
fflam *e.b. ll.* **-au, -iau** flame, blaze.
fflamau: fflamiau *gw.* **fflam.**
ffoadur *e.g. ll.* **-iaid, -ion** fugitive, refugee; deserter.
ffoaduriaid: ffoadurion *gw.* **ffoadur.**
ffodus *a.* fortunate, lucky, prosperous.
ffoi *(rhag.) be.* **(ffoaf)** to flee, to escape; to desert.
ffôl *a.* foolish, unwise, silly, foolhardy.
ffolineb *e.g. ll.* **-au** foolishness, folly.
ffon *e.b. ll.* **ffyn** stick, walking-stick, staff; rod; club.
ffôn *e.g. ll.* **ffonau** telephone, phone; *gw.* **teleffon.**
ffonio *be.* **(ffoniaf)** to phone.
fforc *e.b. ll.* **ffyrc** fork.
fforchio *be.* **(forchiaf)** to fork; to straddle.
ffordd *e.b. ll.* **ffyrdd** road, way, street, route: **ffordd allan** exit; **ffordd fawr** highway; **ffordd osgoi** bypass; **priffordd** highway; **traffordd** motorway; **ffordd ddeuol** dual carriageway; **pontffordd** viaduct; **trosffordd** fly-over.
ffortiwn *e.b. ll.* **ffortiynau** fortune.
ffortiynau *gw.* **ffortiwn.**
ffos *e.b. ll.* **-ydd** ditch, trench.
ffosydd *gw.* **ffos.**
ffowls *gw.* **ffowlyn.**
ffowlyn *e.g. ll.* **ffowls** chicken, fowl *(S.W.)*.
ffraeo (â) *be.* **(ffraeaf)** to quarrel, to bicker.
Ffrangeg *e.b.* French (language).
Ffrainc *e.b.* France.
Ffrances *e.b. ll.* **-au** Frenchwoman.
Ffrancod *gw.* **Ffrancwr.**
Ffrancwr *e.g. ll.* **Ffrancwyr, Ffrancod** Frenchman.
Ffrancwyr *gw.* **Ffrancwr.**
Ffrengig *a.* French.
ffrind *e.g. ll.* **-iau** friend.
ffrindiau *gw.* **ffrind.**
ffrio *be.* **(ffriaf)** to fry.
ffroen *e.b. ll.* **-au** nostril.

ffroesen *e.b. ll.* **ffroes** pancake *(S.W.). gw.* **crempog.**
ffrog: ffroc *e.b. ll.* **-iau** frock: **ffrog felen** a yellow frock; **ffrog wen** a white frock.
ffroga *e.g. ll.* **ffrogaod** frog; *gw.* **broga.**
ffrwd *e.b. ll.* **ffrydiau** swift stream; torrent, flood; current.
ffrwydro *be.* **(ffrwydraf)** to explode.
ffrwyth *e.g. ll.* **ffrwythau** fruit; produce; result, effect.
ffrwythlon *a.* fruitful, fertile.
ffrwythloni *be.* **(ffrwythlonaf)** to become or be fruitful; to fertilise.
ffrydiau *gw.* **ffrwd.**
ffrynt *e.g.b. ll.* **-iau** front: **ffrynt gynnes** warm front; **ffrynt oer** cold front; **drws (y) ffrynt** front door; **o'r ffrynt** from the front.
ffug *a.* deceptive, sham, counterfeit, false: **dogfen ffug** forged document.
ffug-bas *e.b. ll.* **-ys** dummy-pass *(rugby).*
ffugenw *e.g. ll.* **-au** pseudonym, nom de plume.
ffugio *be* **(ffugiaf)** to pretend, to disguise, to forge, to feign.
ffuglen *e.b.* fiction.
ffurf *e.b. ll.* **-iau** form, shape; appearance, likeness; substance.
ffurfafen *e.b. ll.* **-nau** sky; heavens.
ffurfiau *gw.* **ffurf.**
ffurfio *be.* **(ffurfiaf)** to form, to fashion, to create.
ffurflen *e.b. ll.* **-ni** form, chart: **ffurflen gais** application form.
ffurflenni *gw.* **ffurflen.**
ffŵl *e.g. ll.* **ffyliaid** fool.
ffwr *e.g. ll.* **ffyrrau** fur.
ffwrdd, i *ad.* away; **ffwrdd-â-hi** slap-dash, precipitate.
ffwrn *e.b. ll.* **ffyrnau** oven, furnace: **ffwrn microdon** microwave oven.
ffws *e.g.* fuss.
ffydd *e.b. ll.* **-iau** faith, belief, confidence.
ffyddlon *a.* faithful, loyal.
ffyliaid *gw.* **ffŵl.**
ffyn *gw.* **ffon.**
ffynhonnau *gw.* **ffynnon.**
ffynhonnell *e.b. ll.* **ffynonellau** source, spring, fount; origin.
ffynidwydden *e.b. ll.* **ffynidwydd** fir-tree, pine-tree.
ffynnon *e.b. ll.* **ffynhonnau** spring, fountain, well; source, origin.
ffynonellau *gw.* **ffynhonnell.**
ffyrc *gw.* **fforc.**
ffyrdd *gw.* **ffordd.**
ffyrnau *gw.* **ffwrn.**
ffyrnig *gw.* fierce, savage, furious, wild.
ffyrnigrwydd *e.g.* ferocity.
ffyrrau *gw.* **ffwr.**

ga i *bf.* may I . . .? *gw.* **cael.**
gaban *gw.* **caban.**
gacen *gw.* **cacen.**
gacwn *gw.* **cacwn.**
gacynen *gw.* **cacynen.**
gadach *gw.* **cadach.**
gadael *be.* **(gadawaf)** to leave, to desert; to allow; **gadewais** I left; **gadewaist** you left.
gadair *gw.* **cadair.**
gadeiriau *gw.* **cadair.**
gadeirio *gw.* **cadeirio.**
gadeiriol *gw.* **cadeiriol.**
gadeirydd *gw.* **cadeirydd.**
gadno *gw.* **cadno.**
gadw *gw.* **cadw.**
gadwyn *gw.* **cadwyn.**
gadwyno *gw.* **cadwyno.**
gae *gw.* **cae.**
gaeaf *e.g.* *ll.* **-au** winter.
gaeau *gw.* **cae.**
gael *gw.* **cael.**
gaer *gw.* **caer.**
Gaer *gw.* **Caer.**
Gaerdydd *gw.* **Caerdydd.**
Gaeredin *gw.* **Caeredin.**
Gaerfyrddin *gw.* **Caerfyrddin.**
Gaergybi *gw.* **Caergybi.**
gaets *gw.* **caets.**
gaf *gw.* **cael.**
gafael (yn) *be.* **(gafaelaf)** to hold tight, to clutch; to grip: **Gafael yn fy llaw** Take my hand.
gafodd *gw.* **cael.**
gafr *e.b.* *ll.* **geifr** goat.
gaffe *gw.* **caffe.**
gangen *gw.* **cangen.**
ganghennau *gw.* **cangen.**
gaiff *gw.* **caiff.**
gair *e.g.* *ll.* **geiriau** word; **gair bach** short address, brief note; **geirda** good report, commendation, reference; **gair drwg** bad reputation; **ar y gair** instantly: **cadw at ei air** to keep his word; **dweud gair** to speak or address (a meeting, etc.); **Gair Duw** God's word; **gair yn ei bryd** timely advice.
gais *gw.* **cais.**
galan *gw.* **calan.**
galar *e.g.* mourning, grief.
galed *gw.* **caled.**
galedi *gw.* **caledi.**
galedwch *gw.* **caledwch.**
galendr *gw.* **calendr.**
galennig *gw.* **calennig.**
galetach *gw.* **caled.**
galetaf *gw.* **caled.**
galeted *gw.* **caled.**
galon *gw.* **calon.**
galw (ar, am) *be.* **(galwaf)** to call, to summon; to visit; to name.
galwad *e.b.g.* *ll.* **-au** a call; vocation, calling, profession: **Cafodd y gweinidog alwad i Lanelli** The minister received a call to Llanelli.
galwyn *e.g.* *ll.* **-i, -au** gallon.
gall *gw.* **call.**
gallach *gw.* **call.**
gallaf *gw.* **call.**
galled *gw.* **call.**
gallu 1 *be.* **(gallaf)** to be able; 2 *e.g.* *ll.* **-oedd** ability, power; wealth.
galluog *a.* able, powerful.
gam *gw.* **cam.**
gamarwain *gw.* **camarwain.**
gamddeall *gw.* **camddeall.**
gamera *gw.* **camera.**
gamp *gw.* **camp.**
gampfa *gw.* **campfa.**
gampfeydd *gw.* **campfa.**
gampus *gw.* **campus.**
gampwaith *gw.* **campwaith.**
gampweithiau *gw.* **campwaith.**
gamsyniad *gw.* **camsyniad.**
gamu *gw.* **camu.**
gan *ardd.* *(followed by soft mutation)* (*personal forms*: **gen i, gen ti, ganddo/ganddi, gennyn, gennych, ganddyn).** with, by, from, since; **gan amlaf** usually, mostly: **gan hynny** therefore; **gan mwyaf** mostly, almost; *gw. At. Arddodiaid;* **can, cant.**
gân *gw.* **cân.**
ganddi: ganddo *gw.* **gan.**
ganddyn *gw.* **gan.**
ganeuon *gw.* **cân.**

ganfed *gw.* **canfed.**
ganhwyllbren *gw.* **canhwyllbren.**
ganiad *gw.* **caniad.**
ganiadaeth *gw.* **caniadaeth.**
ganiadau *gw.* **cân, caniad.**
ganiatâd *gw.* **caniatâd.**
ganiatáu *gw.* **caniatáu.**
ganiedydd *gw.* **caniedydd.**
ganmlwydd *gw.* **canmlwydd.**
ganmlwyddiannau *gw.* **canmlwyddiant.**
ganmlwyddiant *gw.* **canmlwyddiant.**
ganmol *gw.* **canmol.**
ganmoliaeth *gw.* **canmoliaeth.**
gannoedd *gw.* **cant.**
gannwyll *gw.* **cannwyll.**
ganol *gw.* **canol.**
ganolbarth *gw.* **canolbarth.**
ganolbwyntio *gw.* **canolbwyntio.**
ganoldir *gw.* **canoldir.**
ganolfan *gw.* **canolfan.**
ganolwr *gw,* **canolwr.**
ganradd *gw.* **canradd.**
ganran *gw.* **canran.**
ganrif *gw.* **canrif.**
ganrifau: ganrifoedd *gw.* **canrif.**
gant *gw.* **cant.**
gantor *gw.* **cantor.**
gantores *gw.* **cantores.**
ganu *gw.* **canu.**
ganŵ *gw.* **canŵ.**
ganŵio *gw.* **canŵio.**
ganwr *gw.* **canwr.**
ganwriad *gw.* **canwriad.**
ganwyd *bf.* he/she was born: **Ganwyd ef yng Nghymru** He was born in Wales; *gw.* **geni.**
gap *gw.* **cap.**
gapel *gw.* **capel.**
gapten *gw.* **capten.**
gar *gw.* **car.**
garafán *gw.* **carafán.**
garafana *gw.* **carafana.**
garco *gw.* **carco.**
garcus *gw.* **carcus.**
garchar *gw.* **carchar.**
garcharor *gw.* **carcharor.**
garcharu *gw.* **carcharu.**
gardiau *gw.* **cerdyn.**
gardd *e.b. ll.* **gerddi** garden.
garddio *be.* **(garddiaf)** to garden, to cultivate a garden.
garddwr *e.g. ll.* **garddwyr** gardener.
garedig *gw.* **caredig.**
garedigrwydd *gw.* **caredigrywdd.**
garej *e.g. ll.* **-ys** garage.
gariad *gw.* **cariad.**
gariadon *gw.* **cariad.**
gariadus *gw.* **cariadus.**
gario *gw.* **cario.**
garol *gw.* **carol.**
garped *gw.* **carped.**
garreg *gw.* **carreg.**
gartref *ad.* at home: **Mae e'n byw gartref** He's living at home; *gw.* **cartref.**
gartrefi *gw.* **cartref.**
gartrefu *gw.* **cartrefu.**
gartrefydd *gw.* **cartref.**
garw *a. ll.* **geirwon** coarse, rough, harsh.
garu *gw.* **caru.**
gas *gw.* **cas.**
gasáu *gw.* **casáu.**
gasgen *gw.* **casgen.**
gasgenni *gw.* **casgen.**
gasgliad *gw.* **casgliad.**
gasglu *gw.* **casglu.**
Gas-gwent *gw.* **Cas-gwent.**
Gasllwchwr *gw.* **Casllwchwr.**
Gasnewydd *gw.* **Casnewydd.**
gastell *gw.* **castell.**
Gastell-nedd *gw.* **Castell-nedd.**
gât *e.b. ll.* **gatiau, gâts, gatsys** (*never undergoes soft mutation*) gate: **yr hen gât** the old gate; **dwy gât** two gates; **y gât wen** the white gate; *gw.* **clwyd;** *gw.* **iet.**
gath *gw.* **cath.**
gau *a.* (*precedes noun*) false; **gau broffwyd** a false prophet; *gw.* **cau.**
gawl *gw.* **cawl.**
gawod *gw.* **cawod.**
gawr *gw.* **cawr.**
gaws *gw.* **caws.**
gefn *gw.* **cefn.**
gefnder *gw.* **cefnder.**
gefndir *gw.* **cefndir.**
gefndiroedd *gw.* **cefndir.**
gefndyr *gw.* **cefnder.**
gefnu *gw.* **cefnu.**
gefnwr *gw.* **cefnwr.**
geffyl *gw.* **ceffyl.**
geg *gw.* **ceg.**
gegin *gw.* **cegin.**
gei *gw.* **cei.**
geidwad *gw.* **ceidwad.**
geifr *gw.* **gafr.**
geiliog *gw.* **ceiliog.**
Geinewydd *gw.* **Ceinewydd.**
geiniog *gw.* **ceiniog.**
geir *gw.* **car.**
geirfa *e.b. ll.* **-oedd** vocabulary.
geiriadur *e.g. ll.* **-on** dictionary.
geiriau *gw.* **gair.**
geirio *be.* **(geiriaf)** to word, to phrase.

geirwon *gw.* **garw.**
geisiadau: geisiau *gw.* **cais.**
geisio *gw.* **ceisio.**
gelf *gw.* **celf.**
gelfi *gw.* **celficyn.**
gelficyn *gw.* **celficyn.**
gelwydd *gw.* **celwydd.**
gelwyddog *gw.* **celwyddog.**
gelyn *e.g.* *ll.* **-ion** enemy: **gelyn pennaf** chief enemy; *gw.* **celynnen.**
gelynnen *gw.* **celynnen.**
gell *gw.* **cell.**
gellau: gelloedd *gw.* **cell.**
gem *e.b.g.* *ll.* **-au** gem.
gêm *e.b.* *ll.* **gêmau** *(doesn't mutate)* game: **Dyma gêm dda** Here's a good game; **dwy gêm rygbi** two rugby games; **Dewch i gêmau'r ysgol** Come to the school's games.
gemeg *gw.* **cemeg.**
gen *gw.* **gan.**
gên *e.b.* *ll.* **genau** chin, jaw.
genau *e.g.* *ll.* **geneuau** mouth; *gw.* **gên.**
genedigaeth *e.b.* *ll.* **-au** birth.
genedl *gw.* **cenedl.**
genedlaethol *gw.* **cenedlaethol.**
genedlaetholdeb *gw.* **cenedlaetholdeb.**
genedlaetholwr *gw.* **cenedlaetholwr.**
geneth *e.b.* *ll.* **-od** girl *(N.W.)*.
geneuau *gw.* **genau.**
genfigennus *gw.* **cenfigennus.**
genhadaeth *gw.* **cenhadeth.**
genhadol *gw.* **cenhadol.**
genhadu *gw.* **cenhadu.**
genhadwr *gw.* **cenhadwr.**
genhedlaeth *gw.* **cenhedlaeth.**
genhedloedd *gw.* **cenedl.**
genhinen *gw.* **cenhinen.**
geni *be.* to be born, to give birth to: **dyddiad geni** date of birth.
gennin *gw.* **cenhinen.**
gennych *gw.* **gan.**
gennym *gw.* **gan.**
ger *ardd.* at, by, near, before, in front of; **gerllaw** close to.
gêr *e.ll.* gear, tackle; rubbish.
gerbron *gw.* **ger.**
gerdyn *gw.* **cerdyn.**
gerdd *gw.* **cerdd.**
gerdded *gw.* **cerdded.**
gerddi *gw.* **cerdd, gardd.**
gerddor *gw.* **cerddor.**
gerddorfa *gw.* **cerddorfa.**
gerddoriaeth *gw.* **cerddoriaeth.**
gerddorol *gw.* **cerddorol.**
gerddwr *gw.* **cerddwr.**
gerddwyr *gw.* **cerddwr.**
gerflun *gw.* **cerflun.**
gerllaw *gw.* **ger.**
gerrig *gw.* **carreg.**
ges *gw.* **cael.**
gesair *gw.* **cesair.**
gestyll *gw.* **castell.**
gewri *gw.* **cawr.**
gewyn *gw.* *ll.* **-nau, -ion** sinew, tendon, ligament; nerve; *gw.* **cewyn.**
geyrydd *gw.* **caer.**
gi *gw.* **ci.**
gig *gw.* **cig.**
gigydd *gw.* **cigydd.**
gilio *gw.* **cilio.**
gilydd *rhag.* other, another, another of the same class or kind: **ei gilydd** each other; **gyda'i gilydd** together (they); **gyda'ch gilydd** together (you); **gyda'n gilydd** together (we).
ginio *gw.* **cinio.**
gipolwg *gw.* **cipolwg.**
gist *gw.* **cist.**
glaf *gw.* **claf.**
glai *gw.* **clai.**
glan *e.b.* *ll.* **-nau, glennydd** bank, shore: **glan y môr** sea-shore; **glan yr afon** river's bank; **glan y bedd** the grave-side; **gwyliwr y glannau** coast-guard.
glân *a.* clean, pure, holy; beautiful, fair.
glanhau *be.* **(glanhaf)** to clean, to purify; to heal.
glanio *be.* **(glaniaf)** to land, to come or go ashore, disembark; bring to land.
glannau *gw.* **glan.**
glas 1 *a.* *ll.* **gleision** blue, green, grey, silver; wan, pallid; raw: **arian gleision** silver (money), silver coins; **glas y dorlan** kingfisher. 2 *e.g.* blue.
glaswelltyn *e.g.* *ll.* **glaswellt** green grass.
glasur *gw.* **clasur.**
glasurol *gw.* **clasurol.**
glaw *e.g.* *ll.* **-ogydd** rain; **bwrw glaw** to rain; **eirlaw** sleet; **glaw mân** drizzle.
glawdd *gw.* **clawdd.**
glawr *gw.* **clawr.**
glebran *gw.* **clebran.**
glefyd *gw.* **clefyd.**
gleision *gw.* **glas.**
glendid *e.g.* cleanness, cleanliness, purity; beauty; piety, holiness.
glennydd *gw.* **glan.**
glêr *gw.* **cleren.**

glerc *gw.* **clerc.**
gleren *gw.* **cleren.**
glin *e.g.b.* *ll.* **-iau** knee.
glir *gw.* **clir.**
glirio *gw.* **clirio.**
glo *e.g.* coal: **glo brig** open-cast coal; **glo carreg** anthracite coal; **glo mân** small coal; **glo rhwym** bituminous coal; *gw.* **clo.**
gloc *gw.* **cloc.**
gloch *gw.* **cloch.**
glod *gw.* **clod.**
glodfori *gw.* **clodfori.**
gloddiau *gw.* **clawdd.**
glofa *e.b.* *ll.* **glofeydd** colliery.
glofeydd *gw.* **glofa.**
gloff *gw.* **cloff.**
gloffi *gw.* **cloffi.**
glogwyn *gw.* **clogwyn.**
glogyn *gw.* **clogyn.**
gloi *gw.* **cloi.**
glorian *gw.* **clorian.**
glown *gw.* **clown.**
glöwr *e.g.* *ll.* **glowyr** collier, coal-miner.
glöyn byw *e.g.* *ll.* **glöynnod byw** butterfly (*N.W.*).
gloyw *a.* *ll.* **-on** clear, bright, shiny; **Cymro glân gloyw** a thoroughbred Welshman.
glud *e.g.* *ll.* **-ion** glue.
gludio: gludo *be.* **(gludiaf: gludaf)** to glue; to adhere.
glun *gw.* **clun.**
glust *gw.* **clust.**
glustog *gw.* **clustog.**
glwm *gw.* **clwm.**
glwtyn *gw.* **clwtyn.**
Glwyd *gw.* **Clwyd.**
glwyd *gw.* **clwyd.**
glwyf *gw.* **clwyf.**
glychau *gw.* **cloch.**
glymau *gw.* **clwm, cwlwm.**
glymu *gw.* **clymu.**
glyn *e.g.* *ll.* **-noedd** valley, glen.
Glynebwy *e.b.* Ebbw Vale.
glynu (wrth) *be.* **(glynaf)** to adhere, to cling.
glyw *gw.* **clyw.**
glywed *gw.* **clywed.**
gnau *gw.* **cneuen.**
gneuen *gw.* **cneuen.**
gnoc *gw.* **cnoc.**
gnocio *gw.* **cnocio.**
gnoi *gw.* **cnoi.**
go *ad.* (*precedes noun and causes soft mutation*) rather, somewhat; small, little exceeding (*N.W.*): **go ddrud** somewhat expensive.
gobaith *e.g.* *ll.* **gobeithion** hope.
goban *gw.* **coban.**
gobeithio *gw.* **(gobeithiaf)** to hope.
gobeithion *gw.* **gobaith.**
gobennydd *e.g.* *ll.* **gobenyddion** pillow, bolster.
goch *gw.* **coch.**
gochach *gw.* **coch.**
gochaf *gw.* **coch.**
goched *gw.* **coch.**
godi *gw.* **codi.**
godidog *gw.* excellent.
godre *e.g.* *ll.* **-on** edge, hem, fringe; foot or bottom (*of mountain, hill, etc.*); foot (*of page*).
godro *be.* **(godraf)** to milk.
goddef *be.* **(goddefaf)** to suffer, to bear, to endure, to tolerate.
goddrych *e.g.* *ll.* **-au** subject.
Goed-duon *gw.* **Coed-duon.**
goeden *gw.* **coeden.**
goedwig *gw.* **coedwig.**
goes *gw.* **coes.**
gof *e.g.* *ll.* **-aint** smith, blacksmith; *gw.* **cof.**
gofal *e.g.* *ll.* **-on** care; charge.
gofalu (am) *be.* **(gofalaf)** to take care; to worry, to vex.
gofalus *a.* careful, anxious, worried.
gofalwr *e.g.* *ll.* **gofalwyr** caretaker, custodian.
gofid *e.g.* *ll.* **-iau** trouble, sorrow, grief, affliction.
gofidio (am) *be.* **(gofidiaf)** to grieve, to vex.
gofio *gw.* **cofio.**
gofleidio *gw.* **cofleidio.**
gofod *e.g.* *ll.* **-au** space, gap; *gw.* **gwagle.**
gofodwr *e.g.* *ll.* **gofodwyr** astronaut.
gofrestr *gw.* **cofrestr.**
gofrestru *gw.* **cofrestru.**
gofyn (am) 1 *be.* **(gofynnaf)** to ask (for). 2 *e.g.* *ll.* **-ion** request, requirement, demand: **yn ôl y gofyn** according to demand.
goffi *gw.* **coffi.**
gog *gw.* **cog.**
goginio *gw.* **coginio.**
gogledd 1 *e.g.* north. 2 *a.* north, northern: **Pegwn y Gogledd** North Pole.
gogleddol *a.* northern.
gogleddwr *e.g.* *ll.* **gogleddwyr** northerner.
gogoniant *e.g.* *ll.* **gogoniannau** glory.
gogydd *gw.* **cogydd.**

gôl *e.b. ll.* **goliau** goal (*soccer*).
golau 1 *e.g.* light. **2** *a.* light, fair (*colour*); *gw.* **goleuni.**
golchi *be.* **(golchaf)** to wash; to flow over or past.
golchydd *e.g. ll.* **-ion** washer, washing machine.
goleg *gw.* **coleg.**
goler *gw.* **coler.**
goleudy *e.g. ll.* **goleudai** lighthouse.
goleuni *e.g.* light; *gw.* **golau.**
goleuo *be.* **(goleuaf)** to light, to enlighten; to set fire to.
goliau *gw.* **gôl.**
golofn *gw.* **colofn.**
golud *e.g. ll.* **-oedd** wealth, riches.
goluro *gw.* **coluro.**
golwg *e.g.b. ll.* **golygon** sight; appearance, view: **golygon** eyes; **i bob golwg** to all appearances; **o'r golwg** out of sight; **y fath olwg!** what a sight; **rhagolygon y tywydd** weather prospects; **roedd golwg wael arni** she looked ill.
golygfa *e.b. ll.* **golygfeydd** view, scenery, scene.
golygon *gw.* **golwg.**
golygu *be.* **(golygaf)** to view; to mean, to imply, to intend; to edit: **Beth rwyt ti'n ei olygu?** What do you mean?
golled *gw.* **colled.**
gollen *gw.* **collen.**
golli *gw.* **colli.**
gollwng *be.* **(gollyngaf)** to release; to leak.
gonest *a.* honest, sincere.
gopïo *gw.* **copïo.**
gopyn *gw.* **copyn.**
gôr *gw.* **côr.**
gorau *gw.* **côr, da.**
gorchfygu *be.* **(gorchfygaf)** to defeat, to conquer, to subdue.
gorchymyn (i) 1 *be.* **(gorchmynnaf)** to command, to order, to decree, to charge. **2** *e.g. ll.* **gorch(y)mynion, gorch(y)mynnau** commandment, command, decree, order: **Y Deg Gorchymyn** The Ten Commandments.
gordyn *gw.* **cordyn.**
gorfod 1 *e.g.b. ll.* **-au** compulsion, obligation; victory, success. **2** *a.* enforced, compulsory, obligatory; conquering, victorious. **3** *be.* **(gorfodaf)** to be obliged, forced or compelled to, to have (to): **Rwyt ti'n gorfod mynd** You have to go.
gorfodaeth *e.b.g. ll.* **-au** compulsion, obligation; victory success; **gorfodaeth filwrol** military conscription.
gorfodi (i) *be.* **(gorfodaf)** to compel, to oblige; to conquer, to overcome.
gorfodol *a.* compulsory, obligatory.
gorfoleddus *a.* joyful.
gorff *gw.* **corff.**
gorffen *be.* **(gorffennaf)** to finish, to conclude.
Gorffennaf *e.g.* July.
gorffennol 1 *e.g.* the past. **2** *a.* past.
gorfforol *gw.* **corfforol.**
gorffwys *e.g.* rest.
gorffwyso *be.* **(gorffwysaf)** to rest.
gorgi *gw.* **corgi.**
gorlawn *a.* overflowing, overcrowded.
gorllewin *e.g.* west; **Gorllewin Morgannwg** West Glamorgan.
gormod 1 *e.g.* excess; too many. **2** *a.* & *ad.* too much, excessive: **gormod o gwynion** too many complaints; **gormod o straeon** too many stories; **gormod o stŵr** too much noise; **gormod o drafferth** too much trouble; **bwyta gormod** to eat too much.
gorn *gw.* **corn.**
gornel *gw.* **cornel.**
gornest *e.b. ll.* **-au** contest, battle; match.
goron *gw.* **coron.**
goroni *gw.* **coroni.**
gorryn *gw.* **corryn.**
gorsaf *e.b. ll.* **-oedd** station: **gorsaf betrol** petrol station; **gorsaf bŵer** power station; **gorsaf dân** fire station.
gorsedd *e.b. ll.* **-au** throne: **Gorsedd y Beirdd** the Gorsedd of Bards (*bardic institution*).
goruchaf *a.* most high, supreme.
gorwedd *be.* **(gorweddaf)** to lie, to lie down.
gorwel *e.g. ll.* **-ion** horizon.
gosb *gw.* **cosb.**
gosbi *gw.* **cosbi.**
gosi *gw.* **cosi.**
gosod 1 *be.* **(gosodaf)** to put; to plant; to let; to bestow; to fix: **gosod gerbron** to set before; **gosod mewn trefn** to set in order; **gosod pris** to fix a price; **gosod yr ardd** to plant the garden. **2** *a.* false, artificial, applied: **dannedd gosod** false teeth, dentures; **gwallt gosod** false hair, wig.
gostus *gw.* **costus.**

gostwng *be.* **(gostyngaf)** to lower, to reduce; to diminish; to ease.
gostyngedig *a.* humble.
gostyngiad *e.g.* *ll.* **-au** reduction.
gosyn *gw.* **cosyn.**
got: gôt *gw.* **cot.**
gotwm *gw.* **cotwm.**
grac *gw.* **crac.**
grachach *gw.* **crachach.**
gradd *e.b.* *ll.* **-au** step, grade, degree, university degree: **gradd anrhydedd** an honours degree; **i'r fath raddau** to such an extent; **mewn graddau** by degrees, gradually; **o radd i radd** step by step, by degrees.
graddfa *e.b.* *ll.* **graddfâu, graddfeydd** scale; **ar raddfa eang** on a large scale; **graddfa Celsius** Celsius Scale.
graddio *be.* **(graddiaf)** to graduate, to grade, to scale.
graddol *a.* gradual; **yn raddol** by degrees.
graenus *a.* of good quality, glossy, sleek.
grafu *gw.* **crafu.**
gragen *gw.* **cragen.**
graig *gw.* **craig.**
gramadeg *e.g.* *ll.* **-au** grammar; **llyfr gramadeg** grammar book.
grant *e.g.* *ll.* **-iau** grant.
gras *e.g.* *ll.* **-au, -usau** grace; *gw.* **cras.**
grasu *gw.* **crasu.**
gredu *gw.* **credu.**
grefydd *gw.* **crefydd.**
grefft *gw.* **crefft.**
grefftwr *gw.* **crefftwr.**
gregyn *gw.* **cragen.**
greigiau *gw.* **craig.**
greigiog *gw.* **creigiog.**
greision *gw.* **cras, creisionyn.**
grempog *gw.* **crempog.**
gresyn *e.g.* *ll.* **-au** pity (*N.W.*): **Gresyn iddo farw** Pity that he died; **Gresyn o beth** It's a shame.
gresynu *be.* **(gresynaf)** to deplore, to be sorry, to pity.
greulon *gw.* **creulon.**
greulondeb *gw.* **creulondeb.**
gri *gw.* **cri.**
grib *gw.* **crib.**
gribo *gw.* **cribo.**
griced *gw.* **criced.**
gricedwr *gw.* **cricedwr.**
grio *gw.* **crio.**
gris *e.g.* *ll.* **-iau** step, stair.
Gristion *gw.* **Cristion.**
griw *gw.* **criw.**
Groeg 1 *e.b.* Greece. **2** *e.b.* & *a.* the Greek language, Greek; pertaining to the Greek language, to Greece or to the Greeks.
Groegaidd *a.* Grecian, Greek.
Groeges *e.b.* *ll.* **-au** Greek female.
Groegwr *e.g.* *ll.* **Groegwyr** Greek, Grecian.
groen *gw.* **croen.**
groes *gw.* **croes.**
groesair *gw.* **croesair.**
groesawu *gw.* **croesawu.**
groesawus *gw.* **croesawus.**
groesfan *gw.* **croesfan.**
groesffordd *gw.* **croesffordd.**
groesholi *gw.* **croesholi.**
groesi *gw.* **croesi.**
groeso *gw.* **croeso.**
gronfa *gw.* **cronfa.**
grud *gw.* **crud.**
grudd *e.b.g.* *ll.* **-iau** cheek.
grug *e.g.* heather.
grŵp *e.g.* *ll.* **grwpiau** group: **grŵp pop** pop group.
grwst *gw.* **crwst.**
gryd *gw.* **cryd.**
gryf *gw.* **cryf.**
gryfach *gw.* **cryf.**
gryfaf *gw.* **cryf.**
gryfed *gw.* **cryf.**
grym *e.g.* *ll.* **-oedd** force; energy; power.
grymus *a.* powerful, strong, mighty.
grynhoi *gw.* **crynhoi.**
gryno *gw.* **cryno.**
grynodeb *gw.* **crynodeb.**
grynu *gw.* **crynu.**
grys *gw.* **crys.**
grystyn *gw.* **crystyn.**
gu *gw.* **cu.**
guddio *gw.* **cuddio.**
gul *gw.* **cul.**
guro *gw.* **curo.**
gusan *gw.* **cusan.**
gusanu *gw.* **cusanu.**
gwadu *be.* **(gwadaf)** to deny, to disown.
gwaed *e.g.* blood: **yn y gwaed** in the blood as a family trait; **Cymro o waed coch cyfan** a thoroughbred Welshman.
gwaedu *be.* **(gwaedaf)** to bleed: **gwaedu fel mochyn** to bleed like a (slaughtered) pig.
gwaedd *e.b.* *ll.* **-au** shout.
gwael *a.* poor; miserable; sick; vile: **tro gwael â** an unworthy act (with).

gwaelod *e.g.* *ll.* **-ion** bottom, base, foundation: **ar waelod** at the bottom; **yng ngwaelod** in the bottom; **gwaelodion** sediment, dregs.
gwaeth *gw.* **drwg.**
gwaethaf *gw.* **drwg; er gwaethaf** in spite of: **gwaetha'r modd** the more the pity; worse luck.
gwaethed *gw.* **drwg.**
gwag *a.* *ll.* **gweigion** empty; desolate; vacant.
gwagedd *e.g.* *ll.* **-au** vanity; void.
gwagio: gwagu *be.* **(gwagiaf: gwagaf)** to empty.
gwagle *e.g.* *ll.* **-oedd** space, void; *gw.* **gofod.**
gwagu *gw.* **gwagio.**
gwahân *e.g.* separation; difference; **ar wahân** apart; separately; independently: **byw ar wahân** to live apart.
gwahaniaeth *e.g.* difference, separation.
gwahanol *a.* different, various.
gwahodd 1 *be.* **(gwahoddaf)** to invite, to ask. **2** *e.g.* *ll.* **-ion** invitation, bidding.
gwahoddedig *e.g.* *ll.* **-ion** invited, bidden, called; **gwahoddedigion** guests.
gwahoddiad *e.g.* *ll.* **-au** invitation.
gwahoddion *gw.* **gwahodd.**
gwair *e.g.* *ll.* **gweiriau** grass (*grown for harvesting*); hay (*S.W.*).
gwaith 1 *e.g.* *ll.* **gweithiau** work; composition; works: **gwaith annwyd** cold sores; **gwaith cartref** homework; **gwaith glo** coal-mine, colliery; **gwaith tŷ** house work. **2** *e.b.* *ll.* **gweithiau.** time, occasion, turn: **unwaith** once; **dwywaith** twice; **teirgwaith** three times; **canwaith** a hundred times; **y waith honno** that occasion. **3** *c.* for, because.
gwal *e.b.* *ll.* **gwaliau, gwelydd** wall.
gwâl *e.b.* *ll.* **gwalau** lair; bed.
gwall *e.g.* *ll.* **-au** mistake, defect, want.
gwallt *e.g.* *ll.* **-au, -iau** hair; **blewyn** (*one*) hair.
gwallus *a.* faulty, inaccurate, erroneous.
gwan *a.* *ll.* **gweiniaid, gweinion** weak, feeble; **esgus wan** a feeble excuse.
gwanwyn *e.g.* *ll.* **-au** spring.
gwar *e.b.g.* *ll.* **-rau** nape of the neck.
gwarchod *be.* **(gwarchodaf)** to watch, to guard, to baby-sit.
gwaredu *(rhag.) be.* **(gwaredaf)** to save, to redeem, to deliver, to rid.
gwardedwr *e.g.* *ll.* **gwaredwyr** saviour, deliverer.
gwario *be.* **(gwariaf)** to spend (*money*).
gwarrau *gw.* **gwar.**
gwartheg *e.ll.* cattle; *gw.* **buwch, da.**
gwas *e.g.* *ll.* **gweision** servant; boy, lad.
gwasanaeth *e.g.* *ll.* **-au** service; use.
gwasanaethu *be.* **(gwasanaethaf)** to serve, to minister.
gwasg 1 *e.b.* *ll.* **-au, -oedd, gweisg** press, pressure; waist: **gwasg argraffu** printing-press; **gwasg gaws** cheese-press; **gwasg ddillad** clothes-press; **gwŷr y wasg** the press (*reporters*). **2** *e.g.* *ll.* **-au, -oedd** stress; waist.
gwasgedd *e.g.* *ll.* **-au** pressure; **gwasgedd isel** low pressure; **gwasgedd uchel** high pressure.
gwasgfa *e.b.* *ll.* **gwasgfeydd** squeeze.
gwasgod *e.b.* *ll.* **-au** waistcoat.
gwasgu *be.* **(gwasgaf)** to press, to squeeze, to wring, to crush.
gwastad *a.* flat, level, even; constant: **yn wastad** always (*S.W.*).
gwastraff *e.g.* *ll.* **-au, -oedd** waste: **gwastraff niwclear** nuclear waste.
gwastraffu *be.* **(gwastraffaf)** to waste.
gwau *be.* **(gweaf, gweuaf)** to weave; to knit: **dillad gwau** knitted garments *gw.* **gweu.**
gwaun *e.b.* *ll.* **gweunydd** meadow; moor.
gwawd *e.g.* *ll.* **-iau, -ion** scorn, satire.
gwawdio *be.* **(gwawdiaf)** to scorn, to mock, to jeer.
gwawr *e.b.g.* *ll.* **-iau, -oedd** dawn; hue; shade: **ar doriad gwawr** at day-break; **roedd gwawr las yn y brethyn** there was a shade of blue in the material.
gwawrio *be.* **(gwawriaf)** to dawn.
gwawroedd *gw.* **gwawr.**
gwb *gw.* **cwb.**
gwbl *gw.* **cwbl.**
gwcw *gw.* **cwcw.**
gwch *gw.* **cwch.**
gwd *gw.* **cwd.**
gwdihŵ *e.b.* *ll.* **-aid, -s** owl (*S.W.*); *gw.* **tylluan.**

gwdyn *gw.* **cwdyn.**
gwddf *e.g. ll.* **gyddfau** neck, throat; neckline: **gwddf crwn** round neck; **gwddf ffrog** neckline; **gwddf sgwâr** square neck; **gwddf V** V neck.
gwddwg *e.g. ll.* **gwddygau** neck, throat; neckline (*S.W.*).
gweddi *e.b. ll.* **gweddïau** prayer: **Gweddi'r Arglwydd** The Lord's Prayer; **cwrdd gweddi** prayer meeting.
gweddill *e.g. ll.* **-ion** remnant.
gweddïo *be.* **(gweddïaf)** to pray.
gweddol 1 *a.* fair: **pris gweddol** a fairly good price; **cyflog gweddol** a fairly good wage. 2 *ad. (precedes the adjective and is followed by soft mutation)*; **yn weddol dawel** fairly quiet; **yn weddol gyflym** fairly quick.
gwefus *e.b. ll.* **-au** lip.
gweiddi *be.* **(gwaeddaf)** to shout.
gweigion *gw.* **gwag.**
gweiniaid *gw.* **gwan.**
gweinidog *e.g. ll.* **-ion** minister, servant: **Gweinidog yr Efengyl** Minister of the Gospel; **Prif Weinidog** Prime Minister; **Gweinidog Gwladol** Minister of State.
gweinion *gw.* **gwan.**
gweinyddes *e.b. ll.* **-au** female attendant; nurse: **gweinyddes feithrin** nursery nurse.
gweiriau *gw.* **gwair.**
gweisg *gw.* **gwasg.**
gweision *gw.* **gwas.**
gweithdy *e.g. ll.* **gweithdai** workshop.
gweithiau *gw.* **gwaith.**
gweithio *be.* **(gweithiaf)** to work; to ferment; to operate.
gweithiwr *e.g. ll.* **gweithwyr** worker.
gweithred *e.b. ll.* **-oedd** act, deed.
gweithredu *be.* **(gweithredaf)** to act, to operate, to execute.
gweithwyr *gw.* **gweithiwr.**
gwelâu *gw.* **gwely.**
gweld: gweled *be.* **(gwelaf)** to see, to perceive; **gweler** see (*when referring to something*).
gwely *e.g. ll.* **-au, gwelâu** bed.
gwelydd *gw.* **gwal.**
gwell *a.* better (*note: nouns following* **gwell** *do not mutate.*).
gwella *be.* **(gwellaf)** to improve, to better; to cure; to mend.
gwellt *e. torf.* grass, sward; straw; *gw.* **gwelltyn.**
gwelltyn *e.g. ll.* **gwellt** blade of grass; a straw; **gw. gwellt.**
gwen *a.b.* white: **ffrog wen** a white frock; **torth wen** a white loaf; *gw.* **gwyn.**
gwên *e.b. ll.* **gwenau** smile.
gwenau *gw.* **gwên.**
gwendid *e.g. ll.* **-au** weakness; wane (*of the moon*): **y lleuad yn ei gwendid** the wane of the moon.
Gwener *e.b.* Venus: **dydd Gwener** Friday.
gwenith *e.ll.* wheat; **gwenithen** a grain of wheat.
gwennol *e.b. ll.* **gwenoliaid** swallow.
Gwent *e.b.* a county in S.E. Wales.
gwenu (ar) *be.* **(gwenaf)** to smile.
gwenwyn *e.g. ll.* **-au, -ion** poison; venom; malice; spite.
gwenwynig: gwenwynol *a.* poisonous.
gwenynen *e.b. ll.* **gwenyn** bee.
gwêr *e.g. ll.* **gwerau** tallow.
gwerdd *a.b.* green: **ffrog werdd** a green frock; **deilen werdd** a green leaf; **y Blaid Werdd** The Green Party; *gw.* **gwyrdd.**
gwerin *e.b. & e.torf. ll.* **-oedd, -edd** ordinary people, peasantry, folk; proletariat: **amgueddfa werin** folk museum; **can werin** folk song; **dawns werin** folk dance.
gweriniaeth *e.b. ll.* **-au** democracy, republic.
Gweriniaeth Iwerddon *e.b.* Eire.
gwers *e.b. ll.* **-i** lesson; stanza of poetry: **gwers Gymraeg** Welsh lesson; **gwers hanes** history lesson.
gwerslyfr *e.g. ll.* **-au** textbook.
gwersyll *e.g. ll.* **-oedd** camp.
gwerth *e.g. ll.* **-oedd** worth, value: **mae'n werth y drafferth** it's worth the trouble; **ar werth** for sale; **mae'n werth punt** It's worth a pound; **Ga i werth pum punt o betrol?** May I have five pounds worth of petrol?
gwerthfawr *a.* valuable, precious.
gwerthfawrogi *be.* **(gwerthfawrogaf)** to appreciate.
gwerthfawrogiad *e.g. ll.* **-au** appreciation.
gwerthiant *e.g. ll.* **gwerthiannau** sale.
gwerthoedd *gw.* **gwerth.**
gwerthu *be.* **(gwerthaf)** to sell.
gwerthwr *e.g. ll.* **gwerthwyr** seller, salesman.
gweryl *gw.* **cweryl.**

gweryla *gw.* **cweryla.**
gwestai *e.g. ll.* **gwesteion** guest; *gw.* **gwesty.**
gwesteion *gw.* **gwestai.**
gwesteiwr *e.g. ll.* **gwesteiwyr** host; **gwesteiwraig** hostess.
gwestiwn *gw.* **cwestiwn.**
gwestiyna *gw.* **cwestiyna.**
gwestiynau *gw.* **cwestiwn.**
gwesty *e.g. ll.* **gwestai, gwestyau** hotel, inn.
gweu *be.* **(gweuaf)** to weave; to knit; *gw.* **gwau.**
gweunydd *gw.* **gwaun.**
gwg *e.g. ll.* **-on, gygau** frown, scowl.
gwgu (ar) *be.* **(gwgaf)** to frown, to scowl, to glower.
gwiail *gw.* **gwialen.**
gwialen *e.b. ll.* **gwiail, gwialennod** rod, cane, stick; **gwialen fedw** birch rod.
gwialennod *gw.* **gwialen.**
gwin *e.g. ll.* **-oedd** wine: **gwin coch** red wine; **gwin gwyn** white wine.
gwir 1 *e.g.* truth: **yn wir** in truth, indeed. 2 *a.* true; real; net: **stori wir** a true story; (*the adjective may also precede a noun and convey additional emphasis, it then causes a soft mutation*); **gwir bwysau** net weight; **gwir Gymro** a real Welshman; **y gwir ystyr** the real meaning.
gwirionedd *e.g. ll.* **-au** truth, reality.
gwisg *e.b. ll.* **-oedd** dress: **gwisg briodas** wedding-dress; **gwisg nos** night-dress.
gwisgo *be.* **(gwisgaf)** to dress; to wear.
gwiwer *e.b. ll.* **-od** squirrel: **y wiwer goch** the red squirrel; **y wiwer lwyd** the grey squirrel.
gwlad *e.b. ll.* **gwledydd** country, land: **gwlad fy nhadau** land of my fathers.
Gwlad Belg *e.b.* Belgium.
gwladfa *e.b. ll.* **gwladfaoedd, gwladfeydd** colony; settlement; **Y Wladfa** Patagonia.
gwladgarwr *e.g. ll.* **gwladgarwyr** patriot.
gwladol *a.* civil; country; state; national: **Ysgrifennydd Gwladol** Secretary of State.
Gwlad Pwyl *e.b.* **Poland.**
Gwlad y Basg *e.b.* Basque Country.
Gwlad yr Haf *e.b.* Somerset.
Gwlad yr Iâ *e.b.* Iceland.
gwlân *e.g. ll.* **gwlanoedd** wool.
gwlanen *e.b. ll.* **-ni** homespun, home-made cloth or flannel: **gwlanen goch** red flannel; **gwlanen wen** white flannel; **gwlanen ymolchi** face-cloth; **crys gwlanen** flannel shirt.
gwledig *a.* rural; rustic; boorish: **Cymru Wledig** Rural Wales.
gwledydd *gw.* **gwlad.**
gwledd *e.b. ll.* **-oedd** feast; **gwledd briodas** marriage-feast.
gwledda *be.* **(gwleddaf)** to feast.
gwleidydd *e.g. ll.* **-ion** politician, statesman.
gwleidyddiaeth *e.b.* politics.
gwleidyddol *a.* political.
gwlff *e.g. ll.* **gylffau** gulf.
gwlith *e.g. ll.* **-oedd** dew.
gwlwm *gw.* **cwlwm.**
gwlyb *a. ll.* **-ion** wet.
gwlybaniaeth *e.g.* moisture, wet, humidity.
gwlychu *be.* **(gwlychaf)** to wet, to moisten; to get wet.
gwm *e.g. ll.* **gymiau** gum; *gw.* **cwm.**
gwmni *gw.* **cwmni.**
gwmnïau *gw.* **cwmni.**
gwmnïoedd *gw.* **cwmni.**
gwmwl *gw.* **cwmwl.**
gwn *e.g. ll.* **gynnau** gun; *gw.* **gwybod.**
gŵn *e.g. ll.* **gynau** gown: **gŵn gwisgo** dressing gown; **gŵn nos** night-gown; *gw.* **ci.**
gwneud: gwneuthur *be.* **(gwnaf)** to make; to do; *gw. At. Berfau.*
gwningen *gw.* **cwningen.**
gwniadyddes: gwniyddes *e.b. ll.* **-au** dressmaker, seamstress.
gwnïo *be.* **(gwnïaf)** to sew, to stitch: **peiriant gwnïo** sewing machine.
gwniyddes *gw.* **gwniadyddes.**
gwobr *e.b. ll.* **-au** prize, reward: **y wobr gyntaf** the first prize; **gwobr gysur** consolation prize.
gwobrwyo *be.* **(gwobrwyaf)** to reward, to award prize to.
gwpan *gw.* **cwpan.**
gwpla *gw.* **cwpla.**
gwpwrdd *gw.* **cwpwrdd.**
gwr *gw.* **cwr.**
gŵr *e.g. ll.* **gwŷr** man; husband: **gŵr dieithr** stranger; **gŵr gwadd** guest, guest speaker; **gwŷr y wasg** pressmen, the press.
gwrach *e.b. ll.* **-od, -ïod** hag, witch.
gwragedd *gw.* **gwraig.**
gwraidd *gw.* **gwreiddyn.**

gwraig *e.b.* *ll.* **gwragedd** wife; woman.
gwrandawiad *e.g.* *ll.* **-au** listening, hearing.
gwrandawr *e.g.* *ll.* **gwrandawyr** listener, hearer.
gwrando (ar) *be.* **(gwrandawaf)** to listen: **Gwrandewais ar** I listened to; **Gwrandewaist ar** You listened to.
gwrdd *gw.* **cwrdd.**
gwreichionen *e.b.* *ll.* **gwreichion** spark.
gwreiddiau *gw.* **gwreiddyn.**
gwreiddio *be.* **(gwreiddiaf)** to root, to ground.
gwreiddiol *a.* original.
gwreiddyn *e.g.* *ll.* **gwraidd, gwreiddiau** root; stock.
gwres *e.g.* *ll.* **-au** heat, warmth; zeal.
gwresog *a.* hot, warm; fervent.
gwresogydd *e.g.* *ll.* **-ion** heater.
gwrido *be.* **(gwridaf)** to blush.
gwridog *a.* rosy-cheeked, ruddy.
gwrol *a.* brave, courageous.
gwrs *gw.* **cwrs.**
gwrtais *gw.* **cwrtais.**
gwrtaith *e.g.* *ll.* **gwrteithiau** manure, fertiliser.
gwrth- *rhagdd. Prefix with the sense 'against, contra-, counter-, anti-' in nouns, adjectives and verbs, and followed by soft mutation;* **gwrth-ddweud** to contradict.
gwrthblaid *e.b.* *ll.* **gwrthbleidiau** opposition (*party*).
gwrthdystio *be.* **(gwrthdystiaf)** to protest.
gwrthod *be.* **(gwrthodaf)** to refuse; to reject: **Fe wrthododd e fynd adref** He refused to go home.
gwrthrych *e.g.* *ll.* **-au** object.
gwrthrychol *a.* objective.
gwrthryfel *e.g.* *ll.* **-oedd** rebellion, mutiny, insurrection.
gwrthwyneb 1 *e.g.* *ll.* **-au** in opposition to. 2 *a.* contrary, opposite: **i'r gwrthwyneb** to the contrary, in the opposite direction.
gwrthwynebu *be.* **(gwrthwynebaf)** to oppose; to object.
gwrthwynebwr: gwrthwynebydd *e.g.* *ll.* **gwrthwynebwyr** opponent; objector; antagonist; **gwrthwynebydd cydwybodol** conscientious objector.
gwrw *gw.* **cwrw.**
gwryw 1 *e.g.* *ll.* **-od** male; **gwryw a benyw** male and female. 2 *a.* male.
gwrywaidd: gwrywol *a.* male;
gwrywgydiwr homosexual; *gw.* **gwryw.**
gwsg *gw.* **cwsg.**
gwsmer *gw.* **cwsmer.**
gwstwm *gw.* **cwstwm.**
gwt *gw.* **cwt.**
gwta *gw.* **cwta.**
gwthiad *e.g.* *ll.* **-au** heave, thrust.
gwthio *be.* **(gwthiaf)** to push, to thrust.
gwthiwr *e.g.* *ll.* **gwthwyr** pusher.
gwybedyn *e.g.* *ll.* **gwybed** gnat.
gwybod (am) *be.* **(gwn)** to know; *gw. At. Berfau; e.g.* *ll.* **-au** knowledge: **heb yn wybod(i)** without knowing, unwittingly.
gwybodaeth *e.b.* *ll.* **-au** knowledge.
gwych *a.* fine, splendid; brilliant.
gwydr *e.g.* *ll.* **-au** glass: **gwydr gwin** wine-glass; **gwydr lliw** coloured glass, stained glass; **gwydr nadd** cut-glass; **tŷ gwydr** glasshouse.
gwydrau *gw.* **gwydr, gwydryn.**
gwydryn *e.g.* *ll.* **gwydrau** drinking-glass.
gŵydd 1 *e.b.* *ll.* **gwyddau** goose; **croen gŵydd** goose-flesh. 2 *e.g.* presence: **yng ngŵydd fy ngelynion** in the presence of my enemies.
gwyddbwyll *e.b.* chess.
Gwyddel *e.g.* *ll.* **-od, Gwyddyl** Irishman.
Gwyddeleg *e.b.* Irish language.
Gwyddeles *e.b.* *ll.* **-au** Irishwoman.
Gwyddelig *a.* Irish.
gwyddoniaeth *e.b.* science.
gwyddonol *a.* scientific.
gwyddonydd *e.g.* *ll.* **gwyddonwyr** scientist.
gwyddor *e.b.* *ll.* **-ion** rudiment, science: **yr wyddor** the alphabet.
gwyfyn *e.g.* *ll.* **-od** moth.
gŵyl *e.b.* *ll.* **gwyliau** feast, festival; holiday: **Gŵyl Dewi** Saint David's Day.
gwylan *e.b.* *ll.* **-od** seagull.
gwyliadwrus *a.* watchful, cautious.
gwyliau *gw.* **gŵyl.**
gwylio (dros) *be.* **(gwyliaf)** to mind; watch (over); to guard.
gwyliwr *e.g.* *ll.* **gwylwyr** sentry, guard, watchman.
gwylnos *e.b.* *ll.* **-au** vigil, watch-night.
gwylwyr *gw.* **gwyliwr.**
gwyll *e.g.* darkness.
gwyllt *a.* wild, mad: **yn wyllt**

gacwn furiously cross, in a mad rage.
gwylltio: gwylltu *be.* **(gwylltiaf: gwylltaf)** to lose one's temper, to excite violently.
gwymon *e.g.* seaweed.
gwymp *gw.* **cwymp.**
gwympo *gw.* **cwympo.**
gwyn *a.* *ll.* **-ion** white; holy: **Gwlad y menig gwynion** Land of the white gloves (*alluding to the frequent presentation of white gloves to assize judges in Wales, when there were no cases for trial*; *gw.* **cwyn, gwen.**
Gwynedd *e.b.* county in N.E. Wales.
gwynegon *e.g.* rheumatism (*S.W.*).
gwynegu *be.* **(gwynegaf)** to ache (*S.W.*).
gwynfa *e.b.* paradise.
gwynfyd *e.g.* *ll.* **-au** blessedness, bliss: **Y Gwynfydau** The Beatitudes.
gwyngalch *e.g.* white-lime, whitewash.
gwynion *gw.* **cwyn, gwyn.**
gwynnu *be.* **(gwynnaf)** to whiten, to bleach.
gwynt *e.g.* *ll.* **-oedd** wind; smell: **a'i wynt yn ei ddwrn** breathless, panting, having one's heart in one's mouth; **prin ei wynt** short of breath.
gwyntog *a.* windy; bombastic; **hirwyntog** longwinded.
gwyr *gw.* **cwyr.**
Gŵyr *e.b.* Gower.
gŵyr 1 *a.* crooked, inclined, aslant. 2 *bf.* he/she/it knows; *gw.* **gwybod.**
gwŷr *gw.* **gŵr.**
gwyrdd 1 *a.* *ll.* **-ion** green. 2 *e.g.* green, *gw.* **gwerdd.**
gwyriad *e.g.* *ll.* **-au** deviation.
gwyro: gwyrio *be.* **(gwyraf: gwyriaf)** to bend, to deviate, to incline, to swerve.
gwyrth *e.b.* *ll.* **-iau** miracle.
gwyrthiol *a.* miraculous: **Roedd hi'n wyrthiol ei weld** It was miraculous to see him.
gwyryf *e.b.* *ll.* **-on** virgin.
gwŷs *e.b.* *ll.* **gwysion** summons.
gwystl *e.g.* *ll.* **-on** hostage; pledge.
gwywo *be.* **(gwywaf)** to wither, to fade.
gychod *gw.* **cwch.**
gychwyn *gw.* **cychwyn.**
gyd, i *ad.* (*always immediately follows the noun to which it refers*) all: **Roedd y plant i gyd yn dost** All the children were ill.
gyda: gydag *ardd.* together with; in company of.
gydadrodd *gw.* **cydadrodd.**
gydio *gw.* **cydio.**
gydnabod *gw.* **cydnabod.**
gyddfau *gw.* **gwddf.**
gyfaill *gw.* **cyfaill.**
gyfan *gw.* **cyfan.**
gyfangwbl *gw.* **cyfangwbl.**
gyfansoddi *gw.* **cyfansoddi.**
gyfansoddwr *gw.* **cyfansoddwr.**
gyfanswm *gw.* **cyfanswm.**
gyfarch *gw.* **cyfarch.**
gyfarfod *gw.* **cyfarfod.**
gyfarwyddiadur *gw.* **cyfarwyddiadur.**
gyfarwyddo *gw.* **cyfarwyddo.**
gyfarwyddwr *gw.* **cyfarwyddwr.**
gyfeilles *gw.* **cyfeilles.**
gyfeillgar *gw.* **cyfeillgar.**
gyfeillgarwch *gw.* **cyfeillgarwch.**
gyfeillion *gw.* **cyfaill.**
gyfeiriad *gw.* **cyfeiriad.**
gyfeirio *gw.* **cyfeirio.**
gyfenw *gw.* **cyfenw.**
gyferbyn (â) *ardd.* opposite: **yn y tŷ gyferbyn** in the opposite house; **gyferbyn â'n tŷ ni** opposite our house.
gyfiawn *gw.* **cyfiawn.**
gyfiawnder *gw.* **cyfiawnder.**
gyfieithiad *gw.* **cyfieithiad.**
gyfieithu *gw.* **cyfieithu.**
gyfieithydd *gw.* **cyfieithydd.**
gyfle *gw.* **cyfle.**
gyfleu *gw.* **cyfleu.**
gyfleus *gw.* **cyfleus.**
gyflog *gw.* **cyflog.**
gyflogi *gw.* **cyflogi.**
gyflogwr *gw.* **cyflogwr.**
gyflwr *gw.* **cyflwr.**
gyflwyno *gw.* **cyflwyno.**
gyflym *gw.* **cyflym.**
gyflymach *gw.* **cyflym.**
gyflymaf *gw.* **cyflym.**
gyflymder *gw.* **cyflymder.**
gyflymed *gw.* **cyflym.**
gyflymu *gw.* **cyflymu.**
gyflymydd *gw.* **cyflymydd.**
gyfnither *gw.* **cyfnither.**
gyfoeth *gw.* **cyfoeth.**
gyfoethog *gw.* **cyfoethog.**
gyfraith *gw.* **cyfraith.**
gyfrannu *gw.* **cyfrannu.**
gyfreithiwr *gw.* **cyfreithiwr.**
gyfres *gw.* **cyfres.**
gyfrif *gw.* **cyfrif.**
gyfrifiadur *gw.* **cyfrifiadur.**
gyfrifol *gw.* **cyfrifol.**

gyfrifoldeb *gw.* **cyfrifoldeb.**
gyfrifydd *gw.* **cyfrifydd.**
gyfrinach *gw.* **cyfrinach.**
gyfrinachol *gw.* **cyfrinachol.**
gyfrol *gw.* **cyfrol.**
gyfrwng *gw.* **cyfrwng.**
gyfrwys *gw.* **cyfrwys.**
gyfun *gw.* **cyfun.**
gyfuwch *gw.* **uchel.**
gyfweld *gw.* **cyfweld.**
gyfweliad *gw.* **cyfweliad.**
gyfyng *gw.* **cyfyng.**
gyfyngu *gw.* **cyfyngu.**
gyfystyr *gw.* **cyfystyr.**
gyfforddus *gw.* **cyfforddus.**
gyffredin *gw.* **cyffredin.**
gyffrous *gw.* **cyffrous.**
gyffur *gw.* **cyffur.**
gyffwrdd *gw.* **cyffwrdd.**
gygau *gw.* **gwg.**
gyngerdd *gw.* **cyngerdd.**
gynghori *gw.* **cynghori.**
gynghorwr *gw.* **cynghorwr.**
gyngor *gw.* **cyngor.**
gyhoedd *gw.* **cyhoedd.**
gyhoeddi *gw.* **cyhoeddi.**
gyhoeddiad *gw.* **cyhoeddiad.**
gyhoeddus *gw.* **cyhoeddus.**
gyhoeddusrwydd *gw.* **cyhoeddusrwydd.**
gyhoeddwr *gw.* **cyhoeddwr.**
gyhyd *gw.* **cyhyd.**
gyhyrog *gw.* **cyhyrog.**
gylch *gw.* **cylch.**
gylchgrawn *gw.* **cylchgrawn.**
gylchlythyr *gw.* **cylchlythyr.**
gyll *gw.* **cyll.**
gyllell *gw.* **cyllell.**
gyllyll *gw.* **cyllell.**
gymaint *gw.* **mawr.**
gymal *gw.* **cymal.**
gymanfa *gw.* **cymanfa.**
gymdeithas *gw.* **cymdeithas.**
gymdogion *gw.* **cymydog.**
gymeriad *gw.* **cymeriad.**
gymeryd *gw.* **cymeryd.**
gymharu *gw.* **cymharu.**
gymhleth *gw.* **cymhleth.**
gymhlethdod *gw.* **cymhlethdod.**
gymhlethu *gw.* **cymhlethu.**
gymoedd *gw.* **cwm.**
gymorth *gw.* **cymorth.**
Gymraeg *gw.* **Cymraeg.**
Gymraes *gw.* **Cymraes.**
Gymreictod *gw.* **Cymreictod.**
Gymreig *gw.* **Cymreig.**
Gymreiges *gw.* **Cymraes.**
Gymro *gw.* **Cymro.**
Gymru *gw.* **Cymru.**
Gymry *gw.* **Cymro.**
gymryd *gw.* **cymryd.**
gymwynas *gw.* **cymwynas.**
gymydog *gw.* **cymydog.**
gymylau *gw.* **cwmwl.**
gymylog *gw.* **cymylog.**
gymysg *gw.* **cymysg.**
gymysgu *gw.* **cymysgu.**
gymysgwch *gw.* **cymysgwch.**
gyn *gw.* **cyn.**
gynaeafau *gw.* **cynhaeaf.**
gynau *gw.* **gŵn.**
gynddrwg *gw.* **cynddrwg.**
gynffon *gw.* **cynffon.**
gynhadledd *gw.* **cynhadledd.**
gynhaeaf *gw.* **cynhaeaf.**
gynhesu *gw.* **cynhesu.**
gynhyrfus *gw.* **cynhyrfus.**
gynigion *gw.* **cynnig.**
gynilion *gw.* **cynilion.**
gynilo *gw.* **cynilo.**
gynllun *gw.* **cynllun.**
gynllunio *gw.* **cynllunio.**
gynlluniwr *gw.* **cynlluniwr.**
gynllunydd *gw.* **cynlluniwr.**
gynnal *gw.* **cynnal.**
gynnar *gw.* **cynnar.**
gynnau *gw.* **gwn.**
gynnes *gw.* **cynnes.**
gynnig *gw.* **cynnig.**
gynradd *gw.* **cynradd.**
gynt *ad.* formerly; *née;* long since; ages ago: **Rhian Smith (gynt Jones)** Rhian Smith (*née* Jones); **yr hen ddyddiau gynt** the old days, ages ago; *gw.* **cynnar.**
gyntaf *gw.* **cynnar.**
gynted *gw.* **cynnar.**
gyntedd *gw.* **cyntedd.**
gynulleidfa *gw.* **cynulleidfa.**
gyrddau *gw.* **cwrdd.**
gyrfa *e.b. ll.* **-oedd, gyrfeydd** race; career; course.
gyrfeydd *gw.* **gyrfa.**
gyrff *gw.* **corff.**
gyrion *gw.* **cwr.**
gyrliog *gw.* **cyrliog.**
gyrn *gw.* **corn.**
gyrraedd *gw.* **cyrraedd.**
gyrrau *gw.* **cwr.**
gyrru *be.* **(gyrraf)** to drive; to send; to push.
gyrrwr *e.g. ll.* **gyrwyr** driver; sender.
gyrwyr *gw.* **gyrrwr.**
gysglyd *gw.* **cysglyd.**
gysgod *gw.* **cysgod.**
gysgodi *gw.* **cysgodi.**
gysgu *gw.* **cysgu.**
gystadleuaeth *gw.* **cystadleuaeth.**

gystadleuwr *gw.* **cystadleuwr.**
gystadleuydd *gw.* **cystadleuwr.**
gystadlu *gw.* **cystadlu.**
gystal *gw.* **da.**
gystymau *gw.* **cwstwm.**
gysur *gw.* **cysur.**
gysuro *gw.* **cysuro.**
gysurus *gw.* **cysurus.**
gywsllt *gw.* **cyswllt.**
gytgan *gw.* **cytgan.**
gytsain *gw.* **cytsain.**
gytundeb *gw.* **cytundeb.**
gytuno *gw.* **cytuno.**
gyw *gw.* **cyw.**
gywaith *gw.* **cywaith.**
gywir *gw.* **cywir.**
gywiriad *gw.* **cywiriad.**
gywiro *gw.* **cywiro.**

ngadael *gw.* **gadael.**
ngaeaf *gw.* **gaeaf.**
ngafael *gw.* **gafael.**
ngafr *gw.* **gafr.**
ngair *gw.* **gair.**
ngalar *gw.* **galar.**
ngalw *gw.* **galw.**
ngalwad *gw.* **galwad.**
ngalwyn *gw.* **galwyn.**
ngallu *gw.* **gallu.**
ngardd *gw.* **gardd.**
ngarddio *nw.* **garddio.**
ngarddwr *gw.* **garddwr.**
ngarej *gw.* **garej.**
ngât *gw.* **gât.**
ngeirfa *gw.* **geirfa.**
ngeiriadur *gw.* **geiriadur.**
ngeiriau *gw.* **gair.**
ngelyn *gw.* **gelyn.**
ngem *gw.* **gem.**
ngên *gw.* **gên.**
ngenau *gw.* **gên, genau.**
ngeneth *gw.* **geneth.**
ngeneuau *gw.* **genau.**
ngeni *gw.* **geni.**
ngêr *w.* **gêr.**
ngewyn *gw.* **gewyn.**
nghaban *gw.* **caban.**
nghacen *gw.* **cacen.**
nghacwn *gw.* **cacynen.**
nghacynen *gw.* **cacynen.**
nghadach *gw.* **cadach.**
nghadair *gw.* **cadair.**
nghadeirio *gw.* **cadeirio.**
nghadeirydd *gw.* **cadeirydd.**
nghadnawes *gw.* **cadno.**
nghadno *gw.* **cadno.**
nghadw *gw.* **cadw.**
nghadwyn *gw.* **cadwyn.**
nghadwyno *gw.* **cadwyno.**
nghae *gw.* **cae.**
nghael *gw.* **cael.**
Nghaer *gw.* **Caer.**
nghaer *gw.* **caer.**
Nghaerdydd *gw.* **Caerdydd.**
Nghaerfyrddin *gw.* **Caerfyrddin.**
Nghaergybi *gw.* **Caergybi.**
Nghaerloyw *gw.* **Caerloyw.**
Nghaersalem *gw.* **Caersalem.**
nghaets *gw.* **caets.**
nghaffe *gw.* **caffe.**
nghangen *gw.* **cangen.**
nghais *gw.* **cais.**
nghalan *gw.* **calan.**
nghaledi *gw.* **caledi.**
nghaledu *gw.* **caledu.**
nghaledwch *gw.* **caledwch.**
nghalendr *gw.* **calendr.**
nghalennig *gw.* **calennig.**
nghalon *gw.* **calon.**
ngham *gw.* **cam.**
nghamarwain *gw.* **camarwain.**
nghamddeall *gw.* **camddeall.**
nghamera *gw.* **camera.**
nghamp *gw.* **camp.**
nghampfa *gw.* **campfa.**
nghampwaith *gw.* **campwaith.**
nghamsyniad *gw.* **camsyniad.**
nghan *gw.* **can.**
nghân *gw.* **cân.**
nghaneuon *gw.* **cân.**
nghanfed *gw.* **canfed.**
nghanhwyllau *gw.* **cannwyll.**
nghanhwyllbren *gw.* **canhwyllbren.**
nghaniad *gw.* **caniad.**
nghaniadaeth *gw.* **caniadaeth.**
nghaniadau *gw.* **cân; caniad.**
nghaniatâd *gw.* **caniatâd.**
nghaniatáu *gw.* **caniatáu.**
nghaniedydd *gw.* **caniedydd.**
nghanmlwydd *gw.* **canmlwydd.**
nghanmol *gw.* **canmol.**
nghanmoliaeth *gw.* **canmoliaeth.**
nghannoedd *gw.* **cant.**
nghannwyll *gw.* **cannwyll.**
nghanol *gw.* **canol.**
nghanolbarth *gw.* **canolbarth.**
nghanoldir *gw.* **canoldir.**
nghanolfan *gw.* **canolfan.**
nghanolwr *gw.* **canolwr.**
nghanradd *gw.* **canradd.**
nghanran *gw.* **canran.**
nghanrif *gw.* **canrif.**
nghanrifau: nghanrifoedd *gw.* **canrif.**
nghant *gw.* **cant.**
nghantor *gw.* **cantor.**
nghantores *gw.* **cantores.**
nghanu *gw.* **canu.**
nghanŵ *gw.* **canŵ.**

nghanŵio *gw.* **canŵio.**
nghanwr *gw.* **canwr.**
nghap *gw.* **cap.**
nghapel *gw.* **capel.**
nghapten *gw.* **capten.**
nghar *gw.* **car.**
ngharafán *gw.* **carafán.**
ngharafana *gw.* **carafana.**
ngharco *gw.* **carco.**
ngharchar *gw.* **carchar.**
ngharcharor *gw.* **carcharor.**
ngharacharu *gw.* **carcharu.**
nghardiau *gw.* **cerdyn.**
ngharedigrwydd *gw.* **caredigrwydd.**
nghariad *gw.* **cariad.**
nghariadon *gw.* **cariad.**
nghariadus *gw.* **cariadus.**
nghario *gw.* **cario.**
ngharol *gw.* **carol.**
ngharped *gw.* **carped.**
ngharreg *gw.* **carreg.**
nghartref *gw.* **cartref.**
nghartrefi *gw.* **cartref.**
nghartrefu *gw.* **cartrefu.**
nghartrefydd *gw.* **cartref.**
ngharu *gw.* **caru.**
nghas *gw.* **cas.**
nghasáu *gw.* **casáu.**
nghasgen *gw.* **casgen.**
nghasgliad *gw.* **casgliad.**
nghasglu *gw.* **casglu.**
Nghas-gwent *gw.* **Cas-gwent.**
Nghasllwchwr *gw.* **Casllwchwr.**
Nghasnewydd *gw.* **Casnewydd.**
nghastell *gw.* **castell.**
Nghastell-nedd *gw.* **Castell-nedd.**
nghath *gw.* **cath.**
nghau *gw.* **cau.**
nghawl *gw.* **cawl.**
nghawod *gw.* **cawod.**
nghawr *gw.* **cawr.**
nghaws *gw.* **caws.**
nghefn *gw.* **cefn.**
nghefnder *gw.* **cefnder.**
nghefndir *gw.* **cefndir.**
nghefndiroedd *gw.* **cefndir.**
nghefndyr *gw.* **cefnder.**
nghefnu *gw.* **cefnu.**
nghefnwr *gw.* **cefnwr.**
nghefnwyr *gw.* **cefnwr.**
ngheffyl *gw.* **ceffyl.**
ngheg *gw.* **ceg.**
nghegin *gw.* **cegin.**
nghei *gw.* **cei.**
ngheidwad *gw.* **ceidwad.**
ngheiliog *gw.* **ceiliog.**
Ngheinewydd *gw.* **Ceinewydd.**
ngheiniog *gw.* **ceiniog.**
ngheisio *gw.* **ceisio.**
nghelf *gw.* **celf.**
nghelfi *gw.* **celficyn.**
nghelficyn *gw.* **celficyn.**
nghelwydd *gw.* **celwydd.**
nghelyn *gw.* **celynnen.**
nghelynnen *gw.* **celynnen.**
nghell *gw.* **cell.**
nghellau: nghelloedd *gw.* **cell.**
nghemeg *gw.* **cemeg.**
nghenedl *gw.* **cenedl.**
nghenedlaetholdeb *gw.* **cenedlaetholdeb.**
nghenedlaetholwr *gw.* **cenedlaetholwr.**
nghenhadaeth *gw.* **cenhadaeth.**
nghenhadon *gw.* **cenhadwr.**
nghenhadu *gw.* **cenhadu.**
nghenhadwr *gw.* **cenhadwr.**
nghenhedlaeth *gw.* **cenhedlaeth.**
nghenhinen *gw.* **cenhinen.**
nghennin *gw.* **cennin.**
ngherdyn *gw.* **cerdyn.**
ngherdd *gw.* **cerdd.**
ngherddor *gw.* **cerddor.**
ngherddorfa *gw.* **cerddorfa.**
ngherddoriaeth *gw.* **cerddoriaeth.**
ngherddwr *gw.* **cerddwr.**
ngherflun *gw.* **cerflun.**
ngherrig *gw.* **carreg.**
nghesair *gw.* **cesair.**
nghestyll *gw.* **castell.**
nghewri *gw.* **cawr.**
nghewyn *gw.* **cewyn.**
ngheyrydd *gw.* **caer.**
nghi *gw.* **ci.**
nghig *gw.* **cig.**
nghigydd *gw.* **cigydd.**
nghinio *gw.* **cinio.**
nghipolwg *gw.* **cipolwg.**
nghist *gw.* **cist.**
nghlaf *gw.* **claf.**
nghlai *gw.* **clai.**
nghlasur *gw.* **clasur.**
nghlawdd *gw.* **clawdd.**
nghlawr *gw.* **clawr.**
nghlebran *gw.* **clebran.**
nghledr *gw.* **cledr.**
nghlefyd *gw.* **clefyd.**
nghleifion *gw.* **claf.**
nghlêr *gw.* **cleren.**
nghlerc *gw.* **clerc.**
nghleren *gw.* **cleren.**
nghlirio *gw.* **clirio.**
nghlo *gw.* **clo.**
nghloc *gw.* **cloc.**
nghloch *gw.* **cloch.**
nghlod *gw.* **clod.**
nghlodfori *gw.* **clodfori.**
nghloddiau *gw.* **clawdd.**

nghloffi *gw.* **cloffi.**
nghlogwyn *gw.* **clogwyn.**
nghlogyn *gw.* **clogyn.**
nghloi *gw.* **cloi.**
nghlorian *gw.* **clorian.**
nghloriau *gw.* **clawr.**
nghlown *gw.* **clown.**
nghlun *gw.* **clun.**
nghlust *gw.* **clust.**
nghlustog *gw.* **clustog.**
nghlwm *gw.* **clwm.**
nghlwtyn *gw.* **clwtyn.**
Nghlwyd *gw.* **Clwyd.**
nghlwyd *gw.* **clwyd.**
nghlwydau: nghlwydi *gw.* **clwyd.**
nghlwyf *gw.* **clwyf.**
nghlychau *gw.* **cloch.**
nghlymau *gw.* **clwm.**
nghlymu *gw.* **clymu.**
nghlytiau *gw.* **clwtyn.**
nghlyw *gw.* **clyw.**
nghlywed *gw.* **clywed.**
nghnau *gw.* **cneuen.**
nghneuen *gw.* **cneuen.**
nghnoc *gw.* **cnoc.**
nghnocio *gw.* **cnocio.**
nghnoi *gw.* **cnoi.**
nghoban *gw.* **coban.**
nghoch *gw.* **coch.**
nghodi *gw.* **codi.**
nghoed *gw.* **coeden.**
Nghoed-duon *gw.* **Coed-duon.**
nghoeden *gw.* **coeden.**
nghoedwig *gw.* **coedwig.**
nghoes *gw.* **coes.**
nghof *gw.* **cof.**
nghofion *gw.* **cof.**
nghofleidio *gw.* **cofleidio.**
nghofrestr *gw.* **cofrestr.**
nghofrestru *gw.* **cofrestru.**
nghoffi *gw.* **coffi.**
nghog *gw.* **cog**
nghoginio *gw.* **coginio.**
nghogydd *gw.* **cogydd.**
ngholeg *gw.* **coleg.**
ngholer *gw.* **coler.**
ngholofn *gw.* **colofn.**
ngholuro *gw.* **coluro.**
ngholled *gw.* **colled.**
ngholfen *gw.* **collen.**
ngholli *gw.* **colli.**
nghopïo *gw.* **copïo.**
nghopyn *gw.* **copyn.**
nghôr *gw.* **côr.**
nghorau *gw.* **côr.**
nghordyn *gw.* **cordyn.**
nghorff *gw.* **corff.**
nghorgi *gw.* **corgi.**
nghorn *gw.* **corn.**
nghornel *gw.* **cornel.**
nghoron *gw.* **coron.**
nghoroni *gw.* **coroni.**
nghorryn *gw.* **corryn.**
nghosb *gw.* **cosb.**
nghosbi *gw.* **cosbi.**
nghot *gw.* **cot.**
nghôt *gw.* **cot.**
nghotwm *gw.* **cotwm.**
nghrac *gw.* **crac.**
nghrachach *gw.* **crachach.**
nghrafu *gw.* **crafu.**
nghragen *gw.* **cragen.**
nghraig *gw.* **craig.**
nghrasu *gw.* **crasu.**
nghredu *gw.* **credu.**
nghrefydd *gw.* **crefydd.**
nghrefft *gw.* **crefft.**
nghrefftwr *gw.* **crefftwr.**
nghregyn *gw.* **cragen.**
nghreigiau *gw.* **craig.**
nghreision *gw.* **creision.**
nghrempog *gw.* **crempog.**
nghreulondeb *gw.* **creulondeb.**
nghri *gw.* **cri.**
nghrib *gw.* **crib.**
nghribo *gw.* **cribo.**
nghriced *gw.* **criced.**
nghricedwr *gw.* **cricedwr.**
nghricsyn *gw.* **cricsyn.**
nghrio *gw.*.**crio.**
Nghristion *gw.* **Cristion.**
Nghristnogion *gw.* **Cristion.**
nghriw *gw.* **criw.**
nghroen *gw.* **croen.**
nghroes *gw.* **croes.**
nghroesair *gw.* **croesair.**
nghroesau *gw.* **croes.**
nghroesawu *gw.* **croesawu.**
nghroesfan *gw.* **croesfan.**
nghroesffordd *gw.* **croesffordd.**
nghroesholi *gw.* **croesholi.**
nghroesi *gw.* **croesi.**
nghroeso *gw.* **croeso.**
nghronfa *gw.* **cronfa.**
nghronfeydd *gw.* **cronfa.**
nghrud *gw.* **crud.**
nghrwst *gw.* **crwst.**
nghrwyn *gw.* **croen.**
nghryd *gw.* **cryd.**
nghrynodeb *gw.* **crynodeb.**
nghrynu *gw.* **crynu.**
nghrys *gw.* **crys.**
nghrystiau *gw.* **crwst, crystyn**
nghrystyn *gw.* **crystyn.**
nghuddio *gw.* **cuddio.**
nghuro *gw.* **curo.**
nghusan *gw.* **cusan.**
nghusanu *gw.* **cusanu.**

nghwb *gw.* **cwb.**
nghwbl *gw.* **cwbl.**
nghwcw *gw.* **cwcw.**
nghwch *gw.* **cwch.**
nghwd *gw.* **cwd.**
nghwdyn *gw.* **cwdyn.**
nghweryl *gw.* **cweryl.**
nghwestiwn *gw.* **cwestiwn.**
nghwestiyna *gw.* **cwestiyna.**
nghwestiynau *gw.* **cwestiwn.**
nghwlwm *gw.* **cwlwm.**
nghwm *gw.* **cwm.**
nghwmni *gw.* **cwmni.**
nghwmnïau: nghwmnïoedd *gw.* **cwmni.**
nghwmwl *gw.* **cwmwl.**
nghŵn *gw.* **ci.**
nghwningen *gw.* **cwningen.**
nghwningod *gw.* **cwningen.**
nghwpan *gw.* **cwpan.**
nghwpla *gw.* **cwpla.**
nghwpwrdd *gw.* **cwpwrdd.**
nghwr *gw.* **cwr.**
nghwrdd *gw.* **cwrdd.**
nghwrs *gw.* **cwrs.**
nghwrw *gw.* **cwrw.**
nghwsg *gw.* **cwsg.**
nghwsmer *gw.* **cwsmer.**
nghwstwm *gw.* **cwstwm.**
nghwt *gw.* **cwt.**
nghwymp *gw.* **cwymp.**
nghwyn *gw.* **cwyn.**
nghwyno *gw.* **cwyno.**
nghwyr *gw.* **cwyr.**
nghychod *gw.* **cwch.**
nghychwyn *gw.* **cychwyn.**
nghydadrodd *gw.* **cydadrodd.**
nghydau *gw.* **cwd, cwdyn.**
nghydnabod *gw.* **cydnabod.**
nghyfaill *gw.* **cyfaill.**
nghyfan *gw.* **cyfan.**
nghyfansoddi *gw.* **cyfansoddi.**
nghyfansoddwr *gw.* **cyfansoddwr.**
nghyfanswm *gw.* **cyfanswm.**
nghyfarch *gw.* **cyfarch.**
nghyfarfod *gw.* **cyfarfod.**
nghyfarfodydd *gw.* **cyfarfod.**
nghyfarwyddiadur *gw.* **cyfarwyddiadur.**
nghyfarwyddo *gw.* **cyfarwyddo.**
nghyfarwyddwr *gw.* **cafarwyddwr.**
nghyfeilles *gw.* **cyfeilles.**
nghyfeillgarwch *gw.* **cyfeillgarwch.**
nghyfeillion *gw.* **cyfaill.**
nghyfeiriad *gw.* **cyfeiriad.**
nghyfeirio *gw.* **cyfeirio.**
nghyfenw *gw.* **cyfenw.**
nghyfiawnder *gw.* **cyfiawnder.**
nghyfieithiad *gw.* **cyfieithiad.**
nghyfieithu *gw.* **cyfieithu.**
nghyfieithydd *gw.* **cyfieithydd.**
nghyfle *gw.* **cyfle.**
nghyflog *gw.* **cyflog.**
nghyflogi *gw.* **cyflogi.**
nghyflogwr *gw.* **cyflogwr.**
nghyflwr *gw.* **cyflwr.**
nghyflwyno *gw.* **cyflwyno.**
nghyflymder *gw.* **cyflymder.**
nghyflymu *gw.* **cyflymu.**
nghyflymydd *gw.* **cyflymydd.**
nghyfnither *gw.* **cyfnither.**
nghyfoeth *gw.* **cyfoeth.**
nghyfraith *gw.* **cyfraith.**
nghyfreithiwr *gw.* **cyfreithiwr.**
nghyfres *gw.* **cyfres.**
nghyfrif *gw.* **cyfrif.**
nghyfrifiadur *gw.* **cyfrifiadur.**
nghyfrifiannell *gw.* **cyfrifiannell.**
nghyfrifoldeb *gw.* **cyfrifoldeb.**
nghyfrifydd *gw.* **cyfrifydd.**
nghyfrinach *gw.* **cyfrinach.**
nghyfrol *gw.* **cyfrol.**
nghyfrwng *gw.* **cyfrwng.**
nghyfweliad *gw.* **cyfweliad.**
nghyfyngu *gw.* **cyfyngu.**
nghyffur *gw.* **cyffur.**
nghyffwrdd *gw.* **cyffwrdd.**
nghyngerdd *gw.* **cyngerdd.**
nghyngori *gw.* **cynghori.**
nghynghorwr *gw.* **cynghorwr.**
nghynghrair*gw.* **cynghrair.**
nghyngor *gw.* **cyngor.**
nghyhoeddi *gw.* **cyhoeddi.**
nghyhoeddiad *gw.* **cyhoeddiad.**
nghyhoeddusrwydd *gw.* **cyhoeddusrwydd.**
nghyhoeddwr *gw.* **cyhoeddwr.**
nghylch *gw.* **cylch.**
nghylchfan *gw.* **cylchfan.**
nghylchgrawn *gw.* **cylchgrawn.**
nghylchgronau *gw.* **cylchgrawn.**
nghylchlythyr *gw.* **cylchlythyr.**
nghyll *gw.* **collen.**
nghyllell *gw.* **cyllell.**
nghyllyll *gw.* **cyllell.**
nghymal *gw.* **cymal.**
nghymanfa *gw.* **cymanfa.**
nghymdeithas *gw.* **cymdeithas.**
nghymdogion *gw.* **cymydog.**
nghymeriad *gw.* **cymeriad.**
nghymharu *gw.* **cymharu.**
nghymhlethdod *gw.* **cymhlethdod.**
nghymoedd *gw.* **cwm.**
nghymorth *gw.* **cymorth.**
Nghymraeg *gw.* **Cymraeg.**
Nghymraes *gw.* **Cymraes.**
Nghymreictod *gw.* **Cymreictod.**
Nghymreiges *gw.* **Cymreiges.**

Nghymro *gw.* **Cymro.**
Nghymru *gw.* **Cymru.**
Nghymry *gw.* **Cymro.**
nghymryd *gw.* **cymryd.**
nghymwynas *gw.* **cymwynas.**
nghymydog *gw.* **cymydog.**
nghymylau *gw.* **cwmwl.**
nghymysgu *gw.* **cymysgu.**
nghymysgwch *gw.* **cymysgwch.**
nghyn- *gw.* **cyn-.**
nghynaeafau *gw.* **cynhaeaf.**
nghynffon *gw.* **cynffon.**
nghynhadledd *gw.* **cynhadledd.**
nghynhaeaf *gw.* **cynhaeaf.**
nghynhesu *gw.* **cynhesu.**
nghynilion *gw.* **cynilion.**
nghynllun *gw.* **cynllun.**
nghynllunio *gw.* **cynllunio.**
nghynlluniwr *gw.* **cynlluniwr.**
nghynnal *gw.* **cynnal.**
nghynnig *gw.* **cynnig.**
nghynnwys *gw.* **cynnwys.**
nghynorthwywr *gw.* **cynorthwywr.**
nghynorthwy-ydd *gw.* **cynorthwy-ydd.**
nghyntaf *gw.* **cyntaf.**
nghyntedd *gw.* **cyntedd.**
nghynulleidfa *gw.* **cynulleidfa.**
nghypyrddau *gw.* **cwpwrdd.**
nghyrddau *gw.* **cwrdd.**
nghyrff *gw.* **corff.**
nghyrn *gw.* **corn.**
nghyrraedd *gw.* **cyrraedd.**
nghyrsau: nghyrsiau *gw.* **cwrs.**
nghysgod *gw.* **cysgod.**
nghysgodi *gw.* **cysgodi.**
nghysgodion *gw.* **cysgod.**
nghysgu *gw.* **cysgu.**
nghystadlaethau *gw.* **cystadleuaeth.**
nghystadleuaeth *gw.* **cystadleuaeth.**
nghystadleuwr *gw.* **cystadleuwr.**
nghystadlu *gw.* **cystadlu.**
nghystymau *gw.* **cwstwm.**
nghysur *gw.* **cysur.**
nghysuro *gw.* **cysuro.**
nghyswllt *gw.* **cyswllt.**
nghytgan *gw.* **cytgan.**
nghytsain *gw.* **cytsain.**
nghytundeb *gw.* **cytundeb.**
nghytuno *gw.* **cytuno.**
nghyw *gw.* **cyw.**
nghywaith *gw.* **cywaith.**
nghywiriad *gw.* **cywiriad.**
nghywiro *gw.* **cywiro.**
nglan *gw.* **glan.**
nglân *gw.* **glân.**
nglanhau *gw.* **glanhau.**
nglanio *gw.* **glanio.**
nglannau *gw.* **glan.**
nglas *gw.* **glas.**
nglaswelltyn *gw.* **glaswelltyn.**
nglaw *gw.* **glaw.**
nglendid *gw.* **glendid.**
nglin *gw.* **glin.**
nglo *gw.* **glo.**
nglofa *gw.* **glofa.**
nglöwr *gw.* **glöwr.**
nglöyn byw *gw.* **glöyn byw.**
nglud *gw.* **glud.**
ngludio *gw.* **gludio.**
ngludo *gw.* **gludio.**
nglyn *gw.* **glyn.**
nglynu *gw.* **glynu.**
ngobaith *gw.* **gobaith.**
ngobeithion *gw.* **gobaith.**
ngobennydd *gw.* **gobennydd.**
ngodre *gw.* **godre.**
ngodro *gw.* **godro.**
ngoddef *gw.* **goddef.**
ngoddrych *gw.* **goddrych.**
ngof *gw.* **gof.**
ngofaint *gw.* **gof.**
ngofal *gw.* **gofal.**
ngofalwr *gw.* **gofalwr.**
ngofid *gw.* **gofid.**
ngofidio *gw.* **gofidio.**
ngofod *gw.* **gofod.**
ngofodwr *gw.* **gofodwr.**
ngofynion *gw.* **gofyn**
ngogledd *gw.* **gogledd.**
ngogogiant *gw.* **gogoniant.**
ngôl *gw.* **gôl.**
ngolau *gw.* **golau.**
ngolchi *gw.* **golchi.**
ngolchydd *gw.* **golchydd.**
ngoleudy *gw.* **goleudy.**
ngoleuni *gw.* **goleuni.**
ngoleuo *gw.* **goleuo.**
ngolud *gw.* **golud.**
ngolwg *gw.* **golwg.**
ngolygfa *gw.* **golygfa.**
ngolygfeydd *gw.* **golygfa.**
ngolygon *gw.* **golwg.**
ngollwng *gw.* **gollwng.**
ngorau *gw.* **gorau.**
ngorchfygu *gw.* **gorchfygu.**
ngorchymyn *gw.* **gorchymyn.**
ngorfodaeth *gw.* **gorfodaeth.**
ngorfodi *gw.* **gorfodi.**
Ngorffennaf *gw.* **Gorffennaf.**
ngorffennol *gw.* **gorffennol.**
ngorffwys *gw.* **gorffwys.**
ngorffwyso *gw.* **gorffwyso.**
ngorllewin *gw.* **gorllewin.**
ngornest *gw.* **gornest.**
ngorsaf *gw.* **gorsaf.**
ngorsedd *gw.* **gorsedd.**
ngorwel *gw.* **gorwel.**

ngosod *gw.* **gosod.**
ngostwng *gw.* **gostwng.**
ngostyngiad *gw.* **gostyngiad.**
ngradd *gw.* **gradd.**
ngraddfa *gw.* **graddfa.**
ngramadeg *gw.* **gramadeg.**
ngrant *gw.* **grant.**
ngras *gw.* **gras.**
ngris *gw.* **gris.**
Ngroeg *gw.* **Groeg.**
ngrudd *gw.* **grudd.**
ngrug *gw.* **grug.**
ngrŵp *gw.* **grŵp.**
ngrym *gw.* **grym.**
ngwadu *gw.* **gwadu.**
ngwaed *gw.* **gwaed.**
ngwaedu *gw.* **gwaedu.**
ngwaedd *gw.* **gwaedd.**
ngwaelod *gw.* **gwaelod.**
ngwaelodion *gw.* **gwaelod.**
ngwaethaf *gw.* **gwaethaf.**
ngwagedd *gw.* **gwagedd.**
ngwagle *gw.* **gwagle.**
ngwahanol *gw.* **gwahanol.**
ngwahodd *gw.* **gwahodd.**
ngwahoddedigion *gw.* **gwahoddedig.**
ngwahoddiad *gw.* **gwahoddiad.**
ngwair *gw.* **gwair.**
ngwaith *gw.* **gwaith.**
ngwal *gw.* **gwal.**
ngwâl *gw.* **gwâl.**
ngwalau *gw.* **gwâl.**
ngwaliau *gw.* **gwal.**
ngwall *gw.* **gwall.**
ngwallt *gw.* **gwallt.**
ngwanwyn *gw.* **gwanwyn.**
ngwar *gw.* **gwar.**
ngwarchod *gw.* **gwarchod.**
ngwaredu *gw.* **gwaredu.**
ngwaredwr *gw.* **gwaredwr.**
ngwario *gw.* **gwario.**
ngwartheg *gw.* **gwartheg.**
ngwas *gw.* **gwas.**
ngwasanaeth *gw.* **gwasanaeth.**
ngwasanaethu *gw.* **gwasanaethu.**
ngwasg *gw.* **gwasg.**
ngwasgedd *gw.* **gwasgedd.**
ngwasgfa *gw.* **gwasgfa.**
ngwasgod *gw.* **gwasgod.**
ngwasgu *gw.* **gwasgu.**
ngwastraff *gw.* **gwastraff.**
ngwastraffu *gw.* **gwastraffu.**
ngwau *gw.* **gwau.**
ngwaun *gw.* **gwaun.**
ngwawdio *gw.* **gwawdio.**
ngwawr *gw.* **gwawr.**
ngwdihŵ *gw.* **gwdihŵ.**
ngwddf *gw.* **gwddf.**
ngwddwg *gw.* **gwddwg.**
ngweddi *gw.* **gweddi.**
ngweddill *gw.* **gweddill.**
ngweddïo *gw.* **gweddïo.**
ngwefus *gw.* **gwefus.**
ngweiddi *gw.* **gweiddi.**
ngweigion *gw.* **gwag.**
ngweiniaid *gw.* **gwan.**
ngweinidog *gw.* **gweinidog.**
ngweinion *gw.* **gwan.**
ngweinyddes *gw.* **gweinyddes.**
ngweiriau *gw.* **gwair.**
ngweisg *gw.* **gwasg.**
ngweision *gw.* **gwas.**
ngweithdy *gw.* **gweithdy.**
ngweithiau *gw.* **gwaith.**
ngweithio *gw.* **gweithio.**
ngweithiwr *gw.* **gweithiwr.**
ngweithred *gw.* **gweithred.**
ngweithwyr *gw.* **gweithiwr.**
ngwelâu *gw.* **gwely.**
ngweld *gw.* **gweld.**
ngwely *gw.* **gwely.**
ngwelyau *gw.* **gwely.**
ngwell *gw.* **da.**
ngwella *gw.* **gwella.**
ngwellt *gw.* **gwellt, gwelltyn.**
ngwelltyn *gw.* **gwelltyn.**
ngwên *gw.* **gwên.**
ngwenau *gw.* **gwên.**
ngwendid *gw.* **gwendid.**
Ngwener *gw.* **Gwener.**
ngwenith *gw.* **gwenith.**
ngwennol *gw.* **gwennol.**
Ngwent *gw.* **Gwent.**
ngwenu *gw.* **gwenu.**
ngwenwyn *gw.* **gwenwyn.**
ngwenynen *gw.* **gwenynen.**
ngwêr *gw.* **gwêr.**
ngwerin *gw.* **gwerin.**
ngweriniaeth *gw.* **gweriniaeth.**
ngwers *gw.* **gwers.**
ngwerslyfr *gw.* **gwerslyfr.**
ngwersyll *gw.* **gwersyll.**
ngwerth *gw.* **gwerth.**
ngwerthfawrogi *gw.* **gwerthfawrogi.**
ngwerthfawrogiad *gw.* **gwerthfawrogiad.**
ngwerthiant *gw.* **gwerthiant.**
ngwerthu *gw.* **gwerthu.**
ngwerthwr *gw.* **gwerthwr.**
ngwestai *gw.* **gwestai, gwesty.**
ngwesteion *gw.* **gwestai.**
ngwesteiwr *gw.* **gwesteiwr.**
ngwesteiwraig *gw.* **gwesteiwr.**
ngwesty *gw.* **gwesty.**
ngweu *gw.* **gweu.**
ngweunydd *gw.* **gwaun.**
ngwg *gw.* **gwg.**

ngwgu *gw.* **gwgu.**
ngwiail *gw.* **gwialen.**
ngwialen *gw.* **gwialen.**
ngwialennod *gw.* **gwialen.**
ngwin *gw.* **gwin.**
ngwir *gw.* **gwir.**
ngwirionedd *gw.* **gwirionedd.**
ngwisg *gw.* **gwisg.**
ngwisgo *gw.* **gwisgo.**
ngwiwer *gw.* **gwiwer.**
ngwlad *gw.* **gwlad.**
ngwladfa *gw.* **gwladfa.**
ngwladgarwyr *gw.* **gwladgarwr.**
ngwlân *gw.* **gwlân.**
ngwlanen *gw.* **gwlanen.**
ngwledydd *gw.* **gwlad.**
ngwledd *gw.* **gwledd.**
ngwledda *gw.* **gwledda.**
ngwleidydd *gw.* **gwleidydd.**
ngwleidyddiaeth *gw.* **gwleidyddiaeth.**
ngwlff *gw.* **gwlff.**
ngwlith *gw.* **gwlith.**
ngwlybaniaeth *gw.* **gwlybaniaeth.**
ngwlychu *gw.* **gwlychu.**
ngwn *gw.* **gwn.**
ngŵn *gw.* **gŵn.**
ngwneud *gw.* **gwneud.**
ngwniadyddes *gw.* **gwniadyddes.**
ngwnïo *gw.* **gwnïo.**
ngwniyddes *gw.* **gwniadyddes.**
ngwobr *gw.* **gwobr.**
ngwobrwyo *gw.* **gwobrwyo.**
ngŵr *gw.* **gŵr.**
ngwrach *gw.* **gwrach.**
ngwragedd *gw.* **gwraig.**
ngwraidd *gw.* **gwreiddyn.**
ngwraig *gw.* **gwraig.**
ngwrandawiad *gw.* **gwrandawiad.**
ngwrandawr *gw.* **gwrandawr.**
ngwrando *gw.* **gwrando.**
ngwreichion *gw.* **gwreichionen.**
ngwreiddiau *gw.* **gwreiddyn.**
ngwreiddio *gw.* **gwreiddio.**
ngwreiddyn *gw.* **gwreiddyn.**
ngwres *gw.* **gwres.**
ngwresogydd *gw.* **gwresogydd.**
ngwrtaith *gw.* **gwrtaith.**
ngwrthblaid *gw.* **gwrthblaid.**
ngwrthdystio *gw.* **gwrthdystio.**
ngwrthod *gw.* **gwrthod.**
ngwrthrych *gw.* **gwrthrych.**
ngwrthryfel *gw.* **gwrthryfel.**
ngwrthwyneb *gw.* **gwrthwyneb.**
ngwrthwynebu *gw.* **gwrthwynebu.**
ngwrthwynebwr *gw.* **gwrthwynebwr.**
ngwrthwynebydd *gw.* **gwrthwynebwr.**
ngwthiad *gw.* **gwthiad.**
ngwthio *gw.* **gwthio.**
ngwthiwr *gw.* **gwthiwr.**
ngwybod *gw.* **gwybod.**
ngwybodaeth *gw.* **gwybodaeth.**
ngwydr *gw.* **gwydr.**
ngwydrau *gw.* **gwydr, gwydryn.**
ngwydryn gw. gwydryn.
ngŵydd *gw.* **gŵydd.**
ngwyddbwyll *gw.* **gwyddbwyll.**
Ngwyddel *gw.* **Gwyddel.**
Ngwyddeleg *gw.* **Gwyddeleg.**
ngwyddoniaeth *gw.* **gwyddoniaeth.**
ngwyddonydd *gw.* **gwyddonydd.**
ngwyddor *gw.* **gwyddor.**
ngwyfyn *gw.* **gwyfyn.**
ngŵyl *gw.* **gŵyl.**
ngwylan *gw.* **gwylan.**
ngwyliau *gw.* **gŵyl.**
ngwylio *gw.* **gwylio.**
ngwyliwr *gw.* **gwyliwr.**
ngwylnos *gw.* **gwylnos.**
ngwylwyr *gw.* **gwyliwr.**
ngwyll *gw.* **gwyll.**
ngwylltio *gw.* **gwylltio.**
ngwymon *gw.* **gwymon.**
ngwyn *gw.* **gwyn.**
Ngwynedd *gw.* **Gwynedd.**
ngwynegon *gw.* **gwynegon.**
ngwynfa *gw.* **gwynfa.**
ngwynfyd *gw.* **gwynfyd.**
ngwyngalch *gw.* **gwyngalch.**
ngwynt *gw.* **gwynt.**
ngwŷr *gw.* **gŵr.**
ngwyrdd *gw.* **gwyrdd.**
ngwyriad *gw.* **gwyriad.**
ngwyro *gw.* **gwyro.**
ngwyrth *gw.* **gwyrth.**
ngwŷs *gw.* **gwŷs.**
ngwystlon *gw.* **gwystl.**
ngynnau *gw.* **gwn.**
ngyrfa *gw.* **gyrfa.**
ngyrfeydd *gw.* **gyrfa.**
ngyrru *gw.* **gyrru.**
ngyrrwr *gw.* **gyrrwr.**
ngyrwyr *gw.* **gyrrwr.**

In certain circumstances **h** is prefixed to words beginning with a vowel. If the word you require does not appear in this section ignore the initial **h** and look it up in the appropriate section, for example, ll. **hawr**, see **awr**. See Appendix Pronouns.

had *e, torf.* seed; *gw.* **hadyn, hedyn.**
hadu *be.* **(hadaf)** to sow, to propagate; to run to seed.
hadyn: hedyn *e.g. ll.* **had** a seed; *gw.* **had.**
haearn 1 *e.g. ll.* **heyrn** iron. **2** *a.* of iron, iron.
haeddu *be.* **(haeddaf)** to deserve, to merit: **haeddu ennill** to deserve to win; **haeddu clod** to deserve praise.
hael *a.* generous, liberal.
haelioni *e.g.* generosity, liberality.
haelionus *a.* generous, liberal.
haenen *e.b. ll.* **-nau** layer, strata, seam (*of rock*).
haerllug *a.* impudent.
haerllugrwydd *e.g.* impudence.
haeru *be.* **(haeraf)** to assert, to affirm.
haf *e.g. ll.* **-au** summer, summer-time.
hafaidd *a.* summer-like, summery.
hafaliad *e.g. ll.* **-au** equation: **hafaliad cydamserol** simultaneous equation; **hafaliad dwyradd** quadratic equation; **hafaliad syml** simple equation; **hafaliad unradd** linear equation.
hafan *e.b. ll.* **-au** haven, port, harbour.
hafdy *e.g. ll.* **hafdai** summer-house: **tŷ haf** holiday cottage.
hafddydd *e.g. ll.* **-iau** summer's day.
hafod *e.b. ll.* **-ydd** (*often seen in place names*) summer residence formerly occupied by the family and its stock during the summer months only; *gw.* **hendref.**
hafoty *e.g. ll.* **hafotai** chalet, holiday cottage.
Hafren *e.b.* Severn.
Afon Hafren River Severn, the Severn. **Pont Hafren** Severn Bridge.
hagr *a.* ugly, unsightly (*N.W.*).
hagrwch *e.g.* ugliness.
haid *e.b. ll.* **heidiau** swarm, flock, drove; **haid o wenyn** swarm of bees.
haidd *e. torf.* barley; *gw.* **heidden.**
haig *e.b. ll.* **heigiau** shoal: **haig o bysgod** shoal of fish.
haint *e.b. ll.* **heintiau** disease, infection, plague; faint, fit: **Fe ges i haint pan welais i'r ysbryd** I had a fit when I saw the ghost.
hala *be.* **(halaf)** to spend; to send; to drive; to spread (*S.W.*).
halen *e.g. ll.* **-au** salt, brine: **halen y ddaear** salt of the earth.
hallt *a.* salty, briny; harsh, severe: **talu'n hallt** to pay dearly.
halltu *be.* **(halltaf)** to salt, to cure.
hamdden *e.g.b.* leisure, respite: **canolfan hamdden** leisure centre; **oriau hamdden** leisure hours, spare time.
hamddena *be.* **(hamddenaf)** to concern oneself with leisure pursuits.
hamddenol *a.* leisurely.
hances *e.b. ll.* **-i** handkerchief.
hanerau *gw.* **hanner.**
haneri *gw.* **hanner.**
hanerwr *e.g. ll.* **hanerwyr** half-back (games).
hanes *e.g. ll.* **-ion** history; story of the past, tale, record, report: **Glywaist ti'r hanes am Wil?** Did you hear the tale about Wil?.
haneswyr *gw.* **hanesydd.**
hanesydd: haneswr *e.g. ll.* **hanesyddion: haneswyr** historian.
hanesyn *e.g. ll.* **-nau** anecdote.
hanfodol *a.* essential; integral.
haniaethol *a.* abstract.
hanner *e.g. ll.* **hanerau, haneri** half: **hanner-awr** half an hour; **hanner-call** foolish, half-witted; **hanner-cylch** semicircle; **hanner-dydd** midday, noon; **hanner-munud!** half a minute! half a moment! **hanner**

nos midnight; **hanner-pan** half-soaked; half-wit; **hanner-pris** half-price.
hap *e.b. ll.* **-au, -iau** chance, luck, fortune: **chwarae hap** to gamble.
ar hap a damwain by chance, by luck.
hapus *a.* happy, cheerful.
hapusrwydd *e.g.* happiness, bliss, blessedness.
harbwr *e.g. ll.* **-s** harbour, port.
hardd *a. ll.* **heirdd** beautiful, comely, handsome, fine, splendid (*of person or object*).
harddwch *e.g.* beauty, fairness, comeliness.
hau: heu *be.* **(heuaf)** to sow, to scatter; to disseminate.
haul *e.g. ll.* **heuliau** sun.
hawdd *a.* easy; **Mae'n hawdd gweld** It is easy to see **Mae'n hawdd nofio** It is easy to swim **Mae'n hawdd siopa** It is easy to shop; *gw. At. Ansoddeiriau.*
hawl *e.b.g. ll.* **-au, -iau** legal claim, right, demand; question: **hawliau dyn** the rights of man, human rights; **hawliau sifil** civil rights.
hawlfraint *e.b. ll.* **hawlfreintiau** privilege; copyright.
hawlio *be.* **(hawliaf)** to claim, to demand.
haws *gw.* **hawdd.**
hawsaf *gw.* **hawdd.**
hawsed *gw.* **hawdd.**
heb *ardd.* (*followed by soft mutation*) **hebddo, hebddot, hebddo/hebddi, hebddon, hebddoch, hebddyn)** without, minus, free from, besides; *gw. At. Arddodiaid.*
heblaw *ardd.* besides, without.
hebog *e.g. ll.* **-au, -iaid. -ion** hawk, falcon: **gwylio fel hebog** to watch like a hawk, to watch intensely.
Hebraeg *e.b.* Hebrew language.
Hebreig *a.* Hebrew.
Hebrëwr *e.g. ll.* **Hebrëwyr** Hebrew; **Hebrëes** female Hebrew.
hebrwng *be.* **(hebryngaf)** to lead, to accompany, to escort: **cynhebrwng** funeral, funeral procession; **tŷ hebrwng** funeral home, 'chapel of rest'.
hecsagon *e.g. ll.* **-au** hexagon.
hedeg *be.* **(hedaf)** to fly; *gw.* **ehedaf.**
hedfan *be.* **(hedfanaf)** to fly.
hedydd *e.g. ll.* **-ion** lark; *gw.* **ehedydd.**
hedyn *gw.* **hadyn.**
hedd *e.g.b. ll.* **-au** peace, tranquillity, serenity, calm.
heddiw *ad.* today.
heddlu *e.g. ll.* **-oedd** police force.
heddwas *e.g. ll.* **heddweision** policeman.
heddwch *e.g.* peace, tranquillity, stillness.
heddweision *gw.* **heddwas.**
hefo *gw.* **efo** (*N.W.*).
hefyd *c. & ad.* also, too, in addition; likewise.
heibio *ad.* past; aside, beside, by: **heibio i'r tŷ** past the house.
heidiau *gw.* **haid.**
heidden *e.b. ll.* **haidd** grain of barley.
heigiau *gw.* **haig.**
heini *a.* active, lively, agile, nimble: **dosbarth cadw'n heini** keep fit class.
heintiau *gw.* **haint.**
heintus *a.* diseased, infectious, contagious.
heirdd *gw.* **hardd.**
hel: hela *be.* **(heliaf: helaf)** to drive; to chase, to pursue; to send; to hunt; to gather, to collect; to fetch; **hel achau** to genealogise (*N.W.*) **hel straeon** to gossip (*N.W.*).
helaeth *a.* ample, large, broad; plentiful.
helfa *e.b. ll.* **helfâu, helfeydd** a hunting, hunt, chase, catch: **helfa drysor** treasure hunt; **helfa dda** a good catch.
helgi *e.g. ll.* **helgwn** hound.
heliwr *e.g. ll.* **helwyr** huntsman, gatherer.
help *e.g.b. ll.* **-iau, -oedd** help, aid; assistance; support: **help llaw** helping hand.
helpu (i) *be.* **(helpaf)** to help, to assist.
helygen *e.b. ll.* **helyg** willow.
helynt *e.g. ll.* **-ion** course or way (*of life, etc.*); fuss, bother; business; **Beth yw ei hynt a'i helynt?** What has become of him?
hem *e.b. ll.* **-iau** hem, border, seam.
hen *a.* old, aged; ancient *(Precedes the noun and causes soft mutation.)*: **hen bryd** high time; **hen ddigon** quite enough; **henffasiwn** old-fashioned; **hen gariad** former sweetheart, 'old flame'; **hen gownt** outstanding account, debit; grudge; **hen lanc** (old) bachelor; **wedi hen farw** long since dead; **yr Hen Wlad** the Old Country, term of

endearment for Wales; *gw. At Ansoddeiriau.*
henach *gw.* **hen.**
henaf *gw.* **hen.**
henaidd *a.* oldish, old-fashioned.
henaint *e.g.* old age; senility.
hendaid *e.g. ll.* **hendeidiau** great-grandfather; forefather, ancestor.
hendeidiau *gw.* **hendaid.**
hendref *e.b. ll.* **hendrefi, hendrefydd** winter dwelling located in the valley, to which the family and its stock returned after the summer months in the **hafod** on the mountain; *gw.* **hafod.**
hendrefi *gw.* **hendref.**
hendrefydd *gw.* **hendref.**
henebion *e.ll* ancient monuments.
hened *gw.* **hen.**
heneiddio *be.* **(heneiddiaf)** to grow old, to become old.
heneiniau *gw.* **hennain.**
henffasiwn *gw.* **hen.**
hennain *e.b. ll.* **heneiniau** great-grandmother (*N.W.*).
heno *ad.* tonight, (on) this night.
henoed *e.g. & e.torf. & a.* old age, great age; old person; old people, old, elderly: **cartref henoed** old people's home.
henwr *e.g. ll.* **henwyr** old man.
heol: hewl *e.b. ll.* **-ydd** street, road, way; **heol ddeuol** dual carriageway; **heol fawr** highway; **heol gefn** back-road, by-way.
heolydd *gw.* **heol.**
her *e.b. ll.* **-iau** challenge, defiance, a provoking.
hercyd *be.* **(hercaf)** to fetch, to reach (*S.W.*).
herio *be.* **(heriaf)** to challenge, to defy, to dare.
herwfilwr *e.g. ll.* **herwfilwyr** guerilla.
herwgipiad *e.g. ll.* **-au** hijack.
herwgipio *be.* **(herwgipiaf)** to hijack.
herwgipiwr *e.g. ll.* **herwgipwyr** hijacker.
herwgydiad *e.g. ll.* **-au** kidnap.
herwgydio *be.* **(herwgydiaf)** to kidnap.
herwgydiwr *e.g. ll.* **herwgydwyr** kidnapper.
herwydd *ardd.* according to, by: **o'r herwydd** on account of that.
het *e.b. ll.* **-au, -iau** hat.
heu *gw.* **hau.**
heuad *e.g.* a sowing.
heulog *a.* sunny.
heuliau *gw.* **haul.**
heulwen *e.b.* sunshine; a girl's name. **Heulwen ydy enw'r ferch** The girl's name is Heulwen.
heuwr *e.g. ll.* **heuwyr** sower.
hewl *gw.* **heol.**
hewlydd *gw.* **heol.**
heyrn *gw.* **haearn.**
hi *rhag.* she, her, it.
hidio (am) *be.* **(hidiaf)** to heed, to care, to mind (*S.W.*).
hil *e.b. ll.* **-ion, -iau** race, lineage; offspring, descendants.
hiliol *a.* racial.
hin *e.b. ll.* **-oedd** weather.
hindda *e.b.* fine weather. **hindda a drycin** fair weather and foul.
hinsawdd *e.b. ll.* **hinsoddau** climate.
hir *a. ll.* **-ion** long, lengthy; *gw. At. Ansoddeiriau.*
hirach *gw.* **hir.**
hiraeth *e.g. ll.* **-au** longing, nostalgia, homesickness, grief.
hiraethu (am) *be.* **(hiraethaf)** to long (for), to yearn (for), to sorrow, to grieve.
hiraf *gw.* **hir.**
hirbell *a.* distant, remote; **o hirbell** from afar; **dysgu o hirbell** distance learning.
hired *gw.* **hir.**
hirgylch *e.g. ll.* **-au, -oedd** ellipse.
hirion *gw.* **hir.**
hirlwm *e.g.* lean period at the end of winter.
hirnod *e.g. ll.* **-au** circumflex accent (ˆ).
hithau *rhag.* she, she too.
hiwmor *e.g.* humour.
hoe *e.g. ll.* **-au** pause, break, respite: **Sioni hoe** a layabout (*S.W.*).
hoel: hoelen *e.g.b. ll.* **hoelion, hoelon** nail: **taro'r hoelen ar ei phen** to comment appropriately with a fitting remark; to hit the nail on the head.
hoelio *be.* **(hoeliaf)** to nail.
hofrennydd *e.g. ll.* **hofrenyddion** helicopter.
hoff *a.* (*precedes the noun and causes soft mutation*) dear, beloved, favourite: **fy hoff le bwyta** my favourite eating place.
hoffi *be.* **(hoffaf)** to like, to be pleased (with).
hoffter *e.g. ll.* **-au** liking, fondness.
hogen *e.b. ll.* **-nod** girl, lass (*N.W.*).
hogi *be.* **(hogaf)** to sharpen, to whet:

carreg hogi whetstone.
hogiau *gw.* **hogyn.**
hogyn *e.g. ll.* **hogiau, hogynnau** boy, lad *(N.W.).*
hongian *be.* **(hongiaf)** to hang, to suspend.
hôl *be.* **(holaf)** to fetch (*S.W.*); *gw.* **holi, nôl.**
holi *be.* **(holaf)** to question, to inquire, to ask (about); **holi am** to ask about, to ask after.
holiadur *e.g. ll.* **-on** questionnaire.
holwr *e.g. ll.* **holwyr** questioner, examiner, interrogator.
holwyddoreg *e.b. ll.* **-au** catechism.
holl *a.* (*precedes the noun and causes soft mutation*) all, whole: **yr holl bobl** all the people; **yr holl fyd** the whole world.
hollalluog *a.* almighty.
hollfyd *e.g.* universe.
holliach *a.* whole, sound (of health).
hollol *a. & ad.* (*precedes the adjective and causes soft mutation*) whole, entire, complete; **yn hollol dawel** completely quiet; **yn hollol gywir** wholly correct.
hon *a.b. & rhag.* this (one), she (her), it.
honedig *a.* alleged, reputed.
honiad *e.g. ll.* **-au** assertion, claim.
honni *be.* **(honnaf)** to allege, to assert, to profess, to pretend, to claim.
honno, honna *a.b. & rhag.* that (one), she (her), it; *gw.* **hwnnw.**
hosan *e.b. ll.* **-au** stocking, sock.
hoyw *a.* lively, sprightly; gay, homosexual.
hud *e.g. ll.* **-ion** magic, charm, spell.
hudo *be.* **(hudaf)** to charm, to allure.
hudol *a.* enchanting.
huddygl *e.g.* soot.
hufen *e.g. ll.* **-nau** cream; **hufen iâ** ice-cream.
hugain *gw.* **ugain.**
hun: hunan 1. *rhag. ll.* **hunain** self; **fi fy hun(an)** I myself; **ti dy hun(an)** you yourself; **ef ei hun(an)** he himself; **nhw eu hunain** they themselves; **ei hunan bach** alone. **2** *rhagdd.* self-.
hunain *gw.* **hun.**
hunan-barch *e.g.* self-respect.
hunangofiant *e.g.* autobiography.
hunanladdiad *e.g. ll.* **-au** suicide.
hunanol *a.* selfish.
hunllef *e.b.* nightmare.
huno *be.* **(hunaf)** to sleep, to fall asleep.
Hunodd, 5 Mai 1940 Died 5 May 1940 *(on gravestones).*
hurt *a.* stupid, dull, stunned; **hurtyn** stupid person, blockhead.
hwch *e.b. ll.* **hychod** sow. **Mae hi'n hen hwch** She is slovenly.
hwiangerdd *e.b. ll.* **-i** lullaby; nursery-rhyme.
hwn *a.g. & rhag.* this (one).
hwnnw, hwnna *a.g. & rhag.* that (one); *gw.* **honno.**
hwnt *ad.* beyond, aside, away: **tu hwnt** beyond; **yn gyflym tu hwnt** exceedingly fast.
hwp *e.g.* push, thrust, shove.
hwrdd *e.g. ll.* **hyrddod.** ram (*S.W.*).
hwrê *ebych. & e.b.* hooray!
hwy: hwynt: nhw *rhag.* they, them; *gw.* **hir.**
hwyaf *gw.* **hir.**
hwyad: hwyaden *e.b. ll.* **hwyaid** duck.
hwyaid *gw.* **hwyad.**
hwyl *e.b. ll.* **-iau** sail; journey; religious fervour; mood; fun; goodbye: **mewn hwyliau da** in a good mood; **hwyl!** bye! **Pob hwyl ichi** All the best.
hwyliau *gw.* **hwyl.**
hwylio *be.* **(hwyliaf)** to sail, to set out on a journey.
hwylus *a.* ease, comfortable, expedient, convenient.
hwyluso *be.* **(hwylusaf)** to facilitate.
hwylustod *e.g.* easy, convenience, facility, expediency.
hwynt *gw.* **hwy.**
hwyr 1 *a.* late. **2** *e.g.* (late) evening.
hwyrach *ad.* perhaps (*N.W.*).
hwythau *rhag.* they, they also.
hyblyg *a.* flexible, pliable, pliant.
hybu *be.* **(hybaf)** to recover; to promote.
hychod *gw.* **hwch.**
hyd 1 *ardd.* (*followed by soft mutation*) to, till, for, as far as; **hyd yn hyn** up till now; **hyd at bum punt** up to £5; *gw. At Treigladau.* **2** *e.g. ll.* **-au, -oedd, -ion** length; while.
hyder *e.g.* confidence, trust.
hyderu *be.* **(hyderaf)** to be confident; to trust, rely or depend (on).
hyderus *a.* confident.
Hydref *e.g.* October.
hydref *e.g. ll.* **-au** autumn.
hydrefol *a.* autumnal.
hydrogen *e.g.* hydrogen.

hydd *e.g.* *ll.* **-od** stag.
hyddysg *a.* learned, well-versed.
hyf *a.* bold.
hyfdra *e.g.* boldness.
hyfryd *a.* pleasant, delightful, fine, agreeable.
hyfrydwch *e.g.* delight, pleasure.
hyfforddi *be.* **(hyfforddaf)** to train, to direct, to instruct.
hyfforddiant *e.g.* *ll.* **hyfforddiannau** training, instruction.
hyfforddwr *e.g.* *ll.* **hyfforddwyr** instructor, guide, trainer, coach.
hyhi *rhag.* she, her (*emphatic*).
hylif *a.* & *e.g.* *ll.* **-au** liquid, flowing; fluid; a liquid, a fluid; a flow.
hyll *a.* ugly, hideous.
hyn *a.* & *rhag.* this, these.
hŷn *gw.* **hen.**
hynaf *gw.* **hen.**
hynafiad *e.g.* *ll.* **hynafiaid** ancestor.
hynafol *a.* ancient.
hyned *gw.* **hen.**
hynny *a.* & *rhag.* that, those.
hynod *a.* remarkable, notable; exceptional: **yn hynod o dda** exceptionally well; **yn hynod o gyfoethog** exceptionally rich.
hynt *e.b.* *ll.* **-iau, -oedd** way, course, journey; career; (one's) fate or lot, condition, state: **Beth yw ei hynt erbyn hyn?** What's his fate by now?
hyrddod *gw.* **hwrdd.**
hysbyseb *e.b.g.* *ll.* **-ion** advertisement, announcement.
hysbysebiad *e.g.* *ll.* **-au** advertisement.
hysbysebu *be.* **(hysbysebaf)** to advertise.
hysbysebwr *e.g.* *ll.* **hysbysebwyr** advertiser.
hysbysfwrdd *e.g.* *ll.* **hysbysfyrddau** noticeboard.
hysbysiad *e.g.* *ll.* **-au** announcement, notice, advertisement.
hysbysu *be.* **(hysbysaf)** to announce, to inform; to advertise.
hytrach *ad.* rather; more so.

i 1 *ardd. (followed by soft mutation.)* **(i fi/mi, i ti, iddo/iddi, i ni, i chi, iddyn nhw)** to, into, for: **i'r dim** exactly, precisely; **i fyny** up, upwards; **i ffwrdd** away; **i gyd** all; **i lawr** down; **i mewn** into; *gw. At. Arddodiaid.* **2** *rhag.* I, me; *gw. At. Rhagenwau Personol.*
iâ *e.g.* ice; **cloch iâ** icicle.
iach *a.* healthy, well.
iacháu *be.* **(iachâf)** to heal, to cure.
iachawdwr *e.g. ll.* **iachawdwyr** saviour.
iachawdwriaeth: iechydwriaeth *e.b.* salvation, healing.
iachus *a.* healthy, wholesome.
iaith *e.b. ll.* **ieithoedd** language: **iaith lafar** spoken language; **iaith gyntaf** first language, mother tongue; **ail iaith** second language; **dwyieithog** bilingual.
iâr *e.b. ll.* **ieir** hen; **iâr fach yr haf** butterfly.
iard *e.b. ll.* **ierdydd** yard (of school, etc.).
iarll *e.g. ll.* **ieirll** earl.
iarlles *e.b. ll.* **-au** countess.
ias *e.b. ll.* **-au** thrill, shiver; temper.
iasol *a.* thrilling; intensely cold.
Iau *e.g.* Thursday.
iau 1 *e.g. ll.* **ieuau** liver. **2** *e.b. ll.* **ieuau** yoke; *gw.* **ieuanc.**
iawn 1 *ad.* very; **yn dda iawn** very good. **2** *e.g.* rightness, truth; compensation; atonement; **talu'r iawn am** to compensate. **3** *a.* right, true, correct.
iawndal *e.g. ll.* **-oedd** compensation, damages, indemnity.
iawnder *e.g. ll.* **-au** justice, right, rightness: **iawnderau dynol: iawnderau sifil** civil rights, civil liberties.
idiom *e.b. ll.* **-au** idiom.
Iddew *e.g. ll.* **-on** Jew.
Iddewes *e.b. ll.* **-au** Jewess.
Iddewig *a.* Jewish.
Iddewaeth *e.b.* Judaism.
ie *ad.* yes (*(positive response to a question that does not begin with a verb).*
iechyd *e.g.* health, soundness, well-being.
iechyd da! good health *(in drinking a toast).*
ieir *gw.* **iâr.**
ieirll *gw.* **iarll.**
ieithoedd *gw.* **iaith.**
ierdydd *gw.* **iard.**
Iesu *e.g.* **Jesus: Iesu Grist** Jesus Christ; **Iesu Mab Duw** Jesus Son of God.
iet *e.b. ll.* **-au, -iau** gate; *gw.* **clwyd.**
ieuangach *gw.* **ieuanc.**
ieuangaf *gw.* **ieuanc.**
ieuanged *gw.* **ieuanc.**
ieuainc *gw.* **ieuanc.**
ieuanc: ifanc *a. ll.* **ieuainc: ifainc.** young; *gw. At. Ansoddeiriau.*
ieuau *gw.* **iau.**
ieuenctid *e.g. & e.ll.* youth; **côr ieuenctid** youth choir.
ifainc *gw.* **ieuanc.**
ifanc *gw.* **ieuanc.**
ifancach *gw.* **ieuanc.**
ifancaf *gw.* **ieuanc.**
ig *e.b. ll.* **-ion** hiccup.
igam-ogam *a.* zigzag.
igian *be.* **(igiaf)** to hiccup.
ing *e.g. ll.* **-oedd** anguish, agony, distress.
ildio *be.* **(ildiaf)** to yield.
ill *rhag.* both, they, them; **ill dau (dwy)** both of them.
imwnedd *e.g.* immunity.
imwneiddiad *e.g. ll.* **-au** immunisation.
imwneiddio *be.* **(imwneiddiaf)** to immunise.
incwm *e.g.* income; **Treth Incwm** Income Tax.
India, Yr *e.b.* India.
indiad *e.g. ll.* **Indiaid** an Indian; **Un o'r India yw e/hi** He/she is Indian.
injan: injin *e.b. ll.* **-s** engine.
Ionawr *e.g.* January.
iorwg *e.g.* ivy *(S.W.).*

iro *be.* **(iraf)** to grease; to anoint; to oil; to lubricate.
is 1 *ardd.* below, under; *gw.* **isel. 2** *rhagdd. (followed by soft mutation)* sub-, under-, vice-.
isaf *gw.* **isel.**
ised *gw.* **isel.**
isel *a.* low; humble; base; depressed; *gw. At. Ansoddeiriau.*
Iseldiroedd, Yr *e.b.* The Netherlands.
is-etholiad *e.g. ll.* **-au** by-election.
is-gadeirydd *e.g. ll.* **-ion** vice-chairman.
islaw *ardd.* below, beneath.
is-lywydd *e.g. ll.* **-ion** vice-president.
israddol *a.* inferior; subordinate.
isymwybod *e.g.* subconscious.
Iwerddon Ireland: **byw yn Iwerddon** to live in Ireland; **dod o Iwerddon** to come from Ireland; **mynd i Iwerddon** to go to Ireland.

jac: Jac *e.g. ll.* **-s** jack.
jac-codi-baw *e.g.* 'J.C.B.', mechanical excavator.
jac-do: jac-y-do *e.g. ll.* **-s** jackdaw.
jac-y-do *gw.* **jac-do.**
jam *e.g. ll.* **-iau** jam.
Japán Japan.
Japanëad *e.g. ll.* **Japanëaid** a Japanese.
Japanëaidd *a.* Japanese.
Japanëeg *e.b.* Japanese (language).
jar: jâr *e.b. ll.* **jariau, jarrau** jar.
jas *e.g.* jazz.
jeli *e.g. ll.* **-s, jeliau** jelly.
jersi: jyrsi: siersi *e.b. ll.* **-s** jersey.
jet *e.g. ll.* **-iau** jet (of water, gas, etc); jet (nozzle); jet plane: **awyren jet** jet aircraft, jet plane; **peiriant jet** jet engine.
ji-binc *e.b. ll.* **-od** chaffinch.
jig-so *e.g.* jigsaw: **pos jig-so** jigsaw puzzle.
jîns *e.g.* jeans.
jîp *e.g.* jeep.
jiráff *e.g. ll.* **jiraffod** giraffe.
jiwbilî: jubilî *e.b. ll.* **jiwbilïau** jubilee, occasion or season of rejoicing.
job *e.g.b. ll.* **-iau, -s** job, piece of work; occupation.
jobyn *e.g. ll.* **jobiau** a small job: **Jobyn da!** Good job!
jôc *e.b. ll.* **-s** a joke, witticism; object of ridicule.
jocan *bf.* **(jocaf)** to joke *(S.W.).*
joio *bf.* **(joiaf)** to enjoy.
jubilî *gw.* **jiwbilî.**
jwg: siwg *e.b. ll.* **jygiau: siygiau** jug: **jwg laeth** milk jug.
jygiau *gw.* **jwg.**
jyngl *e.b. ll.* **-oedd** jungle.
jyrsi *gw.* **jersi.**

labed *gw.* **llabed.**
labordy *e.g. ll.* **labordai** laboratory.
labrwr *e.g. ll.* **labrwyr** labourer.
lac *gw.* **llac.**
lacio *gw.* **llacio.**
lacs *gw.* **llacs.**
lacsog *gw.* **llacsog.**
lachar *gw.* **llachar.**
Ladin *gw.* **Lladin.**
ladrad *gw.* **lladrad.**
ladrata *gw.* **lladrata.**
ladron *gw.* **lleidr.**
ladd *gw.* **lladd.**
ladd-dy *gw.* **lladd-dy.**
laes *gw.* **llaes.**
laesu *gw.* **llaesu.**
laeth *gw.* **llaeth.**
lafant *e.g.* lavender.
lafar *gw.* **llafar.**
lafariad *gw.* **llafariad.**
lafn *gw.* **llafn.**
lafur *gw.* **llafur.**
lafurio *gw.* **llafurio.**
lafurus *gw.* **llafurus.**
lafurwr *gw.* **llafurwr.**
lai *gw.* **llai.**
lain *gw.* **llain.**
lais *gw.* **llais.**
laith *gw.* **llaith.**
lam *gw.* **llam.**
lamp *e.b. ll.*-**au** lamp: **lamp ôl** rear-lamp, tail-light of vehicle; **lamp olew** oil lamp.
lamplen *e.b.* lampshade.
lamu *gw.* **llamu.**
lan *ad.* up; *gw.* **glan, llan.**
lân *gw.* **glân.**
lanc *gw.* **llanc.**
lances *gw.* **llances.**
lanciau *gw.* **llanc.**
lanhau *gw.* **glanhau.**
lanio *gw.* **glanio.**
lannau *gw.* **glan, llan.**
lanw *gw.* **llanw.**
lapio (am) *be.* **(lapiaf)** to lap, to wrap: **papur lapio** wrapping paper.
larwm *e.g.* alarm: **cloc larwm** alarm clock.
las *gw.* **glas.**
laswelltyn *gw.* **glaswelltyn.**
lathen *gw.* **llathen.**
lau *gw.* **lleuen.**
law *gw.* **glaw, llaw.**
lawen *gw.* **llawen.**
lawenhau *gw.* **llawenhau.**
lawenydd *gw.* **llawenydd.**
lawer *gw.* **llawer.**
lawes *gw.* **llawes.**
lawfeddyg *gw.* **llawfeddyg.**
lawfeddygaeth *gw.* **llawfeddygaeth.**
lawfeddygol *gw.* **llawfeddygol.**
lawlif *gw.* **llawlif.**
lawlyfr *gw.* **llawlyfr.**
lawn *gw.* **llawn.**
lawnder *gw.* **llawnder.**
lawnt *e.g.b. ll.* **-iau, -ydd** lawn.
lawr, i *ad.* down; *gw.* **llawr.**
lawysgrif *gw.* **llawysgrif.**
lawysgrifen *gw.* **llawysgrifen.**
le *gw.* **lle.**
lecyn *gw.* **llecyn.**
lechen *gw.* **llechen.**
lechi *gw.* **llechen.**
led *gw.* **lled.**
ledled *gw.* **lledled.**
ledr *gw.* **lledr.**
ledrith *gw.* **lledrith.**
ledu *gw.* **lledu.**
lef *gw.* **llef.**
lefain *e.g.b.* leaven; *gw.* **llefain.**
lefaru *gw.* **llefaru.**
lefarwr *gw.* **llefarwr.**
lefarwyr *gw.* **llefarwr.**
lefarydd *gw.* **llefarydd.**
lefau *gw.* **llef.**
lefel *e.b.g. ll.* **-au, -ydd, leflau** level; **lefel y môr** sea-level.
lefelyn *gw.* **llefelyn.**
leflau *gw.* **lefel.**
lefrith *gw.* **llefrith.**
lefydd *gw.* **lle.**
leiaf *gw.* **bach.**
leiafrif *gw.* **lleiafrif.**
leian *gw.* **lleian.**
leidr *gw.* **lleidr.**
leihau *gw.* **lleihau.**
lein *e.b. ll.* **-au, -iau, leins** line, cord; telephone line; line-out; **lein ddillad** clothes line; **lein**

fach narrow-gauge railway.
leiniau *gw.* **lein, llain.**
leinio *be.* **(leiniaf)** to line up; to form a line-out; to thrash, to give (one) a hiding *(N.W.).*
leisiau *gw.* **llais.**
leisio *gw.* **lleisio.**
leithder *gw.* **lleithder.**
len *gw.* **llen.**
lên *gw.* **llên.**
lencyndod *gw.* **llencyndod.**
lendid *gw.* **glendid.**
lenni *gw.* **llen.**
lennydd *gw.* **glan.**
lenor *gw.* **llenor.**
lenwi *gw.* **llenwi.**
lenyddiaeth *gw.* **llenyddiaeth.**
lenyddol *gw.* **llenyddol.**
leoedd *gw.* **lle.**
leol *gw.* **lleol.**
Lerpwl *e.b.* **Liverpool.**
leoli *gw.* **lleoli.**
leoliad *gw.* **lleoliad.**
les 1 *e.b. ll.* **-oedd** lease. 2 *e.b. ll.* **-au** lace; *gw.* **lles.**
lesol *gw.* **llesol.**
lestr *gw.* **llestr.**
letchwith *gw.* **lletchwith.**
lety *gw.* **llety.**
letya *gw.* **lletya.**
letys *gw.* **letysen.**
letysen *e.b. ll.* **letys** lettuce.
leuad *gw.* **lleuad.**
leuen *gw.* **lleuen.**
lew *gw.* **llew.**
lewygu *gw.* **llewygu.**
lewyrch *gw.* **llewyrch.**
lewyrchu *gw.* **llewyrchu.**
lewyrchus *gw.* **llewyrchus.**
lewys *gw.* **llawes.**
liain *gw.* **lliain.**
lid *gw.* **llid.**
lieiniau *gw.* **lliain.**
lif *gw.* **llif.**
lifio *gw.* **llifio.**
lifo *gw.* **llifo.**
lifogydd *gw.* **llif.**
lifft *e.g. ll.* **-iau** lift.
lili *e.b. ll.* **-s, liliau** lily; **lili wen fach** snowdrop.
lin *gw.* **glin.**
lindysyn *e.g. ll.* **lindys** caterpillar.
linell *gw.* **llinell.**
linyn *gw.* **llinyn.**
lipa *gw.* **llipa.**
litr *e.g. ll.* **-au** litre.
lithren *gw.* **llithren.**
lithriad *gw.* **llithriad.**
lithrig *gw.* **llithrig.**
lithro *gw.* **llithro.**
liw *gw.* **lliw.**
liwgar *gw.* **lliwgar.**
liwiau *gw.* **lliw.**
liwio *gw.* **lliwio.**
liwiog *gw.* **lliwiog.**
liwo *gw.* **lliwo.**
lo *gw.* **glo, llo.**
loches *gw.* **lloches.**
lochesu *gw.* **llochesu.**
Loegr *gw.* **Lloegr.**
loer *gw.* **lloer.**
loeren *gw.* **lloeren.**
lofa *gw.* **glofa.**
lofnod *gw.* **llofnod.**
lofnodi *gw.* **llofnodi.**
lofrudd *gw.* **llofrudd.**
lofruddiaeth *gw.* **llofruddiaeth.**
lofruddio *gw.* **llofruddio.**
lofft *gw.* **llofft.**
log *gw.* **llog.**
logi *gw.* **llogi.**
long *gw.* **llong.**
longddrylliad *gw.* **llongddrylliad.**
longwr *gw.* **llongwr.**
loi *gw.* **llo.**
lol *e.b.* frivolity; nonsense: **Paid â siarad lol!** Don't talk nonsense!.
lolfa *e.b. ll.* **lolfeydd** lounge, sitting-room.
lolan: lolian *be.* **(lolaf: loliaf)** to lounge; to joke, to talk nonsense *(S.W.).*
lon *gw.* **llon.**
lôn *e.b. ll.* **lonydd** lane, road: **y Lôn Goed** the Tree-Lined Way *(place name in N.W. Wales);* **y lôn gefn** the back lane; **lôn ddianc** escape lane.
loncian *be.* **(lonciaf)** to jog.
lonciwr *e.g. ll.* **loncwyr** jogger.
lond *gw.* **llond.**
longyfarch *gw.* **llongyfarch.**
longyfarchiad *gw.* **llongyfarchiad.**
lonydd *gw.* **lôn, llonydd.**
lonyddwch *gw.* **llonyddwch.**
loriau *gw.* **llawr.**
lorïau *gw.* **lorri.**
lorri *e.b. ll.* **lorïau, lorris** lorry: **lorri laeth** milk-lorry; **lorri lo** coal-lorry; **lorri wartheg** cattle-lorry.
losg *gw.* **llosg.**
losgi *gw.* **llosgi.**
losin *gw.* **losinen.**
losinen: losen *e.b. ll.* **losin** sweet, lozenge.
löwr *gw.* **glöwr.**
löyn byw *gw.* **glöyn byw.**
loyw *gw.* **gloyw.**

lu *gw.* **llu.**
lud *gw.* **glud.**
ludio: ludo *gw.* **gludio.**
ludw *gw.* **lludw.**
Lun *gw.* **Llun.**
lun *gw.* **llun.**
Lundain *gw.* **Llundain.**
luniaidd *gw.* **lluniaidd.**
lunio *gw.* **llunio.**
luoedd *gw.* **llu.**
luosi *gw.* **lluosi.**
luosog *gw.* **lluosog.**
lusern *gw.* **llusern.**
lusgo *gw.* **llusgo.**
luwch *gw.* **lluwch.**
luwchfa *gw.* **lluwchfa.**
lw *gw.* **llw.**
lŵans: lwfans *e.g.b.* allowance, concession.
lwc *e.b.g.* luck, fate, chance: **Pob lwc i ti!** Good luck to you! **Lwc dda!** Good luck! prosperity, success.
lwcus *a.* lucky, fortunate.
lwch *gw.* **llwch.**
lwfans *gw.* **lŵans.**
lwfr *gw.* **llwfr.**
lwgu *gw.* **llwygu.**
lwnc *gw.* **llwnc.**
lwncdestun *gw.* **llwncdestun.**
lwon *gw.* **llw.**
lwy *gw.* **llwy.**
lwybr *gw.* **llwybr.**
lwyd *gw.* **llwyd.**
lwydo *gw.* **llwydo.**
lwydrew *gw.* **llwydrew.**
lwydrewi *gw.* **llwydrewi.**
lwydd *gw.* **llwydd.**
lwyddiannus *gw.* **llwyddiannus.**
lwyddiant *gw.* **llwydd.**
lwyddo *gw.* **llwyddo.**
lwyfan *gw.* **llwyfan.**
lwyfannu *gw.* **llwyfannu.**
lwyn *gw.* **llwyn.**
lwynog *gw.* **llwynog.**
lwyr *gw.* **llwyr.**
lwyrymwrthodwr *gw.* **llwyrymwrthodwr.**
lwyth *gw.* **llwyth.**
lwytho *gw.* **llwytho.**
lwythog *gw.* **llwythog.**
lydan *gw.* **llydan.**
lydanu *gw.* **llydanu.**
Lydaw *gw.* **Llydaw.**
lyfelyn *gw.* **llyfelyn.**
lyfn *gw.* **llyfn.**
lyfr *gw.* **llyfr.**
lyfrgell *gw.* **llyfrgell.**
lyfrgellydd *gw.* **llyfrgellydd.**
lyfryn *gw.* **llyfryn.**
lyfu *gw.* **llyfu.**
lyffant *gw.* **llyfant.**
lygad *gw.* **llygad.**
lygadu *gw.* **llygadu.**
lygaid *gw.* **llygad.**
lygod *gw.* **llygoden.**
lygoden *gw.* **llygoden.**
lygredig *gw.* **llygredig.**
lygredd *gw.* **llygredd.**
lygru *gw.* **llygru.**
lynges *gw.* **llynges.**
lyn *gw.* **glyn, llyn.**
lynciau *gw.* **llwnc.**
lyncu *gw.* **llyncu.**
lynnau *gw.* **llyn.**
lynnoedd *gw.* **glyn, llyn.**
lynu *gw.* **glynu.**
lys *gw.* **llys.**
lysenw *gw.* **llysenw.**
lysenwi *gw.* **llysenwi.**
lysfam *gw.* **llysfam.**
lysgenhadaeth *gw.* **llysgenhadaeth.**
lysgennad *gw.* **llysgennad.**
lysiau *gw.* **llysieuyn.**
lysieuyn *gw.* **llysieuyn.**
lythrennau *gw.* **llythyren.**
lythrennog *gw.* **llythrennog.**
lythyr *gw.* **llythyr.**
lythyren *gw.* **llythyren.**
lyw *gw.* **llyw.**
lywio *gw.* **llywio.**
lywodraeth *gw.* **llywodraeth.**
lywodraethu *gw.* **llywodraethu.**
lywodraethwr *gw.* **llywodraethwr.**
lywydd *gw.* **llywydd.**
lywyddu *gw.* **llywyddu.**

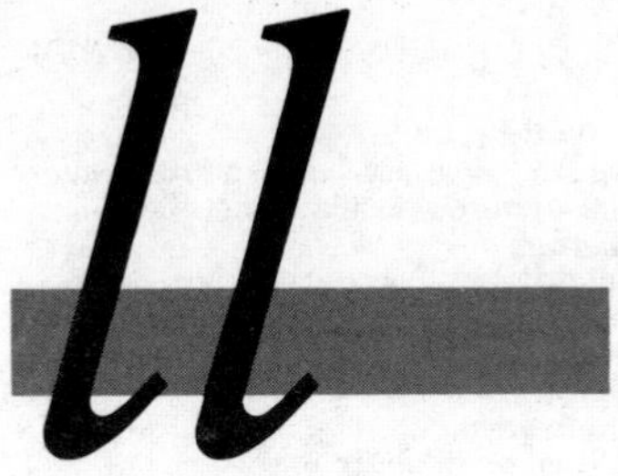

llabed *e.b.* *ll.* **-au** lapel, flap.
llac *a.* slack, loose; lax.
llacio *be.* **(llaciaf)** to slacken; to loosen; to relax.
llacs *e.g.* mud, dirt *(S.W.).*
llacsog *a.* muddy, dirty *(S.W.).*
llachar *a.* bright, brilliant, dazzling.
Lladin *e.b.* & *a.* Latin. **America Ladin** Latin America.
lladrad *e.g.* *ll.* **-au** theft, robbery.
lladrata *be.* **(lladrataf)** to rob, to steal, to thieve.
lladron *gw.* **lleidr.**
lladd *be.* **(lladdaf)** to kill, to stay, to slaughter; to cut, to mow, to fell: **lladd ar** to run down, to criticise adversely; **lladd gwair** to mow *(hay);* **lladd mawn** to cut peat; **fel lladd nadroedd** at full speed, with might and main *(lit. like killing snakes).*
lladd-dy *e.g.* *ll.* **lladd-dai** slaughter-house.
llaes *a.* loose, long, flowing.
llaesu *be.* **(llaesaf)** to slacken, to loosen, to relax; **llaesu dwylo** to become idle, weak or indifferent, to stay one's hand(s).
llaeth *e.g.* *ll.* **-au** milk *(S.W.); gw.* **llefrith.**
llafar 1 *e.g. (verbal)* expression, spoken or colloquial language; **iaith lafar** the spoken language. **2** *a.* loud, clear, vociferous; pertaining to the voice; oral; **arholiad llafar** oral *(as opposed to written)* examination.
llafariad *e.b.* *ll.* **llafariaid** vowel.
llafn *e.g.* *ll.* **-au** blade.
llafur *e.g.* *ll.* **-iau** labour, toil; tillage, corn: **llafur cariad** labour of love; **Y Blaid Lafur** The Labour Party.
llafurio: llafuro *be.* **(llafuriaf: llafuraf)** to labour, to toil, to work.
llafurus *a.* laborious, painstaking, industrious.
llafurwr *e.g.* *ll.* **llafurwyr** labourer, worker, husbandman.
llai *gw.* **bach.**
llain *e.b.* *ll.* **lleiniau** *(long narrow)* strip of land, cloth &c., piece, patch, pitch, wicket *(cricket)*, plot *(of land)*: **llain galed** hard shoulder *(of motorway);* **llain glanio** landing-strip, airstrip; **llain o dir** strip of land, isthmus.
llais *e.g.* *ll.* **lleisiau** voice, sound.
llaith *a.* damp, moist, dank.
llall *rhag.* *ll.* **lleill** the other *(one)*, another: **y llall** the other *(person, thing);* **y lleill** the others, the other persons/things.
llam *e.g.* *ll.* **-au** leap, jump, bound, stride.
llamu *be.* **(llamaf)** to leap, to jump, to bound, to stride.
llan *e.b.* *ll.* **-nau** (parish) church, churchyard; enclosure, yard.
llanc *e.g.* *ll.* **-iau** youth, lad.
llances *e.b.* *ll.* **-i, -au** young woman, lass.
llanciau *gw.* **llanc.**
llannau *gw.* **llan.**
llanw 1. *e.g.* *ll.* **-au** flow (of tide): **trai a llanw** ebb and flow. **2** *be.* **(llanwaf)** to fill, to fill up.
llathen *e.b.* *ll.* **-ni** yard, yardstick: **Doedd e ddim yn llawn llathen** He wasn't all there.
llau *gw.* **lleuen.**
llaw *e.b.* *ll.* **dwylo** hand; **i law** to hand: **llawchwith** left handed; **llawdde** skilful, dextrous; **llawfer** shorthand; **llaw galed** trouble, rough time, hard time *(especially with sick person);* **llaw yn llaw** hand in hand; **ail-law** second-hand; **hen law ar** one who possesses the 'know how', *(lit. an old hand);* **rhoi help llaw** to give a helping hand.
llawen *a.* cheerful, merry, glad.
llawenhau (yn) *be.* **(llawenhaf)** to rejoice, to be joyful.
llawenydd *e.g.* joy, jubilation, rejoicing.
llawer *e.g.* *ll.* **-oedd** many, much; abundant. **2** *ad.* by far, much *(with comparative adjective).* **o lawer** by far, by a great deal, by

much; **llawer gwaith** many times; **yn llawer gwell** much better; **llawer tro** many a time.
llawes e.b. ll. **llewys** sleeve.
llawfeddyg *e.g. ll.* **-on** surgeon.
llawfeddygaeth *e.b.* surgery.
llawfeddygol *a.* surgical.
llawlif *e.b. ll.* **-iau** hand-saw.
llawlyfr *e.g. ll.* **-au** handbook, manual.
llawn *a. ll.* **-ion** full; **yn llawn bryd** high time.
llawnder *e.g.* abundance, fullness.
llawnion *gw.* **llawn.**
llawr *e.g. ll.* **lloriau** floor, ground; storey; earth: **ar lawr** down, exhausted, on (to) the ground, on the ground floor, downstairs, up *(from bed),* not yet gone to bed; **ar lawr gwlad** on the lowlands; **y llawr cyntaf** the first floor.
llawysgrif *e.b. ll.* **-au** manuscript.
llawysgrifen *e.b. ll.* **llawysgrifennau** handwriting.
lle *e.g. ll.* **-oedd, llefydd** place, room, accommodation.
lle bwyd café, restaurant: **lle chwech** toilet; **lle tân** fireplace; **o'i le** out of (its) place or order, wrong, inappropriate.
llecyn *e.g. ll.* **-nau** spot, place.
llechen *e.b. ll.* **llechi** slate.
llechi *gw.* **llechen.**
lled 1 *e.g. ll.* **-au** breadth, width. **Mae stori ar led yn a pentref** There is a story going around the village. 2 *ad.* rather, partly, almost.
lledled *ardd.* throughout; **lledled y byd** throughout the world.
lledr *e.g. ll.* **-au** leather.
lledrith *e.g. ll.* **-oedd** magic, enchantment; spectre; fantasy: **hud a lledrith** magic and fantasy.
lledu *be.* **(lledaf)** to spread, to widen, to open, to expand.
llef *e.b. ll.* **-au** voice, cry.
llefain *be.* **(llefaf)** to cry *(S.W.).*
llefaru *be.* **(llefaraf)** to speak, to utter.
llefarwr *e.g. ll.* **llefarwyr** speaker.
llefarwyr *gw.* **llefarwr.**
llefarydd *e.g. ll.* **-ion** speaker, spokesman: **Y Llefarydd** (the) Speaker of the House of Commons.
llefau *gw.* **llef.**
llefelyn *e.g. ll.* **-od** stye *(in eye); gw.* **llyfelyn, llefrithen.**
llefrith *e.g.* milk *(N.W.); gw.* **llaeth.**
llefrithen *e.b.* stye (in eye) *(N.W.); gw.* **llefelyn, llyfelyn.**
llefydd *gw.* **lle.**
lleiaf *a.* smallest, least: **o leiaf** at least; **gorau po leiaf** least the better.
lleiafrif *e.g. ll.* **-au, -oedd** minority.
lleian *e.b. ll.* **-od** nun.
lleidr *e.g. ll.* **lladron** thief, robber, bandit: **lleidr pen ffordd** highwayman.
lleihau *be.* **(lleihaf)** to become smaller, to diminish, to shrink.
lleill *gw.* **llall.**
lleiniau *gw.* **llain.**
lleisiau *gw.* **llais.**
lleisio *be.* **(lleisiaf)** to use the voice *(in speaking, shouting, etc.),* to sound, to cry out.
lleithder *e.g. ll.* **-au** damp, moisture.
llen *e.b. ll.* **-ni** curtain, veil, sheet: **Y Llen Haearn** The Iron Curtain.
llên *e.b.* literature; **llên gwerin** folklore; **ffuglen** fiction.
llencyndod *e.g.* adolescence.
llenni *gw.* **llen.**
llenor *e.g. ll.* **-ion** author, writer, literary person.
llenwi *be.* **(llenwaf)** to fill.
llenyddiaeth *e.b. ll.* **-au** literature.
llenyddol *a.* literary.
lleoedd *gw.* **lle.**
lleol *a.* local; **llywodraeth leol** local government.
lleoli *be.* **(lleolaf)** to locate, to localise, to place.
lleoliad *e.g. ll.* **-au** location, setting.
lles *e.g. ll.* **-au** benefit, profit, advantage, welfare: **er lles** for the benefit of, to the advantage of; **o les** of benefit; **Y Wladwriaeth Les** The Welfare State.
llesol *a.* beneficial, profitable, advantageous.
llestr *e.g. ll.* **-i** vessel; cup, dish, pot.
lletchwith *a.* awkward, clumsy.
llety *e.g. ll.* **-au** lodging(s).
lletya *be.* **(lletyaf)** to lodge.
lleuad *e.b. ll.* **-au** moon: **lleuad lawn** full moon; **lleuad newydd** new moon; *gw.* **lloer.**
lleuen *e.b. ll.* **llau** louse.
llew *e.g. ll.* **-od** lion; **llewes** lioness.
llewygu *be.* **(llewygaf)** to faint, to swoon.
llewyrch *e.g.* brightness, light, gleam, lustre.
llewyrchu *be.* **(llewyrchaf)** to shine, to gleam.
llewyrchus *a.* bright, prosperous.
llewys *gw.* **llawes.**

lliain *e.g. ll.* **llieiniau** linen, cloth, towel, napkin.
llid *e.g. ll.* **-iau, -ion** wrath; irritation, inflammation; passion: **llid yr ymennydd** meningitis.
llieiniau *gw.* **lliain.**
llif 1 *e.g. ll.* **-ogydd** stream, flow, flood, deluge, current. 2 *e.b. ll.* **-iau** saw; **llif gadwyn** chain saw.
llifio *be.* **(llifiaf)** to saw; to rasp, to file.
llifo *be.* **(llifaf)** to flow, to stream, to flood.
llifogydd *gw.* **llif.**
llinell *e.b. ll.* **-au** line, axis; line-out: **llinell gam** crooked line; **llinell syth** straight line.
llinyn *e.g. ll.* **-nau** line, string, cord, tape, twine: **llinyn mesur** measuring tape.
llipa *a.* limp, flaccid, weak.
llithren *e.b. ll.* **-nau** chute, slide.
llithriad *e.g. ll.* **-au** a slip, glide, slur; error, mistake.
llithrig *a.* slippery; fluent.
llithro *be.* **(llithraf)** to slip, to slide; to slur.
lliw *e.g. ll.* **-iau** colour, countenance, hue: **lliw dydd** by day; **lliw nos** by night; **lliwiau'r hydref** autumn colours.
lliwgar *a.* colourful.
lliwiau *gw.* **lliw.**
lliwio: lliwo *be.* **(lliwiaf: lliwaf)** to colour, to dye.
lliwiog *a.* coloured, tinted.
lliwo *gw.* **lliwio.**
llo *e.g. ll.* **lloi, lloeau** calf; **fel llo** gormless.
lloches *e.g. ll.* **-au** refuge, shelter, lair.
llochesu *be.* **(llochesaf)** to harbour, to shelter.
lloeau *gw.* **llo.**
Lloegr *e.b.* England.
lloer *e.b. ll.* **-au** moon *(literary usage); gw.* **lleuad.**
lloeren *e.b. ll.* **-ni, -nau** satellite, sputnik.
llofnod *e.g. ll.* **-au, -ion** signature.
llofnodi *be.* **(llofnodaf)** to sign.
llofrudd *e.g. ll.* **-ion** murderer.
llofruddiaeth *e.g. ll.* **-au** murder.
llofruddio *be.* **(llofruddiaf)** to murder.
llofft *e.b. ll.* **-ydd** loft, upstairs; gallery; bedroom: **ar y llofft** upstairs; **lan llofft** upstairs *(S.W.)*.
llog *e.g. ll.* **-au** interest, hire; **ar log** for hire.
llogi *be.* **(llogaf)** to hire.
llong *e.b. ll.* **-au** ship: **llong hwyliau** sailing ship; **llong danfor** submarine; **llong ryfel** warship.
llongddrylliad *e.g. ll.* **-au** shipwreck.
llongwr *e.g. ll.* **llongwyr** sailor.
lloi *gw.* **llo.**
llon *a.* merry, cheerful.
llond *e.g.* as much as something will hold; fullness, sufficiency: **llond llwy de o siwgr** a teaspoonful of sugar; **llond tŷ o blant** a houseful of children.
llongyfarch (ar) *be.* **(llongyfarchaf)** to congratulate.
llongyfarchiad *e.g. ll.* **-au** congratulation; **llongyfarchiadau!** congratulations!.
llonydd *a.* quiet, still, calm; **gad lonydd i fi!** let me have some peace!.
llonyddwch *e.g.* stillness, tranquillity, quietness; peace.
lloriau *gw.* **llawr.**
llosg 1 *e.g. ll.* **-iadau** burning, arson. 2. burning, burnt; **llosgfynydd** volcano; **pwnc llosg** burning issue.
llosgi *be.* **(llosgaf)** to burn, to scorch, to smart.
llosgydd *e.g. ll.* **-ion** incinerator, burner.
llu *e.g. ll.* **-oedd** host, multitude, *(follows plural noun and undergoes soft mutation)* crowd: **Daeth milwyr lu o rywle** A host of soldiers came from somewhere.
lluched *e. torf.* flash of lightning; lighting flashes.
lludw *e.g.* ash, ashes: **Lludw i ludw** Ashes to ashes; **dydd Mercher y Lludw** Ash Wednesday; **lorri ludw** ashcart.
Llun *e.g.* Monday: **Llun y Pasg** Easter Monday.
llun *e.g. ll.* **-iau** picture, drawing, image.
Llundain *e.b.* London.
lluniaidd *a.* shapely, graceful.
lluniau *gw.* **llun.**
llunio *be.* **(lluniaf)** to form, to fashion, to shape.
lluoedd *gw.* **llu.**
lluosi *be.* **(lluosaf)** to multiply.
lluosog *a.* numerous, plural.
llusern *e.b. ll.* **-au** lamp, lantern.
llusgo *be.* **(llusgaf)** to drag, to trail, to draw, to crawl: **llusgo traed** to drag (one's) feet.

lluwch *e.g.* *ll.* **-au** snow-drift; dust, specks.
lluwchfa *e.b.* *ll.* **lluwchfeydd** snow-drift.
llw *e.g.* *ll.* **-on** oath; curse: **ar fy llw** on oath, on my word; **cymryd llw** to take an oath.
llwch *e.g.* *ll.* **llychau** dust, powder; ashes; lake, loch.
llwfr *a.* cowardly, timid.
llwgu *be.* **(llwgaf)** to starve, to be ravenously hungry.
llwm *a.* poor, bare.
llwnc *e.g.* *ll.* **llynciau** gullet, throat; draught, gulp.
llwncdestun *e.g.* *ll.* **-au** toast (health).
llwon *gw.* **llw.**
llwy *e.b.* *ll.* **-au** spoon: **llwy bren** wooden spoon; **llwy de** teaspoon; **llwy gawl** soup-spoon; **llwy garu** love-spoon.
llwybr *e.g.* *ll.* **-au** path, track, route: **llwybr tarw** straight path, short cut; **ar y llwybr iawn** on the right track.
llwyd *a.* grey, pale, hoary; **Brawd Llwyd** Grey Friar, Cistercian Friar.
llwydo *be.* **(llwydaf)** to turn grey; to become mouldy.
llwydrew *e.g.* *ll.* **-ogydd** hoar-frost *(S.W.).*
llwydrewi *be.* **(llwydrewaf)** to cast a hoar-frost, to be frosty *(S.W.).*
llwydd: llwyddiant *e.g.* *ll.* **llwyddiannau** success, prosperity.
llwyddiannus *a.* successful, prosperous.
llwyddo (i) *be.* **(llwyddaf)** to succeed, to prosper.
llwyfan *e.g.b.* *ll.* **-nau** platform, stage: **llwyfan olew** oil rig.
llwyfannu *be.* **(llwyfannaf)** to stage.
llwyn 1 *e.g.* *ll.* **-i** grove, bush: **o lech i lwyn** furtively, stealthily, slyly *(literally from rock to bush).* **2** *e.b.* *ll.* **-au** loin.
llwynog *e.g.* *ll.* **-od** fox *(N.W.);* **llwynoges** vixen.
llwyr 1 *a.* complete, entire, utter, total. **2** *ad.* entirely, altogether. **3** *rhag.* total.
llwyrymwrthodwr *e.g.* *ll.* **llwyrymwrthodwyr** teetotaller.
llwyth *e.g.* *ll.* **-au** tribe, clan; *e.g.* *ll.* **-i** load, burden, freight.
llwytho *be.* **(llwythaf)** to load, to burden.
llwythog *a.* laden, burdened.
llydan *a.* wide, broad.
llydanu *be.* **(llydanaf)** to widen.
Llydaw *e.b.* Britanny.
Llydawr *e.g.* Breton.
Llydawes *e.b.* Breton woman.
Llydaweg *e.b.* Breton language.
llyfelyn *e.g.* *ll.* **llyfelod** stye (in eye; *gw.* **llefelyn, llefrithen.**
llyfn *a.* smooth, sleek.
llyfr *e.g.* *ll.* **-au** book: **llyfr emynau** hymn book; **llyfr gosod** set book *(in syllabus);* **llyfr lloffion** scrap-book; **llyfr lluniau** picture book; **llyfr sieciau** cheque book; **llawlyfr** handbook, manual.
llyfrgell *e.b.* *ll.* **-oedd** library: **llyfrgell y sir** county library.
llyfrgellydd *e.g.* *ll.* **-ion, llyfrgellwyr** librarian.
llyfryn *e.g.* *ll.* **-nau** booklet, pamphlet.
llyfu *be.* **(llyfaf)** to lick.
llyffant *e.g.* *ll.* **-od, llyffaint** toad; **caws llyffant** toadstool.
llygad *e.g.b.* *ll.* **llygaid** eye: **llygad tro** squint; **llygad y fynnon** fountain head, original source of information; **yn llygad ei le** perfectly right, quite correct. **yn llygaid i gyd** all eyes, all attention; **(dim ond) dau lygad a thrwyn** '(only) two eyes and a nose', said of a thin person.
llygadu *be.* **(llygadaf)** to eye, to watch, to have (one's) eye upon.
llygaid *gw.* **llygad.**
llygod *gw.* **llygoden.**
llygoden *e.b.* *ll.* **llygod** mouse: **llygoden fach** mouse; **llygoden fawr/Ffrengig** rat.
llygredig *a.* corrupt, degraded, defiled.
llygredd *e.g.* *ll.* **-au** corruption; pollution, contamination.
llygru *be.* **(llygraf)** to corrupt, to pollute, to contaminate.
llynges *e.b.* *ll.* **-au** fleet, navy: **Y Llynges** The Navy.
llym *a.* sharp, keen, severe.
llyn *e.g.b.* *ll.* **-noedd, -nau** lake, pool.
llynciau *gw.* **llwnc.**
llyncu *be.* **(llyncaf)** to swallow, to devour, to gulp.
llynedd *ad.* *(the definite article is used with the adverb).* last year: **Gwelais ef y llynedd** I saw him last year.
llynnau *gw.* **llyn.**
llynnoedd *gw.* **llyn.**
llyo *be.* **(llyaf)** to lick *(S.W.).*

llys *e.g.* *ll.* **-oedd** court, hall, palace: **Llys y Goron** The Crown Court; **Llys yr Ynadon** The Magistrates' Court; **Yr Uchel Lys** The High Court.
llysenw *e.g.* *ll.* **-au** nickname.
llysenwi *be.* **(llysenwaf)** to nickname.
llysfam *e.b.* *ll.* **-au** stepmother.
llysgenhadaeth *e.b.* *ll.* **llysgenadaethau** embassy.
llysgennad *e.g.* *ll.* **llysgenhadon** ambassador.
llysiau gw. **llysieuyn.**
llysieuyn *e.g.* *ll.* **llysiau** vegetable, herb.
llythrennau *gw.* **llythyren.**
llythrennog *a.* literate.
llythyr *e.g.* *ll.* **-au, -on** letter, epistle: **llythyr caru** love-letter; **llythyr cyfreithiwr** solicitor's letter.
llythyren *e.b.* *ll.* **llythrennau** letter of the alphabet: **llythrennau'r abiec** letters of the alphabet; **priflythrennau** capital letters; **llythyren y ddeddf** letter of the law.
llyw *e.g.* *ll.* **-iau** leader, ruler; rudder, helm.
(bod) wrth y llyw (to be) at the helm, (to be) in charge.
llywio *be.* **(llywiaf)** to govern, to rule; to steer, to pilot.
llywodraeth *e.b.* *ll.* **-au** government: **llywodraeth ganolog** central government; **llywodraeth leol** local government.
llywodraethu *be.* **(llywodraethaf)** to govern, to rule, to control.
llywodraethwr *e.g.* *ll.* **llywodraethwyr** governor.
llywydd *e.g.* *ll.* **-ion** president *(of society); gw.* **arlywydd.**
llywyddu *be.* **(llywyddaf)** to preside.

mab *e.g. ll.* **meibion** boy, son, man, male.
maban *gw.* **baban.**
mabi *gw.* **babi.**
mabolgamp *e.b. ll.* **-au** game, sport, feat: **mabolgampau'r ysgol** school sports.
mach *gw.* **bach.**
machau *gw.* **bach; bachyn.**
machgen *gw.* **bachgen.**
machlud *e.g. ll.* **-oedd** setting *(of the sun)*, going down; **machlud haul** sunset.
machu *gw.* **bachu.**
machyn *gw.* **bachyn.**
mad *gw.* **bad.**
madarch *e. torf.* mushrooms; **madarchen** *e.b.* a mushroom.
mae *gw.* **bae, bod.**
maer *e.g. ll.* **meiri** mayor; **maer y dre** the town mayor.
maeres *e.b. ll.* **-au** mayoress.
maes *e.g. ll.* **meysydd** field, square; syllabus: **maes chwarae** playing field; **maes o law** shortly.
maestref *e.b. ll.* **-i, -ydd** suburb.
mafonen *e.b. ll.* **mafon** raspberry.
mag *gw.* **bag.**
magiau *gw.* **bag.**
magu *be.* **(magaf)** to breed, to nurse, to gain: **magu bola** to acquire a pot belly; **magu hyder** to gain confidence.
Mai *e.g.* May.
mai *c.* that *(emphatic)*: **Rwy'n sicr mai Tom yw e** I'm sure that it is *Tom (and nobody else); gw.* **bai.**
maich *gw.* **baich.**
main *a.* thin, lean, slim, shrill, fine.
maint *e.g.b. ll.* **meintiau** size, dimension; magnitude; amount, quantity; extent.
malchder *gw.* **balchder.**
maldod *e.g.* indulgence, pampering, spoiling; caresses; affectation.
maldodi *be.* **(maldodaf)** to pamper, to fondle, to pet.
maled *gw.* **baled.**
maledwr *gw.* **baledwr.**
malot *gw.* **balot.**
malu *be.* **(malaf)** to grind, to crush, to smash; **malu awyr** to talk nonsense, to talk idly.
malŵn *gw.* **balŵn.**
malwen: *(N.W.)* **malwoden** *(S.W.) e.b. ll.* **malwod** snail, slug.
malwoden *(S.W.) gw.* **malwen.**
mam *e.b. ll.* **-au** mother: **mamfaeth** foster-mother; **mam-yng-nghyfraith** mother-in-law.
mam-gu *e.b.* grandmother *(S.W.); gw.* **nain.**
mân *a.* tiny, small, minute; fine; petty: **arian mân** small change, small coin; **glaw mân** fine rain, drizzle; **glo mân** small coal, slack; **yn fân ac yn fuan** quickly and in short gasps *(of breath)*; with small quick steps or movements.
man *e.g.b. ll.* **-nau** place, spot; mark; blemish; **man a man (i fi, i ti . . .)** (it is) all the same (to me, to you . . .), (it makes) no difference; **man cychwyn** starting-point; **man cyfarfod** meeting place; **man gwan** weak spot; **yn y fan a'r lle** in the (very) place, on the (very) spot; **yn y man** soon, before (very) long, presently; on the spot, immediately, at once, now; *gw.* **ban.**
manana *gw.* **banana.**
manc *gw.* **banc.**
mancio *gw.* **bancio.**
mand *gw.* **band.**
mandiau *gw.* **band.**
maneg *e.b. ll.* **menig** glove, gauntlet; **Gwlad y menig gwynion** Land of the white gloves (alluding to the frequent presentation of white gloves to assize judges in Wales, when there were no cases for trial).
maner *gw.* **baner.**
mannau *gw.* **ban, man.**
mans *e.g.* manse.
mantais *e.b. ll.* **manteision** advantage: **o fantais** of advantage; **cymryd mantais (ar)** to take advantage (of).

manteisio (ar) *be.* **(manteisiaf)** to take advantage to profit (from).
manteision *gw.* **mantais.**
mantell *e.b.* *ll.* **-oedd, mentyll** mantle, cloak, robe.
manwl *a.* exact, careful, strict; fine; particular; **yn fanwl** in detail.
manylion *e.ll.* details, particulars.
manylu (ar) *be.* **(manylaf)** to particularise, to go into detail (about), to be exact.
manylyn *e.g.* *ll.* **manylion** detail.
map *e.g.* *ll.* **-iau** map.
mar *gw.* **bar.**
mara *gw.* **bara.**
marc *e.g.* *ll.* **-iau, -au** mark; **gwneud marc** to make one's mark.
marcio *be.* **(marciaf)** to mark, to mark out.
marchnad *e.b.* *ll.* **-oedd** market: **y Farchnad Gyffredin** the Common market; **y farchnad rydd** the free market.
marchog *e.g.* *ll.* **-ion** horseman, rider; knight.
mardd *gw.* **bardd.**
marddoniaeth *gw.* **barddoniaeth.**
marf *gw.* **barf.**
marn *gw.* **barn.**
marnwr *gw.* **barnwr.**
mart *e.g.* *ll.* **-iau** mart *(S.W.).*
marw 1 *be.* **(marwaf)** to die; **wedi marw: yn farw** dead. 2 *a.* *ll.* **meirw, meirwon** dead, deceased. 3 *e.g.* *ll.* **meirw, meirwon** the dead.
marwaidd *a.* lifeless, listless, sluggish.
marwol *a.* deadly, fatal, mortal: **ergyd farwol** mortal blow.
marwolaeth *e.b.* *ll.* **-au** death.
mas *gw.* **bas.**
masged *gw.* **basged.**
masn *gw.* **basn.**
masnach *e.b.* *ll.* **-au** trade, commerce.
masnachwr *e.g.* *ll.* **masnachwyr** merchant, tradesman, dealer.
masnau: masnys *gw.* **basn.**
maswr *e.g.* *ll.* **maswyr** outside-half *(rugby).*
mat *e.g.* *ll.* **-iau** mat; *gw.* **bat.**
mater *e.g.* *ll.* **-ion** matter, subject.
matsen: matsien *e.b.* *ll.* **matsys** match: **fel matsien** wild tempered, fiery *(lit. like a match).*
math *e.g.* *ll.* **-au** sort, kind, species; *gw.* **bath.**
mathemateg *e.g.* mathematics.
mathemategol *a.* mathematical.
mathemategwr *e.g.* *ll.* **mathemategwyr** mathematician.
mathodyn *gw.* **bathodyn.**
maw *gw.* **baw.**
mawd *gw.* **bawd.**
mawl *e.g.* praise.
mawn *e.g.* peat; **lladd mawn** to cut peat.
mawnog *e.b.* *ll.* **-ydd** a peat bog.
mawr *a.* *ll.* **-ion** great, big, large; *gw. At. Ansoddeiriau.*
mawredd *e.g.* greatness, majesty, grandeur; **Mawredd mawr!** Good gracious!
Mawrth *e.g.* March; Tuesday; Mars.
mecso *gw.* **becso.**
mechan *gw.* **bechan.**
mechgyn *gw.* **bachgen.**
mechnïaeth *e.b.* bail, suretyship.
Medi *e.g.* September.
medi *be.* **(medaf)** to reap, to harvest, to cut.
medru *be.* **(medraf)** to be able to do or accomplish *(a thing)*; to be able to speak, know *(a language)*; to hit, to strike, to shoot: **medru'r Gymraeg** to know Welsh, to be able to speak Welsh.
medrus *a.* skilful, able, clever *(with one's hands)*; correct.
medw *gw.* **bedwen.**
medwen *gw.* **bedwen.**
medyddio *gw.* **bedyddio.**
medd *e.g.* mead; *gw.* **bedd, meddaf.**
meddaf *bf.* I say, I said; **meddwn i** I would say; **medd** he/she/it says/said; *gw.* **meddu.**
meddai *bf.* he/she/it was saying, he/she/it was used to saying.
meddal *a.* soft, tender, pliable.
meddalu *be.* **(meddalaf)** to soften, to become soft; to thaw.
meddu *be.* **(meddaf)** to possess, to own.
meddw *a.* *ll.* **-on** drunk; **yn feddw gaib** blind drunk.
meddwi (ar) *be* **(meddwaf)** to be drunk, to become drunk.
meddwl (am) 1 *be.* **(meddyliaf, meddylaf)** to think, to mean, to intend: **meddwl y byd o** to think the world of. 2 *e.g.* *ll.* **meddyliau** thought, mind, meaning, opinion.
meddyg *e.g.* *ll.* **-on** doctor of medicine.
meddygfa *e.b.* *ll.* **meddygfeydd** surgery.
meddyginiaeth *e.b.* *ll.* **-au** remedy, medicine.

meddylgar *a.* thoughtful, pensive.
meddyliau *gw.* **meddwl.**
mefusen *e.b.* *ll.* **mefus** strawberry.
Mehefin *e.g.* June.
meiau *gw.* **bai.**
meibion *gw.* **mab.**
Meibl *gw.* **Beibl.**
meic *e.g.* *ll.* **-iau** microphone; *gw.* **beic.**
meicrodon *gw.* **microdon.**
meichiau *gw.* **baich.**
meiddio *be.* **(meiddiaf)** to dare, to venture; *gw.* **beiddio.**
meim *e.g.b.* *ll.* **-iau** mime.
meinir *e.b.* maiden.
meintiau *gw.* **maint.**
meio *gw.* **beio.**
meirdd *gw.* **bardd.**
meiri *gw.* **maer.**
meirioli *be.* **(meiriolaf)** to thaw, to melt.
meirniad *gw.* **beirniad.**
meirniadu *gw.* **beirniadu.**
meirniaid *gw.* **beirniad.**
meistr *e.g.* *ll.* **-i, -iaid** master, owner.
meistres *e.b.* *ll.* **-i** mistress.
meistri: meistriaid *gw.* **meistr.**
meithrin *be.* **(meithrinaf)** to nurture, to rear, to foster: **meithrinfa** nursery; **ysgol feithrin** nursery school.
mêl *e.g.* honey: **mis mêl** honeymoon; **yn fêl ar ei fysedd** music to his ears, to his extreme gratification.
melen *a.b.* yellow: **ffrog felen** yellow frock; *gw.* **melyn.**
melin *e.b.* *ll.* **-au** mill: **melin ddŵr** water mill; **melin wlân** woollen mill; **melin wynt** windmill; **gwneud melin ac eglwys** to make a great to-do of, to make a fuss about nothing.
melyn *a.g.* yellow: **crys melyn** yellow shirt, **cyw melyn olaf** youngest child of family, last of the brood; **melynwy** yolk of an egg; *gw.* **melen.**
melys *a.* sweet; **melysion** sweets.
mellt *gw.* **mellten.**
mellten *e.b.* *ll.* **mellt** lightning: **fel mellten** like a flash *(of lightning)*, fast.
melltith *e.b.* *ll.* **-ion** curse: **Melltith arno!** Curse him!.
menig *gw.* **maneg.**
menter *e.b.* *ll.* **mentrau** venture, hazard.
mentrau *gw.* **menter.**
mentro (ar)*be.* **(mentraf)** to venture.
mentrus *a.* venturesome.
mentyll *gw.* **mantell.**
menthyca *gw.* **benthyca.**
menyn: ymenyn *e.g.* butter; **blodau menyn** buttercups.
menyw 1 *e.b.* *ll.* **-od** woman. 2 *a.* female *(S.W.).*
mêr *e.g.* *ll.* **merion** marrow.
merch *e.b.* *ll.* **-ed** girl.
Mercher *e.g.* Wednesday; Mercury: **Dydd Mercher Lludw** Ash Wednesday.
merchetaidd *a.* effeminate.
merf *gw.* **berf.**
merfa *gw.* **berfa.**
merfenw *gw.* **berfenw.**
merlod *gw.* **merlyn.**
merlota *bf.* to go pony-trekking.
merlotwr *e.g.* *ll.* **merlotwyr** pony-trekker.
merlyn *e.g.* *ll.* **-nod, merlod** pony.
merthyr *e.g.* *ll.* **-on** martyr: **Merthyr Tudful** valley town in South Wales.
merw *gw.* **berw.**
merwi *gw.* **berwi.**
mesen *e.b.* *ll.* **mes** acorn.
mesul *ad.* in the measure of: **Daeth y plant ymlaen fesul un** The children came in one by one; **fesul tri** three at a time.
mesur *e.g.* *ll.* **-au** 1 measure, metre; **ffon fesur** rule, ruler. 2 *be.* to measure.
mesurydd *e.g.* *ll.* **-ion** measurer, meter, gauge: **mesurydd glaw** rain gauge.
metel *e.g.* *ll.* **-oedd, -au** metal; mettle.
metr *e.g.* *ll.* **-au** metre: **metr sgwâr** square metre.
metrig *a.* metric.
methiant *e.g.* *ll.* **methiannau** failure.
methu (â) *be.* **(methaf)** to fail.
meudwy *e.g.* *ll.* **-aid, -od** hermit, recluse.
mewian *be.* **(mewiaf)** to mew.
mewn *ardd.* in, within; **i mewn: i fewn** in, inward(s): **mewn a maes** in and out; **mewn bod** in being, extant; **mewn cariad** in love; **mewn eiliad** in a moment, at once, instantly; **mewn gwaith** in work, employed; **mewn llaw** in hand, receiving attention, under consideration; **mewn trefn** in order; **o fewn y mis** within the month; **y tu mewn: y tu fewn** inside.
mewnwr *e.g.* *ll.* **mewnwyr** scrum-

half *(rugby)*, inside-forward *(soccer)*.
meysydd *gw.* **maes.**
mha *gw.* **pa.**
Mhab *gw.* **Pab.**
mhabell *gw.* **pabell.**
mhabi *gw.* **pabi.**
mhabydd *gw.* **pabydd.**
mhac *gw.* **pac.**
mhaced *gw.* **paced.**
mhacio *gw.* **pacio.**
mhadell *gw.* **padell.**
mhader *gw.* **pader.**
mhaent *gw.* **paent.**
mhafiliwn *gw.* **pafiliwn.**
mhafin *gw.* **pafin.**
mhagan *gw.* **pagan.**
mhais *gw.* **pais.**
mhâl *gw.* **pâl.**
mhalas *gw.* **palas.**
mhalau: mhalod *gw.* **pâl.**
mhalu *gw.* **palu.**
mhamffled *gw.* **pamffled.**
mhamffledyn *gw.* **pamffledyn.**
mhanasen *gw.* **panasen.**
mhanel *gw.* **panel.**
mhannas *gw.* **panasen.**
mhant *gw.* **pant.**
mhapur *gw.* **papur.**
mhapuro *gw.* **papuro.**
mhâr *gw.* **pâr.**
mharagraff *gw.* **paragraff.**
mharatoi *gw.* **paratoi.**
mharc *gw.* **parc.**
mharch *gw.* **parch.**
mharchu *gw.* **parchu.**
mharchus *gw.* **parchus.**
mhardwn *gw.* **pardwn.**
mharhad *gw.* **parhad.**
mharsel *gw.* **parsel.**
mharti *gw.* **parti.**
Mhasg *gw.* **Pasg.**
mhasiant *gw.* **pasiant.**
mhatrwm *gw.* **patrwm.**
mhatrwn *gw.* **patrwn.**
mhatrymau *gw.* **patrwm.**
mhatrynau *gw.* **patrwn.**
mhawb *gw.* **pawb.**
mhawen *gw.* **pawen.**
mhebyll *gw.* **pabell.**
mhecyn *gw.* **pecyn.**
mhechadur *gw.* **pechadur.**
mhechod *gw.* **pechod.**
mhedair *gw.* **pedair.**
mhedol *gw.* **pedol.**
mhedwar *gw.* **pedwar.**
mhedwaredd *gw.* **pedwaredd.**
mhedwerydd *gw.* **pedwerydd.**
mheg *gw.* **peg.**
mhegwn *gw.* **pegwn.**
mhegynau *gw.* **pegwn.**
mheilot *gw.* **peilot.**
mheint *gw.* **peint.**
mheintio *gw.* **peintio.**
mheintiwr *gw.* **peintiwr.**
mheiriannau *gw.* **peiriant.**
mheiriant *gw.* **peiriant.**
mheisiau *gw.* **pais.**
mhêl *gw.* **pêl.**
mhelydr *gw.* **pelydr.**
mhellter *gw.* **pellter.**
mhen *gw.* **pen.**
mhenaethiaid *gw.* **pennaeth.**
mhenawdau *gw.* **pennawd.**
mhen-blwydd *gw.* **pen-blwydd.**
mhencadlys *gw.* **pencadlys.**
mhencampwr *gw.* **pencampwr.**
mhenderfyniad *gw.* **penderfyniad.**
mhenelin *gw.* **penelin.**
mhen-glin *gw.* **pen-glin.**
mhenillion *gw.* **pennill.**
mhen-lin *gw.* **pen-glin.**
mhennaeth *gw.* **pennaeth.**
mhennau *gw.* **pen.**
mhennawd *gw.* **pennawd.**
mhennill *gw.* **pennill.**
mhennod *gw.* **pennod.**
mhenodau *gw.* **pennod.**
mhenodi *gw.* **penodi.**
mhenodiad *gw.* **penodiad.**
mhenrhyn *gw.* **penrhyn.**
mhensaer *gw.* **pensaer.**
mhensil *gw.* **pensil.**
mhensiwn *gw.* **pensiwn.**
mhensiynwr *gw.* **pensiynwr.**
mhenteulu *gw.* **penteulu.**
mhentref *gw.* **pentref.**
mhentwr *gw.* **pentwr.**
mhêr *gw.* **pêr.**
mherchen: mherchennog *gw.* **perchen.**
mheren *gw.* **peren.**
mhererin *gw.* **pererin.**
mherfedd *gw.* **perfedd.**
mherffaith *gw.* **perffaith.**
mherffeithio *gw.* **perffeithio.**
mheri *gw.* **peri.**
mherl *gw.* **perl.**
mherllan *gw.* **perllan.**
mhersli *gw.* **persli.**
mherson *gw.* **person.**
mhersonoliaieth *gw.* **personoliaeth.**
mherth *gw.* **perth.**
mherthynas *gw.* **perthynas.**
mherygl *gw.* **perygl.**
mheswch *gw.* **peswch.**
mhesychiad *gw.* **pesychiad.**
mheth *gw.* **peth.**

mhiano *gw.* **piano.**
mhianydd *gw.* **pianydd.**
mhib *gw.* **pib.**
mhiben *gw.* **piben.**
mhicil *gw.* **picil.**
mhictiwr *gw.* **pictiwr.**
mhicwn *gw.* **picwnen.**
mhicwnen *gw.* **picwnen.**
mhigiad *gw.* **pigiad.**
mhigo *gw.* **pigo.**
mhil *gw.* **pil.**
mhiler *gw.* **piler.**
mhilion *gw.* **pil.**
mhili-pala *gw.* **pili-pala.**
mhilsen *gw.* **pilsen.**
mhilyn *gw.* **pilyn.**
mhin *gw.* **pin.**
mhîn *gw.* **pîn.**
mhinnau *gw.* **pin.**
mhinsio *gw.* **pinsio.**
mhinwydden *gw.* **pinwydden.**
mhioden *gw.* **pioden.**
mhisyn *gw.* **pisyn.**
mhlaid *gw.* **plaid.**
mhlan *gw.* **plan.**
mhlanced *gw.* **blanced, planced.**
mhlanhigyn *gw.* **planhigyn.**
mhlannu *gw.* **plannu.**
mhlant *gw.* **plant.**
mhlas *gw.* **plas.**
mhlasty *gw.* **plasty.**
mhlât *gw.* **plât.**
mhlatiau *gw.* **plât.**
mhleidiau *gw.* **plaid.**
mhleidlais *gw.* **pleidlais.**
mhleidleisiau *gw.* **pleidlais.**
mhleidleisio *gw.* **pleidleisio.**
mhleidleisiwr *gw.* **pleidleisiwr.**
mhlentyn *gw.* **plentyn.**
mhleser *gw.* **pleser.**
mhleserus *gw.* **pleserus.**
mhlesio *gw.* **plesio.**
mhlisgyn *gw.* **plisgyn.**
mhlisman: mhlismon *gw.* **plisman.**
mhlu *gw.* **pluen.**
mhluen *gw.* **pluen.**
mhluf *gw.* **plufyn.**
mhlufyn *gw.* **plufyn.**
mhlwc *gw.* **plwc.**
mhlwg *gw.* **plwg.**
mhlwm *gw.* **plwm.**
mhlwyf *gw.* **plwyf.**
mhlygu *gw.* **plygu.**
mhob *gw.* **pob.**
mhobi *gw.* **pobi.**
mhobl *gw.* **pobl.**
mhoblogaeth *gw.* **poblogaeth.**
mhobman *gw.* **pobman.**
mhobydd *gw.* **pobydd.**
mhoced *gw.* **poced.**
mhoen *gw.* **poen.**
mhoeni *gw.* **poeni.**
mhoenus *gw.* **poenus.**
mhoenydio *gw.* **poenydio.**
mhoer: mhoeri *gw.* **poer, poeri.**
mhoethi *gw.* **poethi.**
mholyn *gw.* **polyn.**
mhont *gw.* **pont.**
mhopeth *gw.* **popeth.**
mhopty *gw.* **popty.**
mhorfa *gw.* **porfa.**
mhorfeydd *gw.* **porfa.**
mhorffor *gw.* **porffor.**
mhortread *gw.* **portread.**
mhorth *gw.* **porth.**
mhorthladd *gw.* **porthladd.**
mhôs *gw.* **pôs.**
mhosibilrwydd *gw.* **posibilrwydd.**
mhost *gw.* **post.**
mhostman: mhostmon *gw.* **postman.**
mhostyn *gw.* **postyn.**
mhotel *gw.* **potel.**
mhowdr: mhowdwr *gw.* **powdr.**
mhowdrau *gw.* **powdr.**
mhowlen *gw.* **bowlen.**
mhraidd *gw.* **praidd.**
mhram *gw.* **pram.**
mhrawf *gw.* **prawf.**
mhregeth *gw.* **pregeth.**
mhregethu *gw.* **pregethu.**
mhregethwr *gw.* **pregethwr.**
mhreiddiau *gw.* **praidd.**
mhren *gw.* **pren.**
mhrennau *gw.* **pren.**
mhrentis *gw.* **prentis.**
mhrentisiaeth *gw.* **prentisiaeth.**
mhrentisiaid *gw.* **prentis.**
mhres *gw.* **pres.**
mhreseb *gw.* **preseb.**
mhresennol *gw.* **presennol.**
mhresenoldeb *gw.* **presenoldeb.**
mhresgripsiwn *gw.* **presgripsiwn.**
mhreswyl: mhreswylfod *gw.* **preswyl.**
mhridwerth *gw.* **pridwerth.**
mhridd *gw.* **pridd.**
mhrifardd *gw.* **prifardd.**
mhrifathrawes *gw.* **prifathrawes.**
mhrifathro *gw.* **prifathro.**
mhrifddinas *gw.* **prifddinas.**
mhrifeirdd *gw.* **prifardd.**
mhrifysgol *gw.* **prifysgol.**
mhriffordd *gw.* **priffordd.**
mhrinder *gw.* **prinder.**
mhrintio *gw.* **printio.**
mhriod *gw.* **priod.**
mhriodas *gw.* **priodas.**
mhriodi *gw.* **priodi.**

mhriodol *gw.* **priodol.**
mhris *gw.* **pris.**
mhroblem *gw.* **problem.**
mhrofi *gw.* **profi.**
mhrofiad *gw.* **profiad.**
mhrofion *gw.* **prawf.**
mhrofocio: mhryfocio *gw.* **profocio.**
mhroffid *gw.* **proffid.**
mhroffwyd *gw.* **proffwyd.**
mhryd *gw.* **pryd.**
Mhrydain *gw.* **Prydain.**
mhrydau *gw.* **pryd.**
mhryder *gw.* **pryder.**
mhrydferthwch *gw.* **prydferthwch.**
mhrydiau *gw.* **pryd.**
mhryf: mhryfedyn: mhryfyn *gw.* **pryf.**
mhryfocio *gw.* **profocio.**
mhrynhawn *gw.* **prynhawn.**
mhrynu *gw.* **prynu.**
mhrynwr *gw.* **prynwr.**
mhrysurdeb *gw.* **prysurdeb.**
mhulpud *gw.* **pulpud.**
mhum: mhump *gw.* **pum.**
mhunnau *gw.* **punt.**
mhunnoedd *gw.* **punt.**
mhunt *gw.* **punt.**
mhupur *gw.* **pupur.**
mhurfa *gw.* **purfa.**
mhuro *gw.* **puro.**
mhwdin *gw.* **pwdin.**
mhwdryn *gw.* **pwdryn.**
mhŵer *gw.* **pŵer.**
mhwll *gw.* **pwll.**
mhwllyn *gw.* **pwllyn.**
mhwmp *gw.* **pwmp.**
mhwnc *gw.* **pwnc.**
mhwrpas *gw.* **pwrpas.**
mhwrs *gw.* **pwrs.**
mhwyll *gw.* **pwyll.**
mhwyllgor *gw.* **pwyllgor.**
mhwynt *gw.* **pwynt.**
mhwys *gw.* **pwys.**
mhwysedd *gw.* **pwysedd.**
mhwysigrwydd *gw.* **pwysigrwydd.**
mhwyslais *gw.* **pwyslais.**
mhwyso *gw.* **pwyso.**
mhwyth *gw.* **pwyth.**
mhyllau *gw.* **pwll** *gw.* **pyllau.**
mhyllyn *gw.* **pyllyn.**
mhymtheg *gw.* **pymtheg.**
mhymthegfed *gw.* **pymthegfed.**
mhynciau *gw.* **pwnc.**
mhyped *gw.* **pyped.**
mhyrsau *gw.* **pwrs.**
mhyrth *gw.* **porth.**
mhys *gw.* **pysen.**
mhysen *gw.* **pysen.**
mhysgodyn *gw.* **pysgodyn.**
mhysgota *gw.* **pysgota.**
mhysgotwr *gw.* **pysgotwr.**
mhyst *gw.* **postyn.**
mhythefnos *gw.* **pythefnos.**
mi *gw.* **fi;** *geiryn (particle used before a verb) (N.W.); gw.* **fe.**
microdon: meicrodon *e.b.g.* micro-wave; microwave oven.
migwrn *e.g. ll.* **migyrnau.** ankle, knuckle.
mil *e.b. ll.* **-oedd** thousand.
mil *gw.* **bil.**
milfeddyg *e.g. ll.* **-on** veterinary surgeon.
milgi *e.g. ll.* **milgwn** greyhound: **fel milgi** swift, like a greyhound.
miliwn *e.b. ll.* **miliynau** million; **miliynydd** millionaire.
miloedd *gw.* **mil.**
milwr *e.g. ll.* **milwyr** soldier.
milltir *e.b. ll.* **-oedd** mile: **milltir sgwâr** square mile; immediate locality.
min *e.g. ll.* **-ion** lip; side, bank; (cutting) edge (of blade): **min y gyllell** the edge of the knife; **min y ffordd** the wayside; **min y môr** the sea-shore, seaside; **byw wrth fin y gyllell** to live from hand to mouth; *gw.* **bin.**
miniog *a.* sharp, keen, edged.
minlliw *e.g.* lipstick.
minnau *rhag.* I also, me.
mioleg *gw.* **bioleg.**
miri *e.g.* merriment, fun.
mis *e.g. ll.* **-oedd** month: **Mis Bach** February.
misged *gw.* **bisged.**
misgedi *gw.* **bisged.**
misgïen *gw.* **bisgïen.**
misglwyf *e.g.* menstruation, period.
misoedd *gw.* **mis.**
misol *a.* monthly.
misolyn *e.g. ll.* **misolion** monthly (magazine).
miwsig *e.g.* music.
mlaen *gw.* **blaen.**
mlaenor *gw.* **blaenor.**
mlaenwr *gw.* **blaenwr.**
mlagur *gw.* **blaguryn.**
mlaguryn *gw.* **blaguryn.**
mlaidd *gw.* **blaidd.**
mlanced *gw.* **blanced.**
mlas *gw.* **blas.**
mlasu *gw.* **blasu.**
mlawd *gw.* **blawd.**
mleiddiaid *gw.* **blaidd.**
mlew *gw.* **blewyn.**
mlewyn *gw.* **blewyn.**
mlinder *gw.* **blinder.**

mlino *gw.* **blino.**
mlodau *gw.* **blodyn.**
mlodeugerdd *gw.* **blodeugerdd.**
mlodfresychen *gw.* **blodfresychen.**
mlodyn *gw.* **blodyn.**
mloedd *gw.* **bloedd.**
mloeddio *gw.* **bloeddio.**
mlows *gw.* **blows.**
mlwch *gw.* **blwch.**
mlwydd *gw.* **blwydd.**
mlwyddyn *gw.* **blwyddyn.**
mlychau *gw.* **blwch.**
mlynedd *gw.* **blwyddyn.**
mlynyddoedd *gw.* **blwyddyn.**
mocs *gw.* **bocs.**
moch *gw.* **boch, mochyn.**
mochyn *e.g. ll.* **moch** pig. **fel mochyn** dirty, filthy, fat, like a pig.
mod *gw.* **bod.**
modfedd *e.b. ll.* **-i** inch.
modiau *gw.* **bawd.**
modloni *gw.* **bodloni.**
modrwy *e.b. ll.* **-on** ring: **modrwy aur** gold ring; **modrwy briodas** wedding-ring; **modrwy glust** ear-ring.
modryb *e.b. ll.* **-edd** aunt.
modur *e.g. ll.* **-on** motor.
modurwr *e.g. ll.* **modurwyr** motorist.
modd *e.g. ll.* **-ion** manner; means, wealth: **gwaetha'r modd** worse luck; **modd bynnag** however; **pa fodd?** how? *gw.* **bodd.**
moddhad *gw.* **boddhad.**
moddi *gw.* **boddi.**
moddion *e. ll.* means; medicine: **moddion gras** means of grace; *gw.* **modd.**
moel *a.* bare; bald.
moelni *e.g.* bareness; baldness.
moes *e.b. ll.* **-au** usual behaviour, habit, wont; *in plural:* manners; morals: **moesau da** good manners; good morals.
moesol *a.* ethical; moral.
moethus *a.* luxurious, comfortable.
mogi *be.* **(mogaf)** to suffocate, to smother: **Brawd mogi yw tagu** Suffocating is akin to choking, one is as bad as the other.
mol *gw.* **bol.**
mola *gw.* **bola.**
moli *be.* **(molaf)** to praise.
moliau *be.* **bol.**
mollt *gw.* **bollt.**
mom *gw.* **bom.**
Môn, Ynys *e.b.* Anglesey: **Môn Mam Cymru** Anglesey Mother of Wales.
môn *gw.* **bôn.**
moneddiges *gw.* **boneddiges.**
moneddigion *gw.* **bonheddwr.**
monheddwr *gw.* **bonheddwr.**
môr *e.g. ll.* **moroedd** sea, ocean: **Y Môr Canoldir** Mediterranean Sea; **Môr Iwerydd** Atlantic Ocean; **Môr Tawel** Pacific Ocean.
mor *ad. (followed by soft mutation, except for adjectives beginning with* **ll** *and* **rh***)* as, so, how: **mor dew â mochyn** as fat as a pig; **mor ddu â'r nos** as black as the night; **mor goch â thân** as red as fire; **mor wyn ag eira** as white as snow.
mord *gw.* **bord.**
mordau: mordydd *gw.* **bord.**
morddwyd *e.b. ll.* **-ydd** thigh.
more *gw.* **bore.**
morfa *e.b.g. ll.* **morfeydd** sea-marsh, bog, fen.
morfeydd *gw.* **morfa.**
morfil *e.g. ll.* **-od** whale.
morgais *e.g. ll.* **morgeisiau** mortgage.
Morgannwg *e.b.* Glamorgan: **De Morgannwg** South Glamorgan; **Gorllewin Morgannwg** West Glamorgan; **Morgannwg Ganol** Mid Glamorgan.
morgeisiau *gw.* **morgais.**
morgrugyn *e.g. ll.* **morgrug** ant.
morio *be.* **(moriaf)** to sail.
môr-leidr *e.g. ll.* **môr-ladron** pirate.
morlo *e.g. ll.* **morloi** seal.
moroedd *gw.* **môr.**
moron *gw.* **moronen.**
moronen *e.b. ll.* **moron** carrot.
morthwyl *e.g. ll.* **-ion** hammer.
morwr *e.g. ll.* **morwyr** sailor, seaman.
morwyn *e.b. ll.* **morynion** maid, girl, virgin: **y Forwyn Fair** the Virgin Mary.
morwyr *gw.* **morwr.**
mos *gw.* **bos.**
mosys *gw.* **bos.**
motwm *gw.* **botwm.**
motymau *gw.* **botwm.**
mowlen *gw.* **bowlen.**
mraich *gw.* **braich.**
mrain *gw.* **brân.**
mraint *gw.* **braint.**
mrân *gw.* **brân.**
mraslun *gw.* **braslun.**
mraster *gw.* **braster.**
mraw *gw.* **braw.**

mrawd *gw.* **brawd.**
mrawddeg *gw.* **brawddeg.**
mrecwast *gw.* **brecwast.**
mrech *gw.* **brech.**
mrechdan *gw.* **brechdan.**
mrechiad *gw.* **brechiad.**
mreichiau *gw.* **braich.**
mreichled *gw.* **breichled.**
mrenhines *gw.* **brenhines.**
mrenin *gw.* **brenin.**
mres *gw.* **bres.**
mrest *gw.* **brest.**
mresychen *gw.* **bresychen.**
mrethyn *gw.* **brethyn.**
mreuddwyd *gw.* **breuddwyd.**
mreuddwydio *gw.* **breuddwydio.**
mreuddwydion *gw.* **breuddwyd.**
mrifo *gw.* **brifo.**
mrig *gw.* **brig.**
mrigau *gw.* **brig, brigyn.**
mrigyn *gw.* **brigyn.**
mriwsionyn *gw.* **briwsionyn.**
mro *gw.* **bro.**
mrodorion *gw.* **brodor.**
mrodyr *gw.* **brawd.**
mroga *gw.* **broga.**
mron *gw.* **bron.**
mronfraith *gw.* **bronfraith.**
mronnau: mronnydd *gw.* **bron.**
mrown *gw.* **brown.**
mröydd *gw.* **bro.**
mrws: mrwsh *gw.* **brws.**
mrwsio: mrwsho *gw.* **brwsio.**
mrwsys: mrwshys *gw.* **brws.**
mrwydr *gw.* **brwydr.**
mrwydrau *gw.* **brwydr.**
mryd *gw.* **bryd.**
mryn *gw.* **bryn.**
mryniau *gw.* **bryn.**
mrys *gw.* **brys.**
mrysio *gw.* **brysio.**
muarth *gw.* **buarth.**
muchod *gw.* **buwch.**
mud *a.* dumb, mute.
mudiad *e.g. ll.* **-au** movement: **Mudiad Ysgolion Meithrin** (Welsh) Nursery Schools' Movement.
muddugoliaeth *gw.* **buddugoliaeth.**
mugail *gw.* **bugail.**
mugeiliaid *gw.* **bugail.**
mugeilio *gw.* **bugeilio.**
mul *e.g. ll.* **-od** donkey; mule.
munud *e.g.b. ll.* **-au** minute: **Arhoswch funud!** Wait a minute!
mur *e.g. ll.* **-iau** wall.
musnes *gw.* **busnes.**
muwch *gw.* **buwch.**
mwced *gw.* **bwced.**
mwg *e.g.* smoke.
mwgwd *e.g. ll.* **mygydau** mask.
mwlch *gw.* **bwlch.**
mwnci *e.g. ll.* **mwncïod** monkey.
mwrdeistref *gw.* **bwrdeistref.**
mwrdd *gw.* **bwrdd.**
mwriad *gw.* **bwriad.**
mws *gw.* **bws.**
mwstwr *e.g. ll.* **mystyrau** noise, commotion, bustle *(S.W.).*
mwthyn *gw.* **bwthyn.**
mwy 1 *a.* bigger, larger, greater, more, louder, longer, further. **2** *ad.* more. *Often followed by* **na** **(mwy na** more than): **mwy na digon** too much, excessive; **mwy na mwy** a lot, a great deal, very many, too much, exceedingly; **mwy na thebyg** more than likely; **mwy neu lai** more or less; *gw.* **mawr.**
mwyach *ad.* any more, any longer, again, henceforth.
mwyaf *gw.* **mawr.**
mwyar *gw.* **mwyaren.**
mwyaren *e.b. ll.* **mwyar** blackberry.
mwyd *gw.* **bwyd.**
mwydlen *gw.* **bwydlen.**
mwydo: mwyda *gw.* **bwydo.**
mwydod *gw.* **mwydyn.**
mwydyn *e.g. ll.* **mwydod** worm.
mwyn 1 *e.g. ll.* **-au** mineral; ore. **2** *e.g.* sake: **er mwyn** for the sake of: **er mwyn Duw** for God's sake. **3** *a.* gentle, mild, dear.
mwynhad *e.g.* enjoyment, pleasure.
mwynhau *be.* **(mwynhaf)** to enjoy; to become mild.
mwyta: myta *gw.* **bwyta.**
mychan *gw.* **bychan.**
myd *gw.* **byd.**
myddin *gw.* **byddin.**
myfi *rhag.* I, me, myself.
myfyrdod *e.g. ll.* **-au** meditation.
myfyrio *be.* **(myfyriaf)** to study, to meditate.
myfyriwr *e.g. ll.* **myfyrwyr** student: **myfyriwr hŷn** mature student.
myglyd *a.* smoky, close, stifling.
mygu *be.* **(mygaf)** to smoke; to smother; to suffocate.
mygydau *gw.* **mwgwd.**
mylchau *gw.* **bwlch.**
mynach *e.g. ll.* **-od, mynaich** monk.
mynachlog *e.b. ll.* **-ydd** monastery.
mynachod *gw.* **mynach.**
mynaich *gw.* **mynach.**
mynd: myned *be.* **(af)** to go, to proceed; *gw. At. Berfau.*
mynedfa *e.b. ll.* **mynedfeydd** entrance, passage.

mynedfeydd *gw.* **mynedfa.**
mynediad *e.g. ll.* **-au** admission, access, entry, going: **mynediad am ddim** admission free.
mynegai *e.g. ll.* **mynegeion** index, concordance.
mynegeion *gw.* **mynegai.**
mynegi (i) *be.* **(mynegaf)** to tell, to indicate.
mynnu *be.* **(mynnaf)** to will, to insist, to wish, to obtain.
mynwent *e.b. ll.* **-ydd** graveyard, churchyard, cemetery.
mynydd *e.g. ll.* **-oedd** mountain; **llosgfynydd** volcano.
mynyddig: mynyddog *a.* mountainous.
myrbryd *gw.* **byrbryd.**
myrddau *gw.* **bwrdd.**
myrfodd *gw.* **byrfodd.**
myrfoddau *gw.* **byrfodd.**
myrr *e.g.* myrrh.
mys *gw.* **bys.**
mysedd *gw.* **bys.**
mysiau *gw.* **bws.**
mystyrau *gw.* **mwstwr.**
mysys *gw.* **bws.**
myta *gw.* **bwyta.**
myth *e.g. ll.* **-au** myth.
mythynnod *gw.* **bwthyn.**
myw *gw.* **byw.**
mywyd *gw.* **bywyd.**
mywydeg *gw.* **bywydeg.**

na 1 *c.* (*followed by spirant mutation*) nor, neither, than. 2 *ad.* no, not; *gw.* **da.** *At. Treigladau.*
nabod *gw.* **adnabod.**
nac 1 *c.* neither, nor. 2 *ad.* no, not.
nad *ad.* not.
nadansoddi *gw.* **dadansoddi.**
nadl *gw.* **dadl.**
nadlau *gw.* **dadlau.**
Nadolig *e.g.* *ll.* **-au** Christmas: **Nadolig llawen** Merry Christmas.
nadredd: nadroedd *gw.* **neidr.**
naddo *ad.* no (*negative answer to questions using verbs in the past tense*): **Fuest ti yn y dre ddoe? Naddo.** Were you in the town yesterday? No. **Ganodd e gyda'r côr? Naddo.** Did he sing with the choir? No. **Fuoch chi yn Rhos erioed? Naddo.** Were you ever in Rhos? No.
naddu *be.* **(naddaf)** to chip, to hew, to whittle.
naear *gw.* **daear.**
naeareg *gw.* **daeareg.**
naeargryn *gw.* **daeargryn.**
naearyddiaeth *gw.* **daearyddiaeth.**
nafad *gw.* **dafad.**
nag *c.* than.
nage *ad.* not so, no.
nagrau *gw.* **deigryn.**
nai *e.g.* *ll.* **neiaint** nephew.
naid *e.g.* *ll.* **neidiau** jump, leap, bound.
nail *gw.* **dalen, deilen.**
naill *rhag.* the one, either: **y naill neu'r llall** the one or the other; **naill ai Ebrill neu Fai** either April or May.
nain *e.b.* *ll.* **neiniau** grandmother (*N.W.*); *gw.* **mam-gu.**
naioni *gw.* **daioni.**
nal: nala *gw.* **dal.**
nalen *gw.* **dalen.**
nalgylch *gw.* **dalgylch.**
nallu *gw.* **dallu.**
nam *e.g.* *ll.* **-au** flaw, blemish, mark.
nameg *gw.* **dameg.**
namhegion *gw.* **dameg.**
namwain *gw.* **damwain.**
nanfon *gw.* **danfon.**
nangos *gw.* **dangos.**
nannedd *gw.* **dannedd.**
nannoedd *gw.* **dannoedd.**
nant *e.b.* *ll.* **nentydd** brook, stream; *gw.* **dant.**
narganfod *gw.* **darganfod.**
narlith *gw.* **darlith.**
narlithio *gw.* **darlithio.**
narlithiwr: narlithydd *gw.* **darlithiwr.**
narlun *gw.* **darlun.**
narlunio *gw.* **darlunio.**
narlledu *gw.* **darlledu.**
narllen *gw.* **darllen.**
narllenwr: narllenydd *gw.* **darllenwr.**
narn *gw.* **darn.**
natblygiad *gw.* **datblygiad.**
natblygu *gw.* **datblygu.**
natgan *gw.* **datgan.**
natganiad *gw.* **datganiad.**
natganoli *gw.* **datganoli.**
natguddio *gw.* **datguddio.**
natod *gw.* **datod.**
natrys *gw.* **datrys.**
natur *e.b.* nature; temper.
naturiol *a.* natural.
nathlu *gw.* **dathlu.**
nau *gw.* **dau.**
naw 1 *a.* nine. 2 *e.g.* nine: **naw deg** ninety; **naw deg un** ninety one; **deunaw** eighteen; **naw wfft ichi!** blow you!
nawdd *e.g.* refuge; patronage, support.
nawns *gw.* **dawns.**
nawnsio *gw.* **dawnsio.**
nawr *ad.* now: *gw.* **rŵan.**
naws *e.b.* *ll.* **-au** feeling, nature, tingle, disposition, nuance: **naws y gaeaf** feeling of winter; **naws oer** cold feeling.
ne *gw.* **de.**
neall *gw.* **deall.**
neb *e.g.* anyone, no one: **Does neb yma** There's no one here.
nechrau *gw.* **dechrau.**
nechreuad *gw.* **dechreuad.**
neddf *gw.* **deddf.**
neddfu *gw.* **deddfu.**
nef: nefoedd *e.b.* heaven: **Nefoedd**

Wen! Good heavens!
nefol: nefolaidd *a.* heavenly.
nefnydd *gw.* **defnydd.**
nefnyddio *gw.* **defnyddio.**
neffro *gw.* **deffro.**
neg: neng *gw.* **deg.**
negawd *gw.* **degawd.**
neges *e.b.* *ll.* **-au** message, errand; **negesydd** messenger.
negyddol *a.* negative.
neiaint *gw.* **nai.**
neialog *gw.* **deialog.**
neidiau *gw.* **naid.**
neidio *be.* **(neidiaf)** to jump, to leap.
neidiwr *e.g.* *ll.* **neidwyr** jumper, leaper.
neidr *e.b.* *ll.* **nadroedd, nadredd** snake.
neidwyr *gw.* **neidiwr.**
neigryn *gw.* **deigryn.**
neilen *gw.* **deilen.**
neilliaid: neillion *gw.* **dall.**
neilltu *e.g.* one side; **o'r neilltu** apart, aside.
neilltuo *be.* **(neilltuaf)** to reserve, to set aside, to earmark.
neilltuol *a.* special, particular, peculiar: **yn neilltuol o oer** particularly cold.
neiniau *gw.* **nain.**
neintydd *gw.* **deintydd.**
neis *a.* nice.
neiseb *gw.* **deiseb.**
neithiwr ad. last night.
nelw *gw.* **delw.**
nen *e.b.* *ll.* **-nau, -noedd** ceiling; heaven, sky.
nenfwd *e.g.* *ll.* **nenfydau** ceiling.
nentydd *gw.* **nant.**
nenu *gw.* **denu.**
nerbyn *gw.* **derbyn.**
nerbynneb *gw.* **derbynneb.**
nerf *e.b.* *ll.* **-au** nerve.
nerfus *a.* nervous.
neri *gw.* **deri.**
nerth *e.g.* *ll.* **-oedd** strength, might, power.
nerthoedd *gw.* **nerth.**
nerw *gw.* **derw.**
nerwen *gw.* **derwen.**
nes *c.* & *ardd.* until; *gw.* **agos.**
nesaf *a.* next; *gw.* **agos.**
nesáu (at) *be.* **(nesâf)** to approach, to draw near.
nesed *gw.* **agos.**
nesg *gw.* **desg.**
netholiad *gw.* **detholiad.**
neu *c.* (*followed by soft mutation*) or: **bachgen neu ferch** boy or girl; **eira neu law** rain or snow.
Note: conjugated forms of verbs do not *mutate after* ***neu:*** **Rhedodd neu cerddodd** He walked or ran; **Holais neu gofynnais** I questioned or asked.
neuadd *e.b.* *ll.* **-au** hall: **Neuadd Gyhoeddus** Public Hall; **Neuadd Les** Welfare Hall.
neuawd *gw.* **deuawd.**
neuddeg *gw.* **deuddeg.**
neuddegfed *gw.* **deuddegfed.**
neugain *gw.* **deugain.**
neunaw *gw.* **deunaw.**
neuoedd *gw.* **dau.**
newid 1 *be.* **(newidiaf)** to change, to alter. **2** *e.g.* *ll.* **-iadau** change.
newin *gw.* **dewin.**
newis *gw.* **dewis.**
newydd 1 *a.* new; **newydd sbon** brand new. **2** *e.g.* *ll.* **-ion** news; **papur newydd** newspaper.
newydd-ddyfodiad *e.g.* *ll.* **newydd-ddyfodiaid** newcomer.
newyddiadurwr *e.g.* *ll.* **newyddiadurwyr** journalist.
newyddion *gw.* **newydd.**
newyn *e.g.* famine, hunger.
nhabl *gw.* **tabl.**
nhabled *gw.* **tabled.**
nhacl *gw.* **tacl.**
nhaclo *gw.* **taclo.**
nhaclu *gw.* **taclu.**
nhaclwr *gw.* **taclwr.**
Nhachwedd *gw.* **Tachwedd.**
nhad *gw.* **tad.**
nhad-cu *gw.* **tad-cu.**
nhafarn *gw.* **tafarn.**
nhafarnwr *gw.* **tafarnwr.**
nhafell *gw.* **tafell.**
nhaflegryn *gw.* **taflegryn.**
nhaflen *gw.* **taflen.**
nhaflu *gw.* **taflu.**
nhafod *gw.* **tafod.**
nhafodiaith *gw.* **tafodiaith.**
nhafol *gw.* **tafol.**
nhagfa *gw.* **tagfa.**
nhagu *gw.* **tagu.**
nhangnefedd *gw.* **tangnefedd.**
nhai *gw.* **tŷ.**
nhaid *gw.* **taid.**
nhair *gw.* **tair.**
nhaith *gw.* **taith.**
nhâl *gw.* **tâl.**
nhalai *gw.* **talai.**
nhalaith *gw.* **talaith.**
nhalcen *gw.* **talcen.**
nhaleb *gw.* **taleb.**

nhalent *gw*. **talent.**
nhaloedd *gw*. **tâl.**
nhalu *gw*. **talu.**
nhalwr *gw*. **talwr.**
nhalwrn *gw*. **talwrn.**
nhamaid *gw*. **tamaid.**
nhameidiau *gw*. **tamaid.**
nhân *gw*. **tân.**
nhanau *gw*. **tân.**
nhancer *gw*. **tancer.**
nhanio *gw*. **tanio.**
nhannau *gw*. **tant.**
nhanseilio *gw*. **tanseilio.**
nhant *gw*. **tant.**
nhanwydd *gw*. **tanwydd.**
nhap *gw*. **tap.**
nhâp *gw*. **tâp.**
nhapiau *gw*. **tap, tâp.**
nharan *gw*. **taran.**
nharddiad *gw*. **tarddiad.**
nharged *gw*. **targed.**
nharian *gw*. **tarian.**
nhariannau *gw*. **tarian.**
nharo *gw*. **taro.**
nharw *gw*. **tarw.**
nhasg *gw*. **tasg.**
nhasgu *gw*. **tasgu.**
nhaten *gw*. **taten.**
nhato: nhatws *gw*. **taten.**
nhawelu *gw*. **tawelu.**
nhawelwch *gw*. **tawelwch.**
nhawelydd *gw*. **tawelydd.**
nhawelyn *gw*. **tawelyn.**
nhe *gw*. **te.**
nhebot *gw*. **tebot.**
nhebygrwydd *gw*. **tebygrwydd.**
nhecell *gw*. **tecell.**
nhechneg *gw*. **techneg.**
nhechnegwr *gw*. **technegwr.**
nhechnoleg *gw*. **technoleg.**
nhegan *gw*. **tegan.**
nhegell *gw*. **tecell.**
nhegwch *gw*. **tegwch.**
nhei *gw*. **tei.**
nheiar *gw*. **teiar.**
nheidiau *gw*. **taid.**
nheigr *gw*. **teigr.**
nheiliwr *gw*. **teiliwr.**
nheilsen *gw*. **teilsen.**
nheilwres *gw*. **teilwres.**
nheilyngdod *gw*. **teilyngdod.**
nheimlad *gw*. **teimlad.**
nheimlo *gw*. **teimlo.**
nheipiadur *gw*. **teipiadur.**
nheisen *gw*. **teisen.**
nheitl *gw*. **teitl.**
nheithiau *gw*. **taith.**
nheithio *gw*. **teithio.**
nheithiwr *gw*. **teithiwr.**
nhelediad *gw*. **telediad.**
nheledu *gw*. **teledu.**
nheleffon *gw*. **teleffon.**
nhelyn *gw*. **telyn.**
nhelyneg *gw*. **telyneg.**
nhelynor *gw*. **telynor.**
nhelynores *gw*. **telynores.**
nhelynorion *gw*. **telynor.**
nheml *gw*. **teml.**
nherfyn *gw*. **terfyn.**
nherfysg *gw*. **terfysg.**
nherfysgaeth *gw*. **terfysgaeth.**
nherfysgwr *gw*. **terfysgwr.**
nherm *gw*. **term.**
nhes *gw*. **tes.**
nhestun *gw*. **testun.**
nheulu *gw*. **teulu.**
nheyrnas *gw*. **teyrnas.**
nhiced *gw*. **ticed.**
nhîm *gw*. **tîm.**
nhip *gw*. **tip.**
nhipyn *gw*. **tipyn.**
nhir *gw*. **tir.**
nhirlun *gw*. **tirlun.**
nhiroedd *gw*. **tir.**
nhlodi *gw*. **tlodi.**
nhlws *gw*. **tlws.**
nhlysau *gw*. **tlws.**
nho *gw*. **to.**
nhocyn *gw*. **tocyn.**
nhocynnwr *gw*. **tocynnwr.**
nhoddi *gw*. **toddi.**
nhoes *gw*. **toes.**
nhoiled *gw*. **toiled.**
nholc *gw*. **tolc.**
nholl *gw*. **toll.**
nhon *gw*. **ton.**
nhôn *gw*. **tôn.**
nhonau *gw*. **tôn.**
nhonfedd *gw*. **tonfedd.**
nhonnau *gw*. **ton.**
nhorch *gw*. **torch.**
nhorf *gw*. **torf.**
nhorfeydd *gw*. **torf.**
nhoriad *gw*. **toriad.**
nhorri *gw*. **torri.**
nhors *gw*. **tors.**
nhorth *gw*. **torth.**
nhosau *gw*. **tosyn.**
nhost *gw*. **tost.**
nhostrwydd *gw*. **tostrwydd.**
nhosyn *gw*. **tosyn.**
nhrachwant *gw*. **trachwant.**
nhraddodiad *gw*. **traddodiad.**
nhraed *gw*. **troed.**
nhraeth *gw*. **traeth.**
nhraethau *gw*. **traeth.**
nhraethawd *gw*. **traethawd.**
nhrafnidiaeth *gw*. **trafnidiaeth.**

nhrafod *gw.* **trafod.**
nhrafferth *gw.* **trafferth.**
nhrafferthu *gw.* **trafferthu.**
nhraffordd *gw.* **traffordd.**
nhraffyrdd *gw.* **traffordd.**
nhrai *gw.* **trai.**
nhrais *gw.* **trais.**
nhrallod *gw.* **trallod.**
nhrallwysiad *gw.* **trallwysiad.**
nhrap *gw.* **trap.**
nhraul *gw.* **traul.**
nhrawsblannu *gw.* **trawsblannu.**
nhrawst *gw.* **trawst.**
nhrechu *gw.* **trechu.**
nhref: nhre *gw.* **tref.**
nhrefn *gw.* **trefn.**
nhrefnu *gw.* **trefnu.**
nhrefnydd *gw.* **trefnydd.**
nhrefydd *gw.* **tref.**
nhreial *gw.* **treial.**
nhreiglad *gw.* **treiglad.**
nhreiglo *gw.* **treiglo.**
nhreisio *gw.* **treisio.**
nhrên *gw.* **trên.**
nhrenau *gw.* **trên.**
nhreth *gw.* **treth.**
nhrethdalwr *gw.* **trethdalwr.**
nhrethu *gw.* **trethu.**
nhreuliau *gw.* **traul.**
nhreulio *gw.* **treulio.**
nhri *gw.* **tri.**
nhriawd *gw.* **triawd.**
nhric *gw.* **tric.**
nhrigain *gw.* **trigain.**
nhrigfan *gw.* **trigfan.**
nhrigolion *gw.* **trigolion.**
nhrin *gw.* **trin.**
nhrindod *gw.* **trindod.**
nhrioedd *gw.* **trioedd.**
nhriongl *gw.* **triongl.**
nhristwch *gw.* **tristwch.**
nhro *gw.* **tro.**
nhrochi *gw.* **trochi.**
nhroeau *gw.* **tro.**
nhroed *gw.* **troed.**
nhroedfedd *gw.* **troedfedd.**
nhroedffordd *gw.* **troedffordd.**
nhröedigaeth *gw.* **tröedigaeth.**
nhroedio *gw.* **troedio.**
nhroeon *gw.* **tro.**
nhrogylch *gw.* **trogylch.**
nhroi *gw.* **troi.**
nhrosedd *gw.* **trosedd.**
nhroseddwr *gw.* **troseddwr.**
nhrosgais *gw.* **trosgais.**
nhrosglwyddo *gw.* **trosglwyddo.**
nhrosiad *gw.* **trosiad.**
nhroswr *gw.* **troswr.**
nhrothwy *gw.* **trothwy.**
nhrowsus *gw.* **trowsus.**
nhruan *gw.* **truan.**
nhrueni *gw.* **trueni.**
nhrugaredd *gw.* **trugaredd.**
nhrwbl *gw.* **trwbl.**
nhrwser *gw.* **trwser.**
nhrwsiwr *gw.* **trwsiwr.**
nhrwydded *gw.* **trwydded.**
nhrwyn *gw.* **trwyn.**
nhrychineb *gw.* **trychineb.**
nhrydan *gw.* **trydan.**
nhrydanwr *gw.* **trydanwr.**
nhrydedd *gw.* **trydedd.**
nhrydydd *gw.* **trydydd.**
nhrysor *gw.* **trysor.**
nhrysorfa *gw.* **trysorfa.**
nhrysori *gw.* **trysori.**
nhrysorydd *gw.* **trysorydd.**
nhrywydd *gw.* **trywydd.**
nhudalen *gw.* **tudalen.**
nhueddiad *gw.* **tueddiad.**
nhun *gw.* **tun.**
nhunnell *gw.* **tunnell.**
nhw: hwy *rhag.* they, them: **Ble maen nhw?** Where are they? **Gwelodd nhw** He/she saw them.
nhwlc *gw.* **twlc.**
nhwll *gw.* **twll.**
nhwmpath *gw.* **twmpath.**
nhwndis *gw.* **twndis.**
nhwnel *gw.* **twnel.**
nhwpsyn *gw.* **twpsyn.**
nhŵr *gw.* **tŵr.**
nhwr *gw.* **twr.**
nhwrci *gw.* **twrci.**
nhwristiaeth *gw.* **twristiaeth.**
nhwrw *gw.* **twrw.**
nhwyll *gw.* **twyll.**
nhwyllo *gw.* **twyllo.**
nhwymo *gw.* **twymo.**
nhwymyn *gw.* **twymyn.**
nhŷ *gw.* **tŷ.**
nhybied: nhybio *gw.* **tybied.**
nhyddyn *gw.* **tyddyn.**
nhyddynnwr *gw.* **tyddynnwr.**
nhyfiant *gw.* **tyfiant.**
nhyfu *gw.* **tyfu.**
nhynged *gw.* **tynged.**
nhyle *gw.* **tyle.**
nhylwyth *gw.* **tylwyth.**
nhyllau *gw.* **twll.**
nhyllu *gw.* **tyllu.**
nhylluan *gw.* **tylluan.**
nhymer *gw.* **tymer.**
nhymestl *gw.* **tymestl.**
nhymheredd *gw.* **tymheredd.**
nhymhorau *gw.* **tymor.**
nhymor *gw.* **tymor.**
nhyner *gw.* **tyner.**

nhynerwch *gw.* **tynerwch.**
nhynnu *gw.* **tynnu.**
nhyrfa *gw.* **tyrfa.**
nhyst *gw.* **tyst.**
nhystiolaeth *gw.* **tystiolaeth.**
nhystysgrif *gw.* **tystysgrif.**
nhywel *gw.* **tywel.**
nhywod *gw.* **tywod.**
nhywydd *gw.* **tywydd.**
nhywyllu *gw.* **tywyllu.**
nhywyllwch *gw.* **tywyllwch.**
nhywys *gw.* **tywys.**
nhwysog *gw.* **tywysog.**
nhywysoges *gw.* **tywysoges.**
ni *rhag.* we, us.
ni: nid *ad.* not.
niacon *gw.* **diacon.**
niafol *gw.* **diafol.**
nial *gw.* **dial.**
nianc *gw.* **dianc.**
niawl *gw.* **diawl.**
niawliaid *gw.* **diafol, diawl.**
niben *gw.* **diben.**
nid *gw.* **ni.**
niddordeb *gw.* **diddordeb.**
nieithryn *gw.* **dieithryn.**
nifer (o) *e.g.b. ll.* **-oedd, -i** number, quantity: **nifer o fechgyn** a number of boys.
niferyn *gw.* **diferyn.**
nifetha *gw.* **difetha.**
nifyrru *gw.* **difyrru.**
niffiniad *gw.* **diffiniad.**
niffinio *gw.* **diffinio.**
niffodd *gw.* **diffodd.**
niffyg *gw.* **diffyg.**
nigon *gw.* **digon.**
nigonedd *gw.* **digonedd.**
nigwyddiad *gw.* **digwyddiad.**
nihareb *gw.* **dihareb.**
niheintydd *gw.* **diheintydd.**
nihuno *gw.* **dihuno.**
nileu *gw.* **dileu.**
nilyn *gw.* **dilyn.**
nillad *gw.* **dilledyn.**
nilledyn *gw.* **dilledyn.**
nim *gw.* **dim.**
ninas *gw.* **dinas.**
ninasyddion *gw.* **dinesydd.**
ninesydd *gw.* **dinesydd.**
ninistrio *gw.* **dinistrio.**
ninnau *rhag.* we also.
niod *gw.* **diod.**
nioddef *gw.* **dioddef.**
niogi *gw.* **diogi.**
niogyn *gw.* **diogyn.**
niolch *gw.* **diolch.**
niolchgarwch *gw.* **diolchgarwch.**
nirgelwch *gw.* **dirgelwch.**
nirprwy *gw.* **dirprwy.**
nirprwyaeth *gw.* **dirprwyaeth.**
nirwy *gw.* **dirwy.**
nis *ad.* not . . . him/her/it/them; **nis gwelais** I did not see him/etc.
nisg *gw.* **disg.**
nisgrifiad *gw.* **disgrifiad.**
nisgrifio *gw.* **disgrifio.**
nisgwyl *gw.* **disgwyl.**
nisgybl *gw.* **disgybl.**
nisgyblaeth *gw.* **disgyblaeth.**
nisgyn *gw.* **disgyn.**
nistawrwydd *gw.* **distawrwydd.**
nistewi *gw.* **distewi.**
niswyddo *gw.* **diswyddo.**
nith *e.b. ll.* **-oedd** niece.
niwallu *gw.* **diwallu.**
niwed *e.g. ll.* **niweidiau** harm, damage, injury: **gwneud niwed i** to harm.
niwedd *gw.* **diwedd.**
niweddglo *gw.* **diweddglo.**
niweidiau *gw.* **niwed.**
niwl *e.g. ll.* **-oedd** mist, haze; **niwl trwchus** fog.
niwlog *a.* misty, foggy, hazy.
niwrnod *gw.* **diwrnod.**
niwydiant *gw.* **diwydiant.**
niwygiad *gw.* **diwygiad.**
niwygio *gw.* **diwygio.**
niwylliant *gw.* **diwylliant.**
noc *gw.* **doc.**
noctor *gw.* **doctor.**
nod *e.g.b. ll.* **-au, -ion** note; mark, token, aim.
nodau *gw.* **nod, nodyn.**
nodedig *a.* remarkable, noted, appointed, specified.
nodi *be.* **(nodaf)** to note, to mark, to appoint, to state; *gw.* **dodi.**
nodrefn *gw.* **dodrefnyn.**
nodrefnyn *gw.* **dodrefnyn.**
nodwedd *e.b. ll.* **-ion** character, feature, characteristic: **rhaglen nodwedd** feature programme.
nodweddiadol *a.* characteristic, typical.
nodwydd *e.b. ll.* **-au** needle.
nodyn *e.g. ll.* **nodau** note.
noddwr *e.g. ll.* **noddwyr** protector, patron.
noe *gw.* **doe.**
noeth *a.* naked, bare, exposed, raw, sheer.
noethineb *gw.* **doethineb.**
nofel *e.b. ll.* **-au** novel.
nofelwr: nofelydd *e.g. ll.* **nofelwyr** novelist.
nofiad *e.g.* a swim.

nofio *be.* **(nofiaf)** to swim.
nogfen *gw.* **dogfen.**
nol *gw.* **dol.**
nôl: hôl *be.* **(nolaf: holaf)** to fetch; *gw.* **dôl.**
nolen *gw.* **dolen.**
nolur *gw.* **dolur.**
Norman *e.g. ll.* **-iaid** Norman: **castell Normanaidd** Norman castle.
nos *e.b. ll.* **-au** night: **nos da** good night; **nos Sul** Sunday night; **nos yfory** tomorrow night.
nosbarth *gw.* **dosbarth.**
noson: noswaith *e.b. ll.* **nosweithiau** evening: **noswaith dda** good evening; **noson lawen** merry evening; **am ddwy noson** for two evenings.
nosweithiau *gw.* **noson.**
nraen: nraenen *gw.* **draen.**
nraenog *gw.* **draenog.**
nraig *gw.* **draig.**
nrain *gw.* **draen.**
nrama *gw.* **drama.**
nramodwr *gw.* **dramodwr.**
nramodydd *gw.* **dramodwr.**
nreigiau *gw.* **draig.**
nreser: nresel *gw.* **dreser.**
nrewdod *gw.* **drewdod.**
nringwr *gw.* **dringwr.**
nrudwy *gw.* **drudwy.**
nrwg *gw.* **drwg.**
nrwm *gw.* **drwm.**
nrws *gw.* **drws.**
nrych *gw.* **drych.**
nrychiolaeth *gw.* **drychiolaeth.**
nrygioni *gw.* **drygioni.**
nryll *gw.* **dryll.**
nryllau *gw.* **dryll.**
nrysau *gw.* **drws.**
nrysu *gw.* **drysu.**
nryw *gw.* **dryw.**
null *gw.* **dull.**
nuo *gw.* **duo.**
nur *gw.* **dur.**
nuw *gw.* **duw.**
nuwies *gw.* **duwies.**
nwfr *gw.* **dŵr**
nŵr *gw.* **dŵr.**
nwrn *gw.* **dwrn.**
nwsin *gw.* **dwsin.**
nwy *e.g. ll.* **-on, -au** gas: **Nwy Môr y Gogledd** North Sea gas; *gw.* **dwy.**
nwyau *gw.* **nwy.**
nwydd *e.g. ll.* **-au** material, article: **nwyddau** goods (*note: only the plural form is used*).
nwyon *gw.* **nwy.**
nwyieithrwydd *gw.* **dywieithrwydd.**
nwylo *gw.* **dwylo.**
nwyn *gw.* **dwyn.**
nwyrain *gw.* **dwyrain.**
nychmygion *gw.* **dychymyg.**
nychmygu *gw.* **dychmygu.**
nychymyg *gw.* **dychymyg.**
nydd *gw.* **dydd.**
nyddiad *gw.* **dyddiad.**
nyfarniad *gw.* **dyfarniad.**
nyfarnu *gw.* **dyfarnu.**
nyfarnwr *gw.* **dyfarnwr.**
nyfnder *gw.* **dyfnder.**
nyfodol *gw.* **dyfodol.**
nyfroedd *gw.* **dŵr.**
nyfyniad *gw.* **dyfyniad.**
nyffryn *gw.* **dyffryn.**
nylanwad *gw.* **dylanwad.**
nyled *gw.* **dyled.**
nyletswydd *gw.* **dyletswydd.**
nymuniad *gw.* **dymuniad.**
nyn *gw.* **dyn.**
nynes *gw.* **dynes.**
nyni *rhag.* we, us.
nyrnaid *gw.* **dyrnaid.**
nyrnau *gw.* **dwrn.**
nyrs *e.g.b. ll.* **-ys** nurse.
nyrsio *be.* **(nyrsiaf)** to nurse.
nysgl *gw.* **dysgl.**
nysgu *gw.* **dysgu.**
nysgwr *gw.* **dysgwr.**
nyth *e.b. ll.* **-od** nest: **nyth y dryw** the wren's nest.
nywediad *gw.* **dywediad.**
nyweddïad *gw.* **dyweddïad.**

o *ardd. (followed by soft mutation) (personal forms:* **ohono, ohonot, ohono/ohoni, ohonon, ohonoch, ohonyn)** from, of, out of: **o amgylch** around; **o chwith** wrongly, the wrong way about; **o flaen** before, ahead of; **o gwbl** at all; **o gwmpas** about, at all; **o hyd** still; **o'r blaen** beforehand, earlier, previously; **o'r diwedd** at last; **o'r gloch** o'clock; **o'r gorau** very well; *gw. At. Arddodiaid; gw.* **ef.**
obaith *gw.* **gobaith.**
obeithio *gw.* **gobeithio.**
obeithion *gw.* **gobaith.**
obennydd *gw.* **gobennydd.**
oblegid *c. & ardd* because, for.
ochenaid *e.b. ll.* **ocheneidiau** sigh.
ochneidio *be.* **(ochneidiaf)** to sigh, to groan.
ochr *e.b. ll.* **-au** side: **ochr yn ochr** side by side; **wrth ochr** beside; **yr ochr draw i** (on) the other side to.
od *a.* odd, bizarre; remarkable.
odidog *gw.* **godidog.**
odl *e.b. ll.* **-au** rhyme; ode, song.
odli *be.* **(odlaf)** to rhyme.
odre *gw.* **godre.**
odro *gw.* **godro.**
oddef *gw.* **goddef.**
oddeutu *ardd. & ad.* about, around.
oddi *ardd.* out of, from: **oddi allan** outside; **oddi ar** from off; since; **oddieithr** except, unless; **oddi mewn** within; **oddi wrth** from; **oddi yma** from here.
oddrych *gw.* **goddrych.**
oed *e.g. ll.* **-au** age; time: **blwydd oed** year old; **saith oed** seven years of age; **gwneud oed â** to arrange a tryst, to make a date.
oedfa *e.b. ll.* **-on, oedfeuon** service, meeting.
oedi *be.* **(oedaf)** to delay, to postpone; to linger.
oedolion *gw.* **oedolyn.**
oedolyn *e.g. ll.* **oedolion** adult.
oedran *e.g. ll.* **-nau** age.
oedrannus *a.* aged, elderly.
oedd *bf.* was, were; *gw.* **bod.**
oen *e.g. ll.* **ŵyn** lamb.
oer *a.* cold, chill, chilly; frigid.
oerfel *e.g.* cold.
oeri *be.* **(oeraf)** to cool, to become cold.
oes 1 *eb. ll.* **-au, -oedd** age, lifetime: **ers oes** from an age; **o oes i oes** from age to age; **yn oes oesoedd** for ever and ever. **2** *bf.* is, are; *gw.* **bod.**
of *gw.* **gof.**
ofal *gw.* **gofal.**
ofalu *gw.* **gofalu.**
ofalus *gw.* **gofalus.**
ofalwr *gw.* **gofalwr.**
ofer *a.* vain; prodigal; waste; **ymgais ofer** a vain attempt.
oferedd *e.g.* vanity, dissipation, frivolity.
ofergoel *e.b. ll.* **-ion** superstition.
ofergoeledd: ofergoeliaeth *e.g.* superstition.
ofergoelus *a.* superstitious.
ofid *gw.* **gofid.**
ofidio *gw.* **gofidio.**
ofn *e.g. ll.* **-au** fear, terror, dread: **Mae ofn arno fe** He is afraid; **Mae ofn llygod arna i** I am afraid of mice.
ofnadwy *a.* awful, dreadful, horrendous.
ofnau *gw.* **ofn.**
ofni *be.* **(ofnaf)** to fear, to dread.
ofnus *a.* timid, nervous.
ofod *gw.* **gofod.**
ofodwr *gw.* **gofodwr.**
ofyn *gw.* **gofyn.**
offeiriad *e.g. ll.* **offeiriaid** priest, parson.
offer *gw.* **offeryn.**
offeryn *e.g. ll.* **-nau, offer** instrument, tool, apparatus, equipment: **offeryn cerdd** musical instrument; **offeryn chwyth** wind instrument; **offeryn llinynnol** stringed instrument; **offerynnau taro** percussion instruments.
offerynnol *a.* instrumental; **darn offerynnol** instrumental piece *(of music).*
ogledd *gw.* **gogledd.**

ogleddol *gw.* **gogleddol.**
ogleddwr *gw.* **gogleddwr.**
ogof *e.b. ll.* **-au, -âu** cave, cavern; den.
ogoniant *gw.* **gogoniant.**
ogylch *ardd.* about.
ongl *e.b. ll.* **-au** angle: **ongl sgwâr** right angle; **triongl** triangle.
onglog *a.* angular.
oherwydd *c.* & *ardd.* because, for.
ôl 1 *e.g. ll.* **olion** mark, print; track; trace: **ôl bysedd** finger-marks; **ôl traed** footprints. **2** *a.* back, hint: **ar ôl** after; **pen ôl** behind, bottom *(buttocks);* **yn ôl** according to; ago; **y tu ôl i** behind.
olaf *a.* last *(the very last); gw.* **hwyr.**
olau *gw.* **golau.**
olchi *gw.* **golchi.**
olchydd *gw.* **golchydd.**
oleudy *gw.* **goleudy.**
oleuni *gw.* **goleuni.**
oleuo *gw.* **goleuo.**
olew *e.g. ll.* **-au** oil; **maes olew** oilfield.
olion *gw.* **ôl.**
ôl-nodiad *e.g. ll.* **ôl-nodiadau** postscript.
ôl-ofal *e.g. ll.* **ôl-ofalon** after-care.
olrhain *be.* **(olrheiniaf)** to trace, to track.
olud *gw.* **golud.**
olwg *gw.* **golwg.**
olwr *e.g. ll.* **olwyr** back *(rugby, etc.)*
olwyn *e.b. ll.* **-ion** wheel: **cadair olwynion** wheelchair; **olwyn fesur** trundle wheel.
olwyr *gw.* **olwr.**
olygfa *gw.* **golygfa.**
olygon *gw.* **golwg.**
olygu *gw.* **golygu.**
oll *ad.* all, wholly; ever, at all.
ollwng *gw.* **gollwng.**
ond 1 *c.* but, only. **2** *ardd.* except; save; but.
onest *gw.* **gonest.**
oni: onid 1 *ad.* not? is it not? **2** *c.* if not, unless. **3** *ardd.* except; save; but: **onid e?** otherwise; else; is it not?
onibai (am) *c.* were it not (for).
onid gw. **oni.**
onnen *e.b. ll.* **ynn** ash-tree.
opera *e.b. ll.* **operâu** opera: **opera ddigri** comic opera; **opera fawreddog** grand opera; **opera ysgafn** light opera; **opera sebon** soap opera.
optegwr: optegydd *e.g. ll.* **optegwyr** optician.
orau *gw.* **da.**
orchfygu *gw.* **gorchfygu.**
orchymyn *gw.* **gorchymyn.**
oren *e.g. ll.* **-au** orange.
orfod *gw.* **gorfod.**
orfodaeth *gw.* **gorfodaeth.**
orfodi *gw.* **gorfodi.**
orfodol *gw.* **gorfodol.**
orfoleddus *gw.* **gorfoleddus.**
orffen *gw.* **gorffen.**
Orffennaf *gw.* **Gorffennaf.**
orffennol *gw.* **gorffennol.**
orffwys *gw.* **gorffwys.**
orffwyso *gw.* **gorffwyso.**
organ *e.g.b. ll.* **-au** organ; **organ geg** mouth-organ.
organig *a.* organic.
organydd *e.g. ll.* **-ion** organist.
oriau *gw.* **awr.**
oriel *e.b. ll.* **-au** gallery.
orlawn *gw.* **gorlawn.**
orllewin *gw.* **gorllewin.**
ormod *gw.* **gormod.**
ornest *e.b. ll.* **-au** contest, combat, duel, match; *gw.* **gornest.**
orsaf *gw.* **gorsaf.**
orsedd *gw.* **gorsedd.**
oruchaf *gw.* **goruchaf.**
orwedd *gw.* **gorwedd.**
orwel *gw.* **gorwel.**
os *c.* if *(definite not conjecture).* **Os daw Tom, dof i hefyd** If Tom comes, I will come too.
osgoi *be.* **(osgoiaf)** to avoid, to swerve, to evade; to shirk: **ffordd-osgoi** bypass.
osod *gw.* **gosod.**
ostwng *gw.* **gostwng.**
ostyngedig *gw.* **gostyngedig.**
ostyngiad *gw.* **gostyngiad.**
owns *e.b. ll.* **-ys** ounce; **dwy owns** two ounces.

pa *a.* Which? What? **(Pa) beth?** What (thing)? **Pa bryd? Pryd?** When? **Pa fodd?** How? **P'un?** Which one? *gw.* **pam.**
Pab *e.g. ll.* **-au** Pope.
pabell *e.b. ll.* **pebyll** tent, pavilion.
pabi *e.b. ll.* **pabïau** poppy.
pabydd *e.g. ll.* **-ion** papist.
pac *e.g. ll.* **-au, -iau** pack, bundle.
paced *e.g. ll.* **-i** packet, package.
paciau *gw.* **pac.**
pacio *be.* **(paciaf)** to pack.
padell *e.b. ll.* **-i** bowl, pan.
pader *e.g. ll.* **-au** the Lord's prayer, prayers: **dweud pader/dysgu pader i berson** 'to teach your grandmother to suck eggs'.
paent *e.g. ll.* **-iau** paint.
pafiliwn *e.g.* pavilion.
pafin *e.g. ll.* **-au** pavement *(S.W.).*
pagan *e.g* **-iaid** pagan.
paham *gw.* **pam.**
pais *e.b. ll.* **peisiau** petticoat.
pâl 1 *e.b. ll.* **palau** spade *(S.W.).* 2 *e.g. ll.* **palod** puffin.
palas *e.g. ll.* **-au, -oedd** palace.
palau *gw.* **pâl.**
palmant *e.g. ll.* **-au** pavement *(N.W.).*
palod *gw.* **pâl.**
palu *be.* **(palaf)** to dig over *(not down).*
pallu *be.* **(pallaf)** to refuse, to fail, to cease, to lack.
pam: paham: pa *ad.* why?
pamffled *e.g. ll.* **-i, -au** pamphlet.
pamffledyn *e.g.* pamphlet.
pan *c.* when.
panasen *e.b. ll.* **pannas** parsnip.
panel *e.g. ll.* **-i** panel.
pannas *gw.* **panasen.**
pant *e.g. ll.* **-au, -iau** valley, hollow; dent: **Mae e bant** He's away; **o bant i bentan** from pillar to post.
papur *e.g. ll.* **-au** paper; **papur newydd** newspaper; **papur deg punt** ten-pound note; **papur wal** wall-paper.
papuro *be.* **(papuraf)** to paper.
pâr *e.g. ll.* **parau** pair.
para (i): parhau (i) *be.* **(paraf)** to continue (to).
paragraff *e.g. ll.* **-au** paragraph.
paratoi (i) *be.* **(paratoaf)** to prepare (to): **paratoi i fynd** to prepare to go.
parau *gw.* **pâr.**
parc *e.g. ll.* **-au, -iau** park; field *(S.W.W.).*
parch *e.g.* respect: **dillad parch** Sunday best, best clothes *(lit. the clothes of respect).*
parchedig *a. ll.* **-ion** *(often abbreviated to* **y parchg.** reverend, reverent: **Y Parchedig Ifan Rhys** Reverend Ifan Rhys.
parchu *be.* **(parchaf)** to respect.
parchus *be.* respectable, respectful.
pardwn *e.g. ll.* **pardynau** pardon.
parhad *e.g.* continuation.
parhau *gw.* **para.**
parod *a.* ready, willing, prepared: **yn barod** already; **arian parod** ready cash.
parsel *e.g. ll.* **-au, -i** parcel.
parti *e.g. ll.* **-ion** party.
Pasg *e.g.* Easter: **Dydd Llun y Pasg** Easter Monday; **wy Pasg** Easter egg; **y Pasg** Easter.
pasiannau *gw.* **pasiant.**
pasiant *e.g. ll.* **pasiannau** pageant.
patrwm *e.g. ll.* **patrymau** pattern.
patrwn *e.g. ll.* **patrynau** pattern.
patrymau *gw.* **patrwm.**
patrynau *gw.* **patrwn.**
pawb *e.g.* everybody, all.
pawen *e.b. ll.* **-nau** paw.
pe *cys.* if: **Pe bawn i yno** If I were there.
pebyll *gw.* **pabell.**
pecyn *e.g. ll.* **-nau** package, packet.
pechadur *e.g. ll.* **-iaid** sinner.
pechod *e.g. ll.* **-au** sin: **Dyna bechod!** What a pity!
pechu *be.* **(pechaf)** to sing; **pechu yn erbyn** to sin against.
pedair *e.b. & a.b. (adjective placed before feminine noun)* four: **pedair merch** four girls; **pedair cadair** four chairs; *gw.* **pedwar.**

pedol *e.b.* *ll.* **-au** horse-shoe.
pedwar *e.g.* *ll.* & *a.g.* four: *gw.* **pedair.**
pedwaredd *a.b.* fourth: **y bedwaredd ferch** the fourth girl.
pedwerydd *a.g.* fourth: **y pedwerydd bachgen** the fourth boy.
peg *e.g.* *ll.* **-iau** peg.
pegwn *e.g.* *ll.* **pegynau** pole: **Pegwn y De** South Pole; **Pegwn y Gogledd** North Pole.
pegynau *gw.* **pegwn.**
peidio (â) be. **(peidiaf)** to cease, to stop: **Paid (â) siarad** Don't talk.
peilot *e.g.* *ll.* **-iaid** pilot.
peint *e.g.* *ll.* **-iau** pint: **peint a hanner** a pint and a half.
peintio *be.* **(peintiaf)** to paint.
peintiwr *e.g.* *ll.* **peintwyr** painter.
peiriannau *gw.* **peiriant.**
peiriant *e.g.* *ll.* **peiriannau** engine, machine: **peiriant golchi** washing machine; **peiriant car** car engine; **peiriant gwnïo** sewing machine.
peisiau *gw.* **pais.**
pêl *e.b.* *ll.* **peli, pelau** ball: **pêl-droed** football; **pêl rygbi** rugby ball.
pelydr *e.g.* *ll.* **-au** ray, beam: **pelydr X** X ray.
pell *a.* far; *gw. At. Ansoddeiriau.*
pellach *gw.* **pell.**
pellaf *gw.* **pell.**
pelled *gw.* **pell.**
pellter *e.g.* *ll.* **-au, -oedd** distance: **yn y pellter** in the distance; **o bellter** from a distance.
pen 1 *e.g.* *ll.* **-nau** head, top, end, mouth: **ar ben** on top of, ended; **ar ei phen ei hun** by herself; **pen y bryn** top of the hill; **pen ôl** behind, bottom *(buttocks).* **2** *a.* chief, supreme.
penaethiaid *gw.* **pennaeth.**
penawdau *gw.* **pennawd.**
pen-blwydd *e.g.* *ll.* **-i** birthday.
pencadlys *e.g.* *ll.* **-oedd** headquarters.
pencampwr *e.g.* *ll.* **pencampwyr** champion.
pendant *a.* positive, definite, emphatic.
penderfyniad *e.g.* *ll.* **-au** resolution, determination.
penderfynol *a.* resolute, determined: **yn benderfynol o** determined to.
penderfynu *be.* **(penderfynaf)** to decide, to resolve: **Fe benderfynodd fynd** He decided to go.
penelin *e.g.b.* *ll.* **-oedd** elbow.
penfoel *a.* bald-headed.
pen-glin: pen-lin *e.b.* *ll.* **pengliniau: penliniau** knee.
penigamp *a.* splendid, excellent.
penillion *gw.* **pennill.**
pen-lin *gw.* **pen-glin.**
penlinio *be.* **(penliniaf)** to kneel.
pennaeth *e.g.* *ll.* **penaethiaid** chief.
pennaf *a.* principal, chief.
pennau *gw.* **pen.**
pennawd *e.g.* *ll.* **penawdau** heading: headline: **penawdau'r newyddion** the news headlines.
pennill *e.g.* *ll.* **penillion** stanza, verse.
pennod *e.b.* *ll.* **penodau** chapter.
penodau *gw.* **pennod.**
penodi *be.* **(penodaf)** to appoint.
penodiad *e.g.* *ll.* **-au** appointment.
penrhyn *e.g.* *ll.* **-au** promontory, headland.
pensaer *e.g.* *ll.* **penseiri** architect.
penseiri *gw.* **pensaer.**
pensil *e.g.* *ll.* **-iau** pencil.
pensiwn *e.g.* *ll.* **pensiynau** pension.
pensiynau *gw.* **pensiwn.**
pensiynwr *e.g.* *ll.* **pensiynwyr** pensioner.
penteulu *e.g.* *ll.* **-oedd** head of family.
pentref *e.g.* *ll.* **-i** village.
pentwr *e.g.* *ll.* **pentyrrau** heap, mass, pile.
pentyrrau *gw.* **pentwr.**
pêr *a.* sweet *(of sound); gw.* **peren.**
perchen: perchennog *e.g.* *ll.* **perchenogion** owner, proprietor: **Roedd e'n berchen ar dŷ** He was a house owner.
perchenogaeth *e.b.* ownership.
perchenogi *be.* to own.
peren *e.b.* *ll.* **pêr** pear.
pererin *e.g.* *ll.* **-ion** pilgrim.
perfedd *e.g.* *ll.* **-ion** entrails, guts, middle: **perfedd gwlad** heart of countryside; **perfedd nos** dead of night.
perffaith *a.* perfect.
perffeithio *be.* **(perffeithiaf)** to perfect.
peri (i) *be.* **(peraf)** to cause.
perl *e.g.* *ll.* **-au** pearl.
perllan *e.b.* *ll.* **-nau** orchard.
persawr *e.g.* *ll.* **-au** perfume, fragrance.
persli *e.g.* parsley.
person *e.g.* *ll.* **-au** person. *e.g.*

ll. **-iaid** parson.
personol *a.* personal.
personoliaeth *e.b. ll.* **-au** personality.
pert *a.* pretty.
perth *e.b. ll.* **-i** bush; hedge *(S.W.).*
perthnasau *gw.* **perthynas.**
perthnasol *a.* relevant.
perthyn (i) *be.* **(perthynaf)** to belong, to be related.
perthynas *e.b.g. ll.* **perthnasau** relation; relationship.
perygl *e.g. ll.* **peryglon** danger.
peryglus *a.* dangerous.
peswch 1 *be.* **(pesychaf)** to cough. **2** *e.g.* a cough.
pesychiad *e.g. ll.* **-au** cough.
petai *bf.* if it were *(conjecture);* **pe bai** if; **pe basai** if.
petrol *e.g. ll.* **-au** petrol: **petrol di-blwm** unleaded petrol.
peth *e.g. ll.* **-au** thing, some, part: **pa beth?** what (thing)? **oes peth ar ôl** is there some left?
piano *e.g.b. ll.* **-s** piano.
pianydd *e.g. ll.* **-ion** pianist.
pib *e.b. ll.* **-au: pibell** *e.b. ll.* **-au, -i** pipe *(smoking, musical variety)*: **canu'r pibau** to play the pipes; **tanio pib** to light a pipe.
piben *e.b. ll.* **-ni** pipe *(drainpipe, etc.).*
picil *e.g.* pickle, trouble; **mewn picil** in trouble.
pictiwr *e.g. ll.* **pictiyrau** picture.
picwn *gw.* **picwnen.**
picwnen *e.b. ll.* **picwn** wasp *(S.W.).*
pigfain *a.* tapering.
pigiad *e.g. ll.* **-au** prick, sting; injection.
pigo *be.* **(pigaf)** to pick, to sting, to prick, to peck.
pigog *a.* prickly, irritable.
pil *e.g. ll.* **-ion** peel.
piler *e.g. ll.* **-au, -i** pillar, column: **o biler i bost** from pillar to post.
pilio *be.* **(piliaf)** to peel.
pilion *gw.* **pil.**
pili-pala *e.g. ll.* **pili-palod** butterfly *(S.W.).*
pilsen *e.b. ll.* **pils** pill.
pilyn *e.g. ll.* **-nau** garment *(S.W.):* rag: **pilyn gorau** best garment; **pilyn parch** Sunday garment, best garment.
pin *e.g. ll.* **-nau** pin; pen: **pin ysgrifennu** writing pen; **pinnau bawd** drawing pins.
pîn *gw.* **pinwydden.**
pinc *a.* pink: **yn y pinc** in very good health.
pinnau *gw.* **pin.**
pinsio *be.* **(pinsiaf)** to pinch.
pinwydden *e.b. ll.* **pîn, pinwydd** pine.
piod *gw.* **pioden.**
pioden *e.b. ll.* **piod** magpie.
pisyn *e.g. ll.* **-nau** piece *(S.W.)*: **Mae hi'n bisyn!** She's good looking!
piti *e.g.* pity.
plaid *e.b. ll.* **pleidiau** party, side; **o blaid** in favour: **Y Blaid Geidwadol** The Conservative Party; **Y Blaid Lafur** The Labour Party; **Y Blaid (Plaid Cymru)** The Welsh Nationalist Party; **Y Blaid Werdd** The Green Party.
plan *e.g. ll.* **-nau, -iau** plan.
planced *gw.* **blanced.**
planhigyn *e.g. ll.* **planhigion** plant.
planiau *gw.* **plan.**
plannau *gw.* **plan.**
plannu *be.* **(plannaf)** to plant.
plant *gw.* **plentyn.**
plas *e.g. ll.* **-au** palace, mansion.
plastai *gw.* **plasty.**
plasty *e.g. ll.* **plastai** palace, mansion.
plât *e.g. ll.* **platiau** plate.
platiau *gw.* **plât.**
pleidiau *gw.* **plaid.**
pleidlais *e.b. ll.* **pleidleisiau** vote.
pleisleisiau *gw.* **pleidlais.**
pleidleisio *be.* **(pleidleisiaf)** to vote; **bwrw pleidlais** to cast a vote.
pleidleisiwr *e.g. ll.* **pleidleiswyr** voter.
plentyn *e.g. ll.* **plant** child.
plentynnaidd *a.* childish.
pleser *e.g. ll.* **-au** pleasure: **rhoi pleser i** to give pleasure to.
plesurus *a.* pleasant, pleasurable.
plesio *be.* **(plesiaf)** to please.
plisgyn *e.g. ll.* **plisg** shell, pod, casing.
plisman: plismon *e.g. ll.* **plismyn** policeman.
plismyn *gw.* **plisman.**
plith *e.g.* midst: **i blith** into the midst of; **o blith** from among; **ymhlith** among; **blith draphlith** in confusion, intermingled.
plu *gw.* **pluen.**
pluen *e.b. ll.* **plu** feather; fly *(fishing-bait)*: **clymu plu** to fashion fishing-flies; **yn ysgafn fel pluen** light as a feather.
pluf *gw.* **plufyn.**

plufyn *e.b. ll.* **pluf** feather *(S.W.).*
plwc *e.g. ll.* **plyciau** pull, jerk.
plwg *e.g. ll.* **plygiau** plug.
plwm 1 *e.g.* lead; 2 *a.* leaden, vertical.
plwyf *e.g. ll.* **-i** parish: **ar y plwyf** on the parish, destitute.
plyciau *gw.* **plwc.**
plygiau *gw.* **plwg.**
plygu *be.* **(plygaf)** to fold, to bend, to stoop, to bow, to submit.
pob *a.* each, every, all; roast: **pob cynnig** every attempt, every offer; **pob dydd** every day; **pob tro** every occasion; **pob un** everyone; **tatws pob** roast potatoes.
pobi *be.* **(pobaf)** to bake, to roast.
pobl *e.b. ll.* **-oedd** people; **y bobl hyn** these people.
poblogaeth *e.b. ll.* **-au** population.
poblogaidd *a.* popular.
pobman *ad.* everywhere.
pobydd *e.g. ll.* **-ion** baker.
poced *e.b. ll.* **-i** pocket.
poen *e.g.b. ll.* **-au** pain, ache, agony.
poeni *be.* **(poenaf)** to pain, to worry, to tease: **Paid poeni!** Don't worry!
poenus *a.* painful.
poenydio *be.* **(poenydiaf)** to torture, to torment.
poer: poeri *e.g.* spittle, saliva.
poeri (at, i'r) *be.* **(poeraf)** to spit; *gw.* **poer.**
poeth *a.* hot.
poethi *be.* **(poethaf)** to heat, to be heated.
polion *gw.* **polyn.**
politicaidd *a.* political.
polyn *e.g. ll.* **polion** pole, stake.
pont *e.b. ll.* **-ydd** bridge.
pontydd *gw.* **pont.**
Pont-y-pŵl *e.b.* Pontypool.
popeth *e.g.* everything.
poptai *gw.* **popty.**
popty *e.g. ll.* **poptai** bakehouse; oven.
porfa *e.b. ll.* **porfeydd** pasture; grass *(S.W.).*
porfeydd *gw.* **porfa.**
porffor *e.g. ll. & a.* purple.
pori *be.* **(poraf)** to graze.
portread *e.g. ll.* **-au** portrait, portrayal.
porth *e.g. ll.* **pyrth** door; porch.
porthladd *e.g. ll.* **-oedd** harbour.
pôs *e.g. ll.* **posau** puzzle, riddle: **pôs croeseiriau** crossword puzzle.
posibilrwydd *e.g.* possibility.
posibl *a.* possible.
post 1 *e.g. ll.* **pyst** post, pillar. 2 *e.g. ll.* **-iau** post, mail.
postio *be.* **(postiaf)** to post.
postman: postmon *e.g. ll.* **postmyn** postman.
postmyn *gw.* **postman.**
postyn *e.g. ll.* **pyst** post: **fel postyn** deaf *(as a post).*
potel *e.b. ll.* **-i** bottle: **potel ddŵr poeth** hotwater bottle.
powdr: powdwr *e.g. ll.* **powdrau** powder.
powdrau *gw.* **powdr.**
powlen *gw.* **bowlen.**
praidd *e.g. ll.* **preiddiau** flock.
pram *e.g. ll.* **-iau** pram.
prawf *e.g. ll.* **profion** trial, test, proof: **prawf darllen** reading test; **prawf gyrru** driving test; **ar brawf** on trial, on probation; **blwyddyn brawf** probationary year; **Gwasanaeth Prawf** Probation Service; **swyddog prawf** probation officer.
pregeth *e.b. ll.* **-au** sermon.
pregethu *be.* **(pregethaf)** to preach.
pregethwr *e.g. ll.* **pregethwyr** preacher.
preiddiau *gw.* **praidd.**
preifat *a.* private.
pren *e.g. ll.* **-nau** tree, wood, timber: **pren afalau** apple tree; **pren caled** hardwood; **pren meddal** softwood; **llwy bren** a wooden spoon.
prennau *gw.* pren.
prentis *e.g. ll.* **-iaid** apprentice.
prentisiaeth *e.b. ll.* **-au** apprenticeship.
prentisiaid *gw.* **prentis.**
pres 1 *e.g.* brass, bronze; money. 2 *a.* brass: **band pres** brass band; **jwg bres** brass jug.
preseb *e.g. ll.* **-au** crib, stall, manger.
presennol *a.* present: **yr amser presennol** the present tense.
presenoldeb *e.g. ll.* **-au** presence, attendance.
presgripsiwn *e.g. ll.* **presgripsiynau** prescription.
preswyl: preswylfod *e.g. ll.* **preswylfeydd** dwelling place: **ysgol breswyl** boarding school; **neuadd breswyl** hall of residence.
pridwerth *e.g.* ransom.
pridd *e.g. ll.* **-oedd** soil, earth.
prif *a. (precedes the noun it qualifies and is followed by soft mutation)* prime, chief, major, principal: **prif**

ddiddordeb chief interest; **prif westeion** principal guests; **prif lyfrgell** main library.
prifardd *e.g. ll.* **prifeirdd** chief bard *(one who has won chair or crown at National Eisteddfod).*
prifathrawes *e.b. ll.* **-au** headmistress, principal.
prifathro *e.g. ll.* **prifathrawon** headmaster, principal.
prifddinas *e.b. ll.* **-oedd** capital city.
prifeirdd *gw.* **prifardd.**
prifio *be.* **(prifiaf)** to grow *(S.W.).*
prifysgol *e.b. ll.* **-ion** university: **Prifysgol Cymru** University of Wales.
priffordd *e.b. ll.* **priffyrdd** highway.
priffyrdd *gw.* **priffordd.**
prin *a.* rare, scarce.
prinder *e.g. ll.* **-au** scarcity.
printio *be.* **(printiaf)** to print.
priod 1 *a.* own, proper; married. 2 *e.g.b.* husband or wife: **ei phriod** her husband; **fy mhriod** my partner *(husband/wife);* **ei briod le** his proper place; **priodfab** bridgeroom; **priodferch** bride; **gŵr priod** married man; **gwraig briod** married woman; **Ydych chi'n briod?** Are you married?
priodas *e.b. ll.* **-au** marriage, wedding.
priodi (â) *be.* **(priodaf)** to marry.
priodol *a.* appropriate, proper.
pris *e.g. ll.* **-iau, -oedd** price.
problem *e.g. ll.* **-au** problem.
profi *be.* **(profaf)** to prove, to test, to taste.
profiad *e.g. ll.* **-au** experience.
profiadol *a.* experienced.
profion *gw.* **prawf.**
profocio: pryfocio *be.* **(profociaf: pryfociaf)** to provoke.
proffid *e.b. ll.* **-iau** profit.
proffiddiol *a.* profitable.
proffwyd *e.g. ll.* **-i** prophet; **proffwydes** prophetess.
proffwydo *be.* **(proffwydaf)** to prophesy.
Protestant *e.g. ll.* **Protestaniaid** Protestant.
prudd *a.* sad, grave, serious.
pryd 1 *e.g. ll.* **-au** meal: **byrbryd** snack; **tamaid i aros pryd** temporary provision whilst awaiting arrival of something more substantial. 2 *e.g. ll.* **-iau** time, season: **Pryd? Pa bryd?** What time? **mewn pryd** in time; **ar y pryd** at the time; impromptu; **hen bryd** about time.
Prydain *e.b.* Britain.
prydau *gw.* **pryd.**
Prydeinig *a.* British.
pryder *e.g. ll.* **-on** anxiety, care, worry.
pryderu *be.* **(pryderaf)** to be anxious.
pryderus *a.* anxious.
prydferth *a.* beautiful, handsome.
prydferthwch *e.g.* beauty.
prydiau *gw.* **pryd.**
prydlon *a.* **punctual.**
pryf: pryfedyn: pryfyn *e.g. ll.* **pryfed** insect; vermin; animal; worm: **pryf copyn** spider *(N.W.).*
pryfed *gw.* **pryf.**
pryfocio *gw.* **profocio.**
pryfyn *gw.* **pryf.**
prynhawn *e.g. ll.* **-au** afternoon: **prynhawn da!** good afternoon!.
prynu *be.* **(prynaf)** to buy.
prynwr *e.g. ll.* **prynwyr** buyer, redeemer.
prysur *a.* busy, hasty; diligent, serious.
prysurdeb *e.g.* haste, hurry; busyness.
prysuro (i) *be.* **(prysuraf)** to hasten (to), to hurry: **Rwy'n prysuro i esbonio** I hasten to explain.
pulpud *e.g. ll.* **-au** pulpit.
pum: pump *e.g. ll. & a.* five: **pumed** fifth.
p'un *gw.* **pa.**
punnau *gw.* **punt.**
punnoedd *gw.* **punt.**
punt *e.b. ll.* **punnau, punnoedd** pound *(£).*
pupur *e.g. ll.* **-au** pepper; **fel melin bupur** very talkative.
pur 1 *a.* pure, sincere; **Yr eiddoch yn bur** Yours sincerely. 2 *ad.* very, fairly: **yn bur wael** very poorly; **yn bur dda** fairly good.
purfa *e.b. ll.* **purfeydd** refinery; **purfa olew** oil refinery.
puro *be.* **(puraf)** to purify.
pwdin *e.g. ll.* **-au** pudding, sweet *(after dinner).* **Bydd pwdin yn dilyn** There's a sweet to follow.
pwdr *a.* rotten, corrupt, lazy *(S.W.).*
pwdryn *e.g.* idler, sluggard *(S.W.).*
pwdu *be.* **(pwdaf)** to sulk, to pout.
pŵer *e.g. ll.* **-au** power.
pwll *e.g. ll.* **pyllau** pit, pool. pond: **pwll glo** coal-pit, coal-mine.

pwmp *e.g.* *ll.* **pympiau** pump.
pwnc *e.g.* *ll.* **pynciau** subject, topic: **pynciau craidd** core subjects; **pynciau sylfaen** foundation subjects; **Cymanfa Bwnc** assembly for cathechising and discussing prepared portions of Scripture.
pwrpas *e.g.* *ll.* **-au** purpose.
pwrs *e.g.* *ll.* **pyrsau** purse.
pwy *rhag. gof.* who?: **pwy bynnag** whosoever.
pwyll *e.g.* sense, discretion: **colli ei bwyll** to lose his senses, to become enraged; **cymryd pwyll** to take time; **mynd gan bwyll** to go steadily.
pwllgor *e.g.* *ll.* **-au** committee: **pwllgor addysg** education committee; **pwyllgor brys** emergency committee; **pwyllgor gwaith** executive committee.
pwyllo *be.* **(pwyllaf)** to pause, to consider, to reflect.
pwynt *e.g.* *ll.* **-iau** point: **dau pwynt pump** 2.5 *(two point five)*; **rhewbwynt** freezing-point.
pwys 1 *e.g.* *ll.* **-au** weight; importance: **ar bwys** near; **ennill pwysau** to put on weight; **o bwys** important; **codi pwys ar** to make one feel sick. 2 *e.g.* *ll.* **-i** pound *(lb)*.
pwysedd *e.g.* pressure: **pwysedd gwaed** blood pressure.
pwysig *a.* important.
pwysigrwydd *e.g.* importance.
pwyslais *e.g.* *ll.* **pwysleisiau** emphasis.
pwyso (ar) *be.* **(pwysaf)** to weigh, to lean (on), to rest.
pwyth *e.g.* *ll.* **-au** stitch; **talu'r pwyth** to avenge; retaliate.
pydru *be.* **(pydraf)** to rot, to decay.
pyllau *gw.* **pwll. pyllyn.**
pyllyn *e.g.* *ll.* **pyllau** pool, pond.
pympiau *gw.* **pwmp.**
pymtheg 1 *e.g.* *ll.* **-au** fifteen. 2 *a.* fifteen.
pymthegfed *a.* fifteenth.
pynciau *gw.* **pwnc.**
pyped *e.g.* *ll.* **-au** puppet.
pyrsau *gw.* **pwrs.**
pyrth *gw.* **porth.**
pys *gw.* **pysen.**
pysen *e.b.* *ll.* **pys** pea: **pys pêr** sweetpeas.
pysgod *gw.* **pysgodyn.**
pysgodyn *e.g.* *ll.* **pysgod** a fish: **pysgodyn aur** a goldfish.
pysgota *be.* **(pysgotaf)** to fish.
pysgotwr *e.g.* *ll.* **pysgotwyr** fisherman.
pyst *gw.* **post, postyn.**
pythefnos *e.g.b.* *ll.* **-au** fortnight.

pha *gw.* **pa.**
Phab *gw.* **Pab.**
phabell *gw.* **pabell.**
phabi *gw.* **pabi.**
phabydd *gw.* **pabydd.**
phac *gw.* **pac.**
phaced *gw.* **paced.**
phacio *gw.* **pacio.**
phadell *gw.* **padell.**
phader *gw.* **pader.**
phaent *gw.* **paent.**
phafiliwn *gw.* **pafiliwn.**
phafin *gw.* **pafin.**
phagan *gw.* **pagan.**
phaham *gw.* **paham.**
phais *gw.* **pais.**
phâl *gw.* **pâl.**
phalas *gw.* **palas.**
phalau *gw.* **pâl.**
phalod *gw.* **pâl.**
phalu *gw.* **palu.**
phallu *gw.* **pallu.**
pham *gw.* **pam.**
phamffled *gw.* **pamffled.**
phamffledyn *gw.* **pamffled.**
phan *gw.* **pan.**
phanasen *gw.* **panasen.**
phanel *gw.* **panel.**
phannas *gw.* **panasen.**
phant *gw.* **pant.**
phapur *gw.* **papur.**
phapuro *gw.* **papuro.**
phâr *gw.* **pâr.**
phara *gw.* **para.**
pharagraff *gw.* **paragraff.**
pharatoi *gw.* **paratoi.**
pharc *gw.* **parc.**
pharch *gw.* **parch.**
pharchedig *gw.* **parchedig.**
pharchu *gw.* **parchu.**
pharchus *gw.* **parchus.**
phardwn *gw.* **pardwn.**
pharhad *gw.* **parhad.**
pharhau *gw.* **parhau.**
pharod *gw.* **parod.**
pharsel *gw.* **parsel.**
pharti *gw.* **parti.**
Phasg *gw.* **Pasg.**
phasiannau *gw.* **pasiant.**
phasiant *gw.* **pasiant.**
phatrwm *gw.* **patrwm.**
phatrwn *gw.* **patrwn.**
phatrymau *gw.* **patrwm.**
phatrynau *gw.* **patrwn.**
phawb *gw.* **pawb.**
phawen *gw.* **pawen.**
phe *gw.* **pe.**
phebyll *gw.* **pabell.**
phecyn *gw.* **pecyn.**
phechadur *gw.* **pechadur.**
phechod *gw.* **pechod.**
phechu *gw.* **pechu.**
phedair *gw.* **pedair.**
phedol *gw.* **pedol.**
phedwar *gw.* **pedwar.**
phedwaredd *gw.* **pedwaredd.**
phedwerydd *gw.* **pedwerydd.**
pheg *gw.* **peg.**
phegwn *gw.* **pegwn.**
phegynau *gw.* **pegwn.**
pheidio *gw.* **peidio.**
pheilot *gw.* **peilot.**
pheint *gw.* **peint.**
pheintio *gw.* **peintio.**
pheintiwr *gw.* **peintiwr.**
pheiriannau *gw.* **peiriant.**
pheiriant *gw.* **peiriant.**
pheisiau *gw.* **pais.**
phêl *gw.* **pêl.**
phelydr *gw.* **pelydr.**
phell *gw.* **pell.**
phellach *gw.* **pell.**
phellaf *gw.* **pell.**
phelled *gw.* **pell.**
phellter *gw.* **pellter.**
phen *gw.* **pen.**
phenaethiaid *gw.* **pennaeth.**
phenawdau *gw.* **pennawd.**
phen-blwydd *gw.* **pen-blwydd.**
phencadlys *gw.* **pencadlys.**
phencampwr *gw.* **pencampwr.**
phendant *gw.* **pendant.**
phenderfyniad *gw.* **penderfyniad.**
phenderfynol *gw.* **penderfynol.**
phenderfynu *gw.* **penderfynu.**
phenelin *gw.* **penelin.**
phenfoel *gw.* **penfoel.**
phen-glin *gw.* **pen-glin.**
phenigamp *gw.* **penigamp.**

phenillion *gw.* **pennill.**
phen-lin *gw.* **pen-glin.**
phenlinio *gw.* **penlinio.**
phennaeth *gw.* **pennaeth.**
phennaf *gw.* **pennaf.**
phennau *gw.* **pen.**
phennawd *gw.* **pennawd.**
phennill *gw.* **pennill.**
phennod *gw.* **pennod.**
phenodau *gw.* **pennod.**
phenodi *gw.* **penodi.**
phenodiad *gw.* **penodiad.**
phenrhyn *gw.* **penrhyn.**
phensaer *gw.* **pensaer.**
phenseiri *gw.* **pensaer.**
phensil *gw.* **pensil.**
phensiwn *gw.* **pensiwn.**
phensiynau *gw.* **pensiwn.**
phensiynwr *gw.* **pensiynwr.**
phenteulu *gw.* **penteulu.**
phentref *gw.* **pentref.**
phentwr *gw.* **pentwr.**
phêr *gw.* **pêr.**
pherchen *gw.* **perchen.**
pherchennog *gw.* **perchen.**
pheren *gw.* **peren.**
phererin *gw.* **pererin.**
pherfedd *gw.* **perfedd.**
pherffaith *gw.* **perffaith.**
pherffeithio *gw.* **perffeithio.**
pheri *gw.* **peri.**
pherl *gw.* **perl.**
pherllan *gw.* **perllan.**
phersli *gw.* **persli.**
pherson *gw.* **person.**
phersonol *gw.* **personol.**
phersonoliaeth *gw.* **personoliaeth.**
phert *gw.* **pert.**
pherth *gw.* **perth.**
pherthnasau *gw.* **perthynas.**
pherthnasol *gw.* **perthnasol.**
pherthyn *gw.* **perthyn.**
pherthynas *gw.* **perthynas.**
phergyl *gw.* **perygl.**
pheryglus *gw.* **peryglus.**
pheswch *gw.* **peswch.**
phesychiad *gw.* **pesychiad.**
phetai *gw.* **petai.**
phetrol *gw.* **petrol.**
pheth *gw.* **peth.**
phiano *gw.* **piano.**
phianydd *gw.* **pianydd.**
phib *gw.* **pib.**
phiben *gw.* **piben.**
phicil *gw.* **picil.**
phictiwr *gw.* **pictiwr.**
phicwn *gw.* **picwnen.**
phicwnen *gw.* **picwnen.**
phigfain *gw.* **pigfain.**
phigiad *gw.* **pigiad.**
phigo *gw.* **pigo.**
phigog *gw.* **pigog.**
phil *gw.* **pil.**
philer *gw.* **piler.**
philio *gw.* **pilio.**
philion *gw.* **pil.**
phili-pala *gw.* **pili-pala.**
philsen *gw.* **pilsen.**
philyn *gw.* **pilyn.**
phin *gw.* **pin.**
phîn *gw.* **pîn.**
phinc *gw.* **pinc.**
phinnau *gw.* **pin.**
phinsio *gw.* **pinsio.**
phinwydden *gw.* **pinwydden.**
phioden *gw.* **pioden.**
phisyn *gw.* **pisyn.**
phiti *gw.* **piti.**
phlaid *gw.* **plaid.**
phlan *gw.* **plan.**
phlanced *gw.* **blanced.**
phlanhigyn *gw.* **planhigyn.**
phlaniau *gw.* **plan.**
phlannau *gw.* **plan.**
phlannu *gw.* **plannu.**
phlant *gw.* **plant.**
phlas *gw.* **plas.**
phlastai *gw.* **plasty.**
phlasty *gw.* **plasty.**
phlât *gw.* **plât.**
phlatiau *gw.* **plât.**
phleidiau *gw.* **plaid.**
phleidlais *gw.* **pleidlais.**
phleidleisiau *gw.* **pleidlais.**
phleidleisio *gw.* **pleidleisio.**
phleidleisiwr *gw.* **pleidleisiwr.**
phlentyn *gw.* **plentyn.**
phlentynnaidd *gw.* **plentynnaidd.**
phleser *gw.* **pleser.**
phleserus *gw.* **pleserus.**
phlesio *gw.* **plesio.**
phlisgyn *gw.* **plisgyn.**
phlisman: phlismon *gw.* **plisman.**
phlismyn *gw.* **plisman.**
phlu *gw.* **pluen.**
phluen *gw.* **pluen.**
phluf *gw.* **plufyn.**
phlufyn *gw.* **plufyn.**
phlwc *gw.* **plwc.**
phlwg *gw.* **plwg.**
phlwm *gw.* **plwm.**
phlwyf *gw.* **plwyf.**
phlyciau *gw.* **plwc.**
phlygiau *gw.* **plwg.**
phlygu *gw.* **plygu.**
phob *gw.* **pob.**
phobi *gw.* **pobi.**
phobl *gw.* **pobl.**

phoblogaeth *gw.* **poblogaeth.**
phoblogaidd *gw.* **poblogaidd.**
phobman *gw.* **pobman.**
phobydd *gw.* **pobydd.**
phoced *gw.* **poced.**
phoen *gw.* **poen.**
phoeni *gw.* **poeni.**
phoenus *gw.* **poenus.**
phoenydio *gw.* **poenydio.**
phoer *gw.* **poer.**
phoeri *gw.* **poer, poeri (at, i'r).**
phoeth *gw.* **poeth.**
phoethi *gw.* **poethi.**
pholion *gw.* **polyn.**
pholiticaidd *gw.* **politicaidd.**
pholyn *gw.* **polyn.**
phont *gw.* **pont.**
phontydd *gw.* **pont.**
Phont-y-pŵl *gw.* **Pont-y-pŵl.**
phopeth *gw.* **popeth.**
phoptai *gw.* **popty.**
phopty *gw.* **popty.**
phorfa *gw.* **porfa.**
phorfeydd *gw.* **porfa.**
phorffor *gw.* **porffor.**
phori *gw.* **pori.**
phortread *gw.* **portread.**
phorth *gw.* **porth.**
phorthladd *gw.* **porthladd.**
phôs *gw.* **pôs.**
phosibilrwydd *gw.* **posibilrwydd.**
phosibl *gw.* **posibl.**
phost *gw.* **post.**
phostio *gw.* **postio.**
phostman: phostmon *gw.* **postman.**
phostmyn *gw.* **postman.**
phostyn *gw.* **postyn.**
photel *gw.* **potel.**
phowdr: phowdwr *gw.* **powdr.**
phowdrau *gw.* **powdr.**
phowlen *gw.* **bowlen.**
phraidd *gw.* **praidd.**
phram *gw.* **pram.**
phrawf *gw.* **prawf.**
phregeth *gw.* **pregeth.**
phregethu *gw.* **pregethu.**
phregethwr *gw.* **pregethwr.**
phreiddiau *gw.* **praidd.**
phreifat *gw.* **preifat.**
phren *gw.* **pren.**
phrennau *gw.* **pren.**
phrentis *gw.* **prentis.**
phrentisiaeth *gw.* **prentisiaeth.**
phrentisiaid *gw.* **prentis.**
phres *gw.* **pres.**
phreseb *gw.* **preseb.**
phresennol *gw.* **presennol.**
phresenoldeb *gw.* **presenoldeb.**
phresgripsiwn *gw.* **presgripsiwn.**
phreswyl: phreswylfod *gw.* **preswyl.**
phridwerth *gw.* **pridwerth.**
phridd *gw.* **pridd.**
phrif *gw.* **prif.**
phrifardd *gw.* **prifardd.**
phrifathrawes *gw.* **prifathrawes.**
phrifathro *gw.* **prifathro.**
phrifddinas *gw.* **prifddinas.**
phrifeirdd *gw.* **prifardd.**
phrifio *gw.* **prifio.**
phrifysgol *gw.* **prifysgol.**
phriffordd *gw.* **priffordd.**
phriffyrdd *gw.* **priffordd.**
phrin *gw.* **prin.**
phrinder *gw.* **prinder.**
phrintio *gw.* **printio.**
phriod *gw.* **priod.**
phriodas *gw.* **priodas.**
phriodi *gw.* **priodas.**
phriodol *gw.* **priodol.**
phris *gw.* **pris.**
phroblem *gw.* **problem.**
phrofi *gw.* **profi.**
phrofiad *gw.* **profiad.**
phrofiadol *gw.* **profiadol.**
phrofion *gw.* **prawf.**
phrofocio *gw.* **profocio.**
phroffid *gw.* **proffid.**
phroffidiol *gw.* **proffidiol.**
phroffwyd *gw.* **proffwyd.**
phroffwydo *gw.* **proffwydo.**
Phrotestant *gw.* **Protestant.**
phrudd *gw.* **prudd.**
phryd *gw.* **pryd.**
Phrydain *gw.* **Prydain.**
phrydau *gw.* **pryd.**
Phrydeinig *gw.* **Prydeinig.**
phryder *gw.* **pryder.**
phryderu *gw.* **pryderu.**
phryderus *gw.* **pryderus.**
phrydferth *gw.* **prydferth.**
phrydferthwch *gw.* **prydferthwch.**
phrydiau *gw.* **pryd.**
phrydlon *gw.* **prydlon.**
phryf: phryfedyn: phryfyn *gw.* **pryf.**
phryfed *gw.* **pryf.**
phryfocio *gw.* **profocio.**
phryfyn *gw.* **pryf.**
phrynhawn *gw.* **prynhawn.**
phrynu *gw.* **prynu.**
phrynwr *gw.* **prynwr.**
phrysur *gw.* **prysur.**
phrysurdeb *gw.* **prysurdeb.**
phrysuro *gw.* **prysuro.**
phulpud *gw.* **pulpud.**
phum: phump *gw.* **pum.**
ph'un *gw.* **pa.**
phunnau *gw.* **punt.**
phunnoedd *gw.* **punt.**

phunt *gw.* **punt.**
phupur *gw.* **pupur.**
phur *gw.* **pur.**
phurfa *gw.* **purfa.**
phuro *gw.* **puro.**
phwdin *gw.* **pwdin.**
phwdr *gw.* **pwdr.**
phwdryn *gw.* **pwdryn.**
phwdu *gw.* **pwdu.**
phŵer *gw.* **pŵer.**
phwll *gw.* **pwll.**
phwllyn *gw.* **pwllyn.**
phwmp *gw.* **pwmp.**
phwnc *gw.* **pwnc.**
phwrpas *gw.* **pwrpas.**
phwrs *gw.* **pwrs.**
phwy *gw.* **pwy.**
phwyll *gw.* **pwyll.**
phwyllgor *gw.* **pwyllgor.**
phwyllo *gw.* **pwyllo.**
phwynt *gw.* **pwynt.**
phwys *gw.* **pwys.**
phwysedd *gw.* **pwysedd.**
phwysig *gw.* **pwysig.**
phwysigrwydd *gw.* **pwysigrwydd.**
phwyslais *gw.* **pwyslais.**
phwyso *gw.* **pwyso.**
phwyth *gw.* **pwyth.**
phwytho *gw.* **pwytho.**
phydru *gw.* **pydru.**
phyllau *gw.* **pwll, pyllyn.**
phyllyn *gw.* **pyllyn.**
phympiau *gw.* **pwmp.**
phymtheg *gw.* **pwmtheg.**
phymthegfed *gw.* **pymthegfed.**
phynciau *gw.* **pwnc.**
phyped *gw.* **pyped.**
phyrsau *gw.* **pwrs.**
phyrth *gw.* **porth.**
phys *gw.* **pysen.**
physgod *gw.* **pysgodyn.**
physgodyn *gw.* **pysgodyn.**
physgota *gw.* **pysgota.**
physgotwr *gw.* **pysgotwr.**
physt *gw.* **post, postyn.**
phythefnos *gw.* **pythefnos.**

raca *gw.* **rhaca.**
raced *e.b.g.* *ll.* **-i** racket.
racs *gw.* **rhecsyn.**
rad *gw.* **rhad.**
radio *e.g.* *ll.* **-s** radio.
radd *gw.* **gradd.**
raddfa *gw.* **graddfa.**
raddio *gw.* **graddio.**
raddol *gw.* **graddol.**
raeadr *gw.* **rhaeadr.**
raenus *gw.* **graenus.**
raff *gw.* **rhaff.**
ragair *gw.* **rhagair.**
ragbrawf *gw.* **rhagbrawf.**
ragbrofion *gw.* **rhagbrawf.**
ragenw *gw.* **rhagenw.**
ragfarn *gw.* **rhagfarn.**
ragfarnllyd *gw.* **rhagfarnllyd.**
ragflas *gw.* **rhagflas.**
Ragfyr *gw.* **Rhagfyr.**
raglen *gw.* **rhaglen.**
raglenni *gw.* **rhaglen.**
ragor *gw.* **rhagor.**
ragori *gw.* **rhagori.**
ragorol *gw.* **rhagorol.**
rai *gw.* **rhai.**
raid *gw.* **rhaid.**
ramadeg *gw.* **gramadeg.**
ramantaidd *gw.* **rhamantus.**
ramantus *gw.* **rhamantus.**
ran *gw.* **rhan.**
ranbarth *gw.* **rhanbarth.**
randir *gw.* **rhandir.**
raniad *gw.* **rhaniad.**
rannau *gw.* **rhan.**
rannu *gw.* **rhannu.**
ras *e.b.* *ll.***-ys** race (*competitive*): **ras-gyfnewid** relay race; *gw.* **gras.**
raw *gw.* **rhaw.**
record *e.b.* *ll.***-iau** record.
recsyn *gw.* **rhecsyn.**
redeg *gw.* **rhedeg.**
redwr *gw.* **rhedwr.**
redyn *gw.* **rhedynen.**
redynen *gw.* **rhedynen.**
reg *gw.* **rheg.**
regfeydd *gw.* **rheg.**
regi *gw.* **rhegi.**
reidiau *gw.* **rhaid.**
reilffordd *gw.* **rheilffordd.**
reilffyrdd *gw.* **rheilffordd.**
reis *e.g.* rice: **pwdin reis** rice pudding.
reol *gw.* **rheol.**
reolaidd *gw.* **rheolaidd.**
reoli *gw.* **rheoli.**
reolwr *gw.* **rheolwr.**
reolwyr *gw.* **rheolwr.**
res *gw.* **rhes.**
resi *gw.* **rhes.**
restr *gw.* **rhestr.**
restrau *gw.* **rhestr.**
restri *gw.* **rhestr.**
reswm *gw.* **rheswm.**
resymau *gw.* **rheswm.**
resynu *gw.* **gresynu.**
rew *gw.* **rhew.**
rewgell *gw.* **rhewgell.**
rewi *gw.* **rhewi.**
rewlif *gw.* **rhewlif.**
rëydr *gw.* **rhaeadr.**
riant *gw.* **rhiant.**
rieni *gw.* **rhiant.**
rif *gw.* **rhif.**
rifau *gw.* **rhif.**
rifo *gw.* **rhifo.**
rifyddeg *gw.* **rhifyddeg.**
rifyn *gw.* **rhifyn.**
rifynnau *gw.* **rhifyn.**
riffl *e.g.* *ll.* **-au** rifle.
rigwm *gw.* **rhigwm.**
rigymau *gw.* **rhigwm.**
rihyrsal *e.b.* *ll.* **-s** rehearsal.
rinwedd *gw.* **rhinwedd.**
ris *gw.* **gris.**
risiau *gw.* **gris.**
riw *gw.* **rhiw.**
robin goch *e.g.* robin.
roced *e.b.* *ll.* **-i** rocket.
rodd *gw.* **rhodd.**
roddi *gw.* **rhoddi.**
roddion *gw.* **rhodd.**
roedd -e/-hi *bf.* he/she/it/was; *gw.* **bod.**
Roeg *gw.* **Groeg.**
Roegaidd *gw.* **Groegaidd.**
Roegwr *gw.* **Groegwr.**
rofiau *gw.* **rhaw.**
roi *gw.* **rhoddi.**

Romania *e.b.* Romania.
rolio *gw.* **rholio.**
ros *gw.* **rhos.**
rosydd *gw.* **rhos.**
rosyn *gw.* **rhosyn.**
rosynnau *gw.* **rhosyn.**
ruban *e.g.* *ll.* **-au** ribbon.
rudd *gw.* **grudd.**
Rufain *gw.* **Rhufain.**
Rufeinig *gw.* **Rhufeinig.**
rug *gw.* **grug.**
ruo *gw.* **rhuo.**
ruthro *gw.* **rhuthro.**
rŵan *ad.* now *(N.W.): gw.* **nawr.**
rwbio *gw.* **rhwbio.**
rwber *e.g.* rubber.
Rwsia *e.b.* Russia.
Rwsiad *e.g.* *ll.* **Rwsiaid** a Russian.
Rwsieg *e.g.* Russian (language).
rwyd *gw.* **rhwyd.**
rwydi *gw.* **rhwyd.**
rwydd *gw.* **rhwydd.**
rwyfo *gw.* **rhwyfo.**
rwyfus *gw.* **rhwyfus.**
rwygo *gw.* **rhwygo.**
rwymo *gw.* **rhwymo.**
rwystr *gw.* **rhwystr.**
rybudd *gw.* **rhybudd.**
rybuddio *gw.* **rhybuddio.**
ryd *gw.* **rhyd.**
rydw i *bf.* I am; *gw.* **bod.**
Rydychen *gw.* **Rhydychen.**
rydd *gw.* **rhydd.**
ryddhau *gw.* **rhyddhau.**
ryddid *gw.* **rhyddid.**
ryddion *gw.* **rhydd.**
ryfedd *gw.* **rhyfedd.**
ryfeddod *gw.* **rhyfeddod.**
ryfeddol *gw.* **rhyfeddol.**
ryfeddu *gw.* **rhyfeddu.**
ryfel *gw.* **rhyfel.**
ryngwladol *gw.* **rhyngwladol.**
rym *gw.* **grym.**
rymus *gw.* **grymus.**
rysáit *eb.* *ll.* **-s.** recipe, prescription.
ryw *gw.* **rhyw.**
rywbeth *gw.* **rhywbeth.**
rywbryd *gw.* **rhywbryd.**
rywdro *gw.* **rhywdro.**
rywfaint *gw.* **rhywfaint.**
rywiol *gw.* **rhywiol.**
rywle *gw.* **rhywle.**
rywrai *gw.* **rhywun.**
rywsut *gw.* **rhywsut.**
rywun *gw.* **rhywun.**

rhaca *e.b. ll.* **-nau** rake; **fel rhaca** very thin, like a rake.
rhacs *gw.* **rhecsyn.**
rhad 1 *a.* cheap; free: **yn rhad ac am ddim** absolutely free. 2 *e.g. ll.* **-au** blessing, grace.
rhaeadr *e.b. ll.* **-au, rhëydr** cataract, waterfall.
rhaff *e.b. ll.* **-au** rope.
rhag 1 *ardd.* before; lest; against, from. 2 *rhag.* pre-, for-, ante-.
rhagair *e.g.* preface.
rhagbrawf *e.g. ll.* **rhagbrofion** preliminary test; foretaste.
rhagbrofion *gw.* **rhagbrawf.**
rhagenw *e.g. ll.* **-au** pronoun: **rhagenw gofynnol** interrogative pronoun; **rhagenw perthynol** relative pronoun.
rhagfarn *e.b. ll.* **-au** prejudice.
rhagfarnllyd *a.* prejudiced.
rhagflas *e.g.* foretaste.
Rhagfyr *e.g.* December.
rhaglen *e.b. ll.* **-ni** programme: **rhaglen deledu** television programme; **rhaglen fyw** live programme; **rhaglen nodwedd** feature programme.
rhaglenni *gw.* **rhaglen.**
rhagor *e.g. ll.* **-au, -ion** difference, more, excess; **rhagor o fwyd** more food.
rhagori (ar) *be.* **(rhagoraf)** to excel, to surpass.
rhagorol *a.* excellent, splendid.
rhai 1 *rhag.* ones: **y rhai da** the good ones. 2 *a.* some: **Mae rhai pobl yn oer** Some people are cold.
rhaid *e.g. ll.* **rheidiau** necessity, need: **Mae rhaid i ti fynd** You must go.
rhain, y *rhag.* these: **Ble mae'r rhain i fod?** Where are these to go?
rhamantus: rhamantaidd *a.* romantic.
rhan *e.b. ll.* **-nau** part, spare; rôle: **y rhan fwyaf** the greatest part.
rhanbarth *e.g. ll.* **-au** division, region, area, district.
rhandir *e.g. ll.* **-oedd** region, division, district; allotment.
rhandiroedd *gw.* **rhandir.**
rhaniad *e.g. ll.* **-au** division; parting.
rhannau *gw.* **rhan.**
rhannu *be.* **(rhannaf)** to divide, to share, to distribute.
rhaw *e.b. ll.* **-iau, rhofiau** shovel; spade.
rhecsyn *e.g. ll.* **rhacs** rag.
rhedeg *be.* **(rhedaf)** to run; to flow.
rhedwr *e.g. ll.* **rhedwyr** runner.
rhedyn *e.ll.* fern, bracken; *gw.* **rhedynen.**
rhedynen *e.b. ll.* **rhedyn** fern.
rheg *e.b. ll.* **-feydd** curse, swear-word.
rhegfeydd *gw.* **rheg.**
rhegi *be.* **(rhegaf)** to curse, to swear.
rheidiau *gw.* **rhaid.**
rheilffordd *e.b. ll.* **rheilffyrdd** railway.
rheilffyrdd *gw.* **rheilffordd.**
rheini, y: rheiny, y *rhag.* those (*not present*).
rheol *e.b. ll.* **-au** rule, order: **Rheolau'r Ffordd Fawr** the Highway Code.
rheolaidd *a.* regular, constant, orderly, proper.
rheoli *be.* **(rheolaf)** to control, to manage.
rheolwr *e.g. ll.* **rheolwyr** manager, ruler, controller, governor; referee.
rheolwyr *gw.* **rheolwr.**
rhes *e.b. ll.* **-i** row, rank; stripe, line.
rhesi *gw.* **rhes.**
rhestr *e.b. ll.* **-au, -i** row, rank; list: **rhestr fer** short list.
rhestrau *gw.* **rhestr.**
rhestri *gw.* **rhestr.**
rheswm *e.g. ll.* **rhesymau** reason, cause: **y rheswm dros** the reason for.
rhesymau *gw.* **rheswm.**
rhew *e.g. ll.* **-iau, -ogydd** frost, ice: **rhewbwynt** freezing point; **rhewfwyd** frozen food; **rhewlif** glacier; **Siôn Rhew** Jack Frost.
rhewgell *e.b. ll.* **-oedd** deep freeze cabinet, freezer.

rhewi *be.* **(rhewaf)** to freeze.
rhewiau *gw.* **rhew.**
rhewlif *e.g.* *ll.* **-iau** glacier.
rhewogydd *gw.* **rhew.**
rhëydr *gw.* **rhaeadr.**
rhiant *e.g.* *ll.* **rhieni** parent.
rhieni *gw.* **rhiant.**
rhif *e.g.* *ll.* **-au** number, numeral.
rhifau *gw.* **rhif.**
rhifo *be.* **(rhifaf)** to count, to number, to reckon.
rhifyddeg *e.b.g.* arithmetic.
rhifyn *e.g.* *ll.* **-nau** number (*of magazine*).
rhifynnau *gw.* **rhifyn.**
rhigwm *e.g.* *ll.* **rhigymau** rhyme; rigmarole.
rhigymau *gw.* **rhigwm.**
rhinwedd *e.b.g.* *ll.* **-au** virtue.
rhiw *e.b.* *ll.* **-iau** hill, ascent, slope (*S.W.*).
rhodd *e.b.* *ll.* **-ion** gift, donation.
rhoddi: rhoi *be.* **(rhoddaf: rhoiaf)** to give, to bestow, to put; **rhoi benthyg** to lend; **rhoi'r gorau i** to relinquish; *gw. At. Berfau.*
rhoddion *gw.* **rhodd.**
rhofion *gw.* **rhaw.**
rhoi *gw.* **rhoddi.**
rholio *be.* **(rholiaf)** to roll.
rhos *e.b.* *ll.* **-ydd.** moor, heath, plain; *gw.* **rhosyn.**
rhosod *gw.* **rhosyn.**
rhosydd *gw.* **rhos.**
rhosyn *e.g.* *ll.* **-nau, rhos, rhosod** rose.
rhosynnau *gw.* **rhosyn.**
Rhufain *e.b.* Rome.
Rhufeinig *a.* Roman.
rhuo *be.* **(rhuaf)** to roar, to bellow.
rhuthro *be.* **(rhuthraf)** to rush.
rhwbio *be.* **(rhwbiaf)** to rub.
rhwng *ardd.* (*personal forms:* **rhyngo, rhyngot, rhyngddo/ rhyngddi, rhyngom rhyngoch, rhyngddyn)** between, among; *gw. At. Arddodiaid.*
rhwyd *e.b.* *ll.* **-au, -i** net, snare.
rhwydd *a.* easy; fluent; generous; fast (*S.W.*).
rhwyfo *be.* **(rhwyfaf)** to row.
rhwyfus *a.* restless.
rhwygo *be.* **(rhwygaf)** to tear, to rip.
rhwym *a.* bound, tied; constipated.
rhwymo *be.* **(rhwymaf)** to bind, to tie; to constipate.
rhwystr *e.g.* *ll.* **-au** hindrance, obstacle.
rhwystrau *gw.* **rhwystr.**
rhy 1 *e.g.* excess. 2 *ad.* too: **yn rhy drwm** too heavy.
rhybudd *e.g.* *ll.* **-ion** warning, notice, caution.
rhybuddio *(rhag) be.* **(rhybuddiaf)** to warn, to caution.
rhyd *e.b.* *ll.* **-au** ford.
Rhydychen *e.b.* Oxford.
rhydd *a.* *ll.* **-ion** free, liberal: **Y Seiri Rhyddion** Freemasons.
rhyddhau *be.* **(rhyddhaf)** to free, to release, to loose.
rhyddid *e.g.* freedom, liberty.
rhyddion *gw.* **rhydd.**
rhyfedd: rhyfeddol *a.* wonderful, strange.
rhyfeddod *e.g.* *ll.* **-au** wonder, surprise.
rhyfeddol *gw.* **rhyfedd.**
rhyfeddu (at) *be.* **(rhyfeddaf)** to wonder, to marvel.
rhyfel *e.g.b.* *ll.* **-oedd** war, warfare: **Rhyfel y Gwlff** The Gulf War; **Yr Ail Ryfel Byd** The Second World War; **Y Rhyfel Fawr** The Great War.
rhyngo i *gw.* **rhwng.**
rhyngwladol *a.* international.
rhyw 1 *e.b.g.* *ll.* **-iau** sort, kind; sex; gender. 2 *a.* some, certain: **Roedd rhyw ddyn yma ddoe** A certain man was here yesterday.
rhywbeth *e.g.* something.
rhywbryd *ad.* sometime.
rhywdro *ad.* sometime.
rhywfaint *e.g.* some amount.
rhywiol *a.* sexual.
rhywle *ad.* somewhere, anywhere.
rhywrai *gw.* **rhywun.**
rhywsut *ad.* somehow, anyhow.
rhywun *e.g.* *ll.* **rhywrai** someone, anyone: **rhywun neu'i gilydd** someone or other; **rhywrai** some.

Sabath: Saboth *e.g. ll.* **-au** Sabbath.
sach *e.b. ll.* **-au** sack; **sach gysgu** sleeping bag.
Sadwrn *e.g. ll.* **Sadyrnau.** Saturn; Saturday.
saer *e.g. ll.* **seiri** carpenter, joiner; wright; mason: **saer coed** carpenter; **saer maen** stonemason; **pensaer** architect.
Saesneg 1 *e.b.* English (*language*). 2 *a.* English (*in language*).
Saesnes *e.b. ll.* **-au** Englishwoman.
Saeson *gw.* **Sais.**
saeth *e.b. ll.* **-au** arrow.
saethu (at) *be.* **(saethaf)** to shoot, to fire.
saethwr *e.g. ll.* **saethwyr** shooter; archer; goal shooter.
safbwynt *e.g. ll.* **-iau** standpoint, viewpoint, perspective.
safle *e.g. ll.* **-oedd** position, station, situation, rank.
safon *e.b. ll.* **-au** standard, class; criterion: **Safon Dau** Standard Two; **Safon A** A level.
safonol *a.* standard.
saib *e.g. ll.* **seibiau** pause, rest.
sail *e.b. ll.* **seiliau** base, foundation; ground; **ar sail** on the basis of.
saim *e.g. ll.* **seimiau** grease, fat: **saim gŵydd** goose grease.
sain *e.b. ll.* **seiniau** sound, tone.
saint *gw.* **sant.**
Sais *e.g. ll.* **Saeson** Englishman.
saith *a. & e.g.* seven.
sâl 1 *a.* poorly, sick; mean. 2 *e.g.* sale (*N.W.*).
salm *e.b. ll.* **-au** psalm; **salm-dôn** chant.
salw *a.* ugly, vile, mean (*S.W.*).
salwch *e.g.* illness.
sanctaidd *a.* holy.
sant *e.g. ll.* **saint, seintiau** saint: **Dewi Sant** Saint David; **Sant Ioan** Saint John.
santes *e.b. ll.* **-au** female saint: **Santes Dwynwen** Saint Dwynwen, patron saint of lovers.
sarff *e.b. ll.* **seirff** serpent.
sarhad *e.g. ll.* **-au** insult, disgrace.
sarnu (ar) *be.* **(sarnaf)** to trample, to litter, to spill (*S.W.*).
sathru (ar) *be.* **(sathraf)** to trample, to tread: **sathru dan draed** to trample underfoot; **sathru ar gyrn** to offend.
sawdl *e.g.b. ll.* **sodlau** heel.
sawl *rhag. & a.* (*followed by a singular noun*) he that, (*the one*) that, whose; how many? many: **Sawl car sy 'da chi?** How many cars do you have? **Sawl tŷ sy ar y bryn?** How many houses are there on the hill? **Roedd sawl llyfr yn y pentwr** There were many books in the pile; **Y sawl a gododd a gollodd ei le** The one that got up lost his seat.
saws *e.g. ll.* **-iau** sauce.
Sbaen *e.b.* Spain.
Sbaeneg *e.b.* Spanish language.
Sbaenes *e.b. ll.* **-au** Spanish woman.
Sbaenwr *e.g. ll.* **-wyr** Spanish man, Spaniard.
sbectol *e.b.* spectacles.
sbon *ad.* (*as used with the adjective* **newydd**) wholly: **newydd sbon** brand new.
sbot: sbotyn *e.g. ll.* **sbotiau** spot.
sebon *e.g. ll.* **-au** soap: **sebon dannedd** toothpaste.
sedd *e.b. ll.* **-au** seat, pew; **sedd fawr** deacon's pew.
sef *c.* namely, that is to say.
sefydliad *e.g. ll.* **-au** establishment, institution, induction.
sefydlog *a.* fixed, settled, stationary.
sefydlu *be.* **(sefydlaf)** to establish, to settle.
sefyll (am) *be.* **(safaf)** to stand; to stop; to stay, to wait (for) (*S.W.*): **sefyll arholiad** to sit an examination.
sefyllfa *e.b. ll.* **-oedd** situation, position.
segur *a.* idle.
segura *be.* **(seguraf)** to idle.
segurdod *e.g.* idleness.
sengl *a.* single.

seiat *e.b. ll.* **seiadau** fellowship, meeting, society.
seibiant *e.g. ll.* **-au, seibiannau** leisure, respite, pause.
seibiannau *gw.* **seibiant.**
seibiau *gw.* **gw. saib.**
seicoleg *e.b.g.* psychology.
seiliau *gw.* **sail.**
seilio *be.* **(seiliaf)** to base, to found, to ground.
seimiau *gw.* **saim.**
seimlyd: seimllyd *a.* greasy.
seiniau *gw.* **sain.**
seintiau *gw.* **sant.**
seirff *gw.* **sarff.**
seiri *gw.* **saer.**
Seisnig *a.* English, pertaining to England.
Seisnigeiddio: Seisnigo *be.* **(Seisnigeiddiaf: Seisnigaf)** to Anglicise.
seithfed *a.* seventh.
sêl *e.b.* zeal.
Seland Newydd *e.b.* New Zealand.
seld *e.b. ll.* **-au** dresser.
sen *e.b. ll.* **-nau** rebuke, snub, censure; **bwrw sen ar** to cast a rebuke at.
senedd *e.b. ll.* **-au** parliament, senate.
sennau *gw.* **sen.**
sêr *gw.* **seren.**
serch 1 *e.g. ll.* **-iadau** love. 2 *c. & ardd.* although, notwithstanding: **serch ei fod e'n briod** although he was married.
serchog *a.* affectionate, loving.
serchus *a.* affectionate, loving; pleasant.
seremoni *e.b. ll.* **seremonïau** ceremony.
seren *e.b. ll.* **sêr** star; asterisk: **seren wib** shooting star.
serennog *a.* starry.
serth *a.* steep; unclean; obscene.
set *e.b. ll.* **-iau** set: **set deledu** television set.
sêt *e.b. ll.* **seti** seat, pew: **sêt fawr** deacon's seat.
seti *gw.* **sêt.**
setiau *gw.* **set.**
setlo *be.* **(setlaf)** to settle.
sgarff *e.b. ll.* **-iau** scarf.
sgert *e.b. ll.* **-i** skirt; *gw.* **sgyrt.**
sgets *e.b. ll.* **-ys** sketch.
sgi *e.b.g.* ski.
sgil *e.g. ll.* **-iau** skill, device, trick.
sgil *ad.* in the wake of behind: **Daeth tlodi yn sgil y rhyfel** There was poverty in the wake of the war.
sgïo *be.* **(sgïaf)** to ski.
sgipio *be.* **(sgipiaf)** to skip.
sgiw 1 *e.b. ll.* **-iau** settle. 2 *a.* askew.
sgïwr *e.g. ll.* **sgïwyr** skier.
sglefrio *be.* **(sglefriaf)** to skate, to slide.
sglodion *gw.* **sglodyn.**
sglodyn *e.g. ll.* **sglodion** chip: **pysgod a sglodion** fish and chips.
sgôr *e.b. ll.* **sgoriau** score.
sgorio *be.* **(sgoriaf)** to score.
sgrech *e.b. ll.* **-iadau** yell, scream: **sgrech y coed** jay.
sgrechain: sgrechian *be.* **(sgrechaf: sgrechiaf)** to yell, to scream.
sgrifennu: ysgrifennu (ar, at) *be.* **(sgrifennaf: ysgrifennaf)** to write.
sgript *e.b. ll.* **-iau** script.
sgrym *e.b. ll.* **-iau** scrum (*rugby*).
sgrymio *be.* **(sgrymiaf)** to scrum.
sgubo *be.* **(sgubaf)** to sweep, to brush.
sgwâr *e.g.b. ll.* **-iau** square.
sgwd *e.g. ll.* **sgydau** waterfall, cataract.
sgwrs *e.b. ll.* **sgyrsiau** talk, chat; conversation.
sgwrsio (â) *be.* **(sgwrsiaf)** to talk, to chat.
sgydau *gw.* **sgwd.**
sgyrsiau *gw.* **sgwrs.**
sgyrt *e.b. ll.* **-au, -i** skirt; *gw.* **sgert.**
si *e.g. ll.* **sïon** buzz, rumour, murmur.
siaced *e.b. ll.* **-i** jacket, coat.
sialc *e.g. ll.* **-iau** chalk: **sialciau lliw** coloured chalks.
siampl *e.b. ll.* **-au** example.
sianel *e.b. ll.* **-i** channel: **Sianel Pedwar Cymru** S4C (Welsh T.V. Channel 4).
siâp *e.g. ll.* **-iau** shape.
siâr *e.b.* share: **Ga i siâr o'r bwyd?** May I have a share of the food?
siarad *be.* **(siaradaf)** to talk, to speak: **siarad â** to speak with; **siarad am** to speak about.
siaradwr *e.g. ll.* **siaradwyr** talker, speaker.
sibrwd *be.* **(sibrydaf)** to whisper.
sicr: siŵr *a.* sure, certain; secure.
sicrhau *be.* **(sicrhaf)** to assure, to confirm, to obtain, to fix, to secure.
sicrwydd *e.g.* certainty, assurance, security.
sidan *e.g. ll.* **-au** silk.

siec *e.b.* *ll.* **-iau** cheque: **llyfr sieciau** cheque book.
sied *e.b.* *ll.* **-iau** shed.
siersi *e.b.* *ll.* **-s** jersey.
sigâr *e.b.* *ll.* **sigarau** cigar.
sigarét *e.b.* *ll.* **sigaretau** cigarette.
sigledig *a.* shaky, rickety.
siglen *e.b.* *ll.* **-ni, -nydd** swing.
siglo *be.* **(siglaf)** to shake, to quake; to swing; to wag.
silff *e.b.* *ll.* **-oedd** shelf: **silff lyfrau** bookshelf.
silindr *e.g.* *ll.* **-au** cylinder.
silindrog *a.* cylindrical.
silwair *e.g.* *ll.* **silweiriau** silage.
sillaf *e.b.* *ll.* **-au** syllable.
sillafu *be.* **(sillafaf)** to spell: **prawf sillafu** spelling test.
simdde: simnai *e.b.* *ll.* **simneiau** chimney.
simneiau *gw.* **simdde.**
simsan *a.* unsteady, shaky, tottering.
sinema *e.b.* *ll.* **sinemâu** cinema.
sïo *be.* **(sïaf)** to hum, to whiz, to murmur; *gw.* **suo.**
sioc *e.g.* *ll.* **-iau** shock.
sioe *e.b.* *ll.* **-au** show: **sioe amaethyddol** agricultural show; **sioe flodau** flower show; **sioe gŵn** dog show.
sioeau *gw.* **sioe.**
siôl *e.b.* *ll.* **siolau** shawl.
siom *e.g.* *ll.* **-au** disappointment.
siomedig *a.* disappointing, disappointed.
siomedigaeth *e.b.* *ll.* **-au** disappointment.
siomi *be.* **(siomaf)** to disappoint: **siomi ar yr ochr orau** to be pleasantly surprised.
sïon *gw.* **si.**
Siôn Corn *e.g.* Father Christmas.
siop *e.b.* *ll.* **-au** shop; **siop bapurau** newsagent's; **siop ddillad** clothes shop; **siop fara** bread shop, baker's; **siop fwyd** food shop; **siop lyfrau** bookshop; **siop trin gwallt** hair-dresser's, hair salon.
siopa *be.* **(siopaf)** to shop.
siopau *gw.* **siop.**
siopwr *e.g.* *ll.* **siopwyr** shopkeeper.
sipsi *e.g.b.* *ll.* **sipsiwn** gipsy.
sir *e.b.* *ll.* **-oedd** county, shire (*in Wales*); *gw.* **swydd.**
siriol *a.* cheerful, bright, pleasant.
sisial 1 *be.* **(sisialaf)** to whisper. 2 *e.g.* *ll.* **-au** a whisper.
siswrn *e.g.* *ll.* **sisyrnau** scissors.
siwd *gw.* **sut.**
siwg: jwg *e.g.* *ll.* **-iau** jug: **siwg laeth** milk jug.
siwgr *e.g.* sugar; **siwgr brown** brown sugar.
siŵr *gw.* **sicr.**
siwrnai 1 *e.g.* *ll.* **siwrneiau, siwrneion** journey: **Siwrnai dda ichi!** Have a good trip! 2 *ad.* once: **Siwrnai roedd tawelwch, fe gododd i siarad** Once there was silence he rose to speak *(S.W.)*.
sliper *e.b.* *ll.* **-i** slipper.
smotyn *e.g.* *ll.* **smotiau** spot.
sodlau *gw.* **sawdl.**
sôn (am) 1 *be.* **(soniaf)** to mention, to talk, to rumour. 2 *e.g.* mention, talk, rumour: **Does dim sôn amdani** There is no sign of her.
sosban *e.b.* *ll.* **-au, sosbenni** saucepan.
sosbenni *gw.* **sosban.**
soser *e.b.* *ll.* **-i** saucer.
sosialaeth *e.b.* socialism.
sosialaidd *a.* socialist.
sosialwyr *gw.* **sosialydd.**
sosialydd *e.g.* *ll.* **sosialwyr** socialist.
sothach *e.torf.* trash, rubbish.
stabl *e.b.* *ll.* **-au** stable.
stafell: ystafell *e.b.* *ll.* **-oedd** room: **stafell ffrynt** front room; **stafell gefn** back room; **stafell wely** bedroom; **stafell ymolchi** bathroom.
stamp *e.g.* *ll.* **-iau** stamp.
stampio *be.* **(stampiaf)** to stamp.
stôl *e.b.* *ll.* **stolau** stool.
stondin *e.b.* *ll.* **-au** stall: **stondin farchnad** market stall.
stopio *be.* **(stopiaf)** to stop.
stôr *e.g.* *ll.* **storau** store; **stôr celfi** furniture store.
stordy *e.g.* *ll.* **stordai** storehouse, warehouse.
storfa *e.b.* *ll.* **storfeydd** store; storage.
stori *e.b.* *ll.* **storiáu, storïau, straeon** story: **stori arswyd** horror story; **stori fer** short story.
storiáu: storïau *gw.* **stori.**
storïwr *e.g.* *ll.* **storïwyr** story-teller.
storm *e.b.* *ll.* **-ydd** storm.
stormus *a.* stormy, tempestuous.
stormydd *gw.* **storm.**
straeon *gw.* **stori.**
strategaeth *e.b.* strategy.
streic *e.b.* *ll.* **-iau** strike.

strwythur *e.g. ll.* **-au** structure.
strwythuro *be.* **(strwythuraf)** to structure.
stryd *e.b. ll.* **-oedd** street.
stumog *e.b. ll.* **-au** stomach.
stumogi *be.* **(stumogaf)** to stomach.
stŵr *e.g.* stir, noise, bustle, fuss.
su *e.g. ll.* **suon** buzz, murmur, rumour; *gw.* **si.**
suddo *be.* **(suddaf)** to sink, to dive; to invest.
sugno *be.* **(sugnaf)** to suck, to absorb.
Sul *e.g. ll.* **-iau** Sunday: **Dydd Sul** Sunday; **Sul y Blodau** Palm Sunday; **Sul y Mamau** Mothering Sunday.
Sulgwyn *e.g.* Whitsunday.
Suliau *gw.* **Sul.**
suo *be.* **(suaf)** to hum, to buzz; to lull.
suon *gw.* **su.**
sur *a. ll.* **-ion** sour, bitter, acid.
suro *be.* **(suraf)** to sour.
sut: siwd *rhag. gof.* how?: **Sut/Siwd mae?** How are things?
sw *e.g.* zoo.
swil *a.* shy, bashful.
Swistir Y, *e.b.* Switzerland.
swm *e.g. ll.* **symiau** sum.
sŵn *e.g. ll.* **synau** sound, noise.
swnio *be.* **(swniaf)** to sound, to pronounce.
swper *e.g.b. ll.* **-au** supper: **Y Swper Olaf** The Last Supper.
sws *e.g.* kiss (*N.W.*).
swydd *e.b. ll.* **-i, -au** post, office, job; county (*in England*); *gw.* **sir: Swydd Gaerloyw** Gloucestershire; **Swydd Buckingham** Buckinghamshire.
swyddfa *e.b. ll.* **swyddfeydd** office: **Y Swyddfa Gymreig** The Welsh Office.
swyddfeydd *gw.* **swyddfa.**
swyddi *gw.* **swydd.**
swyddog *e.g. ll.* **-ion** officer, official; **swyddog prawf** probation officer; **swyddog y llys** officer of the court.
swyddogol *a.* official; **llythyr swyddogol** official letter.
swyn *e.g. ll.* **-ion** charm, magic, spell.
swyno *be.* **(swynaf)** to charm, to enchant, to bewitch.
swynol *a.* charming, fascinating.
sy: sydd *bf.* is, are; *gw.* **bod.**
sych *a.* dry; **tywydd sych** dry weather.
syched *e.g.* thirst: **Mae syched ar Tom** Tom is thirsty.
sychedig *a.* thirsty, parched.
sychu *be.* **(sychaf)** to dry, to dry up; to wipe.
sydyn *a.* sudden, abrupt.
sydd *gw.* **sy.**
syfrdanol *a.* stupefying, stunning.
sylfaen *e.b. ll.* **sylfeini** foundation, base.
sylfaenol *a.* basic, fundamental.
sylfeini *gw.* **sylfaen.**
sylw *e.g. ll.* **-adau** notice, remark, observation, attention: **Gadewch e dan sylw.** Don't take notice of him.
sylwadau *gw.* **sylw.**
sylwebaeth *e.b. ll.* **-au** commentary.
sylwebu (ar) *be.* **(sylwebaf)** to give a commentary (on).
sylwebydd: sylwebwr *e.g. ll.* **sylwebwyr** commentator.
sylwedd *e.g. ll.* **-au** substance, foundation.
sylweddol *a.* substantial.
sylweddoli *be.* **(sylweddolaf)** to realise.
sylwi (ar) *be.* **(sylwaf)** to observe, to notice: **Sylwch arnyn nhw.** Notice them.
syllu (ar) *be.* **(syllaf)** to gaze.
symiau *gw.* **swm.**
syml *a.* simple.
symud 1 *be.* **(symudaf)** to move, to remove; **2** *e.g.* movement, action.
symudiad *e.g. ll.* **-au** movement, removal.
syn *a.* amazed, astonishing, surprising.
synau *gw.* **sŵn.**
syndod *e.g. ll.* **-au** surprise, amazement.
synhwyrau *gw.* **synnwyr.**
synhwyro *be.* **(synhwyraf)** to sense; to sniff, to smell.
synhwyrol *a.* sensible.
syniad *e.g. ll.* **-au** idea, notion, thought.
synnu (at) *be.* **(synnaf)** to be surprised, to marvel, to wonder: **Rwy'n synnu atoch chi** I'm surprised at you.
synnwyr *e.g. ll.* **synhwyrau** sense.
syr *e.g.* sir: **Annwyl Syr** Dear Sir.
syrcas *e.b. ll.* **-au** circus.
syrffed *e.g.* surfeit.
syrffedu (ar) *be.* **(syrffedaf)** to surfeit, to be fed up (with).
syrthio *be.* **(syrthiaf)** to fall: **syrthio mewn cariad** to fall in love; **syrthio**

ar fai to admit to blame.
syth *a.* stiff, straight, erect: **Dewch yn syth** Come at once.
sythlyd *a.* cold, chilled.
sythu *a.* to become chilled, to straighten (*S.W.*): **Rwyf bron â sythu** I'm perished.

tabl *e.g. ll.* **-au** tabl.
tabled *e.b. ll.* **-au, -i** tablet.
tacl *e.b.g. ll.* **-au** tackle, gear.
taclo *be.* **(taclaf)** to tackle.
taclu *be.* **(taclaf)** to put in order; to dress *(S.W.)*.
taclus *a.* neat, tidy.
tacluso *be.* **(taclusaf)** to trim, to tidy.
taclwr *e.g. ll.* **taclwyr** tackler *(rugby)*.
Tachwedd *e.g.* November.
tad *e.g. ll.* **-au** father: **tadmaeth** foster-father; **llystad** stepfather; **tad-yng-nghyfraith** father-in-law.
tad-cu *e.g. ll.* **tadau-cu** grandfather *(S.W.). gw.* **taid** *(N.W.)*.
tafarn *e.g.b. ll.* **tafarnau** tavern, public house, inn.
tafarnwr *e.g. ll.* **tafarnwyr** publican, inn-keeper.
tafell *e.b. ll.* **-au, -i, tefyll** slice, slab.
taflegryn *e.g. ll.* **taflegrau** missile.
taflen *e.b. ll.* **-ni** leaflet, list, table: **taflen amser** timetable.
taflu (at) *be.* **(taflaf)** to throw (to), to fling, to cast; to dislocate.
tafod *e.g. ll.* **-au** tongue, tang, spit.
tafodiaith *e.b. ll.* **tafodieithoedd** dialect.
tafodieithoedd *gw.* **tafodiaith.**
tafol *e.b. ll.* **-au, -ion** scales.
tagfa *e.b. ll.* **tagfeydd** strangulation, choking, bottleneck.
tagu *be.* **(tagaf)** to strangle, to choke.
tangnefedd *e.g.b.* peace.
tai *gw.* **tŷ.**
taid *e.g. ll.* **teidiau** grandfather *(N.W.); gw.* **tad-cu** *(S.W.)*.
tair *a.b. & e.b.* three: **tair merch** three girls; *gw.* **tri.**
taith *e.b. ll.* **teithiau** journey, tour, voyage.
tal *a.* tall, lofty, high.
tâl 1 *e.g. ll.* **taloedd, taliadau** pay, payment, charge, rates: **Tâl Cymunedol** Community Charge. 2 *e.g. ll.* **talau** forehead, front, end.
talai *e.g. ll.* **taleion** payee.
talaith *e.b. ll.* **taleithiau** province, state: **Yr Unol Daleithiau** The United States.
talcen *e.g. ll.* **-nau, -ni** forehead; gable, pine-end: **talcen tŷ** pine-end of house.
talcennau *gw.* **talcen.**
talcenni *gw.* **talcen.**
taleb *e.b. ll.* **-au, -ion** receipt.
taleion *gw.* **talai.**
taleithiau *gw.* **talaith.**
talent *e.b. ll.* **-au** talent.
talentog *a.* gifted, talented.
talfyriad *e.g. ll.* **-au** abbreviation.
taliadau *gw.* **tâl.**
taloedd *gw.* **tâl.**
talu (am) *be.* **(talaf)** to pay.
talwr *e.g. ll.* **talwyr** payer.
talwrn *e.g. ll.* **talyrnau** spot, place; cock-fighting pit: **Talwrn y Beirdd** the Poet's Place *(for competition)*.
tamaid *e.g. ll.* **tameidiau** piece, bit bite: **tamaid i aros pryd** temporary provision whilst awaiting arrival of something more substantial.
tameidiau *gw.* **tamaid.**
tan *ardd.* (followed by soft mutation) until, as far; under; *gw.* **dan.**
tân *e.g. ll.* **tanau** fire, light: **tân siafins** short-lived enthusiasm and transitory zeal (lit. a blaze of wood shavings).
tanau *gw.* **tân.**
tanbaid *a.* hot, fervent, fiery, brilliant.
tanc *e.g. ll.* **-iau** tank.
tancer *e.g. ll.* **-i** tanker.
tanddaear: tanddaearol *a.* subterranean, underground.
tanfor *a.* submarine: **llong danfor** submarine.
tanio *be.* **(taniaf)** to ignite, to fire, to stoke, to light: **tanio'r dychymyg** to fire the imagination.
tanlinellu *be.* **(tanlinellaf)** to underline.
tanlwybr *e.g. ll.* **-au** subway.
tanllyd *a.* fiery, fervent.

tannau *gw.* **tant.**
tanseilio *be.* **(tanseiliaf)** to sap, to undermine.
tant *e.g. ll.* **tannau** chord, string: **tant telyn** harp string.
tanwydd *e.g. ll.* **-on, -au** fuel, firewood.
tap *e.g. ll.* **-iau** tap; **tap dŵr oer** cold water tap.
tâp *e.g. ll.* **tapiau** tape.
tapiau *gw.* **tap, tâp.**
taran *e.b. ll.* **-au** (peal of) thunder; **mellt a tharanau** thunder and lightning.
taranu *be.* **(taranaf)** to thunder, to threaten.
tarddiad *e.g. ll.* **-au** source, derivation.
tarddu *be.* **(tarddaf)** to spring, to sprout, to derive from, to issue.
targed *e.g. ll.* **-i, -au** target.
tarian *e.b. ll.* **tariannau** shield.
tariannau *gw.* **tarian.**
taro 1 *be.* **(trawaf)** to strike, to hit, to tap; to suit: **Mae e'n dy daro'n iawn** It suits you well. 2 *e.g.* difficulty, crisis; **mewn taro** in an emergency.
tarw *e.g. ll.* **teirw** bull: **llwybr tarw** a short cut.
tasg *e.b. ll.* **-au.**
tasgu *be.* **(tasgaf)** to splash, to start, to bolt; to spark; to lose one's temper: **Roedd e'n tasgu pan glywodd e** He was mad when he heard.
taten *e.b.* **tatws, tato** potato: **tatws drwy'r croen/pil** jacket potatoes; **tatws rhost** roast potatoes; **tatws wedi'u berwi** boiled potatoes; **tatws wedi'u ffrio** fried potatoes; **creision tatws** potato crisps.
tato: tatws *gw.* **taten.**
tawel *a.* quiet, calm, still, peaceful.
tawelu *be.* **(tawelaf)** to calm, to grow calm.
tawelwch *e.g.* quiet, calm, stillness, tranquillity.
tawelydd *e.g. ll.* **-ion** silencer.
tawelyddion *gw.* **tawelydd.**
tawelyn *e.g. ll.* **-ion** tranquilliser.
tawelynion *gw.* **tawelyn.**
te *e.g* tea.
tebot *e.g. ll.* **-au** teapot.
tebyg *a.* like, similar, likely: **yn debyg i** like, similar to; **yn debyg o** likely to.
tebygol *a.* likely, probable; **yn debygol o ennill** likely to win.
tebygrwydd *e.g.* likeness, similarity, resemblance.
tecell: tegell *e.g. ll.* **-au, -i** kettle.
techneg *e.b. ll.* **-au** technique.
technegol *a.* technical.
technegwr *e.g. ll.* **technegwyr** technician.
technoleg *e.b.* technology.
teg *a.* fair, fine, beautiful: **chwarae teg** fair play; **teg o bryd** beautiful in appearance.
tegan *e.g. ll.* **-au** toy, plaything.
tegell *gw.* **tecell.**
tegwch *e.g.* beauty, fairness.
tei *e.g.b. ll.* **teis, -au** tie.
teiar *e.g. ll.* **-s** tyre.
teiau *gw.* **tei.**
teidiau *gw.* **taid.**
teigr *e.g. ll.* **-od** tiger.
teiliwr *e.g. ll.* **teilwriaid** tailor.
teilsen *e.b. ll.* **teils** tile.
teilwng *a.* worthy, deserved: **yn deilwng o** worthy of.
teilwres *e.b. ll.* **-au** tailoress.
teilwriaid *gw.* **teiliwr.**
teilyngdod *e.g. ll.* **-au** merit, worthiness.
teimlad *e.g. ll.* **-au** feel, emotion, feeling, sensation.
teimlo *be.* **(teimlaf)** to feel, to handle, to touch; **teimlo fel** to feel like.
teipiadur *e.g. ll.* **-on** typewriter.
teirgwaith *ad.* three times.
teirw *gw.* **tarw.**
teis *gw.* **tei.**
teisen *e.b. ll.* **-nau** cake, tart: **teisen ddwbl** sandwich cake; **teisen ffrwythau** fruit cake; **teisennau cri** Welsh cakes.
teitl *e.g. ll.* **-au** title.
teithiau *gw.* **taith.**
teithio *be.* **(teithiaf)** to travel, to journey.
teithiwr *e.g. ll.* **teithwyr** traveller.
telediad *e.g. ll.* **-au** telecast.
teledu 1 *be.* **(teledaf)** to televise. 2 *e.g.* television; **set deledu lliw** colour televison set.
teleffon *e.g. ll.* **-au** telephone; gw. **ffôn.**
teleffonio: ffonio *be.* **(teleffoniaf: ffoniaf)** to telephone, to phone.
telyn *e.b. ll.* **-au** harp.
telyneg *e.b. ll.* **-ion** lyric.
telynor *e.g. ll.* **-ion** harpist.
telynores *e.b. ll.* **-au** female harpist.
telynorion *gw.* **telynor.**
teml *e.b. ll.* **-au** temple.
tenau *a.* thin, slender, lean; rare.

terfyn *e.g. ll.* **-au** end, boundary, extremity.
terfynol *a.* ultimate, last: **y taliad terfynol** the last instalment.
terfysg *e.g. ll.* **-oedd** tumult, commotion, riot.
terfysgaeth *e.g.* terrorism.
terfysgwr *e.g. ll.* **terfysgwyr** terrorist.
term *e.g. ll.* **-au** term: **termau technegol** technical terms.
tes *e.g. ll.* **-au, -oedd** heat, sunshine, haze.
tesog *a.* hot, sunny.
testun *e.g. ll.* **-au** text, subject: **testun sgwrs** subject for debate; **testun siarad** subject of gossip.
teulu *e.g. ll.* **-oedd** family.
tew *a.* fat.
teyrnas *e.b. ll.* **-oedd** kingdom: **Teyrnas Nefoedd** Kingdom of Heaven; **Y Deyrnas Unedig** The United Kingdom.
ti *rhag.* you *(singular).*
ticed *e.g. ll.* **-i** ticket.
tîm *e.g. ll.* **timau** team.
tip *e.g. ll.* **-iau** tip.
tipiau *gw.* **tip, tipyn.**
tipyn *e.g. ll.* **-nau, tipiau** little, bit; **tipyn bach** a little; **bob yn dipyn** little by little.
tir *e.g. ll.* **-oedd** land, earth, ground, territory. **tir neb** no man's land; **colli tir** to lose ground.
tirion *a.* tender, kind, gentle, gracious.
tirlun *e.g. ll.* **-iau** landscape.
tiroedd *gw.* **tir.**
tisian *be.* **(tisiaf)** to sneeze.
tithau *rhag.* you also *(singular).*
tlawd *a. ll.* **tlodion** poor, needy: **y tlodion** the poor.
tlodi *e.g.* poverty.
tlodion *gw.* **tlawd.**
tlos *a.b.* pretty: **merch dlos** a pretty girl *(N.W.); gw.* **tlws.**
tlws 1 *e.g. ll.* **tlysau** gem, jewel, brooch: **tlws aur** a gold brooch; **tlws yr eira** snowdrop; **clustlysau** ear-rings. 2 *a.g.* pretty; *gw.* **tlos.**
tlysau *gw.* **tlws.**
to 1 *e.g. ll.* **-eau, -eon** roof. 2 *e.g.b.* generation: **y to sy'n codi** the rising generation.
tocyn *e.g. ll.* **-nau** ticket, token; **tocyn dychwel** return ticket.
tocynnau *gw.* **tocyn.**
tocynnwr *e.g. ll.* **tocynwyr** ticket collector, conductor.
tocynwyr *gw.* **tocynnwr.**
toddi *be.* **(toddaf)** to melt, to thaw, to dissolve.
toeau *gw.* **to.**
toeon *gw.* **to.**
toes *e.g.* dough: **toesenni** doughnuts; **tylino toes** to knead dough.
toiled *e.g. ll.* **-au** toilet.
tolc *e.g. ll.* **-iau** dent.
tolcio *be.* **(tolciaf)** to dent.
toll *e.b. ll.* **-au** toll, custom, duty: **tollborth/tollglwyd** toll-gate.
ton *e.b. ll.* **tonnau** wave, breaker.
tôn *e.b. ll.* **tonau** tune: **tôn gron** a round (tune).
tonau *gw.* **tôn.**
tonfedd *e.b. ll.* **-i** wavelength.
tonnau *gw.* **ton.**
torch *e.b. ll.* **-au** wreath, coil, torque.
toreithiog *a.* abundant, teeming.
toreth *e.b.* abundance.
torf *e.b. ll.* **-eydd** crowd, multitude.
torfeydd *gw.* **torf.**
torfol *a.* collective, mass: **enw torfol** collective noun.
torheulo *be.* **(torheulaf)** to sunbathe.
Tori *e.g. ll.* **Torïaid** Tory.
toriad *e.g. ll.* **-au** break, cut.
Torïaid *gw.* **Tori.**
Torïaidd *a.* Tory, Conservative.
torri *be.* **(torraf)** to break, to cut, to sever; to go bankrupt: **torri ar draws** to interrupt; **torri enw** to sign; **torri gwynt** to break wind.
tors *e.g.b. ll.* **tyrs** torch.
torth *e.b. ll.* **-au** loaf; **torth wen** white loaf.
tosau *gw.* **tosyn.**
tost 1 *a.* severe, sharp, sore; ill *(S.W.).* 2 *e.g. ll.* **-ys** toast (bread).
tostrwydd *e.g.* illness, severity.
tosyn *e.g. ll.* **tosau** pimple *(S.W.).*
trachefn *gw.* **drachefn.**
trachwant *e.g. ll.* **-au** lust, greed, covetousness.
trachwantus *a.* covetous, lustful.
traddodiad *e.g. ll.* **-au** tradition; delivery.
traddodiadol *a.* traditional.
traed *g.w.* **troed.**
traeth *e.g. ll.* **-au** beach, shore.
traethau *gw.* **traeth.**
traethawd *e.g. ll.* **traethodau** essay, treatise, tract.
traethodau *gw.* **traethawd.**
trafnidiaeth *e.b.* traffic, commerce.
trafod *be.* **(trafodaf)** to handle, to discuss, to negotiate, to transact:

cylch trafod discussion group.
trafferth *e.b.g. ll.* **-ion** trouble, toil, bother.
trafferthu (i) *be.* **(trafferthaf)** to trouble, to bother, to take pains.
trafferthus *a.* troublesome, laborious; troubled.
traffordd *e.b. ll.* **traffyrdd** motorway.
traffyrdd *gw.* **traffordd.**
tragwyddol *a.* eternal, everlasting: **o dragwyddol bwys** of everlasting importance.
trai *e.g. ll.* **treiau** ebb, decrease: **llanw a thrai** ebb and flow.
trais *e.g. ll.* **treisiau** violence, oppression; rape.
trallod *e.g. ll.* **-au, -ion** tribulation, trouble.
trallodau *gw.* **trallod.**
trallodion *gw.* **trallod.**
trallwysiad *e.g. ll.* **-au** transfusion: **Gwasanaeth Trallwyso Gwaed** Blood Transfusion Service.
tramor *a.* overseas, foreign.
trannoeth *ad.* next day: **Daeth e drannoeth** He came the next day.
trap *e.g. ll.* **-iau** trap.
traul *e.b. ll.* **treuliau** wear; cost, expense.
trawsblannu *be.* **(trawsblannaf)** to transplant.
trawst *e.g. ll.* **-iau** beam, crossbar.
tre *gw.* **tref.**
trechu *be.* **(trechaf)** to overcome, to defeat.
tref: tre *e.b. ll.* **-i, -ydd** town, home: **tua thre** homeward; **tre farchnad** market town.
trefi *gw.* **tref.**
trefn *e.b. ll.* **-au** order, arrangement, system, method: **dweud y drefn** to scold.
trefnu (i) *be.* **(trefnaf)** to order, to arrange, to organise, to sort.
trefnus *a.* orderly, methodical.
trefnydd *e.g. ll.* **-ion** organiser.
trefol *a.* urban.
trefydd *gw.* **tref.**
treial *e.g. ll.* **-on** trial, contest: **treialon cŵn defaid** sheepdog trials.
treiau *gw.* **trai.**
treiglad *e.g. ll.* **-au** mutation; rolling: **treiglad llaes** spirant mutation; **treiglad meddal** soft mutation; **treiglad trwynol** nasal mutation.
treiglo *be.* **(treiglaf)** to mutate; to roll.
treisiau *gw.* **trais.**
treisio *be.* **(treisiaf)** to force, to violate, to oppress; to rape.
trem *e.b. ll.* **-iau** sight, look.
trên *e.g. ll.* **trenau** train.
trenau *gw.* **trên.**
trennydd *ad.* two days hence.
treth *e.b. ll.* **-i** rate, tax, levy; strain: **treth ar werth** value added tax; **treth incwm** income tax; **treth y pen** community charge/poll tax; **treth cyngor** council tax; **Roedd e'n dreth ar fy amynedd** He was a strain on my patience.
trethdalwr *e.g. ll.* **trethdalwyr** ratepayer.
trethu *be.* **(trethaf)** to tax, to rate.
treuliau *gw.* **traul.**
treulio *be.* **(treuliaf)** to wear; to spend; to digest.
tri *a.g. & e.g. ll. (followed by spirant mutation)* three: **tri chap** three caps; **tri pheint** three pints; **tri thŷ** three houses; **tri chynnig i Gymro** three tries for a Welshman; *gw. At. Treigladau,* **tair.**
triawd *e.g. ll.* **-au** trio, threesome.
tric *e.g. ll.* **-iau** trick.
tridiau *e.ll.* three days.
trigain *a. & e.g.* sixty: **trigain mlynedd yn ôl** sixty years ago; *gw. At. Treiglad Trwynol.*
trigfan *e.b. ll.* **-nau** dwelling-place.
trigo *be.* **(trigaf)** to dwell, to reside; to die (of animal).
trigolion *e.ll.* inhabitants.
trin *be.* **(triniaf)** to treat; to handle; to dress; to till; to revile: **siop trin gwallt** hairdresser's shop; **trin y tir** to cultivate the land.
trindod *e.b. ll.* **-au** trinity: **Coleg y Drindod** Trinity College.
trioedd *e.ll.* triads.
triongl *e.g.b. ll.* **-au** triangle.
trist *a.* sad, sorrowful, unhappy.
tristwch *e.g.* sadness, sorrow: **tristwch o'r mwyaf** the greatest sorrow.
tro *e.g. ll.* **troeau, troeon** turn, twist, bend; conversion: **gweld tro ar fyd** to experience a change in circumstances.
llygad tro a squint: **tro gwael** an unworthy act; **tro yn ei gwt** a twist in his tail.
trochi *be.* **(trochaf)** to dip, to plunge; to soil *(S.W.)*; to bathe *(N.W.)*.
troeau *gw.* **tro.**
troed *e.g.b. ll.* **traed** foot, base; handle.

troedfedd *e.b. ll.* **-i** foot *(measure).*
troedffordd *e.g. ll.* **troedffyrdd** footpath.
troëdig *a.* turned, converted.
tröedigaeth *e.b. ll.* **-au** conversion, turning.
troedio *be.* **(troediaf)** to walk, to tread, to trudge.
troednoeth *a.* barefooted.
troeon *gw.* **tro.**
trogylch *e.g. ll.* **-oedd, -au** roundabout.
troi *be.* **(troaf)** to turn, to revolve, to convert; to plough; to translate; *gw. At. Berfau.*
tros *gw.* **dros.**
trosedd *e.b. ll.* **-au** crime, offence, transgression.
troseddu *be.* **(troseddaf)** to offend, to transgress.
troseddwr *e.g. ll.* **troseddwyr** criminal, transgressor.
trosgais *e.g. ll.* **trosgeisiau** converted try *(rugby).*
trosglwyddo *be.* **(trosglwyddaf)** to convey, to transfer.
trosi *be.* **(trosaf)** to turn, to translate, to transfer; to convert *(rugby).*
trosiad *e.g. ll.* **-au** translation; conversion *(rugby).*
troswr *e.g. ll.* **troswyr** switch *(electricity).*
trothwy *e.g. ll.* **-au, -on** threshold: **ar drothwy'r Nadolig** on the threshold of Christmas.
trowsus *e.g. ll.* **-au** trousers: **trowsus byr** short trousers.
truan *e.g. ll.* **trueiniaid** wretch: **Druan ohono!** Poor fellow! **Jac druan!** Poor Jack!.
trueiniad *gw.* **truan.**
trueni *e.g.* wretchedness, pity, misery: **trueni ei fod** a pity that; **trueni iddo** a pity that.
truenus *a.* wretched, miserable.
trugaredd *e.g. ll.* **-au** mercy, compassion: **drwy drugaredd** fortunately.
trugarhau (wrth) *be.* **(trugarhaf)** to be merciful (to), to take pity (on).
trwbl *e.g.* trouble.
trwchus *a.* thick; dense.
trwm *a. ll.* **trymion** heavy, sad, wretched.
trwser *e.g. ll.* **-i** trousers: *gw.* **trowsus.**
trwsio *e.* **(trwsiaf)** to mend, to trim, to dress.
trwsiwr *e.g. ll.* **trwswyr** repairer.
trwy *gw.* **drwy.**
trwydded *e.b. ll.* **-au** licence, dispensation: **trwydded yrru** driving licence.
trwyn *e.g. ll.* **-au** nose, snout; point, cape.
trwynol *a.* nasal.
trychineb *e.g.b. ll.* **-au** disaster, calamity.
trydan 1 *e.g.* electricity. 2 *a.* electric; **Y Bwrdd Trydan** The Electricity Board.
trydanwr *e.g. ll.* **trydanwyr** electrician.
trydedd *a.b. (used before feminine nouns)* third: **y drydedd bennod** the third chapter.
trydydd *a.g. (used before masculine nouns)* third: **Y trydydd tro** The third time.
trydyddol *a.* tertiary: **Coleg Trydyddol** Tertiary College.
tryloyw *a.* transparent.
trymaidd *a.* heavy, close, sultry.
trymion *gw.* **trwm.**
trysor *e.b. ll.* **-au** treasure.
trysorfa *e.b. ll.* **trysorfeydd** treasury, fund.
trysori *be.* **(trysoraf)** to treasure.
trysorydd *e.g. ll.* **-ion** treasurer.
trywydd *e.g. ll.* **-ion** scent, trail: **ar drywydd** on the trail of.
tu *e.g.* side, region: **tu draw i: tu hwnt** beyond; **tu fewn: tu mewn** inside; **tu faes** *(S.W.):* **tu allan** *(N.W.)* outside.
tua: tuag *ardd. (followed by spirant mutation)* towards; about: **tua thre: adre** homewards; **tuag at** towards; **tua mis** about a month.
tudalen *e.g.b. ll.* **-nau** page: **tudalen flaen** front page; *gw.* **dalen.**
tueddiad *e.g. ll.* **-au** tendency, proneness.
tun 1 *e.g.* **-iau** tin, can. 2 *a.* tin.
tunnell *e.g. ll.* **tunelli** ton.
twlc *e.g. ll.* **tylciau** sty: **twlc mochyn** pigsty.
twll *e.g. ll.* **tyllau** hole.
twmpath *e.g. ll.* **-au** tump, hillock: **Twmpath Dawns** Folk Dancing event.
twndis *e.g. ll.* **-au** funnel.
twnel *e.g. ll.* **-au, -i** tunnel.
twp *a.* dull, stupid *(S.W.).*
twpsyn *e.g.* stupid person.
twr *e.g. ll.* **tyrrau** heap; group; crowd.
tŵr *e.g. ll.* **tyrau** tower.

twrci *e.g. ll.* **twrcïod, tyrcwn** turkey.
twristiaeth *e.b.* tourism: **Y Bwrdd Croeso** The Tourist Board.
twrw *e.g. ll.* **tyrfau** noise, tumult, roar, crash: **tyrfau: taranau** thunder.
twt *a.* neat, tidy: **tŷ bach twt** a Wendy house *(lit. a neat little house);* **twt a lol** nonsense, rubbish.
twyll *e.g.* deceit, fraud, treachery.
twyllo *be.* **(twyllaf)** to deceive, to cheat, to defraud.
twyllodrus *a.* deceitful, false, fraudulent.
twym *a.* warm *(S.W.);* **twym iawn** hot *(S.W.).*
twymo *be.* **(twymaf)** to warm.
twymyn *e.b. ll.* **-au** fever.
tŷ *e.g. ll.* **tai** house: **tŷ newydd** new house; **tŷ bach** toilet; **tŷ tafarn** public house; **tŷ cwrdd** religious meeting house.
tybed *ad.* I wonder: is that so? **Tybed a ddaw hi?** I wonder whether she will come?
tybied: tybio *be.* **(tybiaf)** to suppose, to think, to imagine.
tydi *rhag.* you yourself.
tyddyn *e.g. ll.* **-nod, -nau** small holding, small farm, croft: **tŷ'n cwm: tyddyn y cwm** the valley smallholding; **tŷ'n y waun** the moor croft.
tyddynnwr *e.g. ll.* **tyddynwyr** smallholder, crofter.
tyddynwyr *gw.* **tyddynnwr.**
tyfiannau *gw.* **tyfiant.**
tyfiant *e.g. ll.* **tyfiannau** growth, increase.
tyfu *be.* **(tyfaf)** to grow, to increase.
tynged *e.b. ll.* **tynghedau** destiny, fate.
tyngedfennol *a.* fateful, fatal.
tynghedau *gw.* **tynged.**
tyngu *be.* **(tyngaf)** to swear, to vow.
tylciau *gw.* **twlc.**
tyle *e.g. ll.* **-au** hill, ascent, slope *(S.W.).*
tylino *be.* **(tylinaf)** to knead *(dough).*
tylwyth *e.g. ll.* **-au** family, ancestry, kindred: **Tylwyth Teg** fairies.
tyllau *gw.* **twll.**
tyllu *be.* **(tyllaf)** to hole, to bore, to perforate.
tylluan *e.b. ll.* **-od** owl *(N.W.); gw.* **gwdihŵ.**
tymer *e.b. ll.* **tymherau** temper, temperament.
tymereddau *gw.* **tymheredd.**
tymestl *e.b. ll.* **tymhestloedd** tempest, storm.
tymherau *gw.* **tymer.**
tymheredd *e.g. ll.* **tymereddau** temperature, temperament.
tymhestloedd *gw.* **tymestl.**
tymhestlog *a.* tempestuous, stormy.
tymhorau *gw.* **tymor.**
tymor *e.g. ll.* **tymhorau** season, term: **Tymor yr Haf** Summer Term; **yn ei thymor** in season *(of animal).*
tyn 1 *a.* tight, mean, perverse. 2 *bf.* pull! tighten! *gw.* **tynnu.**
tyner *a.* gentle, tender.
tynerwch *e.g.* gentleness, tenderness.
tynnu *be.* **(tynnaf)** to pull, to draw, to remove; take off: **Tynnwch eich cot** Take off your coat.
tyrau *gw.* **tŵr.**
tyrfa *e.b. ll.* **-oedd** crowd, multitude.
tyrfau *gw.* **twrw.**
tyrrau *gw.* **twr.**
tyst *e.g. ll.* **-ion** witness.
tystio *be.* **(tystiaf)** to testify, to witness; **tystio bod** to testify that.
tystiolaeth *e.b. ll.* **-au** evidence; testimony.
tystion *gw.* **tyst.**
tystysgrif *e.b. ll.* **-au** certificate: **tystysgrif geni** birth certificate; **tystysgrif marwolaeth** death certificate; **tystysgrif priodi** marriage certificate.
tywel *e.g. ll.* **-ion** towel.
tywod *e.g.* sand.
tywydd *e.g.* weather: **tywydd mawr** stormy weather: **tywydd teg** fair weather.
tywyll *a.* dark, obscure; blind, sad.
tywyllu *be.* **(tywyllaf)** to darken.
tywyllwch *e.g.* darkness.
tywys *be.* **(tywysaf)** to lead, to guide.
tywysydd *e.g. ll.* **-ion** guide.
tywysog *e.g. ll.* **-ion** prince: **Tywysog Cymru** Prince of Wales.
tywysoges *e.b. ll.* **-au** princess: **Tywysoges Cymru** Princess of Wales.

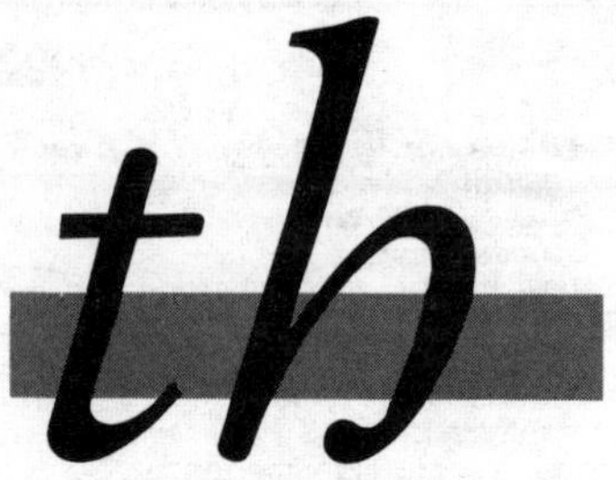

thabl *gw.* **tabl.**
thabled *gw.* **tabled.**
thacl *gw.* **tacl.**
thaclo *gw.* **taclo.**
thaclu *gw.* **taclu.**
thaclus *gw.* **taclus.**
thacluso *gw.* **tacluso.**
thaclwr *gw.* **taclwr.**
Thachwedd *gw.* **Tachwedd.**
thad *gw.* **tad.**
thad-cu *gw.* **tad-cu.**
thafarn *gw.* **tafarn.**
thafarnwr *gw.* **tafarnwr.**
thafell *gw.* **tafell.**
thaflegryn *gw.* **taflegryn.**
thaflen *gw.* **taflen.**
thaflu *gw.* **taflu.**
thafod *gw.* **tafod.**
thafodiaith *gw.* **tafodiaith.**
thafodieithoedd *gw.* **tafodiaith.**
thafol *gw.* **tafol.**
thagfa *gw.* **tagfa.**
thagu *gw.* **tagu.**
thangnefedd *gw.* **tangnefedd.**
thai *gw.* **tŷ.**
thaid *gw.* **taid.**
thair *gw.* **tair.**
thaith *gw.* **taith.**
thal *gw.* **tal.**
thâl *gw.* **tâl.**
thalai *gw.* **talai, talu.**
thalaith *gw.* **talaith.**
thalau *gw.* **tâl.**
thalcen *gw.* **talcen.**
thalcennau: thalcenni *gw.* **talcen.**
thaleb *gw.* **taleb.**
thalent *gw.* **talent.**
thalentog *gw.* **talentog.**
thaliadau: thaloedd *gw.* **tâl.**
thalu *gw.* **talu.**
thalwr *gw.* **talwr.**
thalwrn *gw.* **talwrn.**
thamaid *gw.* **tamaid.**
thameidiau *gw.* **tamaid.**
than *gw.* **dan.**
thân *gw.* **tân.**
thanau *gw.* **tanau.**
thanbaid *gw.* **tanbaid.**
thanc *gw.* **tanc.**
thancer *gw.* **tancer.**
thanddaear *gw.* **tanddaear.**
thanddaearol *gw.* **tanddaear.**
thanfor *gw.* **tanfor.**
thanio *gw.* **tanio.**
thanlinellu *gw.* **tanlinellu.**
thanlwybr *gw.* **tanlwybr.**
thanllyd *gw.* **tanllyd.**
thannau *gw.* **tant.**
thanseilio *gw.* **tanseilio.**
thant *gw.* **tant.**
thanwydd *gw.* **tanwydd.**
thap *gw.* **tap.**
thâp *gw.* **tâp.**
thapiau *gw.* **tap, tâp.**
tharan *gw.* **taran.**
tharanu *gw.* **taranu.**
tharddiad *gw.* **tarddiad.**
tharddu *gw.* **tarddu.**
tharged *gw.* **targed.**
tharian *gw.* **tarian.**
tharianau *gw.* **tarian.**
tharo *gw.* **taro.**
tharw *gw.* **tarw.**
thasg *gw.* **tasg.**
thasgu *gw.* **tasgu.**
thaten *gw.* **taten.**
thato *gw.* **taten.**
thatws *gw.* **taten.**
thawel *gw.* **tawel.**
thawelu *gw.* **tawelu.**
thawelwch *gw.* **tawelwch.**
thawelydd *gw.* **tawelydd.**
thawelyddion *gw.* **tawelydd.**
thawelyn *gw.* **tawelyn.**
thawelynion *gw.* **tawelyn.**
the *gw.* **te.**
theatr *e.b. ll.* **-au** theatre, playhouse.
thebot *gw.* **tebot.**
thebyg *gw.* **tebyg.**
thebygrwydd *gw.* **tebyrgwydd.**
thecell *gw.* **tecell.**
thechneg *gw.* **techneg.**
thechnegol *gw.* **technegol.**
thechnegwr *gw.* **technegwr.**
thechnoleg *gw.* **technoleg.**
theg *gw.* **teg.**
thegan *gw.* **tegan.**
thegell *gw.* **tecell.**

thegwch *gw.* **tegwch.**
thei *gw.* **tei.**
theiar *gw.* **teiar.**
theiau *gw.* **tei.**
theidiau *gw.* **taid.**
theigr *gw.* **teigr.**
theiliwr *gw.* **teiliwr.**
theilsen *gw.* **teilsen.**
theilwng *gw.* **teilwng.**
theilwres *gw.* **teilwres.**
theilwriaid *gw.* **teiliwr.**
theilyngdod *gw.* **teilyngdod.**
theimlad *gw.* **teimlad.**
theimlo *gw.* **teimlo.**
theipiadur *gw.* **teipiadur.**
theirgwaith *gw.* **teirgwaith.**
theirw *gw.* **tarw.**
theis *gw.* **tei.**
theisen *gw.* **teisen.**
theitl *gw.* **teitl.**
theithiau *gw.* **taith.**
theithio *gw.* **teithio.**
theithiwr *gw.* **teithiwr.**
thelediad *gw.* **telediad.**
theledu *gw.* **teledu.**
theleffon *gw.* **teleffon.**
theleffonio *gw.* **teleffonio.**
thelyn *gw.* **telyn.**
thelyneg *gw.* **telyneg.**
thelynor *gw.* **telynor.**
thelynores *gw.* **telynores.**
thelynorion *gw.* **telynor.**
thema *e.b.* *ll.* **themâu** theme.
theml *gw.* **teml.**
thenau *gw.* **tenau.**
therapydd *e.g.* *ll.* **-ion** therapist.
therfyn *gw.* **terfyn.**
therfysg *gw.* **terfysg.**
therfysgaeth *gw.* **terfysgaeth.**
therfysgwr *gw.* **terfysgwr.**
therm *gw.* **term.**
thermomedr *e.g.* *ll.* **-au** thermometer.
thes *gw.* **tes.**
thesog *gw.* **tesog.**
thestun *gw.* **testun.**
theulu *gw.* **teulu.**
thew *gw.* **tew.**
theyrnas *gw.* **teyrnas.**
thi *gw.* **ti.**
thiced *gw.* **ticed.**
thîm *gw.* **tîm.**
thipiau *gw.* **tip, tipyn.**
thipyn *gw.* **tipyn.**
thir *gw.* **tir.**
thirion *gw.* **tirion.**
thirlun *gw.* **tirlun.**
thiroedd *gw.* **tir.**
thisian *gw.* **tisian.**
thithau *gw.* **tithau.**
thlawd *gw.* **tlawd.**
thlodi *gw.* **tlodi.**
thlodion *gw.* **tlawd.**
thlos *gw.* **tlos.**
thlws *gw.* **tlws.**
thlysau *gw.* **tlws.**
tho *gw.* **to.**
thocyn *gw.* **tocyn.**
thocynnau *gw.* **tocyn.**
thocynnwr *gw.* **tocynnwr.**
thocynwyr *gw.* **tocynnwr.**
thoddi *gw.* **toddi.**
thoeau *gw.* **to.**
thoeon *gw.* **to.**
thoes *gw.* **toes.**
thoiled *gw.* **toiled.**
tholc *gw.* **tolc.**
tholcio *gw.* **tolcio.**
tholl *gw.* **toll.**
thon *gw.* **ton.**
thôn *gw.* **tôn.**
thonau *gw.* **tôn.**
thonfedd *gw.* **tonfedd.**
thonnau *gw.* **ton.**
thorch *gw.* **torch.**
thoreithiog *gw.* **toreithiog.**
thoreth *gw.* **toreth.**
thorf *gw.* **torf.**
thorfeydd *gw.* **torf.**
thorfol *gw.* **torfol.**
thorheulo *gw.* **torheulo.**
Thori *gw.* **Tori.**
thoriad *gw.* **toriad.**
Thorïaid *gw.* **Tori.**
Thorïaidd *gw.* **Torïaidd.**
thorri *gw.* **torri.**
thors *gw.* **tors.**
thorth *gw.* **torth.**
thosau *gw.* **tosyn.**
thost *gw.* **tost.**
thostrwydd *gw.* **tostrwydd.**
thosyn *gw.* **tosyn.**
thrachefn *gw.* **trachefn.**
thrachwant *gw.* **trachwant.**
thrachwantus *gw.* **trachwantus.**
thraddodiad *gw.* **traddodiad.**
thraddodiadol *gw.* **traddodiadol.**
thraed *gw.* **traed.**
thraeth *gw.* **traeth.**
thraethau *gw.* **traeth.**
thraethawd *gw.* **traethawd.**
thraethodau *gw.* **thraethawd.**
thrafnidiaeth *gw.* **trafnidiaeth.**
thrafod *gw.* **trafod.**
thrafferth *gw.* **trafferth.**
thrafferthu *gw.* **trafferthu.**
thrafferthus *gw.* **trafferthus.**
thraffordd *gw.* **traffordd.**

thraffyrdd *gw.* **traffordd.**
thragwyddol *gw.* **tragwyddol.**
thrai *gw.* **trai.**
thrais *gw.* **trais.**
thrallod *gw.* **trallod.**
thrallodau *gw.* **trallod.**
thrallodion *gw.* **trallod.**
thrallwysiad *gw.* **trallwysiad.**
thramor *gw.* **tramor.**
thrannoeth *gw.* **trannoeth.**
thrap *gw.* **trap.**
thraul *gw.* **traul.**
thrawsblannu *gw.* **trawsblannu.**
thrawst *gw.* **trawst.**
thre *gw.* **tref.**
threchu *gw.* **trechu.**
thref *gw.* **tref.**
threfi *gw.* **tref.**
threfn *gw.* **trefn.**
threfnu *gw.* **trefnu.**
threfnus *gw.* **trefnus.**
threfnydd *gw.* **trefnydd.**
threfol *gw.* **trefol.**
threfydd *gw.* **tref.**
threial *gw.* **treial.**
threiau *gw.* **trai.**
threiglad *gw.* **treiglad.**
threiglo *gw.* **treiglo.**
threisiau *gw.* **trais.**
threisio *gw.* **treisio.**
threm *gw.* **trem.**
thrên *gw.* **trên.**
threnau *gw.* **trên.**
thrennydd *gw.* **trennydd.**
threth *gw.* **treth.**
threthdalwr *gw.* **trethdalwr.**
threthu *gw.* **trethu.**
threuliau *gw.* **traul.**
threulio *gw.* **treulio.**
thri *gw.* **tri.**
thriawd *gw.* **triawd.**
thric *gw.* **tric.**
thridiau *gw.* **tridiau.**
thrigain *gw.* **trigain.**
thrigfan *gw.* **trigfan.**
thrigo *gw.* **trigo.**
thrigolion *gw.* **trigolion.**
thrin *gw.* **trin.**
thrindod *gw.* **trindod.**
thrioedd *gw.* **trioedd.**
thriongl *gw.* **triongl.**
thrist *gw.* **trist.**
thristwch *gw.* **tristwch.**
thro *gw.* **tro.**
throchi *gw.* **trochi.**
throeau *gw.* **tro.**
throed *gw.* **troed.**
throedfedd *gw.* **troedfedd.**
throedffordd *gw.* **troedffordd.**
throëdig *gw.* **troëdig.**
thröedigaeth *gw.* **tröedigaeth.**
throedio *gw.* **troedio.**
throednoeth *gw.* **troednoeth.**
throeon *gw.* **tro.**
throgylch *gw.* **trogylch.**
throi *gw.* **troi.**
thros *gw.* **tros.**
throsedd *gw.* **trosedd.**
throseddu *gw.* **troseddu.**
throseddwr *gw.* **troseddwr.**
throsgais *gw.* **trosgais.**
throsglwyddo *gw.* **trosglwyddo.**
throsi *gw.* **trosi.**
throsiad *gw.* **trosiad.**
throswr *gw.* **troswr.**
throthwy *gw.* **trothwy.**
throwsus *gw.* **trowsus.**
thruan *gw.* **truan.**
thrueiniaid *gw.* **truan.**
thrueni *gw.* **trueni.**
thruenus *gw.* **truenus.**
thrugaredd *gw.* **trugaredd.**
thrugarhau *gw.* **trugarhau.**
thrwbl *gw.* **trwbl.**
thrwchus *gw* **trwchus.**
thrwm *gw.* **trwm.**
thrwser *gw.* **trwser.**
thrwsio *gw.* **trwsio.**
thrwsiwr *gw.* **trwsiwr.**
thrwy *gw.* **drwy.**
thrwydded *gw.* **trwydded.**
thrwyn *gw.* **trwyn.**
thrwynol *gw.* **trwynol.**
thrychineb *gw.* **trychineb.**
thrydan *gw.* **trydan.**
thrydanwr *gw.* **trydanwr.**
thrydedd *gw.* **trydedd.**
thrydydd *gw.* **tryddydd.**
thrydyddol *gw.* **trydyddol.**
thryloyw *gw.* **tryloyw.**
thrymaidd *gw.* **trymaidd.**
thrymion *gw.* **trwm.**
thrysor *gw.* **trysor.**
thrysorfa *gw.* **trysorfa.**
thrysorydd *gw.* **trysorydd.**
thrywydd *gw.* **trywydd.**
thu *gw.* **tu.**
thua *gw.* **tua.**
thuag *gw.* **tua.**
thudalen *gw.* **tudalen.**
thueddiad *gw.* **tueddiad.**
thun *gw.* **tun.**
thunnell *gw.* **tunnell.**
thus *e.g.* frankincense.
thwlc *gw.* **twlc.**
thwll *gw.* **twll.**
thwmpath *gw.* **twmpath.**
thwndis *gw.* **twndis.**

thwnel *gw.* **twnel.**
thwp *gw.* **twp.**
thwpsyn *gw.* **twpsyn.**
thwr *gw.* **twr.**
thŵr *gw.* **tŵr.**
thwrci *gw.* **twrci.**
thwristiaeth *gw.* **twristiaeth.**
thwrw *gw.* **twrw.**
thwt *gw.* **twt.**
thwyll *gw.* **twyll.**
thwyllo *gw.* **twyllo.**
thwyllodrus *gw.* **twyllodrus.**
thwym *gw.* **twym.**
thwymo *gw.* **twymo.**
thwymyn *gw.* **twymyn.**
thŷ *gw.* **tŷ.**
thybied *gw.* **tybied.**
thybio *gw.* **tybied.**
thydi *gw.* **tydi.**
thyddyn *gw.* **tyddyn.**
thyddynnwr *gw.* **tyddynnwr.**
thyddynwyr *gw.* **tyddynnwr.**
thyfiannau *gw.* **tyfiant.**
thyfiant *gw.* **tyfiant.**
thyfu *gw.* **tyfu.**
thynged *gw.* **tynged.**
thyngedfennol *gw.* **tyngedfennol.**
thynghedau *gw.* **tynged.**
thyngu *gw.* **tyngu.**
thylciau *gw.* **twlc.**
thyle *gw.* **tyle.**
thylino *gw.* **tylino.**
thylwyth *gw.* **tylwyth.**
thyllau *gw.* **twll.**
thyllu *gw.* **tyllu.**
thylluan *gw.* **tylluan.**
thymer *gw.* **tymer.**
thymereddau *gw.* **tymheredd.**
thymestl *gw.* **tymestl.**
thymherau *gw.* **tymer.**
thymheredd *gw.* **tymheredd.**
thymhestloedd *gw.* **tymestl.**
thymhestlog *gw.* **tymhestlog.**
thymhorau *gw.* **tymor.**
thymor *gw.* **tymor.**
thyn *gw.* **tyn.**
thyner *gw.* **tyner.**
thynerwch *gw.* **tynerwch.**
thynnu *gw.* **tynnu.**
thyrau *gw.* **tŵr.**
thyrfa *gw.* **tyrfa.**
thyrfaoedd *gw.* **tyrfa.**
thyrfau *gw.* **twrw.**
thyrrau *gw.* **twr.**
thyst *gw.* **tyst.**
thystio *gw.* **tystio.**
thystiolaeth *gw.* **tystiolaeth.**
thystion *gw.* **tyst.**
thystysgrif *gw.* **tystysgrif.**
thystysgrifau *gw.* **tystysgrif.**
thywel *gw.* **tywel.**
thywod *gw.* **tywod.**
thywydd *gw.* **tywydd.**
thywyll *gw.* **tywyll.**
thywyllu *gw.* **tywyllu.**
thywyllwch *gw.* **tywyllwch.**
thywys *gw.* **tywys.**
thywysog *gw.* **tywysog.**
thywysoges *gw.* **tywysoges.**

uchaf *a.* uppermost, highest; loudest: **am yr uchaf** for the loudest.
uchafbwynt *e.g. ll.* **-iau** climax; zenith.
uchder *e.g. ll.* **-au** height, altitude.
uchel *a.* high; loud.
uchelder *e.g. ll.* **-au** highness.
ucheldir *e.g. ll.* **-oedd** highland.
uchelgais *e.g.b. ll.* **uchelgeisiau** ambition.
uchelgeisiol *a.* ambitious.
uchelion *e.ll.* heights.
uchelwr *e.g. ll.* **uchelwyr** gentleman, nobleman.
uchod *ad.* above: **yn y rhestr uchod** in the above list.
udo *be.* **(udaf)** to howl, to moan, to wail.
ufudd *a.* obedient.
ufuddhau (i) *be.* **(ufuddhâf)** to obey.
uffern *e.b. ll.* **-au** hell: **Uffern dân!** Hell fire!
uffernol *a.* infernal, hellish: **Roedd hi'n ddrud uffernol** It was extremely expensive.
ugain *a. & e.g. ll.* **ugeiniau** twenty: **tri ar hugain** twenty-three; **deg ar hugain** thirty.
ugeinfed *a.* twentieth: **yr ugeinfed ganrif** the 20th century.
ugeiniau *gw.* **ugain.**
un *a. & e.g. ll.* **-au** one: **un tro** one turn; once; **yr un** the one, the same; **yr un faint** as much, the same; **yr un pryd** the same time.
unawd *e.g. ll.* **-au** solo.
unawdwr: unawdydd *e.g. ll.* **unawdwyr** soloist.
unben *e.g. ll.* **-iaid** dictator, despot.
undeb *e.g. ll.* **-au** union, unity: **Undeb yr Athrawon** the Teacher's Union; **Undeb y Mamau** the Mother's Union.
undebwr *e.g. ll.* **undebwyr** unionist.
undod *e.g. ll.* **-au** unit, unity.
Undodwr *e.g. ll.* **Undodwyr** Unitarian.
undonog *a.* monotonous.
undydd *a.* one-day: **ysgol undydd** a one-day school.
uned *e.b. ll.* **-au** unit.
unedig *a.* united.
unfarn *a.* unanimous.
unfryd: unfrydol *a.* unanimous.
unffordd *a.* one-way: **stryd unffordd** one-way street.
uniaethu (â) *be.* **(uniaethaf)** to identify (with).
unig *a.* (*precedes noun and causes soft mutation*) only, sole; alone, lonely: **yr unig fab** the only son; **mab unig** lonely son.
unigol *a.* singular; individual.
unigolyn *e.g. ll.* **unigolion** individual.
unigrwydd *e.g.* loneliness.
unigryw *a.* unique.
union *a.* direct, straight; exact: **yr union fan** the exact place.
unioni *be.* **(unionaf)** to rectify, to straighten.
unman *ad.* anywhere.
unnos *a.* of or for one night: **tŷ unnos** habitable cabin built between dusk and dawn.
uno *be.* **(unaf)** to unite, to join.
unrhyw *a.* same; any; homogeneous: **mewn unrhyw wlad** in any country.
unwaith *ad.* once: **ar unwaith** at once; **unwaith ac am byth** once and for all.
urdd *e.b. ll.* **-au** order, guild: **Urdd Gobaith Cymru** Welsh League of Youth.
urddas *e.g. ll.* **-au** dignity, honour.
urddo *be.* **(urddaf)** to ordain, to bestow honour on.
us *e.ll.* chaff.
ustus *e.g. ll.* **-iaid** magistrate.
uwch *a.* higher, senior, superior; advanced: **uwchgapten** major (army officer); **uwchnormal** superior; *gw.* **uchel.**
uwchben *ardd. & ad.* above.
uwchfarchnad *e.b. ll.* **-oedd** supermarket.
uwchlaw *ardd.* above.
uwchradd *a.* secondary: **ysgol uwchradd** secondary school.
uwd *e.g. ll.* **-iau** porridge.

wadu *gw.* **gwadu.**
waed *gw.* **gwaed.**
waedu *gw.* **gwaedu.**
waedd *gw.* **gwaedd.**
wael *gw.* **gwael.**
waelod *gw.* **gwaelod.**
waeth *gw.* **drwg.**
waethaf *gw.* **drwg.**
waethed *gw.* **drwg.**
wag *gw.* **gwag.**
wagedd *gw.* **gwagedd.**
wagio *gw.* **gwagio.**
wagle *gw.* **gwagle.**
wagu *gw.* **gwagio.**
wahân *gw.* **gwahân.**
wahaniaeth *gw.* **gwahaniaeth.**
wahanol *gw.* **gwahanol.**
wahodd *gw.* **gwahodd.**
wahoddedig *gw.* **gwahoddedig.**
wahoddedigion *gw.* **gwahoddedig.**
wahoddiad *gw.* **gwahoddiad.**
wahoddion *gw.* **gwahodd.**
wair *gw.* **gwair.**
waith *gw.* **gwaith.**
wal *e.b.* *ll.* **-iau** wall; *gw.* **gwal.**
wâl *gw.* **gwâl.**
walau *gw.* **gwâl.**
waliau *gw.* **gwal, wal.**
wall *gw.* **gwall.**
wallt *gw.* **gwallt.**
wallus *gw.* **gwallus.**
wan *gw.* **gwan.**
wanwyn *gw.* **gwanwyn.**
war *gw.* **gwar.**
warchod *gw.* **gwarchod.**
waredu *gw.* **gwaredu.**
waredwr *gw.* **gwaredwr.**
wario *gw.* **gwario.**
warrau *gw.* **gwar.**
wartheg *gw.* **gwartheg.**
was *gw.* **gwas.**
wasanaeth *gw.* **gwasanaeth.**
wasanaethu *gw.* **gwasanaethu.**
wasg *gw.* **gwasg.**
wasgedd *gw.* **gwasgedd.**
wasgfa *gw.* **gwasgfa.**
wasgod *gw.* **gwasgod.**
wasgu *gw.* **gwasgu.**
wastad *gw.* **gwastad.**
wastraff *gw.* **gwastraff.**
wastraffu *gw.* **gwastraffu.**
wats *e.g.* *ll.* **-ys** watch.
wau *gw.* **gwau.**
waun *gw.* **gwaun.**
wawd *gw.* **gwawd.**
wawdio *gw.* **gwawdio.**
wawr *gw.* **gwawr.**
wawrio *gw.* **gwawrio.**
wawroedd *gw.* **gwawr.**
wdihŵ *gw.* **gwdihŵ.**
wddf *gw.* **gwddf.**
wddwg *gw.* **gwddwg.**
wedi *ardd.* after: **wedi deg** after ten; **Mae wedi chwech arno** He has lost his chance; *the preposition is also used as follows:* (forms of **bod**) + **(wedi)** + *(be.);* **Rydw i wedi blino** I am tired; **Dwyt ti ddim wedi cysgu** You have not slept; **Roedd ef wedi troi** He had turned; **Maen nhw wedi marw** They are dead.
wedyn *ad.* afterwards, then.
weddi *gw.* **gweddi.**
weddïau *gw.* **gweddi.**
weddill *gw.* **gweddill.**
weddïo *gw.* **gweddïo.**
weddol *gw.* **gweddol.**
wefus *gw.* **gwefus.**
weiddi *gw.* **gweiddi.**
weigion *gw.* **gwag.**
weiniaid *gw.* **gwan.**
weinidog *gw.* **gweinidog.**
weinion *gw.* **gwan.**
weinyddes *gw.* **gweinyddes.**
weiriau *gw.* **gwair.**
weisg *gw.* **gwasg.**
weision *gw.* **gwas.**
weithdy *gw.* **gweithdy.**
weithiau *ad.* sometimes; *gw.* **gwaith.**
weithio *gw.* **gweithio.**
weithiwr *gw.* **gweithiwr.**
weithred *gw.* **gweithred.**
weithredu *gw.* **gweithredu.**
weithwyr *gw.* **gweithiwr.**
wel *ebych.* well!
welâu *gw.* **gwely.**
weld *gw.* **gweld.**
wele *ebych.* behold!
weled *gw.* **gweld.**
wely *gw.* **gwely.**
welyau *gw.* **gwely.**

welydd *gw.* **gwal.**
well *gw.* **gwell.**
wella *gw.* **gwella.**
wellt *gw.* **gwellt.**
welltyn *gw.* **gwelltyn.**
wen *gw.* **gwen.**
wên *gw.* **gwên.**
wenau *gw.* **gwên.**
wendid *gw.* **gwendid.**
Wener *gw.* **Gwener.**
wenith *gw.* **gwenith.**
wennol *gw.* **gwennol.**
Went *gw.* **Gwent.**
wenu *gw.* **gwenu.**
wenwyn *gw.* **gwenwyn.**
wenwynig *gw.* **gwenwynig.**
wenwynol *gw.* **gwenwynig.**
wenyn *gw.* **gwenynen.**
wenynen *gw.* **gwenynen.**
wêr *gw.* **gwêr.**
werdd *gw.* **gwerdd.**
werin *gw.* **gwerin.**
weriniaeth *gw.* **gweriniaeth.**
wers *gw.* **gwers.**
werslyfr *gw.* **gwerslyfr.**
wersyll *gw.* **gwersyll.**
werth *gw.* **gwerth.**
werthfawr *gw.* **gwerthfawr.**
werthfawrogi *gw.* **gwerthfawrogi.**
werthfawrogiad *gw.* **gwerthfawrogiad.**
werthiant *gw.* **gwerthiant.**
werthu *gw.* **gwerthu.**
werthwr *gw.* **gwerthwr.**
werthwyr *gw.* **gwerthwr.**
westai *gw.* **gwestai, gwesty.**
westeion *gw.* **gwestai.**
westeiwr *gw.* **gwesteiwr.**
westeiwyr *gw.* **gwesteiwr.**
westy *gw.* **gwesty.**
weu *gw.* **gweu.**
weunydd *gw.* **gwaun.**
wg *gw.* **gwg.**
wgu *gw.* **gwgu.**
whilber *e.b. ll.* **-au** wheelbarrow, **berfa:** *gw.* **berfa.**
wiail *gw.* **gwialen.**
wialen *gw.* **gwialen.**
wialennod *gw.* **gwialen.**
wiced *e.b. ll.* **-i** wicket.
wicedwr *e.g. ll.* **wicedwyr** wicket-keeper.
widw *e.b. ll.* **-od** widow (*S.W.*).
win *gw.* **gwin.**
wir *gw.* **gwir.**
wirionedd *gw.* **gwirionedd.**
wisg *gw.* **gwisg.**
wisgo *gw.* **gwisgo.**
wiwer *gw.* **gwiwer.**
wlad *gw.* **gwlad.**
wladfa *gw.* **gwladfa.**
wladgarwr *gw.* **gwladfarwr.**
wladol *gw.* **gwladol.**
wlân *gw.* **gwlân.**
wlanen *gw.* **gwlanen.**
wledig *gw.* **gwledig.**
wledydd *gw.* **gwlad.**
wledd *gw.* **gwledd.**
wledda *gw.* **gwledda.**
wleidydd *gw.* **gwleidydd.**
wleidyddiaeth *gw.* **gwleidyddiaeth.**
wleidyddol *gw.* **gwleidyddol.**
wlith *gw.* **gwlith.**
wlyb *gw.* **gwlyb.**
wlybaniaeth *gw.* **gwlybaniaeth.**
wlychu *gw.* **gwlychu.**
wn *gw.* **gwn.**
ŵn *gw.* **gŵn.**
wneud *gw.* **gwneud.**
wneuthur *gw.* **gwneud.**
wniadyddes *gw.* **gwniadyddes.**
wnïo *gw.* **gwnïo.**
wniyddes *gw.* **gwniadyddes.**
wobr *gw.* **gwobr.**
wobrwyo *gw.* **gwobrwyo.**
ŵr *gw.* **gŵr.**
wrach *gw.* **gwrach.**
wragedd *gw.* **gwraig.**
wraidd *gw.* **gwreiddyn.**
wraig *gw.* **gwraig.**
wrandawiad *gw.* **gwrandawiad.**
wrandawr *gw.* **gwrandawr.**
wrando *gw.* **gwrando.**
wreichion *gw.* **gwreichionen.**
wreichionen *gw.* **gwreichionen.**
wreiddiau *gw.* **gwreiddyn.**
wreiddio *gw.* **gwreiddio.**
wreiddiol *gw.* **gwreiddiol.**
wreiddyn *gw.* **gwreiddyn.**
wres *gw.* **gwres.**
wresog *gw.* **gwresog.**
wresogydd *gw.* **gwresogydd.**
wrido *gw.* **gwrido.**
wridog *gw.* **gwridog.**
wrol *gw.* **gwrol.**
wrtaith *gw.* **gwrtaith.**
wrth *ardd.* by; with; to; because; since: **wrth gwrs** of course; **wrth law** at hand, in reserve; **wrth lwc** luckily.
wrthblaid *gw.* **gwrthblaid.**
wrthdystio *gw.* **gwrthdystio.**
wrthod *gw.* **gwrthod.**
wrthrych *gw.* **gwrthrych.**
wrthrychol *gw.* **gwrthrychol.**
wrthryfel *gw.* **gwrthryfel.**
wrthwyneb *gw.* **gwrthwyneb.**
wrthwynebu *gw.* **gwrthwynebu.**

wrthwynebwr *gw.* **gwrthwynebwr.**
wryw *gw.* **gwryw.**
wrywaidd *gw.* **gwrywaidd.**
wrywol *gw.* **gwrywaidd.**
wthiad *gw.* **gwthaid.**
wthio *gw.* **gwthio.**
wthiwr *gw.* **gwthiwr.**
wy *e.g. ll.* **-au** egg: **wy clwc** addled egg; **wy Pasg** Easter egg; **wy wedi'i falu** beaten egg; **wy wedi'i ferwi** boiled egg; **wy wedi'i ffrio** fried egg.
wybedyn *gw.* **gwybedyn.**
wybod *gw.* **gwybod.**
wybodaeth *gw.* **gwybodaeth.**
wybren *e.b. ll.* **-nau, -nydd** sky, firmament (*literary usage*).
wybrennau *gw.* **wybren.**
wybrennydd *gw.* **wybren.**
wych *gw.* **gwych.**
wydr *gw.* **gwydr.**
wydrau *gw.* **gwydr, gwydryn.**
wydryn *gw.* **gwydryn.**
ŵydd *gw.* **gŵydd.**
wyddau *gw.* **gŵydd.**
wyddbwyll *gw.* **gwyddbwyll.**
Wyddel *gw.* **Gwyddel.**
Wyddeleg *gw.* **Gwyddeleg.**
Wyddeles *gw.* **Gwyddeles.**
Wyddelig *gw.* **Gwyddelig.**
Wyddfa, Yr *e.b.* Snowdon.
Wyddgrug, Yr *e.b.* Mold.
wyddoniaeth *gw.* **gwyddoniaeth.**
wyddonol *gw.* **gwyddonol.**
wyddonydd *gw.* **gwyddonydd.**
wyddor *gw.* **gwyddor.**
wyf (i) *bf.* I am; *gw.* **bod.**
wyfyn *gw.* **gwyfyn.**
ŵyl *gw.* **gŵyl.**
wylan *gw.* **gwylan.**
wyliadwrus *gw.* **gwyliadwrus.**
wyliau *gw.* **gŵyl.**
wylio *gw.* **gwylio.**
wyliwr *gw.* **gwyliwr.**
wylnos *gw.* **gwylnos.**
wylo *be.* **(wylaf)** to weep, to cry (*N.W.*).
wylwyr *gw.* **gwyliwr.**
wyll *gw.* **gwyll.**
wyllt *gw.* **gwyllt.**
wylltio *gw.* **gwylltio.**
wylltu *gw.* **gwylltio.**
wymon *gw.* **gwymon.**
wyn *gw.* **gwyn.**
ŵyn *gw.* **oen.**
wyneb *e.g. ll.* **-au** face; surface: **dauwynebog** deceitful; **wynebddalen** title-page; **wynebgaled** barefaced; **wyneb i waered** upside-down.
wynebu *be.* **(wynebaf)** to face, to confront.
Wynedd *gw.* **Gwynedd.**
wynegon *gw.* **gwynegon.**
wynegu *gw.* **gwynegu.**
wynfa *gw.* **gwynfa.**
wynfyd *gw.* **gwynfyd.**
wyngalch *gw.* **gwyngalch.**
wynion *gw.* **gwyn.**
wynnu *gw.* **gwynnu.**
wynt *gw.* **gwynt.**
wyntog *gw.* **gwyntog.**
wŷr *gw.* **gwŷr.**
ŵyr *e.g. ll.* **wyrion** grandson.
wyrion *gw.* **ŵyr.**
wyrdd *gw.* **gwyrdd.**
wyres *e.b. ll.* **-au** grand-daughter.
wyresau *gw.* **wyres.**
wyriad *gw.* **gwyriad.**
wyrio *gw.* **gwyro.**
wyro *gw.* **gwyro.**
wyrth *gw.* **gwyrth.**
wyrthiol *gw.* **gwyrthiol.**
wyryf *gw.* **gwyryf.**
wŷs *gw.* **gwŷs.**
Wysg *e.b.* Usk (river).
wystl *gw.* **gwystl.**
wyt (ti) *bf.* you are (*singular*); **Wyt ti gartref?** Are you at home? *gw.* **bod.**
wyth *a. & e.g.* eight; **wyth deg** eighty.
wythawd *e.g. ll.* **-au** octave; octet.
wythfed *a.* eighth.
wythnos *e.b. ll.* **-au** week: **yr wythnos diwethaf** last week; **yr wythnos hon** this week; **yr wythnos nesaf** next week.
wythnosol *a.* weekly: **cyfarfod wythnosol** weekly meeting; **papur wythnosol** weekly paper.
wythwr *e.g. ll.* **wythwyr** number eight (*rugby forward*).
wythwyr *gw.* **wythwr.**
wywo *gw.* **gwywo.**

y: yr: 'r, 1 *y fan.* the: **y** *before a consonant:* **y dyn** the man; **y ferch** the girl; **y tai** the houses; **yr** *before a vowel and h:* **yr afal** the apple; **yr esgid** the shoe; **yr haul** the sun; **yr heol** the road; **'r** *after a vowel:* **a'r plant** and the children; **o'r llyfr** from the book; **i'r cae** to the field; **y** *and* **'r** *are followed by soft mutation of feminine singular nouns:* **y dorth** the loaf; **tŷ'r fam** the mother's house; **gyda'r gath** with the cat; *nouns beginning with ll and rh do not mutate after* **y** *and* **'r**; *gw. At. Treiglad Meddal.* **2** *geir. used with forms of the verb* **bod: y mae . . .; yr oedd . . .; rwyf . . .**
y: yr *geir. perth.* **Dyma'r tŷ y trigaf ynddo** Here is the house in which I live.
ychwaith *gw.* **chwaith.**
ychwaneg *gw.* **chwaneg.**
ychwanegu: chwanegu *be.* **(ychwanegaf: chwanegaf)** to add, to augment.
ychydig *a.* little, few: **ychydig o lyfrau** few books; **ychydig fara** a little bread; **ychydig lai** a little less.
ŷd *e.g. ll.* **ydau** corn: **creision ŷd** cornflakes.
ydy *bf.* is, are; *gw.* **bod.**
yddfau *gw.* **gwddf.**
yfed *be.* **(yfaf)** to drink.
yfory: fory *ad.* tomorrow.
yfflon *e.ll.* fragments, pieces, bits (*S.W.*): **yn yfflon racs** in smithereens; *gw.* **yfflyn.**
yfflyn *e.g. ll.* **yfflon** fragment, piece, bit: **heb yfflyn o wahaniaeth** without a scrap of difference.
ygau *gw.* **gwg.**
yng *gw.* **yn.**
ynghanol *ardd.* in the midst of.
ynghyd *ad.* together: **ynghyd â** together with.
ynghylch *ardd.* about, concerning.
ynglŷn (â) *ad.* in connection (with), concerning.
ym *gw.* **yn.**
yma *ad.* here, this.
ymadael (â) *be.* **(ymadawaf)** to depart.
ymadrodd *e.g. ll.* **-ion** speech, saying, expression.
ymaelodi (â) *be.* **(ymaelodaf)** to become a member, to join.
ymaith *ad.* away.
ymarfer (â) 1 *be.* **(ymarferaf)** to practise. **2** *e.b.g. ll.* **-ion** practice, exercise: **ymarfer corff** physical training.
ymarferiad *e.g. ll.* **-au** practice, exercise.
ymarferol *a.* practical.
ymateb 1 *be.* **(ymatebaf)** to respond. **2** *e.g. ll.* **-ion** reaction; response.
ymbelydredd *e.g.* radiation.
ymbelydrol *a.* radioactive.
ymchwil *e.b.* research, search, quest.
ymchwiliad *e.g. ll.* **-au** investigation, inquiry.
ymchwilio (i) *be.* **(ymchwiliaf)** to research, to search.
ymdaith 1 *e.b. ll.* **ymdeithiau** journey, march. **2** *be.* **(ymdeithiaf)** to travel, to march.
ymdrech *e.b. ll.* **-ion** effort, endeavour, struggle: **ymdrech deg** valiant effort.
ymdrechu (i) *be.* **(ymdrechaf)** to strive, to endeavour.
ymddangos (i) *be.* **(ymddangosaf)** to appear, to seem.
ymddangosiad *e.g. ll.* **-au** appearance.
ymddeol *be.* **(ymddeolaf)** to retire.
ymddeoliad *e.g. ll.* **-au** retirement.
ymddiheuriad *e.g. ll.* **-au** apology.
ymddiheuro *be.* **(ymddiheuraf)** to apologise.
ymddiried (yn) *be.* **(ymddiriedaf)** to trust, to confide *(in).*
ymddiriedaeth *e.b. ll.* **-au** trust, confidence.
ymddiriedolaeth *e.b. ll.* **-au** trust *(charity).*
ymddiriedolwr *e.b. ll.* **ymddiriedolwyr** trustee.
ymddiswyddiad *e.g. ll.* **-au** resignation.

ymddiswyddo *be.* **(ymddiswyddaf)** to resign.
ymddwyn *be.* **(ymddygaf)** to behave.
ymddygiad *e.g.* *ll.* **-au** behaviour.
ymennydd *e.g.* *ll.* **ymenyddion** brain.
ymenyddion *gw.* **ymennydd.**
ymenyn: menyn *e.g.* butter: **bara menyn** bread and butter.
ymerodraeth *e.b.* *ll.* **-au** empire.
ymestyn (at) *be.* **(ymestynnaf)** to stretch, to reach, to extend.
ymfudo *be.* **(ymfudaf)** to emigrate.
ymfudwr *e.g.* *ll.* **ymfudwyr** emigrant.
ymfudwyr *gw.* **ymfudwr.**
ymffrost *e.g.* boast.
ymffrostio (yn) *be.* **(ymffrostiaf)** to boast.
ymffrostiwr *e.g.* *ll.* **ymffrostwyr** boaster.
ymffrostwyr *gw.* **ymffrostiwr.**
ymgais *e.b.* effort, attempt.
ymgeiswyr *gw.* **ymgeisydd.**
ymgeisydd *e.g.* *ll.* **ymgeiswyr** candidate, applicant: **ymgeisydd seneddol** parliamentary candidate.
ymgeledd *e.g.* *ll.* **-au** care, succour: **ymgeledd parod** first aid.
ymgom *e.b.* *ll.* **-iau, -ion** conversation, chat: **ymgom â** a conversation with.
ymgomio (â) *be.* **(ymgomiaf)** to chat, to converse.
ymgorffori *be.* **(ymgorfforaf)** to incorporate.
ymgrymu *be.* **(ymgrymaf)** to stoop, to bow down.
ymgynghori (â) *be.* **(ymgynghoraf)** to consult, to confer.
ymgymryd (â) *be.* **(ymgymeraf)** to undertake.
ymgyrch *e.g.b.* *ll.* **-oedd** campaign, expedition.
ymhel (â) *be.* **(ymhelaf)** to be concerned; to meddle *(with).*
ymhell *ad.* far, afar.
ymhellach *ad.* furthermore, further.
ymhlith *ardd.* among.
ymholi *be.* **(ymholaf)** to inquire.
ymholiad *e.g.* *ll.* **-au** inquiry.
ymlacio *be.* **(ymlaciaf)** to relax.
ymladd (â) 1 *be.* **(ymladdaf)** to fight (with). 2 *e.g.* *ll.* **-au** fight, battle.
ymladdwr *e.g.* *ll.* **ymladdwyr** fighter.
ymlaen *ad.* on, onward; **yn ôl ac ymlaen** backward and forward.
ymolch: ymolchi *be.* **(ymolchaf)** to wash oneself.
ymosod (ar) *be.* **(ymosodaf)** to attack.
ymosodiad *e.g.* *ll.* **-au** attack: **ymosodiadau awyr** air attacks.
ymosodwr *e.g.* *ll.* **ymosodwyr** attacker.
ymosodwyr *gw.* **ymosodwr.**
ymostwng (i) *be.* **(ymostyngaf)** to stoop; to submit, to capitulate.
ymryson (â) 1 *be.* **(ymrysonaf)** to contend, to strive, to compete. *2 e.g.* *ll.* **-au** competition, rivalry; strife, contention: **Ymryson y Beirdd** poets' contest.
ymuno (â) *be.* **(ymunaf)** to unite; to join.
ymweld (â) *be.* **(ymwelaf)** to visit.
ymweliad *e.g.* *ll.* **-au** visit, visitation.
ymwelwr: ymwelydd *e.g.* *ll.* **ymwelwyr** visitor.
ymwelwyr *gw.* **ymwelwr.**
ymwelydd *gw.* **ymwelwr.**
ymwneud (â) *be.* **(ymwnaf)** to deal (with), to be connected (with).
ymyl *e.g.b.* *ll.* **-au, -on** edge, border, margin: **ymyl y ddalen** edge of the page; **yn ymyl** close by, near.
ymyrraeth *e.b.* *ll.* **ymyrraethau** interference, intervention.
ymyrru: ymyrryd (â) *be.* **(ymyrraf)** to interfere, to intervene, to meddle.
ymysg *ardd.* among, amid.
yn: yng: ym, 1 *ardd.* (*personal forms:* **yno, ynot, ynddo/ynddi, ynom, ynoch, ynddyn)** in, at, into; for: *the preposition* **yn** *is followed by nasal mutation:* **yn** + Corwen **yng Nghorwen** in Corwen; **yn** + Pen-bre **ym Mhen-bre** in Pen-bre; **yn** + Treorci **yn Nhreorci** in Treorchy; **yn** + Gŵyr **yng Ngŵyr** in Gower; **yn** + Dinbych **yn Ninbych** in Denbigh; **yn** + Bangor **ym Mangor** in Bangor; *gw. At. Treiglad Trwynol. geiryn.* (not translated). *An adjective or noun following the predicative particle yn takes soft mutation:* **Mae Twm yn ddoniol** Tom is amusing; **Ydy Alun yn ddyn da?** Is Alun a good man? *gw. At. Treiglad Meddal. No mutation occurs when yn is followed by a be.* (verb-noun): **Mae'r ci yn neidio** The dog is jumping; **Mae'r gath yn cysgu** The cat is sleeping; **Mae Mair yn canu** Mair is singing; **Rydw i'n darllen** I am reading; **Maen nhw'n gwrando** They are listening.

yna *ad.* there; then; thereupon; that.
ynad *e.g. ll.* **-on** judge, justice, magistrate.
Ynad Heddwch (Y.H.) Justice of the Peace (J.P.).
Llys yr Ynadon the Magistrates' Court.
ynau *gw.* **gŵn.**
yn awr *ymadrodd ad.* now, at present; *gw.* **rwan.**
ynn *gw.* **onnen.**
ynnau *gw.* **gwn.**
ynni *e.g.* energy, vigour.
yno *ad.* there; *gw.* **yn.**
yntau *rhag.* he, he also.
ynte: ynteu *c.* or, or else, otherwise; then.
ynys *e.b. ll.* **-oedd** island: **Ynys Bŷr** Caldey Island; **Ynys Enlli** Bardsey Island; **Ynys Wyth** Isle of Wight; **Ynysoedd Heledd** the Hebrides.
ynysoedd *gw.* **ynys.**
yr *gw.* **y.**
yrfa *gw.* **gyrfa.**
yrfeydd *gw.* **gyrfa.**
yrru *gw.* **gyrru.**
yrrwr *gw.* **gyrrwr.**
yrwyr *gw.* **gyrrwr.**
ysbardun *e.g. ll.* **-au** spur, accelerator (*in car*).
ysbïo *be.* **(ysbïaf)** to spy, to look.
ysbïwr *e.g. ll.* **ysbïwyr** spy.
ysbïwyr *gw.* **ysbïwr.**
ysblander *e.g.* splendour, glory.
ysbryd *e.g. ll.* **-ion, -oedd** spirit, ghost: **Yr Ysbryd Glân** The Holy Spirit.
ysbrydion *gw.* **ysbryd.**
ysbrydoedd *gw.* **ysbryd.**
ysbrydol *a.* spiritual; high-spirited.
ysbrydoli *be.* **(ysbrydolaf)** to inspire; to spiritualise.
ysbwriel *e.g.* refuse, rubbish.
ysbytai *gw.* **ysbyty.**
ysbyty *e.g. ll.* **ysbytai** hospital, hospice.
ysfa *e.b. ll.* **ysfeydd** itching; hankering; urge.
ysfeydd *gw.* **ysfa.**
ysgafn *a.* light (*weight*).
ysgafnhau: ysgafnu *be.* **(ysgafnhaf: ysgafnaf)** to lighten.
ysgall *gw.* **ysgallen.**
ysgallen *e.b. ll.* **ysgall** thistle.
ysgariad *e.g. ll.* **-au** divorce.
ysgol *e.b. ll.* **-ion** school; ladder: **ysgol annibynnol** independent school; **ysgol arbennig** special school; **ysgol breifat** private school; **ysgol breswyl** boarding school; **ysgol feithrin** nursery school; **ysgol gyfun** comprehensive school; **ysgol Gymraeg** Welsh medium school; **ysgol gynradd** primary school; **ysgol iau** junior school; **ysgol nos** night-school; **ysgol Sul** Sunday school; **ysgol uwchradd** secondary school.
ysgolfeistr *e.g. ll.* **-i** schoolmaster.
ysgolfeistres *e.b. ll.* **-au** schoolmistress.
ysgolhaig *e.g. ll.* **ysgolheigion** scholar.
ysgolheigion *gw.* **ysgolhaig.**
ysgolor *e.g. ll.* **-ion** scholar.
ysgoloriaeth *e.b. ll.* **-au** scholarship.
ysgolorion *gw.* **ysgolor.**
ysgrech *e.b. ll.* **-feydd** scream, shriek.
ysgrechfeydd *gw.* **ysgrech.**
ysgrif *e.b. ll.* **-au** article, essay.
ysgrifennu (ar, at) *be.* **(ysgrifennaf)** to write.
ysgrifennydd *e.g. ll.* **ysgrifenyddion** secretary.
ysgrifenyddes *e.b. ll.* **-au** female secretary.
ysgrifenyddion *gw.* **ysgrifennydd.**
ysgrythur *e.b. ll.* **-au** scripture.
ysgubo *be.* **(ysgubaf)** to sweep.
ysgwyd *be.* **(ysgydwaf)** to shake, to sway, to wag.
ysgwydd *e.b. ll.* **-au** shoulder.
ysgyfaint *e.ll.* lungs.
ysgyfarnog *e.b. ll.* **-od** hare; **codi ysgyfarnog** to raise a red herring (*fig.* – irrelevant diversion).
ysgytwad *e.g. ll.* **-au** shock, shaking.
ysmala *a.* funny, amusing; droll.
ystadegau *e.ll.* statistics.
ystafell *e.b. ll.* **-oedd** room: **ystafell ddosbarth** classroom; **ystafell wely** bedroom; **ystafell ymolchi** bathroom.
ystlum *e.g. ll.* **-od** bat (*animal*).
ystlys *e.b. ll.* **-au** side, flank; touchline.
ystlyswr *e.g. ll.* **ystlyswyr** linesman; sidesman.
ystod *e.b. ll.* **-ion, -au** course, space of time, span, range; swath: **yn ystod** during; **ystod oed** age range.
ystrydeb *e.b. ll.* **-au** cliché; stereotype.
ystwyth *a.* flexible, supple, agile, pliant.

ystyr *e.g.b.* *ll.* **-on** sense, meaning.
ystyriaeth *e.b.* *ll.* **-au** consideration, heed.
ystyried *be.* **(ystyriaf)** to consider, to heed.
ystyriol *a.* heedful, mindful.
ystyrlon *a.* meaningful.
ysu *be.* **(ysaf)** to consume, to crave, to itch: **yn ysu am wybod** itching to know.
yswiriannau *gw.* **yswiriant.**
yswiriant *e.g.* *ll.* **yswiriannau** insurance: **yswiriant cyfun** comprehensive insurance; **yswiriant trydydd person** third party insurance.
yswirio: yswiro *be.* **(yswiriaf: yswiraf)** to insure.
yw *bf.* is, are; *gw.* **bod;** *gw.* **ywen.**
ywen *e.b.* *ll.* **yw** yew.

DICTIONARY
English–Welsh

ABBREVIATIONS
BYRFODDAU

a.	adjective	*ansoddair*
ad.	adverb	*adferf*
c.	conjunction	*cysylltair*
def. art.	definite article	*y fannod*
e.g. (exempli gratia)	for example	*er enghraifft*
i.	interjection	*ebychiad*
int. pn.	interrogative pronoun	*rhagenw gofynnol*
n.	noun	*enw*
coll.	collective	*torfol*
f.	feminine	*benywaidd*
m.	masculine	*gwrywaidd*
n.pl.	noun plural	*enw lluosog*
N.W.	North Wales	*Gogledd Cymru*
pn.	pronoun	*rhagenw*
prp.	preposition	*arddodiad*
px.	prefix	*rhagddodiad*
rel. pn.	relative pronoun	*rhagenw perthynol*
S.W.	South Wales	*De Cymru*
v.	verb	*berf*

If a Welsh noun's gender is not specified, that noun has the same gender as the noun(s) immediately following it in the definition.

abbreviation *n.* byrfodd, talfyriad *m.*
abdomen *n.* bol *m.*
ability *n* gallu *m.*
able *a.* galluog, medrus: **to be able** gallu, medru.
abode *n.* cartref, preswyl, preswylfod *m.*
abolish *v.* dileu.
abort *v.* erthylu.
abortion *n.* erthyliad *m.*
about *prp.* & *ad.* am, o gwmpas, oddeutu, tua, ogylch, ynghylch.
above 1 *prp.* dros, i fyny, uwchben, uwchlaw. 2 *ad.* uchod.
abrupt *a.* sydyn, cwta: **abrupt reply** ateb cwta.
absent *a.* absennol.
abstract *a.* haniaethol.
abundance *n.* toreth *f.*
abundant *a.* helaeth, aml, toreithiog.
accelerate *v.* cyflymu.
accelerator *n.* cyflymydd *m.*
accent *n.* acen *f.*
accept *v.* derbyn, cymryd.
acceptable *a.* derbyniol.
access *n.* mynedfa *f.* mynediad *m.*
accident *n.* damwain *f.*
accommodation *n.* llety, lle *m.*
accomplish *v.* cyflawni, gorffen.
account *n.* cyfrif, cownt; adroddiad *m.*
accountant *n.* cyfrifydd *m.*
accustom *v.* cyfarwyddo, arfer.
ache 1 *n.* poen *mf,* dolur *m.* 2 *v.* poeni, brifo, gwynegu.
acid 1 *n.* asid *m.* 2 *a.* sur.
acknowledge *v.* cydnabod.
acorn *n.* mesen *f.*
acquaintance *n.* cydnabod *m.*
acre *n.* erw, acer *f.*
across *prp.* dros, ar draws.
act 1 *n.* act *(drama)*; deddf *(law)*; gweithred *f.* 2 *v.* actio *(drama)*; gweithredu.
active *a.* bywiog, heini.
actor *n.* actor, chwaraewr *m.*
add *v.* ychwanegu, chwanegu.
address 1 *n.* cyfeiriad. *m.* 2 *v.* annerch.
adequately *ad.* digonol.
adhere *v.* glynu wrth.
adjective *n.* ansoddair *m.*
adjudge *v.* dyfarnu.
adjudicate *v.* beirniadu.
adjudicator *n.* beirniad *m.*
admire *v.* edmygu.
admit *v.* derbyn, cyfaddef.
adolescence *n.* llencyndod *m.*
adult *n.* oedolyn *m.*
advantage *n.* mantais *f:* **to take advantage** manteisio.
advantageous *a.* llesol, manteisiol.
adventure *n.* antur *mf.*
adventurous *a.* anturus.
advertise *v.* hysbysebu.
advertisement *n.* hysbyseb *f.*
advertiser *n.* hysbysebwr *m.*
advice *n.* cyngor *m.*
advise *v.* cynghori.
adviser *n.* ymgynghorwr *m.*
aeroplane *n.* awyren *f.*
afar *ad.* ymhell.
affectation *n.* maldod *m.*
affection *n.* cariad, serch *m.*
affectionate *a.* serchus, serchog, cariadus.
after 1 *ad.* wedyn, yna. 2 *prp.* ar ôl, wedi.
after-care *n.* ôl-ofal *m.*
afternoon *n.* prynhawn *m.*
afterwards *ad.* wedyn, wedi hynny.
again *ad.* eto, drachefn, eilwaith.
against *prp.* erbyn, yn erbyn.
age 1 *n.* oed, oedran *m*; oes *f.* 2 *v.* heneiddio.
aged *a.* hen, oedrannus: **the aged** yr oedrannus, yr henoed.
agency *n.* cyfrwng *m,* asiantaeth *f.*
agent *n.* asiant, cyfrwng *m.*
agile *a.* heini.
agitated *a.* cynhyrfus.
ago *ad.* yn ôl.
agony *n.* ing, poen mawr *m.*
agree *v.* cytuno (â).

agreement *n.* cytundeb *m.*
agriculturalist *n.* ffarmwr, ffermwr, amaethwr *m.*
agriculture *n.* amaethyddiaeth *f.*
aid 1 *n.* cymorth, help *m.* **2** *v.* helpu: **First Aid** Cymorth Cyntaf.
ailment *n.* afiechyd, dolur *m.*
aim *n.* amcan, bwriad, diben, nod *m.*
air *n.* awyr; aer; alaw *f*: **fresh air** awyr iach.
alarm *n.* braw, ofn; larwm *m*: **alarm-clock** cloc larwm.
alien *n.* & *a.* estron *m.*
all 1 *n.* pawb; y cwbl, y cyfan *m.* **2** *a.* holl, i gyd, pob. **3** *ad.* yn hollol.
allege *v.* honni.
alleged *a.* honedig.
alliance *n.* cynghrair *m.*
allotment *n.* rhandir *m.*
allow *v.* caniatáu, goddef, gadael (i).
allowance *n.* lŵans, lwfans *m.*
allure *v.* hudo.
ally *n.* cynghreiriad *m.*
almighty *a.* hollalluog: **Almighty God** Hollalluog Dduw.
almost *ad.* bron, braidd, lled.
alone *a.* unig, ar ei ben ei hun, wrtho'i hun.
along 1 *ad.* ymlaen; ar hyd. **2** *prp.* ar hyd: **all along** o'r cychwyn.
alphabet *n.* yr wyddor, abiéc *f.*
already *ad.* eisoes, yn barod.
also *ad.* & *c.* hefyd.
alter *v.* newid.
although *prp.* & *c.* serch, er.
altitude *n.* uchder *m.*
altogether *ad.* yn gyfan gwbl, i gyd.
always *ad.* bob amser, yn wastad.
am I *v.* rydw i.
amazed *a.* syn.
amazement *n.* syndod *m.*
amazing *a.* rhyfedd, rhyfeddol.
ambassador *n.* llysgennad *m.*
ambition *n.* uchelgais *m.*
ambitious *a.* uchelgeisiol.
ambulance *n.* ambiwlans *m.*
amend *v.* gwella, diwygio, cywiro.
American 1 *n.* Americanwr *m,* Americanes f. **2** *a.* Americanaidd.
amid *prp.* ymhlith, rhwng, ynghanol, ymysg.
among *prp.* rhwng, ymhlith, ymysg.
amount *n.* swm, cyfanswm, cyfrif *m.*
ample *a.* helaeth, digon, digonedd.
amuse *v.* difyrru.
amusing *a.* difyr, difyrrus, digrif, ysmala.
analyse *v.* dadansoddi.
ancestor *n.* hynafiad *m.*
ancient *a.* hynafol, hen iawn: **ancient monument** henebyn.
and *c.* a, ac.
anecdote *n.* hanesyn *m.*
angel *n.* angel *m.*
angle *n.* ongl *m*: **right angle** ongl sgwâr.
Anglesey *n.* Ynys Môn *f.*
Anglicise *v.* Seisnigeiddio, Seisnigo.
Anglo- *a.* Eingl-.
Anglo-Welshman *n.* Eingl-Gymro *m.*
angry *a.* crac, dig.
anguish *n.* ing *m.*
angular *a.* onglog.
animal *n.* anifail *m.*
animate *a.* byw.
ankle *n.* migwrn, pigwrn *m.*
announce *v.* cyhoeddi; datgan; hysbysu.
announcement *n.* cyhoeddiad, hysbysiad *m.*
announcer *n.* cyhoeddwr *m.*
anoint *v.* iro.
another *a.* & *pn.* arall, llall.
answer *n.* & *v.* ateb m.
ant *b.* morgrugyn *m.*
antagonist *n.* gwrthwynebwr, gwrthwynebydd *m.*
anthology *n.* blodeugerdd *f,* detholiad *m.*
anti- *px.* gwrth-, yn erbyn.
anxiety *n.* pryder *m.*
any *a.* unrhyw, rhyw, peth, dim; **any more, any longer** mwyach.
anyone *n.* & *pn.* rhywun, unrhyw un, neb *m.*
anywhere *ad.* unman, rhywle, unrhyw le.
apart *ad.* ar wahân, o'r neilltu.
ape *n.* epa *m.*
aperture *n.* agoriad, twll *m.*
apologise *v.* ymddiheuro.
apology *n.* ymddiheuriad *m.*
apparatus *n.* offer *m.*
apparition *n.* drychiolaeth *f,* ysbryd *m.*
appear *v.* ymddangos.
appearance *n.* ymddangosiad *m.*
appendix *n.* atodiad *m.*
apple *n.* afal *m.*
applicant *n.* ymgeisydd *m.*
appoint *v.* penodi; trefnu, nodi.
appointed *a.* penodedig.
appointment *n.* penodiad *m.*
appreciate *v.* gwerthfawrogi.
appreciation *n.* gwerthfawrogiad *m.*
apprentice *n.* prentis *m.*
apprenticeship *n.* prentisiaeth *f.*

approach *v.* agosáu, nesáu.
appropriate *a.* addas, priodol.
approximate *a.* bras, agos.
April *n.* Ebrill *m.*
archer *n.* saethwr *m.*
architect *n.* pensaer, cynlluniwr, cynllunydd *m.*
are *v.* mae, maen, maent, oes, sy, sydd, ydy, ydynt, ydyw, yw; *see* **bod.**
argue *v.* dadlau.
argument *n.* dadl *f.*
arithmetic *n.* rhifyddeg *f.*
ark *n.* arch *f*: **Noah's Ark** Arch Noa.
arm *n.* braich *f;* arf *m*: **nuclear arms** arfau niwclear.
armed *a.* arfog: **armed forces** lluoedd arfog.
army *n.* byddin *f.*
around *ad.* & *prp.* am, o amgylch, o gwmpas, o gylch.
arrange *v.* trefnu.
arrive at *v.* cyrraedd.
arrow *n.* saeth *f.*
art *n.* celf *f*: **art exhibition** arddangosfa gelf.
article *n.* erthygl, ysgrif *f;* nwydd *m*: **definite article** y fannod (y, yr, 'r).
as *c.* & *ad*,. â, ag, fel, mor, cyn: **as if** fel pe bai, fel petai, fel petasai.
ascent *n.* rhiw *f,* tyle *m.*
ash *n.* lludw *m;* onnen *f.*
ashes *n.* llwch, lludw *m.*
aside *ad.* o'r neilltu.
ask *v.* gofyn, holi, gwahodd.
askew *a.* ar gam, gŵyr.
asleep *ad.* yn cysgu, yng nghwsg.
ass *n.* asyn *m.*
assembly *n.* cymanfa *f.* cynulliad *m.*
assert *v.* honni, haeru.
assertion *n.* honiad *m.*
assess *v.* asesu.
assist *v.* helpu.
assistance *n.* cymorth, help *m.*
assistant *n.* cynorthwywr, cynorthwy-ydd *m.*
association *n.* cymdeithas *f.*
assurance *n.* sicrwydd *m.*
assure *v.* sicrhau.
asterisk *n.* seren *f.*
astonishing *a.* rhyfedd, rhyfeddol, syn.
astronaut *n.* gofodwr *m,* gofodwraig *f.*
at *prp.* am, ar, ger, wrth, yn, yng, ym.
atonement *n.* iawn *m.*
attack 1 *n.* ymosodiad *m.* 2 *v.* ymosod (ar).
attacker *n.* ymosodwr *m.*
attain *v.* ennill, cyrraedd.
attempt 1 *n.* cais, cynnig *m;* ymgais *f.* 2 *v.* ceisio, cynnig.
attendance *n.* presenoldeb *m.*
attention *n.* sylw *m.*
attract *v.* denu, tynnu.
attractive *a.* deniadol, atyniadol.
augment *v.* ychwanegu at, chwanegu at.
August *n.* Awst *m.*
aunt *n.* modryb *f.*
author *n.* awdur, llenor *m.*
authoress *n.* awdures, llenores *f.*
authority *n.* awdurdod *m:* **Education Authority** Awdurdod Addysg.
autobiography *n.* hunangofiant *m.*
autumn *n.* hydref *m.*
autumnal *a.* hydrefol.
avenge *v.* dial (ar).
avoid *v.* osgoi.
awake 1 *v.* deffro, dihuno. 2 *a.* effro.
away *ad.* ymaith, i ffwrdd.
awful *a.* ofnadwy.
awkward *a.* lletchwith; chwithig.

baby *n.* baban, babi *m.*
baby-sit *v.* gwarchod: **babysitter** *n.* gwarchodwr banbanod *m.*
bachelor *n.* dyn dibriod, hen lanc *m.*
back 1 *n.* cefn; cefnwr *m.* **2** *ad.* yn ôl.
background *n.* cefndir *m.*
bacon *n.* cig moch, bacwn *m.*
bad *a.* drwg, drygionus; sâl, gwael.
badge *n.* bathodyn *m.*
bag *n.* bag, cwd, cwdyn *m.*
bail *n.* mechnïaeth *f.*
bake *v.* crasu, pobi.
baked *a.* cras, pob.
bakehouse *n.* popty *m.*
baker *n.* pobydd *m.*
bald *a.* moel, penfoel.
baldness *n.* moelni *m.*
ball *n.* dawns; pêl *f*: **football** pêl droed; **rugby ball** pêl rygbi.
ballad *n.* balad *f*; **ballad monger** baledwr.
ballot *n.* balot *m.*
banana *n.* banana *m.*
band *n.* band *m*: **brass band** band pres.
bangle *n.* breichled *f.*
bank 1 *n.* glan *f.*; clawdd; banc *m.* **2** *v.* bancio: **bank statement** adroddiad banc.
banner *n.* baner *f.*
banquet 1 *n.* gwledd *f.* **2** *v.* gwledda.
Baptist *n.* Bedyddiwr *m.*
baptise *v.* bedyddio.
bar 1 *n.* bar *m.* **2** *v.* atal.
bard *n.* bardd *m.*
bare *a.* noeth, llwm, moel, prin.
barefooted *a.* troednoeth.
barely *ad.* prin.
bareness *n.* moelni *m.*
bark *v.* cyfarth.
barley *n.* haidd *coll*, barlys *m.*
barrel *n.* casgen *f*, baril *mf.*
barrow *n.* berfa, whilber *f.*
base 1 *n.* bôn, gwaelod; sail, sylfaen; canolfan *m.* **2** *a.* isel. **3** *v.* seilio.
bashful *a.* swil.
basic *a.* sylfaenol.
basin *n.* basn *m.*
basket *n.* basged *f.*
Basque Country *n.* Gwlad y Basg *f.*
bass *n.* bas, baswr *m.*
baste *v.* iro.
bat 1 *n.* ystlum; bat *m.* **2** *v.* batio.
bath *n.* bath, baddon *m.*
bathe *v.* ymolch, ymolchi, golchi.
bathroom *n.* ystafell ymolchi *f.*
battle *n.* brwydr *f*, ymladd *m.*
bay *n.* bae *m*: **Swansea Bay** Bae Abertawe.
be *v.* bod.
beach *n.* traeth *m*, glan y môr *f.*
beam *n.* pelydr: trawst *m.*
bean *n.* ffäen, ffeuen *f.*
bear 1 *n.* arth *m*, arthes *f.* **2** *v.* cario; geni; goddef: **polar bear** arth gwyn.
beard *n.* barf *f.*
beautiful *a.* hardd, glân, teg, prydferth.
beauty *n.* harddwch, prydferthwch, tegwch *m.*
because *prp.* er, oherwydd, o achos, gan, am, oblegid.
become *v.* dyfod, dod yn.
bed *n.* gwely *m.*
bedding *n.* dillad gwely *m.*
bedroom *n.* ystafell wely, llofft *f.*
bedsitter *n.* ystafell un gwely *f.*
bee *n.* gwenynen *f.*
been, I have *v.* bues i, fues i, bûm; *see* bod.
beer *n.* cwrw *m.*
bees-wax *n.* cwyr *m.*
beetle *n.* chwilen *f.*
before 1 *prp.* cyn, gerbron, o flaen, rhag. **2** *ad.* o'r blaen: **before long** cyn bo hir.
beforehand *ad.* ymlaen llaw.
beg *v.* erfyn (ar).
begin *v.* cychwyn, dechrau.
beginning *n.* dechreuad *m.*
behave *v.* ymddwyn.
behaviour *n.* ymddygiad *m.*
behind 1 *prp.* tu ôl (i), tu cefn (i). **2** *ad.* ar ôl.
behold 1 *i.* wele! **2** *v.* gweld, edrych.
being *n.* bod *m.*
Belgium *n.* Gwlad Belg *f.*
believe *v.* credu (yn).
bell *n.* cloch *f.*

bellow *v.* rhuo.
belly *n.* bol, bola *m.*
belong *v.* perthyn (i).
beloved 1 *n.* anwylyd *mf.* 2 *a.* annwyl, anwylaf, cariadus, cu, hoff: **beloved ones** anwyliaid.
below *prp.* islaw, dan.
bend 1 *n.* tro *m.* 2 *v.* plygu.
beneath *prp.* islaw, dan.
beneficial *a.* llesol.
benefit 1 *n.* elw, lles *m.* 2 *v.* elwa.
berry *n.* aeronen, mwyaren *f.*
berserk *a.* gwyllt.
beside *prp.* ger, gerllaw, wrth, heibio, yn ymyl.
besides *prp.* heb, heblaw.
best *a.* gorau.
bestow *v.* rhoddi, rhoi, cyflwyno.
betrothal *n.* dyweddïad *m.*
better 1 *a.* gwell. 2 *ad.* yn well.
between *prp.* rhwng.
beverage *n.* diod *f.*
bewitch *v.* swyno.
beyond *prp.* draw, dros, tu hwnt.
Bible *n.* Beibl *m.*
bicker *v.* cweryla, ffraeo.
bicycle *n.* beic *m.*
bid *n.* & *v.* cynnig *m.*
bide *v.* aros, disgwyl.
big *a.* mawr: **bigger** mwy; **biggest** mwyaf.
bilingual *a.* dwyieithog.
bilingualism *n.* dwyieithrwydd *m.*
bill *n.* bil; mesur *m;* rhaglen *f.*
bin *n.* bin *m*: **rubbish bin** bin ysbwriel.
bind *v.* rhwymo, clymu.
biological *a.* biolegol.
biology *n.* bioleg, bywydeg *f.*
birch *n.* bedwen, bedw *f.*
bird *n.* aderyn *m.*
birthday *n.* pen-blwydd *m*: **birthday card** cerdyn pen-blwydd.
biscuit *n.* bisged, bisgïen *f.*
bishop *n.* esgob *m.*
bit *n.* tamaid, darn, tipyn, yfflyn *m.*
bite 1 *n.* tamaid *m.* 2 *v.* cnoi.
bitter *a.* chwerw, sur.
bizarre *a.* od, rhyfedd, chwithig.
black 1 *n.* du; dyn du *m.* 2 *a.* du, tywyll. 3 *v.* duo.
blackberry *n.* mwyaren *f.*
blackbird *n.* aderyn du *m.*
blackboard *n.* bwrdd du *m.*
blacken *v.* duo.
blacksmith *n.* gof *m.*
Blackwood *n.* Y Coed-duon *f.*
blade *n.* eginyn; llafn *m.*
blame 1 *n.* bai *m.* 2 *v.* beio.
blameless *a.* di-fai.
blanch *v.* gwynnu.
blank *a.* gwag; syn: **blank cheque** siec wag.
blanket *n.* blanced *f.*
blaze *n.* fflam *f.*
bleach *v.* gwynnu.
bleed *v.* gwaedu.
blemish *n.* nam; bai *m.*
blend *v.* cymysgu.
blessed *a.* bendigedig.
blessedness *n.* gwynfyd *m.*
blessing *n.* bendith *f.*
blind 1 *a.* dall, tywyll. 2 *n.* person dall *m.* 3 *v.* dallu.
bliss *n.* gwynfyd *f.*
blizzard *n.* storm o wynt ac eira *f.*
blood *n.* gwaed *m*: **blood pressure** pwysedd gwaed.
bloom *n.* blodyn *m.*
blossom *n.* blodyn *m.*
blouse *n.* blows, blowsen *f.*
blow 1 *n.* ergyd *mf.* 2 *v.* chwythu.
blow-dry *v.* chwythu'n sych.
blue *n.* & *a.* glas *m.*
blush *v.* gwrido, cochi.
blushing *a.* gwridog.
blustery *a.* stormus.
board *n.* bwrdd *m,* bord *f;* bwyd *m.*
boarding house *n.* llety *m.*
boast 1 *n.* ymffrost *m.* 2 *v.* ymffrostio.
boaster *n.* ymffrostiwr *m.*
boat *n.* bad, cwch *m.*
bodily *a.* corfforol.
body *n.* corff *m.*
boil *v.* berwi.
boiling *n.* & *a.* berw *m.*
bold *a.* hyf.
boldness *n.* hyfdra *m.*
bolster *n.* clustog hir *f,* gobennydd mawr *m.*
bolt 1 *n.* bollt *m.* 2 *v.* bolltio.
bomb 1 *n.* bom *m.* 2 *v.* bomio.
bone *n.* asgwrn *m.*
book *n.* llyfr *m;* cyfrol *f.*
booklet *n.* llyfryn *m.*
boot *n.* esgid *f.*
booth *n.* caban *m,* stondin *f.*
border *n.* ffin *f,* ymyl *mf;* border *m.*
bordering *a.* ffiniol.
bore 1 *n.* twll; dyn diflas *m.* 2 *v.* tyllu; blino.
boring *a.* diflas.
born *a.* wedi ei eni.
borough *n.* bwrdeistref *f*: **Borough Council** Cyngor Bwrdeistref.
borrow *v.* benthyca, cael benthyg.
boss *n.* meistr, pennaeth, bos *m.*

both *a.* & *ad.* & *pn.* y ddau, y ddwy: **they both** ill dau, ill dwy.
bother 1 *n.* helynt *f,* trafferth *m.* **2** *v.* trafferthu.
bottle *n.* potel *f.*
bottleneck *m.* tagfa *f.*
bottom *n.* gwaelod: godre *m.*
boulder *n.* carreg fawr *f.*
bound 1 *n.* llam; terfyn *m,* ffin *f.* **2** *v.* llamu, neidio; ffinio.
boundary *n.* ffin *f,* terfyn *m.*
bow *v.* plygu, ymgrymu.
bowl 1 *n.* bowlen, powlen *f.* **2** *v.* bowlio.
box *n.* blwch, bocs; pren bocs *m*: **box office** swyddfa docynnau.
boy *n.* bachgen, hogyn, mab; gwas *m.*
boyish *a.* bachgennaidd.
brace *n.* bres; pâr *m.*
braces *n.* bresys *m.*
bracelet *n.* breichled *f.*
brain *n.* ymennydd *m.*
branch *n.* cangen *f.*
brandy *n.* brandi *m.*
brass *n.* pres *m.*
brave *a.* dewr, gwrol.
bread *n.* bara *m*: **daily bread** bara beunyddiol.
breadth *n.* lled *m.*
break 1 *n.* egwyl, hoe *f,* toriad *m.* **2** *v.* torri.
breaker *n.* ton *f.*
breakfast *n.* brecwast *m.*
breast *n.* bron; brest *f.*
breath *n.* anadl *mf,* gwynt *m.*
breathe *v.* anadlu, chwythu.
breed *v.* magu, bridio.
breeze *n.* awel *f.*
bride *n.* priodferch *f.*
bridge 1 *n.* pont *f.* **2** *v.* pontio.
brief *a.* byr, cryno.
bright *a.* disglair, gloyw, llachar, llewyrchus.
brightness *n.* llewyrch, disgleirdeb *m.*
brilliant 1 *n.* gem *f.* **2** *a.* disglair, llachar; gwych.
bring *v.* dwyn, dod (â).
brink *n.* ymyl *mf,* min *m.*
Britain *n.* Prydain *f.*
British *a.* Prydeinig.
Brittany *a.* Llydaw *f.*
broad *a.* llydan, eang, bras.
broadcast 1 *n.* darllediad *m.* **2** *v.* darlledu.
brochure *n.* llyfryn *m.*
bronze *n.* pres, efydd *m.*
brooch *n.* tlws *m.*
brook *n.* nant *f.*
broom *n.* brws, brwsh *m,* ysgub *f.*
broth *n.* cawl *m.*
brother *n.* brawd *m*: **brother-in-law** brawd-yng-nghyfraith.
brow *n.* ael *f,* talcen *m;* crib *mf.*
brown *a.* brown.
brush 1 *n.* brws, brwsh *m,* ysgub *f.* **2** *v.* brwsio, brwshio, sgubo, ysgubo. **paint brush** brws paent, brwsh paent.
bucket *n.* bwced *m.*
bud 1. *n.* blaguryn *m.* **2** *v.* blaguro.
build *v.* adeiladu, codi.
builder *n.* adeiladwr *m.*
building *n.* adeilad *m.*
bull *n.* tarw *m;* **bulldozer** tarw dur.
bungalow *n.* tŷ unllawr, byngalo *m.*
burden 1 *m.* baich, llwyth *m.* **2** *v.* llwytho.
burdened *a.* llwythog.
bureau *n.* swyddfa *f.*
burn 1 *n.* llosg *m;* nant *f.* **2** *a.* llosg. **3** *v.* llosgi.
burner *n.* llosgydd *m.*
burrow 1 *n.* twll cwningen *m.* **2** *v.* tyllu.
bus *n.* bws *m*: **bus-stop** arhosfan *f.*
bush *n.* llwyn *m,* perth *f.*
business *n.* busnes *m.*
busy *a.* prysur.
but *c.* ond, onid.
butcher *n.* cigydd.
butter *n.* menyn, ymenyn *m.*
butterfly *n.* glöyn byw *m,* iâr fach yr haf, pili-pala *f.*
button 1 botwm *m.* **2** *v.* botymu.
buy *v.* prynu.
buyer *n.* prynwr *m.*
buzz 1 si, su, sŵn gwenyn *n.* **2** *v.* sio, suo.
by *prp.* erbyn, ger, gerllaw, drwy, trwy, gan, heibio, wrth, â.
by-election *n.* is-etholiad *m.*
bypass *n.* ffordd osgoi *f.*

cabbage *n.* bresychen; bresych *f.*
cabin *n.* caban *m.*
café *n.* caffe *m.*
cake *n.* cacen, teisen *f*: **birthday cake** teisen pen-blwydd.
calamity *n.* trychineb *mf.*
calculate *v.* cyfrif, rhifo.
calculation *n.* cyfrif *m.*
calculator *n.* cyfrifiannell *m.*
calendar *n.* calendar *m.*
calf *n.* llo (anifail) *m;* croth (coes) *f.*
call 1 *n.* galwad *mf*, galw *m.* **2** *v.* galw, ymweld (â).
calling *n.* galwad *mf;* galwedigaeth *f.*
calm 1 *n.* tawelwch; hedd *m.* **2** *a.* tawel; **3** *v.* tawelu, distewi.
camera *n.* camera *m.*
camp 1 *n.* gwersyll *m.* **2** *v.* gwersyllu.
campaign *n.* ymgyrch *mf.*
can *n.* can, tun *m.*
candidate *n.* ymgeisydd *m.*
candle *n.* cannwyll *f.*
candlestick *n.* canhwyllbren *m.*
cane *n.* gwialen *f.*
canoe 1 *n.* canŵ *m.* **2** *v.* canŵio.
cap *n.* cap *m.*
capital 1 *n.* prifddinas *f;* corff (arian), cyfalaf *m*; priflythyren *f.* **2** *a.* prif, pen.
capitulate *v.* ymostwng.
captain *n.* capten *m.*
captivate *v.* swyno, hudo, denu.
capture *v.* dal, dala.
car *n.* car *m*: **car park** maes parcio.
caravan *n.* carafán *f*: **caravan site** maes carafanau *m.*
card *n.* cerdyn *m*, carden *f.*
Cardiff *n.* Caerdydd *f.*
care 1 *n.* gofal, pryder *m.* **2** *v.* gofalu, carco, hidio, pryderu.
career 1 *n.* gyrfa *f.* **2** *v.* rhuthro.
careful *a.* carcus, gofalus, manwl.
careless *a.* diofal, esgeulus.
caretaker *n.* gofalwr *m.*
caring *a.* gofalus.
Carmarthen *n.* Caerfyrddin *f.*
carol *n.* carol *f.*
carpenter *n.* saer coed *m.*
carpet 1 *n.* carped *m.* **2** *v.* carpedu.
carrot *n.* moronen *f.*
carry *v.* cario.
case *n.* cas; achos; cyflwr *m;* dadl *f.*
cash 1 *n.* arian parod *m.* **2** *v.* newid.
casing *n.* plisgyn; casin *m.*
cast *v.* taflu.
castle *n.* castell *m.*
cat *n.* cath *f.*
catalogue *n.* catalog *m.*
cataract *n.* rhaeadr *f,* sgwd *m*; pilen *(ar lygad) f.*
catch *v.* dal, dala.
catchment *n.* dalgylch.
catechism *n.* holwyddoreg *f.*
caterpillar *n.* lindysen *m.*
cathedral *n.* eglwys gadeiriol *f.*
catholic 1 *n.* pabydd *m.* **2** *a.* pabyddol; catholig.
cattle *n.pl.* gwartheg, da.
cauliflower *n.* blodfresychen *f.*
cause 1 *n.* achos; achlysur; rheswm *m.* **2** *v.* achosi, peri.
caution 1 *n.* pwyll; rhybudd *m.* **2** *v.* rhybuddio.
cautious *a.* gofalus, gwyliadwrus.
cave *n.* ogof *f.*
cavity *n.* gwagle *m.*
cease *v.* peidio (â).
ceiling *n.* nen *f.*
celebrate *v.* dathlu.
celebrated *a.* enwog.
cell *n.* cell *f.*
cemetery *n.* mynwent *f.*
censure *n.* sen *f.*
centenary *n.* canmlwyddiant *m.*
centigrade *a.* canradd, sentigred: **20°C** ugain gradd Celsius.
central *a.* canol, canolog: **central heating** gwres canolog
centre *n.* canol *m;* canolfan *f;* canolwr *m.*
centurion *n.* canwriad *m.*
century *n.* cant *m;* canrif *f.*
ceremony *n.* seremoni *f.*
certain *a.* sicr, siŵr; rhyw, rhai.
certainly *ad.* yn sicr, yn siŵr.
certainty *n.* sicrwydd *m.*
certificate *n.* tystysgrif *f.*
chaff *n.* us *coll.*
chaffinch *n.* ji-binc, asgell fraith *f.*

chain 1 *n.* cadwyn *f.* 2 *v.* cadwyno.
chair 1 *n.* cadair, stôl *f.* 2 *v.* cadeiro: **Chairing of the Bard** Cadeirio'r Bardd.
chaired *a.* cadeiriol.
chairman *n.* cadeirydd *m.*
chalet *n.* hafoty, bwthyn (haf) *m.*
chalk 1 *n.* sialc *m.* 2 *v.* sialcio.
challenge 1 *n.* her *f.* 2 *v.* herio.
chamber *n.* ystafell, siambr *f*: **chamber orchestra** cerddorfa siambr.
champion *n.* pencampwr *m.*
chance 1 *n.* hap, siawns, lwc *f,* cyfle *m,* damwain *f.* 2 *v.* digwydd.
change *n.* & *v.* newid *m.*
changing-room *n.* ystafell newid *f.*
channel *n.* sianel *f,* gwely *m.*
chapel *n.* capel *m.*
chapter *n.* pennod *f.*
character *n.* cymeriad, nod *m;* llythyren *f.*
characteristic 1 *n.* nodwedd *f.* 2 *a.* nodweddiadol.
charge 1 *n.* gofal; gorchymyn; pris, tâl; ergyd *m.* 2 *v.* gofalu, gorchymyn codi.
charm 1 *n.* hud, swyn *m.* 2 *v.* hudo, swyno.
charming *a.* swynol.
chase 1 *n.* helfa *f.* 2 *v.* hel, hela, erlid.
chat 1 *n.* sgwrs *f,* siarad, sôn *m,* ymgom *mf.* 2 *v.* sgwrsio, siarad, ymgomio.
chatter *v.* clebran.
cheap *a.* rhad.
cheat 1 *n.* twyllwr *m.* 2 *v.* twyllo.
cheek *n.* grudd *mf,* boch *f.*
cheerful *a.* llawen, llon, siriol.
cheese *n.* caws *m.*
cheers! *i.* iechyd da!
chemist *n.* fferyllydd; cemegwr *m.*
chemistry *n.* cemeg *f.*
Chepstow *n.* Cas-Gwent *f.*
cheque *n.* siec *f*: **cheque book** llyfr sieciau; **cheque card** cerdyn sieciau.
chest *n.* cist; brest *f.*
Chester *n.* Caer *f.*
chew *v.* cnoi.
chick *n.* cyw *m.*
chicken *n.* cyw iâr *m.* ffowlyn *f*: **chicken pox** brech yr ieir.
chief 1 *n.* pen, pennaeth *m.* 2 *a.* prif, pen, pennaf: **chief bard** prifardd.
child *n.* plentyn *m.*
childish *a.* plentynnaidd.
chill 1 *a.* oer. 2 *v.* oeri.
chilled *a.* sythlyd, wedi ei oeri.
chilly *a.* oer, oerllyd.
chimney *n.* simdde, simnai *f.,* corn (mwg) *m.*
chin *n.* gên *f.*
China *n.* Tseina, China *f.*
china *n.* llestri te *m.*
chip *n.* sglodyn *m*: **fish and chips** pysgod a sglodion.
chocolate *n.* siocled *m.*
choice *n.* dewis *m.*
choir *n.* côr *m.*
choke *v.* tagu.
choose *v.* dewis, ethol.
chop *v.* torri.
chord *n.* tant, cord *m*
chorus *n.* cytgan *f;* côr, corws *m.*
Christ *n.* Crist *m.*
christen *v.* bedyddio, enwi.
Christian 1 *n.* Cristion *m.* 2 *a.* Cristnogol: **Christian Aid** Cymorth Cristnogol; **Christian name** enw bedydd.
Christmas *n.* y Nadolig *m*: **Christmas Day** Dydd Nadolig; **Christmas Eve** Noswyl Nadolig; **Christmas Holidays** gwyliau'r Nadolig; **Christmas presents** anrhegion Nadolig; **Christmas tree** coeden Nadolig.
chum *n.* cyfaill, ffrind *m.*
church *n.* eglwys, llan *f.*
churchyard *n.* mynwent *f.*
chute *n.* llithren *f.*
cigar *n.* sigâr *f.*
cigarette *n.* sigarét *f.*
cinema *n.* sinema *f.*
circle *n.* cylch *m.*
circular 1 *n.* cylchlythyr *m.* 2 *a.* cylchog.
circumflex *n.* hirnod *mf.*
circus *n.* syrcas *f.*
citizen *n.* dinesydd *m.*
city *n.* dinas *f.*
civic *a.* dinesig.
civil *a.* gwladol.
civilian *n.* dinesydd *m.*
civil war *n.* rhyfel cartref *mf.*
claim 1 *n.* hawl *m.* 2 *v.* hawlio.
clamber *v.* dringo.
class 1 *n.* dosbarth *m;* adran *f,* cylch *m,* safon *f.* 2 *v.* dosbarthu.
classic *n.* clasur, campwaith *m.*
classical *a.* clasurol.
classics *n.* clasuron *pl.*
clause *n.* cymal *m;* adnod, adran *f.*
clay *n.* clai *m.*
clean 1 *a.* glân. 2 *v.* glanhau.
cleanliness *n.* glendid *m.*

cleanly *ad.* yn lân.
clear 1 *a.* amlwg, clir, eglur, gloyw. **2** *v.* clirio.
cleff *n.* allwedd *f,* cleff *m.*
clerk *n.* clerc *m.*
clever a. medrus, clyfar.
cliché *n.* ystrydeb *f.*
cliff *n.* clogwyn *m,* craig *f.*
climate *n.* hinsawdd *f.*
climax *n.* uchafbwynt *m.*
climb *v.* dringo.
climber *n.* dringwr *m.*
cling *v.* glynu, cydio.
clinic *n.* meddygfa *f,* clinig *m.*
cloak *n.* clogyn *m,* mantell *f.*
clock *n.* cloc *m;* **o'clock** o'r gloch; **six o'clock** chwech o'r gloch.
close 1 *n.* diwedd, terfyn *m.* **2** *v.* cau.
close 1 *n.* clos, buarth *m,* iard *f.* **2** *a.* agos, clòs, tyn.
cloth *n.* brethyn, defnydd, lliain, clwtyn *m.*
clothes *n.pl.* dillad, gwisgoedd *pl.*
clothing *n.* dillad *m.*
cloud 1 *n.* cwmwl *m.* **2** *v.* cymylu.
cloudy *a.* cymylog.
clown *n.* clown *m.*
clumsy *a.* lletchwith.
coach 1 *n.* hyfforddwr *m;* coets *f.* **2** *v.* hyfforddi.
coal *n.* glo *m.*
coarse *a.* garw, bras.
coast *n.* arfordir *m,* glan môr *f.*
coat *n.* cot, siaced *f.*
cockerel *n.* ceiliog *m.*
coffee *n.* coffi *m.*
coffin *n.* arch, coffin *f.*
cog *n.* dant, còg *m.*
coil 1 *n.* torch *m.* **2** *v.* torchi.
coin 1 *n.* darn arian *m.* **2** *v.* bathu; **pound coin** darn punt.
cold 1 *n.* oerfel; annwyd *m.* **2** *a.* oer, sythlyd: **to become cold** oeri; **to catch a cold** dal annwyd.
collar *n.* coler *f*: **collar bone** pont yr ysgwydd.
collect 1 *n.* colect *m* (*gweddi*). **2** *v.* casglu, crynhoi, hel.
collection *n.* casgliad *m.*
college *n.* coleg *m.*
collier *n.* glöwr *m;* llong lo *f.*
colliery *n.* glofa *f,* pwll glo, gwaith glo *m.*
colloquial *a.* llafar.
colony *n.* gwladfa *f.*
colour 1 *n.* lliw *m.* **2** *v.* lliwio, lliwo, coluro.
coloured *a.* lliwiog.
colourful *a.* lliwgar.
colt *n.* ebol *m.*
column *n.* colofn *f,* piler *m.*
columnist *n.* newyddiadurwr *m.*
comb 1 *n.* crib *mf.* **2** *v.* cribo.
combat *n.* gornest, brwydr *f.*
come *v.* dod, dyfod: **to come across** dod ar draws; **to come to an end** dod i ben.
comely *a.* teg, glân, hardd.
comfort 1 *n.* cysur *m.* **2** *v.* cysuro.
comfortable *a.* cyfforddus, cyffyrddus, cysurus.
command *n. & v.* gorchymyn *m.*
commandment *n.* gorchymyn *m*: **The Ten Commandments** Y Deg Gorchymyn.
commence *v.* dechrau.
commend *v.* canmol.
comment 1 *n.* sylw *m.* **2** *v.* sylwi, esbonio.
commentary *n.* sylwebaeth *f;* esboniad *m*: **to commentate** sylwebu.
commentator *n.* sylwebydd, sylwebwr *m.*
commitee *n.* pwyllgor *m.*
common *a.* cyffredin: **common sense** synnwyr cyffredin.
commons *n.* y cyffredin *pl*: **House of Commons** Tŷ'r Cyffredin.
commotion *n.* terfysg *m.*
community *n.* cymdeithas, cymuned *f.*
compact *a.* cryno: **compact disc** cryno ddisg.
companion *n.* cyfaill *m,* cyfeilles *f.*
company *n.* cwmni *m.*
compare *v.* cymharu (â).
compassion *n.* trugaredd *f.*
compel *v.* gorfodi.
compensate *v.* talu iawn.
compensation *n.* iawn, iawndal *m.*
compete *v.* cystadlu.
competition *n.* cystadleuaeth *f,* ymryson *m.*
competitor *n.* cystadleuwr, cystadleuydd *m.*
complain *v.* cwyno.
complaint *n.* cwyn *mf.*
complete *a.* hollol, llwyr.
completely *ad.* yn hollol, yn llwyr.
complex *a.* cymhleth.
complexity *m.* cymhlethdod *m.*
complicate *v.* cymhlethu *m.*
complicated *a.* cymhleth.
complication *n.* cymhlethdod *m.*
compose *v.* cyfansoddi.
composer *n.* cyfansoddwr *m.*
comprehensive *a.* cyfun,

cynhwysfawr: **Comprehensive School** Ysgol Gyfun.
compulsion *n.* gorfod *m,* gorfodaeth *f.*
compulsory *a.* gorfodol.
computer *n.* cyfrifiadur *m.*
conceal *v.* cuddio.
concentrate *v.* canolbwyntio.
concerning *prp.* ynglŷn â, ynghylch.
concert *n.* cyngerdd *mf.*
concession *n.* lŵans, lwfans *m.*
conclude *v.* gorffen.
conclusion *n.* casgliad; diwedd, diweddglo *m.*
concrete *n.* concrit *m.*
condition *n.* cyflwr *m;* amod *mf.*
conditionally *ad.* ar amod.
conduct 1 *n.* ymddygiad *m.* **2** *v.* arwain.
conductor *n.* arweinydd; tocynnwr *m.*
cone *n.* côn *m.*
confer *v.* ymgynghori.
conference *n.* cynhadledd *f.*
confide *v.* ymddiried (yn).
confidence *n.* hyder *m,* ymddiriedaeth *f*: **self-confidence** hunanhyder.
confident *a.* hyderus: **to be confident** hyderu.
confidential *a.* cyfrinachol.
confine *v.* cyfyngu, carcharu.
confined *a.* cyfyng.
confluence *n.* cymer *m.*
confront *v.* wynebu.
confuse *v.* drysu, cymysgu.
congratulate *v.* llongyfarch.
congratulation *n.* llongyfarchiad *m*: **Congratulations!** Llongyfarchiadau!
congregation *n.* cynulleidfa *f.*
Congregationalist *n.* Annibynnwr *m.*
conjecture *v.* dychmygu, dyfalu.
conjunction *n.* cysylltair *m.*
connection *n.* cysylltiad *m,* perthynas *mf*: **in connection with** ynglŷn â.
conquer *v.* gorchfygu, trechu.
conquest *n.* buddugoliaeth, concwest *f.*
conscription *n.* gorfodaeth filwrol *f.*
consent 1 *n.* caniatâd *m.* **2** *v.* caniatáu.
conservative *n.* ceidwadwr; Tori *m.*
conservatory *n.* tŷ gwydr *m.*
conserve *v.* cadw, amddiffyn.
consider *v.* ystyried.
considerable *a.* cryn.
consideration *n.* ystyriaeth *f.*
considering *prp.* ag ystyried.
consolation *n.* cysur *m*: **consolation prize** gwobr gysur.
console *v.* cysuro.
consonant *n.* cytsain *f.*
constituency *n.* etholaeth *f.*
construct *v.* ffurfio, llunio, adeiladu.
consult *v.* ymgynghori (â).
consume *v.* bwyta; defnyddio; treulio.
contact *v.* cyffwrdd (â).
contain *v.* cynnwys, dal.
contaminate *v.* llygru.
contamination *n.* llygredd *m.*
content *n.* cynnwys *m.*
content 1 *a.* bodlon. **2** *v.* bodloni.
contention *n.* ymryson *m.*
contents *n.* cynnwys *pl.*
contest 1 *n.* gornest, ornest, cystadleuaeth, ymryson *f.* **2** *v.* ymryson; ymladd.
contestant *n.* cystadleuwr, cystadleuydd *m.*
context *n.* cyd-destun *m.*
continual *a.* parhaus.
continually *ad.* byth a hefyd.
continuation *n.* parhad *m.*
continue *v.* para, parhau, dal (ati).
continuous *a.* parhaol.
contra- *px.* gwrth-, croes- (*followed by soft mutation*):
contradiction gwrthddywediad.
contract *n.* cytundeb *m.*
contrary *a.* gwrthwyneb, croes: **on the contrary** i'r gwrthwyneb.
contribute *v.* cyfrannu.
contrite *a.* edifeiriol:
control *v.* rheoli.
controller *n.* rheolwr *m.*
convenient *a.* cyfleus, hwylus.
conversation *n.* ymgom *mf,* sgwrs *f.*
converse 1 *n.* gwrthwyneb *m.* **2** *v.* ymgomio, sgwrsio, ymddiddan.
conversion *n.* trosiad *m;* tröedigaeth *f.*
convert *v.* troi, newid, trosi.
converted *a.* wedi ei addasu: **converted try** trosgais.
convey *v.* cyfleu; trosglwyddo.
cook 1 *n.* cogydd *m;* cogyddes *f.* **2** *v.* coginio, gwneud bwyd.
cool 1 *a.* oer. **2** *v.* oeri.
copy 1 *n.* copi *m.* **2** *v.* copïo.
copyright *n.* hawlfraint *f.*
cord *n.* cordyn *m;* lein *f,* llinyn *m.*
corgi *n.* corgi *m.*
corn *n.* llafur, corn, ŷd *m.*
corner *n.* cornel *mf,* cwr *m,* congl *f.*
cornflakes *n.* creision ŷd *pl.*

corpse *n.* corff *m.*
correct 1 *a.* cywir, iawn, priodol. 2 *v.* cywiro.
correction *n.* cywiriad *m.*
corrupt 1 *a.* llygredig. 2 *v.* llygru.
corruption *n.* llygredd, llygredigaeth *m.*
cost 1 *n.* pris *m,* traul, cost *f.* 2 *v.* costio.
costume *n.* gwisg *f.*
cottage *n.* bwthyn *m.*
cotton *n.* cotwm *m;* edau *f:* **cotton wool** gwlân cotwm.
cough 1 *n.* peswch, pesychiad *m.* 2 *v.* peswch.
council *n.* cyngor *m:* **council house** tŷ cyngor; **county council** cyngor sir.
councillor *n.* cynghorwr *m:* **County Councillor** Cynghorwr Sir.
counsel 1 *n.* cyngor *m.* 2 *v.* cynghori.
count 1 *n.* cyfrif; iarll *m.* 2 *v.* rhifo; cyfrif.
counter- *px.* gwrth- (*followed by soft mutation*): **counteract** gwrthweithio; **counterclockwise** gwrthgloc.
counterfeit *n. & a.* ffug *m.*
counterfoil *n.* bôn *m* (*siec/ derbynneb . . .*).
countess *n.* iarlles *f.*
country *n.* gwlad, bro *f:* **Country Music** Canu Gwlad.
county *n.* sir, swydd (*English county*) *f:* **Carmarthenshire** Sir Gaerfyrddin, Sir Gâr; **Lancashire** Swydd Gaerhirfryn; **Yorkshire** Swydd Efrog; **Buckinghamshire** Swydd Buckingham.
courageous *a.* dewr, gwrol.
course *n.* cwrs *m,* hynt; ystod; gyrfa *f:* **in the course of** yn ystod; **of course** wrth gwrs; **crash course** cwrs carlam.
court 1 *n.* llys *m.* 2 *v.* caru, canlyn.
courteous *a.* cwrtais.
cousin *n.* cefnder *m;* cyfnither *f.*
cover 1 *n.* clawr *m.* 2 *v.* gorchuddio.
covetous *a.* trachwantus.
covetousness *n.* trachwant *m.*
cow *n.* buwch *f.*
cowardly *a.* llwfr.
crack 1 *n.* crac *m.* 2 *v.* cracio.
cradle *n.* crud *m.*
craft *n.* crefft; llong; awyren *f.*
craftsman *n.* crefftwr *m.*
crafty *a.* cyfrwys.
crag *n.* craig *f,* clogwyn *m.*
cream *n.* hufen *m.*
crematorium *n.* amlosgfa *f.*
cress *n.* berw *m.*
crest *n.* brig *m,* crib *mf.*
crew *n.* criw *m.*
crib *n.* preseb *m.*
cricket *n.* criced, cricsyn *m.*
cricketer *n.* cricedwr *m.*
crime *n.* trosedd *f.*
criminal *n.* troseddwr *m.*
crisps *n.* creision (tatws) *pl.*
critic *n.* beirniad *m.*
criticise *v.* beirniadu.
crockery *n.* llestri *pl.*
croft *n.* tyddyn *m.*
crook *n.* troseddwr; ffon fugail *m.*
crooked *a.* cam.
cross 1 *n.* croes *f.* 2 *v.* croesi.
cross-examine *v.* croesholi.
crossing *n.* croesfan *f.*
crossroad *n.* croesffordd *f.*
crossword *n.* croesair, pôs croeseiriau *m.*
crow *n.* brân *f.*
crowd *n.* torf *f,* twr *m,* tyrfa *f,* llu *m.*
crown 1 *n.* coron *f.* 2 *v.* coroni: **Crown land** tir y Goron; **Triple Crown** Coron Driphlyg.
cruel *a.* creulon.
cruelty *n.* creulondeb *m.*
crumb *n.* briwsionyn *m.*
crumble *v.* chwalu; briwsioni.
crush *v.* malu, gwasgu.
crust *n.* crwst, crystyn *m.*
cry 1 *n.* cri *mf,* llef, sgrech *f.* 2 *v.* crio, llefain, wylo.
cuckoo *n.* cog, cwcw *f.*
cunning *a.* cyfrwys.
cup *n.* cwpan *mf,* dysgl *f.*
cupboard *n.* cwpwrdd *m.*
cure *v.* gwella, iacháu.
curly *a.* cyrliog.
current 1 *n.* ffrwd *f,* llif *m.* 2 *a.* cyfoes: **current affairs** materion cyfoes.
currently *ad.* ar hyn o bryd.
curse 1 *n.* llw *m,* melltith, rheg *f.* 2 *v.* rhegi.
curtain *n.* llen *f.*
cushion *n.* clustog *f.*
custom *n.* arfer, cwstwm *m;* toll *f.*
customary *a.* arferol.
customer *n.* cwsmer *m.*
customs *n.* y tollau *pl:* **customs officer** swyddog tollau.
cut 1 *n.* toriad *m.* 2 *v.* torri.
cycle 1 *n.* cylch; beic *m.* 2 *v.* seiclo.
cylinder *n.* silindr *m.*
cylindrical *a.* silindrog.

dad: daddy *n.* tad *m.*
daffodil *n.* cenhinen Bedr *f,* daffodil *m.*
daisy *n.* llygad y dydd *m.*
dale *n.* cwm, dyffryn *m,* dôl, bro *f*: **hill and dale** bryn a dôl.
damage *n.* niwed, difrod *m.*
damages *n.pl.* iawndal, iawn *m.*
damp *a.* llaith.
damson *n.* eirinen ddu *f.*
dance 1 *n.* dawns *f.* **2** *v.* dawnsio: **public folk dance** twmpath dawns.
dandelion *n.* dant y llew *m.*
danger *n.* perygl *m.*
dangerous *a.* peryglus.
dank *a.* llaith, gwlyb.
dare *v.* beiddio, meiddio, mentro.
dark *a.* tywyll.
darkness *n.* tywyllwch, gwyll *m.*
darling 1 *n.* anwylyd *mf,* cariad *m.* **2** *v.* annwyl.
date *n.* dyddiad *m.*
daughter *n.* merch *f.*
dawn 1 *n.* gwawr *f.* **2** *v.* gwawrio.
day *n.* diwrnod, dydd *m*: **day before yesterday** echdoe; **yesterday** doe, ddoe; **today** heddiw; **tomorrow** yfory; **day after tomorrow** trennydd; **three days hence** tradwy; **by day** liw dydd; **next day** trannoeth; **Good day!** Dydd da!.
day break *n.* gwawr *f,* toriad dydd *m.*
daylight *n.* golau dydd *m.*
dazzle *v.* dallu; disgleirio.
dazzling *a.* llachar, disglair.
deacon *n.* diacon; blaenor *m*: **deaconess** diacones.
dead *n.* & *a.* marw, meirw, meirwon *pl.*
deadly *a.* marwol.
deaf *n.* & *a.* byddar *m.*
deal *v.* ymwneud (â), delio (â).
dear 1 *n.* anwylyd *mf,* cariad *m.* **2** *a.* annwyl, bach, cu, ffel, hoff; drud.
dearest *n.* & *a.* anwylaf *mf*: **dearest ones** anwyliaid.
death *n.* angau *m,* marwolaeth *f.*
debate 1 *n.* dadl *f.* **2** *v.* dadlau, ymryson.
debt *n.* dyled *f.*
decade *n.* degawd *m.*
decay *v.* pydru.
deceased *a.* y diweddar.
deceit *n.* twyll *m.*
deceitful *a.* twyllodrus.
deceive *v.* twyllo.
decelerate *v.* arafu.
December *n.* Rhagfyr *m.*
decentralise *v.* datganoli.
decide *v.* penderfynu, dyfarnu.
decision *n.* penderfyniad, dyfarniad *m.*
deck *n.* bwrdd; dec *m.*
declaration *n.* datganiad *m.*
declare *v.* datgan, mynegi.
decompose *v.* pydru.
decree *n.* gorchmyn *m.*
dedicate *v.* cyflwyno; cysegru.
deed *n.* gweithred *f.*
deep 1 *n.* dyfnder *m.* **2** *a.* dwfn: **deep freeze cabinet** rhewgell.
Dee Side *n.* Glannau Dyfrdwy *f.*
defeat *v.* gorchfygu, trechu.
defect *n.* nam, diffyg, gwall *m.*
defence *n.* amddiffyn, amddiffyniad *m;* amddiffynfa *f.*
defend *v.* amddiffyn.
defiance *n.* her *f.*
define *v.* diffinio.
definite *a.* pendant.
definitely *ad.* yn bendant.
definition *n.* diffiniad *m.*
defraud *v.* twyllo.
deft *a.* medrus.
degree *n.* gradd *f.*
de-ice *v.* toddi.
deity *n.* duwdod; duw *m.*
delay *v.* oedi.
delectable *a.* hyfryd.
delegate 1 *n.* dirprwy *m.* **2** *v.* dirprwyo.
delegation *n.* dirprwyaeth *f.*
delete *v.* dileu.
delicious *a.* blasus.
delightful *a.* hyfryd, braf.
deliver *v.* gwaredu (rhag); danfon, trosglwyddo.

deliverer *n.* gwaredwr.
demand 1 *n.* gofyn, galw *m,* arch; gofynneb *f.* 2 *v.* mynnu, gofyn.
demi- *px.* hanner.
demise *n.* marwolaeth *f.*
den *n.* ffau *f.*
denomination *n.* enw, enwad *m.*
dense *a.* trwchus; hurt.
dent 1 *n.* pant, tolc *m.* 2 *v.* tolcio.
dentist *n.* deintydd *m.*
dentures *n.* dannedd gosod, dannedd dodi *pl.*
deny *v.* gwadu, gwrthod.
depart *v.* ymadael (â); cychwyn.
department *n.* adran *f.* dosbarth *m.*
depend *v.* dibynnu (ar).
deplore *v.* gresynu.
depose *v.* diswyddo; tystio.
deposit *n.* ernes *f.*
depressed *a.* isel, digalon.
depth *n.* dyfnder *m.*
deputation *n.* dirprwyaeth *f.*
deputy *n.* dirprwy *m*: **Deputy Director** Dirprwy Gyfarwyddwr; **Deputy Headteacher** Dirprwy Brifathro, Dirprwy Brifathrawes.
derivation *n.* tarddiad *m.*
derive *v.* derbyn, cael; tarddu.
descend *v.* disgyn.
describe *v.* disgrifio, darlunio.
description *n.* disgrifiad *m.*
desert *n.* anialwch *m.*
desert *v.* cilio, ffoi (rhag).
deserter *n.* ffoadur *m.*
deserve *v.* haeddu.
deserved *a.* teilwng.
design 1 *n.* cynllun *m.* 2 *v.* cynllunio.
designer *n.* cynlluniwr, cynllunydd *m.*
desirable *a.* dymunol.
desire 1 *n.* dymuniad, chwant, ewyllys *m.* 2 *v.* dymuno.
desirous *a.* awyddus.
desk *n.* desg *f.*
desolate *a.* gwag.
despite *prp.* er, er gwaethaf.
despot *n.* unben *m.*
dessert *n.* pwdin, melysfwyd *m.*
destiny *n.* tynged *f.*
destroy *v.* dinistrio, difetha.
detached *a.* ar wahân.
detail 1 *n.* manlyn *m.* 2 *v.* manylu: **details** manylion; **in detail** yn fanwl.
detective *n.* ditectif *m;* **detective story** stori dditectif.
determination *n.* penderfyniad *m.*
determine *v.* penderfynu.
determined *a.* penderfynol.
detest *v.* casáu.
develop *v.* datblygu.
development *n.* datblygiad *m.*
deviate *v.* gwyro, gwyrio.
deviation *n.* gwyriad *m.*
devil *n.* diafol, diawl *m.*
devilish *a.* diawledig.
devolution *n.* datganoli *m.*
devolve *v.* datganoli.
devour *v.* llyncu, ysu.
dew 1 *n.* gwlith *m.* 2 *v.* gwlitho.
diagnose *v.* adnabod.
diagnosis *n.* diagnosis *m.*
dialect *n.* tafodiaith *f.*
dialogue *n.* deialog, sgwrs *f.*

diarrhoea *n.* dolur rhydd *m.*
diary *n.* dyddiadur *m.*
dictator *n.* unben *m.*
dictionary *n.* geiriadur *m.*
die *v.* marw, darfod, trigo.
difference *n.* gwahaniaeth *m.*
different *a.* gwahanol.
difficult *a.* anodd, caled.
difficulty *n.* anhawster *m.*
dig *v.* palu.
digest *v.* treulio.
dignity *n.* urddas *m.*
diligent *a.* prysur, diwyd.
dimension *n.* maint *m.*
diminish *v.* lleihau.
diminutive *a.* bychan.
dingle *n.* cwm, glyn, pant *m.*
dinner *n.* cinio *mf.*
dip *v.* trochi, golchi.
direct 1 *a.* union. 2 *v.* cyfeirio.
direction *n.* cyfeiriad; hyfforddiant *m.*
directly *ad.* yn union.
director *n.* cyfarwyddwr *m.*
directory *n.* cyfarwyddiadur *m.*
dirt *n.* baw, llacs *m.*
dirty *a.* brwnt, budr.
disability *n.* anabledd *m.*
disabled *a.* anabl, methedig.
disappear *v.* diflannu.
disappoint *v.* siomi.
disappointed *a.* siomedig.
disappointing *a.* siomedig.
disappointment *n.* siom *mf.*
disarm *v.* diarfogi.
disaster *n.* trychineb *mf.*
disc *n.* disg *mf.*
disciple *n.* disgybl *m.*
discipline *n.* disgyblaeth *f.*
disclaim *v.* gwadu.
disclose *v.* datguddio.
discontented *a.* anfodlon.

discover *v.* darganfod.
discretion *n.* doethineb, pwyll *m.*
discuss *v.* trafod.
discussion *n.* sgwrs *f.*
disease *n.* afiechyd, clefyd, dolur *m.* haint *f.*
disembark *v.* glanio.
dish *n.* dysgl *f.*
disinfectant *n.* diheintydd *m.*
disk *n.* disg *mf.*
dislike *v.* casáu.
dismiss *v.* diswyddo; rhyddau; gwrthod.
disown *v.* gwadu, diarddel.
dispatch 1 *n.* neges *f.* 2 *v.* anfon, danfon.
dispute 1 *n.* dadl *f.* 2 *v.* dadlau, amau, ymryson.
disseminate *v.* hau.
dissimilar *a.* annhebyg, gwahanol.
dissolve *v.* toddi; datod.
distance *n.* pellter *m.*
distant *a.* pell, hirbell: **from far** o hirbell.
distasteful *a.* diflas.
distinct *a.* arbennig; eglur; gwahanol.
distribute *v.* rhannu, dosbarthu.
district *n.* ardal *f,* dosbarth, cylch, rhanbarth, rhandir *m.*
ditch *n.* ffos *f.*
diverse *a.* gwahanol.
divide *v.* rhannu.
diviner *n.* dewin, dyn hysbys *m.*
division *n.* adran, rhan *f,* rhaniad, rhanbarth, rhandir *m.*
divorce *n.* ysgariad *m.*
do *v.* gwneud, gwneuthur.
dock *n.* doc *m.*
doctor *n.* meddyg, doctor *m*: **Dr John Jones** y Dr John Jones.
document *n.* dogfen *f.*
dog *n.* ci *m.*
doll *n.* dol *f.*
domesticated *a.* dof.
donation *n.* rhodd *f,* cyfraniad *m.*
donkey *n.* asyn, mul *m.*
door *n.* drws, porth *m.*
double *a.* dwbl.
doubt *n.* & *v.* amau *m.*
dough *n.* toes *m.*
down *ad.* i lawr.
dozen *n.* dwsin, deuddeg *m.*
drag *v.* llusgo.
dragon *n.* draig *f.*
drama *n.* drama *f*: **drama festival** gŵyl ddrama.
dramatist *n.* dramodydd *m.*
draw *v.* darlunio, llunio; tynnu, llusgo.
drawing *n.* llun *m.*
dread 1 *n.* ofn *m.* 2 *v.* ofni.
dreadful *a.* ofnadwy.
dream 1 *n.* breuddwyd *mf.* 2 *v.* breuddwydio.
dregs *n.* gwaelodion *pl,* gwaddodd *m.*
dress 1 *n.* gwisg *f,* dilledyn *m,* ffrog *f.* 2 *v.* gwisgo, taclu; trin.
dresser *n.* seld, dreser, dresel *f;* gwisgwr *m.*
dressmaker *n.* gwniadyddes, gwniyddes *f.*
drink 1 *n.* diod *f.* 2 v. yfed.
drive 1 *n.* dreif *m.* 2 *v.* gyrru, hala.
driver *n.* gyrrwr *m.*
driving licence *n.* trwydded yrru *f.*
droll *a.* ysmala, digrif.
drop 1 *n.* cwymp; diferyn *m.* 2 *v.* cwympo: **drop goal** gôl adlam.
drown *v.* boddi.
drug *n.* cyffur *m.*
drum *n.* drwm.
drunk *a.* meddw: **to get drunk** meddwi.
drunkard *n.* meddwyn.
dry 1 *a.* sych, cras. 2 *v.* sychu.
Dublin *n.* Dulyn *f.*
duck *n.* hwyad, hwyaden *f*: **duckling** cyw hwyaden *m.*
due 1 *n.* dyled, hawl *f,* tâl *m.* 2 *a.* dyledus.
duel *n.* gornest *f.*
duet *n.* deuawd *mf.*
dull *a.* dwl, hurt; diflas, cymylog: **dull man** dyn dwl; **dull day** diwrnod cymylog.
dumb *a.* mud.
dummy-pass *n.* ffug-bas *f.*
during *prp.* yn ystod.
dust *n.* llwch, dwst *m*: **dustbin** bin ysbwriel *m.*
duty *n.* dyletswydd; toll *f.*
dwell *v.* catrefu, trigo, byw.
dwelling *n.* preswylfa, trigfa, trigfan. *f.*
dye *v.* lliwio, lliwo.
dyke *n.* clawdd, morglawdd *m*: **Offa's Dyke** Clawdd Offa.

each *a.* & *pn.* pob un, pob.
eager *a.* awyddus.
eagle *n.* eryr *m.*
ear *n.* clust *f.*
earl *n.* iarll *m.*
earliest *a.* cyntaf.
early 1 *a.* cynnar, bore, boreol. **2** *ad.* yn fore.
ear-mark 1 *n.* clustnod *mf.* **2** *v.* clustnodi, neilltuo.
earn *v.* ennill.
earner *n.* enillwr, enillydd *m.*
earnings *n.* enillion *pl.*
ear-ring *n.* clustlws *m.*
earshot *n.* clyw *m.*
earth *n.* daear *f,* pridd, tir, y byd *m.*
earthquake *n.* daeargryn *mf.*
earthwork *n.* clawdd *m.*
east 1 *n.* dwyrain *m.* **2** *a.* dwyreiniol.
Easter *n.* y Pasg *m*: **Easter egg** wy Pasg; **Easter holidays** gwyliau'r Pasg.
easy *a.* hawdd, rhwydd.
easy-chair *n.* cadair esmwyth *f.*
eat *v.* bwyta.
ebb *n.* trai *m.*
echo *n.* adlais, atsain *m.* carreg ateb *f.*
economics *n.* economeg *f.*
economise *v.* cynilo.
edge *n.* cwr, blaen, min *m,* ymyl *mf.*
Edinburgh *n.* Caeredin *f.*
edit *v.* golygu.
edition *n.* argraffiad *m.*
editor *n.* golygydd *m.*
education *n.* addysg *f.*
effect 1 *n.* effaith *f.* **2** *v.* effeithio.
effective *a.* effeithiol.
effeminate *a.* merchetaidd.
effort *n.* ymdrech, ymgais *f.*
e.g. *(exempli gratia), ad.* er enghraifft, *e.e.*
egg *n.* wy *m.*
egg cup *n.* cwpan wy *mf.*
eight *n.* & *a.* wyth *m.*
eighteen *n.* & *a.* deunaw, un deg wyth *m.*
eighth *n.* & *a.* wythfed *m.*
eighty *n.* & *a.* wyth deg, pedwar ugain *m.*
either 1 *a.* & *pn.* un o'r ddau, naill ai . . . neu. **2** *ad.* & *c.* na, nac, chwaith, ychwaith.
elbow *n.* penelin *mf.*
elderly *a.* oedrannus.
elect *v.* ethol, dewis.
election *n.* etholiad *m.*
electorate *n.* etholaeth *f.*
electric *n.* & *a.* trydan *m*: **electric fire** tân trydan.
electrician *n.* trydanwr *m.*
electricity *n.* trydan *m.*
element *n.* elfen *f.*
elementary *a.* elfennol.
elephant *n.* eliffant.
eleven *n.* & *a.* un ar ddeg *m.*
eleventh *n.* & *a.* unfed ar ddeg *m.*
ellipse *n.* hirgylch *m.*
else *ad.* arall.
embankment *n.* clawdd, cob *m.*
embassy *n.* llysgenhadaeth *f.*
embrace *v.* cofleidio.
emigrant *n.* ymfudwr *m.*
emigrate *v.* ymfudo.
eminent *a.* enwog, amlwg.
emphasis *n.* pwys, pwyslais *m.*
emphatic *a.* pendant.
empire *n.* ymerodraeth *f.*
employ *v.* cyflogi.
employee *n.* gŵr cyflog *m.*
employer *n.* cyflogwr *m.*
employment *n.* gwaith *m.*
empty 1 *a.* gwag. **2** *v.* gwagio, arllwys: **empty-handed** gwaglaw.
enchant *v.* swyno, hudo.
enchanting *a.* hudol, swynol.
enchantment *n.* lledrith, swyn *m.*
enclose *v.* amgáu.
enclosed *a.* amgaeëdig.
encore 1 *n.* encôr *m.* **2** *ad.* eto.
end 1 *n.* diwedd, diben, pen, terfyn *m.* **2** *v.* dibennu, gorffen.
endeavour 1 *n.* ymdrech *f.* **2** v. ymdrechu.
endless *a.* diddiwedd.
endure *v.* dioddef, goddef.
enemy *n.* gelyn *m.*
energetic *a.* egnïol.

energy *n.* egni, ynni *m.*
enforce *v.* gorfodi.
enforced *a.* gorfod.
enforcement *n.* gorfodaeth *f.*
engagement *n.* dyweddïad; ymrwymiad *m.*
engine *n.* peiriant *m,* injan, injin *f.*
England *n.* Lloegr *f.*
English 1 *n.* Saesneg *f.* 2 *a.* Saesneg, Seisnig.
Englishman *n.* Sais *m.*
Englishwoman *n.* Saesnes *f.*
enjoy *v.* mwynhau, joio.
enjoyment *n.* mwynhad *m.*
enlighten *v.* goleuo; hysbysu.
enormous *a.* enfawr, anferth.
enough 1 *n.* digon, digonedd *m.* 2 *a.* & *ad.* digon.
enquire *v.* gofyn, holi.
entangle *v.* drysu.
enter *v.* mynd i mewn.
entertain *v.* difyrru.
entertaining *a.* difyr, difyrrus.
entertainment *n.* adloniant *m.*
enthusiastic *a.* brwdfrydig.
entice *v.* denu, hudo.
enticing *a.* deniadol, dengar.
entire *a.* cyfan, hollol, llwyr.
entirely *ad.* yn gyfan gwbl, yn hollol, yn llwyr.
entrails *n.* perfedd *pl.*
entrance *n.* mynedfa *f.* mynediad, drws, porth; tâl *m.*
entrance *v.* swyno.
entreat *v.* erfyn.
entry *n.* mynediad *m,* mynedfa *f.*
envelop *v.* amgáu.
envelope *n.* amlen *f.*
environment *n.* amgylchedd *m.*
environs *n.* amgylchoedd *pl.*
envoy *n.* negesydd, cennad *m.*
epilogue *n.* diweddglo, epilog *m.*
epistle *n.* llythyr, epistol *m.*
equation *n.* hafaliad *m*: **simple equation** hafaliad syml.
equipment *n.* offer *pl.*
erase *v.* dileu.
erect 1 *a.* syth. 2 *v.* codi.
errand *n.* neges *f.*
error *n.* camsyniad; bai, gwall *m.*
escape *v.* dianc, ffoi.
escort *v.* hebrwng.
especial *a.* arbennig, enwedig, neilltuol.
especially *ad.* yn arbennig, yn enwedig.
essay *n.* traethawd *m.* ysgrif *mf.*
essential *a.* hanfodol.
establish *v.* sefydlu.
establishment *n.* sefydliad *m.*
estate *n.* eiddo *m,* ystad, stad *f.*
estuary *n.* aber *m.*
eternal *ad.* yn dragwyddol, yn oes oesoedd.
Europe *n.* Ewrob, Ewrop *f.*
evade *v.* osgoi.
eve *n.* min nos *m,* noswyl *f.*
even 1 *n.* yr hwyr *m.* 2 *a.* gwastad, llyfn; tawel. 3 *ad.* hyd yn oed.
evening *n.* hwyr *m,* noson, noswaith *f*: **evening class** dosbarth nos.
event *n.* digwyddiad *m.*
eventually *ad.* o'r diwedd.
ever *ad.* byth, erioed.
evergreen *n.* & *a.* bythwyrdd *m.*
everlasting *a.* tragwyddol.
evermore *ad.* byth, byth bythoedd.
every *a.* pob.
everybody *pn.* pawb, pob un.
everyday *a.* bob dydd.
everyone *pn.* pawb, pob un.
everything *pn.* pob peth, popeth.
everywhere *ad.* ym mhobman.
evidence *n.* tystiolaeth *f,* prawf *m.*
evident *a.* amlwg, eglur.
evil 1 *n.* drwg, drygioni *m.* 2 *a.* drwg, drygionus.
evolve *v.* datblygu; esblygu.
ewe *n.* dafad, mamog *f.*
ex-*px.* cyn.
exact *a.* cywir, manwl, union: **to be exact** manylu.
exactly *ad.* yn union, i'r dim.
examination *n.* arholiad, archwiliad *m.*
examine *v.* arholi, chwilio, archwilio.
examiner *n.* arholwr, holwr *m.*
example *n.* enghraifft, esiampl *f*: **for example, e.g.** er enghraifft, e.e.
excavator *n.* jac-codi-baw *m.*
excel *v.* rhagori.
excellent *a.* ardderchog, campus, godidog, gwych, penigamp, rhagorol.
except 1 *v.* eithrio. 2 *prp.* ac eithrio. 3 *pn.* eithr.
excess *n.* gormod.
exciting *a.* cyffrous, cynhyrfus.
exclaim *v.* llefain, gweiddi, bloeddio.
exclamation *n.* llef, gwaedd *f.*
exclude *v.* eithrio, cau allan.
excuse 1 *n.* esgus *m.* 2 *v.* esgusodi.
execute *v.* gweithredu; dienyddio.
exercise 1 *n.* ymarfer *f,* ymarferiad *m.* 2 *v.* ymarfer: **exercise book** llyfr ymarfer,

llyfr ysgrifennu.
exile 1 *n.* alltud *m.* 2 *v.* alltudio.
exist *v.* bod.
existence *n.* bod *m,* bodolaeth *f.*
exit 1 *n.* allanfa *f,* mynediad allan *m.* 2 *v.* mynd allan.
expect *v.* disgwyl.
expediency *n.* hwylustod *m.*
expedient *a.* hwylus, cyfleus.
expense *n.* traul, cost *f.*
expenses *n.* treuliau *pl.*
expensive *a.* costus, drud.
experience *n.* profiad *m.*
experienced *a.* profiadol.
explain *v.* egluro, esbonio.
explanation *n.* esboniad, eglurhad *m.*
explode *v.* ffrwydro.
expose *v.* amlygu, dinoethi.
exposed *a.* agored, noeth.
exposition *n.* esboniad *m.*
express 1 *a.* cyflym. 2 *v.* mynegi. 3 *n.* trên cyflym *m.*
extend *v.* estyn, ymestyn.
extension *a.* estyniad *m.*
extensive *a.* eang, helaeth.
extent *n.* maint, hyd, mesur *m*: **to some extent** i raddau.
exterior 1 *n.* y tu allan *m.* 2 *a.* allanol.
external *a.* allanol.
extinguish *v.* diffodd; dileu.
extreme 1 *n.* eithaf *m.* 2 *a.* eithafol.
extremely *ad.* dros ben, gor-.
extremity *n.* eithaf, terfyn, pen *m.*
eye 1 *n.* llygad *mf.* 2 *v.* llygadu, sylwi ar.
eyesight *n.* golwg *mf.*
eyewitness *n.* llygad-dyst *m.*

fable *n.* chwedl *f.*
fabric *n.* defnydd *m.*
face 1 *n.* wyneb *m.* **2** *v.* wynebu: **face cloth** clwtyn ymolch.
facilitate *v.* hwyluso.
fact *n.* ffaith *f,* gwirionedd *m*: **as a matter of fact** mewn gwirionedd.
factor *n.* elfen, ffactor *f.*
factory *n.* ffatri *f.*
fade *v.* gwywo, colli lliw.
fail *v.* methu, ffaelu.
failure *n.* methiant *m.*
faint 1 *a.* gwan. **2** *v.* llewygu.
fair 1 *n.* ffair *f.* **2** *a.* teg, glân; gweddol; golau.
fairly *ad.* yn deg, yn lân, yn weddol, eithaf-, go -, lled -: **fairly good** eithaf da, go dda, lled dda: **fairly rare** go brin: **fairly quiet** lled dawel;
see Appendix for mutation of Adjectives following certain Adverbs.
fairness *n.* harddwch; tegwch *m.*
faith *n.* ffydd *f.*
faithful *a.* ffyddlon, cywir.
faithfully *ad.* yn ffyddlon, yn gywir: **yours faithfully** yr eiddoch yn gywir.
fake 1 *a.* ffug. **2** *v.* ffugio.
falcon *n.* hebog *m.*
fall 1 *n.* cwymp *m.* **2** *v.* cwympo, syrthio.
false *a.* ffug, gau, twyllodrus: **false teeth** dannedd gosod, dannedd dodi.
fame *n.* enwogrwydd, clod *m.*
familiarise *v.* cyfarwyddo.
family *n.* teulu *m.*
famine *n.* newyn *m.*
famish *v.* llwgu.
famous *a.* enwog.
fanciful *a.* ffansïol.
fancy 1 *n.* dychymyg *m,* ffansi *f,* serch *m.* **2** *v.* dychmygu, ffansïo, serchu.
fantasy *n.* ffantasi *f.*
far *a.* & *ad.* pell, ymhell: **as far as** hyd at: **from afar** o hirbell.
farewell 1 *n.* ffárwel, ffarwél *f.* **2** *v.* ffarwelio: **to bid farewell** canu'n iach.
farm 1 *n.* ffarm, fferm *f.* **2** *v.* ffarmio, ffermio.
farmer *n.* amaethwr, ffarmwr, ffermwr *m.*
farmhouse *n.* ffermdy, tŷ ffarm *m.*
farming *n.* ffermio, gwaith ffarm *m,* amaethyddiaeth *f.*
farmyard *n.* buarth, clos *m.*
farthest *a.* pellaf, eithaf.
fascinate *v.* hudo, swyno.
fascinating *a.* hudol, swynol.
fashion 1 *n.* llun, ffasiwn *m;* arfer *mf.* **2** *v.* llunio, ffurfio, gwneud.
fast *a.* cyflym, buan; tyn.
fat 1 *n.* braster, saim *m.* **2** *v.* bras, tew: **fat meat** cig bras, cig gwyn.
fatal *a.* marwol.
fatality *n.* marwolaeth *f.*
fate *n.* tynged *f.*
fateful *a.* tyngedfennol.
father *n.* tad *m*: **father-in-law** tad-yng-nghyfraith: **stepfather** llystad.
Father Christmas *n.* Siôn Corn *m.*
fault *n.* bai, nam, diffyg *m.*
faultless *a.* di-fai.
faulty *a.* gwallus.
favour *n.* cymwynas, ffafr *f.*
favourite 1 *n.* ffefryn *m.* **2** *a.* hoff.
fear 1 *n.* ofn, braw *m.* **2** *v.* ofni.
feast 1 *n.* gwledd, gŵyl *f.* **2** *v.* gwledda.
feat *n.* camp *f.*
feather 1 *n.* pluen, plufyn *m.* **2** *v.* pluo, plufio.
feature *n.* nodwedd.
fee *n.* tâl *m,* cyflog *mf,* ffi *f.*
February *n.* Chwefror, Mis Bach *m.*
feeble *a.* gwan, egwan, bregus.
feed *v.* bwydo, bwyda; bwyta.
feel 1 *n.* teimlad *m.* **2** *v.* teimlo, clywed.
feeling *n.* teimlad *m,* naws *f.*
feign *v.* cymryd ar; ffugio.
fell *v.* cwympo, syrthio, torri.
female 1 *n.* benyw, menyw *f.* **2** *a.* benywaidd, menywaidd.
feminine *a.* benywaidd, menywaidd.

fence 1 *n.* clawdd *m,* ffens *f.* 2 *v.* cau, amgáu.
fern *n.* rhedynen *f,* rhedyn *pl.*
ferocious *a.* ffyrnig, gwyllt.
fertile *a.* ffrwythlon, bras, toreithiog.
fertilise *v.* ffrwythloni; gwrteithio.
fertiliser *n.* gwrtaith *m.*
fervent *a.* gwresog, tanllyd, tanbaid, selog.
festival *n.* gŵyl, dydd gŵyl *m*: **singing festival** cymanfa ganu.
fetch *v.* hôl, nôl, hercyd.
fever *n.* twymyn *f,* clefyd, gwres *m.*
few *a.* ychydig.
fiancé *n.* darpar-ŵr *m,* darpar-wraig *f.*
fiction *n.* ffuglen *f.*
fictitious *a.* ffug, ffugiol.
field *n.* cae, maes, parc *m.*
fierce *a.* ffyrnig.
fiery *a.* tanllyd, tanbaid.
fifteen *n.* & *a.* pymtheg *m.*
fifteenth *n.* & *a.* pymthegfed *m.*
fifth *n.* & *a.* pumed *m.*
fifty *n.* & *a.* hanner cant, pum deg *m.*
fight 1 *n.* brwydr *f,* ymladd *m.* 2 *v.* brwydro, ymladd.
fighter *n.* ymladdwr *m.*
fighting *n.* ymladd *m.*
figure 1 *n.* ffigur *mf;* ffurf *f,* llun *m.* 2 *v.* ffurfio; rhifo.
fill *v.* llanw, llenwi.
film 1 *n.* ffilm *f.* 2 *v.* ffilmio.
filth *n.* baw, budreddi, mochyndra *m.*
final 1 *n.* rownd derfynol *f.* 2 *a.* terfynol, olaf.
finally *ad.* o'r diwedd, yn olaf.
find *v.* darganfod, cael, dod o hyd.
fine 1 *n.* dirwy *f.* 2 *v.* dirwyo. 3 *a.* mân, manwl; main; braf; gwych; hardd, hyfryd, teg.
finger *n.* bys *m*: **fingerprint** ôl bys.
finish 1 *n.* diwedd, terfyn *m.* 2 *v.* gorffen, dibennu, cwpla.
fir *n.* ffynidwydden *f.*
fire 1 *n.* tân *m.* 2 *v.* tanio; saethu: **fire-brigade** brigâd dân *f.* **fire exit** allanfa dân *f.*
fireplace *n.* lle tân *m.*
firewood *n.* coed tân *pl.*
fireworks *n.* tân gwyllt *pl.*
firm *n.* cwmni, ffyrm *m.*
firmament *n.* ffurfafen *f.*
first 1 *n.* & *a.* cyntaf *m.* 2 *ad.* yn gyntaf.
fish 1 *n.* pysgodyn *m.* 2 *v.* pysgota.
fisherman *n.* pysgotwr *m.*
fishing *n.* pysgota *m.*
fist *n.* dwrn *m.*
fitting *a.* addas, priodol.
five *n.* & *a.* pump *m.*
fix *v.* gosod, sicrhau, sefydlu.
fixed *a.* sefydlog.
flabby *a.* llac, llipa, llaes.
flag *n.* baner *f*: **Union Jack** Jac-yr-Undeb.
flakes *n.* creision *pl.*: **cornflakes** creision ŷd; **snowflakes** plu eira.
flame 1 *n.* fflam *f.* 2 *v.* fflamio.
flank *n.* ystlys, ochr *f.*
flannel *n.* gwlanen *f.*
flap 1 *n.* llabed *f,* fflap *m.* 2 *v.* fflapio.
flash 1 *n.* fflach *f.* 2 *v.* fflachio.
flat 1 *n.* fflat *f.* 2 *a.* fflat, gwastad.
flavour 1 *n.* blas *m.* 2 *v.* blasu.
flaw *n.* bai, diffyg, nam *m.*
flea *n.* chwannen *f.*
flee *v.* cilio, dianc, ffoi.
fleet *n.* llynges *f.*
flesh *n.* cig, cnawd *m*: **flesh and blood** cig a gwaed.
flexible *a.* hyblyg, ystwyth.
fling *v.* taflu.
flock *n.* haid *f;* praidd *m.*
flood 1 *n.* llif *m.* 2 *v.* llifo, gorlifo.
floor *n.* llawr *m.*
flour *n.* blawd, can *m.*
flow 1 *n.* llif *m.* 2 *v.* llifo, rhedeg.
flower *n.* blodyn *m*: **flower pot** pot blodau.
flowing *a.* llithrig; llaes, llac, rhydd.
fluent *a.* rhwydd, llithrig, rhugl.
fluid *n.* & *a.* hylif *m.*
fly 1 *n.* cleren *f,* pryf, gwybedyn *m.* 2 *v.* hedfan.
foam *n.* ewyn *m.*
focus 1 *n.* canolbwynt, ffocws *m.* 2 *v.* canolbwyntio.
foe *n.* gelyn *m.*
fog *n.* niwl, ffog *m*: **thick fog** niwl trwchus.
foggy *a.* niwlog.
fold *v.* plygu.
folk *n.* gwerin (*coll.*), pobl *f.*
folklore *n.* llên gwerin.
folksong *n.* cân werin *f.*
follow *v.* dilyn.
follower *n.* dilynwr *m.*
folly *n.* ffolineb *m.*
fond *a.* hoff, cu, annwyl.
fondle *v.* anwesu, anwylo.
fondness *n.* hoffter; anwes *m.*
food *n.* bwyd *m.*
fool 1 *n.* ffŵl *m.* 2 *v.* twyllo.
foolish *a.* ffôl, dwl.
foolishness *n.* ffolineb, dwli *m.*
foot *n.* troed *mf;* troedfedd *f.*

football *n.* pêl-droed *f*: **footballer** pêldroediwr *m.*
footpath *n.* troedffordd *f,* llwybr *m*: **public footpath** llwybr cyhoeddus.
footprint *n.* ôl troed *m.*
for 1 *prp.* am, dros, tros, er, ers, erbyn, hyd, i, yn, lle. **2** *c.* achos, gan, oblegid, oherwydd.
force *n.* grym; llu *m*: **armed forces** lluoedd arfog.
ford *n.* rhyd *f*: **Ammanford** Rhydaman: **Oxford** Rhydychen.
forehead *n.* talcen, tâl *m.*
foreign *a.* estron, tramor: **foreign affairs** materion tramor.
foreigner *n.* estron *m.*
forest *n.* coedwig, fforest *f.*
foretaste *n.* rhagflas, rhagbrawf *m.*
forge 1 *n.* gefail *f.* **2** *v.* ffugio, twyllo.
forget *v.* anghofio: **forget-me-not** glas y gors.
forgive *v.* maddau.
fork *n.* fforc, fforch *f.*
form 1 *n.* ffurf *f;* modd, dull *m;* ffurflen *f;* dosbarth *m.* **2** *v.* ffurfio, llunio: **application form** ffurflen gais *f.*
former *px.* cyn.
formerly *ad.* gynt.
fort *n.* caer *f.*
forthcoming *a.* ar ddod, gerllaw.
fortnight *n.* pythefnos *mf.*
fortnightly *ad.* bob pythefnos.
fortunate *a.* ffodus, lwcus.
fortunately *ad.* yn ffodus, yn lwcus.
fortune *n.* ffortiwn *f.*
forty *n.* & *a.* deugain, pedwar deg *m.*
forward 1 *n.* blaenwr *m.* **2** *a.* blaen; eofn. **3** *ad.* ymlaen. **4** *v.* anfon ymlaen: **wing forward** blaenasgellwr: **number eight** wythwr.
foster *v.* meithrin, rhoi ar faeth.
foster-mother n. mamfaeth *f.*
foul *a.* brwnt, budr, ffiaidd.
found *v.* dechrau, sefydlu.
foundation *n.* sail *f,* sylfaen *mf.*
fountain *n.* ffynnon, ffynhonnell *f.*
four *n.* & *a.* pedair, pedwar *m.*
fourteen *n.* & *a.* pedwar ar ddeg, pedair ar ddeg, un deg pedwar *m.*
fourth *n.* & *a.* pedwaredd, pedwerydd *m.*
fowl *n.* ffowlyn *m.*
fox *n.* cadno, llwynog: **vixen** cadnawes, cadnöes, llwynoges.
fraction *n.* ffracsiwn *m.*
fragment *n.* darn, tamaid *m,* yfflyn *m.*
France *n.* Ffrainc *f.*
frankincense *n.* thus *m.*
fraud *n.* twyll *m.*
fraudulent *a.* twyllodrus.
free 1 *a.* rhad, rhydd, di-dâl. **2** *v.* rhyddhau: **free kick** cic rydd.
freedom *n.* rhyddid *m.*
freely *ad.* yn rhydd.
freeze *v.* rhewi.
freezer *n.* rhewgell *f.*
freight *n.* llwyth *m.*
French 1 *n.* Ffrangeg *f.* **2** *a.* Ffrengig.
Frenchman *n.* Ffrancwr *m.*
Frenchwoman *n.* Ffrances *f.*
frequent *a.* aml.
fresh *a.* ffres, newydd.
Friday *n.* dydd Gwener.
friend *n.* cyfaill *m,* cyfeilles *f,* ffrind *m.*
friendly *a.* cyfeillgar.
friendship *n.* cyfeillgarwch *m.*
fright *n.* braw, ofn *m.*
frighten *v.* codi ofn ar, brawychu.
frightful *a.* dychrynllyd.
frigid *a.* oer, rhewllyd.
frivolity *n.* lol *f.*
frock *n.* ffrog *f.*
frog *n.* broga, ffroga *m.*
from *prp.* o, oddi, gan, oddi wrth, rhag.
front 1 *n.* ffrynt, talcen, tu blaen *m.* **2** *a.* ffrynt, blaen: **front door** drws ffrynt: **front page** tudalen flaen; **front room** ystafell flaen: **front row** rhes flaen: **cold front** ffrynt oer: **warm front** ffrynt cynnes.
frontier *n.* ffin *f.*
frost n. rhew *m*: **hoar frost** barrug; **to cast hoar frost** llwydrewi.
frosty *a.* rhewllyd.
froth *n.* ewyn *m.*
frown 1 *n.* gwg *m.* **2** *v.* gwgu.
frozen *a.* wedi rhewi.
fruit *n.* ffrwyth *m,* ffrwythau *pl*: **fruit juice** sudd ffrwythau *m.*
fruitful *a.* ffrwythlon.
fry *v.* ffrio.
frying-pan *n.* padell ffrio *f.*
fuel *n.* tanwydd *m.*
fugitive *n.* ffoadur *m.*
full *a.* llawn.
full-back *n.* cefnwr *m.*
fullness *n.* llawnder, cyflawnder *m.*
fully *ad.* yn gyfan gwbl, yn hollol.
fun *n.* hwyl *f,* miri *m.*
fund *n.* cronfa *f.*
fundamental *a.* sylfaenol.
funeral *n.* angladd *mf.*

funnel *n.* twndis, corn *m.*
funny *a.* digrif, ysmala, doniol.
fur *n.* ffwr, blew *m.*
furious *a.* ffyrnig, yn gacwn wyllt, crac.
furnace *n.* ffwrn, ffwrnais *f.*
furnishings *n.* dodrefn *pl.*
furniture n. celfi, dodrefn *pl*: **piece of furniture** celficyn, dodrefnyn.
furry *a.* blewog.
further *ad.* bellach, ymhellach: **further education** addysg bellach.
fuss *n.* helynt *f*, trafferth, ffws, stŵr *m.*
future *n.* & *a.* dyfodol *m.*

gain 1 *n.* elw, ennill *m,* enillion *pl.* 2 *v.* elwa, ennill.
gale *n.* gwynt cryf *m;* tymestl *f.*
gallery *n.* oriel *f,* galeri *m,* llofft *f.*
gallon *n.* galwyn *m.*
gamble *v.* hapchwarae, gamblo.
game *n.* gêm *f,* chwarae *m,* camp *f.*
gang *n.* mintai *f,* torf, haid, gang *f.*
gaol 1 *n.* carchar *m.* 2 *v.* carcharu.
gap *n.* bwlch, adwy *m.*
garage *n.* garej *f.*
garbage *n.* ysbwriel, sothach *m.*
garden 1 *n.* gardd *f.* 2 *v.* garddio.
gardener *n.* garddwr *m.*
garment *n.* pilyn *m,* gwisg *f,* dilledyn *m.*
gas *n.* nwy *m*: **Gas Board** Bwrdd Nwy **gas-mask** mwgwd nwy.
gate *n.* clwyd, gât, iet, llidiart *f.*
gateway *n.* mynedfa *f.*
gather *v.* casglu, crynhoi, cynnull, hel.
gathering *n.* casgliad, cynulliad *m.*
gaunt *a.* llwm, tenau.
gauntlet *n.* maneg *f.*
gay *a.* llon, bywiog, hoyw.
gaze *v.* edrych, syllu, rhythu.
gear *n.* gêr *mf,* offer *pl.*
gem *n.* gem *f,* tlws *m.*
gender *n.* rhyw *mf,* cenedl *f.*
general 1 *n.* cadfridog *m.* 2 *a.* cyffredin, cyffredinol: **general election** etholiad cyffredinol.
generally *ad.* yn gyffredinol.
generation *n.* cenhedlaeth *m,* to *mf.*
generosity *n.* haelioni *m.*
generous *a.* hael, haelionus.
genial *a.* tyner, tirion, hynaws.
genteel *a.* bonheddig.
gentle *a.* tyner, mwyn.
gentleman *n.* bonheddwr, gŵr bonheddig, uchelwr *m.*
gentleness *n.* tynerwch, addfwynder *m.*
gently *ad.* yn dyner, yn addfwyn; gan bwyll.
gents *n.* toiledau dynion *pl.*
genuine *a.* diffuant, cywir, pur.
geography *n.* daearyddiaeth *f.*
geology *n.* daeareg *f.*
geometry *n.* geometreg *mf.*
German 1 *n.* Almaeneg (*iaith*) *f;* Almaenwr (*person*) *m.* 2 *a.* Almaenaidd.
Germany *n.* yr Almaen *f.*
get *v.* cael, ennill.
ghost *n.* ysbryd *m,* drychiolaeth *f.*
giant *n.* cawr *m.*
gift *n.* anrheg, rhodd *f.*
gifted *a.* talentog, dawnus.
gigantic *a.* anferth.
gipsy *n.* sipsi *m.*
giraffe *n.* jiráff *m.*
girder *n.* trawst *m.*
girl *n.* merch, geneth, croten, hogen, llances *f.*
give *v.* rhoddi, rhoi: **to give generously** rhoi'n hael: **to give up** rhoi'r gorau i.
glad *a.* llawen, llon, balch.
gladly *ad.* yn llawen, â phleser.
Glamorgan *n.* Morgannwg *f*: **Mid Glamorgan** Morgannwg Ganol; **South Glamorgan** De Morgannwg; **West Glamorgan** Gorllewin Morgannwg.
glance *n.* cipolwg *m,* trem *f,* cip *m.*
glass *n.* gwydr, gwydryn *m.*
gleam 1 *n.* llewyrch *m.* 2 *v.* llewyrchu.
glen *n.* glyn, cwm, dyffryn *m.*
glide 1 *n.* llithriad *m.* 2 *v.* llithro dros.
glitter *v.* disgleirio, serennu.
glorious *a.* gogoneddus.
glory *n.* gogoniant, ysblander *m.*
Gloucester *n.* Caerloyw *f.*
glove *n.* maneg *f.*
glower *v.* gwgu, cuchio.
glue 1 *n.* glud *m.* 2 *v.* gludo, gludio, glynu.
gnat *n.* gwybedyn *m.*
go *v.* cer! dos! (*unigol*); cerwch! ewch! (*lluosog*); *see* mynd.
goal *n.* gôl *f*: **goalkeeper** golgeidwad, golwr *m.*
goat *n.* gafr *f.*
god *n.* duw *m*: **God** Duw.
goddess *n.* duwies *f.*

godly *a.* duwiol.
gold *n.* aur *m.*
golden *a.* euraid, euraidd.
goldfish *n.* pysgod aur *pl.*
golf *n.* golff *m*: **golf course** maes golffio.
golfer *n.* golffwr *m.*
good *n.* & *a.* da: **good afternoon** prynhawn da: **good day** dydd da; **good evening** noswaith dda: **good morning** bore da: **good night** nos da: **good luck** lwc dda: **Good gracious!** Bobol annwyl! **Good health!** Iechyd da!
goodbye 1 *n.* ffarwél *m.* **2** *i.* da bo chi! hwyl! yn iach!
goodness *n.* daioni *m.*
goods *n.* eiddo *m,* nwyddau, da *pl.*
goodwill *n.* ewyllys da *m.*
goose *n.* gŵydd *f.*
gosling *n.* cyw gŵydd *m.*
gospel *n.* efengyl *f*: **the Gospel according to John** yr Efengyl yn ôl Ioan.
govern *v.* llywodraethu, rheoli.
government *n.* llywodraeth *f.*
governor *n.* llywodraethwr, rheolwr.
Gower *n.* Gŵyr *f.*
gown *n.* gŵn *f.*
grace *n.* gras *m.*
graceful *a.* lluniaidd, urddasol.
grade 1 *n.* gradd, safon *f.* **2** *v.* graddio.
gradual *a.* graddol.
graduate 1 *n.* gŵr gradd *m.* **2** *v.* graddio.
gram *n.* gram *m.*
grammar *n.* gramadeg *m*: **Grammar School** Ysgol Ramadeg.
grand *a.* mawreddog, ardderchog, crand; prif, uchel: **grand concert** cyngerdd mawreddog.
grandchild *n.* ŵyr *m,* wyres *f.*
granddaughter *n.* wyres *f.*
grandeur *n.* mawredd *m.*
grandfather *n.* tad-cu, taid *m.*
grandmother *n.* mam-gu, nain *f.*
grandson *n.* ŵyr *m.*
grant 1 *n.* rhodd *f,* grant, cymhorthdal *m.* **2** *v.* caniatáu.
grapes *n.pl.* grawnwin.
grass *n.* glaswellt *m,* porfa *f*: **grasshopper** ceiliog y rhedyn, sioncyn y gwair.
grateful *a.* diolchgar.
gratefulness *n.* diolchgarwch *m.*
gratitude *n.* diolchgarwch *m.*
grave 1 *n.* bedd *m.* **2** *v.* difrifol, dwys, prudd.
gravestone *n.* carreg fedd *f.*
graveyard *n.* mynwent *f.*
graze *v.* pori.
grease 1 *n.* saim *m.* **2** *v.* iro.
greasy *a.* seimlyd, seimllyd.
great a. mawr: **a great many** llawer iawn.
great-grandfather *n.* hen dad-cu, hendaid *m.*
great-grandmother *n.* hen fam-gu, hennain *f.*
greatly *ad.* yn fawr.
greatness *n.* mawredd *m.*
Grecian 1 *n.* Groegwr *m.* **2** *v.* Groegaidd.
Greece *n.* Groeg, Gwlad Groeg *f.*
greed *n.* trachwant *m.*
greedy *a.* trachwantus.
Greek 1 *n.* Groeg *f* (*iaith*); Groegwr *m.* (*person*). **2** *a.* Groeg, Groegaidd.
green 1 *a.* gwyrdd, gwerdd, glas. **2** *v.* glasu.
greenhouse *n.* tŷ gwydr *m.*
greet *v.* cyfarch, annerch.
greeting *n.* cyfarchiad *m.*
grey *a.* llwyd, glas: **to turn grey** llwydo.
greyhound *n.* milgi *m.*
grief *n.* galar, gofid, hiraeth *m.*
grievance *n.* cwyn *mf.*
grieve *v.* gofidio, hiraethu.
grievous *a.* gofidus, poenus, blin, difrifol.
grind v. malu.
grip 1 *n.* gafael *f.* **2** *v.* gafael (yn), gwasgu.
groan *v.* ochneidio, griddfan.
gross 1 *n.* gros *m.* **2** *a.* bras: **gross weight** pwysau gros.
ground 1 *n.* daear *f,* tir *m;* sail *f;* cae chwarae *m.* **2** *v.* gwreiddio, seilio.
groundless *a.* di-sail.
group *n.* grŵp, twr *m.*
grove *n.* llwyn *m,* celli *f.*
grow *v.* tyfu, prifio, codi.
growing *a.* yn tyfu.
growth *n.* tyfiant *m.*
grubby *a.* brwnt, budr.
guard 1 *n.* gwyliwr, gard *m.* **2** *v.* gwarchod, gwylio.
guerilla *n.* herwfilwr *m.*
guess 1 *n.* amcan, dyfaliad *m.* **2** *v.* dyfalu.
guest *n.* gwestai, gŵr gwadd *m,* gwraig wadd *f.*
guests *n.* gwesteion, gwahoddedigion *pl.*
guide 1 *n.* arweinydd, hyfforddwr, tywysydd *m.* **2** *v.* arwain, tywys.

guild *n.* cymdeithas, urdd *f.*
guilt *n.* euogrwydd, bai *m.*
guilty *a.* euog.
guitar *n.* gitâr *m.*
gulf *n.* gwlff *m.*
gull *n.* gwylan *f.*
gulp *v.* llyncu, traflyncu.
gum *n.* gwm, glud; cig (y dannedd) *m.*
gun *n.* dryll, gwn *m.*
guts *n.* perfedd *m.*
Gwent *n.* Gwent *f.*
gymnasium *n.* campfa *f.*

habit *n.* arfer *mf;* gwisg *f.*
had, he/she/it *v.* cafodd: **I had** ces i, cefais: *see* cael.
hag *n.* gwrach *f.*
hail 1 *n.* cesair *coll. & pl.* **2** *v.* bwrw cesair; cyfarch, galw. **3** *i.* henffych well!
hailstones *n.* cesair *coll. & pl.*
hair *n.* gwallt; blewyn *m.*
hairbrush *n.* brwsh gwallt *m.*
hairy *a.* blewog.
half *n.* hanner *m.*
half-back *n.* hanerwr *m.*
hall *n.* neuadd *f,* llys, plas; cyntedd *m.*
Hallowe'en *n.* Nos Galan Gaeaf *f.*
hammer 1 *n.* morthwyl *m.* **2** *v.* morthwylio.
hand *n.* llaw *f; (of clock)* bys *m;* **hands** dwylo: **in hand** mewn llaw, ar waith.
handbag *n.* bag llaw *m.*
handbook *n.* llawlyfr *m.*
handful *n.* dyrnaid *m,* llond llaw *f.*
handkerchief *n.* cadach *m,* hances, neisied *f,* macyn *m.*
handle *n.* dolen *f.* **2** *v.* trafod, trin.
handsome *a.* hardd, glân, prydferth, golygus.
handwork *n.* gwaith llaw *m.*
handwriting *b.* llawysgrifen *f.*
hang *v.* hongian; crogi.
hankering *n.* ysfa *f.*
happen *v.* digwydd.
happening *n.* digwyddiad *m.*
happily *ad.* yn hapus.
happiness *n.* hapusrwydd, llawenydd *m.*
happy *a.* dedwydd, hapus, llawen, wrth ei fodd, wrth ei bodd.
harbour 1 *n.* harbwr *m,* hafan *f,* porth, porthladd *m.* **2** *v.* llochesu.
hard *a.* caled, anodd.
harden *v.* caledu.
hardly *ad.* o'r braidd.
hardness *n.* caledwch *m.*
hardship *n.* caledi *m.*
hard shoulder *n.* llain galed *f.*
hard-up *a.* prin o arian.
hardwood *n.* pren caled *m.*
hardy *a.* caled.
hare *n.* ysgyfarnog *f.*
harm *n.* cam, drwg, niwed *m.*
harmless *a.* diniwed.
harp 1 *n.* telyn *f.* **2** *v.* canu'r delyn.
harpist *n.* telynor, telynores *m.*
harsh *a.* llym, garw, cras.
harvest *n.* cynhaeaf.
haste 1 *n.* brys, prysurdeb *m.* **2** *v.* brysio, prysuro, cyflymu.
hasten *v.* brysio.
hastily *ad.* yn frysiog.
hasty *a.* brysiog.
hat *n.* het *f.*
hate 1 *n.* cas, casineb *m.* **2** *v.* casáu.
hatred *n.* cas, casineb *m.*
haul *v.* tynnu, llusgo.
have, I *v.* caf.
he/she/it will have caiff; *see* cael.
haven *n.* hafan *f.*
hawk *n.* hebog *m.*
hawthorn *n.* draenen wen *f.*
hay *n.* gwair *m,* porfa *f.*
hazard *n.* perygl *m,* antur *mf.*
haze *n.* niwl, tawch *m.*
hazel *n.* collen *f.*
hazy *a.* niwlog.
he *pn.* ef, fe, efe, efô, fo, yntau.
head 1 *n.* pen, pennaeth *m.* **2** *a.* prif.
headache *n.* pen tost, cur yn y pen *m.*
heading *n.* pennawd, teitl *m.*
headland *n.* penrhyn *m.*
headline *n.* pennawd, teitl *m:* **news headlines** penawdau'r newyddion.
headmaster *n.* prifathro *m.*
headmistress *n.* prifathrawes *f.*
headquarters *n.* pencadlys *m.*
heal *v.* iacháu, gwella.
health *n.* iechyd: **Health Service** Gwasanaeth Iechyd.
healthy *a.* iach, iachus.
heap *n.* pentwr, twr *m.*
hear *v.* clyw! *(unigol),* clywch! *(lluosog); see* clywed.
hearer *n.* gwrandawr *m.*
hearing *n.* clyw; gwrandawiad *m:* **hearing aid** cymorth clywed.
heart *n.* calon *f:* **heart attack** trawiad ar y galon.

hearth *n.* aelwyd *f.*
heat 1 *n.* gwres *m.* 2 *v.* poethi, twymo.
heater *n.* gwresogydd *m.*
heath *n.* rhos *f,* rhostir *m.*
heather *n.* grug *m.*
heave 1 *n.* gwthiad, hwb *m.* 2 *v.* gwthio, codi.
heaven *n.* nef, nefoedd, nen *f.*
heavenly *a.* nefol, nefolaidd.
heavens *n.* ffurfafen, wybren *f.*
heavy *a.* trwm, trymaidd.
Hebrew 1 *n.* Hebraeg *f. (iaith);* Hebrëwr, *m.* Hebrees *f.* 2 *a.* Hebraeg, Hebreig.
hedge *n.* perth *f,* clawdd *m.*
hedgehog *n.* draenog *m.*
heed 1 *n.* sylw *m,* ystyriaeth *f.* 2 *v.* sylwi, ystyried, hidio.
heedful *a.* ystyriol, gofalus.
heel 1 *n.* sawdl *mf.* 2 *v.* sodli.
height *n.* uchder, uchelder *m.*
heir *n.* aer, etifedd *m.*
heiress *n.* aeres, etifeddes *f.*
helicopter *n.* hofrennydd *f.*
hell *n.* uffern *f.*
hellish *a.* uffernol.
hello *i.* helô! hylô! clyw! grwando!.
helm *n.* llyw *m.*
help 1 *n.* cymorth, help *m.* 2 *v.* cynorthwyo, helpu.
helper *n.* cynorthwywr, cynorthwyydd, helpwr *m.*
hem *n.* hem *f,* godre *m,* ymyl *mf.*
hen *n.* iâr *f.*
henceforth *ad.* mwyach, o hyn ymlaen.
her *pn.* ei, hi, hithau.
herb *n.* llysieuyn *m.*
herd *n.* gyr *m,* cenfaint *f.*
here *ad.* yma, yn y man hwn.
hermit *n.* meudwy *m.*
hero *n.* arwr *m.*
heroine *n.* arwres *f.*
hers *pn.* ei, ei heiddo.
hew *v.* torri, naddu.
hexagon *n.* hecsagon *m.*
hiccup *n.* yr ig *m.*
hide 1 *n.* croen *m.* 2 *v.* cuddio: **hide and seek** chwarae mig.
high *a.* uchel; mawr; cryf; llawn: **most high** goruchaf.
higher *a.* uwch.
highest *a.* uchaf.
highland *n.* ucheldir *m.*
highly *ad.* yn fawr, yn uchel.
highness *n.* uchder, uchelder; mawrhydi *m:* **His Highness** Ei Fawrhydi.
highway *n.* priffordd *f.*
highwayman *n.* lleidr penffordd *m.*
hijack 1 *n.* herwgipiad *m.* 2 *v.* herwgipio.
hill *n.* allt *f,* bryn *m,* rhiw *f,* tyle *m.*
hillock *n.* bryncyn, twmpath *m.*
him *pn.* ef, fe, efe, efô, fo, yntau.
hindrance *n.* rhwystr *m.*
hint 1 *n.* awgrym *m.* 2 *v.* awgrymu.
hip *n.* clun *f.*
hire 1 *n.* cyflog *mf.* 2 *v.* cyflogi, llogi.
his *pn.* ei, ei eiddo.
historian *n.* hanesydd, haneswr *m.*
history *n.* hanes *m:* **History of Wales** Hanes Cymru.
hit 1 *n.* ergyd *mf,* trawiad *m.* 2 *v.* taro.
hoarfrost *n.* llwydrew, barrug *m.*
hoary *a.* llwyd.
hoax 1 *n.* tric, twyll *m.* 2 *v.* twyllo.
hold 1 *n.* gafael *f.* 2 *v.* dal, dala, gafael.
hole 1 *n.* twll *m;* ffrau *f.* 2 *v.* tyllu.
holiday *n.* gŵyl *f.*
holidays *n.* gwyliau *pl:* **Christmas holidays** gwyliau Nadolig: **summer holidays** gwyliau haf.
hollow 1 *n.* pant *m.* 2 *a.* gwag, cau.
holly *n.* celyn *pl,* celynnen *f:* **holly bush** llwyn celyn.
holy *a.* sanctaidd, glân, gwyn: **Holy Spirit** Ysbryd Glân.
Holyhead *n.* Caergybi *f.*
home 1 *n.* cartref *m,* aelwyd *f.* 2 *ad.* adref, tua thref: **at home** gartref: **going home** mynd adref, mynd tua thref.
homeless *a.* digartref.
homesick *a.* hiraethus.
homesickness *n.* hiraeth *m.*
homestead *n.* tyddyn *m.*
homeward *ad.* adref, tua thref.
homework *n.* gwaith cartref *m:* **homework book** llyfr gwaith cartref.
honest *a.* cywir, gonest, onest.
honesty *n.* gonestrwydd, onestrwydd *m.*
honey *n.* mêl *m.*
honeymoon *n.* mis mêl.
honour 1 *n.* anrhydedd *mf.* 2 *v.* anrhydeddu; urddo; cydnabod.
hook 1 *n.* bach, bachyn; cryman *m.* 2 *v.* bachu.
hoop *n.* cylch *m.*
hooray *i.* & *n.* hwrê.
hope 1 *n.* gobaith *m.* 2 *v.* gobeithio.
horizon *n.* gorwel *m.*

horn *n.* corn *m.*
horrendous *a.* dychrynllyd, ofnadwy.
horrible *a.* ofnadwy.
horse *n.* ceffyl, march *m.*
horseman *n.* marchog *m.*
horseshoe *n.* pedol *f.*
hospice *n.* ysbyty, llety *m.*
hospitable *a.* croesawus, lletygar.
hospital *n.* ysbyty *m.*
host *n.* llu *m,* byddin *f;* gwesteiwr, lletywr *m.*
hostage *n.* gwystl *m.*
hostel *n.* neuadd breswyl *f.*
hostess *n.* gwesteiwraig *f.*
hot *a.* twym, poeth, gwresog: **hot-water bottle** potel dŵr twym.
hotel *n.* gwesty *m.*
hotelier *n.* gwestywr *m.*
hound 1 *n.* ci hela, helgi *m.* **2** *v.* hela, erlid.
hour *n* awr *f.*
hourly *ad.* bob awr.
house *n.* tŷ *m.*
housework *n.* gwaith tŷ *m.*
housewife *n.* gwraig tŷ *f.*
housing *n.* tai *pl.*
how *ad.* sut, pa fodd, pa.
however *ad.* sut bynnag, er hynny, pa fodd bynnag.
howl *v.* udo.
hue *n.* lliw *m.* gwawr *f.*
hug *v.* cofleidio, gwasgu.
huge *a.* anferth, enfawr.
hum 1 *n.* si, sibrwd *m.* **2** *v.* mwmian.
humble *a.* gostyngedig, isel.
humorous *a.* doniol.
humour *n.* hiwmor *m,* hwyl *f.*
hundred 1 *n.* cant *m.* **2** *a.* can: **hundred years old** canmlwydd.
hundredth *n.* & *a.* canfed.
hunger 1 n. newyn, chwant bwyd *m.* **2** *v.* newynu.
hunt *n.* helfa *f.* **2** *v.* hel, hela, erlid.
hunter *n.* heliwr; ceffyl hela *m.*
hunting *n.* hela *m*: **hunting-horn** corn hela.
hurricane *n.* corwynt *m.*
hurry 1 *n.* brys, prysurdeb *m.* **2** *v.* brysio, prusuro.
hurt 1 *n.* niwed, dolur *m.* **2** *v.* anafu, brifo.
husband *n.* gŵr, priod, gŵr priod *m.*
hut *n.* caban, cwt *m.*
hutch *n.* cwt, cwb *m.*
hydrogen *n.* hydrogen *m.*
hymn *n.* emyn, hymn *m.*
hymnal *n.* llyfr emynau *m.*
hymn-tune *n.* emyn-dôn *f.*
hypermarket *n.* archfarchnad f.
hyphen *n.* cyplysnod, cysylltnod *m.*

I *pn.* mi, myfi; fi, i; minnau, innau.
ice *n.* iâ, rhew *m.*
Ice Age Oes yr Iâ.
iceberg *n.* mynydd iâ *m.*
ice-cream *n.* hufen iâ *m.*
Iceland *n.* Gwlad yr Iâ *f.*
icy *a.* rhewllyd.
idea *n.* syniad *m.*
identical *a.* yr un *(fath).*
identify *v.* adnabod *(fel yr un un),* enwi, nodi; uniaethu (â).
idiom *n.* priod-ddull, idiom *f.*
idle 1 *a.* segur, diog, dioglyd. 2 *v.* segura, diogi.
idler *n.* diogyn, pwdryn *m.*
idol *n.* delw *f.*
if *c.* os, pe.
ignite *v.* tanio.
ill *a.* claf, gwael, sâl, tost; drwg.
ill-mannered *a.* anfoesgar.
illness *n.* afiechyd, clefyd, dolur, salwch, tostrwydd *m.*
illustrate *v.* darlunio; egluro, esbonio.
illustration *n.* darlun *m.*
image *n.* delw, llun *m.*
imagination *n.* dychymyg *m.*
imagine *v.* dychmygu, tybied, tybio.
immediately *ad.* ar unwaith, yn union, yn y man.
immense *a.* anferth, eang.
imminent *a.* agos, gerllaw, wrth y drws.
immunisation *n.* imwneiddiad *m.*
immunise *v.* imwneiddio.
immunity *n.* imwnedd *m.*
impart *v.* cyfrannu, rhoi.
imperative 1 *n.* gorchymyn *m.* 2 *a.* gorchmynnol, gorfodol.
imperfect *a.* amherffaith.
impinge *v.* taro yn erbyn, cyffwrdd â.
implement 1 *n.* offeryn, arf *m.* 2 *v.* gweithredu.
implore *v.* erfyn (ar).
imply *v.* cyfleu, awgrymu.
importance *n.* pwys, pwysigrwydd *m.*
important *a.* pwysig.
impossible *a.* amhosibl.
impress 1 *n.* argraff *f.* 2 *v.* argraffu, pwyso (ar).
impression *n.* argraff.
imprison *v.* carcharu.
improve *v.* gwella.
impudence *n.* haerllugrwydd *m.*
impudent *a.* haerllug, eofn.
in 1 *prp.* yn, yng, ym, mewn. 2 *ad.* i mewn: **in the midst of** ynghanol: **in time** mewn pryd.
inaccurate *a.* anghywir, gwallus.
inasmuch *ad.* yn gymaint (â).
inch *n.* modfedd *f.*
incident *n.* digwyddiad *m.*
incinerator *n.* llosgydd *m,* ffwrnais *f.*
include *v.* cynnwys.
including *prp.* gan gynnwys.
inclusive *a.* gan gynnwys, cynwysedig.
income *n.* enillion *pl,* incwm *m;* **Income Tax** Treth Incwm.
incorporate *v.* ymgorffori.
incorrect *a.* anghywir.
indebted *a.* dyledus.
indeed *ad.* yn wir, iawn.
indemnity *n.* iawndal *m.*
independence *n.* annibyniaeth *f.*
Independent *n.* Annibynnwr *m.*
independent *a.* annibynnol.
independently *ad.* yn annibynnol, ar wahân.
index *n.* mynegai *m.*
India *n.* Yr India *f.*
Indian 1 *n.* Indiad *m.* 2 *a.* Indiaidd.
indicate *v.* dangos, mynegi.
indigestion *n.* diffyg traul *m.*
individual 1 *n.* un, unigolyn *n.* 2 *a.* unigol.
indolent *a.* diog, dioglyd, segur, pwdr.
indoor *a.* i mewn, dan do.
induct *v.* sefydlu.
induction *n.* sefydliad *m.*
indulgence *n.* maldod *m.*
industry *n.* diwydiant; diwydrwydd *m.*
ineffectual *a.* aneffeithiol.
inevitable *a.* anochel.
inexpensive *a.* rhad.
inexperience *n.* diffyg profiad *m.*

inexperienced *a.* dibrofiad.
infant *n.* baban, maban *m*: **infants' school** ysgol fabanod: **infants' teacher** athrawes fabanod.
infection *n.* haint *f.*
inferior *a.* is, israddol.
infinitive *n.* berfenw *m.*
infirm *a.* gwan.
infirmity *n.* gwendid, llesgedd *m.*
inflammation *n.* llid *m.*
inflate *v.* chwyddo, rhoi awyr yn.
inflation *n.* chwyddiant *m.*
influence 1 *n.* dylanwad *m.* **2** *v.* dylanwadu.
influenza *n.* ffliw *m.*
inform *v.* hysbysu.
information *n.* gwybodaeth *f.*
infrequent *a.* anaml.
ingredients *n.* defnyddiau, cynhwysion *pl.*
inhabitants *n.* trigolion, preswylwyr *pl.*
inhale *v.* anadlu.
inherit *v.* etifeddu.
iniquity *n.* drwg, drygioni, anwiredd *m.*
injection *n.* chwistrelliad, pigiad *m.*
injure *v.* anafu, niweidio.
injury *n.* niwed, cam, clwyf, anaf *m.*
inn *n.* tafarn *mf,* gwesty *m.*
inner *a.* mewnol.
innkeeper *n.* tafarnwr, gwestywr *m.*
innocent *a.* diniwed.
inoculation *n.* brechiad *m.*
inquire *v.* gofyn, holi, ymholi.
inquiry *n.* ymchwiliad, ymholiad *m.*
inquisition *n.* ymchwiliad *m.*
insect *n.* pryf, pryfedyn, pryfyn *m.*
in-service *a.* mewn swydd: **in-service training** hyfforddiant mewn swydd.
inside 1 *n.* tu mewn *m.* **2** *a.* mewnol. **3** *ad.* i mewn, o fewn. **4** *prp.* y tu mewn.
inside-out *ad.* o chwith.
insist *v.* mynnu.
insolence *n.* haerllugrwydd *m.*
insolent *a.* haerllug.
inspire *v.* ysbrydoli.
instantaneous *a.* yn y man.
instead *ad.* yn lle.
institution *n.* sefydliad *m.*
instruct *v.* cyfarwyddo, dysgu, hyfforddi.
instruction *n.* hyfforddiant *m.*
instructor *n.* hyfforddwr *m.*
instrument *n.* offeryn, arf *m*: **musical instrument** offeryn cerdd.
instrumental *a.* offerynol.
insult *n.* sarhad *m.*
insurance *n.* yswiriant *m.*
insure *v.* yswiro, yswirio.
insurrection *n.* terfysg, gwrthryfel *m.*
intellect *n.* deall *m.*
intelligent *a.* deallus.
intelligentsia *n.* y deallus *m,* deallusion *pl.*
intend *v.* bwriadu, golygu.
intense *a.* dwys.
intent *n.* bwriad, amcan; diben *m;* ystyr *f.*
intention *n.* bwriad *m.*
interest *n.* diddordeb; llog; budd *m*: **interest rates** cyfraddau llog.
interests *n.pl.* diddordebau *pl.*
interfere *v.* ymhel, ymyrru, ymyrryd.
interference *n.* ymyrraeth *f.*
interior 1 *n.* tu mewn, canol *m.* **2** *a.* mewnol.
interlude *n.* egwyl *f.*
intermediate *a.* canol, canolradd.
internal *a.* mewnol.
international *a.* rhyngwladol.
interpreter *n.* cyfieithydd *m.*
interrogate *v.* holi.
interrogator *n.* holwr *m.*
interrupt *v.* torri ar, torri ar draws, ymyrru, ymyrryd.
interval *n.* egwyl *f,* saib *m.*
intervene *v.* ymyrru, ymyrryd.
interview 1 *n.* cyfweliad *m.* **2** *v.* cyfweld.
into *prp.* i, i mewn.
intoxicate *v.* meddwi.
invalid *n.* un afiach, un methedig *mf.*
invalid *a.* di-rym.
investigate *v.* ymchilio, chwilio.
investigation *n.* ymchwiliad *m.*
investigator *n.* ymchwiliwr, ymchwilydd *m.*
invisible *a.* anweledig.
invitation *n.* gwahoddiad, gwahodd *m.*
invite *v.* gwahodd.
invited *a.* gwahoddedig.
involved *a.* cymhleth, astrus, cywrain.
inward *a.* mewnol.
Ireland *n.* Iwerddon, Yr Ynys Werdd *f.*
Irish 1 *n.* Gwyddeleg *f. (iaith).* **2** *a.* Gwyddelig.
Irishman *n.* Gwyddel *m.*
Irishwoman *n.* Gwyddeles *f.*
iron 1 *n.* & *a.* haearn *m.* **2** *v.* smwddio.
ironing board *n.* bwrdd smwddio *m.*

irritable *a.* pigog, piwis.
irritation *n.* poen *mf,* llid *m,* enynfa *f.*
is *v.* ydy, yw, mae, oes, sy, sydd.
island *n.* ynys *f.* **Caldy Island** Ynys Bŷr: **Bardsey Island** Ynys Enlli.
Israel *n.* Israel *f.*
Israelite *n.* Israeliad *m.*
issue 1 *n.* llif, tarddiad; plant; cyhoeddiad *m.* **2** *v.* tarddu; cyhoeddi.
it *pn.* ef, efe, fe, efo, fo; hi.
Italian *n.* Eidaleg *f.* (iaith); Eidalwr *m,* Eidales *f.*
Italy *n.* Yr Eidal *f.*
itch 1 *n.* crafu *m,* ysfa *f.* **2** *v* cosi, ysu.
item *n.* eitem *f.*
its *pn.* ei.
itself *pn.* ei hun, ei hunan.
ivy *n.* iorwg, eiddew *m.*

jacdaw *n.* jac-y-do *m.*
jacket *n.* siaced *f.*
jail *n.* carchar *m.*
jam 1 *n.* jam *m.*; tagfa *f.* 2 *v.* gwasgu, tagu.
January *n.* Ionawr *m.*
Japan *n.* Siapan *f.*
Japanese 1 *n.* Siapaneg *f.* (iaith); Siapanead *m.* 2 *a.* Siapaneaidd.
jar 1 *n.* jar, jâr *f.* 2 *v.* ysgwyd.
jaundice *n.* y clefyd melyn *m.*
jaw *n.* gên, cern *f.*
jay *n.* sgrech y coed *m.*
jealous *a.* cenfigennus.
jeer 1 *n.* gwawd *m.* 2 *v.* gwawdio.
jelly *n.* jeli *m.*
jerk 1 *n.* plwc *m.* 2 *v.* plycio.
jersey *n.* jersi, jyrsi, siersi *f.*
Jerusalem *n.* Caersalem, Jerwsalem *f.*
Jesus *n.* Iesu *m*: **Jesus Christ** Iesu Grist: **Jesus Son of God** Iesu Mab Duw.
Jew *n.* Iddew *m.*
Jewess *n.* Iddewes *f.*
jewel *n.* gem *f,* tlws *m.*
Jewish *a.* Iddewig.
jingle *n.* rhigwm; tinc *m.*
job *n.* job, jobyn, gwaith *m,* swydd *f*: **Job Centre** Canolfan Gwaith *mf.*
jobless *a.* diwaith.
jog *v.* loncian.
jogger *n.* lonciwr *m.*
join *v.* cydio; ymuno; uno; ymaelodi.
joiner *n.* saer coed *m.*
joint 1 *n.* cyswllt, cymal *m.* 2 *a.* cyd: **joint of meat** darn o gig *m.*
joke 1 *n.* jôc *f.* 2 *v.* jocan, cellwair.
jolly *a.* braf, llawen, llon.
journalist *n.* newyddiadurwr *m.*
journey 1 *n.* hynt, siwrnai, taith *f.* 2 *v.* teithio.
joy *n.* llawenydd *m.*
joyful 1 *a.* llawen, llon. 2 *v.* llawenhau.
jubilation *n.* llawenydd, gorfoledd *m.*
jubilee *n.* jiwbilî *f.*
Judaism *n.* Iddewaeth *f.*
judge 1 *n.* barnwr; beirniad; dyfarnwr *m.* 2 *v.* beirniadu; dyfarnu.
judgement *n.* barn *f.* dyfarniad *m.*
jug *n.* jwg, siwg *f.*
juice *n.* sudd *m.*
juicy *a.* llawn sudd.
July *n.* Gorffennaf *m.*
jumble 1 *n.* cymysgwch *m,* cymysgfa *f.* 2 *v.* cymysgu: **jumble sale** ffair sborion *f.*
jump 1 *n.* naid *f.* llam *m.* 2 *v.* neidio, llamu.
jumper *n.* neidiwr *m;* jersi, jyrsi, siwmper *f.*
junction *n.* cydiad *m;* cyffordd *f.*
June *n.* Mehefin *m.*
junior *a.* iau; ieuaf: **junior school** ysgol iau.
just 1 *a.* cyfiawn, cywir, iawn, teg. 2 *ad.* braidd, yn union; newydd: **just now** gynnau (fach).
justice *n.* cyfiawnder; ynad *m*: **Justice of the Peace** Ynad Heddwch.
juvenile *a.* ieuanc, ifanc.

kangaroo n. cangarŵ *m.*
keep 1 *n.* cadw *m;* amddiffynfa *f.* **2** *v.* cadw; cynnal.
keeper *n.* ceidwad *m.*
kennel *n.* cwb, cenel *m.*
kerchief *n.* cadach *m,* hances *f,* macyn *m,* neisied *f.*
kettle *n.* tegell *m.*
key *n.* agoriad *m,* allwedd *f;* cywair *m;* **keyhole** twll clo.
kick 1 *n.* cic *f.* **2** *v.* cicio: **drop kick** cic adlam.
kidnap 1 *n.* herwgydiad *m.* **2** *v.* herwgydio.
kidnapper *n.* herwgydiwr *m.*
kidney-beans *n.pl.* ffa dringo, cidnabêns *pl.*
kill *v.* lladd.
killer *n.* lladdwr *m.*
kilogram *n.* kilogram (kgm.) *m.*
kilometre *n.* kilometr (km.) *m.*
kilowatt *n.* kilowat (kW.) *m.*
kin *n.* perthynas *mf.*
kind *n.* math, rhyw *m.*
kind *a.* caredig.
kindergarten *n.* ysgol feithrin *f.*
kindliness *n.* caredigrwydd *m.*
kindly *a.* caredig, tirion.
kindness *n.* caredigrwydd *m;* cymwynas *f.*
kindred *n.* perthynas *mf;* perthnasau *pl.*
king *n.* brenin *m.*
kingdom *n.* teyrnas *f:* **Kingdom of Heaven** Teyrnas Nefoedd: **United Kingdom** Teyrnas Unedig.
kingfisher *n.* glas y dorlan *m.*
kingly *a.* brenhinol.
kipper *n.* ciper *m.*
kiss 1 *n.* cusan *mf,* sws *m.* **2** *v.* cusanu.
kitchen *n.* cegin *f.*
kitchenette *n.* cegin fach *f.*
kitchen-garden *n.* gardd lysiau *f.*
kitten *n.* cath fach *f.*
knead *v.* tylino.
knee *n.* glin *mf,* pen-glin, pen-lin *m.*
kneel *v.* penlinio.
knife n. cyllell *f:* **bread-knife** cyllell fara: **pocket-knife** cyllell boced.
knight *n.* marchog *m.*
knit *v.* gwau.
knock 1 *n.* cnoc, ergyd *mf.* **2** *v.* cnocio, curo, taro.
knot 1 *n.* clwm, cwlwm *m.* **2** *v.* clymu.
know *v.* adnabod; gwybod: **I know** gwn, mi wn, rydw i'n gwybod.
knowing *a.* gwybodus; ffel.
knowingly *ad.* yn fwriadol.
knowledge *n.* gwybodaeth *f.*
knuckle *n.* migwrn, cymal *m.*

label *n.* llabed, label *f.*
laboratory *n.* labordy *m*: **language laboratory** labordy iaith.
laborious *a.* llafurus.
labour 1 *n.* llafur, gwaith *m.* **2** *v.* llafurio, gweithio: **the Labour Party** y Blaid Lafur.
labourer *n.* labrwr, gweithiwr *m.*
lace 1 *n.* les *m.* **2** *v.* cau (*esgidiau*).
lack 1 *n.* eisiau, diffyg *m.* **2** *v.* bod mewn eisiau.
lad *n.* llanc, hogyn, gwas, bachgen *m.*
ladder *n.* ysgol *f.*
laden *a.* llwythog.
ladies *n.* arglwyddesau; boneddigesau; toiledau merched *pl.*
lady *n.* arglwyddes; boneddiges *f.*
lair *n.* ffau, gwâl, lloches *f.*
lake *n.* llyn *m.*
lamb *n.* oen *m*: **Paschal Lamb** Oen y Pasg.
lame 1 *a.* cloff. **2** *v.* cloffi.
lameness *n.* cloffi, cloffni *m.*
lamp *n.* lamp *f*: **lampshade** lamplen *f.*
lamp post *n.* postyn lamp, polyn lamp *m.*
land 1 *n.* tir *m,* daear, gwlad, glan *f.* **2** *v.* glanio.
landlady n. gwraig llety *f.*
landlord *n.* meistr tir, lletywr, tafarnwr *m.*
landscape *n.* tirlun *m.*
lane *n.* lôn *f*: **escape lane** lôn ddianc.
language *n.* iaith *f*: **first language** iaith gyntaf, mamiaith; **second language** ail iaith; **foreign language** iaith dramor, iaith estron.
lantern *n.* llusern *f.*
lap 1 *n.* arffed *f,* glin *mf.* **2** *v.* lapio.
lapel *n.* llabed *f.*
large *a.* mawr; eang; helaeth.
largely *ad.* gan mwyaf.
lark *n.* ehedydd, hedydd, uchedydd *m.*
laryngitis *n.* llwnc tost *m.*
lass *n.* geneth, hogen, llances, merch *f.*
last 1 *a.* diwethaf; olaf. **2** *ad.* yn ddiwethaf, yn olaf. **3** *v.* para, parhau, dal, dala: **last night** neithiwr; **last week** yr wythnos diwethaf; **last month** mis diwethaf; **last year** y llynedd; **at last** o'r diwedd; **the last word** y gair olaf.
late *a.* hwyr; diweddar.
lately *ad.* yn ddiweddar.
later *ad.* wedyn, eto, yn ddiweddarach.
latest *a.* diweddaraf.
Latin *n.* Lladin *f.*
latter *a.* diwethaf, olaf.
laugh *n.* & *v.* chwerthin *m.*
laughable *a.* chwerthinllyd.
laughter *n.* chwerthin *m.*
launderette *n.* golchdy *m.*
lavatory *n.* tŷ-bach *m,* ystafell ymolchi *f,* toiled *m.*
lavender *n.* lafant *m.*
law *n.* cyfraith, deddf *f.*
lawn *n.* lawnt *f.*
lawyer *n.* cyfreithiwr *m.*
lax *a.* llac; esgeulus.
lay *v.* gosod, dodi; dodwy.
layer *n.* haenen *f.*
laze *v.* diogi, segura.
laziness *n.* diogi *m.*
lazy *a.* diog, dioglyd, pwdr.
lead *n.* plwm *m.*
lead *v.* arwain, tywys.
leaden a. plwm.
leader *n.* arweinydd; blaenwr *m.*
leaf n. deilen; dalen *f.*
leaflet *n.* taflen *f.*
league *n.* cynghrair *m.*
leak *v.* gollwng, colli, diferu.
lean 1 *n.* cig coch *m.* **2** *a.* main, tenau. **3** *v.* pwyso (ar).
leap 1 *n.* llam *m,* naid *f.* **2** *v.* llamu, neidio: **leap year** blwyddyn naid.
learn *v.* dysgu.
learned *a.* dysgedig, hyddysg.
learner *n.* dysgwr *m.*
learning 1 *n.* dysg *f.* **2** *v.* dysgu.
lease *n.* les, prydles *f.*
least *a.* lleiaf; *see* bach: **at least** o leiaf.

leather *n.* lledr *m.*
leave 1 *n.* caniatâd *m.* 2 *v.* gadael, ymadael.
leaven *n.* lefain *m.*
lecture 1 *n.* darlith *f.* 2 *v.* darlithio.
lecturer *n.* darlithiwr, darlithydd *m.*
ledge *n.* silff *f;* crib *mf.*
leek *n.* cenhinen *f.*
left *a.* chwith: **left-handed** llawchwith.
leg *n.* coes *f.*
legend *n.* chwedl *f.*
legislate *v.* deddfu.
leisure *n.* hamdden *f.*
leisurely *a.* hamddenol.
lemon *n.* lemwn *m:* **lemonade** diod lemwn; **lemon juice** sudd lemwn.
lend *v.* benthyca, rhoi benthyg.
length *n.* hyd *m:* **at length** o'r diwedd.
lengthen *v.* estyn, ymestyn.
lengthy *a.* hir.
less 1 *a.* & *n.* llai *m.* 2 *ad.* yn llai.
lesson *n.* gwers *f:* **history lesson** gwers hanes; **Welsh lesson** gwers Gymraeg.
lest *c.* rhag, rhag ofn, fel na.
let *v.* caniatáu; gadel; gosod; rhentu.
lethal *a.* marwol.
letter *n.* llythyr *m;* llythyren *f.*
lettuce *n.* letysen *f.*
level *n.* & *a.* gwastad *m,* lefel *f:* **spirit level** lefelydd.
level crossing *n.* croesfan *f.*
liable *a.* agored, atebol.
liar *n.* celwyddgi *m.*
liberal *a.* hael, haelionus.
liberty *n.* rhyddid *m.*
librarian *n.* llyfrgellydd *m.*
library *n.* llyfrgell *f.*
licence *n.* trwydded *f:* **driving licence** trwydded yrru.
lick *v.* llyfu, llyo.
lid *n.* clawr *m.*
lie 1 *n.* celwydd, anwiredd *n.* 2 *v.* dweud celwydd, dweud anwiredd; gorwedd.
life *n.* bywyd, byw *m.*
lifeboat *n.* bad achub *m.*
life insurance *n.* yswiriant bywyd *m.*
lifeless *a.* marwaidd.
lifetime *n.* oes *f.*
lift 1 *n.* lifft *m.* 2 *v.* codi.
ligament *n.* gewyn.
light 1 *n.* golau, goleuni, llewyrch *m.* 2 *a.* golau; ysgafn. 3 *v.* goleuo; tanio.
lighten *v.* ysgafnhau, ysgafnu.
lighthouse *n.* goleudy *m.*
lightning *n.* mellt, lluched *pl.*
like 1 *a.* tebyg. 2 *prp.* fel. 3 *v.* hoffi, caru.
likeable *a.* dymunol.
likely *a.* & *ad.* tebygol, tebyg.
likeness *n.* tebygrwydd *m.*
likewise 1 *n.* yn yr un modd. 2 *c.* hefyd.
liking *n.* hoffter *m.*
lily *n.* lili *f:* **lily of the valley** lili'r dyffrynnoedd.
limb *n.* aelod *m;* cangen *f;* cymal *m.*
limit *n.* ffin *f,* terfyn *m.*
limp 1 *a.* llipa. 2 *v.* cloffi.
line *n.* llinell *f,* llinyn *m,* lein *f.*
linen *n.* lliain *m.*
linesman *n.* llinellwr, ystlyswr *m.*
link 1 *n.* dolen *f.* 2 *v.* cydio.
lion *n.* llew *m.*
lioness *n.* llewes *f.*
lip *n.* gwefus *f,* min *m.*
lipstick *n.* minlliw *m.*
liquid 1 *n.* hylif *m.* 2 *a.* hylif; gwlyb.
list *n.* rhestr *f.*
listen *v.* gwrando.
listener *n.* gwrandawr *m.*
literary *a.* llenyddol.
literate *a.* llythrennog.
literature *n.* llên, llenyddiaeth *f.*
litre *n.* litr *m.*
litter 1 *n.* sbwriel, ysbwriel *m.* 2 *v.* sarnu.
littérateur *n.* llenor *m.*
little *a.* bach, bychan, bechan; mân, tamaid, ychydig.
live *a.&v.* byw.
lively *a.* bywiog, heini.
liver *n.* iau *m,* afu *mf.*
Liverpool *n.* Lerpwl *f.*
living *a.* byw, yn fyw.
load 1 *n.* baich, llwyth *m.* 2 *v.* llwytho.
loaf *n.* torth *f.*
loathsome *a.* ffiaidd.
lobby *n.* cyntedd, porth *m.*
local *a.* lleol: **Local Government** Llywodraeth Leol.
locality *n.* lle *m,* ardal, cymdogaeth *f.*
localise *v.* lleoli.
locate *v.* lleoli, gosod.
location *n.* lleoliad *m.*
loch *n.* loch *m.*
lock 1 *n.* clo *m.* 2 *v.* cloi.
locked *a.* ar glo, dan glo, ynghlo.
lodge 1 *n.* llety *m.* 2 *v.* lletya.
lodger *n.* lletywr *m.*
lodging(s) *n. (pl).* llety *m.*
loft *n.* llofft *f.*
loin *n.* llwyn *f.*

London *n.* Llundain *f.*
loneliness *n.* unigrwydd *m.*
lonely *a.* unig.
long 1 *n.* hir, maith. 2 *v.* hiraethu. **long since** ers amser.
longing *n.* hiraeth *m.*
look 1 *n.* golwg *mf*, trem *f.* 2 v. edrych, ysbîo.
loose 1 *a.* llac, llaes, rhydd. 2 *v.* datod, llacio, rhyddhau.
loosen *v.* llacio, rhyddhau, datod.
lord *n.* arglwydd *m*: **The Lord** Yr Arglwydd; **the Lord's Prayer** Gweddi'r Arglwydd; **House of Lords** Tŷ'r Arglwyddi.
lord mayor *n.* arglwydd faer *m.*
lorry *n.* lorri *f.*
lorry driver *n.* gyrrwr lorri *m.*
lose *v.* colli.
loss *n.* colled *mf.*
loud *a.* uchel.
loudest *a.* uchaf.
Loughor *n.* Casllwchwr *f.*
lounge 1 *n.* lolfa *f.* 2 *v.* lolian.
louse *n.* lleuen *f.*
love 1 *n.* cariad, serch *m.* 2 *v.* caru: **love letter** llythyr caru.
lovely *a.* hyfryd, teg, prydferth; braf.
lover *n.* cariad *mf*, carwr *m.*
loving *a.* cariadus, serchus, serchog.
low *a.* isel.
lower 1 *a.* is. 2 *v.* gostwng, gollwng.
lowest *a.* isaf; lleiaf.
loyal *a.* ffyddlon, teyrngar.
lozenge *n.* losinen, losen *f.*
luck *n.* lwc, ffortiwn *f*: **best of luck** lwc dda, pob hwyl.
luckily *ad.* yn ffodus, yn lwcus.
lucky *a.* ffodus, lwcus.
lull 1 *n.* gosteg *m.* 2 *v.* suo.
lullaby *n.* hwiangerdd *f.*
luminous *a.* golau, disglair, llachar.
lungs *n.* ysgyfaint *pl.*
lupins *n.* bysedd y blaidd *pl.*
lust *n.* chwant, trachwant *m.*
lustful *a.* trachwantus.
lustre *n.* llewyrch *m.*
luxurious *a.* moethus.
lyric *n.* telyneg *f.*

machine *n.* peiriant *m*: **machinery** peiriannau.
mackintosh *n.* cot law *f.*
mad *a.* gwyllt, gwallgof.
magazine *n.* cylchgrawn *m.*
magic *n.* hud, lledrith, swyn *m.*
magician *n.* dewin *m.*
magistrate *n.* ustus, ynad *m.*
magnificent *a.* gwych.
magnifying glass *n.* chwyddwydr *m.*
magnitude *n.* maint, ehangder *m.*
magpie *n.* pioden *m.*
maid *n.* morwyn, merch *f*: **old maid** hen ferch.
mail 1 *n.* y post *m.* **2** *v.* postio.
main *a.* pennaf, prif, mwyaf: **main road** ffordd fawr, priffordd; **mainland** y tir mawr.
mainly *ad.* yn bennaf.
majesty *n.* mawredd; mawrhydi *m:* **Her Majesty** Ei Mawrhydi.
major 1 *n.* uwchgapten *m.* **2** *a.* prif, mwyaf.
majority *n.* mwyafrif; oedran llawn *m.*
make *v.* gwneud, gwneuthur.
make-up *n.* & *v.* coluro *m.*
male *n.* gwryw *m.*
man *n.* dyn, gŵr, mab *m*: **man of letters** llenor.
manage *v.* rheoli, trin; llwydo.
manager *n.* rheolwr m.
manger *n.* preseb *m.*
manifest *v.* dangos, egluro.
manipulate v. trin, trafod.
manner *n.* modd, dull *m.*
manners *n.* moesau *pl*: **good manners** moesau da.
manse *n.* tŷ gweinidog, mans *m.*
mansion *n.* plas, plasty *m.*
mantle *n.* mantell *f.*
manual 1 *n.* llawlyfr *m.* **2** *a.* perthynol i'r llaw.
manure *n.* gwrtaith, tail *m.*
manuscript *n.* llawysgrif *f.*
many 1 *n.* llawer *m.* **2** *a.* llawer, aml, sawl: **how many** sawl: **too many** gormod.
map *n.* map *n.*
March *n.* Mawrth *m.*
march 1 *n.* ymdaith *f.* **2** *v.* ymdeithio.
margin *n.* ffin *f*, ymyl *mf.*
mariner *n.* llongwr, morwr *m.*
mark 1 *n.* nod, nam, ôl, marc *m.* **2** *v.* nodi, marcio.
market 1 *n.* marchnad *f.* **2** *v.* marchnata.
marriage *n.* priodas *f.*
married *a.* priod.
marrow *n.* mêr *m*: **vegetable marrow** pwmpen *f.*
marry *v.* priodi.
Mars *n.* Mawrth *m.*
mart *n.* mart *m.*
martyr *n.* merthyr *m.*
marvel 1 *n.* rhyfeddod *m.* **2** *v.* rhyfeddu, synnu.
marvellous *a.* rhyfeddol, gwych
masculine *n.* gwryw, gwrywaidd, gwrywol.
mask 1 *n.* mwgwd *m.* **2** *v.* cuddio
mass *n.* pentwr *m.*; pwysau *pl.*; offeren *f.*
massive *a.* anferth
master 1 *n.* meistr, capten (*llong*) *m.* **2** *v.* meistroli.
masterpiece *n.* campwaith *m.*
mat *n.* mat *m.*
match *n.* matsien; gêm; gornest; priodas *f.*
material *n.* defnydd, nwydd *m.*
mathematical *a.* mathemategol.
mathematician *n.* mathemategwr *m.*
mathematics *n.* mathemateg *f.*
matrimony *n.* priodas *f.*
matter *n.* mater *m*: **What's the matter?** Beth sy'n bod?
mature 1 *a.* aeddfed. **2.** *v.* aeddfedu
maximum *n.* uchafswm, uchafrif, uchafbwynt *m.*
May *n.* Mai *m:* **May Day** Calan Mai.
maybe *ad.* efallai, hwyrach.
mayor *n.* maer *f.*
mayoress *n.* maeres *f.*
me *pn.* myfi, mi, fi, i; minnau.
mead *n.* medd *m.*
meadow *n.* dôl, gwaun *f*, maes *m.*
meagre *a.* cul, llwm, tenau, prin.

meal *n.* pryd o fwyd; blawd *m.*
mean 1 *n.* cyfrwng, modd; canol *m.* **2** *a.* sâl; gwael; tynn. **3** *v.* bwriadu, golygu, meddwl.
meaning *n.* ystyr *mf,* meddwl *m.*
meaningful *a.* ystyrlon.
means *n.* modd, moddion, cyfrwng; cyfoeth *m*: **by all means** ar bob cyfrif, wrth gwrs.
measles *n.* y frech goch *f.*
measure *n.* mesur *m.*
meat *n.* cig *m.*
medal *n.* bathodyn *m,* medal *f.*
meddle *v.* ymhél, ymyrru, ymyrryd.
media *n.* cyfryngau *pl.*
medicine *n.* moddion, ffisig *m;* meddyginiaeth *f.*
meditate *v.* myfrio.
meditation *n.* myfyrdod *m.*
medium 1 *n.* cyfrwng; canol *m.* **2** *a.* canol.
medley *n.* cadwyn o alawon *f;* cymysgwch *m.*
meet *v.* cyfarfod, cwrdd (â); cyffwrdd.
meeting *n.* cyfarfod, cwrdd *m;* oedfa *f.*
melody *n.* alaw, tôn *f.*
melt *v.* toddi.
member *n.* aelod *m*: **to become a member** ymaelodi: **Member of Parliament (M.P.)** Aelod Seneddol (A.S.)
membership *n.* aelodaeth *f.*
memory *n.* cof *m.*
mend *v.* gwella, trwsio, cyweirio.
meningitis *n.* llid yr ymennydd *m.*
menstruation *n.* y misglwyf *m.*
mention *n.* & *v.* sôn *mf* (am).
menu *n.* bwydlen *f.*
merchant *n.* masnachwr *m.*
merciful *a.* trugarog.
mercifully *ad.* drwy drugaredd.
Mercury *n.* Mercher *m.*
mercury *n.* arian byw, mercwri *m.*
mercy *n.* trugaredd *f*: **to be merciful** trugarhau.
merit 1 *n.* teilyngdod *m.* **2** *v.* haeddu.
mermaid *n.* môr-forwyn *f.*
merriment *n.* miri *m.*
merry *a.* llawen, llon.
message *n.* neges *f.*
messenger *n.* negesydd *m.*
metal *n.* metel *m.*
meteor *n.* seren wib *f.*
meter *n.* mesurydd *m.*
method *n.* dull, modd *m,* trefn *f*: **new methods** dulliau newydd.
methodical *a.* trefnus.
metre *n.* mesur; metr *m*: **kilometre** kilometr (km.).
metric *a.* metrig: **metric scale** graddfa fetrig.
mew *v.* mewian.
micro-chip *n.* meicro-sglodyn *m.*
microphone *n.* meic, meicroffon *m.*
microscope *n.* meicrosgop *m.*
microwave *n.* meicrodon *f.*
mid *a.* canol.
midday *n.* canol dydd, hanner dydd *m.*
middle *n.* canol *m.*
middle-aged *a.* canol oed.
midland *n.* canolbarth *m*: **the Midlands** Canolbarth Lloegr: **Mid Wales** Canolbarth Cymru.
midnight *n.* canol nos, hanner nos *f.*
midst 1 *n.* canol, plith *m.* **2** *prp.* rhwng.
might *n.* nerth, gallu *m.*
mighty *a.* grymus.
mild *a.* mwyn, tyner, meddal, gwan: **become mild** mwynhau, tyneru.
mile *n.* milltir *f*: **milestone** carreg filltir *f.*
milk 1 *n.* llaeth, llefrith *m.* **2** *v.* godro: **milkman** dyn llaeth.
mill *n.* melin *f.*
million *n.* miliwn *m*: **millionaire** miliynydd.
mime 1 *n.* meim *m.* **2** *v.* meimio.
mind 1 *n.* meddwl, bryd, bwriad *m.* **2** *v.* gwylio, gofalu, hidio.
mindful *a.* gofalus, ystyriol.
mine 1 *n.* pwll, mwynglawdd *m.* **2** *pn.* fy, yr eiddof i.
miner *n.* glöwr, mwynwr *m.*
mineral *n.* mwyn *m.*
minimum *n.* lleiafswm, isafrif, isafbwynt *m.*
minister 1 *n.* gweinidog *m.* **2** *v.* gwasanaethu.
minority *n.* lleiafrif *m.*
mint *n.* bathdy; mint, mintys *n*: **Royal Mint** Bathdy Brenhinol.
minute *n.* munud *mf;* cofnod *m*: **minute book** llyfr cofnodion.
minute *a.* bach, mân, manwl.
miracle *n.* gwyrth *f.*
miraculous *a.* gwyrthiol.
mirror *n.* drych *m.*
miscarriage *n.* erthyliad *m.*
miscarry *v.* erthlyu; colli.
mischief *n.* drwg, drygioni *m.*
mischievous *a.* drygionus.
miserable *a.* gwael, truenus, diflas.
misery *n.* trallod, trueni, diflastod *m.*
mislead *v.* camarwain, twyllo.

miss *v.* colli, methu, gweld eisiau.
missile *n.* taflegryn *m.*
mission *n.* cenhadaeth *f.*
missionary 1 *n.* cenhadwr *m;* cenhades *f.* **2** *a.* cenhadol.
mist *n.* niwl *m.*
mistake *n.* camsyniad, gwall, camgymeriad *m.*
mistress *n.* meistres, athrawes *f:* **headmistress** prifathrawes.
misty *a.* niwlog.
misunderstand *v.* camddeall.
mix *v.* cymysgu.
mixed *a.* cymysg.
mob *n.* torf, tyrfa, haid *f.*
mock *v.* gwawdio.
mode *n.* modd, dull *m.*
modern *a.* diweddar, modern.
moist *a.* llaith, gwlyb.
moisten *v.* gwlychu.
moisture *n.* gwlybaniaeth *f.*
Mold *n.* Yr Wyddgrug *f.*
moment *n.* eiliad *f,* ennyd *mf,* moment *f.*
monarch *n.* brenin *m.*
monastery *n.* mynachlog *f.*
Monday *n.* dydd Llun *m.*
money *n.* arian, pres *m.*
monk *n.* mynach *m.*
monkey *n.* mwnci *m.*
monoglot 1 *n.* person uniaith *m.* **2** *a.* uniaith.
monotonous *a.* undonog.
monstrous *a.* anferth.
month *n.* mis *m.*
monthly 1 *n.* misolyn *m.* **2** *a.* misol.
mood *n.* tymer, hwyl *f.*
moon *n.* lleuad, lloer *f:* **moonlight** golau leuad.
moor *n.* rhos *f,* rhostir *m,* gwaun *f.*
moral *a.* moesol.
morals *n.* moesau *pl.*
more 1 *n.* rhagor, ychwaneg, chwaneg *m.* **2** *a.* & *ad.* mwy, mwyach: **more than** mwy na.
morning 1 *n.* bore *m.* **2** *a.* bore, boreol: **Monday morning** bore dydd Llun: **every morning** bob bore; **Morning Service** Gwasanaeth Boreol.
morrow *ad.* trannoeth.
mortal 1 *n.* dyn; un marwol *m.* **2** *a.* marwol.
mortgage *n.* morgais *m.*
most *a.* mwyaf, amlaf.
mostly *ad.* gan mwyaf.
moth *n.* gwyfyn *m.*
mother *n.* mam *f:* **mother-in-law** mam-yng-nghyfraith.
motor *n.* modur, car *m:* **motor bike** beic modur.
motorist *n.* modurwr *m.*
motorway *n.* traffordd *f.*
mountain *n.* mynydd *m.*
mountaineer *n.* mynyddwr *m.*
mountainous *a.* mynyddig.
mourn *v.* galaru.
mourning *n.* galar *m.*
mouse *n.* llygoden *f.*
mouth *n.* ceg *f,* genau *pl.*
move *v.* symud.
movement *n.* mudiad; symudiad, symud *m.*
moving *a.* yn symud, cyffrous.
mow *v.* lladd gwair.
much 1 *n.* llawer *m.* **2** *a.* llawer, mawr. **3** *ad.* yn fawr, llawer (*with comparative a.*): **much better** llawer gwell: **too much** gormod.
mud *n.* llacs *m.*
muddy *a.* llacsog.
multiply *v.* lluosi.
multitude *n.* llu *m,* torf, tyrfa *f.*
munch *v.* cnoi.
murder 1 *n.* llofruddiaeth *f.* **2** *v.* llofruddio.
murderer *n.* llofrudd *m.*
muscular *a.* cyhyrog.
museum *n.* amgueddfa *f.*
mushroom *n.* madarchen *f.*
music *n.* cerddoriaeth, cerdd, caniadaeth, alaw, miwsig *f.*
musical *a.* cerddorol.
musician *n.* cerddor *m.*
must *n.* & *v.* rhaid *m.*
mutate *v.* treiglo.
mutation *n.* treiglad, cyfnewidiad *m.*
mute *a.* mud, distaw.
mutilate *v.* anafu, llurgunio.
mutiny *n.* gwrthryfel, terfysg *m.*
mutton *n.* cig dafad, cig gwedder *m.*
my *pn.* fy; 'm.
myrrh *n.* myrr *m.*
myself *pn.* fy hunan, mi fy hunan, myfi fy hun.
mysterious *a.* rhyfedd, dirgel.
mystery *n.* dirgelwch.
myth *n.* chwedl, dameg, myth *f.*

nail 1 *n.* ewin *mf;* hoel, hoelen *f.* 2 *v.* hoelio.
naked *a.* noeth; llwm: **stark naked** noethlymun, porcyn.
name 1 *n.* enw *m.* 2 *v.* enwi, galw.
namely *ad.* sef.
nape *n.* gwar *m.*
napkin *n.* cewyn, clwt *m.*
narrate *v.* adrodd (hanes).
narration *n.* adroddiad *m.*
narrative *n.* chwedl *f,* hanes *m,* stori *f.*
narrow 1 *a.* cul, cyfyng. 2 *v.* cyfyngu.
narrow-minded *a.* cul.
nasal *a.* trwynol.
nasty *a.* cas, brwnt, budr, ffiaidd.
nation *n.* cenedl *f.*
national *a.* cenedlaethol; gwladol: **National Assistance** Cymorth Gwladol: **National Museum** Amgueddfa Genedlaethol.
nationalism *n.* cenedlaetholdeb *m.*
nationalist *n.* cenedlaetholwr *m.*
nationality *n.* cenedligrwydd *m.*
native 1 *n.* brodor *m.* 2 *a.* brodorol.
nativity *n.* genedigaeth *f.*
natural *a.* naturiol.
nature *n.* natur, naws *f.*
naught *n.* dim; sero *m.*
naughtiness *n.* drygioni *m.*
naughty *a.* drwg, drygionus.
navy *n.* llynges *f:* **navy blue** glasddu.
near 1 *a.* agos. 2 *ad.* yn agos, braidd. 3 *v.* agosáu, nesáu. 4 *prp.* ger, yn agos at.
nearby *a.* & *ad.* yn ymyl, gerllaw.
nearly *ad.* bron.
neat *a.* twt, del, taclus, trefnus.
Neath *n.* Castell-nedd *f.*
necessary *a.* angenrheidiol.
necessitate gwneud yn angenrheidiol, gorfodi.
necessity *n.* anghenraid, rhaid *m.*
neck *n.* gwddf, gwddwg.
necklace *n.* neclis *f,* mwclis *pl.*
née *a.* gynt, cyn priodi: **Mair Puw, née Rhys** Mair Puw, gynt Rhys.
need *n.* eisiau, rhaid. *m.*
needle *n.* nodwydd; gwaell *f.*
needy *a.* tlawd.
negative *a.* negyddol.
neglect *v.* esgeuluso.
negligence *n.* esgeulustod *m.*
negligent *a.* esgeulus.
negotiate *v.* trafod, trefnu.
negro *n.* dyn du, negro *m.*
neighbour *n.* cymydog *m.*
neither 1 *ad.* & *c.* na, nac, chwaith, ychwaith. 2 *pn.* nid y naill na'r llall, nid un o'r ddau.
nephew *n.* nai *m.*
nerve *n.* gewyn, nerf *m.*
nervous *a.* nerfus, ofnus.
nest *n.* nyth *mf.*
nestle *v.* nythu.
nestling *n.* aderyn bach, cyw *m.*
net *n.* rhwyd *f.*
netball *n.* pêl rwyd *f.*
Netherlands, The *n.* Yr Iseldiroedd *f.*
never *ad.* byth, erioed.
nevertheless *ad.* er hynny, eto.
new *a.* newydd: **New Year** Blwyddyn Newydd; **New York** Efrog Newydd; **New Zealand** Seland Newydd; **brand new** newydd sbon.
newcomer *n.* newydd-ddyfodiad *m.*
Newport (Dyfed) *n.* Trefdraeth *f.*
Newport (Gwent) *n.* Casnewydd *f.*
Newquay *n.* Ceinewydd *f.*
news *n.pl.* newyddion *pl,* newydd, hanes *m:* **good news** newyddion da; **six o'clock news** newyddion chwech.
newspaper *n.* papur newydd. *m.*
next 1 *a.* nesaf. 2 *prp.* nesaf at: **next door** y drws nesaf: **Next, please** Y nesaf, os gwelwch yn dda; **next week** wythnos nesaf; **next year** y flwyddyn nesaf.
nice *a.* braf, hyfryd, neis, dymunol.
nickname 1 *n.* llysenw *m.* 2 *v.* llysenwi.
niece *n.* nith *f.*
nigh *a., ad.* & *prp.* agos, gerllaw, yn agos.
night *n.* nos; noson, noswaith *f:* **night and day** nos a dydd; **night**

before last echnos; **last night** neithiwr; **the last night** y noson olaf; **Good night!** Nos da!.
nightdress *n.* gŵn nos, coban *f.*
night-gown *n.* gŵn nos, coban *f.*
nightingale *n.* eos *f.*
nightmare *n.* hunllef *f.*
nil *n.* dim *m.*
nimble *a.* heini, sionc, ystwyth.
nine *n.* & *a.* naw *m.*
nineteen *n.* & *a.* pedwar ar bymtheg, un deg naw *m.*
ninety *n.* & a. naw deg *m.*
ninth *n.* & *a.* nawfed *m.*
no 1 *a.* ni, nid, neb, dim. **2** *ad.* na, nad, ni, nid, nac oes, naddo, nage, nac ydy . . . *(Welsh uses the verb forms to answer yes/no) e.g.* **Nia? No.** Nia? Nage. **Was she there? No.** Oedd hi yno? Nac oedd. **Is Non at home? No.** Ydy Non gartre? Nac ydy. **Is there food here? No.** Oes bwyd yma? Nac oes. **Will they be out? No.** Fyddan nhw allan? Na fyddan.
noble *a.* bonheddig, ardderchog.
nobleman *n.* bonheddwr, uchelwr *m.*
nobody *n.* neb *m.*
noise *n.* sŵn, mwstwr, stŵr, sain, twrw *m.*
noisy *a.* swnllyd, stwrllyd.
nom de plume *n.* ffugenw *m.*
none *pn.* neb, dim, dim un.
nonsense *n.* lol *f.*
nook *n.* cornel, congl *f.*
noon *n.* hanner dydd, canol dydd *m.*
no one *pn.* neb.
nor *ad.* & *c.* na, nac.
Norman 1 *n.* Norman *m.* **2** *a.* Normanaidd: **Norman church** eglwys Normanaidd.
north 1 *n.* gogledd *m.* **2** *a.* gogleddol: **North Pole** Pegwn y Gogledd: **North Wales** Gogledd Cymru.
northerly *a.* gogleddol.
northern *a.* gogleddol: **Northern Ireland** Gogledd Iwerddon.
Northerner *n.* Gogleddwr *m.*
nose 1 *n.* trwyn *m.* **2** *v.* trwyno.
nostalgia *n.* hiraeth *m.*
nostril *n.* ffroen *f.*
not *ad.* na, nac, nad, ni, nid.
notable *a.* hynod, enwog, nodedig.
note 1 *n.* nodyn, nod *m.* **2** *v.* nodi, sylwi: **ten pound note** papur decpunt.
noted *a.* nodedig, enwog, hynod.
nothing *n.* dim *m*: **nothing at all** dim byd, dim o gwbl, dim yn y byd.
notice 1 *n.* rhybudd, hysbysebiad, sylw *m.* **2** *v.* sylwi.
notion *n.* syniad, amcan *m.*
notwithstanding 1 *ad.* er hynny. **2** *prp.* er, er, gwaethaf, serch.
noun *n.* enw *m*: **collective noun** enw torfol; **common noun** enw cyffredin; **plural noun** enw lluosog.
novel 1 *n.* nofel *f.* **2** *a.* newydd.
novelist *n.* nofelwr, nofelydd *m.*
November *n.* Tachwedd *m.*
now *ad.* yn awr, nawr, rŵan, bellach, y pryd hwn: **now and again** nawr ac yn y man.
nowadays *ad.* yn y dyddiau hyn.
nowhere *ad.* dim yn unlle.
nuance *n.* naws *f.*
nuclear *a.* niwclear: **nuclear energy** egni niwclear: **nuclear power station** atomfa.
numb *a.* cwsg.
number 1 *n.* nifer *mf,* rhif; rhifyn *m.* **2** *v.* rhifo, cyfrif.
numeral *n.* rhifol, rhifnod *m.*
numerous *a.* lluosog, niferus; aml.
nun *n.* lleian *f.*
nurse 1 *n.* gweinyddes, nyrs *f.* **2** *v.* magu, nyrsio, meithrin.
nursery *n.* meithrinfa *f*: **nursery class** dosbarth meithrin; **nursery nurse** gweinyddes feithrin; **nursery school** ysgol feithrin.
nurseryman *n.* garddwr *m.*
nursery-rhyme *n.* hwiangerdd *f.*
nurture *v.* meithrin.
nut *n.* cneuen; nyten *f*: **coconut** cneuen goco; **hazel-nuts** cnau cyll; **monkey nuts** cnau mwnci; **walnut** cneuen ffrengig; **hexagonal nut** nyten hecsagonal; **square nut** nyten sgwâr; **nut and bolt** nyten a bollt.

oak 1 *n.* derwen *f.* 2 *a.* derw: **oak trees** derw, deri.
oath *n.* llw *m.*
obedient *a.* ufudd.
obey *v.* ufuddhau.
object 1 *n.* gwrthrych, nod, amcan *m.* 2 *v.* gwrthwynebu.
objective 1 *n.* amcan, nod *m.* 2 *a.* gwrthrychol.
objector *n.* gwrthwynebwr *m.*
obligation *n.* dyletswydd, gorfodaeth *f.*
oblige *v.* gorfodi.
obscene *a.* serth, brwnt.
obscure 1 *a.* aneglur, tywyll. 2 *v.* tywyllu.
observation *n.* sylw *m.*
observe *v.* sylwi, edrych; cadw.
obstacle *n.* rhwystr, maen tramgwydd *m.*
obstruct *v.* cau, tagu; rhwystro.
obtain *v.* cael, ennill.
obvious *a.* eglur, amlwg.
occasion 1 *n.* achlysur, achos *m,* adeg *f.* 2 *v.* achosi, peri.
occasional *a.* ambell.
occasionally *a.* ambell waith.
occupation *n.* gwaith *m,* galwedigaeth *f.*
occur *v.* digwydd, taro.
occurrence *n.* digwyddiad, achlysur *m.*
ocean *n.* môr, cefnfor, eigion *m.*
o'clock *ad.* o'r gloch.
octagon *n.* wythongl *f,* octagon *m.*
octave *n.* wythawd *m.*
octet *n.* wythawd *m.*
October *n.* Hydref *m.*
octogenarian *n.* person pedwar ugain mlwydd oed *m.*
odd *a.* od, hynod, rhyfedd.
ode *n.* cerdd, awdl *f.*
odious *a.* cas, ffiaidd.
odour *n.* arogl, aroglau *m.*
of *prp.* o, gan, am, ynghylch: **of course** wrth gwrs.
off 1 *a.* tu allan, tu faes. 2 *ad.* ymaith, i ffwrdd. 3 *prp.* oddi ar, oddi am, oddi wrth.
offence *n.* trosedd *f.*
offend *v.* troseddu.
offender *n.* troseddwr *m.*
offer *n.* & *v.* cynnig *m.*
office *n.* swydd; swyddfa *f.*
officer *n.* swyddog *m.*
official 1 *n.* swyddogol *m.* 2 *a.* swyddogol.
offspring *n.* hil *f,* plant *pl.*
often *ad.* yn aml.
oil 1 *n.* olew, oel *m.* 2 *v.* iro, oelio: **oil field** maes olew: **oil rig** llwyfan olew.
old *a.* hen, oedrannus: **old age** henoed, henaint: **old fashioned** henffasiwn: **old man** hen ŵr, henwr: **of old** gynt.
omelette *n.* omled *m.*
on 1 *ad.* ymlaen. 2 *prp.* ar.
once *ad.* unwaith, un tro, gynt: **at once** ar unwaith.
one 1 *n.* un, rhywun *m.* 2 *a.* un, naill, unig. 3 *pn.* naill: **one by one** bob yn un.
one-way *a.* un–ffordd, unffordd: **one-way street** heol unffordd.
only 1 *a.* unig. 2 *ad.* yn unig, dim ond: **the only one** yr unig un: **one only** un yn unig.
open 1 *a.* agored, ar agor. 2 *v.* agor: **open air** awyr agored: **wide open** lled y pen.
opening *n.* agoriad *m.*
opera *n.* opera *f.*
operate *v.* gweithredu, gweithio.
operation *n.* gweithred *f.,* gweithrediad *m;* triniaeth lawfeddygol *f.*
opinion *n.* barn *f,* meddwl *m.*
opponent *n.* gwrthwynebwr, gwrthwynebydd *m.*
opportunity *n.* achlysur, cyfle *m,* siawns *f.*
oppose *v.* gwrthwynebu.
opposite *a.* & *prp.* cyferbyn, cyferbyniol.
opposition *n.* gwrthwyneb, gwrthwynebiad *m;* gwrthblaid *f.*
optician *n.* optegwr, optegydd *m.*
option *n.* dewis, dewisiad *m.*

or *c.* neu, ynte, ynteu, ai, naill ai.
oral *a.* llafar: **oral examination** arholiad llafar.
orally *ad.* ar lafar.
orange *n.* & *a.* oren *mf.*
orchard *n.* perllan *f.*
orchestra *n.* cerddorfa *f.*
ordain *v.* ordeinio, urddo; penderfynu.
ordeal *n.* prawf llym *m.*
order 1 *n.* trefn; urdd; rheol *f,* gorchymyn *m;* acheb *f.* **2** *v.* trefnu; gorchymyn; archebu.
orderly *a.* rheolaidd, trefnus.
ordinarily *ad.* fel rheol.
ordinary *a.* cyffredin, arferol.
ore *n.* mwyn *m.*
organ *n.* organ *f,* offeryn *m.*
organic *a.* organig.
organist *n.* organydd *m.*
organisation *n.* trefn; cyfundrefn *f.*
organise *v.* trefnu.
organiser *n.* trefnydd *m.*
origin *n.* ffynnon, ffynhonnell *f,* dechreuad *m.*
original *a.* gwreiddiol.
originate *v.* dechrau, tarddu, hanu.
other 1 *a.* arall, eraill. **2** *pn.* arall, y llall: **each other** ei gilydd.
our *pn.* ein, ein — ni; 'n: **Our Father** Ein Tad: **our house** ein tŷ, ein tŷ ni.
ours *pn.* eiddom ni, yr eiddom.
out *ad.* allan.
outcrop *n.* brig *m.*
outdoor *a.* yn yr awyr agored.
outline *n.* braslun *m.*
outside 1 *n.* tu allan, tu faes. *mf.* **2** *a.* & *ad.* allan, oddi allan. **3** *prp.* tu allan i, tu faes i.
outside-half *n.* maswr *m.*
outskirts *n.* cyrrau, cyrion *pl.*
outward *a.* allanol.
oven *n.* ffwrn *f,* popty *m:* **electric oven** ffwrn drydan: **gas oven** ffwrn nwy: **microwave oven** meicrodon.
over 1 *n.* pelawd *m (criced).* **2** *ad.* dros ben, drosodd. **3** *prp.* dros, uwch, uwchben.
over- *px.* gor-, rhag-, rhy-, tra-.
overcast *a.* cymylog.
overcoat *n.* cot fawr, cot uchaf *f.*
overcome *v.* gorchfygu, trechu, cael y gorau ar.
overcrowded *a.* gorlawn.
overdo *v.* gor-wneud.
overdraw *v.* gordynnu.
overflow 1 *n.* gorlif *m.* **2** *v.* gorlifo.
overflowing *a.* gorlawn.
overhead *a.* & *ad.* uwchben.
overjoyed *a.* llawen iawn.
overlook *v.* esgeuluso; edrych dros.
overnight *ad.* dros nos.
overpower *v.* trechu.
overseas *ad.* dros y môr, tramor.
overshadow *v.* cysgodi.
overweight *a.* gor-drwm.
overwork *v.* gorweithio.
owe *v.* bod mewn dyled.
owing *a.* dyledus.
owl *n.* gwdihŵ *m,* tylluan *f:* **barn owl, white owl** tylluan wen: **little owl** tylluan fechan: **long-eared owl** tylluan glustiog.
own 1 *a.* eiddo dyn ei hun, priod. **2** *v.* meddu (ar).
owner *n.* perchen, perchennog *m.*
Oxford *n.* Rhydychen *f.*
oxygen *n.* ocsigen *m.*

pace 1 *n.* cam *m.* 2 *v.* camu, cerdded.
Pacific Ocean *n.* Môr Tawel *m.*
pack 1 *n.* pac *m.* 2 *v.* pacio.
package *n.* paced, pecyn *m.*
packet *n.* paced, pecyn *m.*
pact *n.* cytundeb, cynghrair *m.*
padlock *n.* clo *m.*
pagan *n.* pagan *m.*
page *n.* tudalen *mf.*
pageant *n.* pasiant *m.*
pail *n.* bwced *m.*
pain 1 *n.* poen *mf,* dolur *m.* 2 *v.* poeni.
painful *a.* poenus.
painstakng *a.* gofalus.
paint 1 *n.* paent, lliw *m.* 2 *v.* peintio, lliwo.
painter *n.* peintiwr, arlunydd *m.*
painting *n.* llun, darlun *m.*
pair *n.* pâr, dau, cwpl *m.*
palace *n.* llys, plas, palas, plasty *m.*
pale *a.* llwyd, glas, gwelw.
Palestine *n.* Palestina *f.*
palm *n.* palmwydden *f*: **Palm Sunday** Sul y Blodau, Sul y Palmwydd.
pamper *v.* maldodi, anwesu.
pampering *n.* maldod, anwes *m.*
pamphlet *n.* pamffled, llyfryn *m.*
pan *n.* padell *f.*
pancake *n.* crempog, ffroesen *f.*
pane *n.* cwarel, chwarel *mf.*
panel *n.* panel *m.*
paper 1 *n.* papur *m.* 2 *v.* papuro. **newspaper** papur newydd: **toilet paper** papur toiled, papur tŷ bach; **wall paper** papur wal; **writing paper** papur ysgrifennu.
paperbacks *n.* llyfrau clawr meddal *pl.*
papist *n.* pabydd *m.*
parable *n.* dameg *f.*
paradise *n.* gwynfa, gwynfyd *m,* paradwys *f.*
paragraph *n.* paragraff *m.*
paramount *a.* pen, pennaf, prif.
parcel *n.* parsel *m.*
parch *v.* crasu, sychu.
parched *a.* cras, crasboeth; sychedig.
pardon 1 *n.* pardwn, maddeuant *m.* 2 *v.* maddau.
parent *n.* tad neu fam, rhiant *mf.*
parish *n.* plwyf *m.*
park 1 *n.* parc *m.* 2 *v.* parcio: **car park** maes parcio; **caravan park** maes carafanau.
parliament *n.* senedd *f*: **Member of Parliament** Aelod Seneddol (A.S.).
parsley *n.* persli *m.*
parsnip *n.* panasen *f.*
parson *n.* offeriad, person *m.*
part 1 *n.* darn *m,* rhan *f;* peth *m.* 2 *v.* rhannu; gwahanu; ymadael.
particular *a.* neilltuol.
particularise *v.* manylu.
parting *n.* ymadael *m.*
party *n.* parti *m;* plaid *f*: **birthday party** parti pen-blwydd; **Christmas party** parti Nadolig; **Conservative Party** Plaid Geidwadol; **Green Party** Plaid Werdd; **Labour Party** Plaid Lafur.
pass 1 *n.* bwlch; caniatâd; pás *m.* 2 *v.* mynd heibio (i); llwyddo.
passion *n.* dioddefaint; nwyd *m.*
past 1 *n.* & *a.* gorffennol *m.* 2 *ad.* heibio.
pastor *n.* bugail (*eglwys*), gweinidog *m.*
pasture *n.* porfa *f.*
path *n.* llwybr *m*: **public footpath** llwybr cyhoeddus.
patience *n.* amynedd *m*: **the patience of Job** amynedd Job.
patient 1 *n.* claf *m.* 2 *a.* amyneddgar.
patriot *n.* gwladgarwr *m.*
patron *n.* noddwr *m.*
patronage *n.* nawdd *m.*
pattern *n.* patrwm, patrwn *m.*
pause 1 *n.* hoe *f,* saib, seibiant *m.* 2 *v.* pwyllo, aros, gorffwys.
pavement *n.* pafin *m.*
pavilion *n.* pabell *f,* pafiliwn *m.*
paw *n.* pawen *f.*
pay 1 *n.* cyflog *mf,* tâl *m.* 2 *v.* talu.
payee *n.* talai *m.*
payer *n.* talwr *m.*
payment *n.* tâl, taliad *m.*
pea *n.* pysen *f.*

peace *n.* hedd, heddwch, llonyddwch *m;* tangnefedd *f.*
peaceful *a.* tawel, llonydd, tangnefeddus.
peak *n.* brig, copa *m.*
pear *n.* peren *f.*
pearl *n.* perl *m.*
peasant *n.* gwerinwr *m.*
peasantry *n.* y werin *f.*
peat *n.* mawn *m.*
peck 1 *n.* pigiad *m.* **2** *v.* pigo.
peculiar *a.* od, hynod, arbennig.
pedestrian 1 *n.* cerddwr *m.* **2** *a.* ar draed: **pedestrian crossing** croesfan *f.*
peel 1 *n.* croen, pil *m.* **2** *v.* pilio.
peep 1 *n.* cipolwg, cip *m.* **2** *v.* cipedrych, sbïo.
peg *n.* peg *m.*
pen *n.* pin ysgrifennu *m.*
penalise *v.* cosbi.
penalty *n.* cosb *f.*
pence *n.* ceiniogau *pl.*
pencil *n.* pensil *m.*
pendulum *n.* pendil *m.*
penitent *a.* edifar, edifeiriol.
penknife *n.* cyllell boced *f.*
penniless *a.* heb geiniog.
penny *n.* ceiniog *f.*
pension *n.* pensiwn *m.*
pensioner *n.* pensiynwr *m.*
pensive *a.* meddyglar.
people *n.* pobl, gwerin *f.*
pepper *n.* pupur *m.*
per *prp.* trwy, wrth, yn ôl.
perceive *v.* deall, gweld, gweled.
percentage *n.* hyn a hyn y cant, canran *m.*
perfect 1 *a.* perffaith. **2** *v.* perffeithio.
perfection *n.* perffeithrwydd *m.*
perfectly *ad.* yn berffaith.
perforate *v.* tyllu.
perforated *a.* tyllog.
perforation *n.* twll *m.*
perfume *n.* arogl; persawr *m.*
perhaps *ad.* efallai, hwyrach.
period *n.* adeg *f,* amser; misglwyf *m.*
permanent *a.* seydlog, parhaol.
permission *n.* caniatâd *m,* hawl *f.*
permit *v.* caniatáu.
perpetuate *v.* parhau.
persecute *v.* erlid.
person *n.* person *m.*
personal *a.* personol.
personality *n.* personoliaeth *f.*
perspective *n.* safbwynt, persbectif *m.*
perspiration *n.* chwys *m.*
perspire *v.* chwysu.
pester *v.* blino, poeni.
petite *a.* bychan, bechan.
petition *n.* deiseb *f.*
petrol *n.* petrol *m*: **petrol pump** pwmp petrol; **petrol station** gorsaf betrol; **unleaded petrol** petrol di-blwm.
petticoat *n.* pais *f.*
petty *a.* bach, bychan, mân, gwael.
pew *n.* sedd, sêt *f,* côr *m.*
pharmacist *n.* fferyllydd *m.*
pharmacy *n.* fferyllfa *f.*
phone 1 *n.* ffôn, teleffon *m.* **2** *v.* ffonio: **phone call** galwad ffôn.
photocopier *n.* llungopïydd, ffotogopïydd *m.*
photocopy *n.* llungopi, ffotogopi *m.*
photograph *n.* llun, ffotograff *m.*
photographer *n.* ffotograffydd *m.*
phrase 1 *n.* cymal, ymadrodd *m.* **2** *v.* geirio, mynegi.
physical *a.* corfforol, materol: **physical education** addysg gorfforol.
physics *n.* ffiseg *f.*
pianist *n.* pianydd *m.*
piano *n.* piano *mf.*
pick *v.* dewis, pigo, casglu (blodau/ffrwythau).
pick up *v.* codi.
picture *n.* darlun, llun, pictiwr *m.*
piece *n.* darn, pisyn *m,* rhan *f,* tamaid *m.*
pig *n.* mochyn *m*: **piglet** mochyn bach.
pile *n.* pentwr *m.*
pilgrim *n.* pererin *m.*
pill *n.* pilsen *f.*
pillar *n.* colofn *f,* piler *m.*
pillow *n.* clustog *f,* gobennydd *m.*
pilot *n.* peilot *m.*
pimple *n.* tosyn, ploryn *m.*
pin 1 *n.* pin *m*: **drawing pin** pin bawd. **2** *v.* pinio, hoelio.
pinch 1 *n.* pinsiad *m,* gwasgfa *f.* **2** *v.* pinsio, gwasgu.
pine *n.* ffynidwydden *f,* ffynidwydd *pl;* pinwydden *f,* pinwydd *pl*: **red pine** ffynidwydd coch.
pineapple *n.* afal pîn *m.*
pine-end *n.* talcen tŷ *m.*
pink *n.* & *a.* pinc *m.*
pint *n.* peint *m*: **pint of milk** peint o laeth.
pious *a.* duwiol, crefyddol.
pipe *n.* pib, piben, pibell *f.*
pirate *n.* môr-leidr *m.*

pit *n.* pwll *m*: **coal pit** pwll glo.
pity *n.* trueni, gresyn, piti *m*: **to take pity** trugarhau.
place 1 *n.* lle, llecyn, man *m.* **2** *v.* dodi, gosod, lleoli.
plague *n.* haint *f*, pla *m.*
plain *a.* amlwg; eglur.
plan 1 *n.* cynllun, plan *m.* **2** *v.* cynllunio.
planet *n.* planed *f.*
planner *n.* cynlluniwr, cynllunydd *m.*
planning *n.* cynllunio *m.*
plant 1 *n.* planhigyn *m;* offer *pl.* **2** *v.* plannu; gosod.
plate *n.* plât *m.*
platform *n.* llwyfan, platfform *m.*
play 1 *n.* chwarae *m,* drama *f*: **play group** grŵp chwarae **fair play** chwarae teg **playtime** amser chwarae. **2** *v.* chwarae, canu (*offeryn*).
player *n.* chwaraewr *m.*
plaything *n.* tegan *m.*
pleasant *a.* pleserus, dymunol, hyfryd, serchus, siriol; braf.
please *v.* bodloni, plesio: **if you please** os gwelwch yn dda.
pleased *a.* bodlon, hapus.
pleasurable *a.* pleserus, dymunol.
pleasure *n.* pleser, boddhad *m.*
pledge 1 *n.* addewid *mf;* ernes *f.* **2** *v.* addo.
plentiful *a.* helaeth.
plenty *n.* digonedd, digon *m.*
pliable *a.* hyblyg.
pliant *a.* ystwyth.
plot 1 *n.* cynllun; cynllwyn; darn o dir *m.* **2** *v.* cynllunio; cynllwynio.
plough *v.* aredig, troi.
plum *n.* eirinen *f.*
plumage *n.* plu *pl.*
plume 1 *n.* pluen *f*, plufyn *m.* **2** *v.* pluo, plufio.
plural *n.* lluosog *m.*
pocket 1 *n.* poced *mf*: **pocket money** arian poced. **2** *v.* pocedu.
pod *n.* plisgyn *m,* coden *f.*
poem *n.* cerdd, cân *f.*
poet *n.* bardd *m.*
poetry *n.* barddoniaeth *f.*
point 1 *n.* pwynt, blaen *m.* **2** *v.* dangos.
pointless *a.* dibwynt.
poison 1 *n.* gwenwyn *m.* **2** *v.* gwenwyno.
poisonous *a.* gwenwynig, gwenwynol.
Poland *n.* Gwlad Pwyl *f.*
pole *n.* polyn; pegwn *m*: **Pole Star** Seren y Gogledd.
police *n.* heddlu *m.*
policeman *n.* heddwas, plisman, plismon.
policewoman *n.* heddferch, pliswraig, plismones *f.*
Polish 1 *n.* Pwyleg *f.* **2** *a.* Pwylaidd.
polish 1 *n.* cwyr *m.* **2** *v.* cwyro.
political *a.* gwleidyddol, politicaidd.
politician *n.* gwleidydd *m.*
politics *n.* gwleidyddiaeth *f.*
pollute *v.* llygru.
polluted *a.* llygredig.
pollution *n.* llygredd *m.*
pond *n.* pwll, pwllyn, pownd *m.*
Pontypool *n.* Pont-y-pŵl *f.*
pony *n.* merlyn *m,* merlen *f*: **pony trekking** merlota; **pony trekker** merlotwr.
pool *n.* pwll, pwllyn *m*: **swimming pool** pwll nofio.
poor *a.* gwael, llwm, tlawd.
poorly *a.* gwael, sâl, tost.
Pope *n.* Pab *m.*
poppy *n.* pabi *f.*
popular *a* poblogaidd.
population *n.* poblogaeth *f.*
porch *n.* cyntedd, porth *m.*
porridge *n.* uwd *m.*
port *n.* porth, porthladd *m.*
portrait *n.* llun, darlun, portread *m.*
portrayal *n.* portread *m.*
pose *v.* sefyll, ymddangos, cymryd ar.
position *n.* safle *m,* sefyllfa, swydd *f.*
positive *a.* pendant, cadarnhaol.
possess *v.* meddu.
possession *n.* eiddo, meddiant *m.*
possessor *n.* perchen, perchennog *m.*
possibility *n.* posibilrwydd *m.*
possible *a.* posibl.
possibly *ad.* efallai.
post 1 *n.* post; postyn *m;* swydd *f;* **post card** cerdyn post; **postcode** côd post. **1** *v.* postio.
postal *a.* post: **postal order** archeb bost.
posthumous *a.* ar ôl marw.
postman *n.* postman, postmon *m.*
postmaster *n.* postfeistr *m.*
post office *n.* swyddfa'r post *f*, llythyrdy *m.*
postpone *v.* oedi.
postscript *n.* ôl-nodiad *m.*
potato *n.* taten *f.*
pound *n.* punt *f* (£1.00); pwys *m* (1lb); ffald *m.*

pour *v.* arllwys; bwrw.
pout *v.* pwdu.
poverty *n.* tlodi, eisiau *m.*
poverty-stricken *a.* tlawd, llwm.
powder *n.* llwch, powdr, powdwr *m.*
power *n.* gallu, nerth, pŵer, grym *m.*
powerful *a.* cryf, galluog, grymus, nerthol.
powerless *a.* dirym.
power station *n.* pwerdy.
pox *n.* brech *f*: **chicken-pox** brech yr ieir.
practical *a.* ymarferol.
practice *n.* ymarfer *f*, ymarferiad, practis *m*, arfer *mf.*
practise *v.* arfer, ymarfer.
practising *a.* ymarferol.
praise 1 *n.* canmoliaeth *f*, clod, mawl *m.* **2** *v.* canmol, clodfori, moli.
pram *n.* pram *m.*
pray *v.* gweddïo.
prayer *n.* gweddi *f.*
preach *v.* pregethu.
preacher *n.* pregethwr.
precarious *a.* ansicr, peryglus.
precious *a.* gwerthfawr, drud, prid; annwyl.
precis *n.* crynodeb *mf.*
precise *a.* manwl.
preface *n.* rhagair, rhagymadrodd *m.*
preference *n.* dewis *m*, ffafraeth, ffafriaeth *f.*
preferential *a.* ffafriol.
prefix *n.* rhagddodiad *m.*
pregnant *a.* beichiog.
prejudice 1 *n.* rhagfarn *f*; niwed *m.* **2** *v.* rhagfarnu; niweidio.
prejudiced *a.* rhagfarnllyd.
premier 1 *n.* prif weinidog *m.* **2** *a.* prif, pennaf, blaenaf.
premium *n.* gwobr *f*, tâl, taliad *m.*
preparation *n.* paratoad *m.*
prepare *v.* paratoi *m.*
prepared *a.* parod.
preposition *n.* arddodiad *m.*
prescription *n.* presgripsiwn, rysáit *m.*
presence *n.* presenoldeb, gŵydd *m.*
present 1 *n.* anrheg, rhodd *f.* **2** *v.* anrhegu, cyflwyno, dangos.
present *n.* & *a.* presennol *m*: **at present** ar hyn o bryd, yn awr, nawr, rŵan.
presently *ad.* yn y man, yn union.
preserve 1 *n.* jam *m.* **2** *v.* cadw.
preside *v.* llywyddu.
president *n.* llywydd, arlywydd *m.*
press 1 *n.* gwasg *f.* **2** *v.* gwasgu.
pressure *n.* gwasgiad, pwysedd *m.*
presumably *ad.* yn ôl pob tebyg.
presume *v.* tybio; beiddio.
pretence *n.* esgus *m.*
pretend *v.* ffugio, cymryd ar; honni.
pretext *n.* esgus *m.*
prevent *v.* atal, rhwystro (rhag).
preview *n.* rhagolwg *m.*
previous *a.* cynt; diwethaf.
price 1 *n.* pris *m*: **price list** rhestr prisoedd. **2** *v.* prisio.
prick 1 *n.* pigiad *m.* **2** *v.* pigo.
prickly *a.* pigog.
pride *n.* balchder *m.*
priest *n.* offeiriad *m.*
primary *a.* cynradd; prif: **primary education** addysg gynradd; **primary school** ysgol gynradd.
prime *a.* prif, cyntaf; gorau.
prince *n.* tywysog *m.*
princess *n.* tywysoges *f.*
principal 1 *n.* pen, prifathro *m*, prifathrawes *f.* **2 a.** prif.
principle *n.* egwyddor *f.*
print 1 *n.* argraff *f*, print, ôl *m.* **2** *a.* argraffu, printio.
printing-press *n.* gwasg argraffu.
prison *n.* carchar *m.*
prisoner *n.* carcharor *m.*
private *a.* cyfrinachol, preifat.
privilege *n.* braint *f.*
prize *n.* gwobr *f.*
probable *a.* tebyg, tebygol.
probation *n.* prawf *m*: **probation officer** swyddog prawf; **probation service** gwasanaeth prawf.
problem *n.* problem *f.*
procedure *n.* trefn *f*, arfer *mf*, dull *m.*
proceed *v.* mynd ymlaen.
proceeds *n.* enillion *pl*, elw *m.*
proclaim *v.* cyhoeddi, datgan *m.*
proclamation *n.* cyhoeddiad *m.*
prodigious *a.* anferth.
professor *n.* athro *m.*
profit 1 *n.* elw, ennill, enillion, proffid *m.* **2** *v.* elwa, ennill, manteisio.
profitable *a.* proffidiol.
profound *a.* dwfn, dwys.
programme *n.* rhaglen *f.*
project 1 *n.* bwriad, cynllun; cywaith; prosiect, project *m.* **2** *v.* bwriadu; ymestyn.
proletariat *n.* y werin *f.*
prologue *n.* rhagair, prolog *m.*
prominent *a.* amlwg.
promise 1 *n.* addewid *mf.* **2** *v.* addo.
promontory *n.* penrhyn, pentir *m.*

proneness *n.* tueddiad *m.*
pronoun *n.* rhagenw *m.*
pronounce *v.* cyhoeddi, datgan.
pronouncement *n.* cyhoeddiad, datganiad *m.*
proof *n.* prawf *m.*
proper *a.* addas, priod, priodol, rheolaidd.
property *n.* eiddo *m.*
prophesy *v.* proffwydo.
prophet *n.* proffwyd *m.*
proportional *a.* cyfrannol: **Proportional Representation** Cynrychiolaeth Gyfrannol.
proposal *n.* cynnig *m.*
propose *v.* cynnig, bwriadu.
proposition *n.* cynigiad; gosodiad *m.*
proprietor *n.* perchennog *m.*
prose *n.* rhyddiaith *f.*
prosecute *v.* erlyn.
prosecution *n.* erlyniad *m.*
prosecutor *n.* erlynydd *m.*
prospect *n.* golwg *mf,* golyfga *f,* rhagolwg *m.*
prosper *v.* llwyddo.
prosperity *n.* llwyddiant *m.*
prosperous *a.* llwyddiannus, llewyrchus.
protect *v.* amddiffyn.
protest v. gwrthdystio.
Protestant 1 *n.* Protestant *m.* 2 *a.* Protestannaidd.
proud *a.* balch.
prove *v.* profi.
proverb *n.* dihareb *f.*
province n. talaith *f;* cylch, maes *m.*
proviso *n.* amod *mf.*
provoke *v.* profocio, pryfocio, procio.
proxy *n.* dirprwy *m.*
prudent *a.* call, doeth, synhwyrol.
pry *v.* chwilota, busnesa.
psalm *n.* salm *f.*
psalter *n.* llyfr salmau *m,* sallwyr *f.*
pseudonym *n.* ffugenw *m.*
psychologist *n.* seicolegwr *m.*
psychology *n.* seicoleg *f.*
public 1 *n.* y cyhoedd *m.* 2 *a.* cyhoeddus: **public hall** neuadd gyhoeddus; **public house** tŷ tafarn; **public place** man cyhoeddus.
publican *n.* tafarnwr *m.*
publication *n.* cyhoeddiad *m.*
publicity *n.* cyhoeddusrwydd *m.*
publicly *ad.* yn gyhoeddus.
publish *v.* cyhoeddi.
publisher *n.* cyhoeddwr *m.*
pudding *n.* pwdin *m*: **Christmas pudding** pwdin Nadolig.
puddle *n.* pwllyn *m.*
pull 1 *n.* plwc *m;* tynfa *f.* 2 *v.* tynnu.
pulpit *n.* pulpud *m.*
pulse *n.* curiad *m.*
pump 1 *n.* pwmp *m.* 2 *v.* pwmpio.
punctual *a.* prydlon.
punctuality *n.* prydlondeb *m.*
puncture 1 *n.* twll *m.* 2 *v.* tyllu.
punish *v.* cosbi; poeni.
punishment *n.* cosb, cosbedigaeth *f.*
pup *n.* ci bach; cenau *m.*
pupil *n.* disgybl *m;* cannwyll llygad *f.*
puppet *n.* pyped *m.*
purchase 1 *n.* pryniant *m.* 2 *v.* prynu.
pure *a.* pur, glân, gwir.
purge *v.* puro, glanhau.
purify *v.* puro.
purple *n.* & *a.* porffor, piws *m.*
purpose *n.* bwriad, pwrpas, amcan, diben *m.*
purr *v.* canu grwndi, canu crwth; grwnan.
purse *n.* cwd, cwdyn, pwrs *m.*
pursue *v.* dilyn, erlid, erlyn, hel, hela.
pursuer *n.* erlidiwr *m.*
puffin *n.* pâl *m.*
push 1 *n.* gwthiad, hwp *m.* 2 *v.* gwthio, hwpio.
pusher *n.* gwthiwr.
put *v.* dodi, gosod, rhoddi, rhoi; mynegi.
puzzle *n.* pôs *m*: **crossword puzzle** pôs croeseiriau.
pyjamas *n.pl.* pyjamas *pl,* gwisg nos *f.*

quagmire *n.* siglen, cors *f.*
quaint *a.* od, henffasiwn.
quake *v.* crynu, ysgwyd.
Quaker *n.* Crynwr *m*: **Quakers Yard** Mynwent y Crynwyr.
qualification *n.* cymhwyster *m.*
qualified *a.* cymwys.
quality *n.* rhinwedd *mf,* ansawdd *m.*
quantity *n.* swm *m,* nifer *mf,* maint, mesur *m.*
quarrel 1 *n.* cweryl, ffrae *f.* **2** *v.* cweryla, ffraeo.
quarry *n.* chwarel *f,* cwar *m.* **quarryman** chwarelwr.
quart *n.* chwart, cwart *m.*
quarter *n.* chwarter, cwarter; cwr, man *m*: **quarter of an hour** chwarter awr.
quay *n.* cei *m*: **New Quay (Dyfed)** Ceinewydd.
queen *n.* brenhines *f.*
queer *a.* od, hynod, ysmala.
quench *v.* diffodd; torri (syched).
query 1 *n.* cwestiwn, ymholiad *m.* **2** *v.* holi, ymholi, amau.
quest *n.* ymchwil *f,* cwest *m.*
question 1 *n.* cwestiwn *m*: **question mark** gofynnod **2** *v.* cwestiyna, holi.
questioner *n.* holwr *m.*
questionnaire n. holiadur *m.*
queue 1 *n.* ciw *m;* cwt *mf.* **2** *v.* ciwio.
quick *a.* cyflym, buan, byw: **to the quick** i'r byw.
quickly *ad.* yn fuan.
quiet 1 *n.* tawelwch, llonyddwch *m.* **2** *a.* tawel, distaw, llonydd. **3** *v.* tawelu.
quietness *n.* tawelwch *m.*
quilt 1 *n.* cwilt, cwrlid *m.* **2** *v.* cwiltio.
quintet *n.* pumawd *m.*
quit *v.* gadael, symud, ymadael.
quite *ad.* hollol, llwyr, eithaf.
quiver *ad.* crynu.
quiz 1 *n.* pos, cwis *m.* **2** *v.* holi, profocio.
quotation *n.* dyfyniad *m*: **quotation marks** dyfynodau.

rabbit *n.* cwningen *f.*
race *n.* gyrfa, ras; hil *f.*
racial *a.* hiliol.
racket *n.* raced *mf.*
radio *n.* radio *m*: **radio programme** rhaglen radio; **radio station** gorsaf radio.
rag *n.* clwytyn, rhecsyn *m*: **rag doll** doli glwt *f.*
rail *n.* cledr, cledren, rheilen; canllaw *f*: **rails (of railway)** cledrau.
railway *n* rheilffordd *f*: **railway station** gorsaf reilffordd.
raiment *n.* dillad *m,* gwisg *f.*
rain 1 *n.* glaw *m.* **2** *v.* glawio, bwrw glaw.
rainbow *n.* enfys *f.*
raincoat *n.* cot law *f.*
rainy a. glawog, glawiog.
rake 1 *n.* rhaca *mf.* **2** *v.* crafu, rhacanu.
ram *n.* hwrdd, maharen *m.*
range *n.* amrediad; cwmpas; ystod *f*: **range of temperature** amrediad tymheredd: **age range** ystod oed.
rank *n.* rhes, rhestr, rheng, gradd *f.*
ransom *n.* pridwerth *m.*
rape 1 *n.* trais *m.* **2** *v.* treisio.
rapid *a.* cyflym, buan, gwyllt.
rare *a.* prin; anaml.
raspberry *n.* afanen, afansen, mafonen *f.*
rat *n.* llygoden fawr, llygoden Ffrengig *f.*
rate 1 *n.* treth *f,* tâl; cyflymder; cyfradd *m.* **2** *v.* trethu.
ratepayer *n.* trethdalwr *m.*
rather *ad.* braidd, go, lled, yn hytrach.
raw *a.* noeth, garw.
ray *n.* pelydr, pelydryn *m.*
re *prp.* ynglŷn â, mewn perthynas â.
re- *px.* ail-; eto.
reach 1 *n.* cyrraedd *m.* **2** *v.* cyrraedd, estyn, hercyd.
reaction *n.* ymateb, adwaith *m.*
read *v.* darllen.
re-address *v.* ailgyfeirio.
reader *n.* darllenwr, darllenydd; llyfr darllen *m.*
readily ad. yn barod, yn union, yn rhwydd.
reading *n.* darllen *m.*
reading-room n. ystafell ddarllen *f.*
ready *a.* parod, rhwydd.
real a. gwir, real, go-iawn.
realise v. sylweddoli; gwerthu.
reality *n.* gwirionedd, realiti *m.*
really *ad.* yn wir, mewn gwirionedd.
realm *n.* teyrnas, gwlad, bro *f.*
reap *v.* medi, cywain.
rear 1 *n.* cefn, pen ôl, y tu ôl *m.* **2** *v.* codi, magu, meithrin.
reason 1 *n.* rheswm, achos *m.* **2** *v.* rhesymu.
reasonably *a.* rhesymol.
rebellion *n.* gwrthryfel *m.*
rebuke 1 *n.* cerydd *m,* sen *f.* **2** *v.* ceryddu.
recall *v.* galw yn ôl, galw i gof, cofio.
receipt *n.* derbynneb, taleb *f.*
receive *v.* derbyn.
recent *a.* diweddar.
receptive *a.* derbyniol.
recipe *n.* rysait *f.*
recitation *n.* adroddiad *m.*
recite *v.* adrodd, datgan.
reckon *v.* cyfrif, rhifo; barnu.
recline *v.* gorwedd, gorffwys.
recluse *n.* meudwy *m.*
recognise *v.* adnabod.
recollect *v.* galw i gof, cofio.
record 1 *n.* record *f.* **2** *v.* cofnodi, recordio.
recording *n.* recordiad *m.*
re-count *v.* ailgyfrif.
recreation *n.* adloniant *m.*
rectify *v.* unioni, cywiro.
recurrence *n.* ailddigwyddiad, ail-ymddangosiad *m.*
recycle *v.* ailgylchu.
red *n.* & *a.* coch *m.*
redeem *v.* gwaredu, achub, prynu (yn ôl).
redeemer *n.* prynwr, gwaredwr *m.*
reduce *v.* gostwng.
reduction *n.* gostyngiad *m.*
redundant *a.* di-swydd.

refer *v.* cyfeirio, cyfarwyddo.
referee 1 *n.* canolwr, rheolwr *m.* 2 *v.* dyfarnu.
reference *n.* cyfeiriad; geirda *m.*
refine *v.* puro.
refinery *n.* purfa *f.*
reflect *v.* meddwl, myfyrio, ystyried.
reform 1 *n.* diwygiad *m.* 2 *v.* diwygio, gwella.
reformation *n.* diwygiad *m*: **Protestant Reformation** Diwygiad Protestannaidd.
refresh *v.* adfywio.
refrigerator *n.* oergell *f.*
refuge *n.* lloches, noddfa *f.*
refugee *n.* ffoadur *m.*
refuse *n.* ysbwriel, sothach *m;* **refuse bin** bin ysbwriel.
refuse *v.* gwrthod, pallu.
region *n.* ardal, cylch; rhanbarth *f;* rhandir *m.*
register 1 *n.* cofrestr *f.* 2 *v.* cofrestru.
registrar *n.* cofrestrydd *m.*
regular *a.* rheolaidd, cyson.
rehearsal *n.* rihyrsal, practis *m.*
reimburse *v.* talu yn ôl, ad-dalu.
rejoice *v.* llawenhau.
rejoicing *n.* llawenydd *m.*
relate *v.* adrodd, mynegi; perthyn.
related *a.* yn perthyn; wedi ei ddweud.
relating to *prp.* yn ymwneud â.
relation *n.* perthynas *mf.*
relationship *n.* perthynas *mf.*
relative 1 *n.* perthynas *mf;* 2 *a.* perthynol; cymharol: **relative pronoun** rhagenw perthynol.
relax *v.* llacio, llaesu, ymlacio.
release *v.* gollwng, rhyddhau.
relevant *a.* perthnasol.
religion *n.* crefydd *f.*
religious *a.* crefyddol.
relish 1 *n.* blas *m.* 2 *v.* blasu, hoffi, mwynhau.
rely *v.* dibynnu (ar).
remain *v.* aros, bod ar ôl.
remainder *n.* gweddill *m.*
remains *n.* olion, gweddillion *pl.*
remark 1 *n.* sylw *m.* 2 *v.* sylwi, dweud.
remarkable *a.* hynod, nodedig; rhyfedd, od.
remedy 1 *n.* meddyginiaeth *f.* 2 *v.* gwella.
remember *v.* cofio.
remembrance *n.* cof, coffa *m.*
remind *v.* atgoffa, atgofio, cofio.
remiss *a.* esgeulus, diofal.
remnant *n.* gweddill *m.*
remote *a.* pell, diarffordd, anghysbell.
remotely *ad.* o bell.
removal *n.* symudiad *m.*
remove *v.* symud.
remunerate *v.* talu, gwobrwyo; cydnabod.
rendering *n.* datganiad; trosiad *m.*
rendezvous *n.* man cyfarfod *m.*
renowned *a.* enwog, adnabyddus.
repairer *n.* trwsiwr, cyweiriwr *m.*
repeat *v.* ailadrodd.
reply 1 *n.* ateb, atebiad *m.* 2 *v.* ateb.
report 1 *n.* adroddiad; sŵn ergyd *m.* 2 *v.* adrodd.
reporter *n.* gohebydd *m.*
representation *n.* cynrychiolaeth *f*: **Proportional Representation** Cynrychiolaeth Gyfrannol.
republic *n.* gweriniaeth *f.*
reputed *a.* honedig.
request 1 *n.* cais, dymuniad *m,* arch *f.* 2 *v.* ceisio, dymuno.
require *v.* ceisio, gofyn.
requirements *n.* gofynion *pl.*
rescue *v.* achub.
research *n.* ymchwil *f*: **research work** gwaith ymchwil. 2 *v.* ymchwilio.
researcher *n.* chwilotwr *m.*
resemblance *n.* tebygrwydd *m.*
reserve *v.* neilltuo, cadw wrth gefn.
reserved *a.* swil; wedi ei gadw; **reserved seats** seddau cadw.
reservoir *n.* cronfa *f.*
reside *v.* trigo, byw, preswylio.
resident *n.* preswylydd *m.*
residential *a.* preswyl: **residential school** ysgol breswyl.
residue *n.* gweddill *m.*
resign *v.* ymddiswyddo.
resignation *n.* ymddiswyddiad *m.*
resist *v.* gwrthwynebu, gwrthsefyll.
resolute *a.* penderfynol.
resolution *n.* penderfyniad *m.*
resolve 1 *n.* penderfyniad *m.* 2 *v.* penderfynu.
resources *n.* adnoddau *pl.*
respect 1 *n.* parch *m.* 2 *v.* parchu.
respectable *a.* parchus.
respectful *a.* boneddigaidd.
respectfully *ad.* yn barchus.
respiration *n.* anadliad *m.*
respire *v.* anadlu.
respite *n.* egwyl *f,* seibiant *m,* hoe *f.*
respond *v.* ateb, ymateb.
response *n.* ateb, atebiad *m.*
responsibility *n.* cyfrifoldeb *m.*
responsible *a.* cyfrifol.

rest 1 *n.* gorffwys, saib *m,* hoe *f.* 2 *v.* gorffwyso, pwyso.
restaurant *n.* tŷ bwyta *m.*
restless *a.* rhwyfus, aflonydd.
restore *v.* adfer.
restrict *v.* cyfyngu.
result *n.* canlyniad, ateb *m.*
retain *v.* cadw, dal; llogi.
retard *v.* arafu.
retire *v.* ymddeol.
retired *a.* wedi ymddeol.
retirement *n.* ymddeoliad *m.*
retiring *a.* swil.
returns *n.* enillion *pl.*
reveal *v.* datguddio, dangos, egluro.
revenge *n.* & *v.* dial *m.*
reverend *a.* parchedig: **Rev. Ifan Puw** Parchg. Ifan Puw.
revise *v.* diwygio, cywiro.
revival *n.* diwygiad *m.*
revive *v.* adfer.
revolution *n.* chwyldro, chwyldroad *m.*
revolve *v.*troi.
reward 1 *n.* gwobr *f,* tâl *m.* 2 *v.* gwobrwyo.
rheumatism *n.* gwynegon, cryd cymalau *m.*
rhyme 1 *n.* odl *f;* rhigwm *m.* 2 *v.* odli; rhigymu.
ribbon *n.* ruban *m.*
rice *n.* reis *m.*
rich *a.* cyfoethog, bras, ffrwythlon.
riches *n.* cyfoeth, golud *pl.*
rickety *a.* simsan, sigledig.
rid *v.* gwaredu, cael gwared o.
riddle *n.* pôs *m.*
ridge *n.* crib *mf,* cefn *m.*
rifle *n.* dryll, reiffl *m.*
right 1 *n.* hawl, iawn *m,* braint *f.* 2 *a.* iawn, cywir; de; 3 *ad.* yn gywir, yn iawn: **right angle** ongl sgwâr; **right hand** llaw dde.
righteous *a.* cyfiawn.
righteousness *n.* cyfiawnder *m.*
rim *n.* ymyl *mf.*
ring 1 *n.* cylch *m;* modrwy *f;* caniad *(ffôn) m*: **wedding ring** modrwy briodas. 2 *v.* canu cloch.
rinse *v.* golchi.
riot *n.* terfysg *m.*
rip *v.* rhwygo.
ripe *a.* aeddfed.
rise 1 *n.* codiad *m.* 2 *v.* codi.
river *n.* afon *f*: **River Severn** Afon Hafren; **River Tawe** Afon Tawe; **River Wye** Afon Gwy.
road *n.* ffordd, heol, hewl *f*: **main road** ffordd fawr, heol fawr; **narrow road** ffordd gul, heol gul; **straight road** heol syth; **winding road** heol droellog; **by-pass** ffordd osgoi.
roar *v.* rhuo.
roast 1 *n.* rhost: **roast potatoes** tatws rhost. 2 *v.* rhostio.
rob *v.* lladrata, dwyn, dwgyd.
robber *n.* lleidr *m.*
robbery *n.* lladrad *m.*
robe *n.* gwisg, gŵn *f.*
robin *n.* robin goch *m.*
rock 1 *n.* craig *f;* roc *m.* 2 *v.* siglo.
rocky *a.* creigiog.
rôle *n.* rhan, rôl *f.*
roll 1 *n.* rhôl, rhestr *f.* 2 *v.* rholio, treiglo.
Roman 1 *n.* Rhufeiniwr *m.* 2 *v.* Rhufeinig.
Roman Catholic Pabydd.
romantic *a.* rhamantus, rhamantaidd.
Rome *n.* Rhufain *f.*
roof *n.* to *m,* nen *f.*
room *n.* lle *m,* ystafell, stafell *f.*
rooster *n.* ceiliog *m.*
root *n.* gwreiddyn *m.*
rope 1 *n.* rhaff *f.* 2 *v.* rhaffu, rhwymo.
rose *n.* rhosyn *m.*
rosy-cheeked *a.* gwridog.
rot *v.* pydru.
rotten *a.* pwdr, drwg, sâl.
rough *a.* garw, bras.
roundabout 1 *n.* cylchfan *f,* trogylch *m.* 2 *a.* o amgylch.
route *n.* llwybr *m,* taith, ffordd *f.*
row 1 *n.* rhes, rhes[illegible] *f.* 2 *v.* rhwyfo; **rowing boat** cwch rhwyfo.
row *n.* ffrae *f,* terfysg *m.*
royal *a.* brenhinol.
rub *v.* rhwbio.
rubber *n.* rwber *m.*
rubbish *n.* ysbwriel, sothach *coll,* lol *f*: **rubbish bin** bin ysbwriel.
rudder *n.* llyw *m.*
ruddy *a.* coch, gwridog.
rude *a.* anfoesgar, haerllug.
rudiment *n.* egwyddor, gwyddor, elfen *f.*
rudimentary *a.* elfennol.
rugby *n.* rygbi *m*: **rugby ball** pêl rygbi; **rugby match** gêm rygbi.
rugged *a.* garw.
ruin 1 *n.* dinistr *m;* adfail *mf.* 2 *v.* dinistrio, difetha.
rule 1 *n.* llywodraeth; rheol *f;* arfer *mf;* riwl, riwler *m.* 2 *v.* llywodraethu, rheoli.
ruler *n.* llywodrodaethwr, llyw,

rheolwr; riwl, riwler *m.*
ruling *n.* dyfarniad *m.*
rummage *v.* chwilota.
rummager *n.* chwilotwr *m.*
rumour *n.* & *v.* si, su *m,* sôn *mf,* chwedl *f.*
run 1 *n.* rhediad *m.* **2** *v.* rhedeg, rheoli.
runaway *n.* ffoadur *m.*
runner *n.* rhedwr *m.*
running *n.* rhediad *m.*
rural *a.* gwledig.
rush 1 *n.* rhuthr *m.* **2** *v.* rhuthro.
Russia *n.* Rwsia *f.*
Russian 1 *n.* Rwsiad *m* (*person*); Rwsieg *f* (*iaith*). **2** *a.* Rwsiaidd.

Sabbath *n.* Sabath, Saboth *m.*
sack *n.* cwd, cwdyn *m,* sach *f.*
sacred *a.* sanctaidd, glân.
sacrifice 1 *n.* aberth *mf.* 2 *v.* aberthu.
sad *a.* trist, blin, truenus, trwm, prudd.
sadly *ad.* yn drist, yn flin, yn brudd.
sadness *n.* tristwch, trymder *m.*
safe 1 *n.* cist, cell *f.* 2 *a.* diogel, saff.
sail 1 *n.* hwyl *f.* 2 *v.* hwylio, morio.
sailing *n.* hwylio *m*: **sailing boat** llong hwylio.
sailor *n.* llongwr, morwr *m.*
saint *n.* sant *m;* santes *f*: **Saint David** Dewi Sant; **Saint John** Sant Ioan; **Saint Mary** y Santes Fair; **Saint David's** Tyddewi.
sake *n.* mwyn *m*: **for the sake of** er mwyn.
salary *n.* cyflog *mf.*
sale *n.* gwerthiant *m;* sâl, sêl *f,* arwerthiant *m*: **For Sale** Ar Werth.
salesman *n.* gwerthwr *m.*
saliva *n.* poer, poeri *m.*
salt 1 *n.* halen *m*: **salt cellar** llestr halen. 2 *a.* hallt; **salt water** dŵr hallt; dŵr y môr. 3 *v.* halltu.
salty *a.* hallt.
salvation *n.* iachawdwriaeth *f*: **Salvation Army** Byddin yr Iachawdwriaeth.
same *a.* yr un, yr unrhyw, yr un fath.
sand *n.* tywod *m*: **sand castles** cestyll tywod.
sandwich 1 *n.* brechdan *f.* 2 *v.* gwthio rhwng.
Santa Claus *n.* Siôn Corn *m.*
sap 1 *n.* sudd 2 *v.* sugno; tanseilio.
satellite *n.* lloeren *f.*
satisfaction *n.* boddhad *m.*
satisfy *v.* bodloni.
Saturday *n.* dydd Sadwrn *m.*
Saturn *n.* Sadwrn *m.*
sauce *n.* saws *m.*
saucepan *n.* sosban *f*: **small saucepan** sosban fach; **big saucepan** sosban fawr.
saucer *n.* soser *f.*
savage 1 *n.* dyn gwyllt *m.* 2 *a.* ffyrnig, gwyllt.
save 1 *v.* achub, arbed, gwaredu; cynilo. 2 *prp.* & *c.* ond.
savings *n.* cynilion *pl.*
saviour *n.* gwaredwr, iachawdwr *m.*
savory *a.* blasus.
saw 1 *n.* llif *f*: **sawdust** blawd llif; **hand-saw** llawlif. 2 *v.* llifio.
say *v.* dweud (wrth): **to tell someone to —** dweud wrth rywun am —.
saying *n.* dywediad, ymadrodd *m.*
scale *n.* graddfa; clorian, tafol *f*: **Celsius scale** graddfa Celsius.
scales *n.* clorian, tafol *f.*
scarce *a.* prin, anaml.
scarcely *ad.* braidd, prin, o'r braidd.
scarcity *n.* prinder *m.*
scare 1 *n.* braw, ofn *m.* 2 *v.* ofni, dychryn.
scarf *n.* sgarff *f.*
scatter *v.* chwalu.
scene *n.* lle, man *m.* golgygfa *f.*
scenery *n.* golygfa *f.*
scent 1 *n.* arogl, aroglau: gwynt; trywydd *m.* 2 *v.* arogli; gwynto; sawru.
scheme 1 *n.* cynllun *m.* 2 *v.* cynllunio.
scholar *n.* ysgolhaig, ysgolor *m.*
scholarship *n.* ysgoloriaeth *f.*
school *n.* ysgol *f*: **bilingual school** ysgol ddwyieithog; **local school** ysgol leol; **night school** ysgol nos; **summer school** ysgol haf; **Welsh school** ysgol Gymraeg; **primary school** ysgol gynradd; **comprehensive school** ysgol gyfun.
schoolboy *n.* bachgen ysgol *m.*
schooldays *n.* dyddiau ysgol *pl.*
schoolgirl *n.* merch ysgol *f.*
schoolhouse *n.* tŷ ysgol *m.*
schoolmaster *n.* athro ysgol, ysgolfeistr *m.*
schoolmistress *n.* athrawes, ysgolfeistres *f.*
science *n.* gwyddoniaeth, gwyddor *f.*

scientific *a.* gwyddonol.
scientist *n.* gwyddonydd *m.*
scissors *n.* siswrn *m.*
scorch *v.* crasu; rhuddo.
scorched *a.* cras.
score 1 *n.* sgôr; ugain *m.* 2 *v.* sgorio.
scorn 1 *n.* gwawd *m.* 2 *v.* gwawdio.
Scotland *n.* Yr Alban *f.*
scowl 1 *n.* gwg *m.* 2 *v.* gwgu.
scratch 1 *n.* crafiad *m.* 2 *v.* crafu.
scream1 *n.* sgrech, ysgrech *f.* 2 *v.* sgrechian, sgrechain.
screw 1 *n.* sgriw *f.* 2 *v.* sgriwio.
script *n.* sgript *f.*
scripture *n.* ysgrythur *f,* y Beibl *m.*
scrum 1 *n.* sgrym *f.* 2 *v.* sgrymio.
scrum-half *n.* mewnwr *m.*
sea *n.* môr *m*: **sea level** lefel y môr; **sea water** dŵr y môr.
seagull *n.* gwylan *f.*
seal *n.* morlo *m;* sêl *f.*
seaman *n.* morwr, llongwr *m.*
sea-marsh *n.* morfa *m.*
seamstress *n.* gwniadyddes, gwniyddes *f.*
search 1 *n.* ymchwil *f.* 2 *v.* chwilio, edrych, ymchwilio.
searcher *n.* chwiliwr *m.*
seashore *n.* glan y môr *f.*
seasickness *n.* salwch (y) môr. *m.*
season *n.* adeg *f,* amser, pryd, tymor *m*: **season ticket** tocyn tymor.
seat 1 *n.* sedd, sêt *f.* 2 *v.* eistedd.
seaweed *n.* gwymon *m.*
second 1 *n.* ail *m;* eiliad *f.* 2 *a.* ail: **second class** ail ddosbarth; isradd; **second-hand** ail-law.
secret 1 *n.* cyfrinach *f.* 2 *a.* cyfrinachol.
secretary *n.* ysgrifennydd *m,* ysgrifenyddes *f.* **Secretary of State** Ysgrifennydd Gwladol.
section *n.* adran, rhan *f.*
secure 1 *a.* diogel, sicr, siŵr. 2 *v.* sicrhau.
security *n.* sicrwydd, diogelwch; ernes: **Social Security** Nawdd Cymdeithasol.
sediment *n.* gwaelodion, gwaddod *m.*
see 1 *n.* esgobaeth *f.* 2 *v.* gweld, gweled.
seed 1 *n.* had *coll,* hadyn, hedyn *m.* 2 *v.* hadu.
seek *v.* ceisio, chwilio.
seem *v.* ymddangos.
seemly *a.* addas.
seething *n.* & *a.* berw *m.*
seize *v.* gafael, dal: **to seize the opportunity** achub y cyfle.
seldom *ad.* anaml.
select *a.* & *v.* dewis, dethol.
selection *n.* detholiad *m.*
self *pn.* & *n.* hun, hunan *m.*
selfish *a.* hunanol.
self-respect *n.* hunan-barch *m.*
sell *v.* gwerthu.
seller *n.* gwerthwr.
semi- *px.* hanner-, go-, lled-.
semicircle *n.* hanner cylch *m.*
semi-final *a.* cynderfynol.
senate *n.* senedd *f.*
send *v.* anfon, danfon, gyrru, hala.
sender *n.* gyrrwr *m.*
senile *a.* oedrannus, hen.
senility *n.* henaint.
senior *a.* hŷn, uwch, uchaf.
sense 1 *n.* synnwyr, pwyll *m,* ystyr *mf.* 2 *v.* synhwyro.
sensible *a.* synhwyrol, call.
sentence 1 *n.* brawddeg; barn *f.* 2 *v.* dedfrydu.
sentry *n.* gwyliwr *m.*
separate *a.* ar wahân.
separately *ad.* ar wahân.
separation *n.* gwahaniad *m.*
September *n.* Medi *m.*
serenity *n.* tawelwch, hedd, heddwch *m.*
serial 1 *n.* cyfres *f.* 2 *a.* cyfresol.
series *n.* cyfres, rhes *f.*
serious *a.* difrifol, prudd, prysur.
seriously *ad.* yn ddifrifol.
sermon *n.* pregeth *f.*
serpent *n.* sarff *f.*
servant *n.* gwas *m,* morwyn *f*: **civil servant** gwas sifil.
serve *v.* gwasanaethu.
service *n.* gwasanaeth *m;* oedfa *f.*
set 1 *n.* set; *f.* 2 *v.* trefnu, gosod, dodi.
setting *n.* machlud; lleoliad *m.*
settle 1 *n.* sgiw, setl *f.* 2 *v.* sefydlu; penderfynu; talu, cytuno, setlo.
settled *a.* sefydlog.
settlement *n.* gwladfa *f.*
seven *n.* & *a.* saith *m.*
seventeen *n.* & *a.* dau ar bymtheg, un deg saith *m.*
seventh *n.* & *a.* seithfed *m.*
seventy *n.* & *a.* deg a thrigain, saith deg *m.*
sever *v.* torri.
several *a.* amryw.
severe *a.* caled, llym, hallt, tost.
severity *n.* caledi *m.*
Severn *n.* Afon Hafren *f.*

sew *v.* gwnïo, pwytho.
sewing machine *n.* periant gwnïo.
sex *n.* rhyw *m.*
sexual *a.* rhywiol.
shade 1 *n.* cysgod *m.* 2 *v.* cysgodi.
shadow *n.* cysgod *m.*
shady *a.* cysgodol.
shake *v.* ysgwyd, siglo, crynu.
shaking *n.* ysgytwad *m.*
shaky *a.* sigledig.
shallow *a.* bas.
sham *a.* ffug, gau.
shape 1 *n.* ffurf *f,* llun *m,* siâp *f.* 2 *v.* ffurfio, llunio.
shapely *a.* lluniaidd.
share 1 *n.* rhan, siâr *f.* 2 *v.* rhannu.
sharp *a.* llym, miniog, siarp.
shawl *n.* siôl *f.*
she *pn.* hi, hithau, hyhi.
shed *n.* sied, cwts *m.*
sheep 1 *n.* dafad *f.* 2 *n.* defaid *pl.*
sheer *a.* pur; glân; noeth.
sheet *n.* llen *f,* lliain *m;* dalen *f,* taflen *f.*
shelf *n.* silff *f.*
shell *n.* cragen *f;* plisgyn *m.*
shelter 1 *n.* cysgod *m,* lloches *f.* 2 *v.* cysgodi, llochesu.
shepherd 1 *n.* bugail *m.* 2 *v.* bugeilio.
shield 1 *n.* tarian *f.* 2 *v.* cysgodi; amddiffyn.
shift 1 *n.* newid, symudiad; tro *m;* shifft *f.* 2 *v.* newid, symud.
shine *v.* disgleirio, llewyrchu.
shiny *a.* gloyw, disglair.
ship *n.* llong *f.*
shipshape *a.* taclus, trefnus, twt.
shire *n.* sir (Wales), swydd (England) *f*: **Pembrokeshire** Sir Benfro (Cymru); **Gloucestershire** Swydd Gaerloyw (Lloegr).
shirk *v.* osgoi.
shirt *n.* crys *m.*
shiver *v.* crynu.
shivering *n.* cryd *m.*
shoal *n.* haig *f.*
shock *n.* ysgytwad, sioc *m.*
shoe *n.* esgid *f*: **pair of shoes** pâr o esgidiau.
shoot 1 *n.* eginyn *m.* 2 *v.* saethu.
shooter *n.* saethwr *m.*
shooting *n.* saethu.
shop 1 *n.* siop *f.* 2 *v.* siopa.
shopkeeper *n.* siopwr *m.*
shopper *n.* prynwr *m.*
shopping *n.* siopa *m.*
shore *n.* glan *f,* traeth *f.*
short *a.* byr, cwta, prin.
shot *n.* ergyd *mf.*
shoulder *n.* ysgwydd *f.*
shout 1 *n.* bloedd *m,* gwaedd *f.* 2 *v.* bloeddio, crio, gweiddi.
shove 1 *n.* hwp *m.* 2 *v.* gwthio.
shovel *n.* rhaw *f.*
show 1 *n.* sioe *f.* 2 *v.* dangos, arddangos.
shower *n.* cawod *f.*
shriek 1 *n.* sgrech, ysgrech *f.* 2 *v.* sgrechian, sgrechain.
shrill *a.* main, llym.
shut *v.* cau.
shy *a.* swil.
sick 1 *n.pl.* cleifion *m.* 2 *a.* claf, gwael, sâl, tost.
sickness *n.* afiechyd, clefyd, dolur, anhwyldeb, anhwylder, tostrwydd *m.*
side 1 *n.* ochr *f,* ymyl, ystylys; tu *mf,* plaid *f.* 2 *v.* ochri.
sidesman *n.* ystlyswr *m.*
sideways *ad.* tua'r ochr.
sigh 1 *n* ochenaid *f.* 2 *v.* ochneidio.
sight 1 *n.* golwg *mf,* golygfa *f.* 2 *v.* gweld, gweled.
sign *1 n.* arwydd *m.* 2 *v.* arwyddo, llofnodi.
signal *n.* arwydd *m.*
signature *n.* llofnod *m.*
silage *n.* silwair *m.*
silence 1 *n.* distarwydd, tawelwch *m.* 2 *v.* distewi.
silencer *n.* tawelydd *m.*
silent *a.* distaw, tawel.
silk *n.* sidan *m.*
silly *a.* ffôl, dwl, twp.
silver *n.* arian *m*: **silversmith** gof arian; **silver wedding** priodas arian.
similar *a.* tebyg.
similarity *n.* tebygrwydd *m.*
simple *a.* syml; diniwed.
sin 1 *n.* pechod *m.* 2 *v.* pechu.
since 1 *c.* am, gan, oherwydd. 2 *prp.* er, ers, er pan.
sincere *a.* diffuant, cywir, pur.
sinew *n.* gewyn *m.*
sing *v.* canu.
singer *n.* canwr, cantwr, cantor *m;* cantores *f.*
singing *n.* caniad, caniadaeth *f,* canu *m.*
single *a.* sengl, un; dibriod.
singular *a.* unigol; hynod.
sink 1 *n.* sinc *m.* 2 *v.* suddo.
sinner *n.* pechadur *m.*
sir *n.* syr *m.*

sister *n.* chwaer *f.*
sister-in-law *n.* chwaer-yng-nghyfraith *f.*
sit *v.* eistedd.
situation *n.* lle, safle *m;* sefyllfa *f.*
six *n.* & *a.* chwe, chwech *m.*
sixteen *n.* & *a.* un ar bymtheg, un deg chwech *m.*
sixth *n.* & *a.* chweched *m.*
sixty *n.* & *a.* trigain, chwe deg *m.*
size *n.* maint *m.*
skate 1 *n.* sgêt *f.* 2 *v.* sglefrio: **skateboard** bwrdd sglefrio.
sketch 1 *n.* llun, braslun *m;* sgets *f.* 2 *v.* braslunio.
ski 1 *n.* sgi *f.* 2 *v.* sgïo.
skier *n.* sgîwr *m.*
skilful *a.* medrus.
skill *n.* sgil *m,* crefft *f.*
skim *v.* tynnu, codi (hufen).
skimmed milk *n.* llaeth glas *m.*
skin 1 *n.* croen *m.* 2 *v.* blingo.
skip *v.* sgipio.
skirt *n.* sgert, sgyrt *f.*
sky *n.* wybren, awyr, ffurfafen, nen *f.*
skylark *n.* ehedydd, uchedydd, hedydd *m.*
slack 1 *n.* glo mân *m.* 2 *a.* llac, diofal, esgeulus.
slacken *v.* llacio, llaesu.
slate *n.* llechen *n.*
slaughter *v.* lladd.
slaughterhouse *n.* lladd-dy *m.*
slave *n.* caethwas *m.*
slay *v.* lladd.
sleek *a.* llyfn.
sleep 1 *n.* cwsg *m.* 2 *v.* cysgu huno; **sleeping bag** sach gysgu.
sleepy *a.* cysglyd.
sleet *n.* eirlaw *m.*
sleeve *n.* llawes *f.*
slender *a.* main, tenau.
slice *n.* tafell, sleisen: **slice of bread and butter** tafell o fara menyn; **slice of bacon** sleisen o gig moch.
slide 1 *n.* llithren *f.* 2 *v.* llithro, sglefrio.
slim *a.* main.
slip 1 *n.* llithriad *m.* 2 *v.* llithro dros.
slipper *n.* sliper *f.*
slippery *a.* llithrig, slic.
slipshod *a.* anniben.
slovenly *a.* anniben.
slope *n.* rhiw *f,* tyle, llethr *m.*
slow 1 *a.* araf. 2 *v.* arafu.
slug *n.* malwoden *f,* slyg *m.*
sluggard *n.* diogyn, pwdryn *m.*
sluggish *a.* diog, dioglyd.
slumber 1 *n.* cwsg *m.* 2 *v.* cysgu.
slur 1 *n.* llithriad *m.* 2 *v.* llithro dros.
sly *a.* cyfrwys.
small *a.* bach, mân, bychan, bechan *f.*
smallest *a.* lleiaf; *see* bach.
smallholder *n.* tyddynnwr *m.*
smallholding *n.* tyddyn *m.*
smash *v.* malu.
smell 1 *n.* arogl *m,* aroglau *pl,* gwynt *m.* 2 *v.* arogli, clywed arogl, gwynto.
smile 1 *n.* gwên *f.* 2 *v.* gwenu.
smith *n.* gof *m*: **smithy** gefail.
smoke 1 *n.* mwg *m.* 2 *v.* mygu, ysmygu.
smoky *a.* myglyd.
smooth *a.* llyfn; esmwyth.
smother *v.* mogi, mygu.
snack *n.* byrbryd *m.*
snag *n.* rhwystr.
snail *n.* malwoden *f.*
snake *n.* neidr *f.*
snarl *v.* chwyrnu.
sneeze *v.* tisian.
snobs *n.pl.* crachach.
snore *v.* chwyrnu.
snout *n.* trwyn *m.*
snow *n.* eira *m.*
snowball pelen eira:
snowdrift lluwch, lluwchfa, lluchfa;
snowflake pluen eira.
Snowdon *n.* Yr Wyddfa *f.*
Snowdonia *n.* Eryri *f.*
snowdrop *n.* eirlys, tlws yr eira, lili wen fach *m.*
snub *n.* sen *f.*
so *ad.* & *c.* fel, felly, mor.
soap *n.* sebon *m*: **soap powder** powdr golchi.
soccer *n.* pêl-droed *f.*
socialism *n.* sosialaeth *f.*
socialist 1 *n.* sosialydd *m.* 2 *a.* sosialaidd.
society *n.* cymdeithas *f.*
sociology *n.* cymdeithaseg *f.*
sock *n.* hosan *f.*
soft *a.* meddal: **soft drinks** diodydd ysgafn.
soften *v.* meddalu.
soil 1 *n.* pridd *m;* daear *f.* 2 *v.* trochi, sarnu.
soldier *n.* milwr *m.*
sole 1 *n.* gwadn *m.* 2 *a.* unig, unigol, un.
solemn *a.* difrifol, dwys.
solicitor *n.* cyfreithiwr *m.*
solo 1 *n.* unawd *m.* 2 *a.* unigol.
soloist *n.* unawdwr, unawdydd *m.*
solve *v.* datrys, datod.

some 1 *a.* rhyw, rhai, peth, ychydig. 2 *pn.* rhai, rhywrai, rhywfaint. 3 *ad.* rhyw, tua, ynghylch.
somebody *n.* & *pn.* rhywun *m.*
someone *n.* & *pn.* rhywun *m.*
Somerset *n.* Glwad yr Haf *f.*
something *n.* rhywbeth *m.*
sometime *ad.* rhywbryd, rhywdro, gynt.
sometimes *ad.* weithiau, ambell waith, ar brydiau.
somewhat *ad.* go, lled, braidd.
somewhere *ad.* rhywle.
son *n.* mab *m.*
son-in-law *n.* mab-yng-nghyfraith *m.*
soon *ad.* yn fuan, ar fyr o dro.
sooner *ad.* yn gynt.
soot *n.* huddygl *m.*
sore *a.* blin, tost.
sorrow 1 *n.* gofid, tristwch, galar *m.* 2 *v.* gofidio, hiraethu.
sorrowful *a.* trist.
sorry *a.* blin, drwg gan, edifar, trist.
sort 1 *n.* math, modd, dosbarth *m.* 2 *v.* dosbarthu, trefnu.
soul *n.* enaid *m.*
sound 1 *n.* sain *f,* sŵn *m.* 2 *a.* iach; cyfan. 3 *v.* swnio, seinio.
soup *n.* cawl *m.*
sour 1 *a.* sur. 2 *v.* suro.
source *n.* ffynhonnell *f,* tarddiad *m.*
south 1 *n.* & *a.* de *mf,* deau *m*: **South Wales** De Cymru. 2 *ad.* tua'r de.
southern *a.* deheuol.
sow *n.* hwch *f.*
sow *v.* hau.
sower *n.* heuwr *m.*
space *n.* gofod, gwagle, bwlch *m.*
spaceman *n.* gofodwr *m.*
spaceship *n.* llong ofod *f.*
spade *n.* pâl, rhaw *f.*
Spain *n.* Sbaen *f.*
Spanish 1 *n.* Sbaeneg *f. (iaith).* 2 *a.* Sbaenaidd.
spare 1 *a.* sbâr. 2 *v.* arbed.
spark *n.* gwreichionen *f.*
speak *v.* llefaru, siarad.
speaker *n.* llefarwr, llefarydd, siaradwr *m.*
special *a.* arbennig, neilltuol.
species *n.* math *m.*
specified *a.* nodedig.
specify *v.* enwi.
spectacle *n.* golygfa *f.*
spectacles *n.* sbectol *pl.*
speech *n.* araith *f;* llafar *m,* ymadrodd *m.*
speechless *a.* mud.
speed *n.* cyflymder *m.*
speedy *a.* buan, cyflym.
spell 1 *n.* egwyl, hoe, sbel *f;* hud, swyn *m.* 2 *v.* cael hoe; sillafu: **to cast a spell** swyno.
spend v. gwario, hala *(arian);* treulio *(amser).*
spider *n.* corryn, pryf copyn *m.*
spill *v.* colli.
spine *n.* asgwrn cefn *m.*
spirit *n.* ysbryd *m.*
spirited *a.* ysbrydol, nwyfus.
spiritual *a.* ysbrydol.
spiritualise *v.* ysbrydoli.
spit *n.* & *v.* poeri *m.*
spittle *n.* poer, poeri *m.*
splash *v.* tasgu.
splendid *a.* rhagorol, ardderchog, penigamp, campus, gwych.
splendour *n.* ysblander *m.*
spokesman *n.* llefarwr, llefarydd *m.*
spoon 1 *n.* llwy *f.* 2 *v.* llwyo.
sport *n.* sbort *f,* chwarae *m,* hwyl *f.*
sports *n.* mabolgampau *pl,* chwaraeon.
spot 1 *n.* man *mf,* lle, llecyn, sbot, sbotyn, smotyn *m.* 2 *v.* adnabod; smotio.
spread *v.* lledu.
spring 1 *n.* ffynnon, ffynhonnell; sbring; gwanwyn; neidio *f.* 2 *v.* tarddu; neidio.
sprout *n.* eginyn *m,* egin *pl*: **Brussels sprouts** ysgewyll Brwsel.
spur *n.* ysbardun; clogwyn *m.*
sputnik *n.* lloeren *f.*
spy 1 *n.* ysbïwr *m.* 2 *v.* ysbïo.
square *n.* sgwâr *f.*
squash 1 *n.* sboncen *f.* 2 *v.* gwasgu.
squirrel *n.* gwiwer *f.*
stable 1 *n.* stabl *f.* 2 *a.* sefydlog, diogel.
staff *n.* ffon; staff *f.*
stag *n.* hydd *f.*
stage 1 *n.* llwyfan *m;* lefel *f.* 2 *v.* llwyfannu.
stair *n.* gris *m,* staer *f.*
stall *n.* stondin *f;* côr *m.*
stamp 1 *n.* stamp *m.* 2 *v.* stampio.
stand 1 *n.* stondin *f.* 2 *v.* sefyll.
standard 1 *n.* safon; baner *f.* 2 *a.* safonol.
standpoint *n.* safbwynt *m.*
stanza *n.* pennill *m.*
star 1 *n.* seren *f.* 2 *v.* serennu.
starlight *n.* golau'r sêr.
starling *n.* drudwy *m.*
starry *a.* serennog.

start *n.* & *v.* cychwyn, dechrau *m.*
starve *v.* llwgu.
state 1 *n.* cyflwr *m,* ffurf; talaith *f.* 2 *v.* mynegi, dweud.
statesman *n.* gwleidydd *m.*
station *n.* gorsaf *f;* safle *m,* sefyllfa *f:* **railway station** gorsaf reilffordd.
stationary *a.* sefydlog.
stationer *n.* gwerthwr papurau *m.*
stationery *n.* papur ysgrifennu *m.*
statistics *n.pl.* ystadegau.
statue *n.* cerflun *m,* delw *f.*
statute *n.* deddf, cyfraith, act *f.*
stay 1 *n.* arhosiad *m.* 2 *v.* aros, oedi, sefyll.
steal *v.* lladrata, dwyn.
steel *n.* dur *m.*
steep *a.* serth.
steer *v.* llywio; cyfeirio.
stench *n.* drewdod, drewi *m.*
step 1 *n.* cam, gris 2 *v.* camu.
step- *px.* llys-.
stepdaughter *n.* llysferch *f.*
stepfather *n.* llystad *m.*
stepmother *n.* llysfam *f.*
stepsister *n.* llyschwaer *f.*
stepson *n.* llysfab *f.*
steward 1 *n.* stiward *m.* 2 *v.* stiwardio.
stick 1 *n.* ffon, gwialen *f,* pren *m.* 2 *v.* glynu.
stiff *a.* syth.
stiffen *v.* sythu.
still 1 *a.* llonydd, tawel. 2 *ad.* eto, er hynny; byth.
stillness *n.* tawelwch, heddwch, llonyddwch *m.*
sting 1 *n.* pigiad *m.* 2 *v.* pigo.
stink 1 *n.* drewdod, drewi *m.* 2 *v.* drewi.
stitch 1 *n.* pwyth *m.* 2 *v.* pwytho, gwnïo.
stocking *n.* hosan *f.*
stoke *v.* tanio, gofalu am dân.
stomach 1 *n.* stumog *f,* bol *m.* 2 *v.* stumogi.
stone *n.* carreg *f.*
stool *n.* stôl *f.*
stoop *v.* plygu, ymostwng.
stop 1 atalfa *f,* stop *m:* **full stop** atalnod. 2 *v.* atal; stopio; cau; aros, sefyll; peidio (â).
storage *n.* stôr *m,* storfa *f.*
store 1 *n.* stôr *m,* storfa *f.* 2 *v.* storio.
storehouse *n.* stordy *m.*
storm *a.* storm, tymestl *f.*
stormy *a.* stormus, tymhestlog.
story *n.* stori *f,* hanes, hanesyn *m,* chwedl *f.*
stove *n.* ffwrn, stof *f.*
straight *a.* syth, union.
straighten *v.* sythu, unioni.
straightway *ad.* yn y man, yn syth.
strange *a.* dieithr, rhyfedd, rhyfeddol, od, estron.
stranger *n.* dieithryn, estron *m.*
strangle *v.* tagu.
straw *n.* gwelltyn; gwellt *m.*
strawberry *n.* mefusen *f.*
stream 1 *n.* ffrwd *f,* llif *m,* nant *f.* 2 *v.* llifo.
streamer *n.* ruban *m,* baner *f.*
street *n.* stryd, heol, hewl, ffordd *f.*
strength *n.* nerth, grym *m.*
stretch *v.* estyn, ymestyn.
strict *a.* cyfyng, llym, manwl.
stride 1 *n.* cam *m.* 2 *v.* camu.
strife *n.* ymryson *m.*
strike 1 *n.* streic *f.* 2 *v.* streicio; taro.
striker *n.* streiciwr *m.*
strip *n.* llain *f:* **landing strip, airstrip** llain glanio.
string *n.* cordyn, llinyn; tant *m.*
strive *v.* ymdrechu.
strong *a.* cryf, grymus.
structure 1 *n.* adeilad; strwythur *m.* 2 *v.* strwythuro.
struggle 1 *n.* ymdrech *f.* 2 *v.* ymdrechu.
student *n.* myfyriwr *m.*
study *v.* myfyrio, astudio.
stump *n.* bôn *m.*
stunning *a.* syfrdanol.
stupefying *a.* syfrdanol.
stupid *a.* twp, dwl, hurt: **stupid person** twpsyn, hurtyn.
sty *n.* twlc *m:* **pigsty** twlc mochyn.
stye *n.* llefelyn, llyfelyn *m,* llefrithen *f.*
subconscious 1 *n.* isymwybod *m.* 2 *a.* isymwybodol.
submarine 1 *n.* llong danfor *f.* 2 *a.* tanfor, tanforol.
submit *v.* ymostwng; anfon; cyflwyno.
subordinate *a.* israddol.
substance *n.* sylwedd *m.*
substantial *a.* sylweddol.
substantiate *v.* profi.
substitute *n.* dirprwy, un yn lle arall *m.*
subterranean *a.* tanddaear, tanddaearol.
suburb *n.* maestref *f.*
subway *n.* isffordd *f,* tanlwybr *m.*
succeed *v.* llwyddo; dilyn, canlyn.
success *n.* llwydd, llwyddiant *m.*
successful *a.* llwyddiannus.

succour *n.* ymgeledd, swcwr *m.*
such *a.* y fath, cyfryw.
suck *v.* sugno.
sudden *a.* sydyn.
sue *v.* erlyn.
suffer *v.* dioddef, caniatáu, goddef.
suffering *n.* dioddef *m,* poen *mf.*
sufficient 1 *n.* digon *m.* 2 *a.* digon, digonol.
sufficiently *ad.* digon.
suffocate *v.* mogi, mygu, tagu.
sugar 1 *n.* siwgr *m.* 2 *v.* siwgro.
suggest *v.* awgrymu.
suggestion *n.* awgrym, awgrymiad *m.*
suicide *n.* hunanladdiad *m.*
suitable *a.* addas, priodol.
suite *n.* cyfres *f.*
sulk *v.* pwdu.
sultry *a.* clòs, trymaidd.
sum 1 *n.* swm *m.* 2 *v.* crynhoi.
summarise *v.* crynhoi.
summary *n.* crynodeb *mf.*
summer *n.* haf *m*: **midsummer** canol haf; **a summer's day** hafddydd; **summer dwelling** hafdy, hafod; tŷ haf.
summery *a.* hafaidd.
summit *n.* brig, pen *m,* ban *mf,* copa *m.*
summon *v.* galw, gwysio.
summons *n.* gwŷs *f.*
sumptuous *a.* moethus.
sun *n.* haul *m.*
sunbathe *v.* torheulo.
sunburn *n.* llosg haul *m.*
Sunday *n.* dydd Sul *m.*
sunflower *n.* blodyn yr haul *m.*
sunglasses *n.* sbectol haul *f.*
sunny *a.* heulog.
sunrise *n.* codiad haul *m.*
sunset *n.* machlud haul *m.*
sunshine *n.* heulwen *f.*
superb *a.* ardderchog, rhagorol.
superior *a.* uwch, gwell.
supermarket *n.* archfarchnad *f.*
superstition *n.* ofergoel, ofergoeledd, ofergoeliaeth *f.*
superstitious *a.* ofergoelus.
supper *n.* swper *m*: **the Last Supper** y Swper Olaf.
supple *a.* ystwyth, hyblyg.
supplement 1 *n.* atodiad *m.* 2 *v.* ychwanegu, atodi.
supplementary *a.* atodol, ychwanegol.
support *v.* cynnal.
suppose *v.* tybied, tybio.
supreme *a.* goruchaf, prif, pennaf.
sure *a.* sicr, siŵr.
suretyship *n.* mechnïaeth *f.*
surface *n.* wyneb, arwyneb, arwynebedd.
surfeit 1 *n.* syrffed *m.* 2 *v.* syrffedi.
surgeon *n.* llawfeddyg *m.*
surgery *n.* llawfeddygaeth; meddygfa *f.*
surgical *a.* llawfeddygol.
surname 1 *n.* cyfenw *nm.* 2 *v.* cyfenwi.
surpass *v.* rhagori ar, trechu.
surprise 1 *n.* rhyfeddod, syndod *m.* 2 *v.* synnu.
surprising *a.* rhyfedd, rhyfeddol, syn.
surround *v.* amgylchynu.
suspect *v.* amau.
suspend *v.* crogi; atal.
suspension bridge *n.* pont grog *f.*
swallow 1 *n.* llwnc *m;* gwennol *f.* 2 *v.* llyncu.
swamp 1 *n.* siglen, cors *f.* 2 *v.* gorlifo.
swan *n.* alarch *m.*
swarm 1 *n.* haid, torf *f.* 2 *v.* heidio, tyrru.
swathe 1 *n.* ystod *f.* 2 *v.* rhwymo.
sway *v.* siglo.
swear *v.* tyngu, rhegi.
sweat 1 *n.* chwys *m;* 2 *v.* chwysu.
swede *n.* erfinen, sweden, meipen *f.*
Swede *n.* Swediad *m.*
Sweden *n.* Sweden *f.*
Swedish *a.* Swedaidd.
sweep 1 *n.* ysgubwr, sgubwr *f.* 2 *v.* ysgubo, sgubo, brwsio, brwshio.
sweet 1 *n.* losinen, losen *f.* 2 *a.* melys.
sweetheart *n.* cariad *mf.*
sweets *n.* losin *pl.*
swell *v.* chwyddo.
swerve *v.* osgoi, gwyro, troi.
swift 1 *n.* gwennol ddu *f.* 2 *a.* buan, cyflym.
swiftness *n.* cyflymder *m.*
swim 1 *n.* nofiad *m.* 2 *v.* nofio.
swimmer *n.* nofiwr *m.*
swimming *n.* nofio *m.*
swimming pool *n.* pwll nofio *m.*
swimsuit *n.* gwisg nofio *f.*
swing 1 *n.* siglen *f.* 2 *v.* siglo.
switch *n.* troswr *f. (trydan),* swits *mf.*
Switzerland *n.* Y Swistir *f.*
swoon *v.* llewygu.
syllable *n.* sillaf *f.*
syllabus *n.* maes llafur *m.*
symptom *n.* arwydd *m.*
synonym *n.* cyfystyr *m.*
synonymous *a.* cyfystyr (â).
system *a.* cyfundrefn; trefn, system *f.*

tabernacle *n.* tabernaci *m,* pabell *f.*
table *n.* bord *f,* bwrdd; tabl *m;* taflen *f;* **tableful** bordaid, byrddaid.
table-cloth *n.* lliain bord, lliain bwrdd *m.*
tablespoon *n.* llwy fawr, llwy fwrdd *f.*
tablet *n.* tabled *m.*
tackle 1 *n.* offer *pl,* gêr, tacl *m.* **2** *v.* taclo.
tackler *n.* taclwr *m.*
tail *n.* cynffon *f.*
tailback *n.* tagfa *f.*
tailor *n.* teiliwr *m.*
tailoress *n.* teilwres *f.*
take *v.* cymryd, cael, dwyn, dal.
take hold *v.* cydio.
tale *n.* chwedl *f,* hanes, hanesyn *m,* stori *f.*
talent 1 *n.* talent, dawn *f.* **2** *a.* talentog, dawnus.
talk 1 *n.* sgwrs *f,* siarad *m,* sôn *mf.* **2** *v.* sgwrsio, siarad, sôn.
talker *n.* siaradwr *m.*
tall *a.* tal, uchel.
tallow *a.* gwêr *m.*
talon *n.* ewin *mf,* crafanc *f.*
tame 1 *n.* dof. **2** *v.* dofi.
tang *n.* tafod *m.*
tank *n.* tanc *m.*
tanker *n.* tancer *m;* llong olew *f.*
tap 1 *n.* tap *m.* **2** *v.* taro, tapio.
tape *n.* tâp, incil *m.*
tape measure *n.* tâp mesur *m.*
tape-recorder *n.* recordydd tâp *m.*
tapering *a.* pigfain.
target *n.* targed, nod *m.*
tart *n.* tarten, pastai *f*: **apple tart** pastai afalau; **jam tart** pastai jam.
task *n.* tasg *m.*
taste 1 *n.* blas *m.* **2** *v.* blasu, clywed, profi.
tasty *a.* blasus.
tavern *n.* tafarn *mf,* tŷ tafarn *m.*
tax 1 *n.* treth *f*: **Income tax** Treth Incwm; **Value Added Tax** Treth Ar Werth. **2** *v.* trethu.
tea *n.* te *m*: **tea-bags** cydau te; **teacup** cwpan te, dysgl de; **tea-leaves** dail te.
teach *v.* dysgu.
teacher *n.* athro *m;* athrawes *f.*
team *n.* tîm *m.*
tea-party *n.* téparti *m.*
teapot *n.* tebot *m.*
tear *n.* deigryn *m.*
tear 1 *n.* rhwyg *m.* **2** *v.* rhwygo.
tease *v.* poeni.
teaspoon *n.* llwy de *f.*
teaspoonful *n.* llond llwy de *m.*
technical *a.* technegol.
technician *n.* technegwr *m.*
technique *n.* techneg *m.*
technology *n.* technoleg *f.*
teddy-bear *n.* tedi *m.*
teenager *n.* un yn yr arddegau *mf.*
teens *n.pl.* arddegau.
teetotaller *n.* llwyrymwrthodwr *m.*
telecast *n.* telediad *m.*
telephone 1 *n.* teleffon, ffôn *m*: **telephone call** galwad ffôn **2** *v.* teleffonio, ffonio.
television *n.* teledu *m.*
tell *v.* dweud (wrth), mynegi: **to tell the truth** dweud y gwir.
temper *n.* tymer, natur *m.*
temperature *n.* tymheredd *m.*
tempest *n.* tymestl *f.*
tempestuous *a.* tymhestlog.
temple *n.* teml; arlais *f.*
ten *n.* & *a.* deg, deng *m.*
tendency *n.* tueddiad *m.*
tender *a.* tyner, mwyn, meddal, tirion.
tenderness *n.* tynerwch *m.*
tendon *n.* gewyn, tendon *m.*
tennis *n.* tenis *m*: **tennis ball** pêl denis; **tennis court** cwrt tenis; **tennis racket** raced denis.
tense 1 *n.* amser *m* (*gramadeg*). **2** *v.* tyn, tynn.
tent *n.* pabell *f.*
tenth *n.* & *a.* degfed *m.*
term 1 *n.* tymor; term; amod *m.* **1** *v.* enwi, galw.
terminus *n.* terfyn *m.*
terrace *n.* rhes dai *f,* teras *m.*
terrible *a.* dychrynllyd, ofnadwy.
terrifying *a.* dychrynllyd.

territory *n.* tir *m.*
terror *n.* braw, ofn *m.*
terrorism *n.* terfysgaeth *f.*
terrorist *n.* terfysgwr *m.*
tertiary *a.* trydyddol: **tertiary college** coleg trydyddol.
test 1 *n.* prawf *m*: **driving test** prawf gyrru; **preliminary test** rhagbrawf; **reading test** prawf darllen; **spelling test** prawf sillafu.
testament *n.* testament *m:* **New Testament** Testament Newydd.
testify *v.* tystio.
testimony *n.* tystiolaeth *f.*
text *n.* testun *m*: **text-book** gwerslyfr.
than *c.* na, nag.
thank *v.* diolch: **Thanks** Diolch! **Thanks very much** Diolch yn fawr.
thankful *a.* diolchgar.
thankfulness *n.* diolchgarwch *m.*
thankless *a.* diddiolch.
thanksgiving *n.* diolchgarwch *m*: **Thanksgiving Service** Gwasanaeth Diolchgarwch.
that 1 *a.* hwnnw, honno, hynny, yna, acw. 2 *pn.* hwn, hon, yna, hwn acw, hon acw, dyna, dacw; a, y, yr. 3 *c.* mai, taw, fel y, fel yr.
thaw *v.* toddi, meddalu, meirioli, dadmer, dadlaith.
the *def. art.* y, yr, 'r.
theatre *n.* theatr *f.*
thee *pn.* ti, tydi, tithau.
theft *n.* lladrad *m.*
their *pn.* eu.
theirs *pn.* eiddynt, yr eiddynt.
them *pn.* hwy, hwynt, hwythau, nhw.
themselves *pn.* eu hunain.
then 1 *ad.* wedyn, yna, y pryd hwnnw. 2 *c.* yna, ynte, ynteu.
thereafter *ad.* wedyn.
thereat *ad.* ar hynny, yna.
thereby *ad.* trwy hynny.
therefore *c.* am hynny, gan hynny, felly.
therefrom *ad.* oddi yno.
therein *ad.* yno, ynddo, yn hynny.
thereupon *ad.* ar hynny.
therewith *ad.* gyda hynny.
thermometer *n.* thermomedr *f.*
these *pn.* & *a.* y rhai hyn, y rhain.
they *pn.* hwy, hwynt, hwythau, nhw.
thick *a.* tew, trwchus.
thief *n.* lleidr *m.*
thieve *v.* lladrata, dwyn, dwgyd.
thigh *n.* clun, morddwyd *f.*
thin *a.* main, tenau, cul.
thing *n.* peth, gwrthrych *m.*
think *v.* meddwl, tybied, tybio.
third *n.* & *a.* trydydd *m;* trydedd *f.*
thirst 1 *n.* syched *m.* 2 *v.* sychedu.
thirsty *a.* sychedig.
thirteen *n.* & *a.* tri ar ddeg, un deg tri *m.*
thirty *n.* & *a.* deg ar hugain, tri deg *m.*
this *a.* & *pn.* hwn, hon, hyn; yma: **this minute** y funud hon, y funud yma; **this hour, (now, at present)** yr awr hon, **this day** y dydd hwn; **this week** yr wythnos hon; **this month** y mis hwn; **this year** eleni.
thistle *n.* ysgallen *f.*
thorn *n.* draen, draenen *f;* **thorns** drain.
those 1 *pn.* hynny, y rhai hynny, y rheini, y rheiny. 2 *a.* hynny, yna.
though 1 *ad.* er, serch hynny. 2 *prp.* er, pe, cyd.
thought *n.* meddwl, syniad *m.*
thoughtful *a.* meddyglar.
thousand *n.* & *a.* mil *f.*
thread *n.* edau *f,* llinyn *m.*
three *n.* & *a.* tri *m,* tair *f*: **three times** teirgwaith.
threesome *n.* triawd *m.*
threshold *n.* trothwy *m.*
thrill *n.* ias *f.*
thrilling *a.* iasol.
throat *n.* gwddf, gwddwg, llwnc *m.*
throne *n.* gorsedd *f.*
through 1 *ad.* trwodd. 2 *prp.* drwy, trwy.
throw 1 *n.* tafliad *m.* 2 *v.* taflu.
thrush *n.* bronfraith *f.*
thrust 1 *n.* gwthiad, hwp *m.* 2 *v.* gwthio.
thumb 1 *n.* bawd *m.* 2 *v.* bodio.
thunder 1 *n.* taran *f,* tyrfau *pl.* 2 *v.* taranu.
thunderbolt *n.* bollt *m,* mellten, llucheden *f.*
thunderclap *n.* taran *f.*
thunderstorm *n.* storm fellt a tharanau *f.*
Thursday *n.* dydd Iau.
thus *ad.* fel hyn, felly.
thy *pn.* dy, 'th.
ticket *n.* tocyn, ticed *m*: **ticket collector** tocynnwr; **ticket office** swyddfa docynnau.
tide *n.* llanw *m*: **high-tide** penllanw; **ebb-tide** trai.
tidy 1 *a.* cryno, taclus, twt. 2 *v.* tacluso.
tie 1 *n.* tei; clwm, cwlwm *m.* 2 *v.* clymu, rhwymo.

tiger *n.* teigr *m.*
tight *a.* tyn, tynn; cyfyng.
tile *n.* teilsen *f.*
timber *n.* coed, pren *m.*
time *n.* adeg *f*, oed; amser, pryd *m*: **at times** ar adegau, ar brydiau; **in time** mewn pryd.
timetable *n.* amserlen *f.*
timid *a.* llwfr, ofnus.
tin *n.* tun; alcam *m*: **tin of paint** tun o baent; **tin of peas** tun o bys.
tinge *n.* naws, gwawr *f.*
tinted *a.* lliwiog.
tiny *a.* bach, bychan, bitw, mân.
tip *n.* tip *m*, tomen *f;* cyngor *m;* gwobr *f;* cil-dwrn *m*: **rubbish tip** tomen ysbwriel, tip ysbwriel.
tire *v.* blino.
tired *a.* blinedig, blin.
title *n.* teitl, enw *m;* hawl *f*: **title-page** wyneb ddalen.
to *prp.* at, hyd at, i, er mwyn, tua, wrth, yn.
toad *n.* llyffant *m.*
toadstools *n.* madarch, caws llyffant, bwyd y boda *pl.*
toast 1 *n.* tost; llwncdestun *m.* 2 *v.* tostio; cynnig llwncdestun.
today *ad.* heddiw.
together *ad.* gyda'i gilydd, ynghyd.
toil 1 *n.* llafur *m.* 2 *v.* llafurio.
toilet *n.* toiled, tŷ-bach, lle chwech, jeriw *m.*
token *n.* arwydd; tocyn *m.*
tolerate *v.* goddef, caniatáu.
toll 1 *n.* toll, treth *f.* 2 *v.* canu cloch.
tollgate *n.* tollborth *m,* tollglwyd *f.*
tomato *n.* tomato *m.*
tomb *n.* bedd, beddrod *m.*
tom-cat *n.* cwrcath, gwrcath, cwrcyn, gwrcyn *m.*
tomorrow *ad.* fory, yfory.
ton *n.* tunnell *f*: **tonne** tunnell fetrig.
tone *n.* tôn; naws *f.*
tongue *n.* tafod *m;* tafodiaith, iaith *f.*
tonight *ad.* heno.
too *ad.* hefyd; rhy: **too much** gormod; **too little** rhy fach; **too late** rhy hwyr.
tool *n.* arf, erfyn, offeryn *m.*
tooth *n.* dant *m.*
toothache *n.* dannoedd *f.*
toothbrush *n.* brwsh dannedd *m.*
toothpaste *n.* sebon dannedd, past dannedd *m.*
top *n.* pen, brig, copa, top *m.*
topic *n.* pwnc, testun *m.*
torch *n.* tors *m.*
torch-light *n.* golau tors *m.*
torment *v.* poeni, poenydio.
tormentor *n.* poenydiwr *m.*
torque *n.* torch *m.*
torrid *a.* cras, poeth, crasboeth.
tortoise *n.* crwban *m.*
torture *v.* poenydio.
Tory 1 *n.* Tori, Ceidwadwr *m.* 2 *a.* Torïaidd.
total 1 *n.* cyfanswm, y cyfan *m.* 2 *a.* cyfan, hollol, llwyr.
tottering *a.* sigledig, simsan.
touch 1 *n.* teimlad *m.* 2 *v.* cyffwrdd (â), teimlo.
touch judge *n.* ystlyswr *m.*
touch-line *n.* llinell ystlys *f.*
tour 1 *n.* taith *f,* tro *m.* 2 *v.* teithio.
tourism *n.* twristiaeth *f.*
tourist 1 *n.* teithiwr, ymwelwr, ymwelydd *m.* 2 *a.* twristaidd: **Tourist Board** Bwrdd Croeso.
towards *prp.* tua, at, tuag at.
towel *n.* lliain, tywel *m.*
tower *n.* tŵr *m.*
town *n.* tref, tre *f*: **Carmarthen Town** Tre Caerfyrddin; **town centre** canol y dre; **town council** cyngor y dre; **town hall** neuadd y dre.
toy 1 *n.* tegan *m.* 2 *v.* chwarae.
trace *v.* olrhain.
track 1 *n.* llwybr, ôl, trac *m.* 2 *v.* olrhain.
tracksuit *n.* tracwisg *f.*
trade *n.* masnach; crefft *f.*
tradesman *n.* masnachwr, siopwr; crefftwr.
tradition *n.* traddodiad *m.*
traditional *a.* traddodiadol.
traffic *n.* trafnidiaeth, traffig *f;* **traffic jam** tagfa.
trail 1 *n.* trywydd *m.* 2 *v.* llusgo.
train 1 *n.* trên *m.* 2 *v.* hyfforddi; ymarfer.
trainer *n.* hyfforddwr.
training *n.* hyfforddiant *m,* ymarfer *f*: **in-service training** hyfforddiant mewn swydd.
tramp 1 *n.* crwydryn *m.* 2 *v.* crwydro.
trample *v.* sathru, sarnu.
tranquillity *n.* hedd, heddwch, tawelwch, llonyddwch *m.*
tranquilliser *n.* tawelyn *m.*
transact *v.* trafod, trin, gwneud.
transfer *v.* trosglwyddo.
transfusion *n.* trallwysiad *m*: **blood transfusion** trallwysiad gwaed.
transgress *v.* troseddu.

transgression *n.* trosedd *f.*
transgressor *n.* troseddwr *m.*
translate *v.* cyfieithu, trosi.
translation *n.* cyfieithiad, trosiad *m.*
translator *n.* cyfieithydd *m.*
transparent *a.* tryloyw.
transplant *v.* trawsblannu.
trap 1 *n.* trap *m.* 2 *v.* dal, trapio.
trash sothach, ysbwriel *m.*
travel *v.* teithio.
traveller *n.* teithiwr *m.*
travelling *a.* teithiol.
treachery *n.* brad, twyll *m.*
treasure 1 *n.* trysor *m.* 2 *v.* trysori.
treasurer *n.* trysorydd *m.*
treasury *n.* trysorfa *f*: **the Treasury** y Trysorlys.
treat 1 *n.* gwledd *m.* 2 *v.* trin.
treatise *n.* traethawd *m.*
tree *n.* coeden *f,* pren *m.*
tremendous *a.* dychrynllyd, ofnadwy, anferth.
trench *n.* ffos *f.*
triad *n.* tri *m.*
triads *n.* trioedd *pl.*
trial *n.* prawf; treial *m*: **sheepdog trials** treialon cŵn defaid.
triangle *n.* triongl *mf.*
triangular *a.* trionglog.
tribe *n.* llwyth, tylwyth *m.*
tribulation *n.* trallod *m.*
trick *n.* tric *m.*
trickery *n.* twyll *m.*
tricky *a.* anodd.
trim *v.* tacluso, trwsio.
trinity *n.* trindod *f.*
trio *n.* triawd *m.*
triplet *n.* tripled *m;* triban *f.*
trouble 1 *n.* gofid *m,* helynt *f,* picil, picl, trafferth, trallod, trwbl *m.* 2 *v.* blino, gofidio, trafferthu.
troublesome *a.* trafferthus.
trousers *n.* trowsus, trwser *pl.*
trowel *n.* trywel *m.*
trudge *v.* troedio, cerdded.
true *a.* gwir, cywir, iawn.
truly *ad.* yn wir, yn gywir: **Yours truly** Yr eiddoch yn gywir.
trunk *n.* bôn *m;* cist *f;* trwnc *m.*
trust 1 *n.* ymddiriedaeth, ymddiriedolaeth *f.* 2 *v.* ymddiried (yn).
trustee *n.* ymddiriedolwr *m.*
trusteeship *n.* ymddiriedolaeth *f.*
trusty *a.* ffyddlon, cywir.
truth *n.* gwirionedd, gwir, iawn *m.*
try 1 *n.* cais (*mewn rygbi*, cynnig *m*: **converted try** trosgais. 2 *v.* ceisio, cynnig, profi.
T-shirt *n.* crys-T *m.*
Tuesday *n.* dydd Mawrth *m.*
tug 1 *n.* plwc; tynfad *m.* 2 *v.* llusgo, tynnu.
tuition *n.* addysg *f,* hyfforddiant *m.*
tumble 1 *n.* cwymp *m.* 2 *v.* cwympo.
tumbler *n.* gwydryn *m.*
tummy *n.* bola *m.*
tumult *n.* twrw, mwstwr, terfysg, cythrwfl *m.*
tune *n.* alaw, tôn *f.*
tunnel *n.* twnnel *m.*
turkey *n.* twrci *m.*
Turkey *n.* Twrci *f.*
Turkish *a.* Twrcaidd.
turmoil *n.* berw, trafferth *m.*
turn 1 *n.* tro *m.* 2 *v.* troi.
turning *n.* tro *m.* tröedigaeth *m.*
turning point *n.* trobwynt *m.*
turnip *n.* erfinen, meipen *f.*
tutor 1 *n.* athro, tiwtor, hyfforddwr *m.* 2 *v.* dysgu, hyfforddi.
twelfth *n.* & *a.* deuddegfed *m.*
twelve *n.* & *a.* deuddeg, un deg dau *m.*
twentieth *n.* & *a.* ugeinfed *m.*
twenty *n.* & *a.* ugain, dau ddeg *m.*
twice *ad.* dwywaith.
twig *n.* brigyn, brig *m.*
twilight *n.* cyfnos, cyfddydd *m.*
twin 1 *n.* gefell *m.* 2 *v.* gefeillio.
twine *n.* llinyn *m.*
twist 1 *n.* tro *m.* 2 *v.* troi.
two *n.* & a. dau *m*: dwy *f;* pâr *m*: **in twos, two by two** yn ddeuoedd, yn ddau a dau.
typescript *n.* teipysgrif *f.*
typewriter *n.* teipiadur *m.*
typhoon *n.* corwynt *m.*
typist *n.* teipydd *m.*
tyre *n.* teiar *m.*

ubiquitous *a.* ym mhob man.
ugliness *n.* hagrwch *m.*
ugly *a.* hagr, hyll, salw.
ultra 1 *a.* eithafol. 2 *px.* gor-, dros ben, tu hwnt i.
ultra-modern *a.* tra modern, modern iawn.
umbrella *n.* ambarél, ymbrarél, ymbrelo *m.*
umpire 1 *n.* dyfarnwr, canolwr *m.* 2 *v.* dyfarnu.
unaccompanied *a.* heb gwmni; heb gyfeiliant.
unaccustomed *a.* anghyfarwydd.
unacquainted *a.* anghyfarwydd.
unanimous *a.* unfryd, unfrydol, unfarn.
unanimously *ad.* yn unfryd.
unceasing *a.* di-baid, diddiwedd.
uncertain *a.* ansicr.
uncivil *a.* anfoesgar.
unclad *a.* noeth.
uncle *n.* ewyrth, ewythr *m.*
unclean *a.* aflan, brwnt, budr.
uncommon *a.* anghyffredin.
uncover *v.* datguddio.
uncultivated *a.* heb ei drin.
under 1 *prp.* dan, tan, o dan, is, islaw. 2 *ad.* danodd, oddi tanodd. 3 *px.* is-, tan-.
underclothing *n.* dillad, isaf *m.*
undercurrent *n.* islif *m.*
undergo *v.* dioddef.
underground *a.* tanddaear, tanddaearol.
underline *v.* tanlinellu, pwysleisio.
undermine *v.* tanseilio.
underneath 1 *prp.* dan, tan, oddi tan. 2 *ad.* oddi tanodd.
underpass *n.* tanffordd *f.*
underskirt *n.* sgert isaf, sgyrt isaf, pais *f.*
understand *v.* deall.
understanding *n.* deall, dealltwriaeth.
undertake *v.* ymgymryd (â).
undertaker *n.* trefnydd angladdau *m.*
undo *v.* datod; difetha.
undress *v.* dadwisgo.
unearned *a.* heb ei ennill.
uneasy *a.* ansmwyth, pryderus.
unemployed 1 *n.* y diwaith *m.* 2 *a.* di-waith, segur.
unemployment *n.* diweithdra *m*: **unemployment benefit** budd-dâl diwaith.
unending *a.* diddiwedd, diderfyn.
unfair *a.* annheg.
unfaithful *a.* anffyddlon.
unfamiliar *a.* anghyfarwydd, dieithr.
unfasten *v.* datod.
unfit *a.* anaddas, anghymwys.
unforunate *a.* anffodus.
unfortunately *ad.* yn anffodus.
unhappy *a.* anhapus, trist.
unhealthy *a.* afiach.
uniform *n.* gwisg swyddogol *f;* *a.* unffurf.
unimportant *a.* dibwys.
uninteresting *a.* anniddorol.
union *n.* undeb *m.*
unionist *n.* undebwr *m.*
unique *a.* unigryw.
unit *n.* uned *f;* un, rhif un; undod *m.*
Unitarian *n.* Undodwr *m.*
unite *v.* uno, cysylltu, cyfuno.
united *a.* unedig, unol: **the United Kingdom** y Deyrnas Unedig; **United States of America** Unol Daleithiau America.
unity *n.* undod *m.*
universe *n.* bydysawd, cyfanfyd.
university *n.* prifysgol *f*: **University of Wales** Prifysgol Cymru.
unjust *a.* anghyflawn.
unjustly *ad.* ar gam.
unkind *a.* angharedig.
unleaded *a.* di-blwm: **unleaded petrol** petrol di-blwm.
unless *c.* oni, onid.
unlike *a.* annhebyg.
unlimited *a.* diderfyn.
unlucky *a.* anffodus, anlwcus.
unmannerly *a.* anfoesgar.
unmarried *a.* dibriod.
unnatural *a.* annaturiol.
unoccupied *a.* gwag, segur.
unopened *a.* heb ei agor.

unprepared *a.* amharod.
unravel *v.* datod, datrys.
unready *a.* amharod.
unreasonable *a.* afresymol.
unsatisfied *a.* anfodlon.
unseen *a.* anweledig.
unsightly *a.* diolwg, hyll, salw.
unsteady *a.* simsan.
unsuitable *a.* anaddas, anghymwys.
untidy *a.* anniben.
untie *v.* datod.
until *prp.* & *c.* hyd, hyd oni, nes, tan.
untrue *a.* celwyddog.
untruth *n.* celwydd, anwiredd *m.*
untruthful *a.* celwyddog.
unusual *a.* anarferol.
unwell *a.* anhwylus, afiach, claf.
unwholesome *a.* afiach.
unwilling *a.* anfodlon.
unwise *a.* annoeth, ffôl.
unworthy *a.* annheilwng.
up *ad.* & *prp.* i fyny.
uphill *ad.* i fyny.
uphold *v.* cynnal.
upon *prp.* ar, ar warthaf, ar uchaf.
upper *a.* uwch, uchaf.
uppermost *a.* & *ad.* uchaf.
upright *a.* syth, union, unionsyth; onest, cywir.
upside-down *ad.* wyneb i waered.
upstairs 1 *n.* llofft *f.* 2 *ad.* ar y llofft.
up-to-date *a.* cyfoes, hyd yn hyn.
upwards *ad.* i fyny.
urban *a.* trefol.
urge *v.* argymell.
urgency *n.* brys *m.*
us *pn.* ni, ninnau, nyni, 'n.
usage *n.* arfer *mf,* defnydd *m.*
use 1 *n.* arfer *mf,* defnydd, gwasanaeth, iws *m.* 2 *v.* arfer, defnyddio.
useful *a.* defnyddiol.
useless *a.* diwerth.
user *n.* defnyddiwr *m.*
Usk *n.* Wysg (river); Brynbuga (town) *f.*
usual *a.* arferol: **as usual** fel arfer.
utilise *v.* defnyddio.
utmost *a.* eithaf, pellaf.

vacancy *n.* lle gwag *m,* swydd wag *f.*
vacant *a.* gwag.
vacation *n.* gwyliau *pl.*
vaccination *n.* brechiad *m,* brech *f.*
vacuum *n.* gwagle *m.*
vain *a.* balch; ofer.
vale *n.* bro *f,* cwm, dyffryn, glyn *m*: **Vale of Glamorgan** Bro Morgannwg.
valiant *a.* dewr.
valley *n.* cwm, dyffryn, glyn *m.*
valuable *a.* drud, gwerthfawr.
value *n.* gwerth *m*: **Value Added Tax (VAT)** Treth Ar Werth.
van *n.* fan, y rheng flaenaf *f.*
vandal *n.* fandal *m.*
vandalise *v.* fandaleiddio.
vandalism *n.* fandaliaeth *f.*
vanish *v.* diflannu.
vanity *n.* gwagedd, oferedd *m.*
various *a.* amryw, gwahanol.
vary *v.* newid.
vast *a.* eang, enfawr, anferth.
veal *n.* cig llo *m.*
vegetable *n.* llysieuyn *m.*
vehicle *n.* cerbyd; cyfrwng *m.*
veil *n.* llen *f.*
velocity *n.* cyflymder *m.*
vengeance *n.* dial, dialedd *m.*
venom *n.* gwenwyn *m.*
venture 1 *n.* antur *m,* menter *f.* 2 *v.* mentro, beiddio, meiddio.
venturesome *a.* mentrus, anturus.
Venus *n.* Gwener *m.*
verb *n.* berf *f.*
verbally *ad.* mewn geiriau.
verb-noun *n.* berfenw *m.*
verdict *n.* dyfarniad, dedfryd *m.*
vermin *n.* pryfed, llygod . . . *pl.*
verse *n.* adnod *f,* pennill *m;* barddoniaeth *f.*
version *n.* fersiwn *m.*
versus *ad.* yn erbyn.
vertical *a.* syth, unionsyth, plwm.
very *a.* & *ad.* gwir, iawn, i'r dim.
vessel *n.* llestr; llong *m.*
vestry *n.* festri *f.*
veterinary surgeon *n.* milfeddyg *m.*
vex *v.* blino, gofidio, poeni, becso.
vexation *n.* blinder, gofid *m.*
via *prp.* trwy, ar hyd.
vicar *n.* ficer *m.*
vicarage *n.* ficerdy *m.*
vice *n.* drygioni *m;* gwasg, feis *f.*
vice-, *px.* is-, rhag-.
vice-chairman *n.* is-gadeirydd *m.*
vice-president *n.* is-lywydd *m.*
victor *n.* buddugwr, y buddugol, enillwr, enillydd *m.*
victory *n.* buddugoliaeth *f.*
view 1 *n.* golygfa *f,* golwg *mf;* barn *f.* 2 *v.* edrych, gweld.
viewer *n.* gwyliwr *m, (teledu).*
viewpoint *n.* safbwynt *m.*
vigil *n.* gwylnos, noswyl *f.*
vigour *n.* grym, nerth, egni, ynni.
vigorous *a.* egnïol.
vile *a.* ffiaidd, gwael, salw.
village *n.* pentref *m.*
villager *n.* pentrefwr.
vinegar *n.* finegr *m.*
viola *n.* fiola *f.*
violate *v.* treisio, troseddu.
violence *n.* trais *m.*
violent *a.* treisiol, gwyllt: **non-violent** di-drais.
violet 1 *n.* fioled *f.* 2 *a.* dulas.
violin *n.* ffidil *f.*
virgin *n.* morwyn, gwyryf *f*: **the Virgin Mary** y Forwyn Fair.
virtually *ad.* i bob pwrpas.
virtue *n.* rhinwedd *f.*
virus *n.* firws *m.*
vision *n.* gweledigaeth *f;* golwg *mf;* gweled *m.*
visit 1 *n.* ymweliad *m.* 2 *v.* ymweld (â), galw.
visitor *n.* ymwelwr, ymwelydd *m.*
vitamin *n.* fitamin *m.*
vivacious *a.* bywiog, heini.
vivid *a.* byw, clir, llachar.
vixen *n.* cadnawes, cadnöes, llwynoges *f.*
vocabulary *n.* geirfa *f.*
vocal *a.* llafar; lleisiol.
vocalist *n.* cantor *m,* cantores *f,* canwr *m.*
vocally *ad.* â'r llais.
vogue *n.* ffasiwn *m,* arfer *mf.*
voice 1 *n.* llais *m,* llef *f.* 2 *v.* lleisio, mynegi.

void 1 *n.* gwagle *m.* **2** *a.* di-rym. **3** *v.* gwacáu.
volcano *n.* llosgfynydd, folcano *m.*
vole *n.* llygoden y maes *f.*
volume *n.* cyfrol *f;* cyfaint; llais, sŵn; foliwm *m.*
voluntary *a.* gwirfoddol.
volunteer 1 *n.* gwirfoddolwr *m.* **2** *v.* gwirfoddoli.
vomit *v.* chwydu.
vote 1 *n.* pleidlais *f.* **2** *v.* pleidleisio.
voter *n.* pleidleisiwr *m.*
vowel *n.* llafariad *f.*
voyage 1 *n.* mordaith *f.* **2** *v.* mordeithio, mordwyo, morio: **Bon voyage** Hwyl dda! Siwrnai dda!
vulgar *a.* cyffredin; isel, brwnt; aflednais; gwerinol.
vulgarity *n.* diffyg moes *m.*

wag *v.* ysgwyd, siglo.
wage *n.* cyflog *mf.*
waist *n.* gwasg *mf,* canol *m.*
waistcoat *n.* gwasgod *f.*
wait *v.* aros, disgwyl; gweini.
waiter *n.* gweinydd *m.*
waitress *n.* gweinyddes *f.*
wake *v.* dihuno, deffro.
Wales *n.* Cymru *f.*
walk 1 *n.* tro *m.* **2** *v.* cerdded, mynd am dro.
walker *n.* cerddwr *m.*
walking-stick *n.* ffon *f.*
wall *n.* gwal, wal *f,* mur *m.*
wallflowers *n.* blodau mam-gu *pl.*
wallpaper *n.* papur wal *m.*
want 1 *n.* eisiau, diffyg *m.* **2** *v.* bod mewn eisiau.
wanting *a.* yn eisiau.
war 1 *n.* rhyfel *mf.* **2** *v.* rhyfela.
warehouse *n.* storfa, stôr *f,* ystordy *m.*
warfare *n.* rhyfel *mf.*
warm 1 *n.* cynnes, gwresog, twym. **2** *v.* cynhesu, twymo.
warmth *n.* gwres, cynhesrwydd *m.*
warn *v.* rhybuddio.
warning *n.* rhybudd *m.*
warship *n.* llong ryfel *f.*
wart *n.* dafaden, dafad *f.*
was, I *v.* bues i, bûm, fues i, fûm, roeddwn; *see* bod.
wash 1 *n.* golch, golchiad *m.* **2** *v.* golchi, ymolch, ymolchi.
washer *n.* golchydd *m.*
washing machine *n.* golchydd *m.*
washing powder *n.* powdr golchi *m.*
wash-house *n.* golchdy *m.*
wasp *n.* cacynen, picwnen *f*: **wasps' nest** nyth cacwn.
waste 1 *n.* gwastraff *m*: **nuclear waste** gwastraff niwclear. **2** *v.* gwastraffu.
wasteful *a.* gwastraffus.
watch 1 *n.* wats *f.* **2** *v.* gwarchod, gwylio.
watchful *a.* gwyliadwrus.
watchman *n.* gwyliwr *m.*
watchnight *n.* gwylnos *f.*
water *n.* dŵr *m.*
waterfall *n.* rhaeadr, sgwd *f,* pistyll *m.*
wave 1 *n.* ton *f.* **2** *v.* chwifio, codi llaw.
wavelength *n.* tonfedd *f.*
wax 1 *n.* cŵyr *m.* **2** *v.* cwyro; cynyddu, tyfu.
way *n.* ffordd, heol, hewl *f,* llwybr *m;* hynt *f;* arfer *fm,* modd *m.*
wayside *n.* ymyl y ffordd *mf.*
we *pn.* ni, ninnau, nyni.
weak *a.* gwan.
weaken *v.* gwanhau.
weakness *n.* gwendid *m.*
wealth *n.* cyfoeth, golud, da, modd *m.*
wealthy *a.* cyfoethog, cefnog.
weapon *n.* arf, erfyn *m*: **nuclear weapons** arfau niwclear.
wear 1 *n.* gwisg; traul *f.* **2** *v.* gwisgo; treulio.
weariness *n.* blinder *m.*
wearisome *a.* blinedig, blin, poenus.
weary 1 *a.* blinedig, blin. **2** *v.* blino, diflasu.
weather *n.* tywydd *m,* hin *f*: **fine weather** tywydd teg, hindda; **tempestuous weather** tywydd mawr.
weave *v.* gwau, gweu.
web *n.* gwe *f.*
wed *v.* priodi.
wedding *n.* priodas *f.*
Wednesday *n.* dydd Mercher *m.*
weed 1 *n.* chwynnyn *m.* **2** *v.* chwynnu.
weeds *n.* chwyn *pl.*
week *n.* wythnos *f*: **the first week** yr wythnos gyntaf: **the second week** yr ail wythnos: **the third week** y drydedd wythnos: **the last week** yr wythnos diwethaf.
weekend *n.* penwythnos *m.*
weekly *a.* wythnosol.
weep *v.* crio, wylo, llefain.
weigh *v.* pwyso.
weight *n.* pwys, pwysau *m.*
weighty *a.* pwysig; trwm.
welcome 1 *n.* croeso *m.* **2** *v.* croesawu.

welfare *n.* lles, budd *m.*
welfare state *n.* gwladwriaeth les *f.*
well 1 *n.* ffynnon *f.* **2** *v.* iach, da, iawn. **3** *v.* llifo, cronni. **4** *ad.* yn dda. **5** *i.* wel! **fairly well** yn lled dda; **very well** o'r gorau.
Welsh *a.* Cymraeg; Cymreig: **Welsh affairs** materion Cymreig; **Welsh books** llyfrau Cymraeg; **Welsh cakes** picau ar y maen; **Welsh office** Swyddfa Gymreig; **Welsh schools** ysgolion Cymraeg; **Welsh water** dŵr Cymru.
Welsh (language) *n.* Cymraeg *f.*
Welsh (people) *n.* Cymry *pl.*
Welshman *n.* Cymro *m.*
Welshness *n.* Cymreictod *m.*
Welshwoman *n.* Cymraes *f.*
west 1 *n.* gorllewin *m.* **2** *a.* gorllewin, gorllewinol: **West Wales** Gorllewin Cymru; **west or westerly wind** gwynt y gorllewin.
western *a.* gorllewinol.
wet 1 *n.* gwlybaniaeth *f.* **2** *a.* gwlyb. **3** *v.* gwlychu.
whale *n.* morfil *m.*
what 1 *n.* pa. **2** *pn.* pa beth. **3** *i.* beth!
whatever *pn.* beth bynnag.
wheat *n.* gwenith *m.*
wheel *n.* olwyn *f*: **front wheel** olwyn flaen; **rear wheel** olwyn gefn; **spare wheel** olwyn sbâr.
wheelbarrow *n.* berfa, whilber *f.*
wheelchair *n.* cadair olwynion *f.*
when *ad., pn.* & *c.* pan, pa bryd.
whenever *ad.* pa bryd bynnag.
where *ad.* ym mha le; yn y lle, lle.
whereabouts *ad.* ymhle.
whereas *c.* gan, yn gymaint â.
whereby *ad.* trwy yr hyn.
wherefore *ad.* paham, am hynny.
wherein *ad.* yn yr hyn.
wherever *ad.* ble bynnag.
which 1 *rel.pn.* a; y, yr. **2** *int.pn.* pa un? p'un? **3** *a.* pa.
whichever *a.* & *pn.* pa un bynnag.
whilst *ad.* cyhyd, tra.
whip 1 *n.* chwip *f.* **2** *v.* chwipio.
whirlpool *n.* pwll tro, trobwll *m.*
whisper 1 *n.* sisial *m.* **2** *v.* sisial, sibrwd.
whistle 1 *n.* chwiban *m.* **2** *v.* chwiban, chwibanu.
white *a.* gwyn, gwen, can.
white-lime *n.* gwyngalch *m.*
whiten *v.* gwynnu.
whitewash 1 *n.* gwyngalch *m.* **2** *v.* gwyngalchu.
Whitsunday *n.* Sulgwyn *m.*
whittle *v.* naddu.
whiz 1 *n.* si, su *m.* **2** *v.* sio, suo.
who *pn.* a, pwy; y, yr.
whole 1 *n.* cwbl, cyfan, holl *m.* **2** *a.* cyfan, holl; iach, holliach.
wholesome *a.* iach, iachus.
wholly *ad.* yn hollol, yn gyfan gwbl, yn llwyr.
whom *rel.pn.* a; y, yr.
whose *pn.* eiddo pwy? pwy biau?
whosoever *pn.* pwy bynnag.
why *ad.* paham, pam.
wicked *a.* drwg, drygionus.
wickedness *n.* drwg, drygioni *m.*
wicket *n.* wiced; clwyd *f*: **wicket-keeper** wicedwr.
wide *a.* llydan, eang.
wide-awake *a.* effro, ar ddihun.
widely *ad.* yn eang.
widen *v.* lledu, llydanu.
widow *n.* gweddw, gwidw *f.*
widower *n.* gwidman *m.*
width *n.* lled *m.*
wife *n.* gwraig, gwraig briod, priod *f.*
wild *a.* gwyllt, ffyrnig.
wilderness *n.* anialwch, diffeithwch *m.*
wildfire *n.* tân gwyllt *m.*
will 1 *n.* ewyllys *m.* **2** *v.* mynnu.
will be, he/she/it *v.* bydd; *see* bod.
willing *a.* bodlon, parod.
willow *n.* helygen *f.*
win *v.* ennill: **to win the day** cario'r dydd.
wind *n.* gwynt *m;* anadl *mf*: **cold wind** gwynt oer; **the north wind** gwynt y gogledd.
wind *v.* troi, dirwyn.
windmill *n.* melin wynt *f.*
window *n.* ffenestr *f*: **window pane** cwarel.
windy *a.* gwyntog.
wine *n.* gwin *m*: **dry red wine** gwin coch sych; **sweet white wine** gwin gwyn melys.
wineglass *n.* gwydr gwin *m.*
wing *n.* adain, aden, asgell *f;* asgellwr *m.*
winner *n.* enillwr, enillydd, y buddugol *m.*
winning *a.* buddugol.
winnings *n.* enillion *pl.*
winter *n.* gaeaf *m*: **winter dwelling** hendref, hendre.
wintry *a.* gaeafol.
wipe *v.* sychu.
wire *n.* gwifren *f.*
wisdom *n.* doethineb *m.*

wise *a.* call, doeth: **the Wise Men** y Doethion.
wish 1 *n.* dymuniad, ewyllys *m.* **2** *v.* dymuno.
witch *n.* gwrach *f.*
with *prp.* â, ag, gyda, gydag, efo, gan.
withdraw *v.* tynnu yn ôl; cilio; codi arian.
wither *v.* gwywo.
withhold *v.* atal, dal yn ôl.
within 1 *prp.* i mewn, o fewn, yn. **2** *ad.* tu mewn.
without 1 *prp.* heb. **2** *a.* tu allan.
witness 1 *n.* tyst *m.* **2** *v.* tystio.
wits *n.* synhwyrau *pl.*
witticism *n.* jôc, ffraethineb *f.*
witty *a.* doniol, ffraeth.
wizard *n.* dewin *m.*
wolf *n.* blaidd *m.*
woman *n.* merch, menyw, gwraig, llances, dynes *f.*
wonder 1 *n.* rhyfeddod *m.* **2** *v.* rhyfeddu, synnu: **I wonder** tybed.
wonderful *a.* rhyfedd, rhyfeddol.
wood *n.* coed *pl,* coedwig *f;* pren *m.*
wooden *a.* o goed, o bren.
woodwork *n.* gwaith coed, gwaith saer *m.*
wool *n.* gwlân *m.*
woollen *a.* gwlân, gwlanog: **woollen industry** diwydiant gwlân.
word *n.* gair *m*: **a good word** gair da; **the last word** y gair olaf; **word for word** gair am air.
work 1 *n.* gwaith, llafur *m.* **2** v. gweithio, llafurio.
worker *n.* gweithiwr *m.*
working *a.* gwaith, yn gweithio: **working class** dosbarth gweithiol; **working clothes** dillad gwaith; **working party** gweithgor.
workshop *n.* gweithdy *m,* siop waith *f.*
world *n.* byd *m.*
worldly *a.* bydol.
worldwide *a.* byd-eang.
worm *n.* mwydyn, pryfyn *m.*
worried *a.* gofidus, pryderus.
worry 1 *n.* gofid *m,* helynt *f,* pryder *m.* **2** *v.* gofido, poeni, pryderu, blino.
worse *a.* gwaeth.
worship *n.* addoliad *m.*
worth *n.* gwerth *m.*
worthiness *n.* teilyngdod, gwerth.
worthless *a.* diwerth.
worthy *a.* teilwng.
wound 1 *n.* clwyf, anaf *m.* **2** *v.* clwyfo, anafu.
wrap *v.* lapio, rhwymo: **wrapping paper** papur lapio.
wrath *n.* llid *m.*
wreath *n.* torch *f.*
wren *n.* dryw *m.*
wretch *n.* truan *m.*
wretched *a.* truan, truenus.
wretchedness *n.* trueni, trallod *m.*
wright *n.* crefftwr, saer *m:* **cartwright** saer certiau; **wheelwright** saer olwynion *(pren).*
wrist *n.* arddwrn *m.*
write *v.* sgrifennu, ysgrifennu: **to write a name** torri enw.
writer *n.* ysgrifennwr, awdur *m,* awdures *f.*
writing *n.* ysgrifen, ysgrifennu *f.*
wrong 1 *n.* cam, bai *m.* **2** *a.* anghywir, rong. **3** *v.* gwneud cam â.
wrongdoer *n.* troseddwr *m.*
wrongdoing *n.* trosedd *f.*

x-ray *n.* pelydr X, pelydryn X *m:*
x-rays pelydrau X.
xylophone *n.* seiloffon *f.*

yard *n.* buarth *m,* iard *f,* clos, cwrt *m;* llathen *f.*
yarn *n.* chwedl, stori; edau *f.*
year *n.* blwyddyn; blwydd (oed) *f;* blynedd *pl (after numerals)*: **the first year** y flwyddyn gyntaf; **the second year** yr ail flwyddyn; **three years old** tair blwydd oed; **four years old** pedair blwydd oed; **for five years** am bum mlynedd; **for six years** am chwe blynedd; **last year** y llynedd; **leap year** blwyddyn naid; **this year** eleni; **next year** y flwyddyn nesaf.
yearly *a.* blynyddol.
yearn *v.* hiraethu, dyheu.
yearning *n.* hiraeth *m.*
yell 1 *n.* sgrech, gwaedd *f.* 2 *v.* sgrechian, sgrechain, gweiddi.
yellow *a.* melyn, melen *af*: **the yellow apple** yr afal melyn; **the yellow dress** y wisg felen.
yes *ad.* ie, byddaf, byddan, do, oes, oedd, oeddwn, ydw, ydy, ydyn . . . (*Welsh uses the verb forms to answer* yes/no) e.g. **Tom? Yes.** Tom? Ie. **Was he there? Yes.** Oedd e yno? Oedd. **Is Huw late? Yes.** Ydy Huw'n hwyr? Ydy. **Are there dogs here? Yes.** Oes cŵn yma? Oes. **Will they be cold? Yes.** Fyddan nhw'n oer? Byddan.
yesterday *n.* & *ad.* doe, ddoe; **the day before yesterday** echdoe.
yet *ad.* eto, er hynny.
yew *n.* ywen *f.*
yield *v.* ildio, rhoddi.
yoke *n.* iau *f.*
yolk *n.* melyn wy, melynwy *m.*
yonder *ad.* acw, draw.
you *pn.* ti; chi, chwi: **you also** tithau, chithau, chwithau; **you yourself** tydi.
young *a.* ieuanc, ifanc.
younger *a.* iau.
youngest *a.* ifancaf.
youngster *n.* crwt, hogyn, plentyn *m.*
your *pn.* dy, 'th; eich, 'ch.
yours *pn.* eiddoch, yr eiddoch: **yours faithfully** yr eiddoch yn ffyddlon; **yours truly** yr eiddoch yn gywir.
yourself *pn.* eich hun, eich hunan.
yourselves *pn.* eich hunain.
youth *n.* llanc; ieuenctid *m.*
youthful *a.* ieuanc, ifanc.
Yuletide *n.* adeg y Nadolig *f.*

zeal *n.* sêl *f.*
zero *n.* dim, sero *m.*
zig-zag *a.* igam-ogam.
zinc *n.* sinc *m.*
zip 1 *n.* sip *m.* **2** *v.* sipio.
zone *n.* cylch, rhanbarth *m.*
zoo *n.* sw *m.*
zoology *n.* sŵoleg *mf.*

SUPPLEMENT
ATODIAD

VERBS
BERFAU

In this short introduction to the study of Welsh verbs, the irregular verb **bod** *(to be)* is conjugated in the Present, Imperfect, Future and Past tenses only. For a fuller discussion of the subject the reader must refer to specific books on Welsh grammar.

Present Tense (**bod** *to be*)

Affirmative Form

	Singular		*Plural*	
1	*Rydw i	*I am*	Rydyn ni	*We are*
2	Rwyt ti	*You are*	Rydych chi	You are
3	Mae e/o	*He/It is*	Maen nhw	*They are*
	Mae hi	*She is*		

Note: 3rd Person *Singular*	**mae, oes, sy, yw, ydyw**	*is, there is, are, there are*
	Oes . . .?	*Is there . . .? Are there . . .?*

*Literary Form: **Yr wyf i, 'Rwyf i.** In spoken Welsh one hears **Rw i/Dw i** and also **Rŷn ni/Dŷn ni; Rych chi/Dych chi.**

Interrogative Form

	Singular		*Plural*	
1	Ydw i?	*Am I?*	Ydyn ni?	*Are we?*
2	Wyt ti?	*Are you?*	Ydych chi?	*Are you?*
3	Ydy e/o?	*Is he/it?*	Ydyn nhw?	*Are they?*
	Ydy hi?	*Is she?*		

**Negative Form

	Singular		Plural	
1	Dydw i ddim	*I am not*	Dydyn ni ddim	*We are not*
2	Dwyt ti ddim	*You are not*	Dydych chi ddim	*You are not*
3	Dydy e/o ddim	*He/It is not*	Dydyn nhw ddim	*They are not*
	Dydy hi ddim	*She is not*		

Also heard in spoken Welsh: **Dw i ddim; Dwyt ti ddim; Dyw e/o/hi ddim; Dŷn ni ddim; Dych chi ddim; Dŷn nhw ddim

Imperfect Tense (**bod** *to be*)

Affirmative Form

	Singular		Plural	
1	*Roeddwn i	*I was/used to*	Roedden ni	*We were/used to*
2	Roeddet ti	*You were/used to*	Roeddech chi	*You were/usesd to*
3	Roedd e/o	*He/It was/used to*	Roedden nhw	*They were/used to*
	Roedd hi	*She was/used to*		

Note: 3rd Person Singular **roedd** *was, there was*
were, there were

*Also heard in spoken Welsh: **Rown i, Roen i; Rôt ti; Roedd e/hi; Rôn ni; Roch chi, Rôn nhw.**

Interrogative Form

	Singular	
1	Oeddwn i?	*Was I/Used I to?*
2	Oeddet ti?	*Were you/Used you to?*
3	Oedd e/o?	*Was he/it/Used he to?*
	Oedd hi?	*Was she/Used she to?*

Plural	
Oedden ni?	*Were we/Used we to?*
Oeddech chi?	*Were you/Used you to?*
Oedden nhw?	*Were they/Used they to?*

Note: 3rd Person Singular **Oedd . . .?** *Was there . . .?*
Were there . . .?

Negative Form

	Singular	
1	Doeddwn i ddim	*I wasn't/I used not to*
2	Doeddet ti ddim	*You weren't/You used not to*
3	Doedd e/o ddim	*He/It wasn't/It used not to*
	Doedd hi ddim	*She wasn't/She used not to*
		Plural
1	Doedden ni ddim	*We weren't/We used not to*
2	Doeddech chi ddim	*You weren't/You used not to*
3	Doedden nhw ddim	*They weren't/They used not to*

Future Tense (bod *to be*)

Affirmative Form

	Singular		Plural	
1	Bydda i	*I shall be*	Byddwn ni	*We shall be*
2	Byddi di	*You will be*	Byddwch chi	*You will be*
3	*Bydd e/o*	*He/It will be*	Byddan nhw	*They will be*
	Bydd hi	*She will be*		

Note: 3rd Person Singular **bydd** *will be*

Interrogative Form

	Singular		Plural	
1	Fydda i?	*Shall I be?*	Fyddwn ni?	*Shall we be?*
2	Fyddi di?	*Will you be?*	Fyddwch chi?	*Will you be?*
3	Fydd e/o?	*Will he/she be?*	Fyddan nhw?	*Will they be?*
	Fydd hi?	*Will she be?*		

Negative Form

	Singular		Plural	
1	Fydda i ddim	*I shall not be*	Fyddwn ni ddim	*We shall not be*
2	Fyddi di ddim	*You will not be*	Fyddwch chi ddim	*You will not be*
3	Fydd e/o ddim	*He/It will not be*	Fyddan nhw ddim	*They will not be*
	Fydd hi ddim	*She will not be*		

Imperative (bod *to be*)

Bydd! Bydda! (singular); **Byddwch!** (plural) *Be!*

Past Tense (bod *to be*)

Affirmative Form

	Singular		Plural	
1	*Bues i	*I was*	Buon ni	*We were*
2	Buest ti	*You were*	Buoch chi	*You were*
3	Buodd e/o	*He/It was*	Buon nhw	*They were*
	Buodd hi	*She was*		

*Literary form of 1st Person Singular Past Tense: **Bûm i**

Interrogative Form

	Singular		Plural	
1	Fues i?	*Was I?*	Fuon ni?	*Were we?*
2	Fuest ti?	*Were you?*	Fuoch chi?	*Were you?*
3	Fuodd e/o?	*Was he/it?*	Fuon nhw?	*Were they?*
	Fuodd hi?	*Was she?*		

Negative Form

	Singular		Plural	
1	Fues i ddim	*I wasn't*	Fuon ni ddim	*We weren't*
2	Fuest ti ddim	*You weren't*	Fuoch chi ddim	*You weren't*
3	Fuodd e/o ddim	*He/It wasn't*	Fuon nhw ddim	*They weren't*
	Fuodd hi ddim	*She wasn't*		

Affirmative and Negative Answers Yes and No

The entries shown in the English-Welsh section of the dictionary under **yes** and **no** may be further supplemented:

Present Tense

	Singular		Plural	
1	Ydw/Nag ydw	*Yes/No*	Ydyn/Nag ydyn	*Yes/No*
2	Wyt/Nag wyt	*Yes/No*	Ydych/Nag ydych	*Yes/No*
3	Ydy/Nag ydy	*Yes/No*	Ydyn/Nag ydyn	*Yes/No*
	Oes/Nag oes	*Yes/No*		

Imperfect Tense

	Singular		Plural	
1	Oeddwn/Nag oeddwn	*Yes/No*	Oedden/Nag oedden	*Yes/No*
2	Oeddet/Nag oeddet	*Yes/No*	Oeddech/Nag oeddech	*Yes/No*
3	Oedd/Nag oedd	*Yes/No*	Oedden/Nag oedden	*Yes/No*

Future Tense

	Singular		Plural	
1	Bydda/Na fydda	*Yes/No*	Byddwn/Na fyddwn	*Yes/No*
2	Byddi/Na fyddi	*Yes/No*	Byddwch/Na fyddwch	*Yes/No*
3	Bydd/Na fydd	*Yes/No*	Byddan/Na fyddan	*Yes/No*

With the past tense **Do** *Yes* and **Naddo** *No* are the forms relating to both singular and plural usages.

For forms such as the Pluperfect **Buaswn i, Fe/Mi faswn i** *I would (be)*, see further works on contemporary Welsh grammar.

Regular Verbs

Welsh verbs have inflected tenses, that is, the tenses have their own endings. These endings are added to the stem of the verbs. Most verbs follow a regular pattern but there are some irregular verbs.
In the Welsh – Engiish section of this dictionary an entry for a verb is shown as follows:

canu *be.* **(canaf)** to sing, to play

The stem derived from the verb-noun **canu** is *can-*. The Present Tense ending for the 1st Person Singular is **af-**, and when the ending is added to the stem, **can + af** becomes **canaf**, which is the form shown in the brackets, frequently written and pronounded **cana.**
The verb **bod** (*to be*) is used as an auxiliary in forming tenses of regular verbs such as **canu, bwyta, cysgu . . .** The Present Tense of **canu** is formed by using the Present Tense of the verb **bod**, that is, **Rydw i, Rwyt ti, Mae e . . .** followed by **yn + canu**. It also exists in compact form as shown below.

Note: **Rydw i yn canu** becomes **Rydw i'n canu**
Rwyt ti yn canu becomes **Rwyt ti'n canu**
Mae e yn canu becomes **Mae e'n canu . . .**

Present Tense (**canu** *to sing, to play*)

Singular

1	Rydw i'n canu	I sing, I am singing
2	Rwyt ti'n canu	*You sing, You are singing*
3	Mae e/o'n canu	*He/It sings, He/It is singing*
	Mae hi'n canu	*She sings, She is singing*

Plural

1	Rydyn ni'n canu	*We sing, We are singing*
2	Rydych chi'n canu	*You sing, You are singing*
3	Maen nhw'n canu	*They sing, They are singing*

The Imperfect Tense is formed by using the Imperfect Tense of **bod**, that is, *Roeddwn i, Roeddet ti, Roedd e* . . . followed by *yn canu.*

Imperfect Tense (**canu** *to sing, to play*)

Singular

1	Roeddwn i'n canu	*I was singing*
2	Roeddet ti'n canu	*You were singing*
3	Roedd e/o'n canu	*He/It was singing*
	Roedd hi'n canu	*She was singing*

Plural

Roedden ni'n canu	*We were singing*
Roeddech chi'n canu	*You were singing*
Roedden nhw'n canu	*They were singing*

The Imperfect Tense also conveys the meaning of continuous action. **Roedd hi'n canu** means not only *She was singing*, but also, *She was **going on** singing.* **Roedd hi'n arfer canu** *She used to sing.*

The Future Tense is formed by using the Future Tense of **bod**, that is, **Bydda i, Byddi di, Bydd e . . .** followed by **yn + canu.**

Future Tense (**canu** *to sing, to play*)

Singular

1	Bydda i'n canu	*I shall be singing*
2	Byddi di'n canu	*You will be singing*
3	Bydd e/o'n canu	*He/It will be singing*
	Bydd hi'n canu	*She will be singing*

Plural

Byddwn ni'n canu	*We shall be singing*
Byddwch chi'n canu	*You will be singing*
Byddan nhw'n canu	*They will be singing*

Imperative (**canu** *to sing, to play*)

Cana! (singular); **Canwch!** (plural) *Sing!*

The Past Tense of **canu** is formed by adding **-ais, -aist, -odd, -on, och, -on** to the stem **can-**, and is used to convey completed action in the past.

Past Tense (**canu** *to sing, to play*)

		Singular		*Plural*
1	*Cenais i	*I sang*	Canon ni	*We sang*
2	*Cenaist ti	You sang	Canoch chi	*You sang*
3	Canodd e/o	He/It sang	Canon nhw	*They sang*
	Canodd hi	*She sang*		

*In those verbs which have 'a' in the stem it is usual in literary Welsh for a > e in the 1st and 2nd Persons Singular Past Tense and Person Singular Future Tense

The particle Fe (S.W.)/Mi (N.W.)

The verb is placed as the first word in the normal construction of the Welsh sentence:

Cerddodd Siôn i'r siop.	*Siôn walked to the shop.*
Rydw i'n darllen llyfr.	*I'm reading a book.*
Mae ci yn a cae.	*There's a dog in the field.*
Dydyn nhw ddim yma.	*They're not here.*

Usually the particle **Fe/Mi** is placed in front of the verb merely to indicate that the verb is affirmative.

Note: The particle **Fe/Mi** is not translated, and is not placed before **mae** or **maen** but may occur before other persons of the verb in speech or informal texts. Both particles are followed by Soft Mutation.

Golchodd Mair y dillad. Fe olchodd Mair y dillad.	*Mair washed the clothes.*
Byddan nhw'n canu heno. Fe fyddan nhw'n canu heno.	*They will be singing tonight.*
Canon ni yn yr eisteddfod. Fe ganon ni yn yr eisteddfod.	*We sang in the eisteddfod.*

Compact Form of Verbs

The Future and Imperfect Tenses of the verb **canu** referred to above also exist in their compact forms. These inflected verb forms are more likely to be found in formal texts than in current conversational Welsh, though they may well appear in both.
The endings for the Future Tense of **canu** are **-af/-a, -i, -iff/ith, -wn, -wch, -an** and are added to the stem *can-*.

Future Tense of **canu** (Compact Form)

	Singular	
1	Fe/Mi ganaf/gana i	*I shall sing*
2	Fe/Mi gani di/geni	*You will sing*
3	Fe/Mi ganiff/ganith e/o	*He/It will sing*
	Fe/Mi ganiff/ganith hi	*She will sing*

Plural

Fe/Mi ganwn ni	*We shall sing*
Fe/Mi ganwch chi	*You will sing*
Fe/Mi ganan nhw	*They will sing*

The endings for the Imperfect Tense of **canu** are **-wn, -et, -ai, -en, -ech, -en** and are added to the stem **can-.**

Imperfect Tense of canu (Compact Form).

Singular

1	Canwn i	*I was singing*
2	Canet ti	*You were singing*
3	Canai fe/fo	*He/It was singing*
	Canai hi	*She was singing*

Plural

Canen ni	*We were singing*
Canech chi	*You were singing*
Canen nhw	*They were singing*

Regular verbs follow the same pattern as **canu**. The Present, Imperfect, Future and Past Tenses of **bwyta** are shown below:

Present Tense (bwyta *to eat*)

Singular

1	Rydw i'n bwyta	*I am eating, I eat*
2	Rwyt ti'n bwyta	*You are eating . . .*
3	Mae e'n bwyta . . .	*He/It is eating . .*, etc.

Imperfect Tense (bwyta *to eat*)

Singular

1	Roeddwn i'n bwyta	*I was eating*
2	Roeddet ti'n bwyta	*You are eating*
3	Roedd e'n bwyta . . .	*He/It was eating . .*, etc.

Future Tense (bwyta *to eat*)

Singular

1	Fe/Mi fydda(f) i'n bwyta	*I shall be eating*
2	Fe/Mi fyddi di'n bwyta	*You will be eating*
3	Fe/Mi fydd e'n bwyta . . .	*He/It will be eating . .*, etc.

Past Tense

	Singular		*Plural*	
1	Fe/Mi fwytais i	*I ate*	Fe/Mi fwyton ni	*We ate*
2	Fe/Mi fwytaist ti	*You ate*	Fe/Mi fwytoch chi	*You ate*
3	Fe/Mi fwytodd e/o	*He/It ate*	Fe/Mi fwyton nhw	*They ate*
	Fe/Mi fwytodd hi	*She ate*		

Future Tense (Compact Form)

	Singular		*Plural*	
1	Fe/Mi fwyta(f) i	*I shall eat*	Fe/Mi fwytwn ni	*We shall eat*
2	Fe/Mi fwytwch chi	*You will eat*	Fe/Mi fwytwch chi	*You will eat*
3	Fe/Mi fwytiff e/o	*He/It will eat*	Fe/Mi fwytan nhw	*They will eat*
	Fe/Mi fwytiff hi	*She will eat*		

Imperative

Bwyta! (singular); **Bwyt(e)wch!** (plural) *Eat!*

Irregular Verbs

Irregular verbs do not follow the same pattern as **canu** and have to be treated separately. Included below are: **cael, dod, gwneud, gwybod, mynd, rhoddi** and **troi.**

Present Tense (**cael** *to have*)

	Singular	
1	Rydw i'n cael	*I am having, I have*
2	Rwyt ti'n cael	*You are having, You have*
3	Mae e'n cael . . .	*He/It is having* . . , etc.

Imperfect Tense (**cael** *to have*)

	Singular	
1	Roeddwn i'n cael	*I was having*
2	Roeddet ti'n cael	*You were having*
3	Roedd e'n cael . . .	*He/It was having* . . , etc.

Future Tense (**cael** *to have*)

	Singular		*Plural*	
1	Fe/Mi ga(f) i	*I shall have*	Fe/Mi gawn ni	*We shall have*
2	Fe/Mi gei ddi	*You will have*	Fe/Mi gewch chi	*You will have*
3	Fe/Mi gaiff e/o	*He/It will have*	Fe/Mi gân nhw	*They will have*
	Fe/Mi gaiff hi	*She will have*		

Past Tense (**cael** *to have*)

	Singular		*Plural*	
1	*Fe/Mi ges i*	*I had*	Fe/Mi gawson ni	*We had*
2	Fe/Mi ges ti	*You had*	Fe/Mi gawsoch chi	*You had*
3	Fe/Mi gafodd/gas e/o	*He/It had*	Fe/Mi gawson nhw	*They had*
	Fe/Mi gafodd/gas hi	*She had*		

Imperative

Cymera! (singular); **Cymerwch!** (plural) *Have!*

Present Tense (**dod** *to come*)

Singular

1 Rydw i'n dod *I am coming*
2 Rwyt ti'n dod *You are coming*
3 Mae e'n dod . . . *He/It is coming* . . , etc.

Imperfect Tense (**dod** *to come*)

Singular

1 Roeddwn i'n dod *I was coming*
2 Roeddet ti'n dod *You were coming*
3 Roedd e'n dod . . . *He/It was coming* . . , etc.

Future Tense (**dod** *to come*)

Singular

1 Fe/Mi ddeuaf/ddo(f) i *I shall come*
2 Fe/Mi ddoi di *You will come*
3 Fe/mi ddaw e/o *He/It will come*
Fe/Mi ddaw hi *She will come*

Fe/Mi ddown ni *We shall come*
Fe/Mi ddewch/ddowch chi *You will come*
Fe/Mi ddôn nhw *They will come*

Past Tense (**dod** *to come*)

Singular

1 Fe/Mi ddes i *I came*
2 Fe/Mi ddest ti *You came*
3 Fe/Mi ddaeth e/o, hi *He/It came, She came*

Plural

Fe/Mi ddaethon ni *We came*
Fe/Mi ddaethoch chi *You came*
Fe/Mi ddaethon nhw *They came*

Imperative

Tyrd! *(N.W.)*/**Dere!** *(S.W.)* (singular); **Dewch!** *(S.W.)*/**Dowch!** *(N.W.)* (plural) *Come!*

Present Tense

Singular

1 Rydw i'n gwneud *I am making, I make*
2 Rwyt ti'n gwneud *You are making, You make*
3 Mae e'n gwneud . . . *He/It is making* . . , etc.

Imperfect Tense (**gwneud** *to make, to do*)

Singular

1 Roeddwn i'n gwneud *I was making*
2 Roeddet ti'n gwneud *You were making*
3 Roedd e'n gwneud . . . *He/It was making* . . , etc.

Future Tense (gwneud *to make, to do*)

	Singular	
1	Fe/Mi wna(f) i	*I shall make*
2	Fe/Mi wnei di	*You will make*
3	Fe/Mi wnaiff e/o	*He/It will make*
	Fe/Mi wnaiff hi	*She will make*

Plural	
Fe/Mi wnawn ni	*We shall make*
Fe/Mi wnewch chi	*You will make*
Fe/Mi wnân nhw	*They will make*

Past Tense (gwneud *to make, to do*)

	Singular		*Plural*	
1	Fe/Mi wnes i	*I made*	Fe/Mi wnaethon ni	*We made*
2	Fe/Mi wnest ti	*You made*	Fe/Mi wnaethoch chi	*You made*
3	Fe/Mi wnaeth e/o	*He/It made*	Fe/Mi wnaethon nhw	*They made*
	Fe/Mi wnaeth hi	*She made*		

Imperative

Gwna! (singular); **Gwnewch!** (plural) *Do! Make!*

Present Tense (gwybod *to know*)

	Singular	
1	Rydw i'n gwybod	*I know*
2	Rwyt ti'n gwybod	*You know*
3	Mae e/o'n gwybod . . .	*He/It knows* . . , etc.

Present Form (Compact Form) (gwybod *to know*)

	Singular		*Plural*	
1	Fe/Mi wn i	*I know*	Fe/Mi wyddon ni	*We know*
2	Fe/Mi wyddost ti	*You know*	Fe/Mi wyddoch chi	*You know*
3	Fe/Mi ŵyr e/o	*He/It knows*	Fe/Mi wyddan nhw	*They know*
	Fe/Mi ŵyr hi	*She knows*		

Imperfect Tense (gwybod *to know*)

	Singular	
1	Roeddwn i'n gwybod	*I knew*
2	Roeddet ti'n gwybod	*You knew*
3	Roedd e'n gwybod . . .	*He/It knew* . . , etc.

Future Tense (gwybod *to know*)

	Singular	
1	Bydda i'n gwybod	*I shall know*
2	Byddi di'n gwybod	*You will know*
3	Bydd e'n gwybod . . .	*He/It will know* . . , etc.

The Compact Forms of the Future and Past Tenses are seldom used in conversation.

Present Tense (**mynd** *to go*)

	Singular	
1	Rydw i'n mynd	*I go, I am going*
2	Rwyt ti'n mynd	*You go, You are going*
3	Mae e'n mynd . . .	*He/It goes, He/It is going* . . , etc.

Present Tense (Compact Form) (**mynd** *to go*)

	Singular	
1	Af/Â i	*I go, I am going*
2	Ei di	*You go, You are going*
3	*Aiff e/o	*He/It goes, He/It is going*
	*Aiff hi	*She goes, She is going* . . , etc.

The Present Tense follows the same pattern as the Compact Form of the Future Tense below.

Imperfect Tense (**mynd** *to go*)

	Singular	
1	Roeddwn i'n mynd	*I was going*
2	Roeddet ti'n mynd	*You were going*
3	**Roedd e'n mynd . . .	*He/It was going* . . , etc.

Future Tense (**mynd** *to go*)

	Singular		*Plural*	
1	Fe/Mi af/â i	*I shall go*	Fe/Mi awn ni	*We shall go*
2	Fe/Mi ei di	*You will go*	Fe/Mi ewch chi	*You will go*
3	*Fe/Mi aiff e/o	*He/It will go*	Fe/Mi ân nhw	*They will go*
	*Fe/Mi aiff hi	*She will go*		

*Literary form: **Â ef/hi** **Literary form: **Âi ef/hi**

Past Tense (**mynd** *to go*)

	Singular		*Plural*	
1	Fe/Mi es i	*I went*	Fe/Mi aethon ni	*We went*
2	Fe/Mi est ti	*You went*	Fe/Mi aethoch chi	*You went*
3	Fe/Mi aeth e/o	*He/It went*	Fe/Mi aethon nhw	*They went*
	Fe/Mi aeth hi	*She went*		

Imperative

Dos! *(N.W.)*/**Cer!** *(S.W.)* (singular); **Ewch!/Cerwch!** *(S.W.)* *Go!*

Present Tense (**rhoi/rhoddi** *to give*)

	Singular	
1	Rydw i'n rhoi/rhoddi	*I am giving, I give*
2	Rwyt ti'n rhoi	*You are giving, You give*
3	Mae e'n rhoi . . .	*He/It is giving, He/It gives* . . , etc.

Imperfect Tense

	Singular	
1	Roeddwn i'n rhoi/rhoddi	*I was giving*
2	Roeddet ti'n rhoi	*You were giving*
3	Roedd e'n rhoi . . .	*He/It was giving* . . . etc.

Future Tense

	Singular	
1	Fe/Mi roia/rodda(f) i	*I shall give*
2	Fe/Mi roddi di	*You will give*
3	Fe/Mi roddiff/rydd e/o	*He/It will give*
	Fe/Mi roddiff/rydd hi	*She will give*

Plural	
Fw/Mi roddwn ni	*We shall give*
Fe/Mi roddech chi	*You will give*
Fe/Mi roddan nhw	*They will give*

Past Tense

	Singular		*Plural*	
1	Fe/Mi roiais i/roddais i	*I gave*	Fe/Mi roddon ni	*We gave*
2	Fe/Mi roddaist ti	*You gave*	Fe/Mi roddoch chi	*You gave*
3	Fe/Mi roddodd e/o	*He/It gave*	Fe/Mi roddon nhw	*They gave*
	Fe/Mi roddodd hi	*She gave*		

Imperative

Rhodda! Rho! (singular); **Rhoddwch!** (plural) *Give!*

troi *to turn*

Present Tense

	Singular	
1	Rydw i'n troi	*I am turning, I turn*
2	Rwyt ti'n troi	*You are turning, You turn*
3	Mae e'n troi . . .	*He/It is turning, He/It turns* . . . etc.

Imperfect Tense

	Singular	
1	Roeddwn i'n troi	*I was turning*
2	Roeddet ti'n troi	*You were turning*
3	Roedd e'n troi	*He/It was turning* . . . etc.

Future Tense

	Singular		*Plural*	
1	Fe/Mi droaf/droia i	*I shall turn*	Fe/Mi droiwn ni	*We shall turn*
2	Fe/Mi droi-i di	*You will turn*	Fe/Mi droiwch chi	*You will turn*
3	Fe/Mi dröiff e/o	*He/It will turn*	Fe/Mi droian nhw	*They will turn*
	Fe/Mi dröiff hi	*She will turn*		

Past Tense

	Singular		*Plural*	
1	Fe/Mi droais i	*I turned*	Fe/Mi droeson ni	*We turned*
2	Fe/Mi droaist ti	*You turned*	Fe/Mi droesoch chi	*You turned*
3	Fe/Mi droiodd e/o	*He/It turned*	Fe/Mi droeson nhw	*They turned*

Imperative

Tro!/Troia! (singular); **Trowch!/Troiwch!** (plural) *Turn!*

cloi, paratoi and **rhoi** follow a similar pattern.

Imperative Mood

Commands – 2nd Person Singular and 2nd Person Plural
The 2nd Person Singular is formed by adding **-a** to the stem of the verb-noun, whilst the 2nd Person Plural is formed by adding **-wch** to the stem:

Cysga! (2nd Person Singular);
Cysgwch! (2nd Person Plural) *Sleep!*
Brysia! (2nd Person Singular);
Brysiwch! (2nd Person Plural) *Hurry!*

Commands – Other Persons
The forms **Gadewch i**-*Allow-/Let* -is usually used to express commands in the other persons of the verb.

Gadewch i fi weithio!	(1st Person Singular)	*Let me work!*
Gadewch iddo fe weithio!	(3rd Person Singular)	*Let him work!*
Gadewch iddi hi weithio!	(3rd Person Singular	*Let her work!*
Gadewch i ni weithio!	(1st Person Plural)	*Let us work!*
Gadewch iddyn nhw weithio!	(3rd Person Plural)	*Let them work!*

Verbs and Mutations

The direct object of a verb in compact form takes a Soft Mutation:

Fe welodd e *g*effyl.	*He saw a horse.*
Fe brynon nhw *f*wyd.	*They bought food.*
Mi gana i *g*arolau 'fory.	*I'll sing carols tomorrow.*
Rhoddaf *b*unt iddi.	*I give her a pound.*

Note: When the periphrastic form of the verb (**bod** + **yn** + verb-noun) is used *no* mutation of the object occurs, as is shown in the following sentences:

Mae e'n darllen **ll**yfr.	*He is reading a book.*
Mae mhw'n chwarae **p**êl-droed.	*They are playing football.*
Roedd Siân yn golchi **ll**estri.	*Siân was washing dishes.*
Rydw i'n rhoddi **p**unt iddo.	*I am giving him a pound.*

For examples involving the mutation of verbs following the particles **Fe** and **Mi**, the relative pronoun **a**, and the personal pronouns **mi, ti, ef . . .** see the section below entitled **A Summary of the Main Rules of Mutation.**

PREPOSITIONS
ARDDODIAID

Prepositions are followed by nouns or pronouns, for example:

gyda *with*	**gyda Mam** *with Mother;* **gyda ni** *with us*
i fyny *up*	**i fyny'r bryn** *up the hill;* **i fyny'r ysgol** *up the ladder*
i lawr *down*	**i law y cwm** *down the valley;* **i lawr y pwll** *down the pit*
mewn *in a*	**mewn cwpan** *in a cup;* **mewn munud** *in a minute*

Some prepositions are conjugated and have personal forms:

am, ar, at, dan follow the same pattern.

at *to, towards* (stem, **at-**)

	Singular		*Plural*	
1	dana i	*under me*	danon ni	*under us*
2	danat ti	*under you*	danoch chi	*under you*
3	dano fe/fo	*under him/it*	danyn nhw	*under them*
	dani hi	*under her/it*		

dan *under* (stem **dan-**)

	Singular		*Plural*	
1	**dana i**	*under me*	danon ni	*under us*
2	**danat ti**	*under you*	danoch chi	*under you*
3	**dano fe/fo**	*under him/it*	danyn nhw	*under them*
	dani hi	*under her/it*		

am *around* (stem **amdan-**)

	Singular		*Plural*	
1	amdana i	*around me*	andanon ni	*around us*
2	amdanat ti	*around you*	amdanoch chi	*around you*
3	amdano fe/fo	*around him/it*	amdanyn nhw	*around them*
	amdani hi	*around her/it*		

ar *on*

(stem **arn-**)

	Singular		*Plural*	
1	arna i	*on me*	arnon ni	*on us*
2	arnat ti	*on you*	arnoch chi	*on you*
3	arno fe/fo	*on him/it*	arnyn nhw	*on them*
	arni hi	*on her/it*		

wrth *by*

(stem **wrth-**)

	Singular		*Plural*	
1	wrtho i	*by me*	wrthon ni	*by us*
2	wrthot ti	*by you*	wrthoch chi	*by you*
3	wrtho fe/fo	*by him/it*	wrthyn nhw	*by them*
	wrthi hi	*by her/it*		

drwy *and* **heb** share a similar pattern:

drwy *through*
(stem **drwydd-**)

	Singular		*Plural*	
1	drwyddo i	*through me*	drwyddon ni	*through us*
2	drwyddot ti	*through you*	drwyddoch chi	*through you*
3	drwyddo fe/fo	*through him/it*	drwyddyn nhw	*through them*
	drwyddi hi	*through her/it*		

heb *without* (stem **hebdd-**)

	Singular		*Plural*	
1	hebddo i	*without me*	hebddon ni	*without us*
2	hebddot ti	*without you*	hebddoch chi	*without you*
3	hebddo fe/fo	*without him/it*	hebddyn nhw	*without them*
	hebddi hi	*without her/it*		

yn *in*
(stem **yn-**)

	Singular		*Plural*	
1	yno i	*in me*	ynon ni	*in us*
2	ynot ti	*in you*	ynoch chi	*in you*
3	ynddo fe/fo	*in him/it*	ynddyn nhw	*in them*
	ynddi hi	*in her/it*		

i *to, for*

	Singular		*Plural*	
1	i fi/mi	*to me, for me*	i ni	*to us, for us*
2	i ti	*to you . . .*	i chi	*to you . . .*
3	iddo fe/fo	*to him/it . . .*	iddyn nhw	*to them . . .*
	iddi hi	*to her . . .*		

o *from* (stem **ohon-**)

	Singular		*Plural*	
1	ohono i	*from me*	ohonon ni	*from us*
2	ohonot ti	*from you*	ohonoch chi	*from you*
3	ohono fe/fo	*from him/it*	ohonyn nhw	*from them*
	ohoni hi	*from her it*		

rhwng *between* (stem **rhyng-**)

	Singular		*Plural*	
1	rhyngo i	*between me*	rhyngon ni	*between us*
2	rhyngot ti	*between you*	rhyngoch chi	*between you*
3	rhyngddo fe/fo	*between him/it*	rhyngddyn nhw	*between them*
	rhyngddi hi	*between her/it*		

dros *over, for*

	Singular	
1	drosto/droso i	*over me, for me*
2	drostot/drosot ti	*over you, for you*
3	drosto fe/fo	*over him/it, for him*
	drosti hi	*over her/it, for her/it*

Plural	
droston/droson ni	*over us, for us*
drostoch/drosoch chi	*over you, for you*
drostyn nhw	*over them, for them*

gan *with*

	Singular		Plural	
1	gen i	*with me*	gennyn/gynnon ni	*with us*
2	gen ti	*with you*	gennych/gynnoch chi	*with you*
3	ganddo fe/fo	*with him/it*	ganddyn nhw	*with them*
	ganddi hi	*with her/it*		

Sometimes the preposition **gyda** is used instead of the conjugated preposition **gan** in South Wales.

The conjugated prepositions **am, ar, at, dan, dros, drwy/trwy, gan, heb, i, o, wrth** are used in their simple form when the object governed by the preposition is a noun or verb-noun. Soft Mutation follows these prepositions:

am dro; ar bapur; at drwyn; dan wely; dros frawd; drwy fôr; heb ddiolch; i regi; o freuddwydio; wrth lusgo

See section below **Treiglad Meddal – Soft Mutation**.
The conjugated preposition **rhwng** is **not** followed by mutation:

rhwng cyfeillion da	*between good friends*
rhwng dau frawd	*between two brothers*
rhwng gŵr a gwraig	*between husband and wife*

The conjugated preposition **yn** in its simple form is followed by Nasal Mutation. It becomes **yng** before **c** and **g**, and **ym** before **p** and **b**:

yng nghornel yr ystafell	*in the corner of the room*
yng nghwrs y flwyddyn	*in the course of the year*
yng Nghorwen	*in Corwen*
yng nghardd yr ysgol	*in the school's garden*
yng nglaw mis Ebrill	*in the April rain*
yng Nglanaman	*in Glanaman*
ym mhoced y bachgen	*in the boy's pocket*
ym mhrofiad y dyn	*in the man's experience*
ym Mhorthaethwy	*in Porthaethwy (Menai Bridge)*
ym mwyd y plant	*in the children's food*
ym masged y fenyw	*in the woman's basket*
ym Mangor	*in Bangor*

yn also becomes *ym* before *m:*

ym Môn; ym Mynwy; ym Môr y Gogledd; ym mynwent y plwyf

For examples of **yn** followed by Soft Mutation or by non-mutation, see section below entitled **A Summary of the Main Rules of Mutation.**

ADJECTIVES
ANSODDEIRIAU

In the Welsh language the adjective usually comes after the noun.

afal **sur**	*a bitter apple*
blodyn **hyfryd**	*a beautiful flower*
cadair **uchel**	*a high chair*
siwrnai **hir**	*a long journey*

When the adjective follows a singular masculine noun no mutation occurs but when the adjective follows the singular feminine noun it takes soft mutation.

bachgen bach	*a small boy*
merch **f**ach	*a small girl*
brawd cariadus	*a loving brother*
chwaer **g**ariadus	*a loving sister*
dyn mawr	*a big man*
menyw **f**awr	*a big woman*
gŵr tenau	*a thin man/husband*
gwraig **d**enau	*a thin woman/wife*
tarw du	*a black bull*
buwch **dd**u	*a black cow*

Note: Adjectives do not mutate when they follow *plural* nouns.

When an adjective precedes a noun the noun is mutated whether it be masculine or feminine.

hen **ŵr**	*an old man*
hen **wraig**	*an old woman*
annwyl **dad**	*a dear father*
annwyl **fam**	*a dear mother*

The noun takes a soft mutation on each occasion.

The feminine form of a few adjectives is still used in everyday speech. Some are listed below:

Masculine	*Feminine*	
gwyn	gwen	*white*
melyn	melen	*yellow*
tlws	tlos	*pretty*
bychan	bechan	*little*
byr	ber	*short*

e.g. cot **wen;** ffrog **felen;** merch **dlos;** ynys **fechan;** stori **fer**

The Comparison of Adjectives
Cymharu Ansoddeiriau

There are four degrees of comparison of adjectives in Welsh. These are: positive, equative, comparative and superlative.

Regular adjectives

With regular adjectives the endings **-ed, -ach, -af** are added respectively to the adjective in its positive form in order to form the other degrees:

Positive	*Equative*	*Comparative*	*Superlative*
*agos *near*	agosed *as near*	agosach *nearer*	agosa(f) *nearest*
caled *hard*	caleted *as hard*	caletach *harder*	caleta (f) *hardest*
call *wise*	called *as wise*	callach *wiser*	calla (f) *wisest*
coch *red*	coched *as red*	cochach *redder*	cocha (f) *reddest*
cryf *strong*	cryfed *as strong*	cryfach *stronger*	cryfa (f) *strongest*
cyflym *quick*	cyflymed *as quick*	cyflymach *quicker*	cyflyma (f) *quickest*
elgur *clear*	eglured *as clear*	elgurach *clearer*	elgura (f) *clearest*
glân *clean*	glaned *as clean*	glanach *cleaner*	glana (f) *cleanest*
glas *blue*	glased *as blue*	glasach *bluer*	glasa (f) *bluest*
hapus *happy*	hapused *as happy*	hapusach *happier*	hapusa (f) *happiest*
oer *cold*	oered *as cold*	oerach *colder*	oera (f) *coldest*
pell *far*	pelled *as far*	pellach *further*	pella (f) *furthest*
tawel *quiet*	taweled *as quiet*	tawelach *quieter*	tawela (f) *quietest*
trwm *heavy*	trymed *as heavy*	trymach *heavier*	tryma (f) *heaviest*
tywyll *dark*	tywylled *as dark*	tywyllach *darker*	tywylla (f) *darkest*

Note: The final **f-** of the Superlative is often omitted in spelling and pronunciation.
*See end of section on Adjectives for alternative forms.

In Welsh, adjectives are compared by two methods:
(i) using **cyn**, and
(ii) using **mor.**

cyn is used to compare adjectives which in their positive forms do not contain more than two syllables and do not end in **-en, -gar, -og, -ol** or **-us.**

cyn and **mor** are both followed by Soft Mutation, except when the adjective begins with **ll** or **rh.**

cyn agosed â/ag *(as near as)*	yn agosach na(g) *(nearer than)*	yr agosaf *(the nearest)*

cyn goched â/ag *(as red as)*	yn gochach na(g) *(redder than)*	y cochaf *(the reddest)*
cyn hapused â/ag *(as happy as)*	yn hapusach na(g) *(happier than)*	yr hapusaf *(the happiest)*
cyn llawned â/ag *(as full as)*	yn llawnach na(g) *fuller than)*	y llawnaf *the fullest)*

When the adjective in its positive form ends in **-g, -b** or **-d** these letters harden to **-c-, -p-,** and **-t-** when the adjective is compared, as is shown below with **caled, teg, gwlyb, rhad:**

cyn gale**t**ed â/ag *(as hard as)*	yn gale**t**ach na(g) *(harder than)*	y cale**t**af *(the hardest)*
cyn de**c**ed â/ag *(as fair as)*	yn de**c**ach na(g) *(fairer than)*	y te**c**af *(the fairest)*
cyn wly**p**ed â/ag *(as wet as)*	yn wly**p**ach na(g) *wetter than)*	y gwly**p**af *the wettest)*
cyn rha**t**ed â/ag *(as cheap/free as)*	yn rha**t**ach na(g) *cheaper/freer than)*	y rha**t**af *the cheapest/freest)*

â in the equative degree and **na** in the comparative degree are used when the following word begins with a consonant, and both cause Spirant Mutation.
ag and **nag** are used when the following word begins with a vowel.

cyn goched **â** thân	*(as red as fire)*
yn drymach **na** phlwm	*(heavier than lead)*
cyn wynned **ag** eira	*(whiter than snow)*
yn dywyllach **nag** uffern	*(darker than hell)*

The other method of comparing adjective in Welsh is by putting **mor. . . mwy. . .** and **mwyfa(f). . .** in front of the adjective.

Positive	*Equative*	*Comparative*	*Superlative*
amlwg *evident*	mor amlwg *as evident*	mwy amlwg *more evident*	mwyaf amlwg *most evident*
amyneddgar *patient*	mor amyneddgar *as patient*	mwy amyneddgar *more patient*	mwyaf amyneddgar *most patient.*
blasus *tasty*	mor flasus *as tasty*	mwy blasus *more tasty*	mwyaf blasus *most tasty*
cyfeillgar *friendly*	mor gyfeillgar *as friendly*	mwy cyfeillgar *more friendly*	mwya(f) cyfeillgar *most friendly*
diolchgar *thankful*	mor ddiolchgar *as thankful*	mwy diolchgar *more thankful*	mwyfa(f) diolchgar *most thankful*
doniol *witty*	mor ddoniol *as witty*	mwy doniol *more witty*	mwya(f) doniol *most witty*
dyledus *indebted*	mor ddyledus *as indebted*	mwy dyledus *more indebted*	mwya(f) dyledus *most indebted*
dymunol *desirable*	mor ddymunol *as desirable*	mwy dymunol *more desirable*	mwya(f) dymunol *most desirable*
gwerthfawr *valuable*	mor werthfawr *as valuable*	mwy gwerthfawr *more valuable*	mwya(f) gwerthfawr *most valuable*
peryglus *dangerous*	mor beryglus *as dangerous*	mwy peryglus *more dangerous*	mwya(f) peryglus *most dangerous*
llawen *cheerful*	mor llawen *as cheerful*	mwy llawen *more cheerful*	mwya(f) llawen *most cheerful.*

Note: **mor** *(as, so, how)* is followed by Soft Mutation.* An alternative translation in the above context would read:
mor amlwg so evident; **mor amyneddgar** *so patient;* **mor flasus** *so tasty;* **mor gyfeillgar** *so friendly . . .*

* **ll** and **rh** do not mutate after **mor.**

Irregular adjectives

There are only a few irregular adjectives in Welsh and the most important of them are listed below:

Positive	*Equative*	*Comparative*	*Superlative*
bach/bychan *small*	mor fach/fychan cyn lleied	llai	lleia(f)
buan/cynnar *swift/early*	mor fuan cynt	cynted	cynta(f)
da *good*	mor dda cystal	gwell	gorau
drwg *bad*	mor ddrwg cynddrwg	gwaeth	gwaetha(f)
hawdd *easy*	mor hawdd cyn hawsed	haws	hawsa(f)
hen *old*	mor hen cyn hyned	hŷn	hyna(f)
hir *long*	mor hir cyn hired	hirach	hira(f)
ifanc/ieuanc *young*	mor ifanc cyn ieuanged	ifancach ieungach	ifanca(f) ieuanga(f)
isel *low*	mor isel cyn ised	is	isa(f)
llawer/mawr *many/big*	mor fawr cymaint	mwy	mwya(f)
uchel *high*	mor uchel cyn uched	uwch	ucha(f)

Note: **cyn** *(as)* is also used in the Equative Degree of comparison with the appropriate **-ed** ending. (It is already contained in such forms as **cynt, cystal, cynddrwg** and **cymaint.**) **cyn** is followed by Soft Mutation.
Exception: **ll** and **rh** do not mutate after **mor** and **cyn.**

The adjective **agos** aldo has irregular equative, comparative and superlative forms:

agos *near*	cyn nesed â *as near as*	yn nes na *nearer than*	y nesaf *the nearest*

PERSONAL PRONOUNS
RHAGENWAU PERSONAL

There are two classes of personal pronouns in Welsh: independent and dependent.

Independent Personal Pronouns

These pronouns are not dependent on any other word in a sentence and may stand entirely alone.

Simple

	Singular		*Plural*	
1	fi, mi	*I, me*	ni	*we, us*
2	ti, di	*you*	chi	*you*
3	fe/e, fo/o	*he, him*	nhw	*they, them*
	hi	*she, her*		

Reduplicated

	Singular	
1	myfi, y fi	*I, I myself*
2	tydi, y chdi (G.C.)	*you, you yourself*
3	efe, efô, y fe, y fo	*he*
	hyhi, y hi	*she, it, she herself, it itself*

Plural	
nyni, y ni	*we, we ourselves*
chychi, y chi	*you, you yourselves*
y nhw	*they, them, they themselves*

The reduplicated forms are often placed at the beginning of a sentence for emphasis.

Myfi sy'n magu'r baban.	*It is I who nurses the baby.*
Tydi, O Dduw, sy'n maddau.	*It is You, O Lord, who forgives.*
Nyni sy'n troi y meysydd.	*It is we who plough the fields.*

Conjunctive

		Singular	*Plural*	
1	finnau, minnau	*I, me*	ninnau	*we, us*
2	tithau	*you*	chithau	*you*
3	yntau	*he, him*	nhwthau	*they, them*
	hithau	*she, her*		

The conjunctive forms frequently possess an extra meaning beyond that of the mere pronoun, the additional meaning being expressed in English by a conjunction:

minnau may mean *I (me) also; even I (me); I (me) on the other hand; I (me) for my part; then I; but I . . .*

ninnau may mean *we (us) too, we (us) also; even we (us); we (us) on the other hand; we (us) on the contrary; we (us) for our part . . .*

Dependent Personal Pronouns

These pronouns are dependent on either a noun, another pronoun or personal ending of a verb or preposition, or a verb-noun.

Prefixed

	Singular		*Plural*	
1	fy, f'	*my*	ein	*our*
2	dy, d'	*your*	eich	*your*
3	ei	*his/her*	eu	*their*

The prefixed forms, which are always in the genitive case, are used before nouns and verb-nouns:

Darllenodd y bachgen ei lyfr.	*The boy read his book.*
Clywais fy nhad yn galw.	*I heard my father calling.*
Cafodd y gân ei chanu ar y radio.	*The song was sung on the radio.*

Affixed

	Singular		*Plural*	
1	i, fi	*I, me*	ni	*we, us*
2	di, ti	*you*	chi	*you*
3	e, fe, o, fo	*he, him*	nhw	*they, them*
	hi	*she, her*		

For examples of Infixed forms and a fuller discussion of the subject of Welsh pronouns the reader is referrd to specific works on Welsh grammar.

Words beginning with the vowels **a, e, i, o, u, w** and **y** are aspirated and acquire an initial **h** when preceded by the following pronouns (or their abbreviated forms):

1	ei, 'i, 'w	*her* (feminine singular)
2	eu, 'u, 'w	*their*
3	ein, 'n	*our*

ysgol > **ei hysgol** (hi) *her school;*
*Dyma'***i hysgol** *Here is her school;*
Dewch i'**w hysgol** *Come to her school.*

ardal > **eu hardal** (nhw) *their district;*
Dyna'**u hardal** *That is their district;*
Mi af i'**w hardal** *I shall go go their district.*

ewyllys > **ein hewyllys** *our will;* a'**n hewyllys** da *and our goodwill.*

annwyl > **ein hannwyl** blentyn *our dear child;* **eu hannwyl** wlad *their dear country;* **ei hannwyl** fam *her dear mother.*

For the mutations after the dependent personal pronouns:
fy, dy, ei (masculine) and **ei** (feminine)
see the section below entitled **A Summary of the Main Rules of Mutation.**

A SUMMARY OF THE MAIN RULES OF MUTATION RHEOLAU TREIGLO

Nine initial consonants mutate. They are:
c, p, t, g, b, d, ll, m, rh.
They mutate in the manner shown in the box below:

Initial consonant	*Soft*	*Nasal*	*Spirant*
cath *cat*	dy **g**ath di *your cat*	fy **ngh**ath i *my cat*	ei **ch**ath hi *her cat*
pen *head*	dy **b**en di *your head*	fy **mh**en i *my head*	ei **ph**en hi *her head*
tad *father*	dy **d**ad di *your father*	fy **nh**ad i *my father*	ei **th**ad hi *her father*
gardd *garden*	dy **ardd** di *your garden*	fy **ng**ardd i *my garden*	
bys *finger*	dy **f**ys di *your finger*	fy **m**ys i *my finger*	
dant *tooth*	dy **dd**ant di *your tooth*	fy **n**ant i *my tooth*	
llyfr *book*	dy **l**yfr di *your book*		
mam *mother*	dy **f**am di *your mother*		
rhaff *rope*	dy **r**aff di *your rope*		

Soft Mutation
Treiglad Meddal

Nine consonants are affected by Soft Mutation:

c > **g; p** > **b; t** > **d; g** > (disappears); **b** > **f; d** > **dd; ll** > **l; m** > **f; rh** > **r.**

Nouns

1 Femine singular nouns after the definite article **y, yr, 'r:**
y **g**ot, y **b**êl, y **d**aith, yr **a**rdd, y **f**raich, o'r **dd**afad, i'r **f**am.
ll and **rh** do not mutate after the definite article:
y llaw, y llwy, y rhaglen, y rhaff, i'r rhos.

2 Nouns when preceded by adjectives:
hen **ŵ**r *(an old man)*; annwyl **f**rawd *(a dear brother)*; hoff **l**e *(a favourite place)*; unig **f**erch *(an only daughter)*.

3 Nouns and verb-nouns after the prepositions **am, ar, at, dan, dros, drwy, gan, heb, hyd, i, o, wrth:**
am **fl**wyddyn *(for a year);* ar **f**wrdd *(on a table);* at **dd**rws *(towards a door);* dan **g**oeden *(under a tree);* dros **G**ymru *(for/over Wales);* drwy **dd**ŵr *(through water);* gan **dd**weud *(by saying);* heb **g**ysgu *(without sleeping);* wrth **g**anu *(by singing).* The verb-nouns **dweud, cysgu** and **canu** mutate as nouns in this context.

4 Nouns after **dyma, dyna, dacw, wele:**
Dyma **l**e da *(Here's a good place).* Dyna **d**ŷ hyfryd *(There's beautiful house).* Dacw **g**i defaid *(There's a sheepdog yonder).* Wele **f**aban! *(Behold a babe!)*

5 Feminine singular nouns after the numeral **un** except those nouns beginning in **ll** and **rh;** nouns after the numerals **dau** and **dwy;** and nouns after the numerals **saith** and **wyth** beginning in **c,p,t,ll** and **rh:**
un **f**erch *(one girl);* un **w**raig *(one woman);* un **g**adair *(one chair);* dau **f**achgen *(two boys);* dau **g**ae *(two fields);* dwy **g**ath *(two cats);* dwy **d**ref *(two towns);* saith **g**ant (seven hundred); wyth **d**udalen *(eight pages).* Exceptions remain: **un llaw** *(one hand);* **un llong** *(one ship);* **un rhwyd** *(one net);* **un rhaw** *(one shovel).*

6 A noun when it is the direct object of an inflected verb (Compact Form):

Prynais **l**yfr.	*I bought a book.*
Gwelaf **g**astell.	*I see a castle.*
Agorodd **dd**rysau'r car.	*He opened the car's doors.*
Fe ganon nhw **g**ân hapus.	*They sang a happy song.*

When the verb is in a periphrastic form the object does *not* mutate:

Mae Siôn yn canu cân.	*Siôn is singing a song.*
Rydw i'n ysgrifennu llythyr.	*I'm writing a letter.*

7 Nouns after the predicative **yn:**

Mae Siân **yn f**erch hyfryd.	*Siân is a lovely girl.*
Mae'r gwaith **yn f**raint.	*The work is a privilege.*
Bydd hwn **yn d**rysor am byth.	*This will be a treasure for ever.*

Exceptions: Nouns beginning in **ll** and **rh.**
Roedd Alun yn llawen. *Alun was happy.*

8 Nouns after the personal pronouns **dy** and **ei** (masculine) together with **'i** (masculine) and **'w** (masculine):
dy **g**ot *(your coat);* dy **b**oced *(your pocket);* dy **d**afod *(your tongue);* ei **o**lwg *(his sight);* ei **f**raich *(his arm);* Dyma Ifan a'i **g**ŵn. *(Here is Ifan and his*

dogs.); Collodd ei **f**rawd a'i **d**ad. *(He lost his brother and his father.)*; Aeth e i'w **d**ŷ. *(He went to his house.)*; Chwythodd y llwch i'w **l**ygaid. *(The dust blew into his eyes.)*

9 Nouns and verb-nouns after the conjunction **neu** *or:*
te neu **g**offi *(tea or coffee)*; mab neu **f**erch *(a son or daughter)*; ci neu **g**ath *(a dog or a cat)*; ennill neu **g**olli *(win or lose)*. Infected verbs (Compact forms) are not mutated after **neu.**

10 Feminine singular nouns after ordinal numerals:
y drydedd **f**erch *(the third girl)*; y chweched **b**ennod *(the sixth chapter)*; y nawfed **g**yfrol *(the ninth volume)*; y ddegfed **w**ers *(the tenth lesson)*.

11 The numerals **dau** and **dwy** after the definite article **y:**
y **dd**au fachgen *(the two boys)*; y **dd**wy ferch *(the two girls)*.

12 Nouns used as adjectives after feminine singular nouns:
llwy **d**e *(teaspoon)*; gwisg **b**riodas *(wedding dress)*; gardd **l**ysiau *(a vegetable garden)*; cadair **f**reichiau *(an armchair)*.

13 Nouns in the vocative case:
Fam annwyl! *(Mother dear!)*; **F**rodyr a chwiorydd! *(brothers and sisters!)* **L**öwyr, gwrandewch! *(Miners listen!)*; **W**eithwyr y byd! *(Workers of the world!)*

14 After a break in the normal order of words:

Roedd croeso yno.	Roedd yno **g**roeso.
Mae merch newydd yn yr ysgol.	Mae yna **f**erch newydd yn yr ysgol.

15 Nouns after **amryw, cyfryw, pa, pa fath, pa ryw, rhyw, unrhyw:**
amryw **l**iwiau *(several colours)*; cyfryw **b**ethau *(such things)*; Pa **l**e? *(what place?)*; Pa fath **f**achgen ydy e? *(What kind of a boy is he?)*

16 Nouns after **ambell, aml, holl, naill, ychydig, y fath:**
ambell **w**aith *(sometimes)*; aml **d**ro *(frequently)*; yr holl **b**entref *(the whole village)*; y naill **g**ynllun *(the one plan)*; ychydig **f**wyd *(a little food)*; y fath **dd**yn *(such a man)*.

17 Nouns after the prefix **cyn(-)** *(former, past, ex-, pre-)*:
cyn-**b**rifathro *(former headteacher)*; cyn-**l**ywydd *(past president)*; cyn-**w**einidog *(former minister)*; cyn-**l**öwr *(ex-miner)*.

Adjectives

1 Adjectives after feminine singular nouns:
cadair **f**ach *(a small chair)*; ffordd **g**ul *(a narrow way)*; heol **f**awr *(a big road)*; merch **d**enau *(a thin girl)*; stori **dd**a *(a good story)*.

2 Adjectives after the predicative **yn:**

Mae Nia yn **g**aredig.	*Nia is kind.*
Roedd y saer yn **dd**a.	*The carpenter was good.*
Mae'r bwyd yn **dd**iflas.	*The food is distasteful.*

ll and **rh** do *not* mutate after **yn.**

3 Adjectives in comparison after **cyn** and **mor:**
cyn **g**yflymed â *(as fast as)*; mor **g**yfeillgar â *(as friendly as)*; cyn **w**ynned â *(as white as)*; mor **d**yner â *(as tender as)*. **ll** and **rh** do not mutate after **cyn** and **mor:**
cyn llawned â *(as full as)*; mor rhad â *(as cheap as)*; mor llawen â'r gog *(as happy as the cuckoo)*.

4 Adjectives after the conjunction **neu:**
da neu **dd**rwg *(good or bad)*; gwyn neu **dd**u *(white or black)*.

5 Adjectives after the adverbs **go, gweddol, lled, mor, rhy:**

go **dd**rwg *quite/fairly bad*
gweddol **d**awel *fairly quiet*
lled **dd**a *quite good/fairly well*
mor **b**wysig *so important*
rhy **l**awen *too merry*

ll and **rh** do *not* mutate after **mor:**

mor llwyddiannus *so successful*
mor rhwydd *so easy*

Verbs

1 Interrogative forms of inflected verbs (Compact Forms):

Weloch chi'r papur? *Did you see the paper?*
Fuest ti allan heddiw? *Were you out today?*
Ddaeth e i'r ysgol mewn pryd? *Did he come to school in time?*

2 Verbs after the particles **Fe**(S.W.) and **Mi**(N.W.):

Fe **g**anodd gân. *He sang a song.*
Mi **gl**ywais ei llais hi. *I heard her voice.*
Fe **l**anwon nhw'r car. *They filled the car.*
Mi **gl**ywson ni'r newyddion. *We heard the news.*

3 Verbs after the relative pronoun **a** and the negative relative pronoun **na:**
Dyma'r ferch **a dd**aeth i'r parti.*Here's the girl who came to the party.*
The relative pronoun **a** is frequently omitted in conversational Welsh but the mutation caused by it is retained.

Dyna'r dyn **(a) w**elais i. *There's the man whom I saw.*

The negative relative pronoun **na** causes Soft Mutation with verbs beginning in **g, b, d, ll, m, rh** and Spirant Mutations with verbs beginning in **c, p, t.**
Dyna'r ferch **na dd**aeth i'r parti. *There's the girl who did not come to the party.*
Dyma'r dyn **na ch**anodd. *Here's the man who did not sing.*

4 After the conjunction **pan:**

Pan **dd**aeth Guto i'r tŷ . . . *When Guto came to the house . . .*
Bydda i'n hapus pan **dd**aw'r haf. *I'll be happy when summer comes.*

5 Negative forms of inflected verbs (Compact Forms):

Ddarllenodd e ddim o'r Beibl. *He didn't read the Bible.*
Welais i ddim yno. *I didn't see anything there.*

In written Welsh, the negative particle **ni** precedes these forms, as in **'Ni dd**arllenodd e ddim o'r Beibl' and **'Ni w**elais i ddim yno', and causes Soft Mutation with verbs beginning in **g, b, d, ll, m, rh.** Inflected verbs beginning in **c, p, t** undergo Spirant Mutation.

6 Verbs after the interrogative pronouns **Beth** and **Pwy:**

Beth **w**eloch chi? *What did you see?*
Pwy **br**ynodd y tocyn? *Who bought the ticket?*

Nasal Mutation
Treiglad Llaes

Six consonants are affected by Nasal Mutation:
c > ngh; p > mh; t > nh; g > nh; b > m; d > n.

1 After the personal pronoun **fy:**
fy **ngh**artref *(my home)*; fy **mh**oced *(my pocket)*; fy **nh**afod *(my tongue)*; fy **ng**obaith *(my hope)*; fy **m**rawd *(my brother)*; fy **n**rws *(my door)*.

2 After the preposition **yn:**
(In certain instances **yn** itself changes to **yng** or **ym**
yn + c > yng ngh-
yn + g > yng ng-
yn + p > ym mh-
yn + b > ym m-
When **yn** precedes **m** it changes to **ym** even though there is no mutation.)
yng nghorff y dyn *(in the man's body)*; **ym mh**lwyf Llangyfelach *(in the parish of Llangyfelach)*; yn **nh**re Caerfyrddin *(in Carmarthen town)*; **yng ng**olau'r gannwyll *(in the candle-light)*; **ym m**reichiau Myfanwy *(in Myfanwy's arms)*; **yn nh**ywyllwch y nos *(in the darkness of the night)*; yng **Ngh**aerdydd; **ym Mh**ontyberem; yn **Nh**reorci; **yng Ng**orseinon; **ym** Miwmaris; yn **N**inbych; **ym** Mynwy; **ym** Maesteg; **ym** mis Mai.

3 **blwydd** *(a year old)*, **blynedd** *(a year)*, and **diwrnod** *(a day)* all mutate after the cardinal numbers **pum, saith, wyth, naw, deng, deuddeng, ugain** (and numbers incorporating **ugain**, such as **trigain**), and **can.**
pum **m**lwydd oed *(five years old)*; saith **m**lynedd *(seven years)*; *wyth* **n**iwrnod *(eight days)*; deng **m**lwydd oed; deuddeng **m**lynedd; ugain **n**iwrnod; can **m**lynedd.
Note: Mae Siôn yn **ddwy fl**wydd oed. — *Siôn is two years old.*
Roedd Nia yma am **ddwy fl**ynedd. — *Nia was here for two years.*
Mae **dau dd**iwrnod cyn y parti. — *There are two days before the party.*
See Soft Mutation – *Treiglad Meddal.*

Aspirate Mutation
Treiglad Llaes

Three consonants are affected by Spirant Mutation:
c > ch; p > ph; t > th.

1 After the personal pronouns **ei** (feminine), **'i** (feminine) and **'w** (feminine):
ei **ch**aws *(her cheese)*; ei **ph**en-blwydd *(her birthday)*; ei **th**ad-cu *(her grandfather)*; o'i **ch**artref *(from her home)*; o'i **ph**en i'w **th**raed *(from her head to her feet)*.

2 After the cardinal numbers **tri, chwe:**
tri **ch**wpan *(three cups)*; tri **ph**erson *(three persons)*; chwe **ph**lentyn *(six children)*; chwe **th**estun *(six subjects)*.

3 After the prepositions **â, gyda, tua:**

torri bara â **ch**yllell	*cutting bread with a knife*
cerdded gyda **th**ad y ferch	*walking with the girl's father*
gweithio gyda **ch**yfaill	*working with a friend*
mynd tua **Ph**entre-Bach	*going towards Pentre-Bach*
aros tua **th**ymor	*waiting about a term*

4 After the conjunctions **a** *(and)*, **na** *(nor, than)*, **oni** *(until, unless):*
dŵr a **th**an *(water and fire)*; ci a **ch**ath *(a dog and a cat)*; na **ph**en na **ch**wt *(nor head nor tail)*; yn fwy na **ph**unt *(more than a pound)*; yn gochach na **th**ân *(redder than fire)*; oni **ch**lywaf *(Unless I shall hear)*

5 After the adverbs **â** *(as)*, **tra** *(very/exceedingly):*

cyn drymed â **ph**lwm	*as heavy as lead*
cyn oered â **ch**lai	*as cold as clay*
tra **ch**aredig	*very kind*
tra **th**ywyll	*exceedingly dark*

6 After the negative form of the relative pronoun **na:**
Dyma'r ferch na **th**alodd am ei llyfr. *This is the girl who did not pay for her book.*

Only verbs beginning in **c, p, t** and following **na** in this context are affected by Spirant Mutatuion. For verbs beginning in **g, b, d, ll, m, rh** after the negative pronoun **na** see Soft Mutation – *Treiglad Meddal.*

7 Negative forms of inflected verbs (Compact Forms):

Chlywais i ddim sŵn.	*I didn't hear a sound.*
Thalodd e ddim.	*He didn't pay.*
Phrynais i ddim o'r esgidiau.	*I didn't buy the shoes.*

In written Welsh, the negative particle ni precedes these forms, as in 'Ni chlywais i ddim sŵn' and 'Ni thalodd e ddim', and causes Spirant Mutation with verbs beginning in c, p, t. Inflected verbs beginning in g, b, d, ll, m and rh undergo Soft Mutation.

Notes: nodiadau

Notes: nodiadau

Notes: nodiadau

Notes: nodiadau

Notes: nodiadau